Elizabeth of York

The First Tudor Queen

Alison Weir

JONATHAN CAPE
LONDON

Published by Jonathan Cape 2013

4 6 8 10 9 7 5 3

Copyright © Alison Weir 2013

Alison Weir has asserted her right under the Copyright, Designs
and Patents Act 1988 to be identified as the author of this work

First published in Great Britain in 2013 by
Jonathan Cape
Random House, 20 Vauxhall Bridge Road,
London SW1V 2SA

www.vintage-books.co.uk

Addresses for companies within The Random House Group Limited can be found at:
www.randomhouse.co.uk/offices.htm

The Random House Group Limited Reg. No. 954009

A CIP catalogue record for this book is available from the British Library

ISBN 9780224089814 (Cased edition)
ISBN 9780224097758 (Trade paperback edition)

The Random House Group Limited supports the Forest Stewardship Council®
(FSC®), the leading international forest-certification organisation. Our books
carrying the FSC label are printed on FSC®-certified paper. FSC is the only
forest-certification scheme supported by the leading environmental organisations,
including Greenpeace. Our paper procurement policy can be found at
www.randomhouse.co.uk/environment

Typeset in Bembo by Palimpsest Book Production Limited,
Falkirk, Stirlingshire
Printed and bound in Great Britain by
CPI Group (UK) Ltd, Croydon CRO 4YY

This book is dedicated to
seven little people:
Neve Marston
Jake Preston
Eleanor Weir
Emily Weir
Piper Weir
Susan Weir
Wren Weir
and to two great friends
Shelley and Burnell

Contents

List of Illustrations

half of the 16th century. (© National Portrait Gallery, London)

The Wedding of Henry and Elizabeth by J. R. Brown, _c._1901. (By kind permission of Blackpool Council)

The Deanery, Winchester Cathedral. (© Dr John Crook)

The birth of a prince, from the Beauchamp Pageant, _c._1483–7. (By permission of the British Library/Cotton Julius E. IV, art. 6, f.22v)

Bermondsey Abbey. (By permission of the British Library/_The History of London_ by Walter Besant, London: Longmans Green & Co, 1893)

The coronation of a queen, from the Beauchamp Pageant, _c._1483–7. (By permission of the British Library/Cotton Julius E. IV, art. 6, f.2v)

'Perspective view of the old Palace of Westminster in the reign of Henry VIII', pen and ink drawing, Henry William Brewer, 1884. (© Palace of Westminster)

Portrait of Perkin Warbeck. (Bibliothèque Municipale, Arras, France/The Bridgeman Art Library)

The great hall at Eltham Palace. (Eltham Palace, Greenwich, London, UK/© English Heritage Photo Library/The Bridgeman Art Library)

Autograph inscriptions and signatures of Henry VII and Elizabeth of York in a Latin missal of 1498. (Private Collection/The Bridgeman Art Library)

Elizabeth's signature in 'The Hours of Elizabeth the Queen'. (By permission of the British Library/Add. 50001, f.22)

The Sudbury Hutch. (Courtesy of St James Church, Louth)

Baynard's Castle. (Private Collection/The Bridgeman Art Library)

A modern reconstruction of Fotheringhay Castle. (From a painting by Andrew Spratt)

Engraving of Lathom House as it existed before the siege of 1630, by E. Finden, from a drawing by G. Pickering. (By permission of the British Library/_Traditions of Lancashire_ by John Roby, London: George Routledge and Sons, 1872)

The Paradise Bed. (Courtesy of the Langley Collection)

Margaret Tudor praying. (ONB Vienna: Cod 1897, fol. 243v)

The tomb of Elizabeth's second daughter, Elizabeth. (© Dean and Chapter of Westminster)

Henry VIII in infancy. (Courtesy of Fonds Bibliothèque Méjanes, Aix-en-Provence)

Terracotta bust of a laughing child, possibly the future Henry VIII, by Guido Mazzoni, _c._1498. (Royal Collection Trust/© Her Majesty Queen Elizabeth II 2013)

Henry VIII mourning his mother, detail from The Vaux Passional, Peniarth MS. 482D. (By permission of The National Library of Wales)

Wooden funeral effigy of Elizabeth of York. (© Dean and Chapter of Westminster)

The funeral of Elizabeth of York. (By permission of the British Library/Additional MS 45131 f.42)

The Henry VII Chapel in Westminster Abbey. (© akg-images/ Monheim)

The coffins of James I, Elizabeth of York and Henry VII, as seen in 1869, by Sir George Scharf. (© Dean and Chapter of Westminster)

Tomb effigies of Elizabeth of York and Henry VII, 1512-19. (© The Granger Collection/Topfoto)

Tomb effigy of Elizabeth of York. (Courtesy of The Warburg Institute)

We will unite the white rose and the red.
Smile Heaven upon this fair conjunction
That long hath frowned upon their enmity! –
What traitor hears me, and says not Amen?
England hath long been mad and scarred herself;
The brother blindly shed the brother's blood,
The father rashly slaughtered his own son,
The son, compell'd, been butcher to the sire:
All this divided York and Lancaster,
Divided in their dire division.
O now let Richmond and Elizabeth,
The true successors of each royal House,
By God's fair ordinance conjoin together!
And let their heirs – God, if Thy will be so –
Enrich the time to come with smooth-faced peace,
With smiling plenty, and fair prosperous days!

William Shakespeare: *Richard III*

Acknowledgements

I should like to express my gratitude to the kind, knowledgeable and enthusiastic people who have supported me in the writing of this book. To Sarah Gristwood, for hours of discussion about Elizabeth of York, and for giving so generously of her time to read the typescript, correct errors and make suggestions; to her and to Josephine Wilkinson for their views on the vexatious matter of the Buck letter; to Nicola Tallis, for sending me academic papers on Elizabeth; to Professor Anthony Goodman, for advice on precontracts in the fifteenth century; to Ian Coulson, for sending me his research on the Paradise State Bed; to Jennifer Scott, Curator of Paintings at The Royal Collection, for information on portraits of Elizabeth owned by Her Majesty the Queen, and for engaging in many enjoyable email exchanges on the subject.

I should like to thank Will Sulkin, my publisher at Jonathan Cape for so many years, for commissioning this book, and indeed for all his wonderful support and friendship during those years. Special thanks are due also to my new publisher, Dan Franklin, for his prompt and professional assistance and expertise; to Clare Bullock, for her work on the illustrations and for administrative support; to Frances Jessop, for her creative input; to Neil Bradford for excellent design and production; and to Clara Womersley, for her enthusiasm and ever-supportive help, way beyond the call of duty! Thanks also to Jane Selley and Mary Chamberlain for work on the manuscript.

I owe a huge debt of gratitude to my editorial director, Anthony Whittome, not only for his creative guidance but also for his original and convincing theory about Elizabeth of York and the Buck letter.

I should add that the conclusions I have reached in this book –
and any errors – are my own. Having researched firstly from primary
sources, I had formulated my own conclusions on many aspects of
Elizabeth's story before I came to read the secondary sources and
found that some historians had evolved similar theories. Those whose
views and insights have had a bearing on my work have been credited in the notes.

Introduction

Elizabeth of York's role in history was crucial, although in a less chauvinistic age it would, by right, have been more so. In the wake of legislation to give women the same rights in the order of succession as male heirs, it is interesting to reflect that England's Elizabeth I would not have been the celebrated Virgin Queen but Elizabeth of York. But in the fifteenth century it would have been unthinkable for a woman to succeed to the throne. Elizabeth lived in a world in which females were regarded as inferior to men physically, intellectually and morally. It was seen as against the laws of God and Nature for a woman to wield dominion over men: it was an affront to the perceived order of the world. Even so, Elizabeth of York was important. She was the daughter, sister, niece, wife, mother and grandmother of monarchs: daughter to Edward IV, sister to Edward V, niece to Richard III, wife to Henry VII, mother to Henry VIII and grandmother to Edward VI, Mary I and Elizabeth I; and she was the mother of two queen consorts. She was also the ancestress of every English monarch since 1509, every Scots monarch since 1513, and every British monarch since 1603, including the present Queen, Elizabeth II.

Her impressive pedigree is not the only reason why I have chosen to write Elizabeth of York's biography. She lived through a momentous, well-documented period of history that saw the beginning of the transition from the medieval to the modern world. She was closely connected to some of England's most controversial figures, among them Richard III, Henry VII, Henry VIII and the notorious – or possibly misunderstood – Wydevilles, her mother's family. I wanted to discover how she interacted with these famous people, and what we could learn of her through those dealings. Above all, what influence, if any, did she have on her son, the future Henry VIII?

I knew that there were conundrums relating to Elizabeth of York, and I suspected that too many assumptions about her had been based on unreliable sources. It seemed to me that there were two Elizabeths: the one who was proactive in intriguing behind the scenes to become queen consort; and, later, the docile, compliant royal wife who effectively lacked a voice. How could one reconcile the two? And was either view accurate?

I was drawn again to the mystery surrounding the disappearance of Elizabeth's brothers, the Princes in the Tower, a subject on which I published a book in 1992. What did she know or believe? How could she apparently have contemplated marrying the man who was widely reputed to have had the boys killed? And later, when a pretender surfaced, claiming to be one of her brothers, how did that impact on Elizabeth? I wanted to investigate whether there was any way of finding out where she stood in the ensuing crises. Writing her biography has given me the opportunity of revisiting and re-researching these controversial issues, and revising in some measure my former conclusions. I have also been fortunate to be writing at a time when Richard III's remains were discovered in Leicester. It has been illuminating to be able to explore the implications of his being found to be the 'Crouchback' of the so-called propagandists.

I was interested too in new views on the Wydevilles. It seemed that they must have influenced Elizabeth enormously. Above all, I was struck by the dramatic dynastic changes with which she had to cope. Born a Plantagenet, of the House of York, she came to be identified with the Wydeville party, which was crushed by Richard III, with dire consequences for her and her relatives; then she married a Tudor, the representative of the rival House of Lancaster – no easy transition, one suspects. What really is striking is how successfully she met the challenge. Yet she has usually been perceived as a queen who had no influence, who was kept in subjection by her husband and dominated by her fearsome mother-in-law, Margaret Beaufort. Again we have a conundrum. Here was an intelligent woman who had suffered frightening events in childhood, and tragedy, dispossession and virtual imprisonment as a teenager, yet was ambitious for herself and protective of her family. What was the truth about her relationship with Henry VII and her role as queen?

I was aware that there was a wealth of source material to be explored.

Having written historical biographies of women whose lives are documented only in fragments, I knew that, when it came to Elizabeth, there would be scope not only for forensic analysis but also for a strong and dramatic narrative, a narrative carried by vivid and very detailed source material. It would be possible to write about the human side of her life. In these aspects, I would be returning to the form of many of my earlier books. As with all medieval biography, particularly of women, there are frustrating gaps in our knowledge; but there is sufficient evidence from which to draw conclusions about Elizabeth's character. A wealth of reliable contemporary quotes underpins the authenticity of her story.

When I embarked on this book, I had no idea if I would find information to solve, or throw light on, all the conundrums, or where my research would lead me. Much remains conjectural, of course, but I have been able to draw new conclusions about Elizabeth, correct some errors and reconcile some apparent contradictions. I did not expect to make one very startling connection between her and the mystery of the Princes, but if one compares the chronology of events with information in her *Privy Purse Expenses*, it is there for all to see. Once that link was made, and I dug deeper, even more significant facts emerged. The connection is open to speculation, but it is too much of a coincidence to be dismissed, and it is evidence that no one has taken into account until now.

What also emerged from the collation of source material was the significance of Elizabeth's final progress in the summer of 1502. Put that in its historical context, and some surprising inferences may be drawn, showing that the story of her last year may be sadder than we knew.

It was Elizabeth of York's 'fortune and grace to be queen'.[1] It is our fortune and grace to have so many surviving insights into the life of this remarkable woman.

Alison Weir
Carshalton, Surrey
February 2013

A NOTE ON MONETARY VALUES

I have used the National Archives Currency Converter to determine the present-day value of sums quoted in the text. The approximate worth of such sums at the time of writing, rounded to the nearest £10, is quoted in brackets. Please note that values could change from year to year. Salaries quoted are annual amounts.

Prologue

'Now Take Heed
What Love May Do'

I n January 1466, Thomas Bourchier, Archbishop of Canterbury, and nine of his fellow bishops were summoned to the Palace of Westminster. The Queen of England, Elizabeth Wydeville,[1] was shortly to bear her first child, and these princes of the Church were to be ready and waiting to baptise the infant 'which the Queen shall bring forth' as soon as it was born.

The birth of a son and heir to assure the continuance and future prosperity of his dynasty was of paramount importance to King Edward IV, first sovereign of the royal House of York. Five years before, he had emerged triumphant after six years of conflict with the rival House of Lancaster, which had ended in a bloody dispute for the crown. The roots of that conflict went back to 1399, when Henry IV, the first Lancastrian sovereign, had usurped the throne. His son, Henry V, had been the respected and feared victor of Agincourt, but the warrior hero's son, the weak and ineffectual Henry VI, had proved a disaster, allowing himself to be dominated by court factions who were concerned chiefly with promoting their own interests. He failed to address the many problems he had inherited: a divided Council; a legal system corrupted by local magnates and their armed retainers; an aristocracy that was growing ever mightier and losing its integrity; and a war with France – the Hundred Years' War, which had been waged since 1337 – that could not be won but was draining the country of its resources. This lack of firm government had led relentlessly to a breakdown of law and order throughout the realm of England, and the weakening of royal authority.

Henry VI's cousin, Richard, Duke of York (Elizabeth of York's grandfather), arguably had a better claim to the throne, being senior to Henry in descent from Edward III, but through the female line. York was wealthy, respected, experienced in warfare and government, and – unlike the King – the father of a large family with healthy sons. To begin with, York's ambitions had not included a crown, but he was dismayed at the misrule of the court faction that controlled Henry VI, which was led by the Queen, Margaret of Anjou, and Henry's kinsman, Edmund Beaufort, Duke of Somerset. York was determined to eliminate the endemic corruption and indiscriminate patronage that characterised their régime. In this, he had the support of his cousin and principal ally, the mighty Richard Neville, Earl of Warwick, who was to become Elizabeth's godfather. Warwick was the archetypal English magnate, whose chief motivations were self-promotion and the acquisition of wealth. He was power-hungry, proud, ruthless, violent and forceful, but a brave commander, and very popular with the people of England. Unlike York, he had the common touch, coupled with lavish, open-handed hospitality. The splendour and extravagance of his household was renowned.

By 1450 the Lancastrian government was bankrupt, milked dry by the court faction. Dissension festered, and the situation was exacerbated in 1453 when Henry VI lapsed into either catatonic schizophrenia or a depressive stupor. His incapacity put an end to any hope of unity between the opposing political factions. It brought Queen Margaret, with her poor understanding of English politics, to the forefront of power, and deprived the country of its head of state, removing the last brake on the rapaciousness of the court party. And while the King was comatose, Queen Margaret bore a son, Edward of Lancaster.

Parliament nominated York as regent, and he began to tackle the vast task of reforming the administration. But he had not made much headway when Henry VI recovered his senses and reasserted his authority. The royal authority was back in the hands of a weak king debilitated by mental illness.

Convinced that the Queen and her party were about to destroy him, York raised an army. The first battle in what later became known as the Wars of the Roses – a term coined by Sir Walter Scott, but which contemporaries called the Cousins' Wars – took place at St Albans in 1455, eleven years before Elizabeth's birth. Somerset was killed, and York quickly re-established his political supremacy. Resentment smouldered, and hostilities broke out again in 1459, with the Queen's faction emerging victorious. But after York won a resounding victory at Northampton in 1460, the nature of the conflict changed.

After decades of misrule, the English people were beginning to view Richard of York as a serious rival for Henry VI's crown, and it was at this point that York openly laid claim to the throne and the Wars of the Roses became a dynastic struggle.

A compromise was reached: Henry VI was to retain the crown for his lifetime, but would be succeeded by York. Queen Margaret was outraged at the disinheriting of her son, and again went to war. In 1460 York and his second son, Edmund, Earl of Rutland, were killed at the Battle of Wakefield.

York's cause was immediately taken up by his capable nineteen-year-old son, Edward, Earl of March. In March 1461, having success-fully routed the Lancastrians, March entered London in triumph and was proclaimed King Edward IV. One Londoner observed: 'The commons love and adore him as if he were their God; the entire kingdom keeps holiday for the event.' Edward's enemies remained at large, but later that month, after a decisive but bloody victory at the Battle of Towton, he emerged as the undoubted ruler of England. Queen Margaret fled to France with her son, and Henry VI remained in hiding until 1465, when he was captured and placed in honourable confinement in the Tower of London. By then, England was enjoying the fruits of firm government.

Edward had not achieved power without the staunch help of his father's ally, Warwick. Next to the King, Warwick was now the greatest man in England and Edward's chief mainstay and supporter. For the first three years of the reign, he virtually controlled the government of the realm, carried along on a tide of popularity. Whenever he showed himself in public, attended by his customary train of 600 liveried retainers, crowds would run to see him, crying, 'Warwick! Warwick!' It seemed that God had 'descended from the skies'.[2]

'Warwick seems to me everything in this kingdom,' observed the Milanese ambassador,[3] but although Edward IV relied on Warwick in many ways, he would not be ruled by him. This was not apparent to everyone, even Warwick himself, who certainly overestimated his influence over the King. Nor was it obvious to foreign observers, such as the citizen of Calais who wrote to King Louis XI of France: 'They tell me that they have two rulers in England: Monsieur de Warwick, and another whose name I have forgotten.'[4] The Milanese ambassador in France had already foreseen discord between the Earl and his master.[5]

Elizabeth's father, Edward IV, was a splendid figure of a king. Sir Thomas More described him as 'princely to behold, of body mighty, strong and clean-made'. According to the Tudor historian Polydore Vergil, who was commissioned by Henry VII to write a history of England, Edward was 'broad-shouldered' and 'his head and shoulders towered above those of nearly all other men'.[6] His skeleton, discovered during excavations in St George's Chapel, Windsor in 1789, measured over six foot three, so he was unusually tall for his time. Above all, he was 'unusually handsome':[7] the chronicler Philippe de Commines, a writer and diplomat who worked for Louis XI, remembered Edward as 'the handsomest prince my eyes ever beheld'. His hair was brown,[8] as it appears in portraits and in the strands found near his skull. According to the chronicler Olivier de la Marche, Edward 'was a handsome prince and had style'.

The young King was well aware of the effect his dazzling good looks had on people. He loved to show off his 'fine stature', displaying it to advantage in rich and revealingly cut clothes.[9] By fifteenth-century standards, he was remarkably clean, having his head, legs and feet washed every Saturday night, and sometimes more frequently.

But it was not just good looks that made Edward IV a popular king. He excelled Henry VI in nearly every way, especially as a statesman and a general. He was a firm and resolute ruler, shrewd and astute, and had real ability and business acumen, as well as the willingness to apply himself. He was successful in his determination to restore the authority of the monarchy and make it an institution that once more inspired reverence and respect.

Edward was 'of sharp wit, high courage and retentive memory, diligent in doing his affairs, ready in perils, earnest and horrible to the enemy, and bountiful to his friends and acquaintances . . . Humanity was bred in him abundantly.' Handsome, affable and accessible, he was also 'given to bodily lust', and consequently 'would use himself more familiarly among private persons than the honour of his majesty required'. Edward's chief vice was his sensuality, and his debaucheries were soon notorious. 'He thought of nothing but upon women, and on that more than reason would, and on hunting, and on the comfort of his person.'[10] Dominic Mancini, an Italian visitor to England, thought him 'licentious in the extreme. It was said that he had been most insolent to numerous women after he had seduced them, for as soon as he had satisfied his lust, he abandoned the ladies, much against their will, to the other courtiers. He pursued with no discrimination the married and unmarried, the noble and the lowly. However, he took none by force. He overcame all by money and promises.' It was not long before lust would lead Edward into a situation that would have far-reaching consequences for himself and his children.

'Now take heed what love may do!'[11] All went well between the King and Warwick until 1464, when Edward – 'led by blind affection and not by rule of reason'[12] – married an impoverished Lancastrian widow, Elizabeth Wydeville, Lady Grey. The Wydevilles were an old-established family in Northamptonshire, where they owned the manor of Grafton Regis. Elizabeth's father, Sir Richard Wydeville, had boldly aspired to wed Jacquetta of Luxembourg, daughter of Peter of Luxembourg, Count of St Pol, and 'of the blood of Charlemagne'. In 1433 she had made a highly prestigious marriage with John of Lancaster, Duke of Bedford (the younger brother of Henry V), who had governed France in the name of the infant Henry VI. Bedford had died in 1435, whereupon the childless Jacquetta inherited all his estates. With almost indecent haste, she married Richard Wydeville, a member of Bedford's staff. Immediately Jacquetta's French relations cut her off, despising Wydeville as a mere 'simple knight', and she was fined £1,000 (£469,350) by the English Council for remarrying without permission. But that scandal was long past now, and Wydeville had been raised to the peerage as Baron Rivers in 1448.

Legend has it that Edward IV first encountered Elizabeth Wydeville under an oak tree in Whittlebury Forest, where she and her two young sons fell on their knees before him, and she begged him to restore to her the lands of her late husband, Sir John Grey of Groby, who had been killed fighting for Henry VI.[13] Sadly, there is no truth in the tale: Grey was never attainted, so his lands had not been confiscated. Even so, a big oak tree at Yardley Hill is still known as the Queen's Oak.

Elizabeth Wydeville was 'a woman more of formal countenance than of excellent beauty, of sober demeanour, lovely looking and feminine smiling, neither too wanton nor too humble. Her tongue was so eloquent and her wit was pregnant.'[14] She was 'moderate of stature, well made and very wise'.[15] Her portraits show a poised, elegant, blonde woman with the shaven forehead fashionable at that time, a slender figure and facial features that would be considered striking in any age.[16] Elizabeth of York was to inherit her mother's looks.

Elizabeth Wydeville wasn't interested in money or promises, but held out for marriage. Rumours abounded in the 1460s and beyond that she had refused to become Edward's mistress, or had threatened to stab herself when he tried to rape her, or that he had held the dagger to her throat to force her to submit, or that her mother had used witchcraft to ensnare him. Whatever the tactics, they proved successful. The marriage took place in secret, probably after 30 August 1464. When it was made public that September, it provoked a furore. In an age in which kings married foreign princesses for political advantage, marrying for love was regarded as akin to insanity, and choosing the widow of a man who had fought for the King's enemies was almost worse. Moreover no English king since the Norman conquest of 1066 had wed a commoner, one of his own subjects, and it was seen as scandalous that Edward had set aside all thought of duty and obligation to marry for love – and to marry beneath him.

His mother, Cecily Neville, Duchess of York, violently disapproved. She was the daughter of Ralph Neville, Earl of Westmorland, by Joan Beaufort, daughter of John of Gaunt, Duke of Lancaster, fourth son of Edward III and founder of the House of Lancaster, by the mistress he later married, Katherine Swynford; Cecily was thus the great-granddaughter of King Edward III, and sufficiently conscious of her high lineage to have earned the nickname 'Proud Cis'. In youth, they had called her 'the Rose of Raby', for she had been born and raised at Raby Castle, County Durham. Her marriage to Richard, Duke of York, seems to have been a happy one. The various locations of the births of their twelve children indicate that Cecily accompanied her husband on his many forays to France and on his travels in England. She had never remarried, and in later life would assume the habit of a Benedictine nun. Now, however, she proudly carried herself as if she were a queen, styling herself in letters 'the rightful inheritor's wife of the realm of England, the King's mother, Duchess of York'.[17] She did not take kindly to having a commoner for a daughter-in-law, and a later tale – probably without foundation – claims she was so furious that she offered to prove her son a bastard and thereby unfit to rule.[18]

Warwick was especially angered by the King's marriage. He had been negotiating for a French matrimonial alliance, and Edward had made him look a fool. Warwick, like other nobles, objected to Elizabeth Wydeville because 'she was not the daughter of a duke or earl, but her mother, the Duchess of Bedford, had married a simple knight, so that though she [Elizabeth Wydeville] was the child of a duchess' – who was also a princess of the House of Luxembourg – 'still she was no wife for him',[19] but an upstart. When Edward began advancing his Queen's numerous relations, Warwick could hardly contain his 'secret displeasure'.[20]

The marriage was unpopular with many of the King's subjects,[21] and now the Wydeville Queen was expecting a child, the arrival of which – especially if it was a son and heir – could only boost the pretensions of her faction. Moreover, 'the King was assured of his physicians that the Queen was conceived with a prince, and especially of one named Master Dominic, by whose counsel great provision was ordained for the christening of the said Prince'.[22] The birth of an heir with Wydeville blood was certain to lead to controversy in the future, as Elizabeth of York was to find to her cost.

1

'The Most Illustrious Maid of York'

The royal palace of Westminster extended along the Thames shore, south-west of the City of London. A royal residence had stood on this site opposite Westminster Abbey since the sainted King Edward the Confessor had rebuilt both in the eleventh century, and the magnificent Westminster Hall had been completed by William II in 1099; in the late fourteenth century, Richard II had increased the height of its walls and added the splendid oak hammerbeam roof. The sprawling palace in which the Queen was to be confined was the work of successive medieval kings, and the chief seat of royal government until much of it was destroyed by fire in 1512. Parliament often met within its walls, usually in the Painted Chamber, the White Hall or St Stephen's Chapel. Westminster Hall was used for state occasions and ceremonies, and also for coronation banquets. Daily it was a hive of industry, housing the busy law courts and stalls selling books and other goods.

The rambling old palace was much in need of upgrading, and Edward IV had set about converting part of it into new royal lodgings, which Elizabeth of York would come to know very well. They included a privy kitchen for the preparation of royal meals, a wardrobe for the storage of royal possessions, and something very traditional in royal domestic arrangements: separate ranges of private apartments for the King and Queen.

The creation of a new 'Queen's side' for Elizabeth Wydeville, which was begun in 1464, may have come about because the King's mother, the disapproving Cecily Neville, was living at court and appropriate accommodation was needed for both ladies. The apartments built for Queen Elizabeth included a withdrawing chamber and wardrobe; a great chamber would be added in 1482.[1] It was in these new lodgings that the Queen was to bear her child.

For married women in those days, pregnancy was often an annual event, with all the risks it entailed. Contraception was rudimentary and would not have been practised by royal couples, for whom a large family meant sons to secure the succession and daughters to forge political marriage alliances. It was a son, naturally, that the King wanted, and although, by medieval custom, male physicians did not attend pregnant women, Dr Dominic de Sirego, Elizabeth Wydeville's physician, was determined to 'be the first that should bring tidings to the King of the birth of the Prince', for messengers conveying such glad news often received 'great thanks and reward'. Only women were allowed into the birth chamber, so when the Queen went into labour, Dr Sirego had perforce to wait in the 'second chamber'. The baby was a girl: 'this year [1466], the 11th day of the month of February, was Elizabeth, first child of King Edward, born at Westminster'.[2] She was the first princess born to an English monarch in over a century.

The waiting physician, hearing the child cry, 'knocked or called secretly at the chamber door' and asked 'what the Queen had', whereupon her attendants, much amused, called back, 'Whatsoever the Queen's Grace hath here within, sure it is that a fool standeth there without!' Whereupon Dr Sirego hastily 'departed without seeing the King that time'.[3]

That same month, 'my lady Princess' was baptised 'with most solemnity' in a new font set up in St Stephen's Chapel in Westminster Palace by her kinsman, George Neville, Archbishop of York,[4] just as if she had been the desired prince. She was given her mother's name; it was a happy coincidence that the Queen had a special devotion for St Elizabeth.[5] The name Elizabeth was not new in the royal line: it had been given to daughters of Henry I and Edward I, and to a granddaughter of Edward III. It had also been borne by Elizabeth de Burgh, the heiress who had married Lionel of Antwerp, Duke of Clarence (Edward III's second son), and brought the rich Ulster inheritance to the royal House of York.

Tradition decreed that the King and Queen did not attend the christening, but Edward IV made it the occasion for a show of solidarity, even though the players were privately at odds or disapproved of his marriage. The baby Princess's sponsors were her grandmothers, the duchesses of York and Bedford, and the Earl of Warwick. Walter Blount, Lord Mountjoy, Treasurer of England, received 1,000 marks (£152,250) for his diligence at the baptism, then was promptly told to resign his office to the Queen's father, Lord Rivers.

The King bought his wife a jewelled ornament costing £125 (£62,550) 'against the birth of our most dear daughter Elizabeth'. Even though she had only borne a daughter, Elizabeth Wydeville's churching ceremony that followed in late March was attended by great magnificence. 'The Queen left her childbed that morning and went to church in stately order, accompanied by many priests bearing relics and by many scholars singing and carrying lights. There followed a great company of ladies and maidens from the country and from London. Then came trumpeters, pipers and players of stringed instruments. The King's choir followed, forty-two of them, who sang excellently. Then came twenty-four heralds and pursuivants, followed by sixty earls and knights. At last came the Queen, escorted by two dukes. Above her was a canopy. Behind her were her mother and maidens and ladies to the number of sixty. Then the Queen heard the singing of an office.' Following the service of purification that marked her return to society after her confinement, 'she returned to the palace in procession, as before. Then all who had joined the procession remained to eat'. So many guests were present – clearly a prince had been anticipated – that they 'filled four great rooms' of an 'unbelievably costly apartment'.[6]

Elizabeth Wydeville might have been deemed an unsuitable bride for the King, but she was determined that no one should remember it, and the etiquette that surrounded her on this occasion was rigorous. 'The Queen sat alone at table on a costly golden chair. The Queen's mother and the King's sister [Anne, Duchess of Exeter] had to stand some distance away. When the Queen spoke with her mother or the King's sister, they knelt down before her until she had drunk water. Not until the first dish was set before the Queen could [they] be seated. The [sixty] ladies and maidens and all who served the Queen at table were of noble birth, and had to kneel so long as the Queen was eating; the meal lasted for three hours. The food which was served to the Queen, the Queen's mother, the King's sister and others was most costly. Everyone was silent and not a word was spoken.' Afterwards, no doubt to everyone's relief, there was dancing, with the ladies curtseying elegantly to the silent Queen, and glorious singing by the King's choristers. A foreign observer noted: 'The courtly reverence paid to the Queen was such as I have never seen elsewhere.'[7]

Like all babies in those days, the infant Princess was swaddled in tight bands with a close-fitting cap on her head, and she would have remained swaddled for the first eight or nine months of her life to ensure that her limbs grew straight. She was assigned a stately household that included a nurse (each of the royal children had a separate nurse) and a wet-nurse, for queens did not suckle their children. The household was under the charge of a lady mistress, or governess, Margaret, Lady Berners,[8] who received a salary of £100 (£50,000). Under her were pages of the chamber, a 'knight of the trencher' and rockers to watch over the Princess in her cradle.

The kingdom into which Elizabeth of York was born was a land of prosperity, according to an Italian observer writing in 1500: 'The riches of England are greater than those of any other country in Europe. This is owing, in the first place, to the great fertility of the soil, which is such that, with the exception of wine, they import nothing from abroad for their subsistence.' The export of tin brought large sums into the realm, 'but still more do they derive from their extraordinary abundance of wool. And everyone who makes a tour in the island will soon become aware of this great wealth, for there is no small innkeeper, however poor and humble he may be, who does not serve his table with silver dishes and drinking cups, and no one who has not in his house silver plate to the amount of £100 [£50,000]. But above all are their riches displayed in the church treasures ... You may therefore imagine what the decorations of these enormously rich Benedictine, Carthusian and Cistercian monasteries must be. These are, indeed, more like baronial palaces than religious houses.'[9] And all, of course, would be swept away within seventy years of Elizabeth's birth, on the orders of her son. But for now, England was celebrated as 'the ringing isle' because of its many churches, abbeys and priories.

Much more of the land was covered by forest and woodland than it is now. The country was largely rural and given over to agriculture; as the Italian perceived, it had become prosperous through the export of wool and, latterly, woollen cloth. The people were often turbulent, unruly and vociferous – especially when it came to new taxes – and it was said that while the French vice was lechery, the English vice was treachery. The latter were perceived to be lazy – 'it is received as a prescript that they should sweat by no means' – and gluttonous: 'though they live in hovels, they eat like lords'. Most people lived in the country and society was generally localised. It was the upper classes and merchants who travelled.

Elizabeth would have learned early on in life that she was a very special little girl. Her father was the King, whose person was regarded as sacred. Divinely appointed to rule, he had been invested at his coronation with a sanctity that set him apart from ordinary mortals and bestowed on him the grace to govern with a wisdom denied to others. The royal prerogative was believed to be the will of God working through the will of the King.

The court over which King Edward presided, and in which Elizabeth grew up, was a magnificent one – 'the most splendid court that could be found in all Christendom'.[10] The royal family were its central focus, so Elizabeth would have grown up with a sense of her importance in the world. It would have seemed a crowded world to a young child – Edward IV's household numbered about 800 persons or more, not counting the members of his Queen's separate establishment. The court was itinerant, with the King dividing his time between a dozen of his palaces (most of them in the Thames Valley) according to the demands of state, the hunting to be had, or the need for cleansing a house after hundreds of courtiers and servants had tested its capacity for drainage to the limits.

Elizabeth would have become used to travel from infancy. The royal household would regularly wend its cumbersome way about the country, taking with it a long train of servants, carts and pack-horses laden with furniture, tapestries, personal belongings and state papers, all packed in chests, coffers and bags. The royal women and children travelled either by barge – the Thames being the main highway through London – or in covered horse-drawn coaches, like wagons, with four wheels, which could not have been very comfortable, as they were unsprung; or in smaller versions called litters, chariots, or 'chairs'. A household could travel an average of twenty-six miles a day, depending on the state of the roads. Most were little more than tracks, with a few surviving Roman exceptions, and their condition depended on the weather and the public-spiritedness of the parish authorities or landowners who were supposed to maintain them. It was for this reason that royalty often preferred, where possible, to travel by river.

In his tastes, King Edward followed the dictates of the court of Burgundy, which at that time led the rest of northern Europe in art, architecture, style, dress, manners and court ceremonial. He understood the value of magnificence that underpinned Burgundian court culture, and spent lavishly on clothing, jewels, plate, and tapestries from the Low Countries, but it was not until later in his reign that he was able to patronise the arts and indulge his passion for building. Today, the Perpendicular glory of St George's Chapel, Windsor, and the great hall at Eltham Palace bear witness to the largely vanished splendours of his reign.

Elizabeth grew up to know these places well, especially the Palace of Westminster. Opposite stood Westminster Abbey, where kings were crowned and many of her royal forebears were buried. Elizabeth would have grown up to know the neighbouring City of London well too. 'All the beauty of this island is confined to London,' wrote the anonymous Italian in 1500.[11] It was one of the greatest cities in Christendom, prosperous and teeming, its skyline dominated by the soaring Gothic edifice of St Paul's Cathedral and the spires of over eighty churches. About 60–75,000 of England's estimated population of three or four million people lived in the City, which possessed 'all the advantages to be desired in a maritime town' and was a flourishing mercantile centre. 'On the banks of the Thames are enormous warehouses for imported goods; also numerous cranes of remarkable size to unload merchandise from ships . . . Whatever there is in the City, it all belongs to craftsmen and merchants',[12] such as would supply Elizabeth with luxury goods all her life.

In buildings of timber or brick, 'the Londoners live comfortably'. The City abounded 'with every article of luxury, as well as with the necessaries of life. In a single street, named the Strand, there are fifty-two goldsmiths' shops.' This was especially remarkable to a foreigner because the citizens were not noblemen or gentlemen, but 'persons of low degree and artificers',[13] many made wealthy by trade. The City authorities were fiercely protective of their liberties.

Around 1500, the Scots poet William Dunbar was so impressed

by London, 'sovereign of cities', that he wrote a long poem in praise of it, of which this is an extract:

> Strong be thy walls that about thee stand;
> Wise be the people that within thee dwell;
> Fresh be thy river with his lusty strands;
> Blithe be thy churches, well sounding be thy bells;
> Rich be thy merchants in substance that excels;
> Fair be their wives, right lovesome, white and small;
> Clear be thy virgins, lusty under kirtles;
> London, thou art the flower of cities all.

The luxurious court in which the Princess grew up was dominated by two opposing factions: Warwick and the Wydevilles. The latter, and their connections, were especially prominent in the Queen's household, and their influence on the young Elizabeth and her siblings should not be underestimated.

Her mother, Queen Elizabeth, was confounding her critics and adapting to her role with grace and dignity. In every respect but her background she was a model consort. As the years passed, she proved that she could fulfil her royal duties as well as any born princess and use her influence in beneficial ways. She was pious and charitable; she ran her household efficiently and lived within her means. She enjoyed the King's absolute trust and, having resolved to turn an unseeing eye to his many infidelities, she retained his respect and affection. Thus she was highly influential behind the scenes – and it was this that Warwick and others continued to resent, along with the power enjoyed by her kinsmen.

Not since the aggrandisement of the Savoyard relatives of Henry III's unpopular consort, Eleanor of Provence, in the thirteenth century had the English court witnessed such large-scale promotion of a queen's relations.[14] For the King was advancing his legion of in-laws by securing for them the best matches the aristocracy could offer. He built up the power of the Wydevilles by these marriages, and by bestowing on them titles and offices, while the Queen 'attracted to her party many strangers, and introduced them to court, so that they alone should manage the public and private business of the Crown' through their power to 'give or sell offices, and rule the very King himself'.[15] That power was steadily increasing, 'to the exaltation of the Queen and the displeasure of the whole realm'.[16] While some nobles were eager to mate with the new Queen's relations, seeing such marriages as a means to advancement and royal favour, others – especially Warwick – were scandalised and resentful, for they regarded the Wydevilles as too lowborn for such honours[17] and influence, which was then considered the privilege of the nobility, not upwardly mobile *parvenus*.

Naturally, the Queen was blamed for leading the King astray; she was seen as grasping and interfering, and responsible for the aggressive promotion of her relations and their undue influence with Edward. The Duke of Milan was informed that, 'since her coronation, [the Queen] has always exerted herself to aggrandise her relations. She has five brothers and as many sisters, and has brought things to such a pass that they have the entire government of this realm, to such an extent that the rest of the lords about the government were one with the Earl of Warwick, who has always been great, and deservedly so.'[18] Even though there may have been some exaggeration in foreign reports of the 1460s, twenty years later we find that the Wydevilles were still 'detested by the nobles because they, who were ignoble or newly made, were advanced beyond those who far excelled them in breeding and wisdom',[19] a viewpoint in keeping with the social and cultural sensibilities of the age.

The unpopularity of the Wydevilles centred chiefly upon the aggrandisement of the Queen's father and elder brothers (and later her sons by her first marriage), which led to the whole family being vilified. Yet the Wydevilles were not without virtues or political strengths, even if they were rapacious. Of Elizabeth's uncles, Anthony, the Lord Treasurer of England, was an erudite man of many talents, and Lionel, who became Bishop of Salisbury, was an Oxford-educated canon lawyer.

The power of the Wydevilles was everywhere acknowledged. Appearing one day in 1469 equipped with walking boots and a staff, King Edward's fool jested to his master's face, 'Upon my faith, Sir, I have passed through many countries of your realm, and in places that I have passed the Rivers have been so high that I could barely scape through them!'[20] Yet the Wydeville men were loyal to Edward IV and served him well in the various capacities to which he appointed them; and they did not dominate in his counsels to the exclusion of all others, for Warwick, William, Lord Hastings, and John Howard, Duke of Norfolk, remained highly influential in Edward's inner circle of advisers.

Elizabeth's grandparents were an attractive couple. Lord Rivers had been 'renowned for being the most handsome knight in England'[21] and Jacquetta of Luxembourg was 'an exceedingly handsome gentlewoman'.[22] She had retained her title and rank, and remained first lady in the land until Henry VI married Margaret of Anjou in 1445. She had borne Wydeville sixteen children, of whom Queen Elizabeth was the eldest. During the first phase of the Wars of the Roses, the Wydevilles had naturally supported the House of Lancaster: Lord Rivers and his eldest son, Anthony, had fought for Henry VI at Towton. After Edward IV became king in 1461, they speedily changed sides, and Edward pardoned Rivers for 'all manner of offences and trespasses done against us'. Jacquetta, Duchess of Bedford, was frequently at court during Elizabeth's childhood, so the Princess must have come to know her grandmother well.

She probably grew up with only dim memories of her maternal grandfather, Richard Wydeville, who died when she was three. He had been created Earl Rivers in the year of her birth, to 'the displeasure of the whole kingdom'.[23] Having distinguished himself fighting in France under Henry V and Bedford, he had since risen high on his own abilities. Yet his enemies never allowed this man whom Warwick's father had sneeringly called 'knave's son' to forget his humble origins, and there were accusations that he had been 'made by marriage'.[24] His reputation was compounded by his being rapacious and vengeful, and he was not above using extortion to get what he wanted.

Elizabeth Wydeville was to bear the King ten children. On 11 August 1467, at Windsor Castle, she was delivered of the second, another daughter, Mary, fair-haired and blue-eyed.[25] The Queen's mother, the Duchess of Bedford, came to court to assist at the lying-in. The new Princess was baptised at Westminster in the presence of the French ambassador, with Thomas Bourchier, Archbishop of Canterbury, acting as one of the sponsors.

On 9 October 1467, at Westminster, the King granted 'for life' to his twenty-month-old elder daughter, 'the Princess Elizabeth, the manor of Great Linford, county of Buckingham, lately belonging to James [Butler], Earl of Wiltshire, and in the King's hands'.[26] Butler had been executed in 1461 and his titles confiscated to the Crown. It is unlikely that Elizabeth ever visited Great Linford; the King would have assigned it to her so that the manor rents could maintain her during her childhood. She held it until 1474, when it was sold to Gerard Caniziani, a London merchant.[27]

The manor of Sheen, a royal palace in Surrey, had been granted to the Queen in 1467, for life, probably as a nursery for her children, and by 9 October 1468, the two little princesses, Elizabeth and Mary, were living at Sheen Palace in the care of Margery, Lady Berners, their lady mistress. On that date, the Queen was granted £400 per annum (£200,200) for their expenses until such time as they married.[28]

The Italian visitor was not the only foreigner struck by 'the want of affection strongly manifested' by the English towards their children; 'for everyone, however rich he be, sends his children into the houses of others . . . And on enquiring the reason for the severity, they answered that they did it in order that their children might learn better manners.'[29] There was some concept of the innocence of childhood, but fifteenth-century parents were more concerned about civilising their children and preventing them from falling into sin and wantonness; they recognised that mothers might not be as strict as others less close to their children: 'let not the feminine pity of your wives destroy your children, and pamper them not at home . . . Dandle them not too dearly lest folly fasten on them.'[30] There were also, of course, many advantages to be gained from placing offspring in great establishments, even as apprentices.

Royal children were not sent into noble households, as aristocratic children were, but at an early age were assigned households of their own, away from the court, and their day-to-day upbringing was supervised, not by their parents, but by the lady mistress. Giving royal children separate establishments not only reflected the magnificence of a ruler, but protected his infant offspring from the health hazards they risked in London and the court. Nursery palaces were usually outside the City 'because, the air [in the country] being somewhat at large, the place is healthy; and the noise not so much, and so consequently quiet'.[31]

Sheen Palace dated from the early fourteenth century, when the original manor house had been owned by Isabella of France, wife of Edward II. After her death in 1358, her son Edward III had spent a fortune converting it into a fabulous palace. It became his favourite residence, and he died there in 1377. Appropriately, the name 'Sheen' meant 'beautiful' or 'bright'. In 1395, after his beloved queen, Anne of Bohemia, had died there of plague the year before, Richard II had the palace 'utterly destroyed'. In 1414, on an adjacent site, Henry V erected what his chronicler, Thomas of Elmham, described as a 'delightful mansion, of skilful and costly architecture, becoming to the royal dignity'. Completed by Henry VI, and moated, it was built of Caen stone around two courts, with the royal Privy Lodgings overlooking the River Thames, and was decorated in brilliant hues with stained-glass windows in azure, red and purple tones. Edward IV's *rose-en-soleil* badge featured prominently in the ceiling mouldings alongside 'antelopes, swans, harts, hinds' and lions.[32] This was the house in which Elizabeth spent part of her childhood.

The daily regimen followed by Elizabeth and Mary was probably similar to that later laid down by the King for their brother, the future Edward V, when he was three years old, and the routine described in the household ordinances of their paternal uncle, George, Duke of Clarence, Edward IV's younger brother.[33] The children would have been roused around 6 a.m., so that they could 'get up at a convenient hour according to [their] age' in time to attend Matins in their bedchamber. Then the bell rang for them to go to Mass, which was sung by the household chaplain in their chapel or their closet. The regular observance of the liturgical services was seen as essential for the children of the King. Immediately after Mass they had breakfast, which might have consisted of bread, ale, fish, meat, butter or eggs. Dinner was at 10 or 11 a.m.; it was 'honourably served' with dishes 'borne by worshipful folks' and liveried esquires, and might have lasted for up to two hours. During mealtimes, edifying and noble tales would have been read out to the royal sisters. That the young princesses lived in some state is evidenced by the appointment of a knight of the trencher and a page of the chamber to be in continual attendance upon them.[34]

After dinner, the girls would have been expected to wash and perhaps have a nap. Later, drinks and bread were served before the bell summoned everyone to Evensong. Supper would be served at 4 p.m. Evening was customarily a time of 'honest disports', recreation such as games and music, until bedtime, which for Elizabeth and Mary was probably at 8 p.m., after a snack called 'all night' (comprising bread, ale or wine) had been served. Although their attendants were no doubt ordered to 'enforce themselves' to make the children 'merry and joyous towards bed', household accounts of the period contain barely any references to toys.[35]

After the traverse – the door curtain – was drawn at 8 p.m., no

one but the princesses' own attendants might enter their chamber.
At night, a candle or cresset would be left burning there, and they
slumbered safely, for the outer gates were barred at 9 p.m. in winter
and 10 p.m. in summer, porters were on watch, and watchmen
patrolled three or four times a night, checking every chamber. Their
brother would have someone watching over him all night, lest disease
rob the King of his 'precious son and gift', and it follows that his
older sisters' attendants watched over them too.[36]

Religious instruction began at a very early age, and children were
expected to know their psalter by the age of four.[37] Feast days –
notably Candlemas, Easter, St George's Day, Whitsun, All Hallows
and Christmas, as well as a crowded calendar of saints' days – were
marked by special services in chapel, sermons and entertainments,
and the children made offerings at Mass on holy days. On Maundy
Thursday the girls would have given gifts to the poor; on Good
Friday they would have been taught to creep to the Cross on their
knees. During Lent and Advent they were expected to fast or abstain
from meat. At New Year they would have received Yuletide gifts, as
was customary; on Twelfth Night they would have been allowed to
join the feasting and revelry; and no doubt they laughed at the antics
of the Lord of Misrule on the Feast of the Epiphany. Such was the
cycle of their year.

Religion played a major role in Elizabeth's upbringing. The great
houses in which she was reared had chapels, oratories and closets with
sumptuous furnishings and tapestries, brilliant stained glass, illuminated
psalters, primers, missals, offices and other devotional books, rich altar
cloths, bejewelled crucifixes, statues of the Virgin and the saints, painted
retables, gleaming vestments, gold and silver chalices and candlesticks,
carpets, chairs for the King and Queen, and an organ. Often the
royal pew was in a gallery above the body of the chapel where
the household worshipped. Elizabeth's day would have been
punctuated by bells announcing Mass and the liturgical hours, her
ears regularly assailed by the singing of antiphons and polyphony,
her nose used to the smell of incense. Small wonder that she grew
up to be deeply pious.

Sometimes the little princesses were brought to court, to be
paraded at festivals and state visits. There they joined their mother's
retinue, learning by her example (and that of her ladies), manners,
music, singing, dancing, embroidery and anything else considered
needful to prepare them for their future roles as royal wives and

mothers and the ornaments of courts. They would have been dressed in miniature versions of the luxurious attire worn by ladies of high rank, learning as they grew older to manage heavy fabrics, long court trains and elaborate headdresses. Good deportment was taught from an early age.

To the young princesses, their parents – whom they did not see often – would have appeared as awe-inspiring figures, distant and worthy of the highest reverence, not only because they were royal, but also because children were brought up to revere, honour and obey their parents, and be dutiful towards them all their lives. How much more daunting that would have been when your parents were the King and Queen. Each evening, whenever they were together, they would kneel before their father and mother and crave their blessing, which was given 'in the name of the Father, the Son and the Holy Ghost'.[38]

Good manners and courtesy were drummed into them. *The Babees' Book* of 1475, a manual of courtesy for the young, exhorts children to cut their bread with a knife, eat quietly, wipe their mouths and hands after drinking, share the dishes served to them with guests, 'and in your feeding look ye appear goodly, and keep your tongue from jangling, and always advance yourself in virtue. Sweet children, always have your delight in courtesy and in gentleness, and eschew boisterousness with all your might.' The young were taught that they must never lean their elbows on the table, pick their noses, teeth or nails at mealtimes, eat food with their knives, or pick up meat with their fingers. The humanist scholar and theologian, Desiderius Erasmus, insisted that a child should have 'a kind, modest and honest look'; it should not speak unless spoken to, have a furrowed brow or a dirty nose – signs of bad breeding – or wipe its nose on its clothing, or suck in or puff out its cheeks, stick out its tongue, yawn, laugh immoderately, spit, or be seen with messy hair or uncleaned teeth. Swearing was seen as particularly offensive, and children and servants were often punished for it. Elizabeth's elders would have enforced rules like these. Naughty children were often beaten, and it was felt that indulging or spoiling a child would lead to the need for physical chastisement later: 'who spareth the rod hateth the child'.[39]

Edward IV's officers were instructed to restrain the chatter of young guests at the King's table. There is some evidence that royal mealtimes were kept in silence, or possibly only a low murmur of conversation was permitted. The King was insistent that no 'custom-able swearer, brawler, backbiter, common hazarder or adulterer' be allowed to work in his children's households, and all conversation in their presence was to be of 'virtue, honour, cunning, wisdom and deeds of worship [renown]'. Those who came late to Matins were punished by being served only bread and water at dinner, and any who drew weapons in the household, or went to law without the permission of the Queen's council, were to be clapped in the stocks or dismissed.[40]

Like most females, the Princess and her sisters would have been reared to an awareness that they had been born of an inferior sex, and that consequently their freedoms were limited – although the example of their mother would have demonstrated that women of rank could be enormously influential, albeit with the consent of their menfolk. Medieval women were regarded variously as weak and passive; or as domineering harridans, temptresses or whores. It was held that young girls needed to be protected from themselves so that they could be nurtured as chaste and submissive maidens and mothers.

The princesses would have grown up thinking it normal that their marriages would be arranged for them, and that it was their duty to render obedience first to their parents, and later to their future husbands. Marriage was seen as a desirable estate for both sexes, and for most women it defined their role in life, for with monasticism in decline, relatively few became nuns in this era. It was expected that royal and aristocratic women would marry, and marry well; and it was rare to find one who died a spinster, unless she had become a nun. Thus the upbringing of girls was geared towards finding a suitable husband, one of the right social class and standing, and it was incumbent largely upon mothers to ensure that they did, and to see that their daughters grew up chaste, discreet, humble, pious and obedient. In the early years, queens, of course, delegated much of this role to the lady mistress of the nursery, but they did usually take a keen interest in preparing their daughters for marriage.

A girl's future status, happiness and success depended largely on the marriage she made, her relationship with her husband, and her ability to perform her wifely duties. Most aristocratic brides brought with them dowries consisting of lands, property and perhaps money; if they were royal, their persons would be used to cement political treaties between princes, to secure peace, prosperity or an ally in war.

A father marrying off his daughter would also look to her future financial security, negotiating a jointure, or living, for her maintenance during her married life and in the event of her widowhood; often it comprised rents from estates, of which even a queen's jointure was largely made up. Upon marriage, a woman's property and title (if she had one) transferred to her husband; she retained no control over any of it.

The desirability of a wife therefore lay not in her looks or character, but in her wealth and breeding. Marriage was essentially a contract. Love was not a prime consideration: it was hoped that it would develop after marriage, and indeed it was the duty of a wife to love her husband and to remain unquestionably faithful. Nevertheless, there is evidence that many parents did care that their children were happily married: they allowed the prospective spouses time to get to know and love each other, and on occasions would not even proceed with the wedding if either objected. At the other end of the scale there were parents who beat their daughters into submission,[41] while nearly all frowned on clandestine marriages, and kept idle hands and minds busy to avoid them being unsuitably diverted by bold and importunate young men.

Once wed, a married woman had no legal identity of her own. She was expected to render obedience to her husband as her lord and head, for he was to be to her as Christ was to the Church, and he had the legal right to punish and chastise her. Towards him she was to show love, gentleness and submission.

Nevertheless, women of Elizabeth's class could exercise power, patronage and authority; they might even venture into politics. Yet all these advantages came only through marriage: what influence and autonomy they enjoyed was entirely at the discretion or behest of their husbands, and not all husbands were prepared to allow their wives such leeway.

Such was the future that awaited Elizabeth of York, but the most important event on her horizon at this time was not some distant marriage but the arrival of her sister, Cecily, on 20 March 1469 at Westminster. The birth of a third daughter, despite her being 'very handsome', was a disappointment to the King. He and his lords 'rejoiced exceedingly, though they would have preferred a son',[42] especially now, when Edward's throne was under threat. With a son to follow him, a monarch's position was invariably more secure. No one imagined for a moment that Elizabeth, the King's eldest daughter, might rule after him as queen. Her value was purely matrimonial.

Events of which the young Elizabeth can have had little awareness, but which would adversely affect her life, were gathering momentum. By 1468, rumours were rife of conflict between 'the Earl [of Warwick] and the Queen's blood'. Warwick could not stomach 'the great rule which the Lord Rivers and his blood bare at that time within the realm',[43] and could not conceal his anger when, in 1468, the King married his sister Margaret to Charles the Bold, Duke of Burgundy. Warwick, who pursued Charles the Bold for years 'with a most deadly hatred',[44] had favoured an alliance with France, Burgundy's enemy, but the Wydevilles had used 'their utmost endeavours to promote the marriage, and were favouring other designs to which he was strongly opposed'. It was this that finally alienated the Earl,[45] and drove him, in 1469, to form an alliance with the King's disaffected younger brother, George, Duke of Clarence, whom Elizabeth had displaced in the line of succession; whereupon the two men began intriguing against Edward IV.

Clarence was then twenty, tall, fair and regal. He had a surface charm and 'a mastery of popular eloquence',[46] but these barely masked a weak, discontented and vicious character. Edward had been very generous to him, but Clarence was jealous and hungry for power. Warwick now bolstered Clarence's pretensions by offering to overthrow Edward, make him king and marry him to Isabella, the elder of his two daughters; as Warwick had no son, these girls were the greatest heiresses in England. Edward's brothers, Clarence and Richard, Duke of Gloucester, had repeatedly sought them in marriage, but the King had consistently refused, foreseeing that such alliances would enhance the already disconcerting power of the Nevilles. Naturally this had given Warwick further cause for grievance.

In July 1469 Clarence openly defied the King and married Isabella Neville in Calais, where Warwick was Captain. Then he and Warwick sailed back to England, where they rose in arms against Edward IV, whom they took prisoner at the Battle of Edgecote in August 1469. They then spread the story that the King was a bastard, the son of Cecily, Duchess of York, and an unnamed English archer.

This story has been much debated in recent years, after historian Dr Michael Jones claimed in 2002 that it was the truth.[47] His theory naturally has a crucial bearing on the legitimate right of Edward IV and his children, including Elizabeth, to inherit the crown. Sensationally, Dr Jones asserted that Edward's bastardy compromised every sovereign's title since 1461, and that the true king of Great Britain should be Michael Abney-Hastings, an Australian forklift-truck driver who is descended from George, Duke of Clarence. But in 1485 Henry VII was confirmed as king by Parliament, *before* he married Elizabeth of York, the Yorkist heiress. His title did not legally depend on hers, and thus he and his descendants were – and still are – the lawful occupants of the throne.

Dr Jones claimed that Edward IV, who was born on 28 April 1442, was conceived when Richard, Duke of York, was away fighting the French at Pontoise, near Paris, at which time Cecily Neville was allegedly having an affair with an English archer called Blaybourne, of the Rouen garrison. What Dr Jones discovered was an entry in the registers of Rouen Cathedral under the year 1441, showing that York's campaign in Pontoise lasted longer than historians had previously thought. The registers also revealed that Edward was christened in the private chapel of Rouen Castle, while his brother, Edmund, born in May 1443, also at Rouen, was afforded a bigger christening in the cathedral – from which Dr Jones inferred that he was probably the true heir.

York must have known about the contrast between the christenings; it was probably his decision to make more of Edmund's, as he had named his second son heir to his French lands, so a high-profile baptism in Rouen was appropriate. It is scarcely credible that, knowing Edward was not his son, he arranged a grander christening for the true-born Edmund – thus publicly proclaiming his cuckoldry to the world. He is more likely to have disowned Edward, and his failure to do so would be incomprehensible in an age in which the laws of inheritance were rigidly observed and enforced by the aristocracy, and blood descent was of prime importance. The landed classes took such a serious view of adultery in a noblewoman that the law provided for her to be executed at her husband's behest, and even kings acknowledged that the husband's word was law, and preferred not to interfere.[48] It is hard to believe that York, who was proud of his royal lineage, would have overlooked the presence of a cuckoo in the nest who stood to inherit everything he had.

The quiet baptism can easily be explained by a need for haste, if there was concern because the infant was premature or too weak or sickly to survive. In support of this, we have Cecily's obstetric history. Before Edward was born, she had produced two children, one of whom had died soon after birth in 1441; four of the children she bore later would also die young. The loss of five children out of twelve, while not uncommon for the time, might suggest that there was a history of premature birth, which may be one reason why Edward was christened quietly.

There are other problems with Dr Jones's theory, not least of which is the fact that Cecily's whereabouts in the crucial period are unknown. There is no primary evidence from the 1440s that mentions Blaybourne. The earliest historical reference to Edward IV's alleged bastardy occurs in 1469,[49] when Warwick and Clarence used – and probably invented – it as propaganda in order to have him deposed. No one seems to have taken their assertion seriously. Warwick had earlier spread false rumours that Margaret of Anjou's son was the fruit of adultery. Clarence, it seems, was ready to seize on any pretext to impugn his brother's line so that he could claim the throne, and even asserted that Edward IV's marriage was invalid because he had violated 'established custom' by marrying a widow.[50]

According to Philippe de Commines, in 1475 a lord entertaining Louis XI of France by impersonating Charles the Bold, Duke of Burgundy, had the Duke asserting that Edward's father had been an archer called Blaybourne; this was in the wake of Edward making a profitable treaty with Louis, Charles's enemy, and it sounds more like a joke or malicious gossip than a statement of fact. In 1478, when Clarence's allegation about Edward's bastardy was raised in Parliament, the King publicly refuted it. In 1483, when Edward's youngest brother, Richard, Duke of Gloucester, raised the matter again and defamed his mother in a bid to seize the throne,[51] Londoners gave the allegation such short shrift that he had quickly to come up with another pretext.

For some the Blaybourne story is bolstered by a tale told by Dominic Mancini, the Italian who visited England in 1483 and wrote that year: 'the story runs' – which suggests he gave it little credence – that in 1464, outraged at Edward IV's marriage to Elizabeth Wydeville, Cecily Neville 'fell into such a frenzy that she offered to submit to a public inquiry, and asserted that Edward was not the offspring of her husband, the Duke of York, but was conceived in adultery, and therefore in no wise worthy of the honour of kingship'. We do not know how Mancini learned of Cecily's outburst of nearly twenty years earlier, but his account reads as if he himself knew it was merely far-fetched gossip. Certainly this was a strange claim for the King's mother to make, however angry: one that compromised her son's title to the throne, her own reputation and the rights of any grandchildren born of the King's marriage; and it seems inconceivable that she would publicly brand herself an adulteress. Maybe Cecily, who was used to 'ruling the King as she pleases'[52] and was incensed at his misalliance, was so hysterical with rage that she said the first thing she could think of that could hurt him – if, of course, she said anything at all, for Mancini probably picked up on propaganda deliberately circulated in 1483 in support of Richard of Gloucester's claim to the throne: the official line then was that Richard was the only true surviving son of his father.

Gloucester, short, slight and dark, was said to have resembled Richard, Duke of York, in looks; Edward, tall and fairer in colouring, did not. This was said to be evidence that he was not York's son. But Edward was very like his sister Elizabeth in appearance, if the similarity between his portraits and her tomb effigy in Wingfield Church, Suffolk, is anything to go by. Possibly they both favoured their mother.

Finally, there is the matter of dates. If Edward was a full-term baby, conception would probably have taken place between 2 and 10 August 1441; but if he was premature, obviously it would have occurred later. York was campaigning in Pontoise from 14 July to 21 August, after which he returned to Rouen in triumph. It is well within the bounds of probability that, in the flush of reunion, he got his wife pregnant with a child who was born prematurely. That is the likeliest theory, given the dates and the quiet, possibly hurried, christening. The fact that Edward survived to be a healthy adult may be due to the fact that he was only about two weeks premature. A margin of what might have been only eleven days cannot have any credible bearing on his paternity.

Without any evidence of her whereabouts, it cannot just be assumed that Cecily was staying in Rouen during the Pontoise campaign. The diverse birthplaces of her twelve children show that she often travelled around with her husband, which suggests that they were close and wanted to be together. Even if York was a hundred miles away, it was possible for a rider to cover that distance in a short time; in 1202, for example, King John marched an army more than eighty miles in two days. Cecily could have travelled to be near her husband, even if he could not visit her.

The most crucial piece of evidence is to be found in Cecily's will, made shortly before her death in 1495, in which she refers to her husband York as 'father unto the most Christian prince my lord and son, King Edward IV'.[53] Her other sons, George and Richard – the ones who had impugned her reputation by publicly alleging her adultery – are not mentioned in that document.[54] It is unlikely that the devout Cecily, knowing she was soon to face divine judgement, would have set forth such a falsehood in her last testament.

At the time of Edgecote Elizabeth Wydeville was visiting Norwich with at least two of her daughters, of whom Elizabeth was probably one. They had been received with pageants, banners, songs and ceremony, and were lodged in the house of the Friars Preachers. There they received the dreadful news that Warwick had not only emerged victorious at Edgecote, but had taken the King prisoner and had the Queen's father, Lord Rivers, and her brother, John Wydeville, beheaded without trial.

Having a grandfather beheaded was shocking enough – although, at three, one hopes that Elizabeth was spared too many details – but the impact on her mother must have been profound, and it was compounded by the arrest that same month of the Duchess Jacquetta, who was accused of witchcraft. It was said she had used leaden images to bring about her daughter's marriage to the King and encompass Warwick's destruction. There was a political agenda to this, of course, but Jacquetta had sufficient friends to take up her cause with the King's Council. Soon afterwards the case was dismissed because a crucial witness refused to come forward to testify to having seen the images, but this unpleasant episode, and Rivers's execution, showed how far Edward's enemies were prepared to go to bring down the Wydevilles. Nevertheless, during Warwick's brief spell of power in August 1469, the Queen and her children were left unmolested, although Elizabeth Wydeville was permitted to keep only 'scant state'.[55]

Before long, however, Edward was a free man. There was little support for Warwick, and early that autumn problems on the Scottish border engaged his attention and his resources, and forced him to release the King. In September, Edward entered London in triumph, then began scheming to regain the support of the nobles. Although Elizabeth was not yet four years old, he had her proclaimed his heiress apparent – a move calculated to upset Clarence[56] – and dangled the carrot of her hand in marriage to his advantage. It was the fate of princesses to be the subject of alliances beneficial to the realm and to their royal fathers, but Elizabeth's marriage was a matter of prime importance, as she was the heiress to the throne until such time as the Queen bore a son. She might normally have been affianced to some great foreign prince, or the heir to a throne, but in the wake of the rebellion, urgent political considerations dictated the King's policy at this time. In the autumn of 1469, in a bid to retain the loyalty of a powerful ally, Edward created Warwick's brother, John Neville, Marquess of Montagu and offered Elizabeth as a bride for Neville's five-year-old son George – all in the hope that, were he himself to be killed, Neville would ensure that Elizabeth and George were crowned before Clarence could seize the throne. But this proposed marriage did not weigh heavily in the balance with Warwick.

By Christmas Warwick and Clarence had been pardoned and were back at Westminster. But Edward clearly did not trust them, and still suspected Clarence of having designs on his crown. On 5 January 1470 Elizabeth was formally betrothed to George Neville, whom Edward created Duke of Bedford the same day.[57] It is unlikely, however, that he ever intended that the marriage should go ahead; it was a desperate measure born of a desperate situation, and scant faith was placed in the union of these two children ever taking place.[58]

By the spring of 1470 the King had regained control of the government and denounced Warwick and Clarence as traitors. They fled abroad, only to begin plotting with Louis XI for the restoration of Henry VI. Louis, known as 'the Universal Spider' because of the skill with which he manipulated his enemies, was always eager to exploit Edward IV's troubles, and persuaded the exiled Margaret of Anjou into an unlikely alliance with Warwick.

On Friday, 8 June 1470, the Queen arrived with Elizabeth, then four, at Canterbury to join the King (who had come two days earlier) for a great celebration of the feast of Pentecost. Prior John Oxney and his monks received them all at the great door of the Abbey of St Augustine, and a service of thanksgiving followed. Elizabeth's uncle, Anthony Wydeville, Earl Rivers, arrived the next day, with other distinguished guests, and on the Sunday the Princess went in procession with her parents to High Mass, celebrated by Thomas Rotherham, Bishop of Rochester. Monday was spent at the abbey, attending High Mass and Vespers, then the Queen travelled back to London with Elizabeth, while Edward journeyed east to inspect the fortifications at Dover and Sandwich before rejoining them.[59]

During her visit to Canterbury, Elizabeth would surely have seen the shrine of St Thomas Becket, the martyred archbishop, which was adorned with jewels and valuable offerings, illuminated by candles and surrounded by a floor bearing the imprints of the knees of thousands of pilgrims. It would have made a lasting impression on a young child, especially if she was told of the many miracles the saint was said to have wrought. There is evidence that Elizabeth's devotion to St Thomas remained with her to the end of her life.[60]

In July, wanting to consolidate his alliance with Margaret of Anjou, Warwick urged the marriage of his fourteen-year-old daughter, Anne Neville, to Prince Edward of Lancaster. But Margaret was reluctant because, she said, 'she should find a more profitable advantage with England. And indeed, she showed unto the King of France a letter which she said was sent to her out of England last week, by the which was offered to her son my lady the Princess.'[61]

Elizabeth was, of course, betrothed to George Neville, and Edward IV would not break that betrothal until later, when George's father had gone over to Warwick;[62] but marrying Elizabeth to Edward of Lancaster would have been one way to prevent the marriage with Anne Neville, and might have averted a further war between Lancaster and York. No doubt Margaret envisaged her son being acknowledged as Edward IV's heir, for want of one of his own, and perhaps ascending the throne on the King's death. But Queen Elizabeth was expecting another child that might, this time, be a son, and there is no other evidence that Edward IV made such an approach to Margaret at this time;[63] her remark was probably a bluff, intended to extract better terms from Warwick. In July 1470, after King Louis and Warwick had put pressure on Margaret, her son married Anne Neville.

Elizabeth was four when her father was forced to flee his realm. In September 1470, as he prepared to deal with an invasion by the combined forces of Warwick and Queen Margaret, she and her sisters were taken by their mother to the Tower of London for safety. Anticipating such a crisis, the Queen had arranged for the Tower to be 'well victualled and fortified'.[64] Elizabeth Wydeville was then seven months pregnant with her fourth child. A luxurious chamber in the royal apartments was made ready for her confinement, but she was destined never to use it, for when Warwick invaded, his brother Montagu deserted Edward, and early in October the news was cried in London that the King and his youngest brother Gloucester had fled to the Low Countries with only the clothes on their backs. Hard on the heels of this came tidings that Warwick and Clarence were marching on London.

It must have been bewildering for Elizabeth and her sisters to be hurried in secrecy and silence by their mother and grandmother into a barge in the middle of the night and rowed upstream to Westminster. There they made their way past the palace to Westminster Abbey, where the distraught Queen 'registered herself as a sanctuary woman'.[65] She was eight months pregnant and must have been 'almost desperate of all comfort'[66] to have come to a place like St Peter's Sanctuary.

The sanctuary building was situated in the north-west corner of the Abbey precincts, at the end of St Margaret's churchyard, where Westminster Guildhall now stands. It had been built in the eleventh century by King Edward the Confessor, and was constructed of thick stone walls strong enough to withstand a siege; they were demolished only with difficulty in 1750, by which time the practice of claiming sanctuary had long fallen into disuse. One stout oak door led into a cruciform-shaped interior consisting of two chapels, one above the other. Debtors used the upper level, common felons the lower. At Westminster, the right of sanctuary extended to the adjoining close and churchyard.

Since the seventh century, anyone fleeing justice, oppression or the hostility of those in power could claim the right of sanctuary in a consecrated place, for there was a strong belief that holy ground was inviolable, and that anyone forcibly removing someone from sanctuary was guilty of sacrilege. Violation of the protection of sanctuary was punishable by excommunication.

The right of sanctuary was originally confined to churches, but later its limits were extended to church precincts, and sometimes even to a larger surrounding area. By Norman times there were two kinds of sanctuary in England: a general right of sanctuary conferred on every church, and a peculiar one granted by royal charter. General sanctuaries afforded forty days' protection only to those guilty of felonies. A convicted felon who sought sanctuary was afforded protection for thirty to forty days, after which, subject to certain severe conditions, he had to leave the kingdom within a specified time and take an oath not to return without the King's leave. Peculiars gave immunity for life, even to those accused of high or petty treason. The latter was enjoyed by at least twenty-two churches, including Westminster Abbey, which was the foremost sanctuary in England. Elizabeth was to spend, in total, more than a year of her life here.

The sanctuary was almost deserted when Elizabeth Wydeville arrived with her three daughters and her mother[67] and placed them and herself in the charge and protection of Thomas Milling, the Abbot of Westminster. A kindly, hospitable man, he would not hear of them lodging in the common sanctuary building, where they would rub shoulders with murderers and thieves; instead, he insisted they stay as his guests in his house, Cheyneygates, by the West Door of the Abbey, placing the three best rooms at their disposal and providing the Queen with several items 'for her comfort'.

Parts of medieval Cheyneygates survive today, notably two splendid rooms over the entrance to the cloisters – sufficient, despite wartime bombing and heavy restoration, to show that the Queen and her daughters were luxuriously housed while in sanctuary – and the sumptuous Jerusalem Chamber, the Abbot's principal apartment, then hung with rich tapestries, which was one of the rooms assigned to Elizabeth Wydeville. All date from the fourteenth century, making Cheyneygates the oldest surviving medieval house in London. The rest of the house, which now comprises the Deanery, has been rebuilt. The stone fireplace in the Jerusalem Chamber is Tudor, with a later overmantel, but the original ceiling displays Richard II's crowned initial. The panelling is nineteenth century. Henry IV, first sovereign of the House of Lancaster, had died in this room in 1413. Now it was to serve as the Queen's great chamber; she also had use of the Abbot's great hall with its minstrels' gallery, a privy chamber, which was probably used as a bedchamber, and the courtyard, which would afford Elizabeth and her sisters their only means of enjoying fresh air for some months to come. Had they but known it, they were effectively prisoners in a gilded cage, for their mother dared not leave – and with good reason.

Law and order had broken down in London, which seethed with unrest as felons left sanctuary to infest the streets, prisons were broken open, and mobs looted and rioted unchecked – all in the name of Warwick. The Queen, alarmed, immediately sent Abbot Milling to entreat the Lord Mayor and aldermen of London not to resist

Warwick's forces or do anything to provoke him, lest he force his way into the Abbey 'to despoil and kill her'.[68]

On 6 October Warwick and Clarence entered the City and took control of the Tower, whereupon the Mayor had no choice but to come to terms with them. They speedily restored order, and proclaimed the feeble Henry VI king once more, transferring him from his prison in the Tower to the opulent rooms vacated by the Queen. He would be formally restored to the throne on 30 October.

Warwick had little reason to love 'the Queen that was',[69] but he did not persecute women. Instead, he issued a proclamation forbidding his followers to defoul churches and sanctuaries in London and elsewhere, upon pain of death.[70] Despite this, the Queen evidently felt it was safer to stay in sanctuary with her daughters for the present; with the situation so volatile and uncertain, no one could predict how long they would have to remain there. Worse still, she was 'in great penury, forsaken of all her friends'[71] and 'in great trouble',[72] lacking even 'such things as mean men's wives have in superfluity'. A London butcher, John Gould, came to her rescue. He loyally donated 'half a beef and two muttons weekly for the sustention of her household'. A kindly fishmonger provided victuals for Fridays and fast days. As the Queen neared her confinement, Elizabeth Greystoke, Lady Scrope, was appointed by Henry VI's Council to wait on her, and paid £10 (£5,000) for her services.[73] Marjory (or Margaret) Cobb, who had delivered Princess Cecily and been rewarded with a pension,[74] was brought in to act as midwife, and the Queen's own physician, Dr Dominic de Sirego, was permitted to attend her.

On the feast of All Saints, 1 November 1470,[75] in Cheyneygates, the Queen 'was delivered of a son, in very poor estate'.[76] It seemed ironic that the long-awaited heir should be born during his father's exile, yet 'from this circumstance derived some hope and consolation for such persons as remained faithful in their allegiance to Edward'. King Henry's adherents, however, 'thought the birth of the child of no importance'.[77]

The little Prince was christened in the Abbot's house by the Sub-Prior, 'without pomp', and 'with no more ceremony than if he had been a poor man's son'; the Duchess of Bedford and Lady Scrope were godmothers at the font, while the Abbot and the Prior, John Eastney – in the absence of anyone of higher rank – stood as godfathers. Young Elizabeth bore the chrisom – the robe put on a child after baptism to symbolise its purification from sin. The infant was named Edward, after his father.

Elizabeth and her mother and siblings 'a long time abode and sojourned at Westminster': they were to endure another five months in sanctuary, 'in right great trouble, sorrow and heaviness'. The Queen was painfully aware that her son might be seen as a threat to the new régime. She knew that 'the security of her person rested solely on the great franchise of that holy place'. But Warwick left them largely unmolested, and the Queen 'sustained' her ordeal 'with all manner of patience belonging to any creature, and as constantly as ever was seen by any person of such high estate to endure'.[78] Yet 'what pain had she, what labour and anguish did she endure? To hear of her weeping it was great pity,' and 'when she remembered the King she was woe'[79] – and doubtless Elizabeth was too, witnessing her mother in such distress.

Spurred on by news of the birth of his heir, and enriched by funds provided by the Duke of Burgundy, Edward IV began gathering a fleet and raising an army, intent on reclaiming his kingdom. In the spring of 1471, he invaded England, which fell to him shire by shire. Clarence abandoned Warwick and made peace with his brother. On 9 April, marching south from Dunstable, Edward sent 'very comfortable messages to his Queen'[80] in sanctuary, giving her great cause for hope that he might prevail over his enemies. Two days later, he marched into London unhindered and reclaimed his throne in St Paul's Cathedral. Henry VI was again deposed, and returned to the Tower.

That day, after Edward had given thanks in Westminster Abbey for his victory, and come in procession to the Palace of Westminster, the Queen and her children were escorted there from the sanctuary. There followed a joyful reunion, which proved almost too much for Elizabeth Wydeville, and Edward had to comfort her, for she had been deeply affected by her long ordeal in sanctuary. 'Ne'theless, she had brought into the world, to the King's greatest joy, a fair son, a prince, wherewith she presented her husband at his coming, to his heart's singular comfort and gladness.'[81] Edward was to refer to his son and heir as 'God's precious sending and gift, and our most desired treasure'.

Elizabeth must have been overjoyed to see her father again. A contemporary poem celebrated this touching reunion:

The King comforted the Queen and other ladies eke [also],
His sweet babes full tenderly he did kiss;
The young Prince he beheld, and in his arms did bear;
Thus his bale [anguish] turned him to bliss.
After sorrow, joy, the course of the world is.
The sight of his babes released part of his woe;
Thus the will of God in everything is do.[82]

In July 1471, the King would appoint Abbot Milling chancellor to Prince Edward in reward for his kindness to the Queen and her children while they were in sanctuary, and in 1474 he made him Bishop of Hereford. In return for his 'true heart', Butcher Gould was given permission to load his ship, *The Trinity of London*, at any port and to trade freely with her for a year. Dr de Sirego was paid £40 (£20,000) for attending the Queen's confinement, and Mother Cobb received a pension of £12 (£6,000) for her services.[83] In 1478, in thanksgiving for the safe delivery of her son in the most difficult circumstances, the Queen founded a chapel in Westminster Abbey dedicated to St Erasmus, the protector of women in childbirth.

That night, 'the King returned to London, and the Queen with him', and their children. They stayed at Baynard's Castle, the London residence of Edward's mother, Cecily Neville, Duchess of York.[84] Here young Elizabeth found herself enjoying her first taste of freedom in over five months. In the evening the King and Queen attended divine service, and the next day, 11 April, the royal family kept Good Friday with all solemnity.[85]

Afterwards the King 'took advice of the great lords of his blood and others of his Council' on his next strategy,[86] and later that day the Queen, her children, her mother and the Duchess of York, accompanied by Earl Rivers and the Archbishop of Canterbury, moved to the royal palace in the Tower of London for safety, while the King marched north to meet his enemies. On Easter Sunday, 13 April, Edward defeated Warwick's forces at the Battle of Barnet, leaving the mighty Warwick, whom men had called 'Kingmaker', dead on the field. Warwick's brother, Lord Montagu, whose son Elizabeth was to have wed, was also slain.

But Queen Margaret and her son were still at large, recruiting men. Relentlessly Edward's forces marched west, pursuing them towards the River Severn, to prevent them from linking up with

Lancastrian supporters in Wales, and on 4 May he decisively defeated them at the Battle of Tewkesbury. Edward of Lancaster was slain after the battle – probably killed by Clarence and Gloucester on King Edward's orders[87] – and Queen Margaret was taken prisoner. The King then marched in triumph to London, his throne secure at last.

Even now 'the fury of many of the malignants was not averted'.[88] The last days of this first phase of the Wars of the Roses were not without terrifying drama – and young Elizabeth was at the centre of it. On 12 May Thomas Neville, the Bastard of Fauconberg, Warwick's cousin, Vice Admiral of the Fleet and one of Queen Margaret's most zealous supporters, made a bid to free Henry VI from the Tower. Having sailed up the Thames with a force of 17,000 men of Kent and 'the remains of Warwick's mercenaries, mariners and pirates',[89] he arrived at the gates of London Bridge – 'a very famous bridge built partly of wood and partly of stone [and on it] houses and several gates'[90] – intending to 'subject this most opulent city to their ravages'.

Declaring that he had come to dethrone the usurper Edward and restore King Henry, he demanded permission from the Lord Mayor to march through the City and promised that his men should commit no disturbance or pillage. Then he showed the Lord Mayor and the citizens his commission from Warwick, only to be told it was no longer in force as Warwick was dead. Fauconberg was stunned by this news; he would not believe it, and persisted in his demands, but the City fathers resisted him, closed their gates and began building barricades. They also, 'with right great instance, moved the King in all possible haste to approach and come to the City, to the defence of the Queen, then being in the Tower of London, my lord Prince and my ladies his daughters, all likely to stand in the greatest jeopardy that ever was'.[91]

The Bastard had his cannon ranged along the shore. He ordered his men to set fire to London Bridge, and simultaneously bombarded Aldgate and Bishopsgate, 'where they made most furious assaults and laid waste everything with fire and sword'. 'God gave the Londoners stout hearts:'[92] they bravely defended their bridge, while the cannon from the Tower thundered out in response to the attack. But the Bastard sailed downstream and unloaded 5,000 men below the Tower, with the intention of attacking the City from the east. There was a real danger that these troops and the Lancastrian artillery might breach the Tower's defences; the Bastard's men had already fired beerhouses near the fortress. In retaliation 'the citizens lodged their great artillery against their adversaries and with violent shot thereof so galled them that they durst not abide in any place along the water side but were driven even from their own ordnance'.[93]

In the Tower, five-year-old Elizabeth would have heard the bombardment and the noise; it was the closest she ever got to a battle. It must have been a terrifying episode – and one she probably never forgot. Outside, men were dying as the rebel assault was repelled, but now her uncle, Earl Rivers, accompanied by the Lieutenant of the Tower, Edmund Grey, Earl of Kent, led forth a force of 500 men out of the Tower Postern and went to the aid of the citizens, 'falling at the head of his horsemen upon the rear of the enemy' until they were overcome, and then chasing them as far as Stratford and Stepney. Seven hundred insurgents were killed in the fighting, and hundreds more taken prisoner afterwards. Fauconberg was forced to retreat across the Thames to where his ships were waiting, and fled.[94] 'Everyone rejoiced' at the vanquishing of these rebels, and soon afterwards 'King Edward entered London in state for the third time, with a retinue far greater than any of his former armies, and with standards unfurled and borne before him. There was now no enemy left for him to encounter.'[95]

But Edward was taking no chances. 'And the same night that King Edward came to London' – 21 May 1471 – 'King Henry was put to death between eleven and twelve o'clock',[96] struck down while at prayer, according to a very old tradition. The chronicler John Warkworth noted that the King's youngest brother, Gloucester, was at the Tower at that time. It was given out that Henry had died 'of pure displeasure and melancholy' on hearing of the fate of his wife and son.[97]

The body of the King was 'chested' and displayed at St Paul's Cathedral, 'and his face was open that every man might see him, and he bled on the pavement there'. Then his corpse was moved to the Blackfriars, where it bled again, before being conveyed to Chertsey Abbey for burial.[98] In 1910 Henry's skull was examined, and it was noted that it was 'much broken' as if it had been crushed by a blow, and still had attached to it hair that was 'apparently matted with blood'.[99]

Richard of Gloucester – who was to play a fateful part in Elizabeth's life – was then eighteen, and while he may not personally have struck the blow that killed Henry VI – for it must have been Edward IV who had 'chosen to crush the seed'[100] – he was probably sent to the Tower by the King to convey the order and ensure that the deed was done. But there were rumours. 'The common fame was that the Duke of Gloucester was not all guiltless.'[101] Gloucester, asserted Commines, 'killed poor King Henry with his own hand, or else caused him to be killed in his presence'.

Richard of Gloucester's formative years had been overshadowed by war, treachery and violent death. He had been eight when his father and brother Edmund were killed in battle. He grew up in an insecure, ever-shifting world, and twice suffered the misery of exile. He had seen the King his brother betrayed by Warwick, who had been as a father to Richard. By now, Richard had become hardened to the realities of political expediency.

It was after Tewkesbury that Richard's ruthlessness first became apparent, when, as Constable of England, he had exercised his right to try and sentence to death Edmund, the last Beaufort Duke of Somerset, and other prominent Lancastrians, including one in holy orders who was entitled to immunity from the death penalty. Whether he struck the fatal blow that killed Henry VI or not, Richard, at an impressionable age, had been shown that it was prudent, even neces-sary, to eliminate the threat posed by the continued existence of a deposed king, and that the end – peace and stable government – justified the means.

Richard was undoubtedly an able man, hard-working and conscientious. He had that in him which inspired loyalty, and his share of the Plantagenet charisma, as well as 'a sharp courage, high and fierce'.[102] In many respects, he was a typical late-medieval magnate: acquisitive, hungry for wealth and power, brave in battle, tough and energetic. He took a keen interest in warfare and heraldry, and loved hunting and hawking. He was loyal to his brother, King Edward, and to his own followers, but would not scruple to ride roughshod over the rights of others.

His treatment of his future mother-in-law, the widowed Anne Beauchamp, Countess of Warwick, was a case in point. In 1471, the Countess sent letters to the five-year-old Elizabeth – 'my lady the King's eldest daughter' (among others) – pleading for the restoration of her lands,[103] which Richard and Clarence were determined to appropriate. She received no reply. Evidently the King did not think it politic for his daughter to respond. Under pressure from Richard, he was soon to sanction the division of the Warwick estates between his brothers as if the Countess were dead.[104]

The deaths of Henry VI and his only son brought to an end the first phase of the Wars of the Roses. Clarence had submitted to Edward IV and, at the mediation of the Duchess their mother, was forgiven. The House of Lancaster had been vanquished. But there remained a distant sprig of the family tree in the person of Henry Tudor, the posthumous son of Edmund Tudor, Earl of Richmond. Henry had inherited his claim to the throne through his mother, Margaret Beaufort.

Born in 1443, Margaret was the daughter of John Beaufort, Duke of Somerset, and through him descended from King Edward III in a line tainted with bastardy. Margaret's grandfather, John Beaufort, Earl of Somerset, had been the oldest son of John of Gaunt, Duke of Lancaster, and Katherine Swynford. Their four Beaufort children had been born before their marriage in 1396, but had been legitimated the following year by a statute of Richard II. Yet in 1407 Henry IV, in letters patent confirming their legitimacy, added a qualification that the Beauforts could not inherit the crown. Although letters patent could not overturn a statute, a doubt remained, and the question of the Beauforts' right to the succession greatly exercised legal minds during the fifteenth century.

Margaret Beaufort was only twelve when she was married to Edmund Tudor in 1455. He did not spare his young bride: he got her pregnant immediately, but died of plague in 1456 before his son was born. Many regarded the Tudors themselves as bastard stock. Edmund Tudor had been the offspring of a liaison – there is no good evidence that it was a marriage – between Queen Katherine of Valois, widow of Henry V, and Owen Tudor, a Welsh squire. Owen Tudor, or Tewdwr, came from an obscure Anglesey family of landed gentry that could trace its descent back only to the thirteenth century. The genealogies later commissioned by Henry Tudor to show that the Tudors were descended from ancient Welsh and British princes through Rhys ap Tewdwr, Prince of Deheubarth, Wales (d. 1093),[105] cannot be substantiated.

The whole procedure of pregnancy and birth seems to have been traumatic for Margaret Beaufort, and the child she bore on 28 January 1457 at Pembroke Castle was to be her only one. She was then thirteen, and had been a widow for twelve weeks. 'Like Moses,

[Henry] was wonderfully born and brought into the world by the noble Princess his mother, who was very small of stature, as she was never a tall woman. It seemed a miracle that, at that age, and of so little a personage, anyone should have been born at all, let alone one so tall and of so fine a build as her son.' But the infant Henry was weak, and it was thanks only to his young mother's devoted care that he survived.[106] He spent his earliest years with her at Pembroke Castle, under the protection of his uncle, Jasper Tudor, Earl of Pembroke.

In 1461, when Edward IV became king, Pembroke Castle fell to the Yorkists, and Margaret Beaufort and her son were placed under the guardianship of William Herbert, a staunch Yorkist. Henry was raised as Herbert's ward at Raglan Castle. He had been earl of Richmond from birth, but the King deprived him of this title in 1462. Already, he recognised the five-year-old boy as a potential rival for the throne.

By then, Margaret Beaufort had grown up to be an erudite, pious and virtuous woman of strong character. By 1464 she had married a loyal Yorkist, Sir Henry Stafford. Because of her Lancastrian affiliations, Edward IV had shown himself hostile towards her, but this new marriage changed things, and she was now treated with the deference due to one of royal blood. Young Henry saw little of her during these years, but Herbert proved a kindly guardian and had the boy well educated; Henry's tutor, Andreas Scotus, observed that he had never seen a child so quick in learning. A marriage was planned between Henry and Herbert's daughter Maud.

But Henry's childhood was not easy. Later, he would recall to Commines that 'from the time he was five years old he had been either a fugitive or a captive'. In 1468, Jasper Tudor having fled abroad, Herbert was given his earldom of Pembroke. In 1469 Warwick, now in rebellion against Edward IV, had Herbert executed for treachery. The following year Henry was reclaimed by Jasper Tudor, who had been returned to favour after the restoration of Henry VI, and who took him to court to meet the King; it was his one and only visit prior to his accession.

In 1471 Margaret Beaufort's husband, Henry Stafford, died, probably of wounds received fighting for Edward IV at the Battle of Barnet. Newly widowed, Margaret had now to face a long parting from her fourteen-year-old son, for after the Lancastrian defeat at Tewkesbury Jasper Tudor fled into exile, taking Henry with him.

Still styling himself 'Earl of Richmond', Henry spent his youth in penury at the court of Brittany. Both he and Jasper remained stoutly loyal to the House of Lancaster, and after the death of Henry VI, Henry Tudor was regarded by some as his natural heir; indeed, he was the only viable Lancastrian claimant. Henry always deferred to his mother, Margaret Beaufort, as the heiress of the House of Lancaster, but neither of them ever contemplated her actually ruling because she was a woman. All Margaret's ambitions were for her son, but clearly Edward IV did not perceive him as much of a threat, since he made only sporadic attempts to capture him. It would be many years before Henry's claim was taken seriously by the Yorkist kings.

2

'Madame la Dauphine'

After Tewkesbury the long-standing rivalry between Lancaster and York was thought to have been consigned to history, and the Christmas of 1471 was kept splendidly at Westminster, with a disguising and a great banquet for the Lord Mayor of London and the City fathers. The Queen was excused from the customary wearing of her crown because she was expecting another child.

Edward IV was finally established on his throne, and settled down to rule England firmly and well. Having seen the splendours of Bruges during his exile, he was even more determined to emulate the Burgundian court, and its influence was greatest during this latter part of his reign. In 1472 he had the 'Black Book' drawn up, the first set of ordinances to regulate English court ceremonial and etiquette, and in them the influence of Burgundy was manifest. Edward's purpose was to create a display of magnificence, as Burgundian custom dictated. From now on, there would be two households at court: above stairs, so to speak, the Lord Chamberlain's department, 'the King's house of magnificence'; and below stairs the Lord Steward's department, the 'house of providence'. Edward IV was determined to impress foreign visitors, and his own subjects, with the outer trappings of majesty, and observers were struck by his extravagance, his luxurious 'chambers of pleasaunce' hung with rich hangings, the ostentatious clothes he wore, the costly jewels, and the sumptuousness of his table. All of this made a lasting impression on the young Elizabeth, who was herself to preside over a splendid court based on the Burgundian model, upon which her own tastes were probably influential.

Mancini described Edward IV as gentle and cheerful by nature. Courtesy and the common touch came as naturally to him as it did to Warwick, his mentor. Elizabeth inherited these qualities from her father, who was 'easy of access to his friends, even the least notable. He was so genial in his greeting that, if he saw a newcomer bewildered at his royal magnificence, he would give him courage to speak by laying a kindly hand upon his shoulder.' But Edward had another side to him: 'should he assume an angry countenance, he could be very terrible to beholders'[1] and as terrifying as his grandson, Henry VIII, who much resembled him.

Gone was the glorious youth of Edward's earlier years. The father Elizabeth came to know as she grew up, and to whom she became close, was losing his handsome looks. By 1475 the athletic warrior was 'a little inclining to corpulence',[2] and thereafter he would become increasingly obese, thanks to a life of unbridled excess and gluttony. 'In food and drink he was most immoderate; it was his habit to take an emetic for the delight of gorging his stomach once more. For this reason, he had grown fat in the loins, whereas previously he had been not only tall, but rather lean and very active.'[3] Elizabeth, herself fond of good living, would also put on weight as she approached her thirties.

Despite his overindulgent habits, Edward did not lose his grip on affairs. 'This Prince, although he was thought to have indulged his passions and desires too intemperately, was still a most devout Catholic, a most unsparing enemy to all heretics, and a most loving encourager of wise and learned men, and of the clergy. Men of every rank and condition wondered that a man of such corpulence, and so fond of boon companionship, vanities, debauchery, extravagance and sensual enjoyments should have had a memory so retentive in all respects.'[4]

Edward kept three mistresses during these later years. Two were 'greater personages' than the third, and 'content to be nameless', suggesting that the King's affairs with them were conducted with discretion. 'But the merriest was Shore's wife, in whom the King therefore took special pleasure, for many he had, but her he loved.'[5]

Elizabeth must have known 'Shore's wife', for she was prominent at court and had captivated the Londoners' imagination, probably because she was one of them. Elizabeth (often inaccurately called Jane) Lambert had been born in the City and was 'well married, somewhat too soon', to 'an honest citizen', a goldsmith called William Shore. The marriage was annulled in 1476 on the grounds of his being 'frigid and impotent', which probably 'the more easily made her incline unto the King's appetite when he required her'. Edward experienced no difficulty in 'piercing' Mistress Shore's 'soft, tender heart. Proper she was, and fair', if rather short in stature, 'yet delighted not men so much in her beauty as in her pleasant behaviour, for a proper wit had she, and could both read and write. She never abused to any man's hurt, but to many a man's comfort and relief.'[6] Sir Thomas More asserted that the Queen hated Elizabeth Shore, which would be understandable, although there is no record of her showing any animosity towards her in public.

Elizabeth could hardly have grown up unaware to some degree of her father's promiscuity, since it was notorious. Her undoubted virtue may have masked a sensual nature like his, since she clearly enjoyed the finer things in life – good food, conspicuous display, rich clothing, jewellery and courtly revels. But no one ever accused Elizabeth of promiscuity.

Edward IV had 'many promoters and companions of his vices, the most important and especial [being] the relatives of the Queen, her two sons and one of her brothers'.[7] This brother, Anthony Wydeville, Earl Rivers, was generally lauded as 'a man of great valour'.[8] Although elegantly fashionable and an accomplished jouster, he 'was always considered a kind, serious and just man, and one tested by every vicissitude of life. Whatever his prosperity, he had injured nobody, though benefitting many.'[9] That is debatable, for Rivers, like his father, could be ruthless in the pursuit of his ambitions.

He was a complex man, ambitious yet deeply pious, to the extent of wearing a hair shirt beneath his fine attire. He travelled in Italy and made pilgrimages to Rome and the shrine of St James at Compostela, and it was his unfulfilled life's ambition to go on a crusade against the Infidel. Such was his reputation that Pope Sixtus IV appointed him Defender and Director of Papal Causes in England. Rivers was also an able military commander and diplomat.

An erudite scholar, the Earl was to patronise William Caxton, who set up the first English printing press at Westminster in 1476. Caxton would print three devotional works that Rivers had translated, including *The Dictes and Sayings of the Philosophers*, the first book ever printed in England. Elizabeth would have grown up to be familiar with Caxton's work, for her father was also his patron, and took the royal family to visit his shop, which originally stood south of Westminster Abbey's Lady Chapel, but was moved in 1482 to premises in the Abbey Almonry, and became known as 'The Red Pale'. No doubt Elizabeth grew up to have much respect and admiration for her highly cultivated and multi-talented uncle Rivers, and he must have been an early inspiration to her.

Elizabeth's half-brothers, Thomas Grey, Marquess of Dorset, and Sir Richard Grey, the King's other companions in his debaucheries, were the sons of her mother's first marriage to Sir John Grey of Groby. William, Lord Hastings, the King's Chamberlain and loyal friend, 'was also the accomplice and partner of [Edward IV's] privy pleasures. He maintained a deadly feud with the Queen's sons', and not just over Mistress Shore, after whom Hastings and Dorset both secretly lusted.[10]

The Wydevilles were riding high, and that was the way they intended things to continue. From the first, the young Prince Edward's household was in their control. The Queen appointed Elizabeth, Lady Darcy, as lady mistress of the King's nursery, with responsibility for the Prince and a large staff of attendants.[11] Lady Darcy had been born Elizabeth Tyrell (c.1436-1507), the daughter of Sir Thomas Tyrell (a distant relation of the Sir James Tyrell who was to play a fateful role in Elizabeth's life); as the widow of Sir Robert Darcy, she had married secondly, after November 1469, Richard Haute, esquire (1434-87), son of Sir Richard Haute of Ightham Mote, Kent, a cousin of the Queen; in 1473 the elder Haute was to be appointed one of the councillors of the Prince of Wales and controller of the Prince's household.

In June 1471 Avice Welles, a widow, was appointed nurse to the infant Prince. The baby had his own household officers, and his chamberlain, Thomas Vaughan, was deputed to carry his young master at public ceremonies. The Queen's brother, Lionel Wydeville, was appointed chaplain to the heir. That June young Edward was created Prince of Wales and Earl of Chester, and on 3 July, King Edward made his privy councillors swear an oath of loyalty to the little boy as the 'very undoubted son and heir of our sovereign lord'; foremost among those who did so were young Edward's uncles, the dukes of Gloucester and Clarence.

The King might have been immersed in debauchery, but unstained virtue was expected of his womenfolk, and his daughters were brought up to be pious and morally irreproachable. The 'blind poet'[12] and friar, Bernard André, Henry VII's admiring chronicler and court poet, could not 'pass over in silence the praiseworthy and commendable acts of [Elizabeth] while she was still a girl. She had manifested from her infancy an admirable fear and devotion towards God; towards her parents a truly wonderful obedience; towards her brothers and sisters an unbounded love; and towards the poor and ministers of Christ a reverent and singular affection, instilled in her from childhood.' This was no mere flattery, for these were qualities and bonds that were to be plainly evident all Elizabeth's life.

By five or six she had begun her formal education, which followed a conventional pattern. Girls, even princesses, were traditionally destined to be wives and mothers, and they were educated to that end. As women were held to be morally and intellectually inferior to men, honesty and chastity were considered far more important than learning. Only slowly was the idea becoming accepted that an educated woman could also be a virtuous one. It was royalty and the aristocracy who led the way: in an age in which most women were illiterate, privileged well-born girls were taught to read and write. Thus they were better equipped to run the great castles and houses of which they would one day be mistress. They could write their own letters and wills; and their minds were broadened by reading manuscripts and the new printed books.

Edward IV was a noted collector of richly illustrated manuscripts and books, and it was arguably he who founded the royal library, or at least re-established it. He encouraged in his eldest daughter a love of books. A devotional volume, now in the British Library, is inscribed in her own hand: 'This book is mine, Elizabeth, the King's daughter.'[13] Edward IV, the patron of Caxton, was also deeply immersed in the Arthurian legends and the cult of St George, both of which under-pinned English court culture; he was interested too in the history of ancient Rome and the medieval science of alchemy. His intel-lectual influence on his daughter was clearly pivotal.

Elizabeth grew up to be 'learned and wise'.[14] She and her sisters were taught the skills and accomplishments that were considered appropriate for future queens, skills that would enable them to grace royal courts and equip them to run great households and extensive estates. Much of this was acquired by observing and learning from their mother, their lady mistresses and the gentlewomen in charge of them. They had to learn what we would today call managerial skills: the ability to wield authority over their servants, manage budgets and delegate to the officers who assisted them in their vast responsibilities. To do this, they needed to be literate and numerate.

Elizabeth was taught to read and write. Her signature bears a strong resemblance to her mother's, suggesting that Elizabeth Wydeville took an active role in her education, much as her daughter would when it came to her own children. Elizabeth seems to have been more literate than her sister Cecily, whose handwriting and spelling were atrocious,[15] even in an age in which spelling and grammar were not uniform.

A much later source, 'The Song of Lady Bessy' (see Chapter 6), asserts that Elizabeth could 'indite' (compose) and 'full well read both English, and also French, and also Spanish', but this was an exaggeration, if not an invention. In 1488 a Spanish ambassador reported that she could not read letters in Spanish, and ten years afterwards she insisted that her future daughter-in-law spoke French when she came to England, as she herself did not understand Latin (which was not taught to women before the reign of her son, Henry VIII), much less Spanish.[16] French was seen as a desirable accomplishment among the upper classes, but the evidence suggests that Elizabeth understood it better than she spoke it, for when she received Italian ambassadors in 1497, she struggled to converse with them in French and needed an interpreter.[17]

Her daily curriculum was probably similar in many respects to that laid down by her father in 1473 for her brother, Prince Edward. Edward was to spend his days 'in such virtuous learning as his age shall suffer to receive' and be read 'such noble stories as behoveth a prince to understand and know'. Afternoons were to be spent at lessons or in such recreation as was suitable for 'the eschewing of idleness'. Elizabeth would not have been expected to practise the 'convenient disports and exercises' thought necessary for a prince, but she would have been taught dancing, horsemanship, music and needlework instead.[18]

Elizabeth Wydeville would also have exercised some intellectual influence on her children, especially her daughters. A patron of education and poor scholars, she re-founded Queen's College, Cambridge, in 1465, when its name was changed to Queens' College.[19] She also patronised William Caxton, who dedicated *The Knight of the Tower* to her in 1484. Books were luxury items, often bequeathed in wills, and Elizabeth Wydeville owned or commissioned several, notably Caxton's *Receuil of the Histories of Troy*, his tale of Jason and the Golden Fleece (which she gave to the Prince of Wales) and an illuminated book of devotions, 'The Hours of the Guardian Angel', dedicated to a queen called Elizabeth. It was once thought that this book was presented to Elizabeth of York, but it has been dated on artistic style to 1475–83.[20]

At Stonyhurst College, Lancashire, there is a beautiful illustrated vellum manuscript of the 'Hours of Our Lady', dating from 1470–85; it is signed 'Elysabeth Plantaegenet' and inscribed in a later hand 'the Queen'. It has been suggested that it was once owned by Elizabeth Wydeville and passed by her to her daughter, but Elizabeth Wydeville would not have used the surname Plantagenet, which is how Elizabeth of York might have signed herself before her father's death. Thus it probably came into the latter's possession prior to 1483; her signature also appears on another page.[21]

Elizabeth may jointly have owned 'The Romance of the San Graal', a costly illuminated manuscript of French romances that included the legends of King Arthur. It dated from c.1315–25 and had once been in the library of King Charles V of France. Acquired by the Roos family, it was bequeathed in 1482 by Sir Richard Roos to his niece, the Queen's damsel and kinswoman, Eleanor Haute. It bears four signatures: one is that of Joan, Elizabeth Wydeville's sister; another is 'E. Wydevyll', who was probably their brother, Sir Edward Wydeville, as the Queen is unlikely to have signed herself thus. The other signatures are those of 'Elysabeth the kyngys dowther' and 'Cecyl the kyngys dowther', probably written before April 1483. Since the book is unlikely to have been owned by all four signatories, it may have been shared by Edward Wydeville with his sister and nieces.[22]

Elizabeth owned another manuscript, the 'Testament de Amyra Sultan Nicchemedy, Empereur des Turcs', which tells the story of the Sultan's attempted conquest of Aleppo and subsequent death and obsequies. It bears the date '12 Sept. 1481' on the title page, and is bound in dark leather stamped with a fleur-de-lis, an appropriate emblem considering that Elizabeth was then Dauphine of France. The title page also bears the signatures 'Elysabeth the kyngys dowghter Boke' and 'Cecyl the kyngys dowghter'.[23]

Elizabeth was thus inculcated from childhood not only with devotional works, but also with the precepts of chivalry and courtly love, which informed the popular romances and histories of the age and heavily influenced aristocratic and court culture. Yet there was laughter as well as learning in the young Princess's life. No doubt she and her siblings enjoyed the antics and jests of her father's fool, the disreputable John Scoggin, as much as the King and Queen did.[24]

Meanwhile the royal family was expanding. On 10 April 1472 Elizabeth Wydeville bore a fourth daughter, Margaret, at Windsor Castle.[25] Three months later, at Westminster, the Duke of Gloucester married Warwick's daughter and co-heiress, Anne Neville, the widow of Prince Edward of Lancaster. Her sister and co-heiress, Isabel, was already the wife of Richard's older brother, George, Duke of Clarence.

Richard and Anne had probably known each other as children, as he had been raised in Warwick's household for some years. She was a great prize in the marriage market, for she brought with her half of the vast Warwick estates. After her first husband had been slain at Tewkesbury, Richard had asked the King for her hand, 'but this did not suit his brother, the Duke of Clarence, who caused the damsel to be concealed, as he was afraid of a division of the Earl's property, which he wished to come to himself alone in right of his wife. Still, however, the craftiness of Gloucester so far prevailed that he discovered the young lady in the City of London, disguised in the habit of a cook-maid.' 'Violent dissension' then arose between the brothers, but the King ruled that Gloucester should marry Anne and that the Warwick estates were to be divided by arbitrators.[26] The settlement Richard received on his marriage gave him a great landed inheritance – much to Clarence's fury.

In September 1472 Elizabeth, now six, was at Windsor Castle, one of the foremost royal residences in England. A great fortress had stood here since the days of William I, the Conqueror, and successive monarchs had embellished and enlarged it, converting it into a splendid palace. In the fourteenth century Edward III had built a stately and luxurious range of stone lodgings on the north side of the quadrangle in the upper ward, and converted the old ones in the lower ward into a college dedicated to St George. To achieve this and create the perfect setting for his court and his new Order of the Garter, he had spent unprecedented sums.

Edward III's palace was rather outdated now, and soon to be modernised by Edward IV. To the south of the main quadrangle, which served as the tournament ground, stood St George's Hall, a masterpiece of Gothic splendour with its seventeen tall arched windows, and the Royal Chapel. To the north there were separate sets of first-floor 'Great Chambers' for the King and Queen, arranged around two inner courtyards, Brick Court and Horn Court. Their children were probably lodged in separate apartments overlooking the quadrangle.[27] In 1475 Edward IV gave orders for work to begin on a new chapel dedicated to St George, inspired perhaps by the collegiate church at Fotheringhay, a Yorkist foundation – and by the desire to eclipse Henry VI's sepulchre at Chertsey.[28] It was here that Edward intended to be buried.

Elizabeth was present with several great lords and ladies at a banquet given at Windsor by the Queen in honour of Louis, Lord of Gruthuyse and Governor of Holland, who had offered the King shelter and hospitality in Bruges during his exile. When Edward brought Gruthuyse to her mother's withdrawing room, Elizabeth was among the ladies with whom the Queen was playing at marteaux (marbles) and 'closheys' (ninepins), 'which sight was full pleasant'. Then 'King Edward danced with my Lady Elizabeth, his eldest daughter'.

The following evening, after the King had dined with his guest, 'the Queen did ordain a grand banquet in her own apartments, at which King Edward, her eldest daughter [Elizabeth], the Duchess of Exeter [Edward IV's sister Anne], the Lady Rivers [Elizabeth's aunt, Mary FitzLewes] and the Lord of Gruthuyse all sat with her at one mess [course]; and at another table sat the Duke of Buckingham, my lady his wife [Katherine Wydeville], my Lord Hastings' and other nobles. 'And when they had supped, my Lady Elizabeth danced with the Duke of Buckingham.' This was her cousin, seventeen-year-old Henry Stafford, who was descended from the youngest son of King Edward III. He was to play a fateful role in Elizabeth's future.

After the dancing, Elizabeth was probably with the ladies who accompanied the King and Queen when they paid their guest the honour of conducting him to the apartments that had been made ready for him. When the ladies withdrew so that Gruthuyse could have a bath, Elizabeth was probably sent to bed. The next day, the court returned to Westminster.[29]

Elizabeth's baby sister Margaret did not thrive. She died, aged eight months, on 11 December 1472, and was buried in Westminster Abbey in an altar tomb of grey marble 'at the altar end before St Edward's shrine', which now stands between the tombs of Edward III and Richard II, having been moved here during the Reformation. The tomb brass and inscription plate have long vanished, but the Latin epitaph read: 'Nobility and beauty, grace and tender youth are all hidden here in this chest of death.'[30]

It was common in those days for children to learn about death at close quarters from an early age. It has been estimated that, even among the aristocracy, one in every five or six children died at birth or within a year.[31] There were no antibiotics, and infections that can be effectively treated today could then be lethal. The risks were higher in crowded cities: with their polluted water supplies and accumulation of sewage they were a breeding ground for diseases such as plague, especially in the summer. This was one of the reasons why royal children were given their own separate establishments in the country, well away from the risk of infection. Despite this precaution, three of Elizabeth's own children would die young.

The high rate of infant mortality meant that Edward IV's succession was not secure with just one male heir, so there was cause for rejoicing when the Queen bore a second son, named Richard, on 17 August 1473 at the Dominican Friary in Shrewsbury. This child lived, and was brought up with his sisters. In May 1474 he was created Duke of York, in honour of the grandfather whose name he bore.

Elizabeth was henceforth to see less of the Prince of Wales. In the autumn of 1473 the Queen took him to Ludlow Castle, where he was now to reside as nominal president of a newly created Council of Wales and the Marches. The little boy, now three, had his own household under the governance of his dependable uncle, Anthony Wydeville, Earl Rivers, to whom the King had 'entrusted the care and direction' of his heir.[32]

In May 1474 Edward IV drew up for Rivers specific rules governing the upbringing and education of his son and the management of his household. Actual responsibility for educating the Prince was delegated to John Alcock, Bishop of Worcester. Young Edward 'was brought up virtuously by virtuous men' and showed himself 'remarkably gifted, and very well advanced in learning for his years'.[33]

Elizabeth Wydeville's influence was clear from the first. 'Everyone as he was nearest of kin unto the Queen, so was planted next about the Prince, whereby her blood might of youth be rooted in the Prince's favour.'[34] She was a member of young Edward's council, which was headed by her brother Rivers and their cousin, Sir Richard Haute, and acted only 'with the advice and express consent of the Queen'. She also had responsibility for nominating the officers who served her son.[35] This domination of the heir and his council by the Wydevilles was intended to secure their continuing power in the next reign,[36] but it would in time prove to be fateful for young Edward – and for Elizabeth and his other siblings.

The Prince was not isolated from his family at Ludlow. He was often at court, especially at Christmas, so he would never have become a stranger to his sisters.[37] However, royal siblings were customarily split asunder, for it was expected that the girls would leave court to marry great princes or lords in pursuance of their father's policies. In October 1474, under the terms of a treaty signed in Edinburgh, Cecily of York, aged five, was betrothed to the future James IV of Scots, then only two years old,[38] 'in the interests of peace'. Edward was planning an invasion of France, and did not want Scotland, France's old ally, to cause trouble, so this betrothal was arranged to pre-empt that. On 26 December the formal ceremony of betrothal took place in Edinburgh with a proxy standing in for Cecily, and from this time she was styled 'the Princess of Scots'.

Elizabeth's destiny seemed settled when she was eleven and the King arranged a most prestigious marriage for her. That summer, having invaded France determined to conquer it, he found himself abandoned by his allies, Charles, Duke of Burgundy, and Francis II, Duke of Brittany, and settled instead for coming to terms with Louis XI, who had dangled the carrot of a lavish pension. On 29 August 1475 the two kings met on a bridge at Picquigny and parleyed through a wooden trellis. The result was the Treaty of Picquigny, which sealed a peace between England and France. One of the conditions of the treaty was that, 'for the inviolate observation of the friendship', 'the most serene Lady Elizabeth' should be contracted in marriage to Louis' son, the 'most illustrious' Dauphin Charles, 'when they shall reach marriageable years'. Another condition was that Edward would surrender to the Dauphin his claim to the duchy of Aquitaine, which had been lost during the Hundred Years War, and that it should be considered as part of Elizabeth's dower. After her marriage the French King would settle upon her rents to the annual value of £60,000 (£30 million) for her maintenance in a manner befitting the future Queen of France. This was fifteen times the dower settled on Elizabeth

Wydeville, so the Princess could look forward to a life of luxury. If she were to die before the wedding, her sister Mary was to take her place.[39]

It was agreed that Elizabeth would go to France when she was twelve. Child marriages were made *per verba de futoro* – as a promise for the future – and it was anticipated that they would be consummated when the couple reached the age of consent, which was twelve for girls and fourteen for boys (unless the contract stipulated that they should be older). These were also the respective minimum ages at which the Church sanctioned marital relations. Most royal and aristocratic girls of the period married between the ages of thirteen and sixteen – snapped up because of the advantages and status they would bring their husbands.

'Both the kings laid one of their hands upon the book, and both of them swore religiously that the marriage between their children should be consummated, as was stipulated by the treaty.'[40] Successfully negotiating this marriage was something of an achievement for Edward, for no English princess had ever become the bride of a king of France. This was the third time that Elizabeth had been offered in marriage as a means of resolving a conflict with one of her father's enemies.

Her future husband was five years old, and four years her junior. He was King Louis' only surviving son; his godfather had been Edward of Lancaster, Prince of Wales. The Dauphin lived at the chateau of Amboise, far from his father's court, for his health, unlike that of his future bride, was poor. Although he had a pleasant disposition, he was stunted in height, feeble in body and mind, and many thought him too foolish to make a good king.

From the time of her betrothal, Elizabeth was addressed as 'Madame la Dauphine' and treated with the honours due to a future queen of France.[41] Edward apportioned part of the hefty pension paid to him by King Louis for her maintenance as Dauphine, and rich gowns in the French fashion were made for her. She was probably told to work harder at her French lessons. Commines says that the King and Queen her parents were deeply committed to this marriage, and that Elizabeth Wydeville's pride was so inflated at the prospect of her daughter becoming Queen of France that she repeatedly enquired of King Louis to know when she should send him 'her Dauphiness'.[42]

Elizabeth had been brought up to know what was expected of her. She was probably familiar with Jacobus de Cessolis' *The Game and Play of Chess*, published by Caxton in 1474 and dedicated to her uncle Clarence, and its description of the qualities expected of a queen: 'A queen ought to be chaste, wise of honest people, well mannered, and not curious [anxious, odd] in nourishing of her children. Her wisdom ought not only to appear in feat and works, but also in speaking: that is, to wit, that she be secret and tell not such things as ought to be holden secret. Amongst all, she ought to be timorous and shamefast.' These were lessons Elizabeth learned well.

Another princess, Anne, was born to the Queen on 2 November 1475 at Westminster.[43] She was baptised in Westminster Abbey and given into the care of a nurse, Agnes Butler.[44] Elizabeth's lady mistress, Lady Berners, died on 18 December.[45]

In July 1476 the King took his family to Fotheringhay in Northamptonshire. The Norman castle there had been granted by Edward III to his fifth son, Edmund of Langley, first Duke of York, in 1377. Edmund had endowed the college and church of St Mary and All Saints, and for the next century and more Fotheringhay was one of the chief seats of the House of York. Edmund's son, Edward of Aumale, Duke of York, had built the choir of the now-vanished church in which he would later be buried, which he intended as a mausoleum for his family. In the early 1430s a parish church was built on to the collegiate church. The latter and the college buildings were demolished in 1553 during the Reformation, and the large parish church is what remains today, along with some unexcavated humps and hollows where the college quadrangle once stood. The Yorkist badge of the falcon and fetterlock can still be seen in the church, and the painted pulpit was probably a gift from Edward IV.

Elizabeth's younger uncle, Gloucester, had been born in Fotheringhay Castle in 1452. Edward IV greatly loved Fotheringhay, which was his favourite residence outside London. He had enlarged the castle, and in building 'very fair lodgings' for himself and his Queen, galleries, privies, turrets and a new kitchen, he had created a palace 'fair and meetly strong' with a double moat and a towering gatehouse.[46]

The royal family had returned to Fotheringhay to give their dead fitting burial. Elizabeth and Mary, the eldest, were probably the two unnamed daughters of the King who, clad in deep mourning – possibly of blue, the colour of royal mourning, like that worn by their mother — were present at the sombre ceremonies on 29–30 July, when the bodies of their grandfather, the Duke of York, and their uncle, the Earl of Rutland, were brought from their humble resting place in the church of the Mendicant friars at Pontefract[47] and reinterred with all due honours in the collegiate church at Fotheringhay. Elizabeth had never known them, for they had been killed at Wakefield in 1460.[48]

On 29 July Elizabeth and her sister stood at the entrance to the churchyard, waiting to receive the cortège with their parents, the Duke of Clarence, the Marquess of Dorset, Earl Rivers, Lord Hastings and other noblemen. An effigy of the late Duke of York, 'garbed in an ermine furred mantle and cap of maintenance, covered with a cloth of gold', lay on his coffin on a bier blazing with candles and guarded by an angel of silver bearing a crown of gold, to signify that he had been the rightful King of England. York's youngest son, Richard of Gloucester, with other lords and officers of arms, all in black, followed the funeral chariot, which was drawn by six horses, wearing caparisons of black charged with the arms of France and England.

When the procession drew to a standstill, the King made an obeisance to his father's coffin 'right humbly and put his hand on the body and kissed it, crying all the time'. Then the processions of prelates and peers advanced into the church where two hearses were waiting, one in the choir for the body of the Duke and one in the Lady Chapel for that of the Earl of Rutland. The King retired to his 'closet' while his brothers and the officers of arms stationed themselves around the hearses. Masses were sung and the King's chamberlain, on his behalf, laid seven palls of cloth of gold 'in a cross on the body'.

The next day, three funeral masses were celebrated. After their parents, the princesses bowed to the catafalques and offered Mass pennies at the altar rail, as did Margaret Beaufort, Countess of Richmond. Then the bodies of York and Rutland were interred in the church, where tombs were later built to their memory.[49] After the committals Elizabeth helped the King and Queen to distribute alms among the 5,000 people who had gathered at the church. It was said that 20,000 were present at the feast that followed, which was served partly in the castle and partly in the King's tents and pavilions. Among the dishes were capons, cygnets, herons and rabbits; the bill came to at least £300 (£151,400).

★

After concluding the treaty with Louis XI, Edward IV had sent an embassy laden with gold to Francis II, Duke of Brittany, asking him to send Henry Tudor back to England, as he purposed to arrange a marriage for him that would unite the rival houses of York and Lancaster. That implied that one of the King's younger daughters was to be the intended bride. In fact Edward's real purpose was to snare 'the only imp now left of Henry VI's brood' into his clutches.[50] In November 1476 Margaret Beaufort, guessing that this was a ruse to lure Henry back to England, and terrified lest he be abducted and killed, warned him not to return in the event of such a marriage being proposed for him.[51] Henry feigned illness, and Duke Francis, divining a plot, committed his guest to sanctuary in a church in St Malo.

Edward knew himself beaten, and for the rest of his life he paid Duke Francis to keep the exile in Brittany. The young man was treated 'reasonably well', but he 'lived the life of a prisoner'.[52] Very little is known about this period of Henry's life, but he may have spent some of his enforced leisure imbuing himself with the Celtic culture of the duchy, which was similar to that of the Wales of his youth, and embracing the legends of King Arthur, set here in the forest of Broceliande, and of Tristan and Yseult.

In the winter of 1476 Edward IV opened negotiations for the marriage of his heir, the Prince of Wales, to the Infanta Isabella, eldest daughter of the Spanish sovereigns, Ferdinand, King of Aragon, and Isabella, Queen of Castile, whose marriage had unified Spain and who were highly regarded in Europe. It was two years before these negotiations foundered, and ultimately it would be the Infanta's youngest sister who married Elizabeth of York's eldest son. A daughter of the Holy Roman Emperor, Frederick III of Habsburg, was then sought for young Edward, but 'the chief difficulty' in regard to arranging a marriage for him was proving to be 'the great quantity of money which the King of England will want'.[53]

It was perhaps in March 1477 that Queen Elizabeth gave birth to a third son, George.[54] Joan, Baroness Dacre, wife of the Queen's chamberlain, was appointed his nurse.[55] In 1478, George was designated Duke of Bedford, the title of which the hapless George Neville, Elizabeth's former betrothed, had been deprived early that year, although there is no record of any formal creation.

In 1477 eleven-year-old Elizabeth, her mother the Queen and

her aunt, Elizabeth Plantagenet, Duchess of Suffolk, were all made Ladies of the Order of the Garter, and participated in the traditional three-day Garter celebrations. Elizabeth no doubt thrilled to see her father the King and his Knights Companions 'all mounted on horseback in their habits of blue', and on the 'Grand Day', St George's Day itself, she and her aunt rode with her mother and a company of ladies to the chapel to hear Mass, all wearing a 'livery of murrey [mulberry red] embroidered with garters'.[56] Stalls were not allocated to Ladies of the Garter, so the royal women watched the service from the rood loft. Afterwards, Elizabeth was present at the annual Garter feast in St George's Hall, Windsor, presided over by Edward IV, who was enthroned in solitary state at the high table. Entering with her mother and the other ladies as the second course was borne in, Elizabeth ascended with them to the gallery at the west end of the hall and observed the proceedings from there.[57]

The outward displays of unity by the Yorkist family masked divisions that would soon tear it asunder. Early in 1477 Charles the Bold, Duke of Burgundy, had been killed at the Battle of Nancy, leaving his duchy in the hands of his only legitimate child, Mary of Burgundy. The dukes of Burgundy were descended from Charles V of France, but they had constantly striven for independence from the French crown. Now Louis XI promptly declared the duchy extinct on the grounds that it properly belonged to France.

Charles the Bold's widow, Margaret of York, now schemed to marry her stepdaughter Mary to her brother George, Duke of Clarence, whom she loved more than any other member of her family; and naturally Clarence leapt at the idea, for if he married Mary, he would gain a great European fiefdom. However, such a scheme would seriously have prejudiced England's alliance with France, Burgundy's enemy, and Elizabeth's marriage plans. It would also have given the untrustworthy, treacherous Clarence a rival power base on the continent, with all the riches of Burgundy at his disposal as well as control over the North Sea coast; these resources could have enabled him to challenge his brother's title to the English throne. Evidently this was what Edward IV feared, not least because a case – admittedly weak – could be made for Mary of Burgundy to claim the English throne, since she was descended from John of Gaunt. But the ambitious and headstrong Clarence was unlikely to bother with legal niceties.

Edward 'threw all possible impediments in the way',[58] but fortunately for him, Clarence's schemes were immediately thwarted when Louis XI invaded the duchy and seized Burgundy 'proper' (roughly the area now known as Burgundy today), Flanders, Artois and Picardy. Edward no more wanted Louis ruling Burgundy than he did Clarence, but he was anxious to maintain the alliance with France, so he reminded Louis of the treaty of amity between them, reiterating his desire for the marriage of Princess Elizabeth to the Dauphin. But Louis failed to respond with enthusiasm; he was suspicious of Edward's motives, and proposed that the Dauphin be wed to Mary of Burgundy instead, to which Edward retaliated by offering her Anthony Wydeville, Earl Rivers, as a husband. This kind of diplomatic manoeuvring was common, even after marriage alliances had been concluded. Nothing was set in stone, and treaties could be broken or ignored if a more advantageous alliance presented itself. Elizabeth's future was by no means certain.

In August 1477, thanks to Margaret's efforts, Mary of Burgundy was married to the husband her father had chosen for her, Maximilian of Austria, son of the Emperor Frederick III. When Maximilian began vigorously resisting French aggrandisement, Louis came to believe that Edward IV – who was striving to remain neutral – meant to marry Elizabeth into the Imperial House with a view to forging a new Anglo-Burgundian alliance against France; and he began to plan strategies to avert that threat.

Thwarted of Burgundy, Clarence had forsaken the court and become aggressive and provocative, showing scant respect for his brother or the law, and before long he and Edward had 'each begun to look upon the other with no fraternal eyes'.[59] On 10 June 1477, amidst rumours that Clarence was again plotting rebellion, Elizabeth learned that her uncle had been arrested on her father's orders and imprisoned in the Tower of London. She was probably too young to understand how he threatened the King politically, but she may have been aware that her father hated and feared him, and she would certainly have heard talk or gossip of the scandals that had preceded his arrest. The year before, Clarence's wife, Isabel Neville, had died in childbirth, but he had subsequently accused the Queen of poisoning her by means of a servant, Ankarette Twynho. Elizabeth Wydeville was beyond his reach, but he had had the unfortunate – and innocent – servant hanged. Then, when one of his affinity was executed for using sorcery against King Edward and the Prince of Wales, Clarence provocatively defended the man before the Council, disparaging the King's justice. That was a step too far, and Edward responded accordingly. Clarence was to languish in the Tower for seven months.

Elizabeth and her sisters Mary and Cecily were present at yet another splendid royal occasion when, on 15 January 1478, their brother Richard, Duke of York, aged four, was married to the late Duke of Norfolk's daughter and heiress, Anne Mowbray, aged five. By this marriage King Edward secured for his son the rich Norfolk estates. The wedding took place in St Stephen's Chapel in the Palace of Westminster. This narrow but beautiful Gothic chapel, built in the late thirteenth century in emulation of St Louis IX's *La Sainte Chapelle* in Paris, was two storeys high, and the upper chapel, which was used by the royal family, had a vaulted ceiling of sky blue with numerous gold stars, which soared a hundred feet above the tiled floor. For this occasion, the chapel walls, adorned with murals of angels, kings and religious scenes in vivid scarlet, green and blue, had been hung with azure cloth embroidered with gold fleurs-de-lis.

The Queen escorted her son to the marble altar, where he waited beneath a cloth-of-gold canopy with the bride's mother, Elizabeth Talbot, Dowager Duchess of Norfolk. Then Lord Rivers and the King's nephew, John de la Pole, Earl of Lincoln, led in red-haired Anne Mowbray.[60] Elizabeth sat with her parents, her brother Edward, her sisters, Mary and Cecily, and her grandmother of York beneath another cloth-of-gold canopy while the Papal dispensation permitting this marriage of cousins was read out. Then the King gave away the bride and the marriage service commenced.

Afterwards Gloucester showered gold and silver coins upon the crowds outside, then spices and wine were served to the wedding party. There were jousts and a lavish banquet in the vast Painted Chamber, at which the little bride was named 'Princess of the Feast'. Apart from the incarcerated Clarence, the entire royal family was present, as well as foreign ambassadors, lords, ladies, knights, squires, and guards and servants in the mulberry and blue livery of the House of York. All but the latter took part in the dancing that lasted until the Kings of Arms entered and asked the bride if she would present the prizes that would be won at the jousts to be held the next day. Elizabeth was appointed to assist her, and a council of ladies was convened to decide what share in the ceremony each should take.

After the tournament on 16 January, the Kings of Arms gave Elizabeth the prizes: gems set with the golden letters A, M and E, standing for Anne, Mowbray and Elizabeth; Clarencieux Herald presented her with the A, set with a diamond, saying: 'Right high and excellent Princess, here is the prize which you shall award to the best jouster of the jousts royal.' Norroy Herald gave her the E, set with a ruby, for the best runner in armour, and March Herald the M, set with an emerald, for the best swordsman.

Elizabeth handed the A to the little 'Princess of the Feast', who bestowed it upon Thomas Fiennes, who had won first prize. The others went to Sir William Truswell and William Say, to the delight of the noble company.[61]

Darker deeds were brewing. Less than a month after the wedding festivities, on 8 February 1478, Clarence was condemned in Parliament. The Act of Attainder passed against him stated that he had 'falsely and traitorously intended and purposed firmly the extreme destruction and disinheriting of the King and his issue'. It accused him of spreading 'the falsest and most unnatural-coloured pretence that man might imagine'. He had 'falsely and untruly noised, published and said that the King our sovereign lord was a bastard and not begotten to reign upon us'.[62]

The King himself sat in judgement on his brother, but the Queen – in the deaths of whose father and brother Clarence had been complicit – was thought to have brought pressure to bear, as she had 'concluded that her offspring by the King would never come to the throne unless the Duke of Clarence were removed, and of this she easily persuaded the King'.[63] This Parliament included an influential Wydeville presence – Earl Rivers was one of the four 'triers' – that was 'easily the most powerful faction'.[64] Clarence's attainder deprived him of his life, titles and estates, and the rights of himself and his heirs to the succession. On the face of it, he was condemned for crimes for which he had already been pardoned and forgiven; but it is possible, of course, that he had recently reiterated his calumnies.

Although the Wydevilles were seen as being responsible for Clarence's fall, Edward had long had reason to believe that Clarence had designs on his throne; he had, after all, joined Warwick in rebellion and in spreading that tale of Edward's bastardy, something the King could neither have forgiven nor forgotten, and recently he had questioned the validity of Edward's marriage. Years later, when Elizabeth of York was queen, the historian Polydore Vergil asked Edward IV's surviving councillors about the reasons for the execution of Clarence, but they were not forthcoming. Possibly they were reluctant to repeat anything Clarence had said that cast doubt on Elizabeth's legitimacy. Clarence's recent scheme to marry the heiress of Burgundy had alone represented a major threat to the King, and he had publicly impugned Edward's justice. All in all, he was a deadly troublemaker, and had proved himself a threat to the realm's stability.

Because the Duchess Cecily had protested against her son being executed in public, Clarence was put to death privately on 18 February 1478 in the Tower of London. It was said that, allowed to choose how he would die, he opted to be drowned in a butt of Malmsey (Madeira) wine.[65] He left behind a three-year-old son, Edward, Earl of Warwick, who was barred by his father's attainder from ever inheriting the throne or any of Clarence's lands and titles; and a five-year-old daughter, Margaret, who would wear a tiny wooden wine butt on a bracelet all her life in commemoration of her father; it can be seen in her portrait in the National Portrait Gallery, London. The wardship and custody of Warwick were granted to Elizabeth Wydeville's son, Dorset,[66] and Edward IV arranged for the boy to go to Sheen to be brought up with Elizabeth and the other royal children.[67] It is likely that Margaret of Clarence was sent there too.

Elizabeth cannot have had a good opinion of her uncle. To her, raised under the influence of the Wydevilles, he was no doubt the *bête noire* of the family; like her mother, she probably saw him as a threat. He bore half the blame for the executions of her grandfather, Earl Rivers, and her uncle, John Wydeville, in 1469, and he had accused her mother of compassing his wife's death by sorcery. But the impact on a twelve-year-old of the judicial killing of her uncle by her father must have been considerable, and a brutal reminder of the dangers inherent in being of the blood royal in this turbulent period of history.

Mancini states that Gloucester was 'overcome with grief' at his brother's execution, and vowed to avenge it. Yet, while he would in time exact a fearful vengeance on Elizabeth Wydeville, there is evidence to suggest that he colluded in, and condoned, Clarence's fate. Some of his retainers had sat in the Parliament that condemned the Duke, and he himself appears to have supported Edward's proceedings.[68] He profited too, more than anyone else. Even before his brother's death, he had requested Clarence's share of the Warwick inheritance, and his son, Edward of Middleham, had received Clarence's forfeited earldom of Salisbury, while he himself was appointed Great Chamberlain of England in place of Clarence, and was granted lands belonging to the latter. It is possible, though, that, knowing that Clarence's fate was a foregone conclusion, and that half the Warwick inheritance was at stake, he gave the King his tacit support, then moved quickly afterwards to pre-empt any designs the Wydevilles may have had on that inheritance. That he was affected by his brother's fall is suggested by a letter he sent much later to James FitzGerald, Earl of Desmond, in which he recalled how he had had to keep his 'inward' feelings hidden.[69] Those inward feelings may very well have included hatred for the upstart Wydevilles who had destroyed a prince of the blood. If Richard really felt such hatred and resentment for the Queen and her kin, it would make more sense of his actions in five years' time.

Mancini states that 'thenceforth Richard came very rarely to court. He kept himself within his own lands and set out to acquire the loyalty of his people through favours and justice. The good reputation of his private life' – in contrast to his brother Edward – 'and public activities powerfully attracted the esteem of strangers. By these arts, Richard acquired the favour of the people, and avoided the jealousy of the Queen, from whom he lived far separated.' Richard's main political focus was the north, where he had his power base, and his responsibilities there tended to isolate him from the court anyway. He did spend most of the last years of Edward's reign in the north, as Mancini states, and although he visited the court in London on state occasions, it is unlikely that Elizabeth and her siblings ever got to know this often-absent uncle very well.

Mancini's testimony – which may have owed something to hindsight, although he used as sources people who would surely have known the truth – is often taken to mean that Richard deliberately avoided the Queen after Clarence's fall. But it is clear that avoiding her jealousy was the consequence of his good reputation, while Mancini merely observes that she lived a long way away, implying that this was to his advantage. Maybe Richard did fear her influence, having seen what it could do; while her behaviour later on might suggest that she had his measure and distrusted and feared him. However, working relations between Richard and her brother, Earl Rivers, remained amicable after 1478[70] – although the catastrophic events of 1483 were to show that Richard saw Rivers too as a threat.

Edward IV 'inwardly repented, very often' of having Clarence executed,[71] and reproached his nobles for not suing for mercy.[72] But ultimately he himself had to bear the responsibility for it; and the young Elizabeth had to come to terms with the knowledge that not even ties of blood were surety against disaster.

It was a superstitious age. Apart from the other reasons for Clarence's fall, Edward had apparently been swayed by a prophecy that 'G' should follow 'E' as king of England.[73] If true, it seems not to have occurred to him that his other brother was Gloucester – or that executing one of his blood had set a dangerous precedent for slaughter within his own House.[74]

That month of February 1478, Elizabeth turned twelve, the age at which she was to go to France and be married. Her dowry was already settled, and it had been agreed that King Louis should meet the expenses of her conveyance into his realm. Soon afterwards Mary, Duchess of Burgundy, appealed to Edward IV for aid against Louis XI, but Edward ignored her pleas, for he would allow nothing to compromise Elizabeth's prospects of marriage with the Dauphin.

On 11 August the King sent Dr Thomas Langton to France, to press Louis XI to conclude the espousals without further delay, and to ask him to endow Elizabeth with her jointure immediately, in advance of the wedding. Louis – by no means as committed to the match as Edward was – stalled. In December his ambassador told the King that he must not expect immediate payment of her jointure, insisting that his proposal was contrary to reason and French custom: Elizabeth could have her jointure only when the marriage took place, but the Dauphin, at eight, was too young to be wed at present, and it was usual for a jointure to be paid only after the consummation of a marriage. Edward's councillors expressed great indignation, and urged him to break the treaty, but he refused, being determined to force Louis to keep to its terms. But the writing was on the wall: France was then relying on England not to intervene on Maximilian's behalf in Burgundy, and if Louis could treat

his ally so dismissively when he needed him, clearly he was not
committed to the marriage.

There was grief in March 1479 when Elizabeth's two-year-old brother
George died at Windsor Castle, and was buried in St George's Chapel.
After his death, his nurse, Joan, Lady Dacre, became lady mistress to
Princess Mary.[75] The loss of her youngest son must have been hard
for the Queen, who was pregnant again; on 14 August 1479 she gave
birth to a healthy sixth daughter, Katherine, at Eltham Palace. It was
here that the infant Princess was christened. Joanna Colson was
appointed her nurse.[76]

Arguments about Elizabeth's jointure grumbled on through the
spring and summer of 1479. Edward's envoys warned the French
that, if there was any further prevarication, England would ally itself
with Maximilian. In August the Burgundians won a victory over
the French, and Maximilian and Mary declared that they would not
betroth their heir, Philip, to anyone except Edward IV's daughter
Elizabeth. In the face of this, late that year, Louis instructed his
envoys to offer 10,000 crowns (£1,261,500) as a maintenance grant
for Elizabeth, but Edward, who had been greedily anticipating the
£60,000 (£30 million) agreed at Picquigny, angrily turned down
the offer because it was contrary to the terms of the treaty.

By now, there were doubts in England as to Louis' sincerity. In
January 1480 the Milanese ambassador at the French court shrewdly
observed that Edward was not deceived by the French King's procrastination, and concluded that Elizabeth's marriage to the Dauphin
depended on Maximilian's ability to repel the French. He reported
that the English envoys had been told 'to press in and out of season
for the conclusion of the marriage. The King here stands in fear of
the King of England, on the supposition that, if he will not pay him
any heed while the Flemings still flourish, England will not be able
to get his desire when this King has accomplished his purpose' – i.e.
the conquest of Burgundy – 'and so diamond cuts diamond.'[77]

While Edward continued to put pressure on Louis, French envoys
were instructed to divert him by discussing only superficial details,
such as the timing and manner of Elizabeth's journey to France; if
she did not come, they said, King Louis would pay 20,000 crowns
(£2,520,000) for her maintenance while she remained in England.
But Edward insisted that he would accept only the £60,000 agreed
as her jointure. In May 1480 John, Lord Howard (later Duke of

Norfolk), and Dr Langton were sent to France to remind Louis of the terms of the marriage contract, but they made little progress. In the wake of this, Edward began seriously considering an alliance with Burgundy against France.

Unknown to Edward IV, Louis, fearing that England would unite with the Habsburgs against him, had begun making overtures to the Scots, England's enemy, for the marriage of James III's daughter Margaret to the Dauphin. Early in 1480 Edward learned of this and threatened James with war, thwarting Louis' schemes. At times like these, it may well have seemed to Elizabeth that her marriage would never take place.

In February 1480 she reached her fourteenth birthday. She was growing up to be 'very handsome'.[78] According to Giovanni de' Gigli, prebendary of St Paul's, writing in 1486, she was 'the illustrious maid of York, the fairest of Edward's offspring, deficient nor in virtue nor descent, most beautiful in form, whose matchless face adorned with most enchanting sweetness shines'.[79] It was almost obligatory for queens to be praised for their looks, but that Elizabeth grew up to be beautiful is borne out by her surviving portraits and her tomb effigy – which reveal a strong resemblance to her mother, especially about the large eyes, straight nose and what must have been a rosebud mouth in youth; while the inscription on her tomb, placed there by her son, Henry VIII, describes her as 'very pretty'. If her tomb effigy is an accurate representation, she grew up to be a graceful woman of five foot six in height.

In the fifteenth century, it was seen as highly desirable for queens to have blonde hair, for the Virgin Mary was increasingly being idealistically portrayed thus in art.[80] Elizabeth conformed to this ideal: she had a fair complexion and long 'golden' or 'fair yellow hair',[81] although it looks reddish-gold in her portraits, and may have been the same colour as her daughter Mary's, a lock of which (taken from Mary's coffin) is preserved in Moyse's Hall Museum in Bury St Edmunds.

In April 1480 Elizabeth's sisters Mary and Cecily were made Ladies of the Garter, and robes were provided for all three princesses for the annual festival.[82]

That year Cecily, Duchess of York, now sixty-five, enrolled herself as a Benedictine oblate and retired to her castle at Berkhamsted to pursue a life of religious devotion. As an oblate she wore sober secular robes and embraced the spirit of the Benedictine vows in her life in the world, dedicating herself to the service of God. Daily she observed the canonical hours, prayed and read the Scriptures, leaving only a little time for enjoying wine and recreation with her ladies. Elizabeth, at an impressionable age, was probably influenced by her grandmother's piety, and would herself grow up to be sincerely devout.

On 10 November 1480 Elizabeth Wydeville gave birth to her tenth and last child at Eltham Palace. It was another girl, who was called Bridget, an unusual choice of name that had no royal precedent but was perhaps chosen by Cecily, Duchess of York, who cherished a special devotion to St Bridget of Sweden, foundress of the Bridgettine order, in which the Duchess took a particular interest.[83] Again Cecily's influence can be detected, for Elizabeth herself would grow up with a deep reverence for St Bridget, a fourteenth-century visionary who was celebrated for her piety and charity.

Choosing the name of a saint who left the royal court of Sweden to found a monastic order suggests that the King and Queen decided from the first that they would devote this daughter to God. It was not unusual for wealthy medieval parents to do that, as a gesture of thanksgiving, or to lay up treasure for themselves in Heaven. Their daughter would have no choice in the matter.

On the morning after the birth, St Martin's Day, Elizabeth stood godmother to her new sister at her christening in the Great Chapel at Eltham. A hundred 'knights, esquires and other honest persons' entered the chapel first, carrying unlit torches, then came Thomas FitzAlan, Lord Maltravers, bearing a basin and towel, Henry Percy, Earl of Northumberland, with an unlit taper, and John de la Pole, Earl of Lincoln, bearing the salt; there followed other peers, among them the young Duke of York, Lord Hastings, Thomas, Lord Stanley, and Richard Fiennes, Lord Dacre, the Queen's chamberlain. Then came the Queen's sister, Margaret Wydeville, Lady Maltravers, wearing 'a rich white cloth pinned over her left side' and carrying the chrisom. Margaret Beaufort, the other godmother – no doubt chosen because in 1472 she had married Lord Stanley, a close associate of the Wydevilles – carried the Princess Bridget beneath a canopy borne by three knights and a baron. Elizabeth followed with Dorset and the Duchess of York. William Wayneflete, the octogenarian Bishop of Winchester, was the godfather, and Edward Story, Bishop of Chichester, officiated. 'My lady the King's mother and my Lady

Elizabeth were godmothers at the font,' and a squire held the basins for them. At the moment of baptism, the knights and esquires lit their torches, and the heralds donned their tabards. The baby was taken up to the altar to be confirmed, and then into an anteroom where the godparents presented their 'great gifts'; whereupon she was borne back in procession to the Queen's chamber to be blessed.[84]

Young York's wife, Anne Mowbray, was not present. Possibly she was unwell, for sometime between 16 January and 19 November 1481 she died at the palace of Placentia at Greenwich, aged only eight. She was given a lavish funeral and buried in the chapel of St Erasmus in Westminster Abbey.

In June 1480 Margaret of Burgundy had visited England with a view to enlisting Edward IV's support against France and arranging a marriage between Maximilian's son Philip and Anne of York. Aware of her intentions, Louis sent envoys to England with Edward's pension and the offer of an extra 15,000 crowns (£1,892,210) a year for Elizabeth's maintenance until her marriage. That placed Edward in an ideal situation for bargaining with Burgundy, and that August he signed a treaty with Maximilian, by the terms of which five-year-old Anne was betrothed to Philip of Habsburg, it being agreed that the marriage would take place when she was twelve.[85]

Before entering into this alliance, Edward had told Margaret of Burgundy that Louis was prepared to concede all his demands in regard to Elizabeth's marriage to the Dauphin. But now Louis faced the prospect of Edward joining forces with Maximilian against him, and he began to strengthen his defences for war. He also stopped paying the pension guaranteed to Edward by the Treaty of Picquigny. Plans for a peace conference broke down, and Maximilian continued to press for English aid against France. The Anglo-French alliance now looked decidedly precarious.

In 1481 Edward IV reached an agreement with Francis of Brittany that Prince Edward should marry the Duke's only child, four-year-old Anne, the heiress of Brittany, when she reached the age of twelve. Fourteen-year-old Princess Mary was betrothed to the future King Frederick I of Denmark, and James III of Scots began pressing Edward IV to send Princess Cecily to Scotland to be betrothed to his son.[86] Among the husbands proposed for Katherine of York were the Infante Juan, Prince of the Asturias and heir to the Spanish throne,[87] and James Butler, Earl of Ormond. Through the unions of his daughters, Edward envisioned English influence extending through France, Scotland, Denmark, Burgundy, the Holy Roman Empire and Spain – and beyond. It seemed that soon Elizabeth and her siblings would all be living in far-off kingdoms, rarely or never to see each other again.

But the Scots now began infringing the peace with England, and putting the marriage treaty at risk. Hearing that his ally, King Louis, was once more weighing Elizabeth's betrothal to the Dauphin in the balance, James III led a raid over the border into England. Edward raised a great army in retaliation, but Maximilian was urging him to come to his aid in Burgundy against Louis. Edward prevaricated, while the ailing Louis waited to see what he would do.

Still wanting to maintain his lucrative friendship with France, Edward assured Louis in March 1481 that troops he had sent to Burgundy were not to be used against the French, and that he would continue to uphold the Treaty of Picquigny, on condition that Louis resumed payment of his pension and sent an embassy to arrange Elizabeth's marriage to the Dauphin. If Louis agreed to this, Edward promised not to send his new army against France, but to Scotland, as he had originally intended. Louis was quick to acquiesce, and in August he sent an envoy with Edward's pension.

At last Edward decided to move against the Scots. In the autumn of 1481, at Nottingham – much to King Louis' relief – he again confirmed the Anglo-French treaty, but on condition that Elizabeth's marriage to the Dauphin would not be delayed further. Immediately, Louis abandoned all thoughts of a Scottish marriage for his son.

Tragedy intervened to prevent the fruition of another of Edward's alliances when, on 23 May 1482, the Thursday before Whitsunday, Elizabeth's sister Mary died at Placentia at Greenwich, aged just fifteen. The following Monday her body was carried to the nearby church of the Observant Friars, founded by her father, where James Goldwell, Bishop of Norwich, sang a dirge over it. Elizabeth and her younger sisters were not present, nor did they or their parents attend a second service the following morning, at which many high-ranking ladies were present, including Joan, Lady Dacre, Princess Mary's lady mistress. Dinner was served at the palace afterwards, after which the mourners returned to the church to attend the coffin as it was laid on a chariot adorned with Mary's arms and drawn by horses trapped with sables to Windsor and burial in St George's Chapel. Here Mary was laid to rest beside 'my lord her brother'

(George), the Prince of Wales being present as chief mourner.[88] The loss of her sister must have affected Elizabeth deeply, for they were only seventeen months apart in age, and had been brought up together from infancy.

The year 1482 saw the arrival at court of a number of foreign ambassadors, come to discuss the marriages of the King's daughters. After June, when Henry Tudor was granted the lands of his maternal grandmother on condition he return from exile 'to be in the grace and favour of the King's Highness',[89] there was some discussion about his marrying one of the princesses, but again it would not have been Elizabeth, as she was already betrothed. However, Henry did not venture into England. He may have suspected another trap; unsurprisingly his life as a fugitive had left him deeply suspicious of others' motives. Yet it does seem that Edward IV at last genuinely intended to receive him into favour, and Margaret Beaufort, who was now held in high esteem at court thanks to two judicious marriages, assured him of the King's good faith.

It was Elizabeth, at just sixteen years old, who was soon to discover just how perfidious princes could be. James III had now apologised for his ill-advised border raid, but his disaffected brother, Alexander Stewart, Duke of Albany, whom he had imprisoned, now escaped to the English court and dripped poison into King Edward's ear, with the result that, in June, Edward broke off Cecily's betrothal to Prince James of Scots, and affianced her to the treacherous Albany, of whose designs on the Scots throne he was well aware.[90] 'King Alexander' now advanced north on Scotland with Gloucester at the head of the English army. They took James III captive, but Albany soon came to terms with his brother, and Gloucester made peace, with the Scots ceding Berwick to England. Cecily found herself once more betrothed to James's son, but that was not the end of it: when an attempt was made on the King of Scots' life, Albany again sought the support of King Edward and secured Cecily as his future bride. In October, Edward finally called off her betrothal to James III.[91]

This was just a prequel to what would follow. Possibly Louis had never had any real intention of allowing Elizabeth's marriage to his heir to go forward,[92] but in March 1482 Mary of Burgundy died after a fall from her horse, and her Flemish subjects, who did not like Maximilian, made overtures to Louis XI, who seized his advantage. On 23 December 1482 an alliance – the Treaty of Arras – was concluded between Louis and the Flemings, providing for the marriage of the Dauphin to three-year-old Margaret of Burgundy, Maximilian's daughter. Edward IV's pension was terminated, while Louis got to keep all of Burgundy but Flanders, which was ceded to Maximilian; and thus French ambitions were satisfied.

The treaty left Edward IV's foreign policy in shreds. Not only had his lucrative pension been abruptly cut off, but his daughter was to suffer the humiliation of being publicly jilted. 'It was very well known that the girl was a great deal too old for Monseigneur the Dauphin,' observed Commines, as if that was the reason for Louis snubbing her.

Unsuspecting, the King presided over a splendid court that Christmas, the last time he would ever do so. 'King Edward kept the feast of the Nativity at his palace at Westminster, frequently appearing clad in a great variety of most costly garments.' His 'most elegant figure overshadowed everyone else' as he 'stood before the onlookers like some new and extraordinary spectacle. In those days you would have seen a royal court worthy of a most mighty kingdom, filled with riches and men from almost every nation, and, surpassing all else, those beautiful and most delightful children, the issue of his marriage with Queen Elizabeth', among them his daughters, five 'most beauteous maidens'.[93] Twelve-year-old Prince Edward had come up from Ludlow to join his siblings, and appeared in a dazzling outfit of white cloth of gold, while Elizabeth and her mother had received fifteen yards of green tissue (taffeta silk) cloth of gold.[94] This was the last recorded occasion on which Elizabeth and her brothers and sisters were all together.

On the face of it, they had bright futures awaiting them, but the well-informed Croyland chronicler observed that, 'although, in earlier years, solemn embassies and pledges of faith in the words of princes had been despatched, with letters of agreement drawn up in due form concerning the marriage of each of the daughters, it was not now thought that any of the marriages would materialise, for everything was susceptible to change, given the unstable relations between England and France, Scotland, Burgundy and Spain'. The news of Louis' perfidy reached England in January, and Edward IV's fury knew no bounds. 'Worried and aggrieved', and 'boldly considering any means of gaining revenge', he summoned Parliament, 'revealed the whole series of gross deceits,'[95] and demanded that England make war on France. On 20 January, in the Lords, Thomas Rotherham, Archbishop of York, denounced Louis XI for his deceitfulness, while Croyland accused him of encouraging the Scots to break Cecily's betrothal too.

Although she could not have been hurt personally, Elizabeth was old enough to feel humiliated and offended by the French King's rejection of her, but that was as nothing compared to the 'evils' that 'shortly afterwards miserably befell the King and his illustrious progeny'.[96] In the meantime – as was later asserted by the Elizabethan chronicler, Raphael Holinshed – Edward IV may seriously have begun considering a marriage between his jilted daughter and the exiled Henry Tudor. It was an effective means of removing Tudor from the dangerous arena of European politics and securing his loyalty. Apparently the King had talks on the matter with Margaret Beaufort, Lord Stanley, John Morton, Bishop of Ely, and John Alcock, Bishop of Worcester, with a view to bringing the marriage to fruition. Time, however, was not on Edward's side.

3

'This Act of Usurpation'

On 9 April 1483, when she was just seventeen, Elizabeth was plunged into 'a tempestuous world'.[1] After a short illness, her father King Edward died at Westminster, aged just forty-one. He was 'neither worn out with old age, nor seized with any known kind of malady', but he 'took to his bed'[2] and succumbed to 'an unknown disease'.[3] Mancini says he had caught a chill at the end of March while out in a small boat fishing at Windsor. 'Being a tall and very fat man, he let the damp cold chill his guts and caught a sickness from which he never recovered.' Possibly it was pneumonia or typhoid, but Edward then suffered an apoplexy, which Commines believed 'was caused by Louis XI rejecting the Princess Royal Elizabeth as a wife for his little Dauphin Charles'. It could also have resulted from Edward being overweight and having high blood pressure. After the stroke he 'perceived his natural strength so sore enfeebled that he despaired all recovery'.[4]

Edward was succeeded by his twelve-year-old son, now Edward V, who was proclaimed king on 11 April. Mancini writes dismissively that the King 'also left behind daughters, but they do not concern us' – a typical medieval view. In his will of 1475, Edward had decreed 'that our daughter Elizabeth have 10,000 marks [£1.5 million] towards her marriage, so that [she] be governed and ruled by our dearest wife the Queen' and the young King. If Elizabeth did 'marry without such advice and assent, so as [she] be thereby disparaged (which God forbid), then she so marrying herself have no payment of her 10,000 marks'.[5] The loss of her father and chief protector was, for Elizabeth, the beginning of two of the most traumatic years of her life.

According to 'The Song of Lady Bessy', on his deathbed Edward commended his daughter Elizabeth – who is incorrectly described as 'a little child' – to the governance, guidance and keeping of Thomas, Lord Stanley. Stanley, a prominent member of the King's Council, Steward of the Household, husband of Margaret Beaufort and the owner of vast estates in Cheshire and north Wales, was then forty-eight. He was one of the King's trusted officers, despite his having earlier switched allegiance from York to Lancaster and back again. He has aptly been described as a 'wily fox' who could 'seemingly extricate himself from the most precarious situations',[6] and he was at the forefront of political affairs and intrigues through five reigns. In January 1486, Stanley was to depose that he had known Elizabeth for fifteen years,[7] from about 1470, when she was five. It is not inconceivable therefore that Edward asked him to look to her welfare and act as her mentor, but there is no corroborating evidence to show that Stanley ever had her person in his keeping.

A bidding prayer was read in churches at the beginning of the new reign, enjoining all to pray for 'our dread King Edward V, the lady Queen Elizabeth his mother [and] all the royal offspring'.[8]

The Wydevilles were then in a strong position. They controlled the young King, the court, the Council, the Tower of London, the fleet, the royal treasure and the late King's other children. Mancini wrote of the hatred in which Rivers, Dorset and Sir Richard Grey were held 'on account of their morals, but mostly because of a certain inherent jealousy. They were certainly detested by the nobles because they, who were ignoble and newly made men, were advanced beyond those who far excelled them in breeding and wisdom.' They still 'had to endure the imputation of causing the death of the Duke of Clarence'.

Mancini heard 'men say' that, in his will or the codicils he added on his deathbed, none of which have survived, Edward IV had expressed the wish that his brother, Richard of Gloucester, should act as Lord Protector during the minority of the young King.[9] For many years now, Richard had been ruling the north loyally on Edward's behalf, and enjoying almost sovereign power there as the King's trusted lieutenant. He was the obvious choice. As events would prove, he was also one of the nobles who detested the *parvenu* Wydevilles and deeply resented the influence they enjoyed. He also apparently held them responsible for the death of his brother Clarence.

The Wydevilles had no intention of allowing Gloucester to seize power; they clearly foresaw the continuance and flowering of their supremacy under Edward V. The late King's councillors were with the Queen at Westminster, and it was agreed that the Council should govern for the young King, with Gloucester being accorded a leading role rather than an autonomous one, 'because it had been found that no regent ever laid down his office, save reluctantly. Moreover, if the entire government were committed to one man, he might easily usurp the sovereignty. All who favoured the Queen's family voted for this proposal, as they were afraid that, if Gloucester took unto himself the crown, or even governed alone, they, who bore the blame of Clarence's death, would suffer death, or at least be ejected from their high estate.'[10] This suggests that the Wydevilles had good reason to believe that Gloucester would vent his hatred on them for contriving his brother's execution.

Speedily the councillors named a day – 4 May – for the young King's coronation, to pre-empt Gloucester assuming the regency.[11] It is sometimes asserted that Edward V would have come of age by the time of his coronation, so that there would have been no need for a regency, but he would have been too young. Henry VI, the last king to succeed as a minor, had been crowned at eight years old and had not assumed personal rule until he was declared of age at nearly sixteen. Upon his coronation in 1429, the office of protector had lapsed and devolved upon the Council – which was what the Wydevilles clearly envisaged happening in 1483. It was the Parliament that would be called in Edward V's name after his crowning that would have the authority finally to determine who should wield power during his minority; any appointment made now would cease with the coronation, hence the haste to have the boy crowned. Influence over the Council was therefore crucial, but while some councillors seem to have been concerned to maintain a balance of power, the Wydevilles were determined to prevent Gloucester from taking control. 'We are so important that, even without the King's uncle, we can make and enforce these decisions,' boasted Dorset.[12]

Mancini believed, probably correctly, that there was already little love lost between Gloucester and the Queen and her faction, and the events that would now unfold gave him no cause to doubt that. Edward IV, for all that he had strengthened the monarchy and restored its prestige, had fatally been unable to unite the two power centres he had created – Gloucester and the Wydevilles. There was enmity too between the Queen's son, Dorset, and William, Lord Hastings, of which Edward had been aware. 'At the command and entreaty of the King, who loved each of them, they had been reconciled two days before he died, yet there still survived a latent jealousy.'[13] That jealousy was fuelled by Hastings taking Elizabeth Shore as his mistress as soon as Edward IV was dead. During Edward's lifetime he had been 'sore enamoured' of her, yet had held back, 'either for reverence or for a certain friendly faithfulness' to his master.[14] Dorset had wanted her too; now he was even more incensed against Hastings.

It was inevitable therefore that Edward IV's death would spark a struggle for control of the government and the young King. Edward V, having been under the influence of his mother's faction from infancy, was unlikely to be well disposed towards anyone who opposed them, and he would come of age in three years' time, so his wishes would be influential.

Significantly, the Wydevilles did not send to inform Gloucester of his brother's death, no doubt because of their intention to exclude him from the regency government; he learned of it from Lord Hastings, Edward IV's loyal councillor and friend, who 'was hostile to the entire kin of the Queen, on account of [his rivalry with] the Marquess [of Dorset]'. He advised the Duke that the late King, on his deathbed, had 'committed to him only [his] wife, children, goods and all that ever he had',[15] and urged him to hasten to the capital 'with a strong force', and to take the young King 'under his protection and authority' on the way.[16]

Gloucester was unwilling to tolerate rule by the hated Wydevilles, and he may have feared the consequences to himself if they remained in control.[17] He immediately took Hastings' advice and rode south to meet his kinsman, Henry Stafford, Duke of Buckingham, who was his natural ally. Like Hastings, 'Harre Bokenham' (as he signed himself) hated the Queen's party,[18] and with good cause: brought up in Elizabeth Wydeville's household, he had been forced against his will and aristocratic instincts to marry her sister Katherine.[19] The young Elizabeth probably knew Buckingham quite well; he was her kinsman and her uncle by marriage, and she had danced with him at court. With Gloucester, Hastings and Buckingham allied in a coalition to bring down the unpopular Wydevilles, the stage was set for a fatal power struggle.

★

One of the chief sources for the events that unfolded next was Dominic Mancini. Some recent historians have questioned his credibility as an objective source, asserting that he was swayed by anti-Wydeville propaganda. Yet he was clearly aware of the existence of such propaganda, and he also warmly praised Earl Rivers, the most influential of the Queen's kin. An astute eyewitness, writing in December 1483 at the latest, he was close to the events of that year, even if his account of those that had happened before his arrival in England is flawed in places. John Argentine, Edward V's physician, was one of Mancini's sources, and he would hardly have conveyed a negative view of the Wydevilles, so his testimony could have counterbalanced the propaganda of Gloucester and others. Moreover, Mancini took a dim view of Gloucester, so he is unlikely to have accepted the Duke's propaganda at face value. He was not hampered by the political constraints imposed on English commentators,[20] so his account is less likely to be biased.

Mancini believed that the Wydevilles and Gloucester went in fear of each other. That the Wydevilles did fear the Duke, and with cause, is borne out by subsequent events and the Queen's response to them. If we reject Mancini's rationale, that genuine fear of the Wydevilles drove Gloucester to act as he did next, then we might conclude that he was spurred by hatred or resentment, and the need to overthrow an unpopular faction who were bent on staying in power. Had he liked and approved of the Wydevilles, and had no cause to fear them, there was no reason why he could not have shared power with them. But, as a prince of the blood royal and the second-highest-ranking duke in the realm (after Edward V's younger brother, the Duke of York), he clearly agreed with Hastings, Buckingham and others that the Wydevilles were not fit to have control of the King and the government of the realm.

All Gloucester's acts, from the time he learned of his brother's death, display a strength and consistency of purpose that is at odds with any theory that he was responding to events rather than driving them.[21] In the light of that, we must also consider a far darker scenario: that he was driven by hatred, and by ambition that had either surfaced or been born when an opportune moment presented itself. Mancini says that from the first, 'there were those who were not unaware of [Gloucester's] ambition and cunning, and who had misgivings about where they would lead'. The Queen certainly shared these misgivings. If Gloucester hated her and her faction sufficiently to seek their overthrow, it is possible that his enmity extended to her son, the young King.

He now wrote to the Council, reminding them 'he had been loyal to his brother Edward', and assuring them 'he would be equally loyal to his brother's son, and to all his brother's issue, even female, if, which God forfend, the youth should die. He would expose his life to every danger that the children might endure in their father's realm.'[22] Already these eventualities had occurred to him. He also wrote 'most loving letters' to the Queen, to console her in her loss, declaring 'his carefulness and natural affection towards his brother's children',[23] but his letter did not allay her fears, or divert her and her faction from their determination to bar him from taking power.

On 18 April, after lying in state at Westminster, Edward IV's body was conveyed up the Thames to Windsor and there, two days later, buried in the new St George's Chapel, 'which he had reverently founded and built'.[24] Elizabeth was not present. The funerals of kings were not attended by their female relations, who by custom mourned in privacy.

Meanwhile, Gloucester had hastened south. Although he had not yet been confirmed as Lord Protector, and had no legal mandate to act as he did, he was determined to seize the person of the young King as he was taken to London by his uncle, Earl Rivers, his half-brother, Sir Richard Grey, Sir Thomas Vaughan, his chamberlain, and Sir Richard Haute, the Queen's kinsman, with an escort of 2,000 men. On 29 April, with his forces bolstered by those of his ally, Buckingham, Gloucester intercepted the King's party at Stony Stratford. The next day at dawn, after sharing a convivial meal with them, he suddenly seized Rivers, Grey, Vaughan and Haute, who were afterwards conveyed north and imprisoned at Sheriff Hutton Castle and Pontefract Castle. It was clear that this was the prelude to the overthrow of Wydeville rule. The lack of any outcry in response to Gloucester's coup shows that he and his allies had calculated correctly that hatred of the Queen's faction was widespread and deeply rooted. Evidently many nobles approved of his decisiveness.[25]

Edward V was staunch in his defence of Rivers and the others, but he was overruled by Gloucester, who now saw at first hand that the King's loyalty lay with his mother and her kin. That did not bode well for the future. The boy insisted that the government be entrusted to the Queen and the lords of the realm, doubtless meaning those of the Wydeville faction, but Buckingham answered 'that it was not women's place to govern the kingdom, but men's, [and] if he hoped for anything from her, he should abandon it'.[26]

Elizabeth must have been aware of the political manoeuvring going on around her; she may have known that her mother's kin were not popular, or liked by Gloucester; but her focus would probably have been on the imminent arrival of her brother the King in London and the coming coronation. It was a terrible shock, therefore, when news of Gloucester's coup reached London 'a little before midnight' on 30 April.[27] 'The unexpectedness of the event horrified everyone.'[28]

Elizabeth would have seen how appalled the Queen was to hear that 'the King her son was taken, her brother, her son and her other friends arrested and sent no man knows wist whither, to be done with God wot what'.[29] At a stroke, the Duke had undermined the power of the Wydevilles, whom he apparently seemed bent on destroying. He would soon be in London, and what would happen to them all then?

There was a flurry of panicked activity at Westminster. Immediately the Queen and her remaining son, Dorset, 'began collecting an army to defend themselves and to set free the young King from the clutches of the dukes. But when they had consulted certain nobles and others to take up arms, they perceived that men's minds were not only irresolute but altogether hostile to themselves. Some even said openly that it was more just and profitable that the youthful sovereign should be with his paternal uncle than with his maternal uncles and uterine brothers.'[30]

Elizabeth Wydeville, 'fearing the sequel of this business',[31] decided there was one course of action open to her – one she had taken before in a crisis. That same night,[32] she resolved to take sanctuary at Westminster, 'to the intent she might deliver her other children from the present danger'.[33] 'In great fright and heaviness, bewailing her child's ruin, her friends' mischance and her own infortune, damning the time that ever she dissuaded the gathering of power about the King, she got herself with all haste possible, with her daughters and her younger son, out of the Palace of Westminster, in which she then lay',[34] and fled into sanctuary at Westminster Abbey. Her youngest child, two-year-old Bridget, had not been well, and may have been brought to Westminster from the royal chambers in the Royal Wardrobe near Baynard's Castle, for after her father's death she had been 'sick in the said Wardrobe'.[35]

The Queen 'and all her children and company were registered as sanctuary persons'.[36] John Eastney, Abbot of Westminster since 1474 and a patron of Caxton, had stood godfather to Prince Edward back in 1470; he took them under his protection, and did not demur at the Queen once more 'lodging herself and her company in the Abbot's palace', Cheyneygates,[37] where the little Elizabeth had stayed in sanctuary with her mother and sisters in 1470–1. They were joined in the sanctuary by Dorset and Lionel Wydeville, Bishop of Salisbury.[38] Dorset, who had forsaken his post as Constable of the Tower, escaped from sanctuary some weeks later, evading the soldiers and dogs that were after him, and went into hiding.[39]

This must have been a traumatic and frightening time for Elizabeth, with her father so lately dead and her mother and kinsmen convinced that Richard of Gloucester intended harm to them all. Helpless herself, she must have known that, in his eyes, she was inextricably linked to her mother's party, and therefore an enemy. Maybe she hated him for what he had done to her family.

Her mother was in a state of near collapse. She had fled the palace precipitately, leaving orders for her stuff to be conveyed across to the Abbey after her. When Thomas Rotherham, Archbishop of York, arrived at the sanctuary in the small hours of that morning, bringing the Great Seal of England to the Queen, he found 'much heaviness, rumble, haste and busyness' surrounding her, for 'the carriage and conveyance of her stuff' was already in hand. The Archbishop was astounded to see 'chests, coffers, packs, fardels, trussed all on men's backs, no man unoccupied, some loading, some coming, some going, some discharging, some coming for more, some carrying more than they ought the wrong way, and some breaking down the walls to bring in the next way'. The scene was total chaos, but amidst all the flurry, 'the Queen sat alone, a-low on the rushes, all desolate and dismayed', knowing that there would be no Edward IV to rescue her and her children from sanctuary this time. 'The Archbishop comforted [her] in the best manner he could, showing her that he trusted the matter was nothing so sore as she took it for', and saying he had been reassured by a message sent to him by Lord Hastings.

'Ah, woe worth him,' the Queen cried, 'for he is one of those that laboureth to destroy me and my blood.'

'Madam,' Rotherham replied, 'be ye of good cheer, for I assure you, if they crown any other king than your son, we shall on the morrow crown his brother.' And he handed her the Great Seal, to hold on behalf of Edward V.[40]

But when the Archbishop left at dawn, and returned to York Place, his London residence, he saw through 'his chamber window all the Thames full of boats of the Duke of Gloucester's servants, watching that no man should go into sanctuary, nor none pass unsearched'.[41] Elizabeth would soon realise that she was now a virtual prisoner, unable to leave the Abbey. And this was only the beginning of her misfortunes.

On 4 May a black-clad Gloucester rode into London with the young King, who was wearing royal mourning of 'blue velvet' for his father, and it was noted with approval by the people that the Duke showed his sovereign much respect and honour. But he and Buckingham 'were seeking at every turn to arouse hatred against the Queen's kin, and to estrange public opinion from her relatives', and 'they took especial pains to do so the day they entered the City. For ahead of the procession they sent four wagons loaded with weapons bearing the devices of the Queen's brothers and sons, besides criers to make generally known that these arms had been collected by the Duke's enemies so as to attack and slay [him].'[42] The weapons had, in fact, been stored against war with the Scots.

Elizabeth, who cherished 'unbounded love' for her siblings,[43] must have been sad not to be reunited with her brother, Edward V. She may have had fears for him. But he was effortlessly winning the love of his subjects. Mancini, who may well have seen the young King at this time, says that 'in word and deed, he gave so many proofs of his liberal education, of polite, nay, rather scholarly attainments far beyond his age. He had such dignity in his whole person, and in his face such charm that, however much they might gaze, he never wearied the eyes of beholders.'

Outwardly, all seemed set fair for the new reign, and it might have appeared that the Queen's flight into sanctuary had been too precipitate. Gloucester saw to it that the laws of the realm were enforced in Edward V's name; coins were struck bearing the boy's image, 'and all royal honours were paid to him'.[44] Given that the Duke was now firmly in control of the young King, the Council had no choice but to recognise him as protector, although they refused to proceed against Rivers, Grey and the rest because Gloucester had not – at the time – had the authority to arrest them; nevertheless, the men remained in prison. A new date, 24 June,[45] was set for the coronation. Everyone, says Croyland, 'was looking forward to the peace and prosperity of the kingdom', and Lord Hastings 'was overjoyed at this new world, saying that nothing more had happened than the transfer of the rule of the kingdom from two of the Queen's relatives to two of the King's'. His jubilation was premature, for the Council had made it clear that the office of protector would still lapse with the coronation, and Gloucester knew that the days of his power might be numbered.

Hastings must have been a man of limited imagination to have passed over so glibly the tragedies that had overtaken Elizabeth and her family. Whether Gloucester was a threat or not, her mother had compelling reasons to believe that he was, and the atmosphere in sanctuary must have been heavy with grief and anxiety, with no end to it in view. It must have been poignant living in such close proximity to the palace where they had spent so much time in former years, heedless of the events that were to overtake them. And although they were housed in some luxury, as guests of the Abbot, they were dependent on him for their security, and, before long, for the very necessities of life. For on 7 May Edward IV's executors declined to administer his will, on the grounds that while the Queen held his daughters in sanctuary, his bequests to them could not be carried out. Accordingly, the Archbishop of Canterbury placed the late King's goods under sequestration. Elizabeth had been deprived not only of her freedom, but of her dowry, and the Queen and her children had been rendered penniless.[46]

The contemporary *Paston Letters* contain a complaint about the 'great cost' of living in sanctuary. There is no mention of a butcher like John Gould supplying meat during this second sojourn, and any store of money that Elizabeth Wydeville had brought with her would rapidly have dwindled, because the merchants who came to sell to sanctuary dwellers often charged 'right unreasonable' prices.[47] It must have been a humbling experience for the Queen and her daughters to be obliged to presume upon the Abbot's charity.

They dared not leave Cheyneygates, even though the boundaries of the Westminster sanctuary extended further, for fear of being seized; yet anyone could enter to see them, which must have been a further source of anxiety. Although sanctuaries were regarded as holy places that must be treated with reverence, there were notorious examples of their being breached, as had happened in 1471, when Edward IV, brandishing his sword, had entered the abbey of Tewkesbury and dragged out the Lancastrians who had sought sanctuary there.[48] The sanctuary at Westminster had long enjoyed the patronage and protection of English kings, who regarded it as an outward symbol of royal power and mercy, but Mancini observed that things had declined since the Queen had sought sanctuary under Henry VI, and that 'sanctuaries are of little avail against the royal authority'.

Little is recorded about the lives of those in sanctuary. Elizabeth was effectively a guest in a monastery, and her life was governed by bells and prayer. It cannot have been a happy existence for a bereaved girl of seventeen – indeed it was perhaps a constant ordeal – but the presence of her younger siblings would have enlivened her days and kept her occupied.

Among the luggage the Queen had brought with her was at least one book – a devotional manuscript, 'Letters and Collects for Vigils of Saturday before Easter and Pentecost', dating from around 1300, with later additions. In the margin of the first folio it is inscribed: 'Westminster Abbey. Elizabeth *dei gratia*. To my good friend Mortimer.' In the fourth folio is the dedication: 'To the victorious and triumphant King Henry', which must have been written after August 1485. The last folio bears the words 'Westminster Abbey'. It is a reasonable assumption that the book was owned and annotated by Elizabeth Wydeville when she was in sanctuary, and that the said Mortimer – who was perhaps Sir John Mortimer of Kyre[49] – supported her in some way while she was there. Tradition has it that she gave the book to her daughter Elizabeth, for either could have written the dedication 'To the victorious and triumphous King Henry [VII]'.[50]

The Council felt that it was not suitable for the young King to stay at the Palace of Westminster because of the proximity of the sanctuary at Westminster Abbey, where his mother and sisters lay. Instead it was decided, at Buckingham's suggestion (which was possibly prompted by Gloucester), that Edward should lodge in the palace of the Tower of London, where monarchs traditionally stayed before their coronations. The Tower had not yet acquired the sinister reputation it was to gain under the Tudors; on the contrary, it had been one of Edward IV's favourite residences, so would have held happy associations for Edward V. But it was also a strong and secure fortress.

By May the Council was becoming uneasy about Elizabeth Wydeville remaining in sanctuary, and the continuing imprisonment of her kinsmen, and concerns were expressed that 'the Protector did not, with a sufficient degree of considerateness, take fitting care for the preservation of the dignity and safety of the Queen'.[51] Gloucester responded to this by making efforts to persuade his sister-in-law to leave sanctuary with her children, appointing a committee to negotiate with her, and sending councillors with assurances of her and the children's safety, but all were met with a barrage of scorn, tears and indignation.[52] In the first week of June, the Council tried again to persuade the Queen to leave sanctuary with her children and go into honourable retirement, but again she refused.

Her obduracy gave Gloucester grounds for treating the Wydeville faction as aggressors. On 10 June he sent a letter to the civic council of York for the muster of troops to march on London against 'the Queen, her blood adherents and affinity, which have intended and daily doth intend to murder and utterly destroy us and our cousin, the Duke of Buckingham, and the old royal blood of this realm'[53] – proof, if any were now needed, of how deeply he hated the Wydevilles. But the latter's wings had been well and truly clipped: the Queen was in sanctuary, powerless, and her kinsmen were scattered, either in prison or in hiding, so clearly Gloucester's accusations were merely an excuse to bolster his power with military force.

Lord Hastings, resentful that Buckingham had usurped his prominence on the Council, and mistrusting Gloucester's intentions, now switched sides to the Queen, although his prime loyalty remained to Edward IV's son. But on 13 June Gloucester found out that Hastings had confided his concerns about the Protector's ambitions to Thomas Rotherham, Archbishop of York, John Morton, Bishop of Ely, and Lord Stanley. Within hours Hastings's 'joy gave way entirely to grief',[54] for Gloucester responded by staging a second illegal coup. It was another pre-emptive strike, a ruthless exercise to eliminate or neutralise his opponents, and with it he embarked on a reign of tyranny in order to silence all those who stood in the way of his ambitions. And his ambitions, as many had suspected, and as would now become clear, focused on the crown. His much-vaunted loyalty to his brother now counted for nothing.

Immediately, that same morning, he summoned Hastings and

others to a council meeting in the Tower, and there – in a dramatic scene later immortalised by Shakespeare – accused him of treason and had him summarily executed, 'without judgement or justice'. In like wise, Stanley, Morton and Rotherham were also arrested, but spared execution 'out of respect for their status' and – again without trial – sent to Wales to be imprisoned in separate castles. In this way, 'the three strongest supporters of the new King had been removed, and – all the rest of his faithful subjects fearing the like treatment – the two dukes did thenceforth just as they pleased'. This was achieved in part by the strong presence of Richard's northern troops, 'in fearful and unheard-of numbers', in the capital.[55]

Richard knew that Stanley was too rich and influential to be alienated, and that his loyalty must be bought. Soon he would restore him to the Council and grant him new lands and high offices. It might have seemed to Elizabeth that 'father Stanley' – as she called him in 'The Song of Lady Bessy' – had abandoned her at this frightening time. But Stanley's first loyalty was to himself.

Even in sanctuary Elizabeth must have heard about Elizabeth Shore doing public penance at St Paul's for her harlotry, clad only in a sheet, before being committed to Ludgate Prison, all on Gloucester's orders. In fact, Mistress Shore had been arrested for her connection with Hastings, and her very public punishment was probably intended to discredit them both and give weight to Gloucester's summary sentence on Hastings. It also proclaimed that the Duke, unlike his late brother, would not tolerate immorality.

Gloucester knew it was not enough to have the young King in his power. He 'foresaw that the Duke of York would by legal right succeed to the throne if his brother were removed'. As the day of the coronation approached, 'he went to the Star Chamber at Westminster and submitted to the Council how improper it seemed that the King should be crowned in the absence of his brother, who ought to play an important part in the ceremony. Wherefore he said that, since this boy was held by his mother against his will in sanctuary, he should be liberated, because the sanctuary had been founded by their ancestors as a place of refuge, not of detention, and this boy wanted to be with his brother.'[56] How true this was is not known; but many lively nine-year-old boys would have chafed against the restrictions imposed by being in sanctuary, and resented being cooped up in a household of women; and maybe young York was eager to join the brother he barely knew, but who must have represented power and glory and freedom, and the chance of some excitement.

Gloucester was prepared to use force to remove York from his mother. On 16 June, 'with the consent of the Council, he surrounded the sanctuary with his household troops' armed with swords and staves, and sent the elderly Cardinal Thomas Bourchier, Archbishop of Canterbury, to persuade Elizabeth Wydeville to give up the young Duke. 'When the Queen saw herself besieged, and preparation for violence, she surrendered her son, trusting in the word of the Cardinal of Canterbury that the boy should be restored after the coronation'. But 'the Cardinal was suspecting no guile, and had persuaded the Queen to do this, seeking as much to prevent a violation of the sanctuary as to mitigate by his good services the fierce resolve of the Duke'.[57] Elizabeth Wydeville's parting from her younger son was later touchingly portrayed in many narrative paintings of the romantic era. 'But the Queen, for all the fair promises to her made, kept her and her daughters within the sanctuary.'[58] Clearly she did not think that any of them would be safe if they left it, so her fears for her sons may be imagined.

Elizabeth was a witness to these events, and they must have caused her great distress, as 'the love she bore her brothers and sisters was unheard of, and almost incredible'.[59] Thereafter, she must have fretted – even agonised – over her absent brothers, and if she had heard what was being reported, she would soon have had even more cause for concern. For, 'after Hastings was removed, all the attendants who had waited upon the King were debarred access to him. He and his brother were withdrawn into the inner apartments of the Tower proper, and day by day began to be seen more rarely behind the bars and windows, till at length they ceased to appear altogether.'[60]

This all happened between mid-June and Mancini's recall from England shortly after 6 July. Some of his information came from Dr John Argentine. His account suggests that the boys were now being held in the White Tower – the keep, or 'Tower proper' – and the mention of bars indicates that they were securely confined as prisoners of state. Dr Argentine, who was 'the last of his attendants whose services the King enjoyed', reported 'that the young King, like a victim prepared for sacrifice, sought remission of his sins by daily confession and penance, because he believed that death was facing him'. Mancini saw 'many men burst forth into tears and lamentations when mention was made of him after his removal from men's sight;

and already there was a suspicion that he had been done away with. Whether, however, he has been done away with, and by what manner of death, so far I have not at all discovered.'

Mancini's evidence is corroborated by the anonymous Croyland chronicler, a privy councillor and canon lawyer – probably John Russell, Bishop of Lincoln,[61] 'a man of great learning and piety'.[62] As Lord Chancellor and a member of the Council, he was in a good position to know what was going on. He too states that after Hastings's execution 'was the Prince and the Duke of York holden more straight, and there was privy talk that the Lord Protector should be king'. He also mentions that 'during this Mayor's year, the children of King Edward were seen shooting and playing in the garden of the Tower by sundry times'. But soon, as Mancini corroborates, they would be seen no more. And after 8 June no more grants were made in the name of Edward V.

Indeed, from the day York was removed from sanctuary, Gloucester and Buckingham 'no longer acted in secret but openly manifested their intentions'[63] – and their intentions boded no good for Elizabeth and her family.

Richard was clearly determined to prevent the Wydeville-dominated boy King from reigning. He later alleged that, on 8 June, someone – Robert Stillington, Bishop of Bath and Wells, according to Commines – had 'discovered to the Duke of Gloucester' that, before Edward IV married Elizabeth Wydeville in 1464, he 'had been formerly in love with a beautiful young lady and had promised her marriage, on condition that he might lie with her. The lady consented and, as the Bishop affirmed, he married them when nobody was present but they two and himself. His fortune depending on the court, he did not discover it, and persuaded the lady likewise to conceal it, which she did, and the matter remained a secret.'[64]

Any bishop or cleric would have known that a ceremony of marriage conducted without any witnesses present was invalid, but even if Stillington had officiated, it seems strange that it had taken him nearly twenty years to speak out, for the existence of a previous secret marriage rendered the second union bigamous, with serious implications for the legitimacy of the children born of it and the royal succession; and there were implications too for the safety of the King's immortal soul,[65] which should have exercised the Bishop's mind. But Stillington was no saint – he had fathered bastards, rarely visited his diocese and switched loyalties like a weathercock, according to which king was ruling, acquiring pardon after pardon along the way. What is more, in 1472 he had sworn allegiance to Edward, Prince of Wales, as Edward IV's 'very and undoubted heir' – a strange thing to do if he knew the boy was not legitimate.[66] He was therefore not a reliable witness.

The lady Edward was said to have married was Eleanor Butler, daughter of the great John Talbot, Earl of Shrewsbury, a military hero of the Hundred Years War. She had married Thomas Butler, heir to Ralph Butler, Lord Sudeley, but had been widowed before 1461, and died in a Norwich convent before 30 June 1468. It is highly unlikely that Edward ever did go through any ceremony of marriage with her. English sources mention only a precontract, a promise before witnesses to marry; once it was cemented by sexual intercourse, it became as binding in the eyes of the Church as a marriage. By the fourteenth century, the Church had reluctantly allowed that such clandestine marriages – with no calling of banns or blessing by a priest at the church door – were valid, but only if the promise had been made before two witnesses, which the law required. In practice, many couples considered themselves married on the basis of a promise alone,[67] but there is no good evidence that Edward IV made any promises to Eleanor Butler, or considered himself precontracted to her. Only after his death did Gloucester assert that he 'stood married and troth-plight' to the lady, 'with whom [he] had made a precontract of matrimony'.[68]

Significantly, Eleanor Butler, a member of a powerful aristocratic family, never joined the chorus of protest when the news broke that the King had married Elizabeth Wydeville, who was of lower rank than herself; nor did her family ever defend her honour when the alleged precontract was made public or later confirmed in Parliament. People were not afraid to speak out against the Wydeville marriage, so there is no reason why she and her kin could not have taken advantage of that and enlisted the support of Warwick, who was affronted by the King's marriage. Moreover, as a notably pious lady,[69] she surely would not have allowed a situation in which her husband was putting his immortal soul at risk to continue. Finally her nephew, Gilbert Talbot, was to fight for Henry Tudor, who had vowed to marry Elizabeth of York – which Talbot surely would not have done if he believed Elizabeth to be illegitmate.

Furthermore, if Elizabeth Wydeville had married Edward IV in good faith, not knowing that he was already under contract to another lady, her children could have been declared legitimate, and her marriage regularised, on Eleanor Butler's death in 1468; then the legitimacy of her sons, who were born later, would never have been in doubt. It seems inconceivable that Edward IV, who lived in an age in which lawful title to the crown was bloodily disputed, would knowingly have made a bigamous marriage, or would not have taken steps to ensure that his heirs' legitimacy could never be disputed. But Gloucester apparently accepted this new evidence as sufficient to render his brother's marriage invalid and his nephews and nieces bastards and unfit to inherit the crown or anything else.[70]

Commines is the only source to name Stillington as Gloucester's informant: he is not mentioned by English writers, so Commines may have been reporting speculation or gossip from diplomatic circles abroad. If Edward IV had indeed married Eleanor Butler in secret, he is hardly likely to have chosen his Keeper of the Privy Seal to perform the ceremony,[71] but an obscure priest such as the one who had married him to Elizabeth Wydeville. And as Commines reports that the Bishop had officiated at an actual marriage, rather than a precontract, and without witnesses being present, the rest of his story must be called into question.

Nevertheless, Stillington's possible involvement has been the subject of much debate. It was he who had persuaded Clarence to submit to Edward IV in 1471.[72] In 1475, after being dismissed as Chancellor of England, he had retired to his diocese of Wells, which bordered on Clarence's lands in Somerset. In 1478, shortly after Clarence's execution, Stillington had been sent to the Tower for uttering words 'prejudicial to the King and his estate', but was released three months later after paying a fine.[73] What he had said to give offence is not recorded, but if it had impugned the legitimacy of the King or his children, then the punishment was lenient. Furthermore, he had defended himself, and it was recorded that he had 'done nothing contrary to his oath of fealty, as he has shown before the King and certain lords'.

From such fragmentary evidence it has sometimes been conjectured that Stillington had entered into a secret alliance with Clarence and confided to him the tale of the precontract. That would have been political dynamite, of course, whether true or not. But Clarence never used the precontract story against Edward IV. He was ready to make wild and subversive claims, such as the one about Elizabeth Wydeville having poisoned his wife, and he had been quick to impugn Edward's own legitimacy, so it follows that he would not have hesitated to act on explosive evidence such as this.

If there had been allegations about a precontract in 1478, it would have been remarkable if Gloucester had not heard of them. If he had, they had not undermined his loyalty to his brother, nor had he ever attempted to have the matter clarified. He had not used them against the Wydevilles back in April and May, even when he was fabricating evidence against them, notably falsely accusing them of stockpiling arms to use against him. Now, facing the likelihood of retribution from the young Edward V when the King achieved his majority, and determined at all costs to prevent the Wydevilles from returning to power, Richard probably fabricated the whole story, in all likelihood with Stillington's assistance, for Commines' mention of him (out of all the bishops of England) and his later prosecution by Henry VII suggests that he was involved in some way. A year book of 1488 asserts that it was Stillington who later drew up the petition in which the lords and commons beseeched Richard to accept the crown of England.[74] However, he received no tangible rewards from Richard.

Given Edward IV's reputation with women, the precontract tale may have sounded sufficiently convincing – at least to Gloucester's supporters. But the sudden emergence of this information, surfacing at a crucially convenient time for the Duke, is not only suspicious but also astonishing. Clearly many regarded it merely as 'the colour for' his seizing the throne – 'this act of usurpation', as the Croyland chronicler scathingly put it – or what More calls a 'convenient pretext'; and it is obvious that many continued to regard Edward IV's children as the rightful heirs of the House of York. Croyland, for one, insisted that the whole precontract story was false: 'there was not a person but what knew very well who was the sole mover of such seditious and disgraceful proceedings'. And, of course, both Edward IV and Eleanor Butler were dead, and could not confirm or deny the allegations.

Gloucester's informant was said to have produced 'instruments, authentic doctors, procters and notaries of the law' as well as the 'depositions of divers witnesses', none of which survive, or were publicly produced at the time. If this evidence had been as compelling as Gloucester claimed, it is odd that he did not immediately act upon it, or refer it to an ecclesiastical court, as the law required, for no secular court had jurisdiction over such cases. Probably he realised that the story would not stand up, and knew that proof of it did not exist. Initially, he ordered Dr Ralph Shaa, the Mayor's brother, to preach at Paul's Cross on the text 'Bastard slips shall not take root', and had him rake up Clarence and Warwick's stale propaganda about Edward IV being 'conceived in adultery'.[75] Elsewhere in London, other clerics, similarly primed, were repeating the same thing.

A shocked Mancini wrote that Gloucester 'had so corrupted the preachers of God's word that they did not blush to say in their sermons to the people, without the slightest regard for decency or religion, that King Edward IV's offspring should be disposed of at once, since he had no right to be king, and no more had they. For they claimed that Edward was conceived in adultery and bore no resemblance to the late Duke of York, although he had been passed off as his son. Rather, Gloucester, who looked just like his father, should come to the throne as the rightful successor.' That was no more believed in 1483 than it had been in 1469, and Shaa found his homily falling on deaf ears. The Londoners were unconvinced: 'such as favoured ye matter were few in number'.[76]

Worse was to come. The Council had refused to sanction the executions of Rivers, Grey, Vaughan and Haute, so Gloucester, 'of his own authority as protector', had sent orders to Pontefract for them to suffer execution,[77] on the patently false charge that they had plotted the death of the Protector.[78] There was 'more of will than justice' involved,[79] for they were beheaded on 25 June 'without any form of trial being observed' – another act of tyranny, theirs being 'the second innocent blood that was shed' as a result of Gloucester's coups.[80] These executions prompted a rising in Kent by Elizabeth Wydeville's outraged kinsmen, the Hautes, and although it proved abortive, it was sufficient to prove to Gloucester that the Wydevilles were still a force to be reckoned with, even though their teeth had been drawn. Tidings of the deaths of her uncle and half-brother must have impacted badly on Elizabeth in sanctuary. She would have had to deal with her mother's fresh grief, and her new fears for the future.

It was only now that, influenced probably by the incredulous reaction to Shaa's sermon, or perhaps by his mother's protests, Gloucester publicly proclaimed the illegitimacy of his brother's children. On 25 June 1483, at the Guildhall, in the presence of the lords (who had been summoned to Parliament), the Lord Mayor and the citizens of

London, Buckingham presented an address to the Protector 'in a certain roll of parchment', asserting for the first time 'that the sons of King Edward were bastards'[81] on the grounds that Edward had been 'legally contracted to another wife' at the time of his marriage to Elizabeth Wydeville.[82] At this, a low whispering broke out, 'as of a swarm of bees'. As the next in line of succession, and the only 'certain and uncorrupted blood of Richard, Duke of York' – Clarence's heir Warwick being barred because of his father's attainder – Gloucester was 'entreated' to accept the crown.[83] The lords, who had been ordered to bring only small escorts to London, found themselves intimidated by the presence of 'unheard of terrible numbers' (estimated at 4–5,000) of Gloucester's and Buckingham's armed retainers in the City, and they and the commons unanimously signalled their approval. Some may anyway have regarded a grown man with a proven record of service in government and in the field of battle as preferable to a child ruler.[84] Even so, unsupported allegations about Edward V's legitimacy and an address made before an assembly of nobles were no substitute for a ruling by an ecclesiastical court, and were a very shaky foundation on which to base a claim to the throne.[85] All the same, the next day, at Baynard's Castle, Gloucester was entreated to bow to the lords' petition; with a show of reluctance he agreed, and was proclaimed King Richard III.

What was so striking, and probably shocking, about Richard's usurpation was that, where previous kings – Edward II, Richard II and Henry VI – had been deposed because of their bad government, Edward V had not even had a chance to prove his ability, while the speed of Gloucester's two coups and his ascent to the throne strongly suggested that he had all along meant to oust his nephew. Moreover, Edward had been deposed, and he and his siblings branded bastards, on highly dubious grounds. These rapidly unfolding events must have been horrifying to Elizabeth and her mother and sisters. In an age in which the illegitimacy rate may have been as low as two per cent,[86] and bastards were legally barred from inheriting property, the loss of her status would have been a terrible blow, coming so soon after the death of her father and the curtailment of her freedom. And now the man whom her mother feared most was king, and they were all at his mercy.

4

'The Whole Design of This Plot'

On 6 July 1483, the new King and Queen were crowned in Westminster Abbey. Cecily Neville was not there to witness her son's consecration; maybe she was furious with him for having publicly impugned her honour. Confined in the Abbot's house, Elizabeth and her sisters must have been aware of the bells ringing in celebration – the three Westminster sanctuary bells were customarily rung whenever a monarch was crowned – and they may have heard the crowds outside and even the music in the Abbey. Their thoughts would surely have turned to their brother Edward, whose day of triumph this was to have been. It was a bitter reminder of all they had lost, one more trial coming fast upon the others they had endured.

After the coronation, Richard III went on a progress through the kingdom. Already there were disturbing reports of agitation and confederacies in the south and west in favour of liberating Edward V. People had begun to 'murmur greatly, to form assemblies and to organise associations; many things were going on in secret for the purpose of promoting this object, others quite openly. There was also a report that it had been recommended by those men who had taken refuge in the sanctuaries that some of the King's daughters should leave Westminster, and go in disguise to parts beyond the sea, in order that, if any fatal mishap should befall the male children of the King [Edward IV] in the Tower, the kingdom might still, in consequence of the safety of the daughters, someday fall again into the hands of the rightful heirs.'[1]

Possibly Elizabeth Wydeville was behind what has become known as the 'sanctuary plot'. Elizabeth and her sisters could not have left sanctuary without their mother's collusion, and the former Queen had good reason to resort to desperate measures. Already her brother and one of her sons had been executed without trial. Her royal sons had disappeared into the Tower, and she and others were probably so fearful for their safety that she was prepared to risk the perils attendant on her daughters escaping abroad in order to ensure the survival of the legitimate royal line.

But the plot was discovered, and when Richard III was informed, he ordered that the Abbey be placed under siege, whereupon 'the noble church of Westminster assumed the appearance of a castle and fortress, while men of the greatest austerity were appointed by King Richard to act as the keepers thereof; the captain and head of these was one John Nesfield, esquire, who set a watch upon all the inlets and outlets of the monastery'.[2]

Nesfield, a Yorkshireman, was also responsible for guarding the Queen and her children while they were in sanctuary. He would have been a constant, perhaps menacing, presence in Elizabeth's life. A soldier who is first mentioned in 1470, when Edward IV appointed him 'riding forester of the forest of Galtres' in Yorkshire, Nesfield had pursued Lancastrian adherents on the King's behalf. In 1480 he had been serving in Calais, where he helped to recapture an English ship that had been seized by the French.[3] He was now a staunch supporter of Richard III, and saw that his men-at-arms kept strict guard over the Queen Dowager and her daughters. 'Not one of the persons there shut up could go forth, and no one could enter, without his permission.'[4] Clearly Richard took seriously the threat of the princesses being spirited abroad, for until now escape by boat along the nearby Thames would have been easy. There is no doubt that he regarded Elizabeth and her sisters as threats to his security, and feared that the older ones were as capable of conspiring against him as the mother with whom they were immured.

Although these conspiracies were so vigorously suppressed that most of the evidence documenting them was destroyed, the fact that they had occurred at all probably convinced Richard that he would never be secure on his throne while his nephews lived. In a few years' time, Edward V would be of an age to fight for his rights, and it was evident he would not lack for supporters; Edward IV had been popular, and the boy was loved for his father's sake. It would have made poor political sense not to have considered eliminating the Princes at this juncture.

★

Disapproval of Richard's usurpation was widespread in the south of England. Before the summer was out, 'people in the vicinity of London, throughout the counties of Kent, Essex, Sussex, Hampshire, Dorset, Devonshire, Somerset, Wiltshire and Berkshire, as well as some others of the southern counties of the kingdom' were determined 'to avenge their grievances'.[5] Indeed, by September even Buckingham, Richard's close ally, had turned on him.

It is strange that a man who had profited so 'spectacularly'[6] from his association with the King should suddenly have abandoned him, especially when he had so much to lose. Only weeks before, Richard had appointed Buckingham Constable of England, and granted him the government of Wales and the Marches and control of all the royal estates in Somerset, Dorset and Wiltshire, an unprecedented delegation of royal power. So Buckingham must have had a compelling reason to decide he could support Richard no longer.

On 2 August he had left the progress and ridden west to his castle at Brecknock, Brecon, where he took charge of John Morton, Bishop of Ely, who had been arrested with Hastings and sent to Wales to be held 'under house arrest'. It was apparently during conversations with the formidable Bishop – a dedicated Lancastrian who was Margaret Beaufort's chaplain but had nevertheless served Edward IV devotedly and been present at his deathbed – that Buckingham decided to rise in rebellion against the King.[7]

Some writers have suggested that Buckingham's initial plan was to seize power for himself, for he was descended from Edward III and had a claim to the throne, albeit a weak one. Morton, an astute politician of great integrity, 'resource and daring',[8] is supposed to have told Buckingham that he had 'excellent virtues meet for the rule of a realm'.[9] There is a tale that, having 'suddenly remembered' that he himself was descended from Edward III, Buckingham had then met Margaret Beaufort on the road to Brecon, and realised that her claim was far superior, although this does not sound very likely. But although he did not at any time press his own claim, one might wonder what he hoped to gain from risking supporting the exiled Henry Tudor, when he was already doing so well for himself under Richard III.

Vergil and More report a story that Buckingham turned against Richard III after the King failed to give him lands he had promised him, but he had actually been granted them on 13 July.[10] It has been suggested that Buckingham, having heard how rumours that Richard had had the Princes murdered were provoking a backlash against the King, was fearful that it would rebound on him also, as Richard's greatest supporter,[11] but such rumours did not surface until late September, and what Buckingham was initially plotting was the rescue and restoration of Edward V.

The likeliest explanation for Buckingham's disaffection is that, prior to his leaving the progress, Richard had confided to this man whom he believed he could trust that his intention was to do away with the Princes, and that, for Buckingham, this was a step too far, in which he wanted no part. This was the opinion of the author of the *Great Chronicle of London*: 'The common fame went that King Richard had within the Tower put unto secret death the two sons of his brother Edward, for the which, and other causes, the Duke of Buckingham conspired against him.' It may be that Morton's propaganda took root in fertile ground – or Buckingham took the Bishop into his confidence, and Morton, appalled, concluded that Richard should be brought down as a matter of urgency.

It is clear that initially Morton was urging the restoration of Edward V, for on 24 September Buckingham wrote appealing for support from Henry Tudor in the 'liberation' of the Princes.[12] But around that time 'a rumour was spread that the sons of King Edward had died a violent death, but it was uncertain how'.[13]

Despite imaginative theories to the contrary, put forward from 1483 to the present day, the weight of evidence[14] overwhelmingly points to the Princes having been murdered on the orders of Richard III, the man who had the strongest motive and the best opportunity; and that, on the night of 3 September 1483, they were suffocated with pillows by assassins hired by one of his trusted retainers, Sir James Tyrell, acting on the King's behalf,[15] as Thomas More describes in his book, *The History of King Richard III* (*c*.1513).

Sir John Harington, in *The Metamorphosis of Ajax* (1596), and Sir George Buck both mention a history of Richard III written by John Morton, later Cardinal and Archbishop of Canterbury. Harington wrote that More's book had been 'written, as I have heard, by Morton'. Buck was Master of the Revels to James I and the author of a well-documented *History of King Richard III*, written in 1619 and based on careful research from original sources in Sir Robert Cotton's library at Ashburnham House, Westminster,[16] and other places, the recently rediscovered *Croyland Chronicle* being one of them.[17] Buck describes this history in a marginal note in his copy of Francis Godwin's *A Catalogue of the Bishops of England*: 'This Morton wrote in Latin the life of K.R.3 which goeth in Sir Thomas More's name – as Sir Edward Hoby saith, and that Sir W[illiam] Roper hath the original.'[18] No source before Harington connects Morton with More's history, which was written several years after Morton's death and includes information he could not have imparted, so if there was such a tract – and neither Harington nor Buck say they actually saw it – then it could only have been one of several sources used by More. Even that theory has been challenged by Raymond Chambers, More's biographer and an authority on his literary works, who states that 'the attribution is impossible, equally from the point of view of chronology, literary history, bibliography, language, style and common sense', and that Harington's assertion should be 'treated with the contempt it deserves'.[19]

Tyrell had been knighted after Tewkesbury, and was appointed Master of the Henchmen and Master of the Horse in 1483. Later, he was made Knight of the Body and given various offices, including those of Steward of the Duchy of Cornwall and Chamberlain of the Exchequer, and appointed to the Council. According to More, whose account was based in part on Tyrell's later confession and the probably first-hand testimony of John Dighton, one of the murderers – those 'that much knew and little cause had to lie' – he was prepared to do much to rise high. We know that Tyrell was delegated to ride to the royal wardrobe at the Tower of London to fetch necessities for the investiture of Edward of Middleham, the new Prince of Wales, which was to take place on 8 September in York Minster, and it was probably during that trip that the deed was carried out. Other evidence fits with this account, and certainly the Princes were never seen alive again. In England, most people seem to have believed that Richard had had them killed, possibly on the advice of Buckingham, and speculation focused mainly on how the deed had been done.

Until the 1950s that opinion generally held, with only a few writers disputing Richard III's guilt; since then, in the wake of Josephine Tey's novel, *The Daughter of Time* (1951), and Paul Murray Kendall's sympathetic biography of Richard (1955),[20] the mystery of the Princes' fate has been endlessly debated, and is still controversial. Nevertheless wishful theories evolved by revisionists lack credibility in the face of the weight of evidence against Richard, both written and circumstantial, and the realities of fifteenth-century realpolitik.

The facts remain: the Princes disappeared from view shortly after his usurpation; he had a compelling motive for doing away with them, and the means; they were never seen again; public opinion at the time was that he had murdered them; there is no credible evidence for their survival, nor did Richard ever produce them alive to counteract the rumours of their murder that were eroding his support. But, as Michael Hicks has so perspicaciously said, the weight of evidence 'cannot convince those who do not wish to believe'.[21] As far as Elizabeth of York is concerned, what matters is what *she* came to believe had become of her brothers – and later evidence strongly suggests that she was convinced that they had been murdered.

Rumours of the murders irrevocably damaged the King's reputation. It was said in London that he had 'put to death the children of King Edward, for which cause he lost the hearts of the people. And thereupon many gentlemen intended his destruction.'[22] Ruthlessness in war and politics was tolerated: child murder was a step too far. The Tudor royal historian, Bernard André, wrote that, in the wake of the rumours, 'the entire land was convulsed with sobbing and anguish. The nobles of the kingdom, fearful of their lives, wondered what might be done against the danger. Faithful to the tyrant in word, they remained distant in heart.' We must allow for a degree of exaggeration from a partisan observer, but this was written less than twenty years later, when many people would have remembered the events of 1483. The rumours were believed as far away as Danzig, as Caspar Weinreich's contemporary chronicle recorded that year: 'Later this summer, Richard, the King's brother, had himself put in power and crowned king of England; and he had his brother's children killed.' Certainly Buckingham – who may have had good cause – and Morton took the rumours seriously.

Richard had written to Buckingham several times after the Duke left the progress, but it is unlikely he had revealed that the Princes actually had been murdered, for Margaret Beaufort (who was soon to be involved in the conspiracy) would certainly have come to hear of it from Buckingham and passed on the information to Henry Tudor; yet the evidence strongly suggests that Henry Tudor did not know for certain that they had been killed – at least, probably, until 1502. So the likelihood is that Buckingham and his associates just assumed that they were dead, which was a reasonable conclusion, given the rumours and how ruthlessly Richard had eliminated everyone else who had stood in the way of his ambitions.

The conspirators had now been joined by large numbers of alienated Yorkists. They realised that they must find a new candidate to replace the usurper. If the Princes were indeed dead, Elizabeth of York was the next heir to Edward IV's throne, but there was no question of an eighteen-year-old girl ruling as sovereign, especially with the realm so unstable and troubled. No one even suggested it, and of course there was a prevalent belief that no woman could rule successfully.

Buckingham and Morton now began seriously to consider the claim of Henry Tudor, the only realistic choice. 'Seeing that if they could find no one to take the lead in their designs, the ruin of all would speedily ensue, all those who had set on foot this insurrection turned their thoughts to Henry, Earl of Richmond, who had been for many years living in exile in Brittany.'[23] Buckingham's alliance with Henry Tudor's supporters in support of the Lancastrian pretender was perhaps Morton's doing. Morton may have reminded Buckingham that the latter's father and grandfather had died fighting for Henry VI and the Lancastrian cause,[24] and that his true loyalty should lie with the only viable Lancastrian heir – although Buckingham may not have needed much convincing. Morton seems to have worked covertly to bring together the Lancastrian party, the Wydevilles and Yorkist dissidents, with the objective of overthrowing Richard III. Possibly he was working on behalf of another interested party.

Margaret Beaufort was prominent at Richard III's court, and had even carried Queen Anne's train at the coronation, but she remained a Lancastrian at heart. She was a formidable woman of strong character and steely resolve, and all her ambitions were for her son, Henry Tudor. She had continued to correspond with him, and perhaps secretly cherished hopes that one day he would be able to pursue his claim to the throne. Should the time ever be opportune, her husband, the pragmatic Lord Stanley, could command a private army in Henry's support. In the meantime, Margaret is said to have pressed Richard III – as soon as he came to the throne – to restore her son to the earldom of Richmond and marry him to one of the daughters of Edward IV with his 'favour'.[25]

It may be that Margaret soon realised that Richard would do nothing for Henry; or Henry had made it clear to her that he would never return to England while Richard was on the throne. Whatever the reason, she was soon working against the King, and it has been suggested that she was even involved in a plot to rescue the Princes from the Tower;[26] how that would have furthered her son's cause is hard to see, unless she thought that Edward V would be less of a threat to Henry than Richard, and that Henry might consequently be induced to return to England.

Vergil asserted that, at the same time as Morton and Buckingham were plotting at Brecknock, 'a new conspiracy was laid in London' between Margaret Beaufort and Elizabeth Wydeville. But possibly Margaret Beaufort was already in league with Buckingham, and in contact with him through the good offices of Morton, her chaplain, and her servant, Reginald Bray, who was 'the chief dealer in this conspiracy' and may have travelled to Brecon on her behalf.

Probably Margaret, perhaps briefed by Buckingham, believed that Richard had done away with the Princes. And 'she, being a wise woman, after the slaughter of King Edward's children was known, began to hope well of her son's fortune'.[27]

According to Vergil, it was Margaret who first conceived the momentous idea of uniting the rival houses of Lancaster and York through a marriage between her son and Elizabeth of York, who was now – in the eyes of many – the Yorkist heiress to the throne. Margaret is said to have realised 'that that deed would without doubt prove for the profit of the commonwealth, if it might chance the blood of King Henry VI and King Edward to be mingled by affinity, and so two most pernicious factions should be at once, by conjoining of both houses, utterly taken away'.

It is possible that Vergil overstated the role of the mother of the King he served, but certainly Margaret was active in the conspiracy once its objectives embraced her son, and it was probably true that she had cherished for years the idea of marrying him to Elizabeth of York. In 1486 Lord Stanley would depose that, during Edward IV's reign, he had often heard his wife and others discussing the consanguinity that existed between Henry and Elizabeth,[28] proof that the possibility of them marrying had long been under discussion. But now, in the eyes of legitimists, Elizabeth was an even greater prize, for marriage with her would immeasurably bolster Henry's dubious claim to the throne and win hearts to his cause; and it would unite the Houses of Lancaster and York and be a means of ending the bloody conflict between them.

The success of the plan depended, of course, on the Princes being dead. There was no point in Henry Tudor marrying Elizabeth and claiming the crown through her if Edward V or York remained alive to challenge that claim. Clearly, Buckingham, Margaret Beaufort and Henry Tudor all believed that the Princes were no longer alive. There have been theories that any one of them might have arranged the murder of the boys, which would have been as advantageous to them as it would to Richard III. But while a handful of contemporaries suggested that Buckingham was involved, none of them – even Margaret of Burgundy, his mortal enemy – ever accused Henry Tudor of the deed, still less Margaret Beaufort.

Apart from the lack of evidence, there are insurmountable obstacles to these revisionist views: the Princes disappeared while they were being securely held in the Tower as the King's chief prisoners of state. If someone – Buckingham, for example, who, even as Constable of England, would have needed the King's permission to breach security at the Tower – had murdered them, Richard would quickly have got to hear about it, and it would have been in his interests to make political capital against his enemies, thus giving the lie to the rumours about his own involvement; indeed, he was adept at using the tool of character assassination most effectively. More pertinently, even though the rumours about his having murdered the Princes continued to damn Richard's reputation and undermine his security as king, he took no measures at all to counteract them, when it was crucially in his interests to do so. Had someone else murdered his nephews, especially one of his enemies, it would have served him well, and retrieved his reputation, to be able to accuse them – and he was soon to have an ideal opportunity to do that, of which he did not take advantage. It would also have been in his interests to make it known if the Princes had died natural deaths. Claims that one or both of them survived are fascinating but unconvincing, and cannot be substantiated by good evidence.

Enlisting Buckingham to her son's cause was a great coup for Margaret Beaufort. All that was needed now was to win over Elizabeth Wydeville. But first, she had to be told about the tragic fate of her sons.

Dr Lewis Caerleon, 'a Welshman born', was Margaret Beaufort's physician, and because he was 'a grave man and of no small experience, she was wont oftentimes to confer freely with him to lament her adversity'. It was during one of their talks that she prayed him to lay the conspirators' plan before the Queen Dowager, who also consulted him, 'for he was a very learned physician'. Margaret told him that 'the time was now come when as King Edward's eldest daughter might be given in marriage to her son, Henry, and therefore prayed him to deal secretly with the Queen of such affair'. In September, 'after the slaughter of King Edward's children was known',[29] Dr Caerleon braved Nesfield's soldiers and visited Elizabeth Wydeville in sanctuary in his official capacity, his real purpose being to break the dread news that her sons were believed to have been murdered on the King's orders.

The impact on the Queen Dowager – and on her daughters – must have been dreadful. The likelihood that the princes had been killed was devastating enough, but not knowing exactly what had happened to them, or being able to lay them decently to rest, would surely have caused more anguish than learning for certain how they had died. There would always have been room for imagining so many dreadful scenarios – and for doubt, even hope.

Vergil gives an account of Elizabeth Wydeville's reaction to the news, which he may have embroidered to underline the dreadful import of the moment, yet it is easy to imagine her responding dramatically to news that any mother would dread to hear, and highly likely that there was a scene of this sort. She 'fell in a swoon and lay lifeless a good while. After coming to herself, she wept, she cried aloud, and with lamentable shrieks made all the house ring. She struck her breast, tore and pulled out her hair and, overcome with dolour, prayed also for her own death, calling by name now and then among her most dear children, and condemning herself for a mad woman for that, being deceived by false promises, she had delivered her younger son out of sanctuary, to be murdered by his enemy.' After long lamentation, says More, 'she kneeled down and cried to God to take vengeance, who, she said, she nothing doubted would remember it'.

Elizabeth and her sisters were probably shocked witnesses to their mother's grief. Given Elizabeth's love for her siblings, the news would have hit her hard too. And soon would come the startling realisation that she was now – or should have been – the rightful Queen of England.

To mitigate the dreadful tidings, and bring the Queen over to the side of Margaret Beaufort and Buckingham, Dr Caerleon came to the real point of his visit, reminding her that her daughter Elizabeth was now the rightful inheritor of the crown. 'If you could now agree and invent the means to couple your eldest daughter with the young Earl of Richmond in matrimony, no doubt the usurper of the realm should be shortly deposed, and your heir again to her right restored.'

Very likely Caerleon, primed by Margaret Beaufort, gave a flattering account of the putative bridegroom, but at this point Henry Tudor was not much of a catch for a young woman whom many regarded as the Yorkist heiress. He was not even *de facto* Earl of Richmond, having been deprived of that title; he was a mere landless exile. But Elizabeth Wydeville saw in him her only hope of revenge on the man whom she was convinced had killed her sons and brought her to her present sorry condition, and readily gave her consent. 'The Queen was so well pleased with this device that she commanded Caerleon to repair to the Countess, who remained in her husband's house in London, and to promise that she would do her endeavour to procure all her husband King Edward's friends to take part with Henry, her son, so that he might be sworn to take in marriage Elizabeth, her daughter, after he should have gotten the realm; or else Cecily the younger if the other should die before he enjoyed the same.'[30] Her agreement to the plan – which was not without considerable risk – is proof that she truly believed that her sons had been murdered.

While the two aspiring mothers-in-law covertly planned for the future, with Dr Caerleon acting 'as a messenger between them, without any suspicion',[31] Buckingham sent word to Henry, 'by advice of the lord Bishop of Ely, inviting him to hasten into the kingdom of England as fast as he could reach the shore, to marry Elizabeth, the eldest daughter of the late King; and with her, at the same time, take possession of the whole kingdom', implying that they should reign jointly. He informed Henry that his supporters would rise on St Luke's Day, 18 October, and that he himself would raise the men of Wales. A proclamation was then made to the confederacies that Buckingham 'had repented of his former conduct and would be the chief mover' in the planned risings.[32] Henry Tudor entered enthusiastically into the conspiracy. Francis II, Duke of Brittany, had offered him his daughter and heiress Anne, who could have brought him a duchy, but now Henry 'decided to yield to Edward IV's wishes to marry Elizabeth',[33] who might just bring him a kingdom.

Margaret Beaufort dispatched Reginald Bray 'to draw unto her party such noble and worshipful men' as were prepared to risk joining them. She also sent Hugh Conway to Henry with 'a good great sum of money' and instructions to join Buckingham in Wales. Word of the proposed marriage between Henry and Elizabeth rapidly won the conspirators the loyalty of Yorkists who had been outraged at Richard's disinheriting of Edward IV's children.

Elizabeth's own views on marrying this exiled pretender whom she had never met are unrecorded, but she probably felt that Henry Tudor represented her best chance of ridding herself of the stain of bastardy and attaining what was rightfully hers: the crown of England. She too seems to have accepted that her brothers were dead, and may have believed – in the words of the chronicler Holinshed – that her 'fortune and grace was to be queen'.

In 1489 Margaret Beaufort was to ask William Caxton to translate and print the text of a thirteenth-century French romance entitled 'Blanchardin and Eglantine', which she had acquired in 1483. It was a highly appropriate romance, for Eglantine's story resonated with Elizabeth's own situation at the time of Buckingham's rebellion. Blanchardin, son of the King of Phrygia, falls in love with Princess Eglantine of Tormadei. While he fights the infidel, she makes the stations of the Cross, garrisons the city and plans for their marriage, which is her heart's desire. Eventually Blanchardin passes unscathed through a series of adventures, disasters and escapes, and claims her as his wife. No doubt Elizabeth, and those in sanctuary with her in 1483, would have appreciated the parallels between the story and the alliance between herself and Henry Tudor. It is not beyond the bounds of probability that Margaret Beaufort sent her the book by the hands of Dr Caerleon, to raise her morale and help while away the tedious hours in sanctuary.[34]

Bishop Morton, meanwhile, had pressed Buckingham to allow him to leave Brecknock for Ely, to raise men in his diocese. The Duke showed himself doubtful about releasing the man who was supposed to be his prisoner, but Morton escaped one night and fled to Ely, a move that may have been planned by both men.[35]

The rebels were supposed to rise on 18 October, but their various groups were poorly co-ordinated, and on 10 October, the Hautes orchestrated premature risings at Maidstone and Ightham Mote, only to be repelled by John Howard, now Duke of Norfolk. Dorset emerged from hiding to rouse the men of Exeter, and Lionel Wydeville stirred the men of Salisbury, his See. The Queen's younger brothers, Sir Edward and Sir Richard Wydeville, were involved, and there were planned risings in Guildford and Newbury, while Buckingham was to raise Brecon and south Wales. In the wake of the rumours about the murder of the Princes, many former members of Edward IV's household had joined the rebels.

Already, though, 'the whole design of this plot had, by means of spies, become perfectly well known to King Richard, who, as ever, did not act sleepily, but swiftly, and with the greatest vigilance'.[36] On 15 October Richard had Buckingham proclaimed a rebel and he offered free pardons to any who surrendered. He 'contrived that, throughout Wales, armed men should be set in readiness around the said Duke as soon as ever he had set a foot from his home'.[37]

Unsuspecting, Buckingham left Brecon on 18 October, as planned, and advanced through the Wye Valley, making for Hereford. But storms and flooding wrecked his plans, his army deserted him, and he was forced to flee to Shropshire, where he sought shelter in the cottage of a poor retainer, who betrayed him for a handsome reward. On arrest, he was led to the city of Salisbury, 'to which place the King had come with a very large army, on the day of the commemoration of All Souls; and [on 2 November], notwithstanding the fact that it was the Lord's day, the Duke suffered capital punishment in the public market place of that city'.[38]

If, as has been suggested, Buckingham had murdered the Princes, with Richard's approval and therefore on his behalf,[39] Richard now had the perfect opportunity to lay the blame at his door and so give the lie to rumour. He did not seize it.

On 31 October, unaware that the rebellion had collapsed, Henry Tudor set sail from Brittany with the intention of invading England, but was blown off course by the foul weather. He was stationed off Plymouth harbour when 'news of the current situation reached him, both of the death of the Duke of Buckingham and the flight of his own faction', and realising that his cause was hopeless, 'hoisted his sails and put out to sea again',[40] fleeing back to Brittany.

Richard III was remarkably lenient with Margaret Beaufort, despite her having treasonably conspired against him; she was lucky to escape being attainted by Parliament. He contented himself with giving her estates to her husband (who had rallied to his King), depriving her of the title Countess of Richmond, and ordering Stanley – who claimed he had known nothing of her subversive activities – to keep his wife a virtual prisoner 'in some secret place' apart from her household. He also extended clemency, and the offer of a pardon, to Dorset and Morton, but they, Lionel Wydeville and other rebels had already fled the kingdom to join Henry Tudor.[41]

What of Elizabeth? André, in a passage that may relate to this time, later wrote that, before the summer of 1485, after Henry Tudor had decided to yield to Edward IV's wishes and marry her, a 'grievous situation nearly brought her noble life to an untimely end. And indeed, as the outcome of the matter later showed, by the pleasure of Edward, his noble and wise daughter was preserved in all her virtue for Henry.'

The context of this passage is unclear, as is André's meaning. It reads as if it was due to her father's pleasure that Elizabeth survived this crisis, but it is more likely that the passage refers to Edward's willing the marriage to take place, rather than to his being responsible for Elizabeth's survival. The 'grievous situation' to which André refers is probably the collapse of Buckingham's rebellion. He may be implying that Elizabeth too could have been penalised for treason, although Richard's leniency with Margaret Beaufort, who had been far more deeply involved, precluded Elizabeth from suffering the death penalty. Or André could have meant that she was so distressed at the dashing of her hopes of freedom and a crown that it severely affected her health.

'The Hours of Our Lady', which bears the signature 'Elizabeth Plantagenet' on the flyleaf, has traces of an inscription containing the name 'Henry' at the top of that page, which someone has evidently tried to erase. Maybe it was Elizabeth herself, realising that her hopes of marrying Henry Tudor were now in the dust, and that it was wiser to delete this evidence of them.[42]

The rebellion had collapsed, but it had demonstrated that Henry Tudor was now a serious contender for the crown. In his native Wales, the bards were claiming that he should rule as the rightful descendant of the near-legendary Cadwaladr, the seventh-century King of Gwynned, and Brutus of Troy, to whom legend attributed the founding of the kingdom of Britain. The support of a growing body of Yorkist dissidents in Brittany – about 400 fled to his base at the Château of l'Hermine after the rebellion failed – had strengthened Henry's cause to the extent that he was now ready to throw down the gauntlet to King Richard. At dawn on Christmas Day 1483, Henry went to Rennes Cathedral and, in the presence of about 500 of his supporters, publicly, 'upon his oath, promised that, as soon as he should be king, he would marry Elizabeth, King Edward's daughter',[43] thus uniting the rival Houses of Lancaster and York.

In so doing he acknowledged Elizabeth as the rightful heiress to the crown – but she could only be that if her brothers were dead; and Henry and all his adherents must have had good reason to believe that they were before announcing his intention of marrying her. In fact Henry described Richard as a homicide in letters he sent to potential allies in England.[44] Effectively, Henry's oath was a public acknowledgement that the sons of Edward IV were dead. Had they been living, Richard III surely would have produced them to scupper the Tudor's ambitions, but – incomprehensibly, if he had not had them killed – he did not.

The oath, optimistic though it was, turned out to be a brilliant masterstroke because it united Lancastrian and Yorkist supporters and again made Henry a rallying point for disaffected Yorkists, many of whom swore homage to him in Rennes Cathedral on that Christmas morning 'as though he had been already created king'.[45] No doubt there were those who did so in the hope that, if he won the crown, he would restore their property. Until now, few had taken Henry's claim to be the Lancastrian claimant seriously, but his vow to wed Elizabeth was a deciding factor for many. It also turned the power-less Elizabeth into one of the most important political figures in England, because marriage to this girl who was regarded by many as the true heir to York would from now on be seen by an increasing number as the key to holding legitimate sovereign power in the realm.

After what must have been a mournful Christmas, compared with the splendid celebrations of the previous year, when her father had been alive, and before so many close to her had died or disappeared, Elizabeth and her mother and sisters now suffered another blow. In January 1484, in Richard III's first Parliament, the Act entitled *Titulus Regius* was passed confirming the King's title to the throne and setting forth the grounds of his claim. It declared how, thanks to 'the ungracious pretended marriage' of Edward IV, 'the order of all politic rule was perverted', and went on to state:

> We consider how the pretended marriage between King Edward
> and Elizabeth Grey was made of great presumption, without

the knowledge and assent of the lords of this land, and also by sorcery and witchcraft committed by the said Elizabeth and her mother, Jacquetta, Duchess of Bedford; and also we consider how that the said pretended marriage was made privily and secretly, without edition of banns, in a private chamber [which was untrue], a profane place, and not openly in the face of the Church after the law of God's Church; and how also, that at the time of the contract of the said pretended marriage, and before and long after, King Edward was and stood troth-plight to one Dame Eleanor Butler, daughter of the old Earl of Shrewsbury, with whom King Edward had made a precontract of matrimony long time before he made the said pretensed marriage with Elizabeth Grey. Which premises being true, as in very truth they been true, it appeareth and followeth evidently that King Edward and Elizabeth lived together sinfully and damnably in adultery, against the law of God and His Church, [and] also it followeth that all th'issue and children of the said King Edward been bastards and unable to inherit or to claim any thing by inheritance.[46]

Croyland fulminated, correctly, that Parliament, being a lay court, had no jurisdiction to pronounce on the validity of a marriage, but 'it presumed to do so, and did do so, because of the great fear [of Richard] that had struck the hearts of even the most resolute'. Elizabeth and her siblings were now legally bastards; the Act had stripped them of their titles and property and barred them from inheriting anything from their parents.

In February Elizabeth turned eighteen, the average age for marriage for upper-class girls at that period.[47] She must have felt that time was passing her by while she was immured in sanctuary, and wondered what the future held for her. Her brothers were dead, her Wydeville relatives murdered or in exile, her mother powerless. It would not be surprising if she was still hoping against hope that Henry Tudor would somehow be able to fulfil his vow and marry her, although the prospect of that probably seemed remote.

Richard III was taking no chances, though. He needed to neutralise the threat posed by the proposed marriage between Elizabeth and Henry Tudor, who was now styling himself King of England, and would, on 27 March, obtain a Papal dispensation sanctioning the union of 'Henry Richmond, layman of the York diocese, and Elizabeth Plantagenet, woman of the London diocese'.[48]

Richard wanted Elizabeth in his power. He could not continue to allow the Queen Dowager and her daughters to go on hiding in sanctuary, as if they were in danger from him; it did not do his already tarnished reputation any good. The rumours about the Princes had proved highly damaging. Early in 1484 the Chancellor of France had publicly accused him of 'murdering with impunity' his nephews, and Commines records that Louis XI believed Richard to be 'extremely cruel and evil' for having had 'the two sons of his brother put to death'. In December 1483 Mancini (who had been recalled to France in July) had written unquestioningly that Richard had 'destroyed his brother's children'. But if the King could secure the persons of Elizabeth and her sisters, he could show the world he had no evil intent towards them, and marry them off to men of his own choosing, thus preventing Henry Tudor from claiming the throne through marriage to any of them.

He knew he faced a struggle to persuade Queen Elizabeth to let her daughters leave sanctuary. He sent 'grave men promising mountains to her' and 'frequent entreaties as well as threats',[49] possibly of removing the girls by force. The ring of steel still surrounding the Abbey was a constant, intimidating reminder that he had the means to carry out such threats. But there was perhaps talk that Richard was thinking of marrying Elizabeth to his son, Edward of Middleham, who was her cousin and could not have been much above ten years old.[50] Vergil says his emissaries to Elizabeth Wydeville prejudiced their arguments at the outset by referring to 'the slaughter of her sons', after which she would not be comforted; if this is true, it amounted to an admission that Richard had had the boys killed. Certainly he had been responsible for the judicial murder of another of her sons, Sir Richard Grey, and he had given abundant proof of his hatred of the Wydevilles. The former Queen had good cause to be afraid of him.

She made her fears so plain that on 1 March the King felt obliged to make an 'oath and promise' in the presence of the lords of the Council and the Lord Mayor and aldermen that, if she would agree to her daughters leaving sanctuary, he would offer them all his protection. This he confirmed in writing, declaring:

I, Richard, by the grace of God, King of England [etc.], in the presence of you my lords spiritual and temporal, and you, Mayor and aldermen of my City of London, promise and swear on the word of a king, and upon these holy evangelies [Gospels] of God, by me personally touched, that if the daughters of Dame Elizabeth Grey, late calling herself Queen of England, that is, Elizabeth, Cecily, Anne, Katherine and Bridget, will come unto me out of the sanctuary of Westminster, and be guided, ruled and demeaned after me, then I shall see that they shall be in surety of their lives, and also not suffer any manner [of] hurt in their body by any manner [of] person or persons to them, or any of them in their bodies and persons by way of ravishment or defouling contrary to their wills, not them or any of them imprison within the Tower of London or other prison; but that I shall put them in honest places of good name and fame, and them honestly and courteously shall see to be founden and entreated, and to have all things requisite and necessary for their exhibitions [display] and findings [domestic arrangements] as my kinswomen; and that I shall marry such of them as now be marriable to gentlemen born, and every of them give in marriage lands and tenements by the yearly value of 200 marks [about £34,000] for term of their lives, and in like wise to the other daughters when they come to lawful age of marriage if they live. And such gentlemen as shall hap to marry with them I shall straitly charge from time to time lovingly to love and entreat them, as wives and my kinswomen, as they will avoid and eschew my displeasure . . . And moreover, I promise to them that if any surmise or evil report be made to me of them by any person or persons, that I shall not give thereunto faith ne credence, nor therefore put them to any manner punishment, before that they or any of them so accused may be at their lawful defence and answer. In witness whereof to this writing of my oath and promise aforesaid in your said presences made, I have set my sign manual the first day of March, the first year of my reign.[51]

While he may have offended his sister-in-law by calling her 'Dame Elizabeth Grey', Richard had at least very publicly guaranteed the future safety and welfare of her daughters. His promises – and his oath made on the Gospels – reflect widespread concerns that he had done away with her sons, for whose safety, as opposed to that of her daughters, there are no reassurances in the document.[52] This strongly suggests that they were dead, while the specific mention of the Tower, and Richard's willingness to give such a public guarantee, amounts to a tacit admittance that she had good cause for concern.

Clearly Elizabeth Wydeville had feared – especially in the wake of the sanctuary plot – that a pretext might be sought to find her daughters guilty of treason and worthy of punishment. But for Elizabeth of York, the King's promises can only have emphasised the shame of her bastardy. He was contemplating marrying her to some gentleman, when, if her brothers really were dead, she was the rightful Queen of England, and might yet be queen consort, if Henry Tudor realised his ambitions. And the dowry Richard was offering was paltry compared with the 10,000 marks (£1.5 million) willed her by Edward IV, and a cruel reminder of her reduced status.

In the circumstances, though, this was a pragmatic way of securing the girls' futures, and Elizabeth Wydeville, 'being strongly solicited to do so', agreed to release them. On 1 March 1484, the same day that her brother-in-law made his public declaration, she 'sent her daughters from the sanctuary at Westminster to King Richard'.[53]

The Tudor chronicler Edward Hall castigated Elizabeth Wydeville for surrendering her daughters to her enemy: 'Putting in oblivion the murder of her innocent children, the infamy and dishonour spoken by the King her husband, the living in adultery laid to her charge, the bastardising of her daughters, forgetting also the faithful prayers and open oath made to the Countess of Richmond, mother of the Earl Henry, blinded by avaricious affection and seduced by flattering words, [she] delivered into King Richard's hands her five daughters as lambs once again committed to the custody of the ravenous wolf.'

Yet what choice had she really had? There were pressing practical realities to be taken into account. Richard III was thirty-one, and might be in power for a very long time. She could not stay in sanctuary for ever, especially in the face of the King's guarantees; her continuing presence there might compromise the Abbot's standing with his monarch, and she had already been dependent on his kindness and charity for nearly a year. Furthermore, the Abbey was still under siege on her account. If she refused to let her daughters leave, then Richard might well take them away, as he had done young York, and on the same pretext. Her capitulation does not necessarily mean that she did not believe the King had murdered the Princes. He had already judicially murdered another of her sons, on the flimsiest of pretexts, yet still she came to terms with him, doubtless hoping she had done the best she could for her remaining children.

Vergil states that 'King Richard received all his brother's daughters out of sanctuary into the court'. Hall follows Vergil, saying that the King caused them 'to be conveyed into his palace [of Westminster] with solemn receiving; as though, with his new, familiar, loving entertainment they should forget, and in their minds obliterate, the old committed injury and late perpetrated tyranny'. Buck also says that Elizabeth Wydeville sent the girls 'to the court', where they were 'very honourably entertained and with all princely kindness'. Even so, it may have been a bitter experience for Elizabeth and her sisters to return to the palace where, just a year before, they had been honoured as royal princesses. Possibly resentment against their uncle, and anxiety about their mother, warred with pleasure and relief at being out of sanctuary and able to enjoy worldly pleasures and freedoms again. They were, after all, only young.

It is likely that they were received into the Queen's household; as unmarried girls of royal birth, it was the only suitable place for them in a court dominated by men. But it seems that, as soon as Elizabeth Wydeville left sanctuary, some time after her daughters did, they joined her. It is clear she did not return to court, as Croyland records that 'the Lady Elizabeth was, with her four younger sisters, sent by her mother to attend the Queen at court' the following Christmas, so obviously they were not lodging there then. If she sent them to court, they must have been living with her.

All that is known of Elizabeth Wydeville's whereabouts after she left sanctuary is that she was residing at Sheen in August 1485. The late Audrey Williamson wrote of an eighteenth-century tradition that the Queen Dowager and her sons had once lived at Gipping Hall near Stowmarket, Suffolk, by permission of 'the uncle', presumably Richard III. Gipping Hall, which was demolished in the 1850s, was the seat of Sir James Tyrell, the man who had probably arranged the murder of the Princes, and had been rebuilt by him in 1474. From this late tradition, for which no earlier corroborating evidence exists, Williamson inferred that the boys had not been murdered at all, but had been sent here in secrecy with their mother by the King. If so, their sisters were with them.

There are obvious problems with this theory, not least the discovery in 1674 in the Tower of London of the bones of two children of approximately the age of the Princes at the time of their disappearance in 1483. But if they had survived, and were taken to Gipping Hall, someone would surely have got to know about it. Late-medieval royal and noble households were teeming places peopled with servants and officials, and privacy would not become a priority until the reign of Henry VIII. It is likely that several of those who served the Queen could have recognised her sons. Thus it would have been virtually impossible to keep the existence of the Princes a secret, especially in the face of rumours of their deaths.

It is inconceivable that Richard, knowing that Elizabeth Wydeville had not hesitated to plot his overthrow, would have entrusted the Princes to her care anyway, let alone in a house fewer than twenty miles from the coast, whence their escape to the Continent could easily have been arranged, even if that house did belong to one of his trusted retainers. The River Gipping flowed nearby, and was navigable all the way down to Ipswich and then, as the River Orwell, to the sea. Many disaffected Yorkists were just across the Channel with Henry Tudor; had it come to their knowledge that the sons of Edward IV still lived, and were at liberty on the Continent, they would surely have switched their allegiance instantly.

Some traditions may have a basis in fact, but even if this one originated with Elizabeth Wydeville retiring to Gipping Hall with her daughters, rather than her sons, it was still near the coast, and the chief objective of the sanctuary plot the previous year had been to spirit the Yorkist heiresses abroad. And it is highly unlikely that, in the wake of his undertaking to Elizabeth Wydeville, Richard would have entrusted her and her daughters to the custody of the man who had had her sons killed.

Elizabeth Wydeville had been deprived of her property by Parliament, which had assigned her a life annuity of 700 marks (£117,750), which Richard had confirmed in his public undertaking. Both he and Parliament had stipulated that it was to be paid, not to her, but to John Nesfield, Squire of the Body to the King, 'for the finding, exhibition and attendance of Dame Elizabeth Grey, late calling herself Queen of England'.[54] Nesfield was to continue as the former Queen's 'attendant', or rather, custodian,[55] and historian David Baldwin has offered the compelling theory that she was sent to live in his charge, possibly at Heytesbury, a Wiltshire manor near Devizes, which he had been granted on 5 April by Richard III after helping to suppress Buckingham's rebellion the previous year.[56] The manor had been confiscated from the Hungerfords after they had supported the Lancastrians during the Wars of the Roses and been attainted.

At Heytesbury, Elizabeth would have resided at East Court, a medieval manor house dating from the fourteenth century, the erstwhile seat of the Hungerfords. It was rebuilt in the sixteenth century and may have occupied the site of Heytesbury House, home of the poet Siegfried Sassoon, which still stands and probably incorporates some fragments of the medieval building.[57]

Nesfield held other properties in the north riding of Yorkshire, where his forebears had been landowners since the fourteenth century: the manors of Amotherby, near Malton, and Broughton. Both had a 'capital messuage' – the chief residence of a lord of the manor, with outbuildings, possibly a courtyard, and a garden – in the thirteenth century,[58] but there is no other record of them, and by 1484 they may not have been suitable residences for the former Queen and her daughters. It is more likely, therefore, that Elizabeth and her daughters went to stay at Heytesbury. Many years later Elizabeth was to make a point of visiting this small village, which suggests she had some link to it.[59]

Maybe it was Nesfield who made certain that Elizabeth Wydeville kept her word and sent messages to Dorset in Brittany, urging him to abandon Henry Tudor and put an end to any idea of a marriage between Henry and her daughter Elizabeth. Her decision struck a blow to the hopes of the pretender, and provoked consternation and censure among his supporters, but it had been both wise and necessary – and she really had no choice in the matter. In January Parliament had attainted Henry Tudor as a traitor, which meant that, if he ever returned to England, he would be arrested and summarily executed. Elizabeth Wydeville must have realised that anyone supporting the mooted marriage between Henry Tudor and her daughter could be deemed guilty of misprision of treason.

We next hear of Nesfield in the summer of 1484, when he was captured whilst in naval combat with French and Scottish ships off Scarborough, and had to be ransomed by Richard III.[60] David Baldwin suggests that, because of his absence, Elizabeth Wydeville was placed in the custody of someone else and moved elsewhere, but it is also possible that Nesfield left someone trustworthy to keep an eye on her in his absence.[61]

★

Elizabeth's cousin, John de la Pole, Earl of Lincoln, had recently been appointed King's Lieutenant in the North. The son of Richard's sister Elizabeth and John de la Pole, Duke of Suffolk, Lincoln's loyalty had never been in doubt, and he now presided over the Council of the North, set up by Edward IV in 1472 to govern the region in the King's name. In July 1484 Richard drew up ordinances for a new royal household – the King's Household of the North – which was to be based at Sandal Castle, Yorkshire, Lincoln's official head-quarters. In September Lincoln was also entrusted with responsibility for another royal household, at Sheriff Hutton Castle, fifty miles away, where the King was establishing a nursery for children of the House of York, notably Clarence's son, Edward, Earl of Warwick, now aged nine, and his own bastard son, John of Gloucester, who was probably about the same age as Warwick. Richard had high hopes of this boy, whose 'quickness of mind, agility of body and inclination to all good customs' he warmly praised.[62] Henry Lovell, Lord Morley, aged eighteen, Lincoln's brother-in-law, also lived in the household. Some historians[63] have conjectured that Elizabeth's brothers were among the children at Sheriff Hutton, having been secretly conveyed there from the Tower, but apart from a reference to 'the Lord Bastard' in the household ordinances,[64] which probably refers to John of Gloucester, there is no evidence for this.

The ordinances laid down for the regulation of the establishment at Sheriff Hutton provided for 'my lord of Lincoln and my Lord Morley to be at one breakfast, [and] the children together at one breakfast. My lord and the children' received the most generous allowances of food and drink. No other boys were allowed in the household apart from those sanctioned by Lincoln and the Council of the North,[65] from which we might infer that at least one daughter of the House of York was living there, probably Warwick's sister Margaret, aged eleven.[66] It is unlikely that Richard III's bastard daughter, Katherine Plantagenet, was present,[67] as she was now married to William Herbert, Earl of Huntingdon.

It has been suggested by some historians[68] that Elizabeth and her sisters were sent to reside at Sheriff Hutton in 1484; certainly Elizabeth was staying there in the summer of 1485. But because she and her sisters were sent by their mother to court at Christmas 1484, and there is no record of Elizabeth Wydeville living at Sheriff Hutton, it is more likely that they were living with her, probably at Heytesbury. Moreover, there is no record of her younger daughters ever being at Sheriff Hutton, and Elizabeth, now eighteen, was too old to be one of the children described in the ordinances.[69]

In 1484, according to Commines, the King offered Elizabeth Bishop Stillington's bastard son, William, in marriage, which would have seemed a mighty insult, especially if she had come to regard Stillington as the arch-enemy of her family and the architect of its ruin. But the young man was shipwrecked off the coast of France, taken prisoner in Paris and 'by mistake' starved to death.[70] No English source mentions this proposed marriage, and it would have contravened the terms of the King's undertaking to Elizabeth Wydeville, so the tale was probably an invention or garbled gossip.

Anne of York's betrothal to Philip of Burgundy had been broken off after her father's death. In 1484 Richard arranged for her to be affianced to Lord Thomas Howard, the eldest grandson of John Howard, Duke of Norfolk,[71] a good match in the circumstances. But Cecily had to endure the humiliation of her cousin, Anne de la Pole, being betrothed by King Richard to Prince James of Scots, her own former fiancé. Hall, the Tudor chronicler, observed: 'Here may well be noted the disordered affection which this kind [King] showed to his blood; for he, not remembering the tyranny that he had executed against his brother's sons, the wrong and manifest injury he had done to his brother's daughters, both in taking from them their dignity, possessions and living, thought it would greatly redound to his honour and fame if he promoted his sister's child to the dignity of a queen, rather than to prefer his brother's daughter, whom he had disinherited.'

Soon after Elizabeth left sanctuary, observed Croyland, 'it was fully seen how vain are the thoughts of a man who desires to establish his interests without the aid of God'. On 9 April 1484 Richard's only son, Edward of Middleham, the hope of his line, died at Middleham Castle 'after an illness of but short duration'.[72] When the news came, 'you might have seen his father and mother in a state almost bordering on madness by reason of their sudden grief'.[73] In the wake of the young Edward's death, 'after Easter' (which fell on 18 April), rumours of the murder of the Princes resurfaced (if they had ever gone away), and 'much whispering was among the people that the King had the childer [sic] of King Edward put to death', with much speculation as to how,[74] prompting More to write, years

later, that 'Englishmen declared that the imprecations of [the Princes']
agonised mother' and her appeal for divine vengeance 'had been
heard'.

The death of Edward of Middleham strengthened Elizabeth's own
position as the rightful Yorkist heir.[75] 'Still yet the King, [Richard]
looked to the defence of his territory, for there was then a report
that the exiles and those who had been proscribed would soon reach
England with their leader, Henry Tudor, to whom all these exiles
had sworn allegiance as if to their King, in the hope that a marriage
could be arranged with King Edward's daughter. King Richard was
better prepared to resist that year than he would be at any time subsequently.'[76] How Elizabeth must have held her breath. But Henry
Tudor did not come that year.

5

'Her Only Joy and Maker'

By Christmas 1484 it was being 'said by many that the King was applying his mind in every way to contracting a marriage with Elizabeth' himself.[1] 'The Lady Elizabeth (who had been some months out of sanctuary) was, with her four younger sisters, sent by her mother to attend the Queen at court, at the Christmas festivals kept with great state in Westminster Hall. They were received with all honourable courtesy by Queen Anne, especially the Lady Elizabeth [who] was ranked most familiarly in the Queen's favour, who treated her like a sister.' But Anne Neville, for all her welcome, was sad and preoccupied: 'neither society that she loved, nor all the pomp and festivity of royalty, could cure the languor or heal the wound in the Queen's breast for the loss of her son'.[2]

Anne was still only twenty-eight, 'in presence seemly, amiable and beauteous, and in conditions full commendable and right virtuous, and full gracious'.[3] Much of Richard's oft-vaunted popularity in the north, where the Nevilles had long had their power base, was due to his marriage to her, but there are few clues as to whether the couple were happy together. In September 1483 Thomas Langton, Bishop of St David's, had said of Richard that 'his sensuality appears to be increasing'. But Anne was no longer able to satisfy those needs. By Christmas 1484 she was ailing and her death was anticipated.[4]

Croyland states that 'the feast of the Nativity was kept with due solemnity at the Palace of Westminster'. He goes on mysteriously: 'There may be many other things that are not written in this book and of which it is shameful to speak, but let it not go unsaid that during this Christmas festival, an excessive interest was displayed in singing and dancing and to vain changes of apparel presented to Queen Anne and the Lady Elizabeth, the eldest daughter of the late King, being of similar colour and shape: a thing that caused the people to murmur and the nobles and prelates greatly to wonder at, while it was said by many that the King was bent either on the anticipated death of the Queen taking place, or else by means of a divorce, for which he supposed he had quite sufficient grounds, on contracting a marriage with the said Elizabeth. For it appeared that in no other way could his kingly power be established, or the hopes of his rival being put an end to.'[5]

Given that Croyland, writing after Anne Neville had died, is refer-ring to the *anticipated* death of the Queen or a divorce, he must have based his account on his inside knowledge of discussions at the time.[6] He states that people were saying that Richard wanted to marry Elizabeth, but reveals that the King (not the gossipers) supposed he had sufficient grounds for an annulment, so evidently Croyland knew that an annulment had been discussed and was privy to the King's intentions.

No wonder he and others murmured and wondered, and that word of Elizabeth's apparel spread beyond the palace to the common people. The fifteenth century was an age of strict sumptuary laws reserving the right to wear luxurious materials to the upper ranks of society; an Act prohibiting all but the King's family from wearing purple silk and cloth of gold had been passed only two years earlier. The Queen's clothes were expected, by law and tradition, to be more sumptuous than those of women of lower rank, so the sight of Anne Neville's bastardised niece 'arrayed like a second queen' in robes to which she had no right would inevitably have prompted comment, even in a court where 'sensual pleasure holds sway to an increasing extent'.[7] It is hardly credible that Anne, welcoming as she was to Elizabeth, would have suggested out of kindness that she wear the same clothes as herself. Born into the higher nobility, she would have known that comment would ensue, and while Elizabeth was at court her reputation was under her aunt's protection, the Queen being effectively the moral guardian of the unmarried girls in her retinue. It could only have been King Richard, eager to discounte-nance Henry Tudor, who ordered that Elizabeth appear dressed as a queen; and in that he showed scant regard for her reputation or for his ailing wife.

But this was not the only cause for gossip and speculation. Croyland's account makes it clear that, in the wake of that Christmas court, 'the King's determination to marry his niece reached the ears of his people, who wanted no such thing'. Naturally many found the notion shocking.

The plan was 'ill-judged, inept, unrealistic'[8] and 'foolish'.[9] Richard surely knew it would be controversial, but he had compelling reasons for pressing ahead with it. Many still recognised Elizabeth as the legitimate, rightful heiress of the House of York. Marriage to her could render Richard's title unassailable. A union with the popular princess whose brothers he was said to have murdered might also help to restore his damaged reputation and win over the loyalty of disaffected Yorkists. Richard desperately needed a son to succeed him, and Elizabeth, who came from fecund stock, was likely to provide one. Above all, their marriage would take her forever beyond the reach of Henry Tudor, and put paid to the latter's designs on the crown.

It may be that Richard was personally attracted to Elizabeth, for she was young and comely, and there is evidence from which we might infer that there was more to this than politics. Aside from Croyland's consistently cynical view of his motives, the King's most trusted advisers, Sir Richard Ratcliffe and Sir William Catesby, were to warn him that people would believe he was pursuing this marriage to 'gratify an incestuous passion for his niece'.[10] Maybe this was purely what people might, or did, infer, but evidently many had a clearer view of what was morally permissible or practically workable than Richard seems to have done, and if he had wanted merely to put Elizabeth beyond Henry Tudor's reach, any bridegroom would have sufficed – it did not have to be himself.

Sir George Buck, Richard III's seventeenth-century apologist, believed that the King's 'counterfeit wooing' was just a political ploy to discountenance Henry Tudor and deflect him from his plans, and that he had no intention of marrying Elizabeth. 'It may not be denied but that he made love to this lady and pretended [to marr]y her, and obtained both the good will of the lady [and] the Queen her mother. But this love was made in policy, and cunningly, to draw her to him [and divert her] from the Earl of Richmond.' This is at variance with what Croyland, Ratcliffe and Catesby believed. If Richard had no real intention of marrying Elizabeth, but merely wanted to discountenance Henry Tudor, he did so with little thought of how it would rebound on Elizabeth or his wife, and he failed to take his advisers into his confidence, even in the face of adverse rumours.

Whatever Richard's initial motivation, he moved quickly – he had to, as Tudor's prospects were looking decidedly brighter. That autumn, having been warned that the Breton chancellor was plotting with Richard III to seize him, Henry had fled to France. His timing was perfect, as the new French King, Charles VIII, Elizabeth's former betrothed, was determined to annexe Brittany by marrying its duchess, and feared that Richard III would support its independence. Thus he was more than willing to offer Henry his support, which made Henry an even greater threat to Richard. Marrying Elizabeth was, for Richard, an effective way of neutralising that threat; thus it was a matter that needed to be advanced with some urgency. As Shakespeare has Richard saying, 'I must be married to my brother's daughter, or else my kingdom stands on brittle glass.'

Obviously the plan was fraught with difficulties. Elizabeth's bastardisation was the grounds of Richard's title to the throne. Either he was being ruthlessly pragmatic, or at heart he knew that Elizabeth was Edward IV's lawful issue and the true heiress of the House of York. If she could supply all that was wanting in Henry Tudor's title, she could also supply all that was lacking in Richard's, although that would have raised awkward issues, for his marriage to her would be seen by many as a tacit admission that the Princes were not only legitimate but also dead. Declaring her and her sisters legitimate would have been tantamount to proclaiming that Edward V was the rightful king but that he and Richard of York were no more, and that would have raised yet more contentious questions, and given rise to further damaging rumours; it would also have made Richard, in the eyes of many, king only in Elizabeth's right. Yet it is hard to see how he could have married her without legitimising her, for kings did not marry bastards, and a queen's lineage was expected to be impeccable, which was why Elizabeth's own mother had been so disparaged by the nobility. When it came down to it, the only political advantage to the union that Richard could actually acknowledge was thwarting Henry Tudor, and the path to that was littered with insurmountable obstacles.

The prime obstacle to the marriage was that Richard already had a wife, and although he and Anne were cousins, a dispensation for their marriage had been granted by the Pope himself on 22 April 1472.[11]

However, the marriage settlement had included a divorce clause allowing Richard to keep Anne's lands if either of them remarried.

Then there was the grave matter of the close blood relationship between Richard and Elizabeth. Marriage between an uncle and niece was frowned upon by the Church and forbidden by canon law, as it was within the third degree of consanguinity; the ban extended to marriages up to the seventh degree of consanguinity. Dispensations for unions within these prohibited degrees could, for 'great and pressing' reasons,[12] be granted by the Pope. In 1528, wishing to marry the sister of his former mistress, Henry VIII obtained a dispensation that (had he been so inclined) would have allowed him to marry his mother or daughter; in 1496 Ferdinand II, King of Naples, was granted a dispensation to marry his aunt, Juana of Aragon;[13] and in 1582 Ferdinand II, Archduke of Austria, was permitted to wed his niece, Anne Gonzaga. Otherwise examples of uncle–niece marriages are rare before the Reformation, after which Parliament banned them in England,[14] and there was no precedent in the English royal houses. In 1560, avunculate marriages were forbidden by the Church of England because they were contrary to Levitical law. It is easy to see why such unions were regarded as incestuous in Elizabeth's day, and why Richard, who had been at pains to show himself an upright, moral ruler, was to be accused of immorality by his contemporaries and later writers. That he risked such a backlash shows how desperate he must have been to put paid to Henry Tudor's pretensions.

It seems likely that Elizabeth Wydeville knew of Richard's intentions before Christmas, for she sent her younger daughters to court to 'colour' their elder sister's appearance there.[15] Stuart and Georgian historians asserted that this proposed marriage was Elizabeth Wydeville's idea, but that is unlikely; she had no influence now, she was not at court, and there is no evidence to support the assertion. Not many months before, Elizabeth and her mother had been told that Richard III had murdered her brothers, and evidently they had believed that. How then could either of them have come to regard a marriage alliance with Richard as desirable? It has been asserted by his apologists that Elizabeth Wydeville would never have consented to her daughter marrying the man she believed had killed her sons, although, again, whether he had murdered the Princes or not, he had executed without trial Sir Richard Grey. Those who believe Richard innocent of the Princes' death often overlook the fact that Elizabeth Wydeville schemed to marry Elizabeth to Henry Tudor, the man whom many revisionists believe was the real murderer.

Probably the former Queen saw marriage with Richard as a means of restoring her daughter's status, rescuing her from the prospect of an undistinguished union with a man of lesser birth, and setting her up in an advantageous position from which she could exercise influence and patronage, which could only benefit her mother and sisters.

Richard was then thirty-two, fourteen years Elizabeth's senior; it was not an unusual age gap in an age of arranged marriages. 'He was of bodily shape comely enough, only of low stature.'[16] A Silesian knight, Nicholas von Poppelau, who visited his court in 1484, described him as lean, with 'delicate arms and legs', while John Rous speaks of 'his little body and feeble strength'. His skeleton, discovered under a car park in Leicester in 2012, was found to have severe scoliosis, or curvature of the spine; this would have accounted for his having one shoulder higher than the other, which was what gave rise to the nickname 'Crouchback', first recorded in 1491. Coincidentally, the Greek word *skoliosis* means crooked. Although five foot eight tall, Richard would have appeared shorter because of the curvature. Only this one source mentions him having any deformity, so clever dressing in padded doublets must have disguised it.

This was probably no easy disability to bear. In all respects severe scoliosis is a serious condition with far-reaching effects impacting on every aspect of life. There was no treatment in Richard's day, and he probably suffered pain and muscle fatigue in the back, chest, head, hips, shoulders, neck and legs as a result of postural problems and limited spinal movement. Severe scoliosis can cause constriction of the chest and restrict breathing capacity. It can also lead to serious emotional and behavioural problems such as low self-esteem, mood swings, depression, difficulty in sleeping, poor sexual relationships and interpersonal skills, and social isolation. Untreated, the condition usually worsens. That Richard III overcame such difficulties to the extent of being able to lead a charge in battle says much for his strength of character. One may speculate as to the ways in which his disability might have impacted on his life and actions, but we can never know that for certain. He appears to have been a man much in command of himself.

The reconstruction of his face, based on scans of his skull, was of necessity partly conjectural, as no soft tissue survived, and makes him look very young and fresh-faced; in those days, a person of thirty-two was nearing middle age. Richard's portraits show a set-faced, serious-looking man with a jutting chin, thin lips and long dark hair. He was no great catch physically, but he was the King, which outweighed that, and that was what mattered to Elizabeth.

Elizabeth was probably present on the feast of the Epiphany, 6 January 1485, when Richard entered Westminster Hall wearing his crown, as was customary, and presided over a great feast. During that feast, word was brought to him from his spies on the coasts that 'his enemies would without doubt invade the kingdom early the following summer, or at least would attempt to do so'. This was welcome news 'as much as it could be seen to be putting an end to all the doubt and misfortune', but it was also worrying because his treasury was short of money. He was to resort to demanding forced loans, or 'benevolences', from his subjects, just as his brother had done, despite the fact that he himself had condemned the practice in Parliament.[17]

It was probably early in 1485 (the date is not recorded) that the King, bearing in mind Henry Tudor's vow to marry Cecily of York if he could not have Elizabeth, ensured that Cecily was found a husband, the relatively lowly Ralph Scrope of Upsall,[18] another intimation that he had reserved Elizabeth for himself. Elizabeth may have felt Cecily's humiliation keenly, for while Ralph Scrope was hardly 'a man found in a cloud, of unknown lineage and family', as Hall asserts, but the second son of Thomas, 5th Baron Scrope of Masham, he was no great match for a girl who had once been a princess.

'In the course of a few days' after Christmas, Croyland recorded, 'the Queen fell extremely sick, and her illness was supposed to have increased still more and more, because the King entirely shunned her bed, declaring that it was by the advice of his physicians that he did so. Why enlarge?'

Several writers have concluded from this passage in Croyland that Anne's doctors believed her illness to be contagious, hence the long-held theory that she was suffering from tuberculosis. But Croyland's cynical aside suggests either that he did not believe Richard's excuse for shunning her bed, or that he thought the King was glad to have such an excuse. In view of the rumours that had proliferated in the year between Anne's death and the writing of his chronicle, he might have been implying something more sinister, a matter of such common currency that he had no need to enlarge.

We do not know what killed Anne Neville. It could have been

cancer, or one of any number of conditions, to which stress over her son's death and her husband's neglect may have undermined her resistance. Tuberculosis can spread rapidly through the lungs – what used to be called galloping consumption – but in view of Croyland's scepticism, Anne may have died of something else entirely. She lingered into the early spring of 1485, attended by many physicians, but they could do nothing to save her, and on 16 March, 'upon the day of a great eclipse of the sun, [she] departed this life'. Soon afterwards she 'was buried at Westminster with no less honours than befitted the interment of a queen'.[19] No provision was ever made for a tomb, and the site of her grave is lost. She is commemorated only by a small bronze wall plaque erected in 1960 in the Abbey.

Vergil asserts that it was now, when he was 'loosed from the bond of matrimony', that Richard began to 'cast an eye upon Elizabeth, his niece, and to desire her in marriage'. As we have seen, Croyland makes it clear that this had been in his mind at least three months earlier. Vergil continues: 'Because the young lady herself, and all others, did abhor the wickedness so detestable, he determined there-fore to do everything by leisure.' But rumours had spread in the wake of the Christmas court, and it was clear that public opinion was against such a marriage, while Richard's enemies had been spreading sedition. For, in the days immediately following Anne's death, there was 'much simple communication among the people by evil-disposed persons, contrived and sown to very great displeasure of the King, showing how that the Queen, as by consent and will of the King, was poisoned, to the intent that he might then marry and have to wife Lady Elizabeth, eldest daughter of his brother'.[20]

Richard was quick to deny it. Within six days of Anne's passing, 'the King's purpose and intention being mentioned to some who were opposed thereto, [he] was obliged, having called a council together, to excuse himself with many words, and to assert that such a thing had never once entered his mind'.[21]

Croyland says 'there were some persons, however, present at that same Council, who very well knew the contrary [as, he implies, he did himself]. Those who were most strongly against the marriage' were Sir Richard Ratcliffe and Sir William Catesby, 'two men whose views even the King himself seldom dared oppose', which shows how much he needed their support. 'By these persons the King was told to his face that if he did not abandon his intended purpose, and deny it by public declaration before the Mayor and commons of the City of London, opposition would not be offered to him merely by the warnings of the voice; for all the people of the north, in whom he placed the greatest reliance, would rise in rebellion and impute to him the death of the Queen, in order that he might, to the extreme abhorrence of the Almighty, gratify an incestuous passion for his niece.'This was the motive imputed to him by Tudor chroniclers such as Hall, who states that Richard 'compassed by all the means and ways that he could invent how carnally to know his own niece under the pretence of a cloaked matrimony'.

To give weight to their protests, Ratcliffe and Catesby 'brought to him more than twelve doctors of divinity who had sat on the case of a marriage of an uncle and niece, and had declared that the kindred was too near for the Pope's bull to sanction'.[22]

These alone were powerful arguments against the match, but 'it was supposed by many' that Ratcliffe, Catesby and others nursed darker, more self-interested concerns, and that they 'threw so many impediments in the way for fear lest, if the said Elizabeth should attain the rank of Queen, it might at some time be in her power to avenge upon them the death of her uncle, Earl Anthony [Rivers], and her brother, Richard [Grey], they having been the King's special advisers in those matters'; Ratcliffe, moreover, had pitilessly supervised the executions of Rivers and Grey. There is no evidence at all that Elizabeth of York had it in her to be vengeful, but she was a Wydeville, so it is credible that Ratcliffe and Catesby believed they had reason to fear that she might seek to avenge her kinsmen's deaths, or would be persuaded to it by her mother's family. Some of Richard's northern councillors had received Wydeville lands and were worried that they might lose them if a queen of Wydeville stock married the King. In the light of this, Vergil's assertion that Ratcliffe and Catesby had suggested the marriage in the first place makes little sense. Vergil claimed that the councillors were now decrying the marriage because 'the maiden herself opposed the wicked act'.

Richard III urgently needed to beget an heir to his throne; he could not afford to observe a decent period of mourning for Anne, for taking a new wife was a priority. On 22 March 1485, having suppressed whatever disappointment he might have felt at being thwarted of his chosen bride, he sent Sir Edward Brampton to Portugal to negotiate two marriages: one for himself with the saintly Infanta Joana, daughter of Alfonso V, King of Portugal, and a woman close to him in age; and the other for 'the daughter of King Edward'[23] with sixteen-year-old Manuel, Duke of Beja – the future King Manuel I, a nephew of King Alfonso.[24] There has been credible speculation that this match was intended for Elizabeth, for it would have made sense now for Richard to have married her off and put her safely beyond Henry Tudor's reach; had she died before the wedding, he doubtless meant to substitute one of her sisters.

Since Alfonso V's death in 1481, Portugal had been ruled by his son, John II, who had a son of his own, so at present there was no prospect of any daughter of Edward IV becoming queen. England had enjoyed an alliance with Portugal for a century. There was close kinship between the two ruling dynasties: both Joana and Manuel descended from John of Gaunt. For Richard, Joana was arguably the next best dynastic choice after Elizabeth, although the Portuguese councillors feared that he might reject her for another of Gaunt's descendants, Isabella, Infanta of Castile, daughter of the Spanish sovereigns, Ferdinand and Isabella. They were therefore keen to conclude the alliance as soon as possible, and aware that 'it suits the King of England to marry straight away'. However, nothing came of these negotiations, which continued until August 1485. The Infanta, at heart, wanted to be a nun, and a much later story has her predicting that Richard III would be dead within a year.[25] No one could have foreseen that John II's son would die in 1491, or that Manuel would become king four years later; had Elizabeth married him, she would have been a queen. Even as things stood this was a prestigious and honourable marriage, far better than she might have expected – and it would have restored her royal status.[26]

Historians have long speculated as to where Elizabeth stood in all this. Writing much later under a régime that wished to eradicate all remembrance of Richard III's plan to marry her, Henry VII's official historian, Polydore Vergil, claimed that 'the young lady herself, and all others, did abhor this wickedness so detestable. To such a marriage the girl had a singular aversion.' Richard Grafton, More's continuator, also asserted that Elizabeth 'abhorred this unlawful desire as a thing most detestable'. In his printed edition of the work of his uncle, Sir George Buck, George Buck Esq. emphasised that 'all men, and the maid herself most of all, detested this unlawful copulation'. In his original manuscript, Vergil says that Elizabeth was 'weighed down for this reason by her great grief' and repeatedly exclaimed,

'I will not thus be married, but, unhappy creature that I am, will rather suffer all the torments which St Katherine is said to have endured for the love of Christ than be united with a man who is the enemy of my family!'[27]

Yet in the early seventeenth century, Sir George Buck wrote that he had seen a letter, now lost, which Elizabeth had sent to Richard III's loyal supporter, John Howard, Duke of Norfolk, at the end of February 1485, the month in which she turned nineteen. The text of the original letter can now only be guessed at, for Buck only summarised it, and although his unfinished, partially holograph manuscript survives, with revisions by himself and his nephew, George Buck Esq., it was badly damaged in 1731 in a fire that ravaged the Cotton library, and parts of the text are missing or illegible. What remains is as follows:

'. . . st she thanked him for his many Curtesies and friendly . . . as before . . . in the cause of . . . and then she prayed him to be a mediator for her to the K . . . ge who (as she wrote) was her onely joy and maker in . . . Worlde, and that she was his . . . harte, in thoughts, in . . . and in all, and then she intimated that the better halfe of Ffe . . . was paste, and that she feared the Queene would neu . . . .'[28]

There are copies of Buck's history in other, later hands, mostly with revisions by George Buck Esq.[29] The younger Buck – who had not hesitated to revise and publish another of his uncle's works as his own – extensively and (in parts) inaccurately rewrote *The History of King Richard III* in a condensed form for publication in 1646, and there are later printed editions based on that.[30]

Only in 1979 did A. N. Kincaid edit what remains of Buck's original text, himself supplying some of the missing text – shown in square brackets below – from B.L. Egerton MS. 2216, the closest manuscript copy to the original. The letter appears there in a passage written by Buck's scribe, in what Kincaid believes to be a fair copy of Buck's original words, and parts of it are probably in Buck's own hand; these are shown in italics below.[31] This edited version reads:

When the midst and more days of February were gone, the Lady Elizabeth, being very desirous to be married and, growing not only impatient of delays, but also suspicious of the [success], wrote a letter to Sir John Howard, Duke of Norfolk, intimating first therein that [he was the] one in whom she most [affied] [i.e trusted], because she knew the King her father much lov[ed] him, and that he was a very faithful servant unto him and to [the King his brother, then reign]ing, and very loving and serviceable [in the sense of rendering service] to King Edward's children. First, she thanked him for his many courtesies and friendly [offices, an]d then she prayed him, as before, to be a mediator for her *in the cause of [the marria]ge* to the K[i]ng, who, as she wrote, was her only joy and maker in [this] world, and that she was his in heart and in thoughts, in [body] and in all. And then she intimated that the better half of Fe[bruary] was passed, and that she feared the Queen would nev[er die].[32]

The younger Buck naturally could not claim to have seen the letter, and his bowdlerised version of it is as follows:

When the midst and last of February was past, the Lady Elizabeth, being more impatient and jealous of the success [of the King's plan to marry her] than anyone knew or conceived, writes a letter to the Duke of Norfolk, intimating first that he was the man in whom she affied [trusted], in respect of that love her father had ever bore him, etc. Then she congratulates his many courtesies and friendly offices, in continuance of which she desires him, as before, to be a mediator for her to the King in the behalf of the marriage propounded between them; who, as she wrote, was her only joy and maker in the world; and that she was his in heart and thought, [the words 'in body and in all' are left out] withal insinuating that the better part of February was past, and that she feared the Queen would never die.

As can be seen, this version differs significantly from Buck's original text.

Sir George Buck – who was praised by his contemporary, the antiquarian scholar William Camden, for his learning – believed that the letter was genuine. 'And all these be her own words, written with her own hand,' he wrote, 'and this is the sum of the letter, whereof I have seen the autograph, or original d[raft], under her [own] hand, and by the special and honourable favour of the mos[t noble] and first count of the realm, and the chief of his family, Sir Thomas Howard, Earl of Arundel and of Surrey, and the immediate and lineal [heir] of this Sir John Howard. And he keepeth that princely letter in his rich and magnificent cabinet, among precious jewels and rare monuments.' The text Buck cites bears similarities to other letters written by noble ladies in Elizabeth's day, notably one by her sister-in-law, Cecily Bonville, Marchioness of Dorset, whose words 'I have none help in the world but him only' are strikingly similar to those in the Buck letter.

Buck was not unbiased: his great-grandfather, Sir John Buck, had been one of Richard III's household officers and would fight for him at Bosworth, suffering decapitation two days later; his children would be raised by Thomas Howard, Earl of Surrey, whose own father, John Howard, had been killed in the battle fighting for Richard.[33] Buck's ancestors had had close ties with the Howard family and enjoyed their patronage since the fifteenth century, and his history was dedicated to his patron and distant kinsman, Thomas Howard, Earl of Arundel, who would have been presented with a copy[34] and could have disputed any inaccuracy.

Thus it is likely that Buck was writing the truth about the letter. As Kincaid has demonstrated, there are relatively few inaccuracies in his long history, and he was at pains to get his facts right. He made some errors of fact, and of judgement, such as accepting *Titulus Regius* at face value, and his memory was sometimes at fault, but he brought integrity to his work, so it is inconceivable that he would have forged or invented the letter.

Arundel was a discerning collector of art, historical artefacts and a great library; he was also the patron of Sir Anthony van Dyck and Inigo Jones, and at the centre of a circle of scholars and literary figures such as Sir Francis Bacon and William Harvey. His magnificent cabinet containing the letter would have stood in one of the galleries at his London residence, Arundel House, where his collections were kept. That he kept the letter in such a prominent place shows that he considered it one of his prized possessions and believed it to be authentic; and Buck's emphasis on having been shown such a treasure may, as Kincaid suggests, be a compliment to the kindness of his patron. Arundel was prominent at court during the reign of James I, whose title to the throne descended from that of Elizabeth of York, which makes it unlikely that Buck invented any calumny about her; indeed, as Master of the Revels, he showed caution in licensing plays that portrayed women or the ancestors of the nobility in a disrespectful light.[35]

On Arundel's death in 1646, his library was divided and given to the Royal Society and the College of Heralds. The Royal Society sold his manuscripts to the British Museum in 1831. A lot of Arundel's papers are in the archives of the Duke of Norfolk at Arundel Castle; some more are in other collections. Others, inherited by his widow, were auctioned in 1720.[36] Elizabeth's letter is one of only eight sources out of the many Buck cites that are no longer extant. Given the widespread dispersal of Arundel's collection, it is not surprising that the letter is missing, and it may still survive somewhere amongst these scattered papers.[37]

Historians have long questioned the authenticity of the letter, pointing out that Buck is the only source to mention it, and that he reports rather than cites the text. It has been suggested that the letter is a forgery by his nephew, but the manuscript versions give the lie to that. Nineteenth-century historians such as Nicholas Harris Nicolas,[38] Caroline Halsted and Agnes Strickland could not believe that their heroine had written such a letter, and scathingly dismissed it as a fiction or hearsay. James Gairdner thought it 'revolting' and 'monstrous' – a 'horrible perversion and degradation of domestic life' – and rejected any suggestion that Elizabeth was capable of 'sentiments so dishonourable and repulsive'.[39] Strickland called the letter 'infamous', insisting that Elizabeth 'detested the idea of the abhorrent union'. Her 'sweet and saintly nature' would never have allowed her to cherish the murderous ambition of her father and uncles, or to wish her kind aunt dead. Why, Strickland asked, did Buck not quote the Princess's words directly? Why had no one else seen the letter? Buck was obviously 'too violent a partisan and too unfaithful a historian to be believed on his mere word'. None of these writers ever consulted Buck's original manuscript.

Recently the historian Rosemary Horrox has concluded that 'one can hardly doubt that Buck saw the letter and that his version is broadly correct'.[40] One can therefore hardly doubt that it did exist. Many historians have inferred from this letter that Elizabeth believed and hoped that her uncle would marry her and make her queen. Kincaid, however, concluded that, while the letter was genuine, it proved only that Elizabeth wanted to be married – but not necessarily to the King.[41] She asks Norfolk to be a suitor 'in the cause of the marriage to the King', which can be read two ways, especially if a comma is inserted after 'marriage'.

Recently it has been suggested that the letter relates not to marriage with Richard III but to that with Manuel of Portugal.[42] In either case, it is credible that Elizabeth approached Norfolk, who had been one of her father's foremost advisers, and was also trusted by Richard; indeed, the letter reveals that he had already acted as a mediator between Elizabeth and the King in regard to the marriage in question, which shows that it had been under discussion for a while. This ties in with Croyland's report of the Christmas court. The letter was written in February, and there is no evidence that there were any discussions about the Portuguese alliances until 22 March, when Richard proposed himself for a Portuguese bride. It follows that he would not have put forward the Portuguese match for himself while there was hope that he might marry his niece – unless, of course, it had been under discussion as an alternative option; the short timescale after Anne's death might suggest that. But if he had considered it, there was no reason why he should have delayed negotiations for Elizabeth's marriage to Manuel until after Anne's death.

The statements of Croyland, the mooted annulment, the rumours, the concerns of Richard's advisers about his marrying Elizabeth, and his public denial, taken together, are sufficient to demonstrate that there was something to deny, and that until the week after Anne Neville's death his intention was to marry Elizabeth. Given its context, the balance of probabilities strongly suggests that her letter relates to that. Indeed, Buck cites it in a discussion of this proposed marriage, so obviously he believed that the letter referred to it.

That being so, Elizabeth was actively pushing for the marriage and apparently ready to promise her all to the man who – she had so recently believed – had had her brothers murdered; indeed, she could not wait for his wife to die. This is not the Elizabeth of York we know in other historical contexts, whose gentle, giving and kind character shines forth. Many have thought it incredible that she could have written such a letter. But it is not irreconcilable with what else we know of her – and it may have been written for her.

With no guarantee that Henry Tudor would ever successfully claim her, Elizabeth must have known that she would be far better off, and more safe and secure, as Richard's queen than in the limbo she now inhabited. She may have been living in dread of an unworthy marriage being arranged for her, and in fear for her own and her family's future. Probably she was ready to give her hand to any man who could put a crown on her head. Pragmatism, necessity and ambition had overcome her mother's scruples, and maybe her own, but in her case there was probably a more altruistic reason for pursuing the marriage with the King.

According to Bernard André, Elizabeth had always shown 'a truly wonderful obedience' to her mother. Even if she personally shrank from doing Elizabeth Wydeville's bidding in this case, she bore 'towards her brothers and sisters an unbounded love', which André says 'was unheard of, and almost incredible'. This is borne out by her kindness and generosity to her sisters later in life. Very probably she consented to the marriage for love of her mother and sisters, sacrificing herself to ensure their futures and prevent their situation from becoming any worse. Her becoming queen would restore their lost prestige; and she would be in a position to use her influence on their behalf, particularly in regard to finding husbands for her sisters. The advantages of such a marriage were sufficiently powerful considerations to outweigh any revulsion or fears that she might have felt, and Elizabeth probably saw it as the only way of ensuring her own and her family's future security. This would explain why she was so eager to have it concluded and so rescue them all from their invidious situation. Her pursuance of the marriage is in keeping with the Elizabeth who is so proactive in 'The Song of Lady Bessy' (see Chapter 6), an Elizabeth who will fade gracefully and wordlessly into the shadows once she achieves her ambition, and of whom there are only tantalising glimpses in later years.

It may seem odd that Norfolk would be interceding with the King on Elizabeth's behalf for a marriage they both knew he wanted. Yet she seems to have been very much in the dark as to what was going on. Buck thought her naïve in thinking that Richard could not marry her while his wife still lived.[43] Evidently she did not know that the subject of an annulment had been raised. Buck observed that 'by this letter, it may be observed that this young lady was inexpert in worldly affairs'. But her mother was not, and the letter may well have been a diplomatic ploy to bring Richard to the point and discover his true intentions, which he may have been reluctant to declare while his wife lived. Indeed, the words could have been dictated by Elizabeth Wydeville,[44] in which case Elizabeth had probably returned to Heytesbury after Christmas, which would explain why she was writing to Norfolk rather than approaching him personally.

Indeed, it is unlikely she would have sent such a letter without her mother's knowledge and approval.[45]

In it she described Richard as 'her only joy and maker in this world' and wrote that 'she was his in heart, in thoughts, in [body] and in all'. The word 'maker' meant one who makes or shapes, who advances or contrives, or even frames a legal document or law, possibly a treaty. That would make sense in the context of arranging a marriage, while the rest was intended as a fulsome declaration of loyalty, rather than something more personal. It was probably a means to an end, calculated to convince the King that Elizabeth was eager to marry him and that he held her happiness in his gift.

Several historians have remarked upon her statement that 'she was his in heart and thoughts, *in body* [author's italics] and in all'. The word 'body' is speculative, as text is missing here, although it does appear in Egerton 2216. This might seem to imply a more intimate involvement, but the passage is probably a declaration that Elizabeth would serve the King with every aspect of her being – the conventional phraseology of late-medieval fealty as well as courtship. Yet her words have also been taken to mean[46] that she had already given herself to Richard. If so, would she have spoken so frankly of it to Norfolk? Sleeping with her uncle without any contract or the dispensation of the Church could seriously have endangered her reputation and her future, not to mention her immortal soul. But speculation on the matter is not just a modern construction; there were rumours at the time, on the Continent, if not in England: the Burgundian chronicler, Jean Molinet, never very reliable, even claimed that Elizabeth bore Richard a child, an assertion that is unsubstantiated by any other source.

There is overwhelming evidence that Elizabeth was virtuous and deeply religious, but even if pragmatism had outweighed moral considerations, an illicit pregnancy could have ruined her. So it is highly unlikely that she took a desperate gamble, hoping that giving herself to a man who was shunning his wife's bed was the best way to a crown. Vergil, no apologist for Richard III, says the King 'had kept her unharmed with a view to marriage'. This chimes with the opinion of his advisers that people would think he was marrying her to gratify an 'incestuous passion',[47] which more or less confirms that he had not already done so.

Elizabeth's letter betrays desperation and a sense of time passing fruitlessly: she is clearly anxious that the matter should be concluded, and apparently ready to display a callous disregard for the dying Queen Anne. In her defence, her sense of urgency may have stemmed from fear that Richard would be dissuaded from marrying her by his advisers – as later happened – and that he might then find her a less acceptable husband, which would put paid to her prospects of ever wearing a crown.

There is no evidence as to her true feelings for Richard III. It appears that at this time she had in her possession two books: a manuscript containing a verse translation in French of Boethius's *Consolatio Philosophiae* (*Consolations of Philosophy*)[48] and 'The Book of Tristram', or 'The Romance of Tristram de Lyonesse', dating from the latter part of the fifteenth century.[49] Both had belonged to Richard when he was Duke of Gloucester. The Boethius bears his motto, '*Loyalte me lye*' ('Loyalty binds me'), possibly written by Elizabeth, and her signature; the Tristram contains the inscription (not necessarily in his hand) '*Iste liber constat Ricardo Duci Gloucestre*'. On the same page Elizabeth wrote the motto she had chosen for herself, '*Sans removyr* [without changing], Elyzabeth'. Her signature appears by itself in both books, not in the form she had used as a princess – 'Elizabeth, the King's daughter' or 'Elizabeth Plantagenet' – or would use as queen: 'Elizabeth ye Queen'. The lack of a title suggests that she owned the books during this period when she had no royal status, while the motto is apposite, given her situation, and may reveal a strength of character that enabled her to cope in adversity with fortitude.

The tale of Tristram of Lyonesse may have had some significance for Elizabeth. Sir Thomas Malory's version of the Arthurian legends has Tristram falling in love with Isode, whose uncle he has killed,[50] just as Richard had had Elizabeth's uncle, Earl Rivers, executed.

Possibly these books were gifts from Richard to Elizabeth, and it has been suggested that they are tangible evidence of a degree of closeness between them.[51] It is more likely that they were merely gifts given – or sent – formally by the King to the woman he hoped to marry, conventional and costly expressions of his esteem. Elizabeth had been at court only over Christmas. There had been no possibility of courtship while Queen Anne lived, and little opportunity for any relationship to develop.

Elizabeth probably never saw Richard again. She may have been at Heytesbury while the momentous events of the spring were taking place. Holinshed, writing much later, states that the King would not permit her to attend the Queen's obsequies, and sent her away from court, presumably to escape the rumours, to stay at Lathom House in Lancashire, Lord Stanley's seat. But it is more likely that Elizabeth was at Heytesbury, itself a good distance from London. It is unlikely that the King would have risked her going to a house where she might come into contact with Margaret Beaufort.

Whether Margaret Beaufort was at Lathom or not, she was still doing her best to bring about Elizabeth's marriage to her son. That spring, when Henry Tudor, busily preparing ships for his invasion, heard a rumour that 'King Richard, his wife being dead, was minded to marry Elizabeth, his brother Edward's daughter', and that he had married Cecily, Edward's other daughter, to the younger son of a peer, it 'pinched him to the very stomach', and left him in fear that his friends would forsake him.[52] He was so insulted that he decided to seek another bride in the person of Katherine Herbert, daughter of his former guardian. While Katherine could not bring him a crown, marriage to her might rally Welsh support to his cause. But the letter he sent to Henry Percy, Earl of Northumberland (who was married to Katherine's sister), containing his proposal never reached its destination,[53] and his mother wrote urging him to set aside his pride, insisting that his marriage to Elizabeth was crucial to his success in winning the crown. By then, Henry had probably heard that Richard had publicly denied ever intending to wed his niece.[54]

In view of the rumours, Richard had no choice but to take his councillors' advice. 'A little before Easter (which fell on 3 April), in the presence of the Mayor and citizens of London, in the great hall of the priory of the Knights Hospitallers of St John in Clerkenwell, in a loud and distinct voice', he publicly denied that he had ever intended to wed his niece. Croyland observed that he made 'the said denial, more, as many supposed, to suit the wishes of those who advised him to that effect, than in conformity with his own'.

But the King needed to placate his critics. He 'showed his grief and displeasure, and said it never came in his thought or mind to marry in such manner wise, nor [was he] willing nor glad of the death of his Queen, but as sorry, and in heart as heavy, as man might be'; and he 'admonished and charged every person to cease of such untrue talking on peril of his indignation'.[55] On 11 April letters containing the text of his public denial were sent to major towns and cities, which shows how widely the gossip had spread. In them the King fulminated against 'divers seditious and evil persons in London and elsewhere within our realm [who] enforce themselves daily to sow seeds of noise and dislander against our person, to abuse the multitude of our subjects and avert their minds from us, some by setting up bills, some by spreading false rumours, some by messages and sending forth of lies, some by bold and presumptuous open speech and communication'; and he ordered that such persons be arrested and questioned.[56]

Richard's humiliating denials did little to quench the gossip; in fact, they fuelled it. Decades later Richard Grafton, in his continuation of More's history, would still state that Richard had 'fancied apace Lady Elizabeth, desiring in any wise to marry with her'. But that was not all that rumour alleged. 'After Easter,' *The Great Chronicle of London* records, 'much whispering was among the people that the King had poisoned the Queen his wife, and intended with a licence purchased to have married the eldest daughter of King Edward. Which rumours and sayings with other things before done caused him to fall in great hatred of his subjects.'

The damning rumours about Anne's death passed into common currency. Commines heard them in France and reported: 'Some say he had her killed.' The chronicler John Rous, a Neville adherent who had been full of praise for Richard but turned vitriolic, possibly after Anne's death, was to state categorically: 'Lady Anne, his Queen, he poisoned.' Later, Vergil wrote cautiously that 'the Queen, whether she was despatched with sorrowfulness or poison, died within a few days after'.

Later writers asserted that Richard had harried Anne to her death by psychological means. Vergil wrote that he abstained from her bed, then lamented bitterly to Archbishop Rotherham that she was unfruitful, whereupon Rotherham spread the word that the Queen 'would suddenly depart from this world'. The King was saying the same, and even spread a rumour that she had died, intending to frighten her to death. When one of her ladies told her of it, Anne was so fearful that she concluded that her days were at an end, and fled to Richard in tears, asking why 'he should determine her death', but he made a show of kissing and comforting her, and bade her 'be of good cheer'. In the late seventeenth century, Thomas Fuller would write that 'this lady, understanding that she was a burden to her husband, for grief soon became a burden to herself and wasted away', her condition worsened by daily quarrels with Richard and his complaints that she was barren. 'Some think she went her own pace to the grave, while others suspect a grain was given her to quicken her in her journey to her long home.'

Of course, these later stories were written at a time when people believed that Richard III had been a tyrant and a monster, but rumours that he had done away with Anne were in circulation very soon after her death, at the same time as it was being said that he was planning to marry Elizabeth. Given that rumours that he had murdered the Princes had now been in circulation for eighteen months, would not die down, and were damaging his reputation, it must have seemed believable that he had murdered an unwanted wife too. He had, after all, destroyed others – Hastings, Rivers and Grey – who stood in the way of his ambitions. And it is possible, given the urgent need to neutralise Henry Tudor, that there was more than just rumour involved, and that the man who had murdered his own nephews had not scrupled to hasten the end of the wife who stood in the way of his plans. That many people – sufficient to merit a public denial – believed this at the time is clear; and it might be that those who had kept silent felt free to voice their suspicions once Richard was dead, about this and other matters.

The rumours, true or not, had done much damage. In southern England and Wales, Richard had lost any popular support he had ever had. This was the man who had ruthlessly manoeuvred his way to the throne, impugning the legitimacy of his brother's children, and his mother's honour in the process, and committing acts of tyranny, justified by what many regarded to be lies; who was widely reputed to have murdered his nephews and even his wife, and was known to have been contemplating a marriage with his niece that most people condemned as incestuous. Only in the north did he retain some of his former popularity and support, but some of it had been due to his marriage to the Neville heiress, and now even that was dwindling. Small wonder that, after the Queen's death, Richard's 'countenance was always drawn'.[57] Someone who had known him later told More that he 'was never quiet in his mind, never thought himself secure, his hand ever on his dagger', and that 'he took ill rest at night'.

One thing Richard III could have done to put paid to Henry Tudor's aspirations was marry off Elizabeth – and her sisters. His failure to do so seems inexplicable, as many Yorkists had attached themselves to Henry in the expectation that he would wed Elizabeth and restore the rightful royal line to the throne. Maybe Richard was hoping that the Portuguese marriage would be speedily concluded. But these things took time – and, for him, time was now running out.

6

'Purposing a Conquest'

Publicly rejected and humiliated by the King after being made a spectacle of at the Christmas court, deprived of the chance to wear the crown that would have brought honour and prosperity to her family, and possibly horrified by rumours that Richard had hastened his Queen's death, Elizabeth had every reason to feel distressed and angry. Now plans were afoot to marry her into Portugal, which would put paid to her aspirations, and left her family without a friend in high places. Small wonder that she now looked to Henry Tudor to deliver her and fulfil her hopes. After all, he had sworn to marry her and rule England with her. Marriage to him probably seemed the best way to satisfy her ambitions, restore her rights and safeguard her kinsfolk – and it would wreak a devastating revenge on Richard.

She had good reason to hope. In 1485 Charles VIII recognised Henry Tudor as king of England and gave him money, ships and French troops for an invasion, with the aim – as Henry put it – of 'the just depriving of that homicide and unnatural tyrant'. Upon this, many Englishmen hastened to France to join the pretender. Even though Richard III had now repudiated his plan to marry Elizabeth, Henry knew he must invade soon lest the King marry her elsewhere; if that happened, his cause would irretrievably be lost. He was as eager as she was for their marriage. Thus the French aid was a godsend.

There is evidence that Elizabeth enlisted the aid of Lord Stanley, Henry's stepfather. Stanley may privately have resented Richard III's treatment of his wife, Margaret Beaufort, and by Christmas 1484 both of them were secretly in contact with Henry Tudor. But Stanley, as ever, would not show his hand until it was safe to do so.

A near-contemporary metrical chronicle, 'The Song of Lady Bessy', describes Elizabeth's involvement in the momentous events of 1485. Although the earliest surviving text dates from c.1600, the song was written in Henry VII's reign, probably before 1500 (see p. 146), and perhaps disseminated as popular propaganda against Richard III. It exists in three different forms: in Harleian MS. 367 ff. 89–100, which dates from c.1600, and Bishop Percy's Folio Manuscript III, which is just slightly later in date; both are probably the most authentic versions and closer to the original, although there is no means of detecting how much the fifteenth-century text has been altered. There is a later seventeenth-century copy, printed with notes by Thomas Heywood in the reign of Charles II, which has suffered by elaborate embellishment.

The song was probably composed by Stanley's squire, or agent, Humphrey Brereton of Cheshire, who himself features in it and was the person best placed to recount the events the ballad describes. Opinions vary as to its historical accuracy. A few parts are demonstrably inventions, and others may be too – although there are not 'numerous anachronisms', as claimed by Gairdner.[1] The inaccuracies probably arise from the author not always being as close to events as he would have liked the reader to think he was, and also no doubt as a result of his partisan zeal. He perhaps exaggerated his own role, and the familiar trust in which he was held by Elizabeth and the other high-ranking people who appear in the poem. He invented speeches for his characters; again that was standard practice at this period, even in the recording of history. Stanley's role in this episode may also have been overstated, for the poem was probably written under his auspices, and with the benefit of hindsight – as well as a good dollop of poetic licence.

There is no way of proving if the substance of the poem is based on fact, as the historical record is silent on Elizabeth's role in the events it describes. Yet despite being mere doggerel, and possibly altered in parts, the minute and exact details in 'The Song of Lady Bessy' suggest a close acquaintance with real people and events, and are unlikely to be entirely imaginary. Even Gairdner admitted that there was 'a great deal of truth in the poem'. Brereton's almost affectionate portrayal of the industrious and committed Lady Bessy appears to come from one who was familiar with her. She is a

Elizabeth of York,
'the most virtuous princess and gracious Queen'.

Edward IV and Elizabeth Wydeville with their children: the future Edward V kneels in front of his brother on the left, and Elizabeth of York heads her sisters, Mary, Cecily, Anne and Katherine, on the right. 'In those days you would have seen a royal court worthy of a most mighty kingdom, filled with riches and, surpassing all else, those beautiful and most delightful children.'

Edward IV, Elizabeth's father.
'The commons love and adore him
as if he were their God.'

Elizabeth Wydeville,
Elizabeth's mother.
'Now take heed what love may do.'

One of the restored rooms at Cheyneygates,
the former house of the Abbot of Westminster, where
Elizabeth lived in sanctuary with her mother and
siblings for eighteen months in total, 'in right great
trouble, sorrow and heaviness'.

Elizabeth and her sisters, Mary, Cecily and Anne.
'She manifested towards her brothers and sisters
an unbounded love.'

Fotheringhay Church, where Elizabeth witnessed the solemn reburial of her grandfather, Richard, Duke of York, in 1476.

Richard III, the uncle who had Elizabeth declared a bastard. She called him 'her only joy and maker in this world'.

Thomas, Lord Stanley, later Earl of Derby, Elizabeth's 'Father Stanley', who intrigued with her against Richard III.

Sheriff Hutton Castle, Yorkshire, where Elizabeth was effectively held prisoner by Richard III in 1485.

Elizabeth's husband, Henry VII, as a young man. 'He was governed by none,' yet there is evidence that he came to respect Elizabeth's judgement and confided in her.

Margaret Beaufort, Countess of Richmond, Elizabeth's mother-in-law.
'Everyone that knew her loved her,' and the two women got on well together.

'The joining of the Houses of Lancaster and York': imaginative painting of the wedding of Henry and Elizabeth by J.R. Brown, c.1901. 'Two titles in one thou didst unify, when the red rose took the white in marriage.'

'The rose both red and white in one rose now doth grow.' The Deanery, Winchester Cathedral, the former Prior's House, where Elizabeth's first child Arthur, was born in 1486.

The birth of a prince, from the Beauchamp Pageant, c.1483-7. 'Behold, the royal child Arthur arises, the second hope of our kingdom.'

Bermondsey Abbey, south of London, where Elizabeth's mother was sent 'for divers considerations' in 1487.

'O Commonwealth, the Queen with joyous heart takes up her glorious crown.' The coronation of a queen, from the Beauchamp Pageant, c.1483-7. Although this drawing depicts Joan of Navarre, wife of Henry IV, it was executed eighty years later, around the time of Elizabeth's coronation.

The Palace of Westminster, with Westminster Abbey in the background, as it would have looked in the reign of Elizabeth's son, Henry VIII. (St Stephen's Chapel can be seen in the centre, with Westminster Hall behind it to the right). Elizabeth was born here. She spent much time at Westminster, which was the foremost of the royal palaces in her day.

Perkin Warbeck, the 'feigned lad', who claimed to be Elizabeth's brother, Richard, Duke of York. He could 'move pity and induce belief, as was like a kind of fascination and enchantment to those that saw or heard him'.

Edward IV's great hall at Eltham Palace, where Henry and Elizabeth's 'right dearly well-beloved' younger children spent much time in their early years.

'Madam, I pray you forget not me to pray
to God that I may have part of your prayers.'
Inscriptions written by Elizabeth and Henry VII in
a Latin missal of 1498, owned by one of her ladies.

Elizabeth's signature appears at
the bottom of this page in
'The Hours of Elizabeth the Queen'.

Carved reliefs of Henry VII and Elizabeth of York on the Sudbury Hutch of *c.*1500.

heroine standing up for the right, busily intriguing to achieve her ambitions, and working actively undercover to aid Henry Tudor's – and her own – cause. It is unlikely that Brereton would have depicted her as such were there not a degree of truth behind his verses. There was no reason to include her if she had not been involved – Lord Stanley's exploits alone justified a ballad.

There can be little doubt that Brereton was privy to much that was going on in Lord Stanley's life at that time, and the details in the song suggest that it is first-hand evidence of Elizabeth's involvement in the conspiracy to put Henry Tudor on the throne. The ballad may exaggerate her role in the intrigues that preceded Henry Tudor's invasion, yet it is conceivable – even credible – that she did participate, perhaps even to the extent the poem portrays. Written probably within eight years of the events it describes so vividly, and by a trusted retainer of her stepfather-in-law, it would have had to appear credible to anyone who read it, especially as it described in detail the deeds of one who was now queen of England. What is striking is that the Elizabeth portrayed in 'The Song of Lady Bessy' is as proactive as the Elizabeth who wrote to John Howard urging his help in progressing her marriage with Richard III.

Politically, much – if not all – of the chronology of 'The Song of Lady Bessy' fits into the context of the known events of 1485. A lot of the information it contains has the ring of authenticity, and affords insights into the kind of intrigues that were secretly at play at this time but otherwise, inevitably, went unrecorded.

If the poem does reflect actual events, given some dramatic licence, it may seem strange that Margaret Beaufort barely earns a mention in it; but Margaret had already courted disaster in supporting Buckingham and Henry Tudor, and had got off lightly. Given the dread penalty for women who committed treason, she probably felt she dared not test Richard's leniency a second time, and kept her dealings with her son as secret as possible.

It may be that, by becoming proactive in Henry's cause, Elizabeth was trying to redeem herself in his eyes and make amends for what he had seen as a betrayal; for she could have learned from Margaret Beaufort of his reaction to rumours that she was to marry Richard III.

The poem begins when 'Lady Bessy' is sojourning in London with Lord Stanley; internal evidence indicates that this is the spring of

1485, after Queen Anne's death. At that time, Elizabeth may have been living at Heytesbury, but there is no actual evidence for her whereabouts. Her age is given by Brereton as twenty-one when in fact she was nineteen. When we first encounter Bessy, she is apparently distressed and frightened, angry even – much as the historical Elizabeth probably felt at that time – and she complains to Stanley about her uncle, King Richard.

'Help, Father Stanley, I do you pray!' she cries, then tells him that the King has had her brothers put to death by drowning them in 'a pipe of wine' in their bed (a garbled description of their fate that owes much to the rumours then in circulation, not only about the Princes' end, but Clarence's also). Then she says that Richard 'would have put away his Queen for to hath lain by my body'. She begs Stanley to 'help that he were put away, for all the royal blood destroyed will be!' She wants to wreak revenge on 'that traitor' and 'help Earl Richmond, that prince so gay, that is exiled over the sea. For if he were king, I should be queen.' She loves him, she declares, even though she has never seen him.

She reminds Stanley that her father, King Edward, on his deathbed, 'put me to thee to govern and to guide'. She says that the King left her a book of prophecy, and that 'he knew that ye might make me a queen, Father, if thy will it be, for Richard is no righteous king', who will destroy 'the royal blood of all this land, as he did the Duke of Buckingham'. Buckingham, she reminds Stanley, 'was as great with King Richard as now are ye'.

Bessy now reveals that she has busily been thinking of ways to overthrow Richard. She knows that Stanley's brother, Sir William, could summon up 500 fighting men, while Stanley's oldest son George, Lord Strange, then at Lathom House, the family seat in Lancashire, could afford to support a thousand men for three months; and his younger sons, Edward and James, a priest who had 'lately' been made Warden of Manchester, could send soldiers too. In fact, James was not appointed warden until July 1485, but Brereton's memory was probably imprecise. James was made Archdeacon of Richmond in 1500, and Bishop of Ely in 1506.[2] Since he is referred to only as Warden of Manchester, and there is mention of Sir William Stanley coming 'under a cloud', a reference to his execution for treason in 1495, the poem must originally have been written between 1495 and 1500.

Bessy persists, telling Stanley that his sister's son, Sir John Savage, could provide 1,500 fighting men, Gilbert Talbot (a younger son of John Talbot, Earl of Shrewsbury) could send a thousand and pay their wages for three months, while Stanley himself could provide another thousand. Historically, Savage was to command the right wing of Henry Tudor's army at the Battle of Bosworth, and Gilbert Talbot the left; Talbot would be knighted for his support of Henry in the battle and would receive several important appointments thereafter. Bessy urges Stanley, 'Thou and thine may bring Richmond o'er the sea, for, an [if] he were king, I should be queen.'

Stanley appears as cautious in the poem as he was in real life. 'An King Richard do know this thing, we were undone, both thou and I,' he warns Bessy. What she is plotting is no less than high treason. If anything went wrong, he continues, 'in a fire you must burn' – burning at the stake being the penalty for women who committed treason – while 'my life and my lands are lost from me. Therefore these words be in vain. Leave and do away, good Bessy!'

Bessy is determined; her ambition is to wear the crown. 'Father Stanley! Is there no grace? No, queen of England, that I must be.' Tears of frustration trickle from her eyes. 'Now I know I must never be queen! All this, man, is long of thee!' She urges Stanley to think of the dreadful Day of Judgement, crying: 'I care not whether I hang or drown, so that my soul saved may be. Make good answer, as thou may, for all this, man, is long of thee.' With that, she pulls off her headdress of pearls and precious stones, throws it to the ground, tears her hair and wrings her hands, saying through her tears: 'Farewell, man, now I am gone; it shall be long ere thou me see!'

Stanley stands 'still as any stone', weeping himself. 'Abide, Bessy! We part not so soon,' he replies. 'Here is none but thee and I. Fields hath eyen and wood hath ears; you cannot tell who standeth us by, but wend forth, Bessy, to thy bower, and look you do as I bid ye.' He tells her to 'put away thy maidens bright, that no person doth us see', and he will come to her bower at nine o'clock at night, when they will talk more of the matter; and she must have ready a charcoal fire – 'that no smoke come in our eye' – wine and spices, pen, ink and papers.

Bessy eagerly complies, and has 'all things full ready'. Waiting for Stanley, she looks at her book of prophecy and realises that, for her to become queen of England, 'many a guiltless man first must die'. When Stanley arrives, he finds her weeping. She bars the door behind him, and when they are seated she gives him wine and spices, saying, 'Blend in, Father, and drink to me.' The fire is hot, and soon 'the wine it wrought wonderfully', mellowing Stanley and making him weep.

'Ask now, Bessy, then, what thou wilt, and thy boon granted shall be,' he says.

'Nothing,' she answers. 'I would have neither of gold nor yet of fee, but fair Earl Richmond, so God me save, that hath lain so long beyond the sea.' Stanley replies that he would grant her that boon, but there is no clerk he can trust to write to Richmond on their behalf.

'Father, it shall not need,' Bessy assures him. 'I am a clerk full good, I say.' And to prove her point she draws 'a paper on her knee' and begins to write 'speedily'. Stanley tells her to write to his brother, Sir William, at Holt Castle, Denbighshire. 'Bid him bring seven sad yeomen all in green clothes, and change his inn at every town where before he was wont to lie; and let his face be towards the bench', to avoid being recognised. He asks Elizabeth to write to his three sons, as well as to John Savage and Gilbert Talbot, who are all to follow the same instructions and be with Stanley by 3 May.

Stanley seals the letters that Bessy has written, then pauses. 'Alas!' he laments. 'All our work is forlorn, for there is no messenger that we may trust.' It is Bessy who suggests Humphrey Brereton. 'He hath been true to my father and me. He shall have the writing in hand. Go to bed, Father, and sleep, and I shall work for thee and me. Tomorrow, by rising of the sun, Humphrey Brereton shall be with thee.'

After Stanley has gone to bed, Bessy works through the night: 'there came no sleep in her eye'. Early the next morning she seeks out Brereton in his 'bower' and calls out to him 'in a small voice'.

'Lady, who are ye that calleth on me ere it be light?' he responds.

'I am King Edward's daughter, the Countess Clare,[3] young Bessy,' she tells him, saying he must come 'with all the haste you can' to speak with Lord Stanley. Humphrey throws on a gown and slippers and emerges from his chamber. He goes with Bessy 'to the bedside' where Stanley is sleeping. When Stanley wakes, he weeps 'full tenderly' at the sight of Brereton.

'My love, my trust, my life, my land – all this, Humphrey, doth lie in thee,' he tells him. 'Thou may make, and thou may mar; thou may undo Bessy and me.'

Brereton evidently assures Stanley of his loyalty, as in the next moment Stanley commands him to take the six letters Bessy has written and deliver them to the people whose names are 'written on the backside'. Brereton is about to depart when Bessy waylays him, saying, 'Abide, Humphrey, and speak with me. A poor reward I shall thee give.' It will be £3 (£1,470). 'If I be queen, and may live, better rewarded shalt thou be.' She advises him, when he sets off on his mission, to take 'no company but such as shall be of the best. Sit not too long drinking thy wine, lest in heat thou be too merry' – and indiscreet. She gives him nine nobles (£1,470) to cover his expenses, and some wine, whereupon he takes leave of her and rides westwards to Holt Castle.

Brereton delivers her letters to Sir William Stanley at Holt, and to Lord Strange at Lathom, both of whom rally to the cause, then to Edward and James Stanley in Manchester. These two praise Bessy for her good counsel. 'We trust in God, full of might, to bring her lord over the sea!' they declare. Sir John Savage, however, pales when he reads her letter. 'Women's wit is wonder to hear!' he exclaims. 'My uncle is turned by your Bessy!' Nevertheless, he promises to do Stanley's bidding. Brereton then rides to Sheffield Castle, where Gilbert Talbot also pays tribute to Bessy's true counsel, and says: 'Commend me to that Countess Clare; tell her I trust in God to bring her love over the sea. In all this land she hath no peer.'

Brereton rides straight back to London, where he finds Lord Stanley walking in a garden with King Richard. Stanley gives him 'a privy twinkle with his eye', and welcomes him warmly as he bends his knee to the King. Brereton pretends he has been visiting the place where he was born and bred, and that support for Richard is strong there; the people will fight for him 'and never flee'. This pleases the King; he thanks Brereton courteously, and assures Stanley: 'Father Stanley, thou art to me near; you are chief of your commonalty.[4] Half of England shall be thine, and equally divided between thee and me. I am thine, and thou art mine.' It is easy to imagine the beleaguered Richard making such extravagant promises to secure the loyalty of the slippery Stanley.

When the King has gone, Stanley and Brereton hasten to Bessy's bower, where they find her alone. She is so pleased to see Brereton safely returned that she kisses him three times – a detail Brereton is unlikely to have included were it not true.

'Welcome home!' she cries. 'How hast thou sped in the west country?' Stanley leaves Brereton with Bessy, so that he can tell her the tidings of his journey, which she is eager to hear. Even so, she is fearful. 'If I should send for yonder prince [Henry Tudor] to come over for the love of me', he might be murdered by his foes. 'Alas, that were full great pity! Forsooth, that sight I would not see for all the gold in Christendom!'

Brereton recounts how Stanley's kinsmen and allies have shown themselves ready to overthrow King Richard. 'By the third day of May, Bessy, in London there will they be. Thou shalt in England be a queen – or else doubtless they will die.'

As the conspirators' plans mature, Stanley withdraws from the City to an old inn in the suburbs, and draws an eagle (part of the Stanley cognisance of the eagle and child) above the doorway – a pre-arranged sign to the men who come to find him. Bessy is there with him to greet them – the Stanleys, Savage and Talbot – and 'when all the lords together' meet over flagons of wine, 'among them all' is 'little Bessy', who asks, 'Lords, will ye do for me? Will ye relieve yonder prince that is exiled beyond the sea?'

Stanley answers, 'Forty pound[s] will I send, Bessy, for the love of thee, and twenty thousand eagle feet [men] a queen of England to make thee.' Sir William Stanley adds, 'Remember, Bessy, another time, who doth the best for thee.' He says he has raised a thousand men, who will be ready at an hour's warning. 'In England thou shall be a queen, or else doubtless I will die.' Savage tells her he is sending a thousand marks to 'thy love beyond the sea', and Strange adds, 'A little money and few men will bring thy love over the sea.' But they decide it is too hazardous to send their gold abroad, and that they will keep it at home to spend on waging war on Richard III. Edward Stanley also reminds Bessy to remember in the future those who are doing their best for her, 'for there is no power that I have, nor no gold to give thee. Under my father's banner will I be, either for to live or die.'

Bessy falls on her knees before the lords, promising to send £10,000 (£4.9 million) 'to my love over the sea'. This seems highly unlikely, as Elizabeth had no money of her own, but it was probably the imagined value of 'a rich ring with a stone' that Brereton was to take to Henry Tudor – although it is unlikely that any ring of the period was worth as much. Brereton tells her he dare not take her gold over the sea for fear of being robbed or drowned.

'Hold thy peace, Humphrey,' she replies. 'Thou shalt carry it without jeopardy. Thou shalt have no basket nor no [chain] mail, no bucket nor sackcloth; three mules that be stiff and strong, loaded with gold shall they be, with saddles side-skirted wherein the gold stowed shall be. If any man says, "Who[se] is the ship that saileth forth upon the sea?" say it is the Lord Lisle's – in England and France well-beloved is he.' This was Edward Grey, who had borne the rod with the dove at Richard III's coronation, and had been created Viscount Lisle by the King.[5]

Stanley scolds Bessy: 'Thou art to blame, to point any ship upon the sea! I have a good ship of my own.' He will send it across the sea with the eagle symbol flying from the top mast, and if anyone asks whose ship it is, the crew must say it is his. It is in this ship that Brereton sails to France with the ring given him by Bessy, which he takes to Henry Tudor at 'Bigeram Abbey'. This was probably Bec Hellouin Abbey, west of Rouen, where Henry was raising mercenaries, and south of Harfleur, whence he would sail to England.

When Brereton comes before Henry Tudor, he falls to his knees and delivers Bessy's letter and her ring. Henry is gladdened at the sight; he takes the ring and kisses it three times. Then he stands silent, leaving Brereton on his knees, perplexed. Eventually, the squire rises.

'Why standeth thou so still?' he asks. 'I am come from the Stanleys bold, king of England to make thee, and a fair lady to thy fere [wife]; there is none such in Christendom. She is a countess, a king's daughter, a lovely lady to look upon, and well she can work by prophecy. I may be called a lewd messenger, for answer of thee I can get none. I may sail hence with a heavy heart. What shall I say when I come home?'

Henry turns to John de Vere, Earl of Oxford, Lord Dorset (who is referred to in the poem by his lesser title, Lord Ferrers) and Lord Lisle, who are standing by, and confers with them. Then he tells Brereton he cannot give him an answer for three weeks. The next day he rides off with his lords to Paris, 'there arms to make ready', and to ask the King of France to lend him ships. Historically, Henry visited Paris in June 1485. Back at Bec Hellouin Abbey, he gives Brereton 100 marks (£16,300), promising he will be 'better rewarded' in time to come.

'Commend me to Bessy, that Countess Clare,' he says. 'I trust in God she shall be my Queen. For her I will travel the sea. Commend me to my father, Stanley. Bring him here a love letter, and another to little Bessy. Commend me to Sir William Stanley. Tell him, about

Michaelmas I trust in God in England to be.' The mention of Michaelmas sounds authentic; Brereton might well have remembered Henry saying that, and if he was writing purely with the benefit of hindsight, he would probably have had Henry predicting his arrival in August.

Brereton returns to Bessy and Stanley in London, with the letters from Henry to both of them. At this point, Stanley prepares to ride to Lathom, and Sir William Stanley, Gilbert Talbot, John Savage and Edward Stanley are raising their levies. The stage is set for the King's destruction.

If 'The Song of Lady Bessy' was pure fiction, Elizabeth may have been at Hetyesbury with her mother all along. But it is also possible that at some point she was residing in Stanley's London house, and there remains a fair chance that Richard III did discover that she was involved in a conspiracy against him – or suspected that she was in league with that proven turncoat, Lord Stanley, or even feared that she would attempt to flee abroad to join his enemy. He may have anticipated that Elizabeth would do much to win the crown she believed was rightfully hers. Even had he nurtured no such suspicions, with Henry Tudor's invasion believed to be imminent, he was taking no chances. He knew that Elizabeth was regarded by many as the rightful heiress to York, and at some stage he decided to move her to a secure place, far out of the reach of Henry Tudor or anyone else who might aspire to a crown by marrying her.

Wherever Elizabeth was, she was vulnerable to intrigue and capture, so the King gave orders that she be escorted to Sheriff Hutton Castle, ten miles north-east of York, to join the household he had set up for her cousins, Edward, Earl of Warwick, and probably Warwick's sister, Margaret Plantagenet, and his own bastard son, John of Gloucester. It has often been suggested that Elizabeth's sisters were sent there too, but there is no evidence for this.

Sheriff Hutton Castle was a feudal fortress dating from the 1140s, but rebuilt in the late fourteenth century by the powerful Nevilles, who held it until it was confiscated by Edward IV in 1471; soon afterwards it was given to Richard of Gloucester. Situated next to a park on a rising bank affording beautiful views across the Forest of Galtres, it had two moats, used as fishponds, while the village of Sheriff Hutton had grown up around it. The castle was built of brown stone around a large rectangular courtyard, or 'base court'. John Leland, who visited Sheriff Hutton during the reign of Henry VIII, recorded that it had 'four great towers with a gatehouse in the middle' – the arched gateway in the Warder's Tower, which probably accommodated the garrison. 'In the second area were five or six small towers.'[6] In fact there were eight or nine square towers over a hundred feet high. The connecting stone walls were five storeys high and contained narrow galleries and chambers.

In Yorkist times the castle was not only a building of strength and security, but also boasted luxurious accommodation. The tower chambers, accessed by spiral stairs, had arched or vaulted ceilings and painted plaster walls, while below were strong cellars that could be used as storerooms or dungeons. There was a great hall in the 'second area', and Leland thought 'the stately stair up to the hall . . . very magnificent, and so is the hall itself, and all the residue of the house, insomuch that I saw no house in the north so like a princely lodging'. In Elizabethan times William Camden called Sheriff Hutton a most elegant castle, pleasantly seated among the woods.[7]

Richard probably felt that it would be safer to lodge Elizabeth in the north, where he could command his greatest support, but Sheriff Hutton cannot have had happy associations for her, for it was the place where her uncle, Earl Rivers, had been imprisoned two years earlier before being borne off to execution at Pontefract; and it was a long way from her mother and sisters, and from Westminster and the palaces of the Thames Valley where she had spent most of her life. Again she found herself effectively a prisoner, in 'safe custody', according to Sir Francis Bacon, whose *History of the Reign of King Henry VII* was published in 1622.[8]

The household at Sheriff Hutton was under the control of John de la Pole, Earl of Lincoln, the King's Lieutenant in the North, who was then twenty-six. As the eldest son of Edward IV's sister Elizabeth and John de la Pole, Duke of Suffolk, he was the heir to a wealthy and noble house, with great establishments at Ewelme, Oxfordshire and Wingfield, Suffolk. Through his grandmother, Alice Chaucer, Lincoln was descended from the poet Geoffrey Chaucer. He was Richard III's closest adult male relative and had carried the orb at his coronation.

After the death of the Prince of Wales, Richard III had considered naming Clarence's son, the Earl of Warwick, as his successor, but it was a choice fraught with difficulties. Warwick was technically barred from the succession by his father's attainder, and although that could have been reversed, it would have left Warwick with a better claim to the throne than Richard. Moreover, he was only a child of nine. Richard decided that Warwick was not the best option and, with the consent of the nobility, named Lincoln as his successor,[9] appointing him Lord Lieutenant of Ireland, a post customarily held by Yorkist heirs to the throne. Lincoln was also granted the reversion of Margaret Beaufort's estates.

Little is recorded of Lincoln's character, saving the conventional praise for his nobility, wisdom and gallantry. Despite his youth, he was experienced in government and respected for his judgement and political sense. He was a committed Yorkist, as events would prove, especially as he had a crown in his sights and stood to lose much if Henry Tudor was victorious.

Elizabeth probably saw little, if anything at all, of her cousin of Lincoln while she was at Sheriff Hutton. His official base was at Sandal Castle, fifty miles away, and in July 1485 he was at Nottingham with the King, preparing to fight for Richard against Henry Tudor. In June, anticipating that Henry would invade soon, Richard had issued a proclamation calling on all true Englishmen to repel a pretender who was 'descended of bastard blood both of the father's side and of the mother's side, for Owen [Tudor], the grandfather, was bastard born, and his mother was daughter to John, Duke of Somerset, son unto John, Earl of Somerset, son unto Dame Katherine Swynford, and of her in double adultery gotten, whereby it evidently appeareth that no title can nor may be in him, which fully intendeth to enter this realm purposing a conquest'.[10]

On 1 August Henry Tudor's invasion fleet set sail from Harfleur in Normandy. Six days later, 'the enemy landed with a fair wind and without opposition at Milford Haven, near Pembroke'.[11] After disembarking, Henry fell to his knees, recited the 43rd Psalm – 'Judge me, O God, and plead my cause against an unworthy nation' – and kissed the ground. Then, calling on the aid of God and St George, he urged his men onwards, marching under a white and green banner proudly displaying the red dragon traditionally attributed to Cadwaladr. He came, as he was at pains to make clear, to reconcile the warring factions.

From his base at Nottingham, Richard had summoned 'his adherents from every quarter' to help him triumph over 'so contemptible a faction',[12] but by now he had lost the support of more than half of his nobility.[13] Estimates vary from six to twelve, but only a few peers answered his summons, and many knights and gentlemen ignored it. Even the Mayor and corporation of York, with whom Richard had enjoyed good relations, sent only eighty men.[14]

Croyland states that Lord Stanley had sought and received permission to go to Lancashire to see his family, but only on condition that he left his heir, Lord Strange, with the King as a hostage for his loyalty. The King had no illusions about Stanley, who had changed sides to suit himself too often, and whose loyalty could not be taken for granted, especially as he was married to Henry Tudor's mother. Richard was afraid 'lest she might induce her husband to go over to the party of her son'.[15]

'The Song of Lady Bessy' also has Stanley taking leave of the King and riding to Lathom, but taking Elizabeth with him. He leaves her at Leicester, bidding her 'lie there in privity', and warns her, 'If King Richard knew thee here, in a fire burnt must thou be.' Then he spurs his horse towards Lancashire, and sends Lord Strange 'to London [sic] to keep King Richard company'.

It has long been assumed that Elizabeth was sent to Sheriff Hutton in June,[16] but in fact no date is recorded. It is possible therefore that she was sent there in August, and not impossible that Richard's men discovered her in hiding at Leicester and, being preoccupied with more pressing matters, he gave orders that she be sent to Sheriff Hutton at this juncture, rather than earlier in the summer, thus deferring the question of what to do with her. What mattered now was that she was safely beyond Henry Tudor's reach at Sheriff Hutton.

As Henry marched his army eastwards, entering England via Shrewsbury on 15 August, the King rode to confront him. The armies met in Leicestershire, near Market Bosworth, on 22 August.

Both Croyland and Vergil state that Richard had suffered nightmares in the dark hours before they met in the field. 'The King, so it was reported, had seen that night, in a terrible dream, a multitude of demons apparently surrounding him, just as he attested in the morning, when he presented a countenance which was always drawn but was then ever more pale and deadly.' In this mood, he 'declared that he would ruin all the partisans of the other side, if he emerged as the victor'.[17] Elizabeth was one of those who stood in deadly danger of her uncle's vengeance – not least because she was seen by many as the legitimate Yorkist heir.

The Battle of Bosworth lasted two hours, with an estimated 20,000 men engaging in combat, with the majority in the royal forces. It was 'a most savage battle'.[18] Henry Tudor – whom Richard dismissed beforehand as 'an unknown Welshman, whose father I never knew, nor him personally saw'[19] – did not engage in the fighting, but remained under his standard behind the lines, leaving the experienced John de Vere, Earl of Oxford, to command his vanguard. Lord Stanley had turned up with his men, but he had secretly met with Henry two days earlier,[20] and when Richard had commanded his presence, had sent word that he 'was suffering an attack of the sweating sickness' and could not attend him.[21] 'The Song of Lady Bessy' has Stanley meeting Henry before the battle, giving him his blessing and Margaret Beaufort's, and promising to come to his aid. But when the historical Stanley turned up at Bosworth, he positioned himself some way off to the north with his forces, waiting to see which way the battle was going before joining it. His brother, Sir William Stanley, also notorious for changing sides, was with him. Even if the Stanleys had intrigued with Elizabeth to set Henry on the throne, they were looking to their own advantage before anyone else's.

On the morning of the battle the King sent a message ordering Stanley to join him at once, if he wanted his son to stay alive. Stanley, taking a terrible gamble, sent back word that he did not feel like joining the King, and he had other sons, whereupon Richard ordered his captains to put Lord Strange to death. When they refused, he told them to keep Strange under close arrest until he could deal with him after the battle.

When the King's side appeared to be losing the day, the Earl of Northumberland, who should have intervened with his men to aid his sovereign, did nothing. Seeing that he had been deserted by those in whom he had trusted, Richard gathered a small band of loyal followers and made one final, desperate charge, bearing down on the red dragon banner of Henry Tudor. He cut down the standard bearer, and was about to swoop on Henry himself, but now Lord Stanley came racing to Henry's aid, which decisively turned the tide of the battle, and 'a glorious victory was granted by Heaven to the Earl of Richmond'.[22]

The Croyland chronicler recorded that it was during the fighting, and not in the act of flight, that Richard fell, 'like a brave and most valiant prince'. The chronicler John Rous, who had once praised Richard, but turned hostile towards him in 1485, was moved to write: 'Let me say the truth to his credit, that he bore himself like a noble soldier and honourably defended himself to his last breath, shouting again and again that he was betrayed, and crying, "Treason! Treason! Treason!"' Even the Tudor historian, Polydore Vergil, conceded that King Richard was killed 'fighting manfully in the thickest press of his enemies'. 'Providence,' declared Croyland, 'gave a glorious victory to the Earl of Richmond.'

Legend has it that the crown fell from the dying Richard's helmet and rolled under a hawthorn bush – later a popular Tudor emblem, which can be seen on Henry VII's tomb and in a window of Westminster Abbey. The crown was lying 'among the spoils in the field',[23] where Sir William Stanley spotted and retrieved it.[24] As 'the soldiers cried, "God save King Henry!"' he placed it on the head of Henry Tudor, 'as though he had been already by the commandment of the people proclaimed king after the manner of his ancestors'.[25] The first sovereign of the celebrated royal House of Tudor was 'replenished with joy incredible'.[26]

With Richard III's death, 331 years of Plantagenet rule had come to an end. Now a new age had begun, and its progenitor, Henry VII, 'began to receive the praises of all, as though he had been an angel sent down from Heaven, through whom God had deigned to visit His people and deliver them from the evils with which they had hitherto, beyond measure, been afflicted'. 'The children of King Edward,' commented Croyland, had been 'avenged' at last 'in this battle: the boar's tusks quailed, and, to avenge the white, the red rose bloomed'.

Richard's body, 'pierced with numerous and deadly wounds', was found under a heap of the dead, for many men had been cut down in that last fatal charge. His corpse was stripped naked, 'with not so much as a clout to cover his privy members'; then, 'with many other insults heaped on it', it was thrown over a horse's saddle with a felon's halter around its neck, and borne, 'besprung with mire and filth', back to Leicester, where it was exhibited for two days in the collegiate church of St Mary in the Newark.[27] 'The Song of Lady Bessy' claims that 'Bessy met him with merry cheer' and addressed the bloody remains: 'How likest thou thy slaying of my brethren twain? Now are we wreaked upon thee here! Welcome, gentle uncle, home!' But there is no other record – as surely there would have been – of Elizabeth being at Leicester on that day; and Sheriff Hutton is nearly 130 miles from Leicester, a journey of at least two days back then. It is inconceivable that she could have escaped Richard's custodians before his defeat at Bosworth, and more likely that Brereton was taking poetic licence to show that she viewed her uncle's defeat as just retribution for the death of her brothers.

The vanquished King's body, which had apparently been mutilated after death, was 'indifferently buried'[28] in a roughly dug grave that was too small for it in the choir of the Grey Friars' church,[29] and in 1502 Henry VII paid out £10.1s. (£4,890) 'for King Richard's tomb' of alabaster.[30] This was destroyed along with the church during the Reformation of the 1530s. In the early seventeenth century, Robert Herrick, a mayor of Leicester, built a house and laid out a garden where once the choir had stood. Here, in 1612, Christopher Wren, father of the architect, saw 'a handsome stone pillar, three foot high', bearing the inscription 'Here lies the body of Richard III, sometime King of England'. In 2012 the grave was found under the car park laid out where the Grey Friars' monastery once stood.[31]

How rapidly news of these momentous events had filtered through to Sheriff Hutton is unknown, but Elizabeth would certainly have been anxious to hear of the outcome of the conflict between the two men who had played for her hand, for it would seal her own fate. She did not have long to wait, for within hours of his victory at Bosworth, even before departing from Leicester, the new King sent Sir Robert Willoughby and Sir John Halewell[32] to Sheriff Hutton to secure her person and that of Edward, Earl of Warwick; they came with 'a noble company to fetch [Elizabeth] to her lady mother'.[33]

André says that when Elizabeth 'learned that Henry had won the victory', she 'exclaimed with gladness of heart: "So even at last, thou hast, O God, regarded the humble and not despised their prayers. I well remember that my most noble father, of famous memory, meant to have bestowed me in marriage upon this most comely Prince! O that I were worthy of him; for, as I have lost my father and protector, I sorely fear me that he will take a wife from foreign parts whose beauty, age, fortune and dignity will more please him than mine! What shall I say? I am alone, and I dare not take counsel. O that I could acquaint my mother, or some of the lords, with my fears, but I dare not, nor have I the courage to discourse with him himself on the subject, lest in so doing I might discover my love. What will be, I cannot divine, but this I know, that Almighty God always succours those who trust in Him. Therefore will I cease to think, and repose my whole hope in Thee. O my God, do Thou with me according to Thy mercy."' And she 'pondered these things privately'.

Allowing for the flowery language, and the likelihood that the speech is invented, there may be some truth in the sentiments expressed; it is unlikely that André would have made all this up. Elizabeth might indeed have come to regard her father's plan to marry her to Henry Tudor as prescient, if not sacrosanct, and these may well have been the sentiments she expressed at the time. It is credible that she herself was one of André's sources, for he wrote his official history during the last years of her life.

Henry wanted Elizabeth and Warwick brought south immediately, and Elizabeth 'received a direction to repair with all convenient speed to London, and there to remain with the Queen her mother; which accordingly she soon after did',[34] escorted under Sir Robert's protection with the honour due to a future queen of England. Warwick, however, was to be conveyed in secret.

Henry was always to regard young Warwick as one of the chief threats to his crown, despite the fact that the Earl, then just ten years old, was barred from the succession and seems to have been mentally backward. But for the attainder against his father, the Duke of Clarence, Warwick would have been the rightful male heir to the House of York; Elizabeth's claim was better, but she was a woman, and Henry, knowing that attainders could be reversed, feared that Yorkists might now look to Warwick in preference to her and the man Richard III had called 'an unknown Welshman'. As soon as Warwick arrived in London, Henry had him confined briefly at Margaret Beaufort's London house, Coldharbour, and then imprisoned in the Tower. Because Henry was fearful lest he escape to 'stir up civil discord',[35] the unfortunate boy was to spend the rest of his life there, bereft of companions, tutors or much in the way of comforts. Thus seriously did the new King regard him as a rival, and with justification, for, captive though Warwick remained, he was to be the focus of several Yorkist plots.

Elizabeth, however, was brought openly to London, attended by an escort of 'many noblemen and ladies of honour'.[36] That was a good sign, yet she might have felt a passing anxiety as to her future, for until Henry married her, she was essentially a rival claimant to his throne, for all that she was a woman; and she could transmit her claim to any man she married. Probably she had read enough history to know that King John had murdered Arthur, Duke of Brittany, a rival claimant to the throne, and then imprisoned Arthur's sister Eleanor for life. But Elizabeth had four sisters, each of whom could replace her in the line of succession, and her proposed marriage was popular, so it was hardly likely that the new King would renege on a promise that had won over so many Yorkists to his cause. And now the courtesy and honour accorded to her must have given her cause to hope that she would soon be queen, although she may have been disconcerted to learn that Henry 'had assumed the style of king in his own name', on the battlefield of Bosworth, 'without mention of the Lady Elizabeth at all',[37] especially as he was supposed to be marrying her to give legitimacy to his title. Furthermore, when she reached London, she might have found it strange that there was no state welcome in the capital, or any celebrations to mark her arrival, as was usual for a royal bride. These were the first indications that her marriage to Henry VII was not to be regarded as the means of his kingship. Had she processed through the City in triumph, it might have looked as if she herself was the rightful sovereign.[38]

Observing the proprieties, Henry had arranged for his prospective bride to be lodged with his mother. Apartments had been made ready for Elizabeth and her mother at Coldharbour, which lay on the foreshore south of Thames Street, just outside the city walls; and it was there that she was reunited with Elizabeth Wydeville. The former Queen had been staying at Sheen at the time of Bosworth, but had hastened to London, and it was to her care that the new King initially entrusted his future bride. It is likely that Elizabeth's sisters joined her, for Henry arranged for Margaret Beaufort to be given 'the keeping and guiding of the ladies daughter of King Edward IIII' along with eight-year-old Edward Stafford, Duke of Buckingham, Ralph Neville, Earl of Westmorland, and the hapless Earl of Warwick.[39] Warwick's sister Margaret probably also joined this bustling household.

Elizabeth spent the following weeks at Coldharbour. In 1484, Richard III had granted the royal heralds this ancient house as a permanent home. It lay by the river Thames on the site now occupied by 89 Upper Thames Street.[40] It was a great mansion, dating from at least the early fourteenth century, and among previous residents were Henry IV, Henry V, Margaret of Burgundy, Sir John de Pulteney, four times mayor of London in the fourteenth century and builder of Penshurst Place, and Alice Perrers, Edward III's mistress, who added a tower. The heralds had held the house for only a year when Richard III was killed and Henry VII cancelled the grant of Coldharbour, which he gave to his mother.

Here Elizabeth anxiously awaited news that she was to become queen of England at last.

7

'Our Bridal Torch'

Henry VII made a triumphal entry into London on 3 September. After giving thanks at St Paul's Cathedral for his victory and his crown, he retired to the nearby Bishop's Palace, and summoned his first Privy Council, declaring to them his intention of marrying Elizabeth of York. The matter was discussed at length, but first there were two obstacles to be overcome.[1] Parliament had to repeal the Act *Titulus Regius* in order to declare Elizabeth legitimate and restore her royal status, for it was unthinkable that the King should found his dynasty by marrying a lady tainted with the stain of bastardy. Then a new dispensation for the marriage had to be obtained, for Henry and Elizabeth were related in the fourth degree of kinship.[2] The dispensation obtained by Henry in 1484 was deemed insufficient because it had been sought without Elizabeth's consent.[3]

It is possible too that Henry VII wanted time to have a search made in the Tower for the bodies of the Princes to assure himself that they really were dead before legitimising their sister and marrying her. Probably Henry did have the Tower searched for any trace of them,[4] but if he gave the order at this time – and it would be surprising if he hadn't – then almost certainly nothing was found, and he was unable to confirm whether they were dead or alive. If their bodies had been discovered, he would surely have made political capital out of it. Proof that they were not may lie in a clause inserted when *Titulus Regius* was repealed, providing that nothing in the reversal should prejudice the Act 'establishing the crown to the King and the heirs of his body'.[5] Even if Henry had got to London and found the Princes alive, then had them murdered – an unlikely theory advanced by some revisionists – it would have been of no benefit to him because their removal was not sufficient in itself to guarantee his security: people had to know they were dead. But Henry never uttered a word on the matter, or accused Richard III of their murder. He could not, because, not having found any bodies, he had no means of knowing what had happened to the Princes. That must have concerned him greatly, as uncertainty about their fate undermined the title of the woman he intended to make his wife, and it was to underscore many of the problems facing him in the years to come.

Legislation and dispensations took time, but there is evidence to suggest that Henry was in no hurry and that the delay suited him well, for it underlined the fact that he was king in his own right, and not by right of marriage to the Yorkist heiress. None should ever say that he owed his crown to his Queen (although many did). He would not be his wife's 'gentleman usher', he said; and he was resolved to be crowned and have Parliament recognise his title before he married. Although marriage to Elizabeth was 'the fairest' claim to the throne he had 'and the most like to give contentment to the people, [who] were become affectionate to that line, it lay plain before his eyes that, if he relied upon that title, he could be but a king at courtesy, and have rather a matrimonial than a regal power, the right remaining in his Queen, upon whose decease, either with issue or without, he was to give place and be removed. And though he should obtain by Parliament to be continued [as king], yet he knew there was a very great difference between a king that holdeth his crown by a civil act of estates, and one that holdeth it originally by the law of nature.'[6]

Back in 1483 Buckingham and his allies had risen on Henry Tudor's behalf on the understanding that he would marry Elizabeth of York and rule jointly with her, as King Ferdinand and Queen Isabella did in Spain. But now Henry was claiming the throne by right of conquest, as the true successor to the House of Lancaster. Wisely he did not stress his Lancastrian descent, as there were about thirty other people who could have been considered to have a better claim, including Elizabeth, her sisters, her Yorkist cousins and his own mother. Instead, he declared it was 'the true judgement of God', expressed in his victory at Bosworth, that gave him the crown by divine right.[7]

Henry was aware that his claim to the throne was weak and open to challenge. As Strickland wrote, not entirely fancifully, 'much of the royal brain was occupied with ballads of the "Mort d'Arthur", with red dragons and green leeks, besides long rolls of Welsh pedigrees, in which Noah figured about midway'. Henry took care to emphasise his descent from the ancient kings of Britain, and in particular the legendary Arthur, and the Welsh prince Cadwaladr, King of Gwynedd, who had fought the Anglo-Saxon invaders in the seventh century. He claimed Cadwaladr as his hundredth progenitor, and had his red dragon emblazoned on his standard and later used as one of the supporters of the Tudor royal arms. It was said that, on his deathbed, Cadwaladr had foretold that a Welsh king would restore the ancient royal line of Britain, and that his descendants would rule the whole island. The message was clear: Henry Tudor was the true successor of these ancient rulers; it was those interlopers who had come since – the Saxon and Norman kings and the Plantagenets – who were the real usurpers. And lest his Welsh heritage make him appear alien to the English, Henry also took care to emphasise his devotion to St George, the patron saint of England. As for his future bride, she was descended from the ancient princes of Wales by virtue of the marriage of her ancestor, Roger Mortimer, to Gladys Ddu, daughter of Prince Llywelyn ap Iorwerth, in 1230. Her father, Edward IV, had also boasted of his descent from Cadwaladr; thus she was, by descent, an eminently suitable wife for a Welsh-born king.

Craftily, Henry VII dated his reign from the day before Bosworth,[8] effectively branding as traitors Richard III and all those who had fought for him, and provoking much comment, including this outraged response from Croyland: 'O God, what security shall our kings have henceforth that in the day of battle they may not be deserted by their subjects?' Richard's remaining adherents scattered, changed sides or prudently disappeared. His heir, John de la Pole, Earl of Lincoln, was one of those who made his peace with the new King and obtained a pardon. Henry VII even gave him a prominent place on his Council, although no doubt he kept an eye on him, given Lincoln's prominence under Richard III, and the fact that he was now the hope of those who wanted to see a Yorkist king on the throne. Henry also issued a general pardon to those who had fought at Bosworth. Peers such as the earls of Northumberland and Surrey (Norfolk's son), who were initially taken into custody, were later pardoned and released.

Possibly there were personal reasons why Henry was in no hurry to marry Elizabeth. By now he could have heard that she had urged Norfolk to further her marriage to Richard III. In Henry's eyes that might have looked like betrayal, after he had publicly vowed to take her as his wife. Of course, Elizabeth could probably have reassured Henry as to why she had pressed for the marriage to Richard, and no doubt did, but history now had to be rewritten. Not for nothing would Henry's official historian, Polydore Vergil, describe Richard's plan to marry her as 'the most wicked to be spoken of, and the foulest to be committed that ever was heard of'. Henry's feelings may perhaps be gauged from the fact that, around 1488–9, his mother commissioned Caxton to print the romance *Blanchardin and Eglantine*, doubtless because of its clear parallels with the story of her son and Elizabeth of York. Its publication may have been intended to quell any persistent rumours about Elizabeth's eagerness to marry his enemy.

Many Yorkists had supported Henry precisely because he had sworn to marry Elizabeth; they were of the opinion that marriage to her would supply all that was lacking in his title to the throne. Most people in England believed that he could only claim the throne through marriage to the Yorkist heiress.[9] Moreover, Henry needed this marriage in order to build support for his rule. He dared not leave the way open for anyone else to wed Elizabeth; unmarried, she would remain a threat to him, and the best way to neutralise it was to honour his word and marry her himself. Such a fortuitous union was seen by many as the best means of bringing peace between the two warring royal houses, and a lot of people, both high and low, were anxious to see it come to pass, to set the seal upon the King's victory. Therefore his delay in marrying Elizabeth must have seemed like a betrayal to many, and certainly there was some murmuring that he had slighted her.

No one, however, could accuse Henry of being tardy while Elizabeth's status remained unsettled and the dispensation needed to be obtained; nor could they have complained that he did not pay court to her. Buck states that he 'came to the Tower to meet [her] there, to whom he was shortly to be married'. 'The Song of Lady Bessy' exults: 'Great solace it was to see, when the red rose of mickle [much] price and our Bessy were met.' But there is no other record of what happened when Henry and Elizabeth encountered each other for the first time, although it is likely to have been a formal occasion with all the courtesies being observed. When Elizabeth came face to face with the man who was to be her husband, it might have struck her, as it did a Spanish ambassador, that 'there is nothing purely English in the English King's face'.[10] That was perhaps not surprising, as Henry was a quarter Welsh, a quarter French and only half English.

Vergil described the King thus: 'His body was slender but well-built and strong; his height above the average. His appearance was remarkably attractive; his eyes were small and blue.' That Henry was tall is borne out by his tomb effigy, which shows him to have been over six feet. Later Tudor chroniclers, Edward Hall and Raphael Holinshed, would extol his good looks. Hall, who took a hagiographic view of the Tudors, says he was 'a man of body but lean and spare, albeit mighty and strong therewith, of personage and stature somewhat higher than the mean sort of men be, of a wonderful beauty and fair complexion, his eyes grey, his teeth single and hair thin'. Holinshed states he was 'so formed and decorated with all the gifts and lineaments of Nature that he seemed more an angelical creature than a terrestrial personage. His countenance and aspect [were] cheerful and courageous, his hair yellow like the burnished gold, his eyes grey, shining and quick'. Both chroniclers were no doubt exaggerating, for certainly Henry's portraits belie their admiring descriptions.

It may have been Henry's manner, rather than his looks, that made an impression on Elizabeth. His expression was normally 'cheerful, especially when speaking',[11] and he had a 'countenance merry and smiling, especially in his communications, [being] of wit quick and prompt, of a princely stomach and high courage'.[12] Holinshed recorded that Henry was 'prompt and ready in answering', but added, more realistically, that he was 'of such sobriety that it could never be judged whether he were more dull than quick in speaking, such was his temperance'. One imagines, given his probable awareness that the young woman before him had schemed to marry his enemy, that it was this wary and cautious side of Henry that came across in his first meeting with Elizabeth. And of course she represented the rival House of York. Yet all the evidence suggests that she gave him no provocation in this regard, but exerted herself to be pleasant and conformable to his wishes, and so impressed him.

There were certainly other meetings after this. For the first two weeks after his arrival in London, the King was staying near Coldharbour at Baynard's Castle, prior to removing to his mother's palace at Woking, Surrey, and that would have facilitated the couple meeting in private, affording them the opportunity to get to know each other.[13] After that, an understanding grew between them, and – on Elizabeth's side at least – affection blossomed. In January Lord Stanley would state that he had 'heard the King and [the] lady often and at divers times treating and communing of, and about, a marriage to be contracted between them'. By the following January, according to the testimony of Lord Stanley, Elizabeth had come to feel 'great and intimate love and cordial affection' for Henry, so the couple must have seen each other reasonably often.[14] During the Michaelmas term of 1485, the King arranged for his Great Wardrobe to supply the Princess with ten yards of crimson velvet and six yards of russet damask, priced at £20.4s. (£9,880) and sixty-four timbers (individual furs) of ermine costing £54.2s. (£26,450), supplied by Gerard Venmar and Hildebrand Vannonhaw (or Vain), furriers.[15]

Henry needed to consolidate his title and be formally acknowledged as king as soon as possible. A 'device' for a joint coronation was drawn up, probably by one of the heralds of the College of Arms, laying out detailed arrangements for the King and 'the noble Princess, Dame [space left blank], his wife, Queen of England', for royal approval. 'Soon after the King is passed out of the Tower, the Queen shall follow upon [a] cushion of white damask cloth of gold, bareheaded, wearing a round circle of gold set with pearls and precious stones, [and] arrayed in a kirtle of white damask cloth of gold furred with miniver, garnished with onlets [aiglettes, or fastenings] of gold . . . The Cardinal [Thomas Bourchier, Archbishop of Canterbury] shall bless the Queen's crown, then he shall set the same crown upon the Queen's head, having then a coif put thereon by a great lady, for conservation of the unction [holy oil]. The Queen, thus crowned, shall be led by the bishops of Exeter and Ely unto her seat of estate near to the King's seat royal.'[16]

But Henry could not afford to defer his coronation until he was married, while a joint ceremony with Elizabeth might have sent out the message that they were equal sovereigns. There was to be no queen at his coronation, and the service was hastily amended to omit all references to one. Elizabeth was not even present at the

solemnities in Westminster Abbey on 30 October. Instead, the Lady
Margaret Beaufort enjoyed a prominent place, visibly overwhelmed
by the occasion: 'in all that great triumph and glory, she wept marvellously'.[17] Those who had lent Henry valuable support – Jasper Tudor,
Bishop Morton, Lord Stanley and John de Vere, Earl of Oxford –
were given prominent roles at the ceremony; Morton would be
consecrated Archbishop of Canterbury the following year, on the
death of Cardinal Bourchier. Possibly the people were dismayed at
Elizabeth's absence. She was popular, the crown was seen as her right,
and public opinion wanted her wed to the King without further
delay. But before that could happen, there was other important business to be attended to.

'After the coronation had been solemnly performed, a parliament
was held at Westminster,' in which Henry VII was hailed as a second
Joshua who had rescued his people from tyranny. 'And the sovereignty
was confirmed to our lord the King as being his due, not by one
but by many titles; so that we are to believe he rules most rightfully
over the English people, and that not so much by right of blood as
of conquest and victory in warfare.'[18]

Parliament then proceeded to repeal Richard III's Act, *Titulus
Regius*, effectively proclaiming Elizabeth and her siblings legitimate.
This Act, which had declared them bastards, was ordered to be
suppressed. The judges deemed it too scandalous even to be read
out, and urged that its recital in Parliament be avoided in order to
pre-empt the perpetuation of its contents. It was also considered
too subversive to be allowed to remain on record, for its 'falseness and
shamefulness' deserved only 'utter oblivion': the very Parliament roll
on which it had been written was burnt by the public hangman,
and orders were given that every copy be surrendered to the
Chancellor before Easter 1486, on pain of imprisonment or a heavy
fine, so that 'all things said and remembered in the said Act may be
forever out of remembrance and forgot'.[19] Fortunately for posterity,
the original draft of the Act was found in the seventeenth century
among the records stored in the Tower, and printed by John Speed
in 1611; the text of it was also preserved in the *Croyland Chronicle*,
most copies of which were also destroyed.

Thus it is unsurprising that Polydore Vergil, an intelligent man
with a humanist approach to history, later declared that the 'common
report that in Shaa's sermon King Edward's children were called
bastards' was 'devoid of all truth'. Thanks to the suppression of *Titulus*

Regius, the finer details of the precontract story – such as the identity of the lady to whom Edward IV had supposedly been contracted (More thought she was Elizabeth Lucy, one of the King's mistresses) – were forgotten; but the scandal was not. As late as 1533, the Spanish ambassador, Eustache Chapuys, when urging his master, the Emperor Charles V, to invade England in the defence of Katherine of Aragon, whom Henry VIII had divorced, suggested he might seize the throne: 'People here say you have a better title than the present King, who only claims by his mother, who was declared by sentence of the Bishop of Bath a bastard, because Edward IV had espoused another wife before the mother of Elizabeth of York.'[20] There were several scions of the House of York then living who were in league with Chapuys and could have passed on that information. Eleanor Butler's name was not to be published until 1646, after the text of *Titulus Regius* had been rediscovered.[21]

Just after Bosworth Henry VII had sent a warrant for Bishop Stillington's arrest to the civic council in York, near to where Stillington was then living. Possibly Henry had heard in France the same gossip that had informed Commines' claim that it was Stillington who had married Edward IV to Eleanor Butler; or he had received information from his supporters in England that Stillington had helped to compromise Elizabeth's legitimacy. Whether any of this was true or not, Stillington could prove a threat or liability, and Henry may have felt he deserved to be punished, or at least frightened into silence.

When the Bishop was brought to York he was found to be 'sore crazed' and too ill to be sent south to London, so the city fathers imprisoned him at York – but not for long. A pardon for 'horrible and heinous offences imagined and done by him to the King' was issued by Henry VII in his first Parliament on the grounds of Stillington's 'great age, long infirmity and feebleness'.[22] After that, the King and the judges appointed to study *Titulus Regius* came to the conclusion that Stillington was either its author or had furnished the information about the precontract, but the King would not allow the Bishop to be examined because he had been pardoned. Thus he blocked any discussion of the alleged precontract.

Henry VII's discretion in regard to *Titulus Regius* and the naming of crimes and offences can be better understood when one remembers that he had publicly committed himself to marrying a princess whose legitimacy had been called into question. He knew there were many who believed he must marry Elizabeth to make good his own claim; therefore her legitimacy must be beyond dispute. He could not risk anyone challenging her title, or that of himself and their heirs. It may be that Henry was unable to disprove the allegations of a precontract between Edward IV and Eleanor Butler, probably because no evidence of one had ever been produced. It was essential therefore that all the evidence that impugned Elizabeth's legitimacy be eradicated. This appears to have been a subject about which Henry VII was especially sensitive.

Elizabeth was now the undisputed heiress of Edward IV. A political poem of 1487 acknowledged that:

> His title is fallen to our sovereign lady,
> Queen Elizabeth, his eldest daughter lineal;
> To her is come all the whole monarchy,
> For the fourth Edward had no issue male.
> The crown therefore and sceptre imperial
> Both she must have without division.

Pietro Carmeliano, an Italian poet who had transferred from Richard III's service to Henry VII's, recognised that, upon the murder of her brothers, Elizabeth – that 'beautiful, marriageable virgin' – had become her father's heiress.[23] Undoubtedly she had a better claim to the throne than Henry did, but there is no record of her resenting Henry relegating her to the role of queen consort instead of queen regnant. Although the Pope himself called her 'the undoubted heir of that famous King of immortal memory, Edward IV'[24] and Giovanni de' Gigli, the Papal collector in England, recognised that Edward's 'firstborn, should of right succeed her mighty sire',[25] and there were those who thought that Henry and Elizabeth should reign as joint sovereigns, no one seriously considered that a woman, even the legitimate, rightful heiress of the House of York, could actually rule alone as queen regnant. On the contrary, her crown was the inheritance she would bring to her husband. As one song would put it, 'the Queen's title, by fortune's adventure, he hath'.[26] Traditionally women could transmit the crown – the royal houses of Plantagenet, York and Tudor derived their claim through the female line – but not wield sovereign power. Even Margaret Beaufort, with all her astute capabilities, had never been regarded – or regarded herself – as a contender for the throne.

There was no Salic law in England barring women from the throne, as there was in France, so there was nothing to prevent a woman from ruling, but memories of female misrule were long. People remembered how, in the twelfth century, the haughty, over-bearing Empress Matilda's attempt to pursue her lawful claim to the throne had resulted in a civil war so bloody that it had been said that 'God and His saints slept'. That experience had left the English with an enduring prejudice against female rulers.

The notion of a woman wielding dominion over men was seen as unnatural and against the laws of God and Nature. As Buckingham had bluntly put it, 'It was not women's place to govern the kingdom, but men's.'[27] Women were regarded as weak, irrational creatures at the mercy of their reproductive cycle, their chief function being the bearing of children. They were seen as unfit to lead armies in battle and interfere in affairs of state. Once wed, they had no control over their own property. In law, they were regarded as infants. Their primary purpose was to be wives and mothers, subordinate to their menfolk, in whose interests their marriages were arranged. Thus it was that no one spoke out in favour of Elizabeth of York ascending the throne in her own right as England's lawful queen, and in this respect, in Parliament, Henry VII 'would not endure any mention of the Lady Elizabeth, no, not in the nature of a special entail' of the crown.[28] It would be left to the granddaughter who was named for her, Elizabeth I, to prove that a woman could rule successfully.

There were those who felt strongly that Henry VII should have become king only through marriage to Elizabeth. He would remain unpopular with several of his nobles 'for the wrong he did his Queen, that he did not rule in her right'.[29] Resentment festered in all ranks of society, and in time it would emerge as one of the chief causes of discontent on the part of his subjects, and provide a convenient pretext for his enemies to move against him.

In an Act attainting Richard III as a traitor, Parliament made no direct mention of Elizabeth's brothers, the Princes in the Tower, but referred to 'homicides and murders, in shedding of infants' blood' among the many crimes attributed to him[30] – the kind of crimes of which traitors were often accused. Some modern historians have commented on the fact that the Princes are not specifically named in the Act. Given that the repeal of *Titulus Regius* had legitimated Edward V and Richard, Duke of York, Henry VII might have been expected to publicise their murders in order to show that Elizabeth was the undoubted heir of York, and to stain Richard's name more foully. The omission of their names has therefore been seen as proof that the Princes still lived.

There is little evidence that the early Tudor monarchs actively pursued a policy of character assassination against Richard III.[31] Henry VII had good reasons for wanting to avoid any mention of the heirs of Edward IV. One was that it was not in his interests to raise the spectre of Elizabeth's bastardy. The other was that, almost certainly, he had no hard evidence of the Princes' murder, and was relying on the assumption made in 1483 that Richard had gone ahead with his plan to destroy them. Had their bodies been found, Henry would surely have publicised the fact; it would have saved him a lot of trouble in the long run, because from the commencement of his reign there were 'secret rumours and whisperings (which afterwards gained strength and turned to great troubles) that the two young sons of King Edward the Fourth, or one of them (which were said to be destroyed in the Tower) were not indeed murdered, but conveyed secretly away, and were yet living; which, if it had been true, had prevented the title of the Lady Elizabeth'.[32] Henry's failure to establish beyond doubt that the Princes were dead probably accounts for his unwillingness to accuse Richard III openly of having them killed; there was then a legal presumption that, without a body, there could be no charge of murder.

In legitimising Edward IV's children, Henry VII could not but have been aware that he was acknowledging Edward V's just title, so he must have been convinced that the Princes were dead, for if they still lived, they posed a serious threat to his crown. Much has been made of two royal pardons granted by Henry to Sir James Tyrell in the summer of 1486, but there is no evidence that these relate to the murder of the Princes. Very likely Henry himself did not know for certain what had happened to the boys, and it would have been highly damaging to the Crown to publicise the fact that the brothers of the Yorkist heiress had effectively disappeared – hence the official silence on the matter.

What Elizabeth felt about the 'secret rumours and whisperings' of the survival of her brothers is not recorded. Maybe she believed that there was no truth in them; but if there was doubt in her mind, then soon would have followed the realisation that she faced a massive conflict of interests in marrying the man who occupied the throne to which they had a better claim, and that his hold on it – not to mention her own position – might then prove precarious. If so, she might have reasoned that she had done well to survive the past two years with her legitimacy restored and a crown within her grasp, and that it was better to accept the status quo than to stir up controversy; and of course she was in no position to challenge Henry Tudor's title. But it may be that her brothers were never far from her mind, and that the possibility of their survival was to haunt her for many years to come.

Now that Parliament had recognised Elizabeth Wydeville as Edward IV's rightful Queen, it restored her 'estate, dignity, pre-eminence and name' and repealed Richard III's Act confiscating her property.[33] This was not returned to her, but she was allowed her widow's jointure of thirty manors plus rents, as well as the rights and privileges normally enjoyed by a queen dowager. Parliament restored to Margaret Beaufort all the estates confiscated in 1483, and granted her rights as a sole person, 'not wife or covert of any husband',[34] which gave her control over her huge fortune. Thereafter the King, grateful for all she had done to further his cause, 'allotted her a share in most of his public and private resources'.[35] Her status at court as 'my lady the King's mother' was to remain unchallenged. It was such that, from 1499, after years of signing herself 'M. Richmond', she began using the royal style 'Margaret R.'. The R stood for Richmond, of course, but it sounded suitably regal, and the Lady Margaret was already enjoying commensurate influence; effectively, she acted as an unofficial queen dowager and wore her countess's coronet whenever she appeared in public, whereas the King and Queen only appeared in their crowns on state occasions.

During this Parliament the King rewarded those who had served him loyally and helped him to win the crown. Lord Stanley was made Earl of Derby and given the offices of Constable of England and Chief Steward of the Duchy of Lancaster. Jasper Tudor, Henry's uncle, was created Duke of Bedford. On 7 November Elizabeth was probably present at Jasper's wedding to her aunt, Katherine Wydeville, widow of the Duke of Buckingham.

Henry Tudor had triumphed. But, 'although all things seemed to be brought to a good and perfect conclusion, yet the harp still needed tuning to set all things in harmony. This tuning was the marriage between the King and Elizabeth.'[36] There was no cause now for any further delay. Elizabeth had been legitimated, and a dispensation for her marriage to the King could be applied for. By 4 November, a new coinage was being minted with a double rose symbolising the union of Lancaster and York on the reverse – proof of Henry's firm resolve to proceed to the marriage.[37] But he still appeared in no hurry to fulfil his vow to wed Elizabeth. He clearly did not want it to be thought that their union was a matter of political necessity.[38]

Bernard André asserts that, as Christmas drew nearer with no sign of any marriage preparations, Elizabeth grew anxious, for she had heard reports that the King had considered marrying Anne, Duchess of Brittany, who could bring him a great duchy coveted by the French King; or, it was said, his personal choice was Katherine, the youngest daughter of his former guardian, William Herbert, Earl of Pembroke, a girl he had known since childhood, and whom he had considered as a bride earlier that year.

There was no substance to these reports, but they 'bred some doubt and suspicion in divers that [the King] was not sincere, or at least not fixed in going on the match England so much desired, which conceit also, though it were but talk and discourse, did much afflict the poor Lady Elizabeth herself'.[39] Bacon says she greatly desired this marriage, and to corroborate that we have Stanley's evidence that her love for Henry had grown on acquaintance during the few weeks they had been seeing each other.[40]

Elizabeth did not know it, but Maximilian of Austria had his sights on her as a bride. His late wife, Mary of Burgundy, had had a claim to the throne of England through her grandmother, Isabella of Portugal, a descendant of John of Gaunt, which Charles the Bold had unsuccessfully asserted in 1471. Now Maximilian had begun entertaining the idea of marrying Elizabeth, which he felt would be sufficient to make good his claim.[41] It is doubtful that Elizabeth would have been interested, with her hopes set on Henry, and certain that the King would not have permitted such a marriage.

In a Latin epithalamium commissioned by Henry as Elizabeth's morning gift, to be given to her after their wedding night, Giovanni de' Gigli tells how Elizabeth was longing to marry her King, and frustrated at being made to wait.[42] Given Lord Stanley's evidence

that she had come to love Henry deeply and intimately,[43] this may
be no fanciful portrayal, and it chimes with her earlier eagerness to
marry Henry Tudor (or Richard III), and with André's testimony to
her anxiety. Possibly she regarded Henry as the chivalrous knight
errant who had rescued her and her family from the slur of bastardy
and the clutches of the man who had spurned her. Gigli imagines
her agonising:

> Oh, my beloved! My hope, my only bliss!
> Why then defer my joy? Fairest of kings,
> Whence your delay to light our bridal torch?
> Our noble House contains two persons now,
> But one in mind, in equal love the same.
> O, my illustrious spouse, give o'er delay,
> Your sad Elizabeth entreats; and you
> Will not deny Elizabeth's request,
> For we were plighted by a solemn pact,
> Signed long ago by your own royal hand.

Gigli then presents a touching picture of Elizabeth whiling away the
waiting time, longing for Henry to name the day:

> How oft with needle, when denied the pen,
> Has she on canvas traced the blessed name
> Of Henry, or expressed it with her loom
> In silken threads, or 'broidered it in gold.
> And now she seeks the fanes [temples] and hallowed shrines
> Of deities propitious to her suit,
> Imploring them to shorten her suspense,
> That she may in auspicious moment know
> The holy name of bride.

This reads convincingly, for we know from her privy purse expenses
how frequently Elizabeth made offerings at shrines, especially in
times of stress.[44]

Her fears were soon to be allayed. The rumbles of discontent
about her delayed nuptials could be ignored no longer. Parliament
wanted her for queen consort and was keen to see the King honour
his vow to wed her. Some members were of the opinion that his
claim to rule by right of conquest rather than by right of blood

'might have been more wisely passed over in silence than inserted in our statutes, the more especially because in that Parliament, a discussion took place with the King's consent, relative to his marriage with the Lady Elizabeth, in whose person it appeared to all that every requisite might be supplied which was wanting to make good the title of the King himself'.[45]

On 10 December, as Henry VII sat enthroned in the Parliament chamber, Sir Thomas Lovell, the Speaker of the Commons, announced that the King wished 'to take for himself as wife and consort the noble Lady Elizabeth, daughter of King Edward the Fourth, from which marriage, by the grace of God, it is hoped by many that there would arise offspring of the race of kings for the comfort of the whole realm'. The emphasis was not on Elizabeth's title, but on her eminent suitability to be queen and bear Henry heirs, for – as the Speaker emphasised – the succession 'is, remains, continues and endures in the person of the lord King, and of the heirs legitimately issuing from his body'. All the Lords Spiritual and Temporal rose to their feet and, facing the throne with bowed heads, urged the King to proceed to this union of 'two bloods of high renown'; to which he replied that 'he was very willing to do so; it would give him pleasure to comply with their request'. And so 'it was decreed by harmonious consent that one house would be made from two families that had once striven in mortal hatred'.[46]

In a Latin oration made to the Pope after the marriage,[47] Henry VII's envoy explained that 'the King of England, to put an end to civil war, had, at the request of all the lords of the kingdom, consented to marry Elizabeth, daughter of Edward IV', on account of her beauty and virtue, 'though he was free to have made a profitable foreign alliance'. This last was a bluff, part of Henry's strategy to show the world that his crown was his by right, not in right of his wife, whose title he omitted to mention. Given the abysmal history of the warring royal houses over the past thirty years, marriage to the Yorkist heiress was probably the most profitable match he could have made, with peace being far more crucial to the future welfare of his kingdom than a fat foreign dowry – and it was surely what he had intended all along. It is highly unlikely that he had ever seriously contemplated marrying anyone else. He was aware that marriage with Elizabeth was a political necessity if he wanted to secure the loyalty of the Yorkists, and that, if he did not fulfil his vow to wed her, and thus publicly humiliated her, he risked alienating the many people who saw her as the true successor of the Plantagenets.

As Lord Stanley was soon to testify, the King was 'moved and led to contract marriage with the lady for the sake of the peace and tranquillity of his realm, and by the entreaties and petitions of the lords and nobles, both spiritual and temporal, and of the whole commonalty of the same realm, who in parliament assembled requested him to do so, and made prayers and great entreaties to him'. William de Berkeley, Earl of Nottingham, would add that he believed in conscience 'that the King intends to contract marriage with the lady, if it can be done by the law of the Church, both on account of the singular love which he bears to her, and also on account of the special prayers and entreaties of the lords and nobles, both spiritual and temporal, and of the whole commonalty of his said realm of England'.[48]

Thus Henry's motives in marrying Elizabeth seem to have been largely political. But there was more to it than that, on both sides. Lord Stanley, under oath, was to tell the Papal legate 'that the aforesaid lady has not been captured nor compelled, but of great and intimate love and cordial affection desires to contract marriage with the said King, to the knowledge of this sworn [witness], as he says in virtue of his oath'.[49] Stanley knew Elizabeth well, so his testimony is good evidence that her heart was involved as well as her ambitions; this being so, it is easier to understand her future relations with Henry. Loving him, she was all the more prepared to mould herself to what he wanted her to be, especially now that her hopes of a crown were to be fulfilled. Sir Richard Edgecombe and Sir William Tyler were also emphatic that Elizabeth had not been 'ravished', or captured, as the word meant then. Nottingham's testimony to 'the singular love' Henry bore Elizabeth[50] is corroborated by André's statement that, even before being petitioned by Parliament, the King 'had come to know [Elizabeth's] purity, faith and goodness', and 'God [had] inclined his heart to love the girl'.

Having made a show of giving in to Parliament's request, Henry, 'like a prince of just faith and true of promise, detesting all intestine and cruel hostility, appointed a day to join in matrimony ye Lady Elizabeth, heir of the House of York, with his noble personage, heir to ye line of Lancaster: which thing not only rejoiced and comforted the hearts of the noble and gentle men of the realm, but also gained the favour and good minds of all the common people'. The latter were soon 'much extolling and praising the King's constant fidelity and his politic device, thinking surely that the day was now come that the seed of tumultuous factions and the fountain of cruel dissension should be stopped, evacuated and clearly extinguished'.[51]

On 10 December, after the date of the wedding had been set for 18 January, the Lord Chancellor prorogued Parliament, announcing that, before it reassembled, 'the marriage of the King and the Princess Elizabeth would take place'.[52]

From that day, Elizabeth was treated as queen of England. On 11 December, the King ordered that preparations for the nuptials were to go ahead: a celebratory tournament was proclaimed, 'then wedding torches, marriage bed, and other suitable decorations were made ready'.[53] Elizabeth was declared duchess of York, as heiress to her father and her other illustrious forebears,[54] a move calculated to please the Yorkist faction.

According to Lord Stanley, Henry and Elizabeth had several discussions about their being 'joined together in the fourth and fourth degrees of kindred', and he heard them say that 'they wished to make use of an apostolic dispensation in the matter of such impediment'.[55] Pope Innocent VIII was now approached for a special dispensation. Giovanni de' Gigli wrote to him, urging the marriage as the best means of establishing peace in England. Henry's emissary to the Vatican was instructed to praise Elizabeth in a formal oration to his Holiness: 'The beauty and chastity of this lady are indeed so great that neither Lucretia nor Diana herself were ever more beautiful or more chaste. So great is her virtue, and her character so fine, that she certainly seems to have been preserved by divine will from the time of her birth right up until today to be consort and queen.'[56] No mention was made of Elizabeth's claim to the throne;[57] again, Henry did not want to be seen to be king in right of his wife. Already he was finding that his bride's royal lineage was proving an embarrassment as well as an advantage.

Henry did not need to wait for the Pope's sanction to arrive. He and 'the most illustrious Lady Elizabeth, eldest legitimate and natural daughter of the late Edward, sometime king of England', drew up a joint petition to the Papal legate, Giacomo Passarelli, Bishop of Imola, 'setting forth that whereas the said King Henry has, by God's providence, won his realm of England, and is in peaceful possession thereof, and has been asked by all the lords of his realm, both spiritual and temporal, and also by the general council of the said realm, called Parliament, to take the said lady Elizabeth to wife, he, wishing to accede to the just petitions of his subjects, desires to take the said lady to wife, but cannot do so without dispensation, inasmuch as they are related in the fourth and fourth degrees of kindred, wherefore petition is made on their behalf to the said legate to grant them dispensation by his apostolic authority to contract marriage and remain therein, notwithstanding the said impediment of kindred, and to decree the offspring to be born thereof legitimate'.[58]

On 14 January, at Westminster, the couple appointed proctors, who presented their petition to the legate in the Chapel of St Mary the Virgin in St Paul's Cathedral. Two days later, after hearing testimony from the mandatory eight witnesses required by the Church, including Lord Stanley, and taking into account the people's impatience to see the marriage concluded, Imola issued an ordinary dispensation allowing Henry and Elizabeth to marry (which was confirmed in a brief issued by the Bishop on 2 March following). Given that this was just two days before the wedding, and that preparations for it were nearing completion, Henry must have been advised that the dispensation would be forthcoming, and that the Pope's bull would be just a formality.[59] The marriage could go ahead. It was now five months since the King had emerged triumphant at Bosworth.

'At last, upon the eighteenth of January [1486] was solemnised the so long expected and so much desired marriage between the King and the Lady Elizabeth',[60] and 'great gladness filled the kingdom'. The wedding took place at Westminster with 'great magnificence displayed to everyone's satisfaction'.[61] It is uncertain whether it was solemnised in the Abbey or in St Stephen's Chapel. Surprisingly, no detailed account survives, which may be because the ceremony took place in the greater privacy of St Stephen's. The bridegroom was twenty-nine, the bride nearly twenty.

'The Pope had opportunely sent a legate to celebrate the nuptials',[62] but it was Cardinal Thomas Bourchier, the aged Archbishop of Canterbury, who performed the ceremony 'in the sight of the Church'.[63] As Bernard André colourfully put it, 'his hand held the sweet posy wherein the white and red roses were first tied together'.

Among the wedding guests were Elizabeth's aunts, Anne Wydeville, Lady Wingfield, and Margaret Wydeville, Lady Maltravers. Her grand-mother, Cecily, Duchess of York, did not attend, but Henry VII evidently approved of her, as in 1486 he granted her an annuity and renewed her licence to export wool.[64]

Elizabeth went to her wedding in a gown of silk damask and crimson satin costing £11.5s.6d. (£5,500),[65] with a 'kirtle of white cloth of gold damask and a mantle of the same suit, furred with ermine'. Giovanni de' Gigli, in his Latin epithalamium, conjures a charming – probably imaginary – portrait of the Princess on her wedding day, as his poem was almost certainly written beforehand. It suggests, however, the kind of jewels that Elizabeth might have worn:

> Your hymeneal torches now unite
> And keep them ever pure. O royal maid,
> Put on your regal robes in loveliness.
> A thousand fair attendants round you wait,
> Of various ranks, with different offices,
> To deck your beauteous form. Lo, this delights
> To smooth with ivory comb your golden hair,
> And that to curl or braid each shining tress
> And wreath the sparkling jewels round your head,
> Twining your locks with gems; this one shall clasp
> The radiant necklace framed in fretted [symmetrically
>   patterned] gold
> About your snowy neck; while that unfolds
> The robes that glow with gold and purple dye,
> And fits the ornaments with patient skill
> To your unrivalled limbs; and here shall shine
> The costly treasures from the Orient sands:
> The sapphire, azure gem that emulates
> Heaven's lofty arch, shall gleam, and softly there
> The verdant emerald shed its greenest light,
> And fiery carbuncle flash forth rosy rays
> From the pure gold.[66]

It was not customary then for a bride to be wholly attired in white – that was a tradition begun centuries later by Queen Victoria – but for her to wear the richest materials. It was her flowing hair, threaded with jewels, not the colour of her clothes, that proclaimed her virginity.

Henry was gorgeously attired in cloth of gold. The clerk of the works of the King's Wardrobe was paid £95.3s.6½d. (£46,500) for 'divers stuffs bought for the day of the solemnisation of the King's marriage'; 23s.4d. (£770) was paid 'for the Queen's wedding ring', which was of gold, weighing two thirds of an ounce, and heavy compared with modern wedding rings; it had been purchased before the beginning of January.[67]

According to the eleventh-century Sarum Rite, the pre-Reformation form of the marriage service then in use, Elizabeth vowed to take Henry for her wedded husband, 'for fairer, for fouler, for better, for worse, for richer, for poorer, in sickness and in health, to be blithe and bonair [amiable] and buxom [obedient, in the sense of obliging] in bed and at board' till death parted them.

André says 'the most wished day of marriage was celebrated by them with all religious and glorious magnificence at court, and by their people, to show their gladness, with bonfires, dancing, songs and banquets throughout all London, both men and women, rich and poor, beseeching God to bless the King and Queen and grant them a numerous progeny'. The 'great triumphs and demonstrations, especially on the people's part, of joy and gladness' were greater 'than the days either of [Henry VII's] entry [into London] or his coronation, which the King rather noted than liked'.[68]

'Gifts flowed freely on all sides and were showered on everyone, while feasts, dances and tournaments were celebrated with liberal generosity to make known and to magnify the joyful occasion and the bounty of gold, silver, rings and jewels. Then everyone, men and women, prayed to God that the King and Queen might have a prosperous and happy issue.'[69]

Giovanni de' Gigli's epithalamium had more of joy and relief in it than mere flattery:

> Hail! Ever-honoured and auspicious day,
> When in blest wedlock to a mighty king,
> To Henry, bright Elizabeth is joined.
> Fairest of Edward's offspring, she alone
> Pleased this illustrious spouse.
> So here the most illustrious maid of York,
> Deficient nor in virtue nor in descent,
> Most beautiful in form, whose matchless face
> Adorned with most enchanting sweetness shines.
> Her parents called her name Elizabeth,
> And she, their firstborn, should of right succeed
> Her mighty sire. Her title will be yours
> If you unite this Princess to yourself
> In wedlock's holy bond.

But now the royal pair were one, and a child, Gigli predicted, would shortly gambol in the royal halls, and grow up a worthy son of the King, emulating the noble qualities of his parents and perpetuating their name in his illustrious descendants for ever.[70]

Inevitably, much was made of this union of the white rose of York and the red rose of Lancaster, which was seen as symbolising the end of the conflict between the two royal houses. 'By reason of which marriage, peace was thought to descend out of Heaven into England, considering that the lines of Lancaster and York were now brought into one knot and connexed together, of whose two bodies one heir might succeed, which after their time should peaceably rule and enjoy the whole monarchy and realm of England.' This was written by the chronicler, Edward Hall, from the perspective of the reign of Henry VIII, whom he greatly admired. Vergil attributed the marriage to 'divine intervention, for plainly by it all things which nourished the most ruinous factions were utterly removed, the two houses of Lancaster and York were united and from the union the true and established royal line emerged which now reigns'. Hall even went so far as to compare this 'godly matrimony' with the union of God and man in Christ.

Most English people believed that the royal wedding would bring an end to the civil wars and herald a new era of peace and stability; consequently it was very popular, and it won for Henry Tudor the loyalty of many who had supported the House of York. Victory had given Henry 'the knee of submission', wrote Bacon, but 'marriage with the Lady Elizabeth gave him the heart; so that both knee and heart did truly bow before him'.

The nuptial union of Lancaster and York was a continuing theme in Tudor propaganda. 'Now may we sing, we two bloods all made in one,' Bessy rejoices in Brereton's poem. Thomas Ashwell, an English composer skilled in polyphony, wrote an early form of the National Anthem, 'God save King Henry, wheresoe'er he be', in honour of the marriage.[71] In 1509, at the coronation of Henry VIII, the court poet, Stephen Hawes, reputed (probably without foundation) to have been a bastard son of Richard III, lauded the King's parentage:

> Two titles in one thou didst unify
> When the red rose took the white in marriage.[72]

More than a century on, the union was still being extolled, indeed, immortalised, by Shakespeare in *Richard III*:

We will unite the white rose and the red.
Smile Heaven upon this fair conjunction
That long hath frowned upon their enmity! –
What traitor hears me, and says not Amen?
England hath long been mad and scarred herself;
The brother blindly shed the brother's blood,
The father rashly slaughtered his own son,
The son, compell'd, been butcher to the sire:
All this divided York and Lancaster,
Divided in their dire division.
O now let Richmond and Elizabeth,
The true successors of each royal House,
By God's fair ordinance conjoin together!
And let their heirs – God, if Thy will be so –
Enrich the time to come with smooth-faced peace,
With smiling plenty, and fair prosperous days!
Now civic wounds are stopped, peace lives again
That she may long live, God say Amen!

And as late as 1603, the accession proclamation of James I would speak of this marriage that had 'brought to an end the bloody and civil wars to the joy unspeakable of this kingdom'.[73]

After the wedding, the King and his new Queen presided over a lavish nuptial feast, at which the guests dined on roasted peacocks, swans, larks and quails, followed by sugared almonds and fruit tarts.

It is often claimed that a medal (now in the British Museum) was struck to commemorate the marriage, embellished with images of the happy couple holding hands; the man wears a garland of roses on his head, while the woman is shown crowned, with her wavy hair loose, as betokened a virgin bride and queen. She wears a round-necked gown beneath a mantle, and a heavy cross suspended from a pearl necklace. The reverse shows a wreath of roses enclosing a legend: *As the rising sun is the ornament of the day, so is a good wife the ornament of her house.* It is the roses that have led to the incorrect assumption that the medal was struck to mark the union of Henry and Elizabeth, but it has now been established that the medal is one of a series made in Prague in the late sixteenth century, and that it has nothing to do with them.[74]

Similarly, a painting formerly at Sudeley Castle (once at Strawberry

Hill), said to be by Jan Gossaert (or Mabuse), has long been said to portray the marriage of Henry VII and Elizabeth of York, and has often been engraved as such. Yet there is no evidence that Gossaert ever visited England, and his style is very different. The setting is an imaginary church, and the attire of the bride appears to date from the late sixteenth century, while the other figures wear late-fifteenth-century dress. A painting, perhaps contemporary, and said to be of the marriage, is in Lady Braye's collection at Stanford Hall, Leicestershire. A modern romanticised painting of *The Joining of the Houses of Lancaster and York*, executed by J. R. Brown around 1901, hangs in Blackpool Town Hall.

At last Elizabeth's ambitions had been crowned with the royal dignity that was rightfully hers. Her wedding night was spent in the King's bedchamber, the Painted Chamber of the Palace of Westminster, a vast room built in the thirteenth century by Henry III, measuring eighty-six by twenty-six feet. Behind the massive four-poster bed was a mural dating from that time, showing the coronation of Edward the Confessor in faded red, blue, silver and gold, and on the walls were huge paintings of Biblical battles. There was a great fireplace in the room, but even so the Painted Chamber must have been difficult to heat in January, and the palace was notoriously damp. Fortunately, the bed-curtains would have afforded a degree of intimacy.

Now, it was Henry's part to assay a second victory: as on the battlefield, so in the bedchamber, for as Ann Wroe points out, the language of love was very much the language of war, and a man was expected to come prepared with his 'weapon' or 'harness' and engage in a 'raid', or 'sweet combat', with his lady, each showing the other mercy in paying 'the sweet due debt of nature'.[75] For all the years of intrigue and political manoeuvring, the blood shed at Bosworth, the pageantry and symbolism of the wedding, and the advantages of this great alliance, what mattered now was what happened when these two young people, divested of their royal finery – for it was customary to sleep naked – got between the sheets together to do their duty to their people and to posterity, and, as Fuller put it, 'the two Houses of York and Lancaster united first hopefully in their bed'. As time would soon prove, this was a most successful mating, not least because the Yorkist claimant to the throne, who could have been Henry Tudor's greatest enemy, had now been rendered neutral in his embrace.

The white and red roses of York and Lancaster combined were from the first the chief symbol of this union, and of the new dynasty. Henry was actively to promote it. The following year, in York on progress, he ordered a pageant to be performed featuring 'a royal rich red rose, unto which rose shall appear another rich white rose, unto whom all flowers shall give sovereignty, and there shall come from a cloud a crown covering the roses'.[76] Here is the origin of the Tudor badge, the rose and crown. The great rose window in the south transept of York Minster, with its intertwined red and white roses, commemorates the marriage of the founders of the Tudor dynasty. The King had the Tudor rose incorporated into the collar of the Garter insignia, and it became customary to surround the royal arms with a garland of Tudor roses.

Popular songs were written about the new emblem, notably 'A Crown-Garland of Noble Roses gathered out of England's loyal Garden: A Princely Song made of the Red Rose and White, royally united together by King Henry VII and Elizabeth Plantagenet', which claimed that 'the owners of these princely flowers in virtues do excel'.[77] And in 1550 the title page of the printed edition of Hall's chronicle, *The Union of the Two Noble and Illustre Families of Lancaster and York*, had the title enclosed between two rose trellises, with Henry VII and Elizabeth of York kneeling, hand in hand, at the top of each, with their son, Henry VIII, in majesty above them – the true inheritor of both strains of royal blood.[78]

8

'In Blest Wedlock'

On the morning after her wedding night, Henry presented Elizabeth with Giovanni de' Gigli's poem, her morning gift, and then there would have been the traditional small ceremony of her 'uprising' as a new wife.[1] Henceforth, as a married woman, she would be expected to bind up her hair and cover it with a hood, although queens were invested with symbolic virginity because they were expected to emulate Mary, the Mother of Christ, so they were allowed the privilege of wearing their hair loose on ceremonial occasions when they wore their crowns.

Waking up as queen of England, Elizabeth would surely have been conscious of the fact that she now occupied the most powerful and socially desirable position to which a woman could aspire.[2] She was the wife of the Lord's Anointed,[3] a status that would from now on be reflected in every aspect of the ritual and ceremonial that surrounded her and governed her life; and she, the daughter of a king and queen, would have been aware of the weight of responsibility that brought with it. She was to be the highest example of virtuous womanhood: the living mirror of the Virgin Mary, as exemplified by her chastity and humility, her anticipated motherhood, her charity and her acts of mercy. A queen had to be the embodiment of piety, the guardian of the royal bloodline, an object of chivalric devotion, a gentle and moderate mediator in the conflicts of men, and an inspiration to her husband's subjects.

Elizabeth now had to prove her worthiness in more practical ways too. She had to bear the heirs so crucial to the Tudor succession and the continuance of the new dynasty. She had a great household to run, and was no doubt thankful that a phalanx of officers had been appointed to help her do it. She had a sophisticated ceremonial role to perform at court and in the realm at large. She had to negotiate the political institution that was the court, which might mean subsuming her private loyalties to her duty to the King her husband. She had to learn to live within her means, yet show herself generous in her charities and make provision for her immediate relations, who would now look to her for support and advancement. She also had to accustom herself to her husband's ways, combine queenly dignity with the docility and submission expected of a wife, and be a loving helpmeet to this man who clearly expected her to play a subordinate role, despite her superior claim to the throne. Then she had to forge good relations with his influential mother. It was daunting, what was expected of her: yet she had been born a royal princess and reared to know what to expect; and she had the example of her mother before her.

The Queen's seal survives in the National Archives at Kew. Elizabeth chose 'Humble and reverent' as her queenly motto, in place of 'Sans removyr', and the white rose of York as her personal emblem. As her father's heiress, she was legally entitled to bear the royal arms of England, but for Henry VII that implied joint sovereignty, so at his instance she and her sisters bore the royal arms quartered with those of their Mortimer and de Burgh forebears. Their maternal Wydeville heritage did not feature at all.[4] Elizabeth's escutcheon can be seen at the foot of her tomb in Westminster Abbey. For public occasions and court ceremonials, her retinue wore her personal livery of mulberry and blue silk, the colours of the House of York.[5] At other times they wore liveries of various colours, such as russet, green, tawny (tan) or black.[6]

Elizabeth now had to adjust to marriage with the complex twenty-nine-year-old man who was her husband. Bacon called Henry VII 'a dark prince and infinitely suspicious', which is not surprising considering that, from early childhood, his life had been overshadowed by war and intrigue. And as king, as Bacon observed, 'his time was full of secret conspiracies'. He was calculating, pragmatic, devious, ruthless and prone to dissimulation, and he never won the love of his people, only their grudging respect.

But Henry was also 'a man of vast ability'[7] and hidden depths. He knew four languages, was well read, good at economics, and well versed in the arts of the period. He was clever, hard-working, subtle, shrewd, caring to his family and possessed of a dry humour. His good qualities would much later be lauded in a funeral oration made by John Fisher, Bishop of Rochester and chaplain and confessor to Margaret Beaufort, who praised 'his politic wisdom in governance' as 'singular', his wit 'always quick and ready, his reason pithy and substantial, his memory fresh, his counsels fortunate and taken by wise deliberation'.

Henry's greatest achievements were to survive on the throne for so long and ultimately to bring stability to England. His aims were a secure throne bolstered by wealth, the maintenance of law, order and peace, the supremacy of the Crown, the future prosperity and standing of his dynasty, and the establishment of his realm as an international power to be reckoned with. He succeeded in them all. He established strong centralised government, a far-flung network of administrators and justices, and effective law and order. He promoted foreign trade and commerce, brought economic prosperity to the merchant classes, and amassed a fortune that made him financially independent of Parliament. By clever alliances, he would substantially enhance England's standing in the arena of European politics.

Henry was haunted by the knowledge that an army as small as the one he had led against Richard III at Bosworth could overthrow him, and by the fear that any of the Yorkist heirs might challenge his title. Yet despite his insecurities, he brought firm government to England. Conscientious and professional, he displayed insight, prudence, patience and understanding. He was well-informed and astute, and his political acumen earned him universal respect. Ever suspicious of his nobles, he outlawed 'bastard feudalism', the system by which great lords had maintained private armies of retainers, which had made the Wars of the Roses possible. Henry reined in the power of the nobility by banning such armies and reviving the Court of Star Chamber,[8] which had power to punish those lords who infringed the new laws. He promoted loyal and energetic 'new men' who had risen through wealth and ability to prominence.

He was a man who liked to keep an eye on details that other kings might have left to others. Notoriously careful with money, he painstakingly initialled each item in his accounts.[9] 'He constantly kept notes and memorials in his own hand, especially touching persons, as whom to employ, whom to reward, keeping a journal of his thoughts.' But he was to be confounded. 'His monkey, set on, as it was thought, by one of his Chamber, tore his principal notebook all to pieces, when by chance he had left it about. Whereat the court, which liked not these pensive accounts, was much tickled with the sport.'[10]

Henry was an intelligent and cultured man who patronised William Caxton, collected books, appreciated poetry and encouraged the new learning of the Renaissance in England. He invited French and Italian scholars such as Bernard André and Polydore Vergil to his court. Like Elizabeth, he was genuinely devout, and would attend Mass up to three times a day. He was also liberal when it came to giving alms to the sick, the poor and the Church.

If Henry lacked the common touch, he liked to give the impression of greatness, and knew when to spend lavishly to project the magnificence expected of monarchs, which would command respect and awe for the new dynasty. Andrea Trevisano, a Venetian envoy, was received by the King in 1497 in 'a small hall hung with very handsome tapestry. Leaning against a tall gilt chair covered with cloth of gold, his Majesty wore a violet-coloured gown lined with cloth of gold, and a collar of many jewels; and on his cap was a large diamond and a most beautiful pearl.'[11] When the King ate, he was served not by his household officers but by peers of the realm. Whenever he ventured out in public, he walked under a canopy of estate and was attended by great ceremonial. He founded the Yeomen of the Guard, the first standing army in English history, as his personal bodyguard. Henry VII's personal magnificence, typical of princes of the age, helped to convince not only his subjects, but also foreign ambassadors and the princes they served, that his throne was secure. Yet an envoy once observed of him: 'He likes to be much spoken of, and to be highly appreciated by the whole world. He fails in this because he is not a great man.'[12]

Henry was often a cheerful, witty and congenial companion. He loved court ceremonial, music, cards, dice, gambling, dancing, disguisings, plays and morris dancers, and delighted in the antics of tumblers, jugglers, acrobats, fire eaters and court fools, pastimes Elizabeth enjoyed also. He was clearly a thoughtful man, and gave generous gifts to his servants and Elizabeth at New Year, and extra to those who could not attend the festivities.[13] To his children, he was an attentive and loving father, 'full of paternal affection, careful of their education, aspiring to their high advancement, regular to see that they should not want of any due honour and respect'.[14] That he loved them too is apparent in two inscriptions he wrote in a book of hours given to his daughter, Margaret, probably on her departure to marry the King of Scots in 1503: 'Remember your kind and loving father in your prayers.' 'Pray for your loving father that gave you this book, and I give you at all times God's blessing and mine.'[15] And he was a faithful and loving husband to Elizabeth.

The carved letters H and E in a lovers' knot on the tower roof of Sherborne Abbey Church, Dorset, are said to be the initials of Henry VII and Elizabeth of York, symbolising their loving wedlock. Touching mentions of Elizabeth in official correspondence and accounts, such as 'the King's most dear bedfellow, the Queen', 'the King's most dear consort' or 'our dearest wife, the Queen',[16] were merely conventional forms of reference, and do not necessarily reflect real affection. That there was affection and tenderness between Henry and Elizabeth cannot be doubted, but evidence about the true nature of their relationship is contradictory. A Spanish envoy, Juan de Matienzo, Sub-Prior of Santa Cruz, claimed in 1498 that Elizabeth 'suffered under great oppression and led a miserable, cheerless life'. He suggested to his sovereigns, Ferdinand and Isabella of Spain, that 'it would be a good thing to write often to her, and to show her a little love'.[17] Evidently he thought love was lacking in her life. Yet there is no other evidence that Elizabeth was deprived of it – rather the opposite, for there are instances of both the King and his mother showing genuine concern for her health and her happiness; and on this one occasion there may have been a very good reason why Elizabeth appeared subdued, even unhappy.

In 1613 Bacon asserted of Henry that 'his Queen (notwithstanding she presented him with divers children, and a crown also, though he would not acknowledge it) could do nothing with him . . . Towards [her] he was nothing uxorious, nor scarce indulgent, but companionable and respective [considerate], and without jealousy . . . And it is true that, all his lifetime, while the Lady Elizabeth lived with him, he showed himself no very indulgent husband to her, though she was beautiful, gentle and fruitful. But his aversion towards the House of York was so predominant in him, as it found place not only in his wars and councils, but in his chamber and bed.' If this were initially true, it could have had much to do with Elizabeth's involvement with Richard III, which had upset Henry at the time, and must have seemed like a betrayal. But was it true?

To begin with, Henry may have resented what Elizabeth was, even while growing to love her for herself. He was clearly wary of her lineage and potential influence. That is evident in his determination not to be seen to owe his crown to her, and his relegating her to a dynastic, ceremonial and domestic role, and placing financial constraints upon her, as will be seen. Above all, it seems, he did not want her to be associated in any way with Richard III, as the matter of Queens' College, Cambridge, shows. It had been founded by Margaret of Anjou and later enjoyed the patronage of Elizabeth Wydeville and Anne Neville, so it might have followed that Elizabeth of York, as queen, would assume that role too. But Richard III had also been a patron of Queens', and on his accession, Henry VII confiscated all the endowments made by Richard and Anne; significantly Elizabeth did not become the college's new royal patron. On her death, however, that role would be taken over by Margaret Beaufort.[18]

Bacon was sometimes apt to draw sweeping conclusions about Elizabeth that jar with other evidence and should be treated with caution. There is little else to support his damning assessment of the marriage, which was based on negative inferences he had made from Henry VII's delay in marrying Elizabeth,[19] and his belief that Henry had wronged her by not ruling in her right. In fact, historians all the way back to John Lingard, whose history of England was published in 1819, have questioned Bacon's observations about the relationship between Henry and Elizabeth.

The years spent as a fugitive had taken their toll on the King. He trusted few and had learned to maintain an autocratic distance. 'He was of a high mind and loved his own will and his own way, as one that revered himself and would reign indeed. Had he been a private man he would have been termed proud: but in a wise prince, it was but keeping of distance, which indeed he did towards all, not admitting any near or full approach, either to his power or to his secrets. For he was governed by none.'[20] Elizabeth may have found this daunting, at least to begin with, and probably soon realised that her husband was not going to treat her as a political confidante, for it was not in his nature. Children, companionship and support seem to have been all he wanted from her, at least at the beginning.

It was for these reasons, and possibly more personal ones, that

Henry began by keeping Elizabeth in her place. The early years of their marriage were probably challenging, for he had to overcome his suspicions of his Yorkist bride and deal with her dangerous relations. Yet it is clear that Elizabeth left him in no doubt as to where her loyalties lay. Her superior title to the throne never proved a threat to him, and probably she herself made sure that he knew he had nothing to fear from her. As time passed, he clearly grew to love, trust and respect her; he was affectionate towards her, and they seem to have become emotionally close. We know that she loved him, and she must have appreciated the stability that marriage to Henry brought her after so many years of tragedy, danger and anxiety.

We will hear how, much later, the couple hastened lovingly to comfort and support each other after losing a child, which argues that, after years of wedlock, they had come to enjoy a close and mutually supportive relationship. Thomas More would write of the 'faithful love' that enabled them 'to continue in marriage and peaceable concord'. Certainly there is no record of any strife between them. Touching references in Henry's letters and privy purse expenses reveal his tenderness towards his wife, while his desperate grief after her death suggests that he had come to cherish her, and perhaps felt remorseful that he had not shown it enough. Probably, after suffering an uncertain youth in captivity or exile, he was grateful for the settled existence he came to enjoy with his virtuous Queen, and for the welcome peace and tranquillity of his domestic life. And no doubt, over the years, he would have been increasingly grateful to Elizabeth for presenting him with the heirs that were so essential to the future of the Tudor dynasty.

In an age in which royal couples often lived separate lives in separate apartments, and kings were frequently absent on business of their own while queens stayed at home, Elizabeth and Henry participated together in a full social life at court and travelled together frequently, spending much time in each other's company. They shared a common piety and, it seems, a sense of humour. Inevitably, over the years, they grew closer. There was a softer side to the King that Elizabeth must have known. His privy purse expenses reveal numerous kindnesses, such as money he gave variously to a man wrongfully arrested, a woman with child, children singing for him in a garden, a Jewess for her marriage, the liberating of prisoners, and 'a little fair maiden that danceth'.[21] A man whose heart was touched by people such as these must have had some kindness and warmth in his character.

We know something of what Henry VII admired in a woman from instructions he was later to give his ambassadors when, as a widower, he considered marrying Joan, Queen of Naples. He could not court her in person, so he asked them to note carefully her age and stature, 'the features of her body; the favour of her visage, whether she be painted or not, and whether it be fat or lean, sharp or round, and whether her countenance be cheerful and amiable, frowning or melancholy, steadfast or light, or blushing in communication; her eyes, brows, lips and teeth; the fashion of her nose, and the height and breadth of her forehead; her arms, whether they be great or small, long or short; her breasts and paps, whether they be big or small; whether there appear any hair about her lips or not; the condition of her breath, whether it be sweet or not; [and] whether she be a great feeder or drinker'.[22] It may be that he had come to regard his late wife as an ideal to which any future wife must conform or be found wanting.

Henry had lived a relatively chaste life. He had only one bastard son, Roland de Velville, conceived during his exile in Brittany; Velville was knighted by Henry VII, who appointed him Constable of Beaumaris Castle in Anglesey.[23] After marriage, the King was apparently faithful to Elizabeth, and no breath of scandal tainted their union. A Spanish ambassador wrote that 'one of the reasons why he leads a good life is that he has been brought up abroad'.[24] He was implying that, had Henry been raised at the licentious court of Edward IV instead of being exiled, he might have succumbed to the temptations on offer there. Yet even an exile can indulge in amorous intrigues, so the likelihood is that Henry was, by nature, a monogamous man. And although there is evidence that, after years of faithful marriage, he was attracted to another lady, that was almost certainly as far as it went.

The sources give an overwhelming impression that the union between Henry and Elizabeth evolved into a true partnership, a relationship based on deep affection, if not love, co-operation, fidelity and trust. She was to show herself devoted to promoting his interests; she never interfered, never openly complained, and proved herself a true helpmeet. In short, this was the most successful and stable marriage made by any of the Tudors.

Kings were not expected to share government with their queens, or to rely on their advice, and certainly they were not supposed to be influenced by them in political matters.[25] Medieval queens were 'generally the passive instruments of policy'[26] and had no formal political identity or power of their own. Queens were applauded, however, when they used their gentle feminine influence to intercede with the King where appropriate, and thus enabled him to rescind a decision without losing face. Instances of queens using their influence probably went largely unrecorded; a queen enjoyed a unique advantage over other petitioners due to her intimate relationship with the King. It was accepted that, because of this, she might be privy to matters of state, but advice that Elizabeth might have read urged that her 'wisdom ought to appear in speaking, that is to wit that she be secret and tell not such things as ought to be holden secret'.[27] If she ever interceded with Henry it was in private, and there are instances of his paying heed to her concerns, but it was not in his nature generally to be swayed by her.

As he almost certainly came to appreciate, Elizabeth performed her queenly role to perfection, understanding exactly what was required of her, and conforming seemingly effortlessly to the late medieval ideal of queenship, which constrained her to a role that was essentially decorous, symbolic and dynastic. She was beautiful, devout, fertile and kind – the traditional good queen.

In the past, historians tended to compare Elizabeth of York favourably to Margaret of Anjou,[28] that 'great and strong laboured woman';[29] yet today, in the wake of a revolution in female emancipation, it is the proactive Margaret, vigorously fighting her husband Henry VI's cause, who earns our admiration, rather than the passive Elizabeth. Gentleness, fruitfulness and piety are no longer qualities esteemed in women. We have learned to admire them for what they do, and for their strengths. But in Elizabeth's day, queens were not expected to do very much beyond exemplifying the humane, feminine side of monarchy – interceding for others, being charming to foreign ambassadors, or winning popularity by their charities, their gifts to the poor, their pilgrimages and their pious example. Getting involved in politics and wars was a step too far. Unlike Margaret of Anjou, Elizabeth never identified herself with factions at court; unlike her mother, she did not promote a horde of ambitious relatives. Certainly she was not as politically inclined, or as politically active, as Elizabeth Wydeville,[30] and she never enjoyed anything approaching Elizabeth Wydeville's influence. If she had been strongly identified with the Wydeville faction prior to her marriage, that was all at an end, for her mother's family were never allowed much influence by Henry VII, who clearly preferred to emphasise Elizabeth's paternal descent.

Yet this was the girl who had schemed to marry her uncle, Richard III, the girl whose vengeance his councillors had feared – that same girl who had probably plotted with the Stanleys on Henry Tudor's behalf. What drove her had doubtless been the desire to be restored to her rightful inheritance and elevated to the throne. But now that she was queen, having made that dynastically crucial marriage and achieved her ambition, she retreated from politics and interested herself largely in affairs that were her legitimate province, such as her household, her estates, her court and her children. Her opinions were seldom to be voiced, and although she would be at the centre of great and tumultuous events that must have affected her personally, probably deeply in some instances, we know little of her role – if any – in them, or her views or her feelings.

It seems strange that she was now apparently ready meekly to accept a passive role as the price of her marriage and her queenship, but probably it was an adjustment she was happy to make, for there is no evidence that she wanted to involve herself in political affairs. Even so, her married life may have been fraught at times. Her Yorkist blood and her superior claim to the throne ensured that she would tread a tightrope of divided loyalties in the coming years, joined as she was to a husband who was deeply suspicious of her House. How she rose to these challenges we do not know specifically, yet we can surely infer, from the emerging harmony of her marital existence, that she took care never to be controversial and always to place her husband's interests first.

Her own concerns were apparently domestic rather than political. From time to time, the King involved her in diplomatic relations, mainly in connection with the marriages of their children, in which traditionally she was supposed to interest herself. It is often said that Henry allowed Elizabeth no power at all, but evidently it was known that she exercised a gentle, unobtrusive influence on him, as is evidenced by the endless stream of gifts to her from powerful persons who clearly believed that her patronage was worth having.[31]

However, given that she wielded such influence only in private, it is hard to assess the extent of it. Certainly there are instances of her exercising authority independently of her husband. We find her intervening in matters of law, and petitioning him on behalf of her servants, London merchants and others. When one of her Welsh tenants complained of the heavy-handedness of Henry's uncle, Jasper Tudor, Earl of Pembroke, Chief Justice of North Wales, she did not refer the matter to the King but sent a sharp reproof to Pembroke herself, which apparently achieved the desired result.[32]

Another letter from Elizabeth, undated but written in 1492, is among the Paston letters, that great collection of fifteenth-century correspondence; in it, she rebukes John de Vere, Earl of Oxford, in regard to disputed ownership of a manor:

> To our right trusty and beloved cousin, the Earl of Oxenford. By the Queen.
>
> Right trusty and entirely beloved cousin, we greet you well, letting you wit [understand] how it is come unto our knowledge that, whereas ye newly entered upon our well-beloved Simon Bryant, gentleman, into the manor of Hemnals [Hempnalls Hall] in Cotton [Suffolk], descended and belonging unto him by right of inheritance, as it is said, ye thereupon desired the same Simon to be agreeable for his part to put all matters of variance then depending atween him and one Sir John Paston, knight, pretending a title unto the said manor, into th'award and judgement of two learned men, by you named and chosen as arbiters atween them; and in case that the same arbiters of and upon the premises neither gave out nor made such award before the breaking up of Pasche [Easter] term, now last passed, ye of your own offer granted and promised unto the said Simon, as we be informed, to restore him forthwith thereupon unto his possession of the said manor; and how it be that the same Simon, at your motion, and for the pleasure of your lordship, as he saith, agreed unto the said compromise, and thereupon brought and showed his evidence concerning, and sufficiently proving, his right in the said manor unto the said arbiters; and that they have not made nor holden out between the said parties any such award. Yet have not ye restored the same Simon unto his possession of the said manor but continually kept him out of the same, which, if it so be, is not only to his right great hurt and hindrance, but also our marvel. Wherefore we desire and pray you right affectuously that ye will rather, at the contemplation of these our letters, show unto the said Simon, in his rightful interest and title in the said manor, all the favourable lordship that ye goodly may, doing

him to be restored and put into his lawful and peaceable possession of the same, as far as reason, equity and good conscience shall require, and your said promise, in such wise that he may understand himself herein to fare the better for our sake, as our very trust is in you.

Given under our signet at my lord's Palace of Westminster, the xxv day of June,

Elesebeth.

Beneath is written: 'Subscribed with the Queen's hand.' The existence of this letter – and there were probably more like it that are lost – proves that Elizabeth did sometimes venture into the world of public affairs. Here we see her being firm, fair and concerned to right a wrong, and her influence must have been known to be effective, or Simon Bryant would surely not have judged it worth appealing to her for help. Two months after the letter was written, John Daubeney sent Sir John Paston, Oxford's councillor, 'a copy of the letter that the Queen sent to my lord of Oxford from the manor of Cotton for Bryant'. He reported that the Archbishop of York wanted Oxford to help Paston keep possession of the manor, and was going to 'inform the Queen of the matter, and because the Queen hath take[n to] her chamber', he had sent a ring to the Lord Treasurer, anxious 'that he should excuse my lord of Oxford to the Queen', for he really had no choice in the matter.[33]

As queen, Elizabeth travelled widely, often with the King, sometimes on her own, showing the gentler face of monarchy to the people, which doubtless enhanced her popularity. Like her father, she had the common touch; like him, she was charming and accessible. Certainly she was generous, and the multiplicity of her many charities and kindnesses bears testimony to a warm and giving heart. Sadly, her privy purse expenses survive for only one year, 1502–3,[34] but they are packed with evidence of her goodness, her open-handedness and her kindnesses, as will be seen; and no doubt those for the missing years would have further served to show why she was such a popular queen.

Elizabeth was seen as 'a very noble woman', 'the most distinguished and the most noble lady in the whole of England', and she was 'much loved'[35] by her husband's subjects, high and low. *The Great Chronicle of London* states that she 'demeaned her[self] so virtuously that she was named the Gracious Queen', while Edward Hall, writing under her son, Henry VIII, was to recall: 'For her great virtue this noble princess was commonly called the good Queen Elizabeth.'

Short of cash though she was, her charities were many. She supported orphans, took children under her wing and raised them, and liberated debtors from London prisons. She gave money, for example, to an anchoress living in St Peter's almshouses in St Albans; in alms to two of her father's former servants; to a friary clerk, so that he could bury pirates who had been hanged at Execution Dock on the Thames at Wapping; to Nicholas Grey, clerk of the works at Richmond, whose house had burned down; to the children of the College of Windsor; to the son of a madman, for his diet and a gown; to the man who had cured himself of syphilis – 'the French pox'; to 'little Anne Loveday', a girl who wanted to be a nun at Elstow Abbey, so that she could have a dowry; to a child christened at Windsor; and as alms to many beggars. She also obtained a letter of pardon 'for the remission of sins' for the friars of the monastery housing St Katherine's shrine on Mount Sinai in the Holy Land.[36] She was the generous patron of several religious establishments, including the austere Carthusian priory of the Charterhouse at Sheen, founded by Henry V in 1414, and lying half a mile north of Sheen Palace; and she gave alms, rewards and cash for repairs to the buildings.[37]

Her privy purse expenses of 1502–3 reveal that she was the recipient of numerous gifts from many of her husband's appreciative subjects. She handsomely rewarded them all, from the poor man who came with apples, to the Lord Mayor of London, who presented her with cherries. A substantial number of the gifts were of food: her son's fool sent her some carp; Lord Stanley sent Malmsey wine; Edith Sandys, Lady Darcy, sent 'a present of seal', the meat of which was then a delicacy; Sir John Williams sent two bucks; Sir John Seymour sent two does; the prothonotary of Spain sent oranges – a costly delicacy only recently introduced into England – 'from Spain to the Queen at Richmond'; Richard Smythe, yeoman of the wardrobe, sent a gift of a fawn 'from the park of Swallowfield', Berkshire, where he was bailiff; the Abbess of Syon sent rabbits and quails; Richard FitzJames, Bishop of Rochester, sent grapes; Henry Deane, Archbishop of Canterbury, sent a 'Llanthony cheese', while Henry, Prior of Llanthony, also sent regular gifts of cheeses and some baked lampreys.[38]

People of all ranks sent gifts for the Queen, and many commoners or poor folk came to the palace gates with humble offerings, such as butter, chickens, wardens (pears), pippins, puddings, apples, peascods, cakes, cherries in season, a conserve of cherries (several gifts of cherries are recorded, so they must have been known to have been among Elizabeth's favourite foods), pomegranates, oranges, comfits (candied fruit), cheeses, several bucks, wild boar, tripes, chines of pork, a goshawk, pheasant cocks, capons, birds, a crane, Rhenish wine, roses, fine ironwork and a cushion. None went away without a handsome reward, usually more than Elizabeth could afford. One man got 13s.4d. (£320) for bringing her a popinjay (parrot).[39]

Some of the gifts may have been expressions of thanks or appreciation, much as flowers are given to royalty today; some were perhaps given in anticipation of queenly favour to come, given Elizabeth's reputation for open-handedness and the influence she was perceived to have with the King. But most are probably testimony to the love and goodwill borne by Henry's subjects for a kind, gentle and generous-hearted queen.

Ballads were sung about Elizabeth, such as the 'White Rose Carol':

> In a glorious garden green
> Saw I sitting a comely queen;
> Among the flowers that fresh been.
> She gathered a flower and sat between;
> The lily-white rose methought I saw,
> And ever she sang,
> This day, day dawns,
> This gentle day, day dawns,
> This gentle day dawns
> And I must home gone.
>
> In that garden be flowers of hue:
> The gillyflower[40] gent that she well knew;
> The *fleur de lis* she did one rue[41]
> And said, 'The white rose is most true
> This garden to rule by righteous law.'
> The lily-white rose methought I saw,
> And ever she sang,
> This day, day dawns,
> This gentle day, day dawns,
> This gentle day dawns
> And I must home gone.[42]

Henry VII did not enjoy that kind of affection, so he was lucky to have such a queen to show to the world the popular face of monarchy.

Elizabeth was 'intelligent above all others, and equally beautiful. She was a woman of such character that it would be hard to judge whether she displayed more of majesty and dignity in her life than wisdom and moderation'. This was written by Polydore Vergil, Henry VII's favoured historian, so one might expect it to be flattering in the extreme, but Vergil was not afraid to offend or criticise his royal patron – Henry was decidedly put out when Vergil dismissed the Arthurian legends as myths – and that Elizabeth had these qualities in good measure is borne out by the praise of other contemporaries. One chronicler called her 'noble and virtuous',[43] and a Venetian report described her as 'a very handsome woman of great ability, and in conduct very able', beloved for her abundant 'charity and humanity'.[44] Erasmus described the Queen in one word – 'brilliant'.

Later writers had little to say about her, though. 'Besides her dutifulness to her husband, and fruitfulness in her children, little can be extracted of her personal character,' observed Thomas Fuller in the 1660s, and his words sum up a problem faced by her biographers today, because much about her has to be inferred from external evidence. That she was gentle, kind and devout is patently clear, and she was demonstrably generous by nature. Alison Plowden describes her as fruitful, beautiful, submissive, a loving mother, a dutiful daughter, chaste after marriage, pious, charitable, placid, kind, sweet-tempered, generous and 'naturally indolent'. In short, she had all the virtues of great ladies in medieval chivalric verse.

Certainly she was pious: her privy purse expenses show that she unfailingly made offerings on all the great feasts of the Church and on numerous saints' days; she had a special devotion to the Virgin Mary and various other saints; she owned religious books that give insights into a conventional, late-medieval piety, and 'a chest of ivory with the Passion of Our Lord thereon'.[45] In 1486 the Pope issued her and Henry with a special dispensation 'to have a portable altar, on which they may have Mass celebrated when necessary before daybreak, and to have Mass and other divine offices celebrated in places' – even 'under interdict, with doors closed, the excommunicate and interdicted being excluded, bells unrung, and in a low voice, in presence of themselves and their household, etc., provided that they are not the cause of such interdict, nor specially interdicted'. His

Holiness also permitted 'each of them and for Margaret, countess of Richmond, the King's mother, not to be bound to fast in Lent, and during that season to eat eggs, cheese, butter and other milk-meats, whenever they shall think fit'.[46]

Elizabeth was hardly indolent. Rather, as Thomas Penn suggests in *Winter King*, she had a natural serenity. She could bestir herself when she needed to, as when she had busily schemed in the months before Bosworth. That serenity made it easy for her to accept the decisions that were made for her, asserting herself with fervour only at a time when important things were at stake, or with anger, as when she intervened to prevent an injustice. Richard III's councillors had feared she had it in her to be vengeful, but they may have been making assumptions, for it is unlikely that they knew her very well. Certainly there is no evidence to give credence to their fears. Elizabeth had neither her mother's robust energy nor her strong will and steely determination, and maybe she felt at a disadvantage beside that practical and capable paragon, Margaret Beaufort. It was fortunate that her serene nature – and no doubt her love for her husband – helped her to survive in a marriage in which she was kept in submission, and in a queenly role that was overshadowed by her mother-in-law. Her love for Henry would have made that easier, too.

The appearance of placidity, even indolence, may stem from the fact that, all her life, Elizabeth was overshadowed by dominant women: her grandmothers, her mother and her mother-in-law – and it is sometimes said that there was friction between the latter, although that can only be an assumption. In her early years Elizabeth had learned that it was her lot to be obedient and conformable, and this was to stand her in good stead in adult life. It is hard to imagine any of those domineering female relations being so mild and self-effacing as she undoubtedly was during her years as queen. She was not domineering and grasping like her mother and mother-in-law, and it was probably because of her dutifulness and her willingness to accept a subordinate role that her marriage was successful, if not happy.

It was not only Henry Tudor to whom Elizabeth had now to accustom herself, but also his devoted, emotional and possibly overbearing mother. Margaret Beaufort's lifelong passion was for her son; he was her 'own sweet and most dear King, and all my worldly joy'.[47] In one letter, she reminded him that it was the feast of St

Agnes, 'the day that I did bring into this world my good and gracious prince, King and only beloved son'.[48] In another letter, from 1501, Margaret addresses Henry as 'my dearest and only desired joy in this world' and calls him 'dear heart' and 'my sweet King', saying 'I trust you shall well perceive I shall deal towards you as a kind, loving mother.'[49]

In 1485 Henry was something of a stranger to his mother – they had been separated since he was fourteen – although he was sensible of what he owed her, and over the years he came to reciprocate her devotion. In 1498 he wrote to her: 'I shall be as glad to please you as your heart can desire it, and I know well that I am as bounden so to do as any creature living, for the great and singular motherly love and affection that it hath pleased you at all times to bear towards me. Wherefore, mine own most loving Mother, in my most hearty manner I thank you, beseeching you of your good continuance of the same.'[50] Even allowing for the extravagant salutations of the period, this was no mere flattery. Sadly, no letters from Henry to Elizabeth survive, so we do not know if he addressed his wife as warmly as he did his mother.

Margaret Beaufort had been a driving force behind the marriage of her son to Elizabeth of York. His earlier years had been ones of anxiety and intrigue, and they had taken their toll. 'Either she was in sorrow by reason of present adversities, or else when she was in prosperity she was in dread of the adversity to come.'[51] Elizabeth also owed a debt of gratitude to her mother-in-law, and was probably conscious of the fact.

Contemporaries were unanimous in their praise of Margaret Beaufort. To Vergil, she was 'a wise woman, a most worthy woman, whom no one can extol too often for her sound sense and holiness of life'. A friend, Henry Parker, Lord Morley, wrote of 'her fame, her honour, her liberality, her prudence, her chastity and her excellent virtues'.[52] According to the funeral oration by her confessor, Bishop Fisher, Margaret was 'a scholar and a saint, unkind to none' and 'never forgetful any kindness or service done to her. Neither was she revengeful or cruel. Everyone that knew her loved her, and everything that she said or did became her.'

Portraits of Margaret Beaufort show a thin-faced, thin-lipped elderly woman with high cheekbones, wearing a black gown and a severe widow's chin-barbe under her long-lappeted white gable hood. Yet they all derive from originals painted late in her life. In earlier years she wore fashionable attire, and it was probably only after she took a vow of chastity in 1499 that she adopted more sombre garb, and only after her husband's death in 1504 that she donned a widow's barbe. Yet however royally or soberly she was robed, she attended Mass six times daily, ate sparingly, observed fast days rigorously and, when in good health, wore a hair shirt next to her skin.[53] She was extremely devout, spending hours in daily prayer, and repeating moral homilies 'many a time'.[54]

She used some of her vast wealth for the benefit of others, not only doing good works but in furthering education. A great scholar herself, she became renowned as a patron of art, learning and religion, and was to found two Cambridge colleges: Christ's and St John's. An intelligent woman, she patronised William Caxton and translated books from French, which he printed; she also translated devotional texts. Her influence over the kingdom's intellectual and spiritual life was considerable.

Yet this was also the woman who sued the widows of her servants for debt, and who ruthlessly pursued her legal and fiscal rights;[55] a woman who was vigorously efficient and a formidable disciplinarian, in whom piety combined with practicality. Margaret Beaufort was the greatest landowner in the realm after the King and Queen, and her expenditure was lavish. She kept almost royal state, had a great affinity of dependents, and was at the centre of a wide network of patronage[56] – just as the Queen should have been, but was not.

Although Bacon later claimed that Henry 'reverenced [his mother] much' but 'heard little' of what she said, Pedro de Ayala, the Spanish ambassador, reported, in July 1498: 'The King is much influenced by his mother', and stated that Margaret Beaufort's influence was greater than that of Lord Chancellor Morton or Henry's Chamberlain, Giles, Lord Daubeney. He added: 'The Queen, as is generally the case, does not like it.' The Sub-Prior of Santa Cruz had written only days earlier: 'The Queen is a very noble woman, and much beloved. She is kept in subjection by the mother of the King.'[57] Yet there is much evidence to show that the relationship between the two women was outwardly one of companionship and co-operation, so if there was any conflict between them, they had concealed it very well for twelve years, and would continue to do so. Indeed, they got on so well that it was said they lived 'in peaceable concord',[58] and they seem also to have developed an affection for each other. This suggests that Elizabeth had quickly learned to defer to her mother-in-law's wisdom and decrees, and wisely did not try to compete with her. Probably she appreciated the support that Margaret so readily gave her, and was happy to co-operate with her.

The two Spanish reports are the first of just three references to conflict between the Queen and her mother-in-law. It may be significant that they were written by Spaniards who were used to seeing their Queen, Isabella, exercising power in her own right, and were startled by Elizabeth's lack of it.[59] Their being written so close together, and independently, suggests that both comments were prompted by something that happened that summer.[60] However in 1500 a yeoman of the crown, John Hewyk of Nottingham, observed during a royal visit to that town 'that he had spoken with the Queen's Grace, and should have spoken more with her said Grace, had [it] not been for that strong whore the King's mother'.[61] Possibly Margaret had intervened to silence an aggravating man, but his remark is in keeping with the Spanish reports, and together they suggest an established balance of power in the relationship. Possibly, on occasion, Elizabeth allowed her irritation to show.

Apart from these isolated observations, all the signs are that Elizabeth and Margaret Beaufort were close. Too much credence has been given to these reports and to Bacon's jaded assumptions, and some modern writers have tended to superimpose their own perceptions of mother-and-daughter-in-law relationships.

The Lady Margaret was often at court, especially in the earlier years of the reign. Although she played no formal role in politics, her influence in the domestic sphere was strong, and Elizabeth rarely acted independently of her – and possibly was glad of her advice. Yet, as she was soon to find, Margaret was frequently at her side, or never very far away. Wherever the King and Queen were, there his mother would usually be too, and she often accompanied Henry and Elizabeth on their travels and progresses around the kingdom. Sometimes she would appear in public with Henry when Elizabeth was absent. His household ordinances provided for lodgings to be kept for his mother at all the royal residences, often next to his private apartments. At Woodstock, their apartments were linked by a shared withdrawing chamber, and at the Tower they adjoined Henry's bedchamber and council chamber.[62] It was soon accepted that the King, the Queen and the King's mother formed an inviolable triumvirate.

The pattern was set less than a month after the wedding when, on 6 February 1486, the King issued a licence jointly to his 'dearest consort, Elizabeth, Queen of England, and his dearest mother, to found a perpetual chantry in the parish church of the Holy and Undivided Trinity of Guildford, Surrey, for one chaplain to perform divine service daily for the healthful estate of the King, his consort and his mother, and for their souls after death'.[63] In conjunction with this, two gentlemen of Guildford persuaded the Queen, the Lady Margaret and two knights of the King's household to assist them in the founding of a guild in honour of the Trinity, the Virgin Mary, St George and All Saints at the same parish church.[64] In December 1487 Elizabeth and Margaret, along with Archbishop Morton and Reginald Bray, were granted the right to present their candidate to the deanery of the college of St Stephen at Westminster.[65]

Whenever the Lady Margaret attended church with the King and Queen, she sat beneath her own cloth of estate. If she entertained a bishop to dinner, he would be treated as if he were in the King's own presence. After Evensong, wine and spices would be served to Margaret as well as to the King and his sons – the Queen was not included. But when Elizabeth went in procession, Margaret had to walk a little behind her, 'aside the Queen's half train'. When Henry and Elizabeth dined in state after Mass, only 'half estate' was accorded to Margaret; and at the Easter Garter ceremonies in chapel, while Elizabeth and Margaret were censed after Henry, only the King and Queen might kiss the Pax,[66] a small tablet adorned with a sacred image, usually the crucifixion, which the devout kissed instead of each other as a sign of peace.

Thus it was soon made clear to Elizabeth that, from now on, she was invariably to be associated with her formidable mother-in-law. It was to be expected that Margaret, an experienced and capable woman of forty-three, would take the young Queen under her wing and act as her mentor. That they enjoyed a harmonious relationship is evident from various sources and the fact that they collaborated on several occasions when they were of one mind about something. The impression one gets is of two women who got on well working in unison together for everyone's benefit. As Fisher testified, everyone who knew Margaret loved her, and there is no reason why Elizabeth should have been an exception. Furthermore the Lady Margaret had a sense of humour and could provide congenial companionship: she kept two fools, Skip and Reginald the idiot, and she enjoyed gambling at cards and chess, as did the Queen.[67]

The affection between the two ladies may have been facilitated to a degree by the fact that they were not continually obliged to enjoy each other's company. The Lady Margaret sometimes resided at Lathom House or Knowsley Hall, the northern seats of the Stanleys; when in London, she would stay at Coldharbour.[68] After 1499, having taken a vow of chastity with Stanley's permission, she was less often at court, having moved into her own house at Collyweston in Northamptonshire, where apartments were permanently kept ready for her husband and her daughter-in-law the Queen.[69] She never visited Lathom after that, but sometimes resided at Woking Palace in Surrey or Hunsdon House in Hertfordshire.

Elizabeth's good relations with her formidable mother-in-law are testimony to her warm heart, her good judgement of character, her peaceable nature and her talent for diplomacy.

The court over which Elizabeth presided as queen was as magnificent as her father's, and like Edward IV's it was modelled on that of Burgundy. Henry VII has gone down in history as a miser, but he spent freely on the outward trappings of wealth such as jewels, on which he paid out upwards of £128,000 (£62.2 million), hundreds of pieces of plate bearing the monogram HE (for Henry and Elizabeth), tapestries, rich furnishings and the rebuilding and decoration of his palaces. His court was imbued with learning, music and pageantry. He deliberately exploited the symbolism of royal pageantry and ceremonial, laying down a new series of ordinances for the regulation of daily royal life and etiquette. Small wonder that Bacon called him 'a wonder for wise men'.

Elizabeth may have been influential in the development of royal pageantry during Henry's reign, which would set a pattern for the Tudor court for the next century and more. As the daughter of Edward IV, who had recognised the value of Burgundian court culture, with its emphasis on magnificence and display, and emulated it, she was ideally placed to advise her husband.

On great occasions, the court was be the setting for the lavish feasts, tournaments, pageants and revelry that were deemed essential for a successful monarchy, but, as we have seen, Henry VII enjoyed simpler pleasures too. No great sportsman himself – although he liked hunting, hawking, cock-fighting, bull baiting, shooting crossbows at the butts and the spectacle of jousting – he nevertheless installed bowling alleys and tennis courts in the grounds of his palaces, and laid on hunting expeditions and lavish musical entertainments, all for the diversion of his courtiers and guests. Elizabeth shared many of these interests, but she also enjoyed hunting and archery; her privy purse expenses record payments for her greyhounds, and for arrows and broadheads (arrow tips). She went hawking too: Oliver Aulferton was keeper of the Queen's goshawks and spaniels, and was paid a salary of £2 (£970).[70]

Where the moral laxity of some European courts was notorious, that presided over by Henry and Elizabeth was a byword for propriety, which was ensured by the marital fidelity of the King and Queen, and no doubt by the guiding moral hand of the Lady Margaret. It was also a great centre of piety and learning, peopled by divines, scholars and poets.

When they were not on display to the court, the royal family enjoyed living in the warmth and intimacy afforded by the warren of small closets beyond the public chambers of their apartments, an arrangement that reflected the increasing desire of European monarchs to achieve some privacy in their otherwise very public lives, although privacy as they understood it invariably meant having many select persons in attendance to look to their every need. It was during Edward IV's reign that this growing taste for seclusion emerged, so Elizabeth would have grown up with the notion of kings and queens enjoying a private life away from the court. That would have been a foreign concept to earlier medieval kings, whose lives had been communally centred on the great hall, and who were incessantly on display.

The court was not just a magnificent domestic and ceremonial institution; it was also the seat of government and the political hub of the kingdom. There were two political entities in the court: the Privy Council, which – presided over by the King – attended to matters of state; and the Privy Chamber, the nerve centre of monarchical power. It was Henry VII who created the Privy Chamber, the department of state comprising the influential and often powerful gentlemen who waited personally upon the sovereign and were thus able to influence him and bestow patronage. There are frequent references to his retiring among them in his private lodgings, which were also called the privy chamber.

Elizabeth had her corresponding private apartments, where she resided with her ladies and other female attendants – a chaste female enclave within the King's 'house of magnificence'. It usually consisted of three distinct parts: a great chamber, a presence chamber for audiences and entertaining, and a privy chamber, which, like the King's, might comprise bedchambers, closets, a privy, a privy wardrobe and some-times a privy kitchen, where the Queen's meals were prepared. Guards were stationed at the entrance to each room, and only the King, Elizabeth's servants and the most privileged guests would be admitted to her privy chamber. Elizabeth would usually dine with her ladies in her presence chamber, rather than with the King.[71] Edward IV's 'Black Book of the Household' had laid down that service to the Queen 'must be nigh like unto the King'.[72]

The Queen was not of course confined to her apartments. She enjoyed the freedom of the court and the King's lodgings, and it was expected that she would be at his side whenever appropriate: at the great religious festivals, when both wore their crowns, at 'days of estate', feasts, courtly celebrations, receptions and entertainments, and when peers were ennobled. When the King sat in his chair of estate, or throne – the actual seat of government – there she would be, seated on a lower chair beside him, with 'the cloth of estate hanging somewhat lower than the King's, by the valance'.[73]

Although he was 'frugal to excess in his own person', Henry VII 'kept a sumptuous table. There might be six to seven hundred persons at dinner. His people say that his Majesty spends upon his table £14,000 [nearly £7 million] annually.'[74] On a 'day of estate' when Henry dined before the court in his great chamber, he would have a bishop and a duke, or two earls, at table with him, and Elizabeth – who arrived in procession preceded by her chamberlain and usher – always sat at her own table with a duchess, a countess and perhaps a baroness. She had her own servers and carver, and her sewer (food taster) to bring her neck-towel, or napkin, which was worn over one shoulder. Everyone else was seated below the high tables according to rank. Once the meal was over, the boards were cleared and the royal sewers spread a clean 'surnap' (tablecloth) across them, which the ushers then smoothed over. Knights or barons would bring covered ewers containing water and basins, and at a sign from the King, everyone washed their hands. The esquires then took up the boards, while the ushers knelt down to 'make clean the King's skirts' of crumbs. Grace was said by a bishop or a royal chaplain.[75]

Music, minstrelsy and disguisings were part of the culture of the Tudor court. Elizabeth loved them all, especially music; she had grown up in a court where her parents had both employed musicians, and she too had her own minstrels and drummers; three of the latter would serve her son, Henry VIII. Among her musicians were Mark Jaket and Janyn Marcazin, who is listed as a minstrel in 1503, Richard Denouse, William Older and a fiddler whom Henry VII rewarded.[76] Late in 1486 Jaket and Older received a reward of £5 (£2,500). In 1502, the Queen's minstrels were headed by 'M. of Lorydon', and each received a salary of £2.6s.8d. (£1,130).[77] These minstrels were professional musicians and their function was to entertain the Queen, her household and her guests, and provide accompaniment for dancing in the privy chamber; they also taught musical skills to the royal children.

Elizabeth was to commission works from those two *virtuosi* of the Tudor court, William Cornish and Richard Fairfax.[78] Her passion for music, which was to be inherited by her children, may be measured by the large sums she was ready to spend on it – money she could ill afford. She would handsomely reward minstrels such as the man who played a drone – possibly an organ or a cornemuse (bagpipes) – before her at Richmond. One of her most lavish purchases was a pair of clavichords for herself, costing £4 (£1,950).[79] Her influence was significant. Her daughters played skilfully upon the lute, and her son, the future Henry VIII, became a notable musician and composer.

Books would have had a prominent place in the Queen's chamber; they were not just there for the pleasure to be obtained from them, but as outward manifestations of magnificence, for they were fabulously expensive objects of desire and proclaimed the erudition and interests of their owners. Elizabeth's love of books had stayed with her from childhood. Hers were a mix of the secular and the devotional. She owned one of the finest manuscripts of the age, the beautifully illuminated 'Hours of Elizabeth the Queen', dating from c.1415–30. It is now thought to have been owned by her, rather than by her mother, as was previously claimed, and had once belonged to her cousin, Cecily Neville, Countess of Warwick (d.1450), daughter of Ralph Neville, Earl of Salisbury. Its colourful pages illustrate the Hours of the Virgin and the Passion of Christ, the Penitential Psalms, the Office of the Dead, the Commendation of Souls and prayers to St Mary. There are eighteen exquisite miniatures, borders lavishly decorated with foliage on solid gold leaf, 423 decorated initials, and roundels showing the signs of the Zodiac. The manuscript bears the inscription 'Elysabeth ye quene' in the lower margin of one folio, beneath a miniature of the Crucifixion.[80]

The beautiful fourteenth-century Bohun Psalter owned by Elizabeth of York as queen is in Exeter College, Oxford, and is inscribed on the first page in her hand:

> Thys book ys myn
> Elysabeth ye quene.

It is also known as 'The Mass Book of King Henry VII's Queen Elizabeth and King Henry VIII's Queen Katherine', and contains calendar notes by Elizabeth and her daughter-in-law, Katherine of Aragon, to whom it came after her death, and a further autograph inscription:

> Thys book ys myn
> Katherine the qwene.

Elizabeth also recorded in it the dates of birth of her children.[81]

An illuminated manuscript of verses written between 1415 and 1440 by Charles, Duke of Orléans,[82] bears the arms of Henry VII and Elizabeth of York. It may have been partly executed for Edward IV at the end of his reign, but was completed by the anonymous Master of the Prayer Books under the direction of Quentin Poulet, Henry VII's librarian, by 1500.[83] It was probably a gift from Henry to Elizabeth. Orléans, a French prince captured at Agincourt, wrote his poems while he was a prisoner in the Tower of London. They tell of love, of spring and of melancholy, and one speaks of jealousy, which may have struck a chord with Henry:

> Strengthen, my Love, this castle of my heart,
> And with some store of pleasure give me aid,
> For Jealousy, with all them of his part,
> Strong siege about the weary tower has laid.
> Nay, if to break his bands thou art afraid,
> Too weak to make his cruel force depart,
> Strengthen at least this castle of my heart,
> And with some store of pleasure give me aid.
> Nay, let not Jealousy, for all his art
> Be master, and the tower in ruin laid,
> That still, ah Love! thy gracious rule obeyed.
> Advance, and give me succour of thy part;
> Strengthen, my Love, this castle of my heart.

Henry may also have presented Elizabeth with the 'Miroir des Dames', a manuscript containing moral instruction for queens and other high-born ladies.[84] Based on a thirteenth-century text, of which copies had been owned by several European queens, and finished in 1428, it contained an addition in the form of a frontispiece showing the crown of England resting on a hawthorn bush – that favoured Tudor symbol – with a salutation to Henry VII, *Vive le noble roy Henry*'; this was perhaps added soon after Bosworth, possibly around the time of the King's marriage. The nature of the text – which reminds queens that, as the image of feminine perfection, they are blessed with a special grace and must be an example to their sex – makes it likely that this book was given by Henry to Elizabeth of York.[85]

Another illuminated manuscript associated with Elizabeth is a lavish 'Legendary', a book of the lives of the saints, dating from c.1250.[86] The flyleaf bears the inscription 'God save King Harry and Queen Elizabeth', which must have been added before 1503, and a mark identifying it as later belonging to Henry VIII's library.[87] A prayer book that had belonged to Elizabeth of York was sold at auction in 1983.[88]

Like her parents, Elizabeth was a patron of William Caxton and his successor at the Westminster printing press, Wynkyn de Worde. In 1490 Caxton's translation of *Eneydos*, a French version of Virgil's *Aeneid*, was dedicated to her eldest son, and around 1491 Caxton printed the *Orationes: Fifteen Oes and Other Prayers* 'by commandments of' the Queen and the Lady Margaret. It was his last publication, and comprised fifteen prayers then believed to have been written by St Bridget of Sweden, all beginning with the letter O.[89] It was probably Elizabeth's grandmother, Cecily Neville, who had nurtured in her a special devotion to St Bridget, which she shared with Margaret Beaufort. Margaret was a regular visitor to the Bridgettine abbey of Syon,[90] where Elizabeth's cousin, Anne de la Pole, was prioress. When Anne died in 1501, her successor maintained good relations with the Queen, sending her quails and rabbits for her table.[91]

Books were valued gifts. In 1494 Margaret Beaufort commissioned from Wynkyn de Worde a weighty book of spiritual exercises entitled *Scala Perfectionis (The Scale of Perfection)* by the Augustinian mystic Walter Hilton, which she and Elizabeth jointly presented to their kinswoman, Mary Roos, who served the Queen as lady-in-waiting.

Elizabeth inscribed it: 'I pray you pray for me. Elysabeth ye quene.'[92] Elizabeth may have been the 'Queen Elizabeth' who gave a book of hours to Katherine Neville, the widow of Lord Hastings, but Elizabeth Wydeville could also have been the donor.[93]

Both the King and Queen wrote inscriptions in a Parisian missal of 1498 owned by one of Elizabeth's ladies. Henry's read: 'Madam, I pray you remember me, your loving master, Henry R.' Elizabeth's was less formal: 'Madam, I pray you forget not me to pray to God that I may have part of your prayers. Elysabeth ye Queene.' Evidently she felt she needed the spiritual consolation these prayers might afford her.[94]

Henry VII was astute when it came to finance. His tough upbringing had taught him the value of money and of enforcing policies that would ensure peace and generate wealth; he understood that the subtle practice of statecraft was infinitely preferable to achieving his aims through war. Yet although he was generous in giving alms to the sick and the destitute, and in enriching the Church, he was to gain a lasting reputation for parsimony. It was said that 'although he professes many virtues, his love of money is too great'.[95] The Milanese ambassador reported in 1495, 'The King is rather feared than loved, and this is due to his avarice.'[96] A Venetian ambassador thought him 'a great miser', and wrote that he 'had accumulated so much gold that he was supposed to have more than well-nigh all the other kings in Christendom'.[97] 'The King's riches augment every day,' the Spanish ambassador observed. 'I think he has no equal in this respect. If gold coin once enters his strongboxes, it never comes out again. He always pays in depreciated coin. All his servants are like him: they have a wonderful dexterity in getting other people's money.'[98] A Papal envoy who came to the English court to raise money for a crusade was disconcerted to find only £11.11s. (£5,650) in his collecting box, 'which result made our hearts sink within us, for there were present the King, the Queen, the mother of the King and the mother of the Queen' and many lords and ladies.

But the description of Henry as a miser, a gloomy, Scrooge-like figure in sober, shabby clothing counting his money is a distorted one. He had known adversity and realised that strength lay in financial security. By amassing a fortune, he was bolstering the future success of his dynasty, and he was determined to live in a style befitting a great prince. But his subjects paid a high price for it. A few years later, Pedro de Ayala, the Spanish ambassador, imputed 'the decrease of trade' to 'the impoverishment of the people by the great taxes laid on them. The King himself said to me that it is his intention to keep his subjects low, because riches would only make them haughty.' He was to pay for this with his popularity. 'He is disliked, but the Queen is beloved because she is powerless.'[99]

Henry's carefulness with money did not extend to the state he kept as king. It was expected of Renaissance sovereigns that they looked and acted the part magnificently, outward display being considered essential to command the respect, confidence and admiration of their subjects and other nations. In this, Henry was following the precepts of the court of Burgundy. Careful in other respects with money, he recognised the value of regal display and spent lavishly on it. 'He knew well how to maintain his royal majesty and all which pertains to kingship.'[100]

As queen, according to Thomas More, Elizabeth enjoyed 'plenty of every pleasant thing'.[101] Rodrigo de Puebla, ambassador from the court of Queen Isabella of Spain, observed: 'There is no country in the world where queens live with greater pomp than in England, where they have as many court officers as the King.'[102]

But that high estate had to be maintained. On marriage, every English queen consort received a dower for the financial support of herself and her household. This took the form of a substantial settlement of lands, manors and other crown property, making her one of the major landowners in the realm.[103]

Elizabeth was co-heiress with her sisters to the lands of the noble families of Mortimer, earls of March, and Clare, which had been inherited by the House of York. These lands, of which Cecily Neville held a share as dower, were not part of the crown estate, and should have been divided between the Yorkist princesses and then passed to their husbands on marriage; but Henry VII appropriated their shares as well as what was his in right of his wife, quietly incorporated them into the Crown lands, and dowered Elizabeth from them.[104] She was in possession of lands of the earldom of March in Herefordshire by September 1486;[105] some of the rest went towards the support of Elizabeth Wydeville and Cecily, Duchess of York; but for Elizabeth's sisters, there would be nothing, not even dowries.

Elizabeth had to wait for the rest of her settlement, for it was not finally assigned to her until November 1487; until then her financial needs were mainly met by the King's household, further – and perhaps deliberately – limiting her sphere of influence and her capacity for patronage. From time to time she received grants from the King, such as the annuity of £100 (£48,900) bestowed on 3 February 1486 at Sheen Palace.[106] When she finally was assigned her dower, for life, no set amount appears formally to have been settled on her. To the Mortimer and Clare estates were added her mother's lands, worth about £1,890 (£924,000), and annuities from fixed rents from the towns of Bristol (amounting to £102.15s.6d., now £50,250) and Bedford. In addition, like her predecessors, she had income from wardships, fines and tax exemptions granted her by the King, and in 1487 Parliament enacted that she could sell and grant leases in her own name, without the King's consent, in consideration of the great expense of her chamber. On 1 February 1492 Henry settled upon her the reversion of the dower lands of her grandmother, Duchess Cecily, which she should have inherited anyway as part of the Mortimer and Clare inheritance.[107]

Henry had not only to maintain his wife but also her mother – effectively, he was supporting two queens, which placed an unusual strain on his finances, as a new queen was usually assigned the dower of her predecessor; as we have seen, Henry had granted other lands to Elizabeth Wydeville. He also gave grants to his own mother, and was responsible for the maintenance of Elizabeth's dowerless sisters, although he expected her to support them out of the income allocated her. It did not help that revenues from the dukedom of York were tied up in her grandmother's generous dower. To boost Elizabeth's income, the King, 'in consideration of the great expenses and charges that his most dear wife, Elizabeth, Queen of England, must of necessity bear in her chamber', obtained the consent of the Lords Spiritual and Temporal in Parliament that she should 'be able to sue in her own name, without the King, by writs &c., all manner of forms [contracts], rents and debts due to her; and sue in her own name in all manner of actions, and plead, and be impleaded, in any of the King's courts'.[108] Queens, unlike other married women, enjoyed the unique privilege of granting and acquiring lands as *femmes sole*, and they could also sue, and be sued, independently of the King.[109] However, Henry VII, like Edward IV, was not above alienating lands he claimed to hold 'in right of Elizabeth, the Queen Consort', as in 1494 when he gave away some Irish estates of Elizabeth's earldom of March to her chamberlain, Thomas Butler, Earl of Ormond.[110]

In 1489 Elizabeth was granted the use of some of the property of her aunt, Isabella Neville, Duchess of Clarence, during the minority of Isabella's son, the Earl of Warwick. In 1495 she inherited Mortimer and Clare property worth £1,400 (£684,500) from her grandmother, Cecily Neville, which she had been granted in reversion in 1492.

Elizabeth had her own auditors. Each year they and her receiver-general would tour her estates, inspect her stewards' accounts, compile valuations of her properties, arbitrate in disputes, and advise their mistress on various issues.[111] There could be a shortfall between what was due to her in rents and what was actually received.[112] There is evidence to show that Elizabeth and her council were obliged to extract as much income as they could from her manors, but that this was resented by her tenants. For example, in 1487 they established a collector of rents at the royal manor of Havering in the hope of ensuring that all moneys due to the Queen would be raised, but the local people made life difficult for every occupant of the post until, in 1497, the then incumbent, Thomas Elrington, was assaulted after ordering the bailiff to seize the goods of the Queen's tenant, local Justice of the Peace Sir Philip Coke, who might have been knighted for valour in the recent Cornish uprising, but had rent outstanding. Coke, whose wife was probably the sister or aunt of Margaret Belknap, one of Elizabeth's gentlewomen, was accused of an act injurious to the honour of the Queen and a dangerous example to her other tenants. Her council fined him £5, whereupon Elrington demanded twelve years' back rent. Coke reacted violently, and was fined a further £5; he never again held office, but in a sense his was the victory, because Elrington was relieved of his post to avoid further violence, and was never replaced.[113]

The Queen had the right to make a new appointment every time a post on one of her estates fell vacant: it was another way in which she could show favour to those who had served her well. Sir Gilbert Talbot, who had been associated with Elizabeth in 'The Song of Lady Bessy' and was now one of Henry VII's privy councillors, was appointed steward of her lands in Feckenham, Worcestershire. A letter from Elizabeth survives in which she acknowledges the good and faithful service he had rendered to her.[114] In November 1502 Talbot sent her a wild boar as a gift.[115]

Margaret of Anjou had received a dower of 10,000 marks (at least £1.5 million), which was later increased. Elizabeth Wydeville's dower was at least £4,500 (£2.1 million). Elizabeth of York's dower lands were ultimately worth only £3,360 (£1.6 million) in 1506, less than two thirds of her mother's income.[116] Although she had brought him a great inheritance (the lands of the Mortimers and the Clares), Henry kept her short of money, which meant that financially she would always be heavily dependent on him for loans and gifts of cash, several of which are recorded.[117] She was obliged to borrow small sums from her sisters and even her servants.[118] For all that she appeared outwardly wealthy,[119] she struggled to make ends meet, and her extant privy purse expenses show that often she could settle her debts only in part, leaving much owing, in several cases over an extended period. One London silk merchant, Henry Bryan, had to submit his account for £107 (£52,000) several times, and in the end was obliged to settle for payment in instalments.[120]

By 1495 Elizabeth was deeply in debt, and had been driven to pawning her plate to Sir Thomas Lovell for £500 (£250,000), and borrowing money from her chamberlain and her ladies. In February 1497 the King ordered £2,000 (£972,200) to be delivered to her 'to repay her debts', but it was only another loan. When he loaned her money, he expected her to pledge her plate as security, and to redeem it on the due date, and took care to see that she did.[121]

She was not extravagant in her personal expenditure. She ran her household economically, better than her mother had run hers. She paid her ladies lower salaries than previous queens, the highest being £33.6s.8d. (£16,200). As well as her dower, she received money from the Exchequer for her chamber expenses, and this she spent on items such as clothes for herself and for her household, horses, repairs to her barge and litters, repeated 'boat hire', household items (such as sheets, baskets, bellows, carving knives, bolts, locks, an axe, brushes, wheels, wax, faggots and barehides), jewels, a small pair of enamelled knives for the Queen's own use, meat for her goshawks and spaniels, offerings in church, barrels of Rhenish wine, bread, ale, butter, eggs and milk, and payments to her physicians and apothecaries. There were a few luxury items too, including chair coverings of crimson and blue cloth of gold and crimson velvet with linings of blue satin; and, for the Queen's litters, twenty-seven cushions of blue cloth of gold, backed with various shades of satin, damask and velvet. Elizabeth herself checked and signed every page of the book wherein details of her income and her privy purse expenses were listed, ensuring that her officers were acting within their means. The most costly items she ever bought for herself

– clothing apart – were the clavichords and the popinjay for which she paid a poor man 13s.4d. (£320).[122]

The small sums of pocket money she apportioned to herself were given by her accountant, Richard Deacons, into the hands of her ladies (usually Lady Anne Percy, Lady Elizabeth Stafford or Elizabeth Lee), who would put them in her privy purse. It was rare for Elizabeth to receive more than 10s. (£250) or 20s. (£500) at a time, and sometimes she got as little as 4s.4d. (£110). She was, however, abundantly generous, which may have been the cause of some of her financial difficulties.[123] The King gave her only a very small allowance for the charities that she was expected to dispense, so she had to make stringent economies in order to give to the poor. Much of her available funds went on gifts – numerous, but not lavish – and donations to religious establishments. That left less for alms, and it has been noted that she outlaid only £9.11s.5d. (£4,650) on those in her last year. Her gambling debts at Christmas 1502 were about half that amount.[124]

She also had to support her unmarried sisters, paying them annuities of £50 (£24,450) each out of her privy purse. When they married, they received no dowries from the King, so she paid their husbands annuities of £120 (£58,350) for their maintenance. In addition, she sent her sisters gifts of cash: in 1502, for example, she gave Anne £6.13s.4d. (£3,250) for pocket money.[125] Often, Elizabeth would go without to do all this. She might have lived in great state and luxury, but the Queen of England had to juggle her financial resources as carefully as any peasant's wife.

9

'Offspring of the Race of Kings'

Early in January 1486, before her wedding, it had been confidently expected that the new Queen would immediately be crowned, and it must have been on the King's orders that a royal official, Piers Curteys, drew up a memorandum listing expenditure for items to be delivered 'against the Queen's coronation': spurs for the henchmen who were to ride in the procession; 'tawing' (treating) of ermines; 'canopy staves and ye timber work of two chairs of estate'; hire of a cart 'to carry in ye Rennes' – a fine linen cloth woven in Brittany, to be dyed scarlet and used as a carpet – 'unto Westminster and six porters' wages for to help to lay the same Rennes from Westminster Hall unto the Abbey'; ermines, miniver and 'powderings for furring of divers of ye Queen's robes' (small spots added to distinguish royal ermine from that worn by the nobility); worsted, 'white bogy [lambskin] for furring of ye henchmen's gowns' and 'scarlet', a fine, expensive wool cloth.[1]

In the event, though, there was no coronation for Elizabeth – not for nearly two years. It is often said that Henry expected her to bear him a son before he outlaid any serious expenditure on her crowning, or that he did not want people to think that the ceremony was an endorsement of her title; but the likeliest explanation for it being deferred is that, by Lent, it was known that Elizabeth was expecting a child.

Loyal subjects had 'prayed to Almighty God that the King and Queen would be favoured with offspring, and that eventually a child might be conceived and a new prince be born, so that they might heap further joys upon present delights'. They had not had long to wait. 'Our Lord Jesus Christ heard their prayers and permitted the joyous Queen to become pregnant with the desired offspring.'[2]

The speed with which Elizabeth conceived – on her wedding night, perhaps – must have seemed to Henry, and no doubt to many of his people, to be the greatest manifestation of divine approval of his marriage. 'Then a new happiness took over the happiest kingdom, great enjoyment filled the Queen, the Church experienced perfect joy, while huge excitement gripped the court and an incredible pleasure arose over the whole country.'[3]

The bodies of queens were effectively public property, for their fertility was of prime importance to the nation and a legitimate object of speculation in courts, diplomatic circles, noble households, taverns and humble hovels. The swift arrival of an heir would go far towards assuring the stability of the Tudor dynasty, and it would immeasurably increase Elizabeth's standing with her husband the King and the country at large.

The news that any high-born lady was to bear a child was cause for great celebration in that dynastically minded age, and it was the subject of much interest on the part of both sexes. It was not expected that the Queen would retire from public view or swathe herself in shawls like Queen Victoria, for there was then no sense of squeamishness or embarrassment about what was regarded as a highly desirable condition; and it was customary for relatives and friends to send good wishes for a safe delivery – a 'happy hour'. Everyone was well aware of the risks involved in childbirth.

Henry VII might have claimed his crown by right of conquest, but now that he had married Elizabeth, it was indisputably his by right. It should have ensured his security and been 'the final end to all dissensions, titles and debates',[4] yet it was already obvious that this marriage, which had been made to heal the breach between the warring royal houses, was insufficient to stifle treason and had not reconciled all the King's opponents. Some diehard Yorkist activists just would not accept it, and they were making their opposition plain.

In the spring of 1486 Henry VII felt it politic to go on a progress to Lincolnshire and Yorkshire to be seen by his northern subjects and to 'weed, root out and purge men tainted with dissension and privy factions', especially in Yorkshire, where Richard III had once been popular.[5] Elizabeth stayed behind at the palace of Placentia at

Greenwich with her mother. It has been suggested that Henry did not take her with him because he wanted to make it clear he did not owe his crown to her or 'seek popularity on her account',[6] yet it is far more likely that she was suffering the nausea and fatigue common in early pregnancy; moreover, the King was visiting areas where pockets of Yorkist resistance were anticipated, so he would not have wanted his expectant Queen to be exposed to any risk.

Henry departed before Easter, which fell on 26 March that year, and he would be away for three months, visiting – among other places – Waltham, Cambridge, Huntingdon, Stamford, Lincoln, Doncaster, Pontefract, York and Worcester. On the way he had to suppress insurrections involving Humphrey Stafford and Francis, Lord Lovell, one of Richard III's closest adherents, and deal with a plot against himself – but generally he was well received, even in York. While he was away, he sent frequent letters to Elizabeth.

Placentia, where she was staying, was a beautiful palace that she had known from childhood. Built around 1437 as 'Bella Court' by Henry V's brother, Humphrey, Duke of Gloucester, who had acquired the large hunting park surrounding it in 1433, this large stone mansion was seized by Margaret of Anjou on his death in 1447. It was she who renamed it 'Placentia', meaning a 'pleasance', or pleasant place, and set about converting it into a palace, building ranges of brick and timber, paving the floors with terracotta tiles bearing her monogram, inserting beautiful glass windows decorated with marguerites and hawthorn buds, adding pillars and arcades adorned with sculpted marguerites, and building a vestry to serve as a jewel house. Tapestries covered the walls of the royal apartments, and in the gardens there was an arbour for ladies to sit in. Queen Margaret's house was arranged around two courtyards, and to the west she ordered a pier to be constructed, so that royal barges could land.[7] In 1465 Placentia was granted to Elizabeth Wydeville as part of her jointure.

The palace lay in a healthy setting, aired by breezes from the Thames, and nestling in 200 acres of rolling parkland. Elizabeth had known this palace from childhood, and it was already one of Henry VII's favourite residences. He was soon to rename it Greenwich Palace.

On 6 March Pope Innocent VIII issued a bull confirming the dispensation issued by the Bishop of Imola. On the 27th, in another bull, he gave his own dispensation addressed to 'thou King, Henry of

Lancaster, and thou, Elizabeth of York', recognising Henry as king, threatening anyone who rose against him with excommunication, and informing the royal couple that, 'as their progenitors had vexed the kingdom of England with wars and clamours, to prevent further effusion of blood it was desirable for them to unite in marriage'. He referred to Elizabeth as 'the undoubted heir of that famous King of immortal memory, Edward IV'. The bull arrived in England in June, and copies of it, printed in Holborn by William Machlin, were distributed.[8]

Henry VII was at Worcester when the dispensation was brought to him, and he was present in Worcester Cathedral on Trinity Sunday to hear John Alcock, Bishop of Worcester, read it out, proclaiming to all that, 'understanding of the long and grievous variance, contentions and debates that hath been in this realm of England between the House of the Duchy of Lancaster on the one party, and the House of the Duchy of York on the other party', and 'willing all such divisions to be put apart, by the counsel and consent of his College of Cardinals', His Holiness had approved, confirmed and established 'the matrimony and conjunction made between our sovereign lord, King Henry the Seventh of the House of Lancaster of that one party, and the noble Princess Elizabeth of the House of York of that other, with all their issue lawfully born between the same'. A copy was presented to the Queen at Sheen, and the text was printed, circulated and read out in pulpits throughout the realm 'for conservation of the universal peace and eschewing of slanders'.[9]

When the King was at Coventry Cathedral on St George's Day, John Morton, the new Archbishop of Canterbury, and many other bishops, all in their pontifical vestments, 'read and declared the Pope's bulls, touching the King's and Queen's right, and there in the choir, in the Bishop's seat, by the authority of the same bulls, cursed with book, bell and candle all those that did anything contrary to their right, and approving their titles good'.[10]

In a third bull of dispensation, issued on 23 July,[11] the Pope confirmed that, 'if it please God that the said Elizabeth (which God forbid) should decease without issue between our sovereign lord and her of their bodies born, then such issue as between [the King] and her whom after that God shall join him to shall be had and born inheritors to the same crown and realm of England'. In other words, Henry's title, and his children's right to the succession, did not depend on his marriage to Elizabeth, but was vested in him independently. It was through him, not his wife, that the crown would descend. Again, Elizabeth's title to the throne had been slighted, while this bull confirmed Henry's title and threatened anyone challenging it with excommunication.

That summer, after suppressing 'tumultuous sedition' in the north,[12] Henry returned south via Worcester, Hereford, Gloucester and Bristol, rejoining Elizabeth at Sheen.[13] By now she would have begun loosening the front laces of her bodice as her pregnancy began to show. There was no concept of antenatal care in those days, and a midwife would not have been engaged until near the time of the expected confinement. On 5 June the royal couple travelled by barge to Westminster for London's official welcome.[14]

André says that, 'while the Queen was close to delivery', Henry was administering affairs from Windsor. At the end of August, the King and Queen moved to Winchester,[15] the ancient capital of England, where Henry wanted his heir to be born, for he believed it to be the site of Camelot, King Arthur's fabled seat, and that being born there would be portentous for the prince who would bring a new golden age to England.

In Winchester Castle there was displayed a round table, said to be King Arthur's, but in fact dating from the mid-thirteenth century; it has been said that the Queen wished to give birth in the castle but that it proved inconvenient, so she moved instead to St Swithun's Priory, the ancient Benedictine monastery founded in A.D. 642–3, attached to Winchester Cathedral. However, the city of Winchester was by then depopulated and run-down, and the castle was in decline, the last major works having been undertaken in the fourteenth century,[16] so it is likely that the Queen had intended all along to be confined in the priory, where most of the buildings dated from the later Middle Ages.

Prior Thomas Hunton gave Elizabeth the use of the luxurious Prior's House, now the Deanery. It was originally built in the thirteenth century, from which time the triple-lancet-arched porch survives, but was largely reconstructed in the seventeenth century after becoming derelict. The Prior's House stood at the south-east corner of the Great Cloister, on the edge of Little Cloister. It had a vaulted ground floor, above which was the Prior's chapel. Adjoining the house was his great hall with its magnificent timber roof, erected in 1459–60. Here, Elizabeth established her small court, with her mother, her sisters and the Lady Margaret in attendance. 'The Prior's great hall was the Queen's chamber.'[17] While Elizabeth rested, the King took advantage of the good hunting to be had nearby in the New Forest, braving the torrential rains that swept the land as autumn approached.[18]

Records survive of the expenditure laid out by the King on items for Elizabeth in preparation for her confinement, 'both for her own use and also for the removal of the Queen to the city of Winchester, and afterwards for the taking of her chamber before the birth, and also towards the birth, as in divers robes and divers other ornaments pertaining to the said lady Queen': lengths of cloth of scarlet and of various other colours, white woollen cloth and cloth of frieze (a coarser woollen cloth); 33 timbers of whole ermines; 39 timbers of ermine backs; 2½ timbers of ermine bellies; one pane (piece) of ermine; 49 timbers and 15 bellies of pure miniver; 13½ timbers of 'lettuce' ('letoux') miniver, which was white or pale grey; powderings of bogy; 66½ yards of cloth of 'doubly set' velvet, probably having a two-pile warp; 42¾ yards of 'singly set velvet'; 1¼ yards and three separate 'nails' (yards) of cloth of gold; 23½ yards of damask; 5¾ yards of satin; 230 yards of sarcanet, to be furred with ermine and miniver; pieces of buckram, worsted and fustian (a thick woven cloth of wool, Egyptian cotton or linen); 440 ells of Holland linen cloth for napkins and kerchiefs; 119¾ ells of canaber cloth, a linen cloth for making hose; 4¼ ounces of silk; 2 pounds and 12 ounces of silk ribbon; one pound of gold-coloured silk ribbon; fringe of silk and Venice gold; thread; cord; down and wool. Among 'divers other things necessary for the said Queen' were a chair of state, two beds, fourteen pommels of cypress wood, gilded; gilt nails; rings of lacquered iron; skins of leather; iron hammers; two pounds of feathers; four fustian cushions; seventeen yards of waxed linen and two saddles covered with velvet.[19] As much importance was accorded to the maintenance of the Queen's royal estate during her confinement as to practical essentials.

Benjamin Digby, page of the Queen's bed, was paid 16s.8d. 'for preparing certain stuffs for the lady Queen against the nativity of the lord Prince', while Thomas Swan, his colleague, received 40s. 'for the making of divers bearing sheets [infant mantles] of Holland cloth'.[20]

There was no question of Elizabeth taking charge of her own confinement. Even though childbirth was an exclusively female preserve, even for queens, it was the King who regulated ceremonial in the royal household. On 31 December 1494, evidently inspired by Olivier de la Marche's *L'Etat de la Maison de Charles de Bourgogne*, commissioned by Edward IV in 1473 to facilitate the establishment of fashionable Burgundian protocols at his court, Henry drew up a series of ordinances governing the running of the royal household and laying down the ceremonial to be observed there. These included 'ordinances as to what preparation is to be made against the deliverances of the Queen, as also for the christening of the child when she shall be delivered'; and those ordinances were to be observed for many decades to come.[21] There is no evidence that they were drawn up by Margaret Beaufort, as is often stated, although it is likely that she was consulted. Elizabeth herself may also have contributed her views.

Little is known of royal birth conventions prior to the late fifteenth century, but Henry's ordinances were modelled on procedures laid down in Edward IV's 'Royal Book'[22] of court ceremonial, which had drawn on English, French and Burgundian court ritual: we know that certain formalities had evolved in regard to royal confinements, for in 1456, Isabella of Portugal, Duchess of Burgundy, had consulted a book about the estates of France before preparing chambers for the confinement of her daughter-in-law.[23]

Henry VII himself expanded on the dictates of the 'Royal Book', which may have been based on the court ceremonial of the Lancastrian kings. Even if Elizabeth's earlier confinements were not conducted according to the 1494 ordinances, she would have been subject to similar provisions laid down in the 'Royal Book' for her mother, with which she was no doubt familiar. These determined the colour and quality of the furnishings for her chamber and bed, which was to be made up with pillows of down and a scarlet counterpane bordered with ermine, velvet or cloth of gold.[24]

Henry VII's ordinances of 1494 reflected and formalised existing practice – it is stated in places that they were laid down 'after the old custom' – and doubtless they embellished it. They provided for 'the furniture of her Highness' chamber, and the furniture appertaining to her bed, how the church shall be arrayed against the christening, [and] how the child shall go to be christened'.[25]

The King decreed: 'As to the deliverance of a queen, it must be known what chamber she will be delivered in, by the Grace of God; and that chamber must be hanged with rich Arras [tapestry], the roof, side and windows, all except one window, and that must be hanged so she may have light when it pleaseth her.' The room was also to have 'a royal bed therein, the floor laid with carpets over and over with a fair pallet bed, with all the stuff belonging thereto, with a rich sperner [bed canopy] hanging over; and there must be a cupboard set fair, covered with the same suit that the chamber is hanged withal'. Over the doorway was to be hung a 'traverse [curtain] of damask'.[26]

The 'stuff for the Queen's bed' consisted of 'two pairs of sheets of Rennes, either of them of four breadths and five yards long; two long pillows and two square, of fustian stuffed with fine down; a pane of scarlet furred with ermines and bordered with velvet or cloth of gold; an head-sheet of like cloth furred in like wise; a counter[pane] of fine lawn of five breadths and six yards long; and hinder [bottom] sheet of the same lawn, four breadths and five yards long'.[27] The bedlinen would have been sweetly perfumed with flowers and herbs. The bed was made according to the King's regulations, which stipulated that the Queen's ladies and gentlewomen must perform the task to a set routine that involved drawing the bed-curtains back, stripping the mattress and shaking it, then laying each cover separately and straightly, and smoothing it down with care, leaving no wrinkles. They would also have tightened the ropes across the bedstead (the origin of the saying 'sleep tight'), then laid upon that a canvas cover before plumping the mattress in place. The curtains would have been drawn to conserve warmth, and the bed sprinkled with holy water.

The pallet bed was to be made up with 'a featherbed with a bolster of fine down; a mattress stuffed with wool; two long and four short pillows; a pane of fustian of six breadths and five yards long; two pair of sheets of Rennes of four breadths and five yards long; two head-sheets of Rennes of two breadths and four yards long; a pane of scarlet furred with ermines, bordered with blue velvet upon blue velvet or cloth of gold; an head-sheet of like colour, furred with ermines; a coverture of fine lawn of five breadths and six yards long, an head-sheet of the same lawn of four breadths and five yards long; a sperne[r] of crimson satin, embroidered with crowns of gold, the [King's and] Queen's arms and other devices, and lined with double tartaron [or tartaire, silk stuff, originally from Tartary] garnished with fringe of silk and gold and blue and russet, with a round bowl of silver and gilt'. Also to be provided were 'four cushions covered with crimson damask or cloth of gold' and 'a round mantle of crimson velvet, plain, furred with ermines, for the Queen to wear about her in her pallet, and all other things necessary for the same'.[28] Thus royally robed, she would give birth on the pallet bed, and then be lifted into the great bed for her lying-in period.

Near the pallet bed was to be placed an altar with relics, so that Elizabeth could hear Mass after being confessed and shriven before facing the dangers of childbirth, and pray for the protection of God and His Holy Mother during her coming labour. A court cupboard laden with gold plate for the service of her meals was also placed in the bedchamber.[29]

The Queen, by custom, withdrew from the world for the duration of her confinement: this was known as 'taking to her chamber'. Precise instructions were given by the King for the ceremonial to be followed, although he would not be present. 'And if it please the Queen to take to her chamber, she shall be brought thither with lords and ladies of estate, and brought into the chapel or church there to be houselled [given Holy Communion].' When Elizabeth took to her chamber in good time for the birth, her mother and Margaret Beaufort headed her attendants, and her elder sisters were probably among their number. Throughout her life, Elizabeth would surround herself with family members, especially her female relations, to whom she was evidently close.[30]

After Mass, attended by these ladies, her household and a throng of courtiers, she processed 'into the great chamber', seated herself on her chair of estate and took 'spice and wine under the cloth of estate'.[31] Her chamberlain, the Earl of Ormond, 'in a very good voice desired in the Queen's name all her people to pray God would send her a good hour', and Elizabeth formally bade farewell to the courtiers. 'Two of the greatest estates [led] her into her chamber where she shall be delivered, and then they [took] their leave of the Queen. Then all the ladies and gentlewomen [went] in with her' and she disappeared from public view.[32]

Childbirth being an exclusively female ritual, 'no man [was] to come into the chamber where she shall be delivered, save women'. All her male officers were temporarily stood down, for 'thenceforth, no manner of officer should come within the Queen's chamber but only ladies and gentlewomen, according to the old custom that women be made all manner of officers, as butlers, panters, sewers, carvers, cupbearers; and all manner of officers shall bring to them all manner of things to the great chamber door'. The only men who might be admitted during the weeks to come were the King and the Queen's chaplains.

It was at this point that the 'gossips' took up residence at court. They were the godparents, or sponsors, of 'such estates both spiritual and temporal as it shall like the King to assign to be gossips', and they were summoned 'to be near the place where the Queen shall be delivered', so that 'they may be ready to attend on the young Prince or Princess to the christening'.[33]

Childbirth was a hazardous event for women in Tudor times. There was a very real chance of either mother or baby dying, and because of the risks life expectancy for women was around thirty years. It has been estimated that one in forty women perished in childbed, and that the average first marriage lasted for five years because of that high mortality rate. There must have been countless other women who were injured or traumatised by childbirth, or left with chronic conditions as a result of it. Male physicians were not normally involved in childbirth, as their presence was thought to upset labouring women; it was the midwife who was in charge of the confinement, but midwives were usually of lowly status, poorly paid, and qualified only by reason of their experience.[34] The midwives who served queens in this period seem to have practised their calling professionally, and were probably more expert at it than most. It was common for female relations, friends and 'gossips' to be present at a birth, to encourage the labouring mother, so it was natural for Elizabeth's own mother, the Queen Dowager, to join her when she took to her chamber, because mothers often assisted at their daughters' confinements, many travelling long distances to do so.

Knowledge of the reproductive process was limited, but the practices employed by midwives could be surprisingly modern. Herbal baths were given to relax the expectant mother during the later months.[35] Documentary evidence suggests that women were encouraged to give birth in a sitting or squatting position. They were encouraged to do breathing exercises for labour, much as they are today, but there was no pain relief beyond opiates such as poppy seeds or infusions made of tansy, parsley, mint, cress, willow leaves and seeds, ivy, birthwort or the bark of the white poplar. Instead, women relied on the protection of female saints such as St Margaret of Antioch, to whom they would offer prayers of supplication. Westminster Abbey owned a precious relic, the girdle of the Virgin Mary, which was sometimes lent to queens and high-ranking women, so that they could tie it around themselves in labour, for it was believed to be of special efficacy at such times; and there were girdles of other saints with similar miraculous properties.[36] Sometimes a prayer on a long scroll of parchment would be wrapped around the mother as a 'birth girdle'.[37] Despite all these practices, many women would have suffered the unmitigated pain of natural labour.

The baby was supposed to arrive within twenty contractions. If it took longer, certain remedies might be essayed to open up the womb, such as opening doors and cupboards, untying knots or unlocking chests.[38] It is hardly surprising that childbirth was an ordeal in those days – and it was an ordeal that many women faced on a yearly basis; Elizabeth was to suffer it seven times.

'Afore one o'clock after midnight' on the morning of St Eustace's Day, 20 September 1486, as Margaret Beaufort's scribe noted in her Book of Hours,[39] 'the Queen was delivered of a fair prince',[40] to the great joy of the King and his subjects high and low. A manuscript drawing in the 'Beauchamp Pageant' of *c*.1483–7 shows the birth of Henry VI to Katherine of Valois, wife of Henry V, in 1421, but the costumes and interior are those of the 1480s and reflect the kind of arrangements in place at the time of Elizabeth's first confinement. The picture depicts the Queen, crowned (although she would not have been in reality), lying in a great bed, tended by four ladies, one of whom holds the swaddled infant, who is also crowned; another smooths the sheets; at the doorway, a third passes on the good news of the birth to a messenger waiting outside.[41]

Bacon states that Elizabeth's son 'was strong and able, though he was born in the eighth month, which the physicians do prejudge', while Fuller describes him as 'vital and vigorous, contrary to the rules of physicians'. To have been born at full term, he would have had to have been conceived between 29 December and 6 January, but his parents had not married until 18 January. It is possible that Henry and Elizabeth had pre-empted their nuptial vows; as we have seen, once a precontract had been made, it was acceptable for couples to consummate their union, after which society regarded them as legally wed. Elizabeth had been honoured as queen from December 1485, so maybe she and Henry began sleeping together at that time. Many couples of lesser rank did not bother with a formal marriage ceremony, but for royalty, of course, it was crucial for the avoidance of doubt over the succession. Even if the King and Queen had waited until after their wedding, their child might have been only about two to three weeks premature.

However, other evidence tends to corroborate the statement that he was born at eight months, and suggests that Bacon and Fuller were making flattering assumptions; the accounts of the bishops of Winchester for 1486–7[42] show that the Prince's nursery household was established for at least the first six months of his life at Farnham, Surrey, halfway between Winchester and London, because he was weak and needed careful nursing until he was strong enough to be moved to London and the palaces of the Thames Valley. William Wayneflete, the Bishop of Winchester, had died the previous month, but the man who was already designated his successor, the aristocratic Peter Courtenay, Bishop of Exeter, was in Winchester for the Prince's christening, and it was probably at his suggestion that the concerned parents decided to send their little son to Farnham. Courtenay, a loyal Yorkist, had been in the service of Edward IV, so may have been familiar to Elizabeth in her younger days. He had joined Buckingham's rebellion against Richard III, then fled to Brittany to join Henry Tudor, who later rewarded him handsomely, making him keeper of the Privy Seal. The King and Queen would have been grateful to entrust the well-being of their heir to such a loyal supporter.

In her hour of triumph, Elizabeth too was in a weak state. She may have caught an infection during parturition, as she is recorded as suffering an ague[43] – an acute fever – during her lying-in period. The importance of hygiene during childbirth was not fully under-stood until the nineteenth century, even in royal households, and unwashed hands and instruments not infrequently gave rise to fatal infections such as puerperal fever.[44] It was not until the sixteenth century that midwives were urged to wash their hands and remove rings before delivering a baby.

Although Henry and Elizabeth must have felt concern over the health of their child, it surely seemed to them that, in vouchsafing the blessing of a male heir, God had smiled upon the marriage that had united Lancaster and York. Henry named his son Arthur, 'in honour of the British race'[45] and after the hero-king of legend, in order to underline his much-vaunted (but mythical) descent from King Arthur and his dynasty's links with the ancient rulers of Britain; and because his infant heir had been born at Winchester, 'where

King Arthur kept his court'.[46] Above all, he chose the name because it epitomised a universally revered heroic and powerful ideal. 'Englishmen no more rejoiced over that name than other nations and foreign princes quaked, so much was the name terrible and formidable to all nations.'[47] It resonated with their burgeoning nationalism, with its promise that the Tudors were ushering in a new Arthurian age of greatness.

The tiny Prince Arthur, already styled Duke of Cornwall, was bathed, swaddled and laid in one of the two cradles that had been made for him, the one that had been 'fair set forth by painter's craft' in fine gold – 'the little cradle of tree' with buckles that could be attached to his swaddling bands. This was in everyday use. The other cradle, which stood in his outer chamber under a cloth-of-gold canopy, was only 'used on state occasion. Furnished with great magnificence', it was five feet six inches long and two feet six inches wide, and was 'graven with the King and Queen's arms' and made up with luxurious bedding of crimson cloth of gold, scarlet, ermine and blue velvet.[48]

Yeomen of the Queen's chamber were immediately dispatched with the 'comfortable and good tidings' of the birth to 'all the estates and cities of the realm', and the King gave orders for church bells to be rung throughout the land. *Te Deum* was sung in churches in thanksgiving, and in the streets people lit bonfires 'in praise and rejoicing' and 'every true Englishman' celebrated the joyful news.[49]

On a cold, wet Sunday, 24 September, four-day-old Arthur was borne to his christening in Winchester Cathedral. Because so many infants died young, it was customary to have them baptised soon after birth. By tradition, the King and Queen did not attend: Elizabeth, of course, was still lying in, and the King kept no 'day of estate' as a christening was seen as 'a deed of alms'.[50] It was the godparents – or sponsors – who had important parts to play, while the ceremonial was ordered by the King. It is a measure of Henry's gratitude to Elizabeth – and no doubt of his desire for a display of amity and unity – that her mother and other members of the Wydeville family were assigned prominent roles, while the high-profile presence of Elizabeth's Yorkist relations was a public acknowledgement of Arthur as the heir to both York and Lancaster, and proclaimed their endorsement of the legitimacy of the Tudor dynasty. It also showed that in return for their loyalty, Henry was ready to treat them with the honour their blood deserved.

The christening was held up because John de Vere, Earl of Oxford, one of the godfathers, had been delayed on his way from Lavenham, Suffolk, because of the stormy weather, which had turned the roads into quagmires. After waiting for him in vain for three hours, the King gave the order for the procession to form in Elizabeth's great chamber. 'My Lady Cecily, the Queen's eldest sister, bare the Prince, [who was] wrapped in a mantle of crimson cloth of gold furred with ermine and with a train' that Sir John Cheyney helped to support. Cecily was attended by her eleven-year-old sister Anne and supported by the Marquess of Dorset and the Earl of Lincoln. It was thought proper that the Prince's train should be borne by an earl, so Lincoln may have been assigned the honour. Two hundred unlit torches, carried by esquires and yeomen, were borne before the Prince as, attended by 'a great company of lords and ladies and divers gentlewomen', Cecily 'proceeded through the cloisters into the church, where Queen Elizabeth [Wydeville] was abiding the coming of the Prince'.[51]

Margaret Beaufort was strangely absent on this important occasion. Possibly she did not wish to be seen to be taking second place to the Prince's other grandmother, Elizabeth Wydeville, who outranked her, yet they had worked together for Henry Tudor's triumph and his marriage to Elizabeth of York, so possibly the Lady Margaret was merely unwell. The Queen Dowager stood godmother to the Prince, and Thomas Stanley, Earl of Derby, who gave a salt cellar, was one of the godfathers. Thomas FitzAlan, Lord Maltravers, stood in to present a coffer of gold on behalf of the Earl of Oxford, who arrived in time to sponsor Arthur at his confirmation. Lionel Wydeville, Bishop of Salisbury, also took part in the ceremony, and Margaret of Clarence was foremost among the ladies in attendance.

Henry VII's ordinances of 1494 specified the manner of the christening of a prince, and it is likely that they reflected the arrangements made for Arthur's baptism. The cathedral door was hung with cloth of gold, and the nave had been magnificently 'hanged with cloths of Arras and red sarsenet' and laid with carpets right to the altar, a sure sign of magnificence, for carpets were costly items that were more commonly placed on tables to preserve them; only the very wealthy put them on floors. In the Lady Chapel 'a solemn font of silver-gilt' costing £5.11s. (£2,700) was placed next to the ancient Norman font on 'a stage of steps with a rich canopy' of cloth of gold, the stage also being laid with carpets. The font was lined with cloth of Rennes, surmounted by 'a great gilt bowl' and 'set on a great height, that the people may watch the christening'. Beside it was 'a step like a block for the Bishop to stand on'.

To one side was a curtained area, behind which was 'a fire of coals', a chafer of water and silver basins. It was here, where he could be kept warm and clean, that the Prince was undressed completely. Then he was carried up the steps and given into the arms of John Alcock, Bishop of Worcester, who immersed him in the font and christened him. Anne of York came forward with a rich chrisom cloth, which she had worn pinned to her breast and draped over her arm on 'a kerchief of fine ermines', and as it was placed on the baby's anointed head the esquires and yeomen lit their torches.

With his little fingers held closed around a lighted taper, Arthur was 'borne in fair order to the High Altar' by his grandmother, as the choir sang *Veni Creator Spiritus* and *Te Deum*. The Queen Dowager laid him on the altar, 'after which the Earl of Oxford took the Prince in his right arm, and Peter Courtenay, Bishop of Exeter, confirmed him'. Afterwards he was taken back behind the curtain to be dressed, and wine and spices were served to the 'gossips', who presented many costly gifts to the child. Elizabeth Wydeville's was 'a rich cup of gold, covered, which was borne by Sir Davy Owen', the King's bastard uncle.

With the gifts being carried aloft in procession by the peers, 'the Prince returned and was borne home by my Lady Cecily, the minstrels playing on their instruments; and then was he borne to the King and the Queen'. Henry sat by Elizabeth's gorgeously hung bed of estate as they waited to receive their son; she was wearing a rich gown and mantle for the occasion. Given that she was still feverish, she must have made an effort to put on such a brave show. Cecily placed young Arthur in her arms, for, following ancient custom, his mother was the person who first called him by his Christian name; then he received 'the blessings of Almighty God, our Lady and Saint George, and of his father and mother'. The christening gifts were presented at the door to the Queen's chamber, after which the infant Prince was returned to his nursery.[52]

The King wanted everyone to share in his joy at having an heir, and to understand the importance of this day. 'In the church yard were set two pipes of wine, that every man might drink enough' to toast the Prince, and three days of celebrations followed the christening, as England rejoiced.[53] The birth of a royal heir who embodied the union of Lancaster and York and would aptly be hailed as 'the rosebush of England, rose in one', had greatly strengthened the King's position, and assured the succession; it was hailed as the beginning of a new golden age, and commemorated in ballads such as this one, 'The Peace of the Roses', by Thomas Phelypps:

> I love the rose both red and white;
> Is that your pure, perfect appetite?
> To hear talk of them is my delight.
> > Joyed may we be
> > Our Prince to see
> > And roses three![54]

Pietro Carmeliano composed a long laudatory poem in honour of the Prince's birth, hailing him as a new Arthur, the manuscript being decorated with red and white roses,[55] and the poet laureate, John Skelton, joined the chorus of celebration:

> The rose both red and white
> In one rose now doth grow.

Bernard André composed 'a poem of one hundred verses', which, thankfully, he omitted from his history because of its length. Yet he could not resist including its opening lines, which begin: 'Come celebrate the child's birth, O Muses, and the noble offspring born of illustrious royalty. To celebrate the festal day, wreath your hair with a comely flower, O English, and crown your brows with garlands. Let the pipe blow, let boys and young girls dance and stir the air with applause, and let happy London celebrate festive games. Behold, the royal child Arthur arises, the second hope of our kingdom.'

It was said that the birth of the new Arthur had been foretold by Merlin,[56] while the Welsh bard, Dafydd Lloyd, celebrated the arrival of this 'descendant' of the ancient Welsh princes in a verse in which he recommended him to the keeping of Dark-Age Welsh saints:

> Let St Mary and St Mwrog secure
> Our Prince and his cradle;
> Let the hand of Beuno and Ilar
> Preserve him from all ill,
> And the hand of Derfel, the great guide,
> And the hand of Christ.[57]

Newly delivered mothers were expected to lie in after the birth; there was no getting up and walking around soon afterwards, as now, and of course no understanding of the risks of blood clots and pulmonary embolisms, which may well have accounted for a number of fatalities in childbed. It was believed that the body needed time to cleanse itself during the period following labour. The lying-in period could be anything from fifteen to sixty days, and it ended with the mother's churching. The new mother might spend up to two weeks on her back before her 'upsitting'. As soon as she could sit up and was well enough to receive visitors, the Queen presided over a ceremony called the *relevailles*, at which she showed off her child to the courtiers whilst sitting up in bed, royally wrapped in her mantle of estate.[58] Afterwards she would remain in her bedchamber, but not necessarily in bed; and for the last few days of her confinement she was allowed to leave her chamber but not go outdoors.[59] Given that childbirth was such an ordeal, and could have painful physical repercussions such as a perineal tear or an obstetric trauma, many women must have needed this time to recuperate.

'After that the Queen was purified and whole of an ague that she had,'[60] she was churched. At the feast of Michaelmas (29 September), at the King's command, Richard Gullefer, merchant of London, supplied 'my lady the Queen' with 'ten yards of crimson velvet at 35s. [£850] the yard [and] six yards of damask russet at 9s. [£220] the yard', at a cost of £20.4s. [£10,000]'.[61] This was for her churching, the solemn purification and thanksgiving service that followed her lying-in period, cleansed her of sexual sin and afforded her the opportunity to offer thanks for her child and her survival. 'And when the Queen shall be purified, she must be richly beseen in tires[62] and rich laces about her neck, and linen cloth [must be laid] upon the bed of estate; and there shall be a duchess or a countess to take her down off ye bed and lead her to her chamber door', where two more duchesses waited to receive her. Then 'a duke shall lead her to the church', carrying a lighted taper, as the choir sang the *Nunc dimittis* and *Lumen ad relevacionem*, antiphons that were associated with the purification of the Virgin Mary.[63]

The ceremony of churching took place at the chapel door, where the bishop intoned, 'Enter the temple of God, adore the Son of the Holy Virgin Mary, who has given you the blessing of motherhood'[64] and sprinkled the Queen with holy water before leading her by the hand into the church, where the Mass of the Trinity was celebrated. The escorting duke, still carrying the lighted taper, would precede the Queen up to the high altar, where she made her offering of it, along with gold and the chrisom cloth used at her infant's baptism; then all her ladies and gentlemen offered too, according to their degrees. Once the ceremony was over, Elizabeth sat enthroned in her great chamber, under her canopy of estate, and had her largesse, or charity, cried. The King, by custom, was not present.[65]

Now Elizabeth was officially ready to resume normal everyday life – and sexual relations with her husband. Queens did not breast-feed their infants, so their periods resumed soon after giving birth, enabling them to conceive again. Whatever her joy in her baby, Elizabeth had already given him into the care of others who would suckle him and see to all his daily needs, leaving her free to fulfil her prime dynastic duty of bearing royal offspring, and to attend to her ceremonial functions and other duties. In the late fifteenth century, a good mother was one who loved her children and looked to their advancement; the term did not imply daily practical care or interaction with them. Royal mothers accepted it as inevitable, indeed normal, that their young would be reared and looked after by other people. Their chief concerns were to oversee and supervise their children's upbringing and education, and, later on, to ensure that they made good marriages.

The infant Prince already had his personal staff, and soon he would have his own establishment headed by a chamberlain. The King laid down the rules for the management of the royal nursery, which was to have a lady governor, a nursery nurse (the term wet-nurse had not yet come into use) and rockers, or chamberers; but it was the Queen who appointed the staff. Before June 1487 – and probably from the time of the Prince's birth – Elizabeth, Lady Darcy, who had been in charge of Edward V's nursery and obviously managed it well, was appointed to run Prince Arthur's as 'lady governor' or 'lady mistress', at a salary of £26 (£12,700) per annum. Under her was Katherine Gibbs, the Prince's nurse, Elizabeth Wood, a gentlewoman, and a staff of yeomen, grooms, sewers and panters. There were also three rockers – Amy Butler, Emmeline Hobbes and Alison Bwimble – whose duty it was to rock Arthur to sleep in his cradle and keep watch over him. Velvet liveries were supplied by the King to the female attendants in 1488.[66] All had sworn solemn oaths of service before the Lord Chamberlain.

Every precaution was taken, for in an age before antibiotics, infants were vulnerable to infection, and clearly Henry VII feared that other dangers might threaten 'the jewel of his household'. He gave orders that, once his son was weaned – which would not have been until he was two[67] – 'it must be seen that the nurse's meat and drink be essayed [for poison] during the time that she giveth suck to the child'; he also commanded that 'a physician do stand over her at every meal, which see what meat or drink she giveth the child'.[68]

The Prince's nursery was furnished with rich stuffs, crimson damask cushions and 'eight large carpets' on the floor, but his father also provided for practical items such as a great chafer (warming dish), a basin of latten (brass), and two large pewter basins for washing laundry.[69]

Elizabeth's ague persisted into the autumn. Her prolonged ill health after the birth of Prince Arthur may have been the reason why she did not conceive another child for nearly two and a half years. When she finally recovered, she gave a substantial offering to Winchester Cathedral in thanksgiving for her return to health and the safe delivery of her son. Prior Hunton and his successor, Prior Thomas Silkestede, used this gift for enlarging and revaulting the fourteenth-century Lady Chapel where Arthur had been christened, installing larger windows with beautiful stained glass, and commissioning a series of wall paintings depicting scenes from the life of the Virgin Mary. The work was completed around 1500, and Elizabeth's arms, surmounted by the legend *In Gloriam Dei,* may be seen there today, alongside those of her son, on decorative shields mounted on the wall. She herself is depicted in a Victorian stained-glass window in the same chapel.[70]

The court left Winchester in the third week of October, arriving on the 26th at Farnham, where Prince Arthur's household was now established, with 1,000 marks (£140,300) being allocated for its upkeep.[71] 'The town of Farnham, where the King's firstborn son, Arthur, is now being nursed',[72] had been in the hands of the bishops of Winchester since the ninth century; the castle dated from 1138 and overlooked the town from its high hill. The Prince's household was probably established in the adjacent bishop's palace, an equally ancient building with many later improvements. Peter Courtenay, the Bishop-elect, was probably in residence in the palace at this time. The constable of Farnham was Thomas FitzAlan, Lord Maltravers (soon to be Earl of Arundel), who was married to Elizabeth's aunt, Margaret Wydeville.

It was no doubt felt that the cleaner air of Farnham would do the premature infant some good, and it was certainly not felt necessary for his mother to be with him. Elizabeth had discharged her chief responsibility, that of appointing trustworthy attendants to care for him, and now she had duties to perform. She was back with Henry at Greenwich by 1 November, when the King held a great court to celebrate the feast of All Hallows, clad magnificently in cloth of gold, 'a very good sight, and right joyous and comfortable to behold'. On 18 November, no doubt grateful for the heir who had arrived so promptly, the King sent £100 (£48,900) to the Queen 'by the hands of the Lord Treasurer'.[73]

This disruption to the bonding process may have affected the relationship between mother and son. A substantial body of modern research has shown that mothers show limited maternal responsiveness towards premature babies when there has been a prolonged period of separation after birth.[74] We cannot say that that was the case with Elizabeth and Arthur – not enough is known, although there is evidence that she would have much more to do with her subsequent children – but it is a possibility. There is no evidence to suggest that Arthur experienced the learning difficulties that can affect premature children, but new research, based on a study of a million births,[75] shows that prematurity can have consequences right into adulthood, and that such children have an increased risk of dying in late childhood compared with babies delivered at full term; in late childhood, boys in particular have a seven-fold increased risk of dying. That may not impact greatly on today's low mortality rates, but it would have had serious implications 500 years ago. And while there is little evidence to support the theory that Arthur was always delicate, it is likely that he had a lifetime risk of poor health because he was premature and there would be concerns about his frailty before he reached his fourteenth birthday.

Arthur's nursery was to remain at Farnham for at least six months, and perhaps the first two years of his life, after which it was apparently relocated to, or near, Ashford, in Kent.[76]

10

'Damnable Conspiracies'

N ow that Elizabeth was the mother of a prince, plans were once again set in hand for her crowning. Late in 1486 Sir Robert Cotton was paid £40 (£19,500) 'for divers necessaries furnished by him towards the coronation of the lady Queen'.[1]

Elizabeth's Wydeville relatives were now held in high favour by the King. On 19 November Thomas Grey was confirmed as Marquess of Dorset and granted an annuity; Elizabeth's uncle, Sir Richard Wydeville, received a similar reward in January, and his brother Edward was made a Knight of the Garter.[2]

The court remained at Greenwich for Christmas, a time for religious observance, festivity and ceremony. Although Elizabeth Wydeville seems to have accompanied Elizabeth back to London from Winchester, she is not recorded at this Christmas court, although Margaret Beaufort was present with her husband, Derby.

On Christmas Day the King customarily went in procession to Mass, wearing his crown and his royal robes. Gifts were exchanged formally on New Year's Day in the King's bedchamber, but Elizabeth did not give hers to her husband in person. Instead, she sent a messenger with it. When the King came to his 'foot-sheet' (the bench at the end of his bed, over which the bedding would have been draped), the usher of his chamber door would say to him, 'Sire, here is a New Year's gift coming from the Queen.' The King would reply, 'Sir, let it come in.' Then his usher admitted the Queen's messenger with the gift, and was rewarded by the customary 10 marks (£1,600) by Henry; one can see why posts in royal service were much sought-after. 'The Queen, in like manner, sat at her foot-sheet' with her chamberlain and usher in attendance, 'and received the King's New Year gift within the gate of her bed railing. When this formal exchange of presents had taken place between the King and his consort, they received, seated in the same manner, the New Year's gifts of their nobles.' It is clear from Elizabeth's privy purse expenses that she gave rewards to those lords and servants who brought her New Year's gifts, and that those payments were carefully graded according to rank, but they were 'not as good as those of the King'.[3]

On New Year's Day the King and Queen always wore their crowns and their royal robes furred with ermine, and went in procession to chapel. Afterwards they presided over a great feast. Normally, after such a feast, they and their special guests would retire to a private chamber or banqueting house for what was known as 'the void' (as it took place when the table was voided), or banquet – the informal serving of sweet or spiced wine known as hippocras, spices, sugared fruits, marchpane or other comfits. But on Twelfth Night, the culmination of the Yuletide celebrations, they took the void in the hall. Then the Lord Steward and the Treasurer of the Household would enter with their staves of office, bearing gold wassail cups containing a kind of mulled fruit punch that was drunk to toast the festive season. The steward would cry, 'Wassail! Wassail! Wassail!' and the choristers of the King's Chapel, waiting at the side of the hall, would 'answer with a good song'.[4]

That Christmas season was perhaps overshadowed by a rumour that had surfaced in November, asserting that more would be heard of the Earl of Warwick before long. There had been other rumours too, that he had escaped, or been murdered in the Tower,[5] like his cousins the Princes; but he was still there and very much alive. These rumours presaged the first serious threat to Henry VII's security.

Again, Elizabeth's coronation had to be deferred, for in January the King received news that a pretender to his throne, one Lambert Simnel, had appeared in Ireland, claiming to be the Earl of Warwick and to have escaped from his prison in the Tower.

Then, as now, the identity of this pretender was something of a mystery; much of the contemporary evidence about him derives from English government sources, so there may have been some spin at play. His very name may have been made up: John Leland[6] gave it as Lambert, but elsewhere it appears as John,[7] while the surname, Simnel, is extremely rare. This suggests that the King and his ministers were much in the dark about the facts behind the conspiracy. Later it emerged that Lambert Simnel, who was about the same age as Warwick, was the bastard son of an organ-maker at the University of Oxford.[8] He was said to have been coached in his role by an ambitious priest, Richard Symonds, who had apparently had a dream that he would be tutor to a king, although it is more likely that he was acting on behalf of more powerful Yorkist interests.

Because the real Warwick was largely unknown, many were taken in by Simnel: the boy was well-spoken, handsome and gracious, and he talked accurately and convincingly of his past, as if he really were Warwick, and scathingly of the 'Welsh milksop' who had seized his crown.

It is highly likely that the driving force behind the Simnel plot was the Earl of Lincoln, the hope of those who wanted a Yorkist king on the throne; and that it was he who had secretly had Simnel groomed as a pretender to mask his own intention of seizing the crown. Once designated to succeed Richard III, Lincoln had seen his ambitions overthrown by the victory of Henry VII, and although he had offered Henry his allegiance, and been outwardly reconciled to the new régime, he had never enjoyed the same income and honours that had been his under King Richard. Probably his loyalty had always been in question, for apparently he had never come to terms with the loss of his hopes of a crown.

It is perhaps significant that the Simnel conspiracy originated in Oxford, not far from Lincoln's house at Ewelme – and that Simnel soon afterwards surfaced in Ireland, of which Lincoln had been Lord Lieutenant under Richard III. His appearance heralded the first serious crisis of Henry VII's reign.

That January Elizabeth visited Arthur at Farnham, and on 1 February, in response to a petition by the townsfolk, the King granted licence to Lord Maltravers 'to found a perpetual chantry' at Farnham 'for the good estate of the King, Elizabeth, Queen of England, Prince Arthur and the King's mother'. On 29 May, Henry would also grant Bishop Peter's nephew, Sir William Courtenay, licence to found a perpetual chantry in the parish church of St Clement at Powderham in Devon, 'to pray for the King, Queen Elizabeth, Arthur, Prince of Wales, the said William Courtenay and Cecily his wife'. In February 1487, licence was granted to Thomas, Abbot of Shrewsbury, 'to celebrate Mass at the altar of St Winifred for the good estate of the King [and] Elizabeth the Queen', and a grant was made to Henry,

Prior of St Mary's at Llanthony in Wales, so that he could perform a similar service.[9] It was common for royal and noble persons to make such provision for the health of their souls and those dear to them: thus did they lay up treasure in Heaven.

On 10 July 1486 Elizabeth Wydeville had taken a forty-year lease on Cheyneygates, the abbot's house at Westminster Abbey; after her previous sojourns there, while in sanctuary, it may have represented a refuge from a court where (in view of what was about to befall her) she may have felt increasingly unwelcome – and it was conveniently situated for worship at the Abbey and for visiting the Palace of Westminster. But she was not to enjoy it for long.

That same month, in negotiating a truce with Scotland, Henry VII had suggested that Elizabeth Wydeville might marry the widowed James III of Scotland, even though she was nearing fifty – to James's thirty-four – and highly unlikely to bear him children. Henry would have been relieved of the burden of providing for the Queen Dowager if she married abroad, but the plan was complicated by the fact that two of her daughters had been proposed as brides for the Scots King's eldest son, James, and his second son, Alexander Stewart, Earl of Ross, and there ensued some discussion about proposing one of her younger girls, Anne or Bridget, for the King instead. Negotiations dragged on until, abruptly, they were halted by James III's assassination in June 1488.[10]

By then, Elizabeth Wydeville was out of the running. Early in February 1487, at Sheen, she was deprived 'by the decree of the Council of all her possessions'.[11] The King took all her property into his hands, and on 20 February Parliament allocated her a pension of 400 marks ($£133.3s.6d.$, now worth £65,100), which was to be paid in instalments to 'our right dear and right well beloved Queen Elizabeth, late wife unto the noble Prince of famous memory, King Edward, and mother unto our dearest wife the Queen'.[12] This was 300 marks fewer than Richard III had assigned Elizabeth Wydeville in 1484.[13]

According to Vergil, the reason given for the confiscation of the Queen Dowager's property was that in 1484 she had imperilled Henry's cause because she had 'made her peace with King Richard, had voluntarily submitted herself and her daughters to the hands of King Richard, whereat there was much wondering, and had, by leaving sanctuary, broken her promise to those (mainly of the nobility) who had, at her own most urgent entreaty, forsaken their own English property and fled to Henry in Brittany, the latter having pledged himself to marry her elder daughter, Elizabeth. She was accordingly deprived of the income from her estates, so that she should offer an example to others to keep faith.' Hall adds: 'Through her double dealings it was likely to have followed that the marriage could not take place, nor might the noblemen who, at her request, took King Henry's part return without danger to their lives.' Undoubtedly that had been a savage blow to Henry Tudor's ambitions at the time. Yet it had been all of three years ago, and none of it was news to him: why wait until now to punish her for it? Far from appearing to harbour resentment, he had restored her to royal status and treated her honourably and well, giving her prominence above his own mother as the godmother of his firstborn son. It is also unlikely that he would have contemplated marrying her to the Scots King if he feared she had it in her to intrigue against him, for the Scots were notoriously unreliable allies. It sounds therefore as if this pretext was contrived.

Elizabeth Wydeville now retired, for 'divers considerations', to St Saviour's Abbey at Bermondsey, across the river from the Tower of London.[14] It has been suggested that she retreated there at her own request, possibly because of ill health, or because she did not wish to marry the Scots King, or because she was broken by the murders of three of her sons, although they had taken place nearly four years before – but subsequent events would suggest otherwise. It could not have been because she wanted to retire from the world to lead a life of piety, because Bermondsey was a house of monks, and her marriage to the Scots King was still being mooted nine months later. And if she had gone willingly, why had she taken a forty-year lease on Cheyneygates less than a year earlier?

Her retirement came at a time when the threat posed by Lambert Simnel and those who were using him to achieve the restoration of the House of York was becoming more acute. Although no contemporary commentator linked Elizabeth Wydeville to the Simnel conspiracy, the two other orders in council passed on that day at Sheen related to that threat: one offered pardon to all rebels who threw themselves on the King's mercy; the other was for the parading of the real Warwick at St Paul's. It has therefore been assumed by some commentators that the order in council banishing the Queen Dowager to Bermondsey was also connected to the Simnel plot – but that does not necessarily follow.

Francis Bacon, writing more than a century later, was the first to assert that Henry VII distrusted his mother-in-law and banished her to Bermondsey because she had been the prime mover behind that plot: 'It cannot be but that some great person that knew [Warwick] particularly and familiarly had a hand in the business. That which is most probable, out of precedent and subsequent acts, is that it was the Queen Dowager from whom this action had the principal source and motion. For certain it is she was a busy negotiating woman, and in her withdrawing chamber had the fortunate conspiracy for the King against King Richard III been hatched, which the King knew and remembered perhaps but too well.' As she had plotted on Henry's behalf, the theory went, so she might decide to plot against him, and apparently she had anticipated that her daughter would enjoy more influence as Queen – the kind of influence she herself had enjoyed in her day – but it had quickly become clear that Elizabeth was to be allowed no real power at all. Therefore the Queen Dowager 'was at this time extremely discontent with the King, thinking her daughter not advanced but depressed'.[15] Thanks to Bacon, there has been speculation ever since that Elizabeth Wydeville was involved in the Simnel conspiracy.

Why would Elizabeth Wydeville have plotted against Henry to the detriment and ruin of her own daughter and grandson? There is absolutely no evidence that she did. She had actively worked for Elizabeth's marriage to the King. If Elizabeth had little power as queen now, she would have even less if Henry were to be deposed and Lincoln became king. Even if the Queen Dowager really believed Simnel to be Warwick, which is highly unlikely, would she have lent her support to the son of Clarence – in whose ruin she and her party had probably been complicit – above the claim of her own grandson? And would she have collaborated with the ever-busy Bishop Stillington, who was suspected of supporting the rebels – the man who had been instrumental in the impugning of her marriage? The only scenario that makes sense of Bacon's assertions is that she believed at least one of her sons to be still alive, but there is no evidence to support this.

Henry VII might be forgiven for being over-cautious, or even slightly paranoid, at this time, and Bacon imagines him thinking that his mother-in-law was involved in the Simnel plot, and that 'none could hold the book so well to prompt and instruct this stage play as she could'. The fact that the King imprisoned her son Dorset in the Tower until the threat from Simnel and his supporters was dealt with appears to support this assumption, but her brother, Sir Edward Wydeville, was to fight for the King against Simnel's forces.[16] No contemporary source mentions Henry voicing the concerns described by Bacon more than a century later.

Yet he did have another, more pressing reason for banishing his mother-in-law. Two queens in one kingdom involved unnecessary expenditure. Throughout the fifteenth century the Queen consort's dower had been paid out of the revenues of the Duchy of Lancaster, but the income assigned by the King to Elizabeth Wydeville had proved a drain on resources that should have supported his wife.[17] Probably his only objective in sending his mother-in-law to Bermondsey was to seize her lands, which could then be used to dower his financially embarrassed Queen.

At Bermondsey, Elizabeth Wydeville was registered as a boarder, which entitled her to free board and lodging as a descendant of the founder. She was lodged in an old range of apartments formerly used by the earls of Gloucester, early benefactors of the monastery, whose line had died out in the fourteenth century; maybe these old rooms did not offer the most comfortable or elegant accommodation. The Benedictine abbey, originally a priory, had been founded in the eleventh century on the site of what had been successively a Saxon monastery and a royal manor recorded in Domesday Book. From the twelfth century onwards it had enjoyed the patronage of royalty, and in 1399 it had become an abbey. In 1437 Queen Katherine of Valois, widow of Henry V, had been sent to Bermondsey after her secret liaison with Owen Tudor (grandfather of Henry VII) was discovered, and died there in childbirth soon afterwards. The present Abbot, John Marlow, had been among the clergy who officiated at the obsequies of Edward IV.[18]

In the fifteenth century Bermondsey was a large and important religious house, but it was not an ideal retreat. It had often been poorly run and allowed to fall into neglect – its history is a long catalogue of debt and mismanagement – and it was located in a damp and unhealthy situation, so if Elizabeth Wydeville retired there solely on account of her failing health, as some writers have suggested, it was a strange choice. For Henry VII, though, it provided a solution to the problem of maintaining his mother-in-law, for a condition of the original royal grant of the land stipulated that the monks must always keep a residence for the use of the monarch. Thus Henry could send the Queen Dowager there at no cost to himself – and he could also provide the more easily for his Queen.

At Easter 1487 (which fell on 15 April) Elizabeth got her dower at last. Royal warrants were issued to officers of the Exchequer to pay 'all profits and issues of all lands, honours and castles lately belonging to Elizabeth, late wife of King Edward IV' to her daughter, 'the lady Queen'. At Coventry, on 1 May, the King confirmed that, 'whereas we have seized into our hands all honours, castles, manors, lordships, etc. by us late assigned unto Queen Elizabeth, late wife to Edward IV', he had formally assigned 'every of the said honours to our dearest wife the Queen'.[19] One of the properties that Henry confiscated from his mother-in-law was Sheen Palace, which he soon proceeded to repair and alter, building two large towers and adding a new lead roof. It was to become one of his and Elizabeth's favourite residences.

Bacon states that Elizabeth Wydeville was now so tainted with treason 'that it was almost thought dangerous to visit her, or even see her'; yet after her retirement she came to court occasionally and was visited by her daughters. The King made grants of money to her from time to time, and they exchanged gifts – in 1488 he rewarded her for sending him a tun of wine, and in 1490 he gave her 50 marks 'against the feast of Christmas'. He referred to her in letters as 'our dear mother, Queen Elizabeth' or 'our right dear and right well beloved Queen Elizabeth, mother of our dear wife the Queen'.[20] This all suggests cordiality and concern rather than antagonism. In November 1487 Henry again put the Queen Dowager forward as a bride for James III, which he is hardly likely to have done if he believed she had been plotting treason and saw her as a threat to him – or if she had retired to Bermondsey because of ill health or a desire to retreat from the world.

Elizabeth Wydeville's wishes for the disposition of her youngest daughter, Bridget, were honoured by the King. Possibly in 1490[21] – between 1486, when Bridget was considered as a potential bride for James III, and 1492, when she is recorded as coming from Dartford to Windsor – the child was sent to the Dominican priory at Dartford, Kent, to join the sisters of the Order of St Augustine, 'a house of close nuns'.[22] Dartford was the only Dominican nunnery in England, and the seventh-richest convent in the land at the time of the disso-lution of the monasteries in the 1530s. It was famous as a centre for prayer, spirituality and education, and had enjoyed royal patronage since its foundation by Edward III in 1349.

Bridget had been destined for the religious life from birth, so possibly she was sent to Dartford soon after her mother had retired to Bermondsey, when she was six. Initially, like other children of noble families, she would have lived in the priory as a boarder before entering the novitiate. The earliest date she could have taken her final vows was November 1493, for girls had to be thirteen to become professed Dominican nuns. Candidates had to be highly educated, and to that end Bridget would have been tutored well in the Priory's school and become familiar with the holy texts in its library. On entry to the Order, she donned the requisite white tunic and scapular and black mantle and veil, and resigned herself to a strict régime of prayer and contemplation. Nevertheless, she continued to correspond regularly with her sister the Queen. Elizabeth paid her a pension of 20 marks (£3,250) a year (less than she provided for her other sisters), and forwarded sums to the Abbess of Dartford 'towards the charges of my Lady Bridget'. In 1495, Cecily, Duchess of York, bequeathed to Bridget three books: the *Legenda Aurea*, a life of St Catherine of Siena and a life of St Hilda.[23]

Elizabeth has been criticised for acquiescing in her husband's treatment of her mother, but she was powerless, and Henry may have ignored any protests she made. As usual, she kept her opinions – and perhaps her objections – private. But even if she was relieved to be in possession of her dower at last, it must surely have troubled her that she had profited by her mother's misfortune.

Elizabeth Wydeville was not the only one to come under suspicion at this time. That same month of February saw Bishop Stillington summoned before the Council to answer charges regarding certain 'damnable conjurations and conspiracies'. Since receiving his pardon in 1485, the Bishop had been living in retirement at the University of Oxford. But Oxford was where the Simnel conspiracy had originated, and these charges may well have related to his suspected involvement. Stillington refused to obey the summons, and claimed the protection of the university. There he remained throughout March, and it was only after he received a royal safe conduct that he agreed to go to Windsor. Here he was interrogated in private. No charges were laid against him, yet he was kept under house arrest at Windsor, and remained more or less in custody for the four years that were left to him.

★

In the first week of February, at Sheen, the Council, having arrested the priest, Symonds, had decided that the threat posed by the pretender in Ireland was sufficiently serious to justify showing the real Warwick to the people.[24] A week after Elizabeth Wydeville retired to Bermondsey, the young Earl was paraded in a stately procession through London to St Paul's Cathedral to attend Mass. Afterwards, he was allowed to mingle freely and converse with the King's councillors and people he knew, including his cousin Lincoln, before being taken in procession to Sheen Palace, where he was received by another cousin, the Queen. Elizabeth would have known him well – they had both lived in the household at Sheriff Hutton less than two years before – so she must have been able to recognise him, as did others, although when the rebels in Ireland heard of the parading of Warwick, they accused Henry of trickery.

Elizabeth and several lords conversed with Warwick but they found the twelve-year-old unresponsive and backward. Vergil says he could not tell a goose from a capon, while Warwick's own nephew, Cardinal Reginald Pole, was to declare that his uncle was as innocent as a year-old child. Almost certainly Warwick was of limited intellectual capacity, but just by living he posed a threat to the King, and at the end of the day he was returned to his dismal existence in the Tower.

Soon afterwards, in March, Elizabeth – like many other people – was probably shocked to hear that the Earl of Lincoln had left court and fled to Flanders, where lived his aunt, Margaret of York, Duchess of Burgundy. Margaret violently disapproved of Henry VII because he had slain her brother, Richard III, and toppled the House of York from the throne, and she was to do everything in her power to undermine his title. She was 'not mindful of the marriage which finally united the two houses of York and Lancaster. She pursued Henry with insatiable hatred.'[25] 'She bare such a mortal hatred to the House of Lancaster, and personally to the King, as she was in no ways mollified by the conjunction of the houses in her niece's marriage, but rather hated her niece as the means of the King's ascent to the crown.'[26]

Possibly her resentment had its roots in the young Elizabeth displacing her as the eldest daughter of the royal House of York, and then becoming betrothed to the heir to France, Burgundy's enemy; her jealousy may also have been fuelled at the prospect of her niece outranking her as queen of France.[27] But after marrying 'this most iniquitous invader and tyrant', who had overthrown the Plantagenet dynasty, Elizabeth was forever damned in Margaret's eyes because she had turned traitor to her House. In 1493 Margaret told Isabella of Castile that her family had 'fallen from the summit'.[28] Henry VII thought Margaret a 'silly and shameless woman',[29] but she was dangerous too, and her meddling would prove a constant threat to him and Elizabeth. One exasperated English envoy was to express the fervent wish that 'the lady would once taste the joys which Almighty God doth serve up to her, in beholding her niece to reign in such honour and with so much royal issue, which she might be pleased to account as her own'.[30]

Lincoln's defection dealt a blow to the Queen, placing her in a difficult situation, because he was the first member of her family to come out in open rebellion against the King, and the first to challenge Henry's title. His treason set a precedent, paving the way for his brothers, Edmund and Richard de la Pole, and, much later, other surviving scions of the House of York, to plot against the Tudors, who inevitably became increasingly paranoid about the loyalty of anyone with Plantagenet blood in their veins, with the inevitable consequence that much of that blood would be spilt on the executioner's block.

At Lincoln's behest, Margaret of Burgundy was only too happy to acknowledge Simnel as the nephew she had barely seen (if at all), and to finance the hiring of German mercenary troops to back his claim. In May, with this force at his back, Lincoln sailed to Ireland to offer his sword to the pretender, take control of the situation and prepare for an invasion of England.

The House of York had long been popular in Ireland, and there was already much support there for the lad who was calling himself Warwick. Waterford alone had declared for Henry VII, on account of Elizabeth's claim to the throne. On Whitsunday, 24 May, Lincoln, the disaffected Gerald FitzGerald, Earl of Kildare, and other dissident Anglo-Irish lords had the pretender crowned as Edward VI in Christ Church Cathedral, Dublin. Soon afterwards, with hordes of half-naked, untrained Irishmen swelling its ranks, the rebel army sailed for England.

Elizabeth apparently feared the rebels as much as Henry did. The evidence for this occurs in the Papal Registers for June 1487, where it is stated that Pope Innocent VIII, who had 'lately inhibited all the inhabitants of the realm and subjects of king Henry to stir up fresh disturbances in the matter of the right of succession, etc., under pain of excommunication and the greater anathema', had learned that 'there is a doubt whether the said inhibition included the inhabitants of Ireland and other places subject to the said king, outside the realm of England, who do not obey the said monition, wherefore the King and Queen Elizabeth fear lest ecclesiastical persons of the said realm and dominions may stir up such new disturbances'. To allay their fears, the Pope declared 'that the secular inhabitants of Ireland and other places and dominions subject to the said King are included in the said monition, and extends it to all ecclesiastical persons in the said realm and in Ireland and other dominions of the said King, under pain of interdict'.[31]

In March 1487 Henry had left Elizabeth behind when he departed on a progress to East Anglia and Warwickshire. He was at Kenilworth when, on 5 May, he received news of the imminent invasion, and on the 13th he wrote to the Earl of Ormond, the Queen's chamberlain, commanding him – 'not failing hereof as ye purpose to do us pleasure' – to escort 'our dearest wife and lady mother' to his presence[32] at Kenilworth, a strongly built, centrally located fortress where Henry was setting up his headquarters, having chosen the castle for its stout defences.

When she received her husband's summons, Elizabeth was staying with Margaret Beaufort at Chertsey Abbey in Surrey.[33] Her first concern was for her child. Accompanied by Bishop Courtenay, she hastened to Farnham Castle to collect Prince Arthur, while emergency plans were made for her to take refuge with him at nearby Romsey Abbey, which was convenient for the coast should they need to be spirited across the sea to safety.[34] But that proved unnecessary, and Elizabeth and Arthur had joined the King at Kenilworth by 29 May.[35] This would not be the only time that the Queen would take one of her children under her protection when danger threatened.

In the fourteenth century Kenilworth had been transformed by John of Gaunt from a feudal stronghold into a luxurious palace with a vast and magnificent great hall. Elizabeth and her baby would have lodged in splendour in this mighty fortress, protected by its massive walls and the great lake, the Mere, which surrounded it on three sides. When news came that Lincoln's army had landed in Lancashire on 4 June, the King marched to Coventry and prepared to defend his kingdom, having ordered Bishop Courtenay to remain with the Queen and Prince Arthur at Kenilworth during his absence. By then, alarm and confusion were spreading throughout England.

Few rallied to the pretender and his supporters. 'Their snowball did not gather as it went,'[36] especially after the King again proclaimed that he would pardon any rebel who surrendered. On 16 June, in a hard-fought battle at Stoke, near Newark, Henry won a great victory, at a cost of at least 4,000 lives. Lincoln was killed and Lambert Simnel taken prisoner. The King was lenient towards him, setting him to menial work in his kitchens; later, Simnel rose to be 'trainer of the King's hawks',[37] and died in 1525.

The Battle of Stoke, which André called 'the second triumph of Henry VII', finally brought the Wars of the Roses to an end, and established the Tudor dynasty more firmly on the throne. But the legacy of those wars – the heirs of the overthrown House of York, whom the Tudors feared because they were too close in blood to the throne – and the memory of the 'treachery' of the 'perfidious Dark Earl',[38] as Henry called Lincoln, would haunt the King and his successors for another eight decades. Stoke taught Henry VII that the elimination of his Yorkist rivals could ensure the stability of his throne and the kingdom, but the implications for Elizabeth were, of course, horrible. Her position depended on her husband's security, yet it was her close kin whose lives were at stake in the years that followed, years that would see conspiracies, plots and rebellions all aimed at toppling Henry VII and restoring the House of York to the throne. Small wonder that, throughout Elizabeth's lifetime, Henry was 'possessed with many secret fears touching his own people', and 'had a settled disposition to depress all eminent persons of the House of York'.[39]

After the victory, Henry gave thanks in Lincoln Cathedral, then rode back to rejoin Elizabeth at Kenilworth in July. In August 1487 the King and Queen visited Oxburgh Hall in Norfolk, where they were entertained by its owner, Sir Edmund Bedingfield. The present King's and Queen's Rooms on the first floor at Oxburgh were those occupied by the royal couple at this time, and were named in honour of them.

Henry had a son to succeed him; he had triumphed over his enemies, and his throne seemed more secure than ever. It was time for a celebration.

11

'Bright Elizabeth'

Elizabeth had still not been crowned, even though her title to the throne had bolstered Henry's own, and she had borne him a son and heir. English queens had customarily been crowned soon after marriage or their husbands' accessions, and Elizabeth was the first uncrowned queen to bear an heir since the Norman Conquest of 1066. The delay was unprecedented, and it had not made Henry popular. 'The root of all was the discountenancing of the House of York, which the general body of the realm still affected. This did alienate the hearts of the subjects from him daily more and more, especially when they saw that after his marriage, and after a son born, the King did nevertheless not so much as proceed to the coronation of the Queen, not vouchsafing her the honour of a matrimonial crown.'[1] Even Simnel's rebels had complained about the delay.[2] But in September 1487, twenty months after his marriage, Henry 'began to find where his shoe did wring him' and, 'being now too wise to disdain perils any longer, and willing to give some contentment in that kind (at least in ceremony), resolved at last to proceed to the coronation of his Queen'.[3]

'It was an act against his stomach, and put upon him by necessity and reason of state',[4] yet he rose magnificently to the occasion, appointing his uncle, Jasper Tudor, Duke of Bedford, to act as Lord High Steward at the coronation, Lord Stanley as High Constable, and the Earl of Oxford as Lord Chamberlain. At Michaelmas 1487 Richard Guildford was put in charge of 'the jousts for the coronation of the lady Queen', and paid 100 marks (£15,500).[5] In September summonses were sent out commanding the nobility to attend the ceremony. Following Henry's consecration, his wedding to Elizabeth and the christening of Prince Arthur, the Queen's coronation was to be an even more spectacular means of proclaiming the legitimacy of the Tudor dynasty to the world. It was also an expression of the high regard in which he now held Elizabeth.

It does seem that Henry was at last coming to appreciate the benefits of his marriage. At this time he sent an envoy to the Pope, 'signifying unto him that, like another Aeneas, he had passed through the floods of his former troubles and travails and was arrived unto a safe haven', by which he meant his marriage to Elizabeth. His ambassador, 'making his oration to the Pope in the presence of the cardinals, did so magnify the King and Queen as was enough to glut the hearers'.[6]

Henry and Elizabeth left Warwick for London on 27 October, celebrating the feast of All Hallows in St Albans a few days later. They lodged at Barnet that night, then she returned ahead of him to the capital, in readiness for her great day.

But for now the glory was to be the King's alone. On 3 November, richly clothed, the Queen 'went secretly' to the hospital of St Mary Spital in Bishopsgate, where she sat in a window with the Lady Margaret and other great lords and ladies 'to behold the fair and goodly sight' of her husband, the victor of Stoke, making his jubilant entry into a capital city 'hugely replenished with people'. Henry, 'a comely and royal prince, apparelled accordingly', was given a rousing welcome by citizens 'that made great joy and exaltation to behold his most royal person after his late triumph and victory against his enemies'. They cheered as he was escorted by Sir William Horne, the Lord Mayor, to St Paul's, where *Te Deum* was sung in honour of his triumph.[7] Elizabeth and Margaret did not attend the service; they travelled down 'to their beds' at Greenwich, where the King joined them two days later.

On 7 November the Court of Common Council of the City of London voted a gift of 1,000 marks for the Queen in honour of her coronation.[8] Three days later a royal commission was issued to the stalwarts of Henry's régime: Jasper Tudor, Duke of Bedford; John de Vere, Earl of Oxford; Thomas Stanley, Earl of Derby; William de Berkeley, Earl of Nottingham, and three others. Stanley, as High Constable, was in overall charge of the arrangements for the ceremony.

Elizabeth's coronation far surpassed her husband's in splendour, and followed time-honoured rituals: a sojourn at the Tower of London, a state entry into London, and the crowning itself in Westminster Abbey. It was timed to coincide with the feast day of the hugely popular virgin martyr, St Katherine of Alexandria, patron saint of royal ladies, who exemplified all the virtues most admired in women and was also a queen by birth.[9]

On Friday, 23 November, a 'royally apparelled' Elizabeth left Greenwich with Margaret Beaufort, attended by a great train of lords and ladies, and boarded the magnificently decorated royal barge that was to convey her to the Tower. The Londoners, as ever, were ready to put on a good show, especially to welcome this popular Queen. The City's streets had been cleaned for the official welcome celebrations; there was a great water pageant, the first recorded at the coronation of a queen; it launched a new tradition of river spectacles, which would become customary in later centuries.

'The Mayor, sheriffs, aldermen and many out of every craft [guild] attended [the Queen] in a flotilla of boats freshly furnished with banners and streamers of silk richly beseen with the arms and badges of their crafts' and rowed by liveried oarsmen. Alongside Elizabeth's boat glided the barge of the bachelors of Lincoln's Inn, 'garnished and apparelled, [sur]passing all other' and containing a model of 'a great red dragon' – the red dragon of Cadwaladr – that 'spouted flames of fire into the Thames'. The symbolism was apt, as Elizabeth, like Henry VII, claimed descent from Cadwaladr. Manned by the handsomest legal graduates, the barge kept pace side by side with the Queen's, entertaining her with sweet music and attracting the excited admiration of the many spectators thronging the riverbanks.

In the barges that followed there were 'many other gentlemanly pageants, well and curiously devised to do her Highness sport and pleasure withal', and she was 'accompanied with the music of trumpets, clarions and other minstrelsy'. When she landed at Tower Wharf, 'the King's Highness welcomed her in such manner and form as was to all the estates, being present, a very goodly sight, and right joyous and comfortable to behold'. Then he led her across the Cradle Tower drawbridge, and so to the old royal apartments in the Lanthorn Tower, where they kept 'open household and frank resort' for all the court. That night, Henry created fourteen new Knights of the Bath, as was customary at coronations, and Elizabeth joined him for a reception in their honour.

After dinner the next day, 24 November, the Queen made her state entry into London. Dressed by her sisters, she was 'royally apparelled, having about her a kirtle of white cloth of gold of damask, and a mantle of the same suit furred with ermine, fastened before her breast with a great lace curiously wrought of gold and silk and rich knots of gold at the end, tasselled. Her fair yellow hair [was] hanging down plain behind her back, with a caul of pipes over it.' This was a coif cross-barred with a network of gold cords, a fashion popular in France and Italy. 'She had a circlet of gold, richly garnished with precious stones upon her head,' resting atop the coif. White symbolised virginity, or in Elizabeth's case chastity and purity, as did loose hair.[10]

Emerging in great state from the Tower, with Cecily of York carrying her train, Elizabeth climbed into an open litter richly hung with white cloth-of-gold damask, and upholstered with matching cushions of down. Eight white horses were harnessed to the litter, and above it was a canopy on gilt staves borne by four of the new Knights of the Bath. Preceded by Bedford and four baronesses riding grey palfreys, and followed by her master of horse, Sir Robert Cotton, leading her horse of estate, Elizabeth was borne into the City, where huge crowds had gathered to see her and watch her progress through the streets. In a chariot behind rode Cecily with Katherine Wydeville, Duchess of Bedford, and following them came another chariot carrying Elizabeth's aunt, Elizabeth, Duchess of Suffolk, and another bearing Margaret Chedworth, Dowager Duchess of Norfolk (widow of John Howard), with six baronesses on palfreys trotting behind. Also in attendance were Lord Stanley and the other new Knights of the Bath. The Queen's squires trotted along on palfreys 'harnessed with cloth of gold' emblazoned with the white roses and suns of York, 'richly embroidered'. It was a magnificent procession, calculated to impress the crowds, enhance the reputation of the Tudor dynasty and proclaim the universal approval of the Queen.

London was *en fête*. The streets were hung with tapestries, and velvet and cloth-of-gold hangings streamed from the windows in Cheapside. Along the processional route children dressed as angels, saints and virgins sang 'sweet songs as her Grace passed by' on her way to the Palace of Westminster.

On 25 November, St Katherine's Day, Elizabeth went to her coronation, sumptuously attired in a kirtle, gown and mantle of purple velvet, furred with ermine bands, and the same circlet of gold garnished with pearls and precious stones that she had worn the day before. This circlet was probably a gift from Henry; from the late fourteenth century at least, it had been customary for the crown worn by a queen in her coronation procession to be given to her by the King.[11]

With Cecily again bearing her train, Elizabeth entered Westminster Hall with her attendants, and took up her position beneath a purple silk canopy of estate supported by silver lances held by the barons of the Cinque Ports. Here she waited for the procession to form. She was attended by her aunt, the Duchess of Suffolk, her fourteen-year-old cousin, Margaret of Clarence, now the wife of Sir Richard Pole, and Margaret Beaufort.

As Elizabeth passed on her way to the Abbey on a 'new bay-cloth' (baize) striped runner, the people surged forward behind her, each one eager to snip off a piece of the stuff on which she had trodden, such valued souvenirs were traditionally their perquisite. But the crowd was too boisterous: 'there was so much people inordinately pressing to cut the bay-cloth that certain persons in the press were slain, and the order of the ladies following the Queen was broken and distroubled'. This tragic incident cannot but have blighted the day for Elizabeth, who must have been painfully aware of the tragedy being enacted in her wake.

In the calm of the Abbey, Cecily was once more train-bearer as Elizabeth walked along the nave, supported on either side by the bishops of Ely and Winchester; going before her were her uncle, John de la Pole, Duke of Suffolk, carrying a gilt sceptre topped with the *fleur-de-lis*,[12] as he had done at her mother's coronation; William FitzAlan, Earl of Arundel, who bore the rod with the dove; and – in his robes of estate – Jasper Tudor, Duke of Bedford, who had the honour of bearing the consort's crown. Also in the procession was the Earl of Oxford, as Lord Great Chamberlain, wearing 'his Parliament robes'. After the Queen and Cecily 'followed the Duchess of Bedford and another duchess and countess, apparelled in mantles and surcoats of scarlet, furred and powdered, the duchesses having on their heads coronets of gold richly garnished with pearl and precious stones, and the Countess on her head circlets of gold in like wise garnished, as doth appear in the book of pictures thereof made' – which, sadly, does not survive.

There was no tradition that prevented kings from attending the coronations of their consorts, but Henry VII allowed his wife to enjoy her hour of glory alone. He watched the whole ceremony with Margaret Beaufort and 'Lady Margaret Pole, daughter to the Duke of Clarence',[13] from behind a 'well-latticed' screen covered with cloth of Arras, which stood on a 'goodly stage' specially erected between the altar and the pulpit. Elizabeth Wydeville was not present to see her daughter's triumph (although, as her biographer Arlene Okerlund imagines, she perhaps saw the river pageant from Bermondsey), nor were Elizabeth's younger sisters; but her half-brother Dorset was there, having been allowed out of the Tower for the occasion. The Abbey was packed with the nobility of England, as well as fifteen bishops and seventeen abbots, demonstrating how beloved a queen Elizabeth was, and how eager people were to see her crowned, as was her right, and to endorse the joining of York and Lancaster.

John Morton, the Archbishop of Canterbury, was waiting to receive the Queen, and prayed over her as she prostrated herself on the carpet before the high altar. She knelt to be anointed with holy oil on the forehead and breast, unlacing her gown for the purpose. Then her coronation ring, symbolising her faithfulness, was blessed, after which she received the sceptre and rod, and was 'with great solemnity crowned'. The ritual followed was that laid out for the crowning of a queen consort in Westminster Abbey's *Liber Regalis*, a late-four-teenth-century illuminated manuscript containing the Latin orders of royal services, including coronations, which was in use from 1399 to 1559. The prayers dated back to the twelfth century, exhorting the Queen to virtuous conduct, so that, like the five wise virgins, she would be worthy of the Celestial Bridegroom – or rather, the King's bed.[14]

It is not known for certain which crown was blessed and placed on Elizabeth's head. 'A crown and two rods for a queen' are first recorded in an inventory of 'precious relics' taken in 1450, but they were probably older than that. 'Queen Edith's crown' is listed in a Commonwealth inventory of 1649.[15] In 1045 Edith of Wessex had married the Saxon King, Edward the Confessor, whose crown was used at the coronation of every monarch, but the crown that bore her name was probably not Saxon in origin. It was apparently the consort's crown added to the regalia in the late fourteenth century, and was recorded in 1649 as being 'of silver gilt enriched with garnets, foul pearl, sapphires and other stones', and valued at £16

(£1,200). It is tempting to conclude that Queen Edith's crown was regarded as being invested with a similar sanctity to her husband's, but there seems to have been no tradition of crowning queens with a hereditary crown.

In a panel painting known as the St George altarpiece, which dates from *c.*1503–9 and is now in the Royal Collection (see Appendix 1), Elizabeth is shown wearing a very ornate imperial crown – a 'closed' crown featuring gold arches. This type of crown – as opposed to a traditional open circlet with crosses and *fleurs-de-lis* – was first worn in England by Henry V (reigned 1413–22). Similar crowns appear in drawings of Richard III and Anne Neville in the Rous Roll, and in various images of Richard III and Edward IV. A drawing of the wedding of Henry V and Katherine of Valois, in the Beauchamp Pageant, dating from *c.*1485, shows them both wearing imperial crowns. The earliest image of an English queen wearing an imperial crown is a medal of Margaret of Anjou, dating from 1463. Henry VII also wears one in the St George altarpiece, but it differs from Elizabeth's so it is unlikely that they were made at the same time; possibly Elizabeth was wearing the one made for Margaret of Anjou, which was probably also worn by Anne Neville and perhaps Elizabeth Wydeville. The King and Queen wear their imperial crowns in an illumination in the 'Ordinances of the Confraternity of the Immaculate Conception' of 1503 (see Appendix 1), and these crowns are probably the same ones that appear in the St George altarpiece. By the fifteenth century, it had become customary for a queen to wear her crown on the anniversary of her coronation, so it is possible that the crown worn by Elizabeth in the painting is the one that had become associated with her, which she had worn for her crowning. As one of the crown jewels, it was normally entrusted to the care of the Master of the Jewel House in the Tower of London.

None of Elizabeth's crowns survive. The ancient crown jewels, as symbols of monarchy, were 'totally broken and defaced' in the seventeenth century under Oliver Cromwell because they symbolised 'the destestable rule of kings'. Detailed inventories were made of what was destroyed, but Elizabeth's imperial crown does not appear to be listed. Almost certainly it was used by at least one later queen. A woodcut showing the coronation of Henry VIII shows Katherine of Aragon being crowned with a very similar crown, probably the one used by her mother-in-law. Like Elizabeth, she wears hers on top of her long-lappeted gable hood in a stained-glass window in St

Margaret's Church, Westminster. This is not the crown that appears in Elizabeth I's coronation portrait (or in any of her numerous portraits), so by 1559 it had probably gone out of fashion; Elizabeth's granddaughter's crowns have wider arches. The likelihood is that her own crown had already been melted down and perhaps remodelled.

While Mass was said, Elizabeth remained seated on the ancient coronation chair, then the Pax was brought to her. She kissed it, and went to the altar, where she prostrated herself again to make her confession. After this, she was given communion, then enthroned once more. The ceremony culminated with the Queen being escorted to St Edward's shrine, where she laid her crown on the altar dedicated to him.

A manuscript drawing of the coronation of Joan of Navarre, wife of Henry IV, in 1403,[16] but dating from *c.*1485–90, might more accurately portray the crowning of Elizabeth of York. It shows a queen seated on a throne on a raised platform beneath a canopy of estate bearing the royal arms, with two bishops placing the crown on her head, and lords and ladies standing at the foot of the steps. The Queen wears traditional ceremonial dress of a style dating back to the fourteenth century: a sideless surcoat with a kirtle beneath, and a mantle fastened across the upper chest with cords and tassels. Her hair, by custom, is loose.

It has been suggested[17] that Thomas Ashwell's anthem may have been sung at Elizabeth's coronation, given the repeated emphasis on her name:

> God save King Henry, whereso'er he be,
> And for Queen Elizabeth now pray we,
> And for all her noble progeny.
> God save the Church of Christ from any folly;
> And for Queen Elizabeth now pray we.[18]

The ceremony over, the procession then re-formed and Elizabeth returned to the Palace of Westminster. While she washed and refreshed herself in preparation for her coronation banquet in Westminster Hall, Bedford acted as the Queen's Champion. Riding a horse trapped with red roses and dragons, he led other mounted lords around the Hall, ensuring that the hordes of spectators were kept well back. Then the Queen and her train entered and the banquet commenced. Again the King and his mother played no part, watching from another latticed closet hung with cloth of Arras, set up on 'a goodly stage' in a window embrasure to the left of the high table, 'that they might privily, at their pleasure, see that noble feast and service'.

Elizabeth, wearing her crown, sat alone at the high table at the top of a flight of steps. 'The Lady Katherine Grey and Mistress Ditton went under [in front of] the table and sat at the Queen's feet; and the countesses of Oxford and Rivers kneeled on either side, and certain times held a kerchief before her Grace.' Archbishop Morton, seated nearest the Queen on her right, was guest of honour. When all were in place, the trumpeters and minstrels standing on a stage at the further end of the hall 'began to blow', and knights entered the hall in procession, carrying a vast array of dishes up to the high table, where the Queen would make her choices before they were offered to others. The first dish was a subtlety, an elaborate sugar sculpture, often with dynastic or political symbolism.

John Ratcliffe, Lord Fitzwalter, the Queen's 'sewer or dapifer, came before her in his surcoat with tabard sleeves, his hood about his neck and a towel over all, and sewed [essayed, or tasted] all the messes' (portions of food sufficient for four people). The royal cooks had excelled themselves: twenty-four dishes were offered to the Queen at the first course: 'shields of brawn in armour'; frumenty (wheat porridge) with venison; a rich 'bruet', or brewet (broth with meat); minced venison with spices and dried fruits; 'pheasant royal'; 'swan with chawdron' (spiced entrails); capons of high grease; 'lampreys in galantine' (eels in a seasoned bread sauce spiced with ginger); crane with cretonne (a thick meat soup with almonds and eggs); pike in Latimer sauce; 'heron with his sique', or sake, another word for sauce; carp 'in foil' (leaves); kid; perch in jelly; 'coneys of high grease'; 'mutton royal richly garnished'; 'Valence baked' (raisins or almonds); 'custard royal'; 'tart poleyn' – probably baked in the shape of the piece of armour that protected the kneecap; 'leyse damask' (lees – residual yeast from ale or wine – in rosewater); ruby-red fruit 'Sinopia'; 'fruit *formage*' – *formage* being old French for cheese; and another subtlety, which is not described.

The tables were then cleared for the second course, which was heralded by another fanfare of trumpets and the parading of a third subtlety, this time served with hippocras (spiced wine). A further twenty-seven dishes were offered: mawmenny (rich beef or chicken broth) garnished with lozenges of gold leaf; roast peacock in hackle, i.e. re-dressed in its plumage; bitterns; pheasants; 'browes' (broth or gravy); 'egrets in beorwetye' (possibly a beer sauce); cocks; partridge; sturgeon with fresh fennel; plovers; suckling rabbit; 'seal in fenyn [leeks] entirely served richly'; red shanks; snipe; quails; 'larks engrailed' (presumably in a pie with an indented crust); crayfish; 'venison in paste royal' (pastry); baked quinces; marchpane royal; cold baked meats; 'lethe of Cyprus' and 'lethe ruby' (milk puddings); fritters; 'castles of jelly in temple-wise made', and a last subtlety.[19] During the meal the King's minstrels 'played a song before the Queen'.

After the feast Elizabeth thrice distributed largesse, as was customary at coronations, and Garter King of Arms, 'with other kings of arms, heralds and pursuivants, did their obeisance, and in the name of all the officers, gave the Queen thanks, saying, "Right high, mighty, most noble and excellent Princess, most Christian Queen, and all our most dread sovereign and liege lady, we, the officers of arms and servants to all nobles, beseech Almighty God to thank you for the great and abundant largesse which your Grace has given us in honour of your most honourable and righteous coronation, and to send your Grace to live in honour and virtue."' And he cried her largesse 'in five places of the hall'.

'Then played the Queen's minstrels, and after them the minstrels of other estates.' A bowl and towel were presented so that the Queen could wash her hands, whereupon the trumpets sounded, 'fruit and wafers' were served to her, and the Lord Mayor, Sir William Horne, came forward and offered her the traditional golden goblet of hippocras – wine infused with costly spices – in return for which she gave him a covered gold cup in fee. 'And after the feast the Queen departed with God's blessing and the rejoicing of many a true Englishman's heart.'

Verses were composed in her honour, such as this one, 'Prophecy for the Crowned Queen', probably written by Bernard André:

> Descend, Calliope, from your sacred ridge, descend, bearing
>   the quill of clean-shaven Apollo, and come with your
>   Pythian lyre, first of the Muses.
> The Queen, progeny of highest Jove, whiter than the roses
>   of spring, bears her crown as Diana leaps brightly from
>   the midst of rose gardens.

Sprung from the noblest gods of heaven, you were joined
by divine majesty to so great a prince, who excels all
the earth with becoming virtues.

O nymph, who gave wondrous birth to such a prince, and
who surpasses the divinities in virtue, you are blessed
more than the mother of Phoebus, begotten of a great
father.

Her chastity, sworn by united compact, restored increased
limits of justice for all ages in which the peaceful Sibyl
reigns in love.

O Commonwealth, the Queen with joyous heart takes up
her glorious crown.

Rejoice for both roses, and ever celebrate them with
honour.

With 'divine inspiration', André 'foretold the success of the happy
Prince', Arthur, while lauding his 'distinguished mother'. Calliope,
the goddess muse of epic poetry, was the inspirer of this panegyric,
along with Apollo, or Phoebus, the god of music and prophecy, light
and the sun. Diana was a huntress but, more importantly here, the
virgin goddess of women and childbirth. The Sibyl had the gift of
prophecy. The theme of the roses predominates.

On the morning after the coronation, the King and Queen, the
Lady Margaret and the princesses heard Mass in St Stephen's Chapel,
'nobly accompanied' by eighty peeresses, ladies and gentlewomen.
Then Elizabeth went in procession to the Parliament chamber, where
'she kept her estate' to receive guests, sitting on her throne under a
canopy of estate, with the Lady Margaret seated firmly at her right
hand, and her aunt, the Duchess of Bedford, and Cecily of York on
her left. They sat together thus at the banquet that followed, with
the Archbishop of Canterbury and many duchesses and baronesses
also at table. After dinner Elizabeth presided over the celebrations at
court, during which she and her ladies danced. On that day, 26
November, Elizabeth was finally assigned her dower as queen of
England. The next day she was conveyed by barge to Greenwich
Palace.

12

'Elysabeth ye Quene'

As queen, Elizabeth had her own household and administrative officers. They were an extension of the King's court, and very much a part of it, although they operated separately, enabling her to fulfil her duties in her husband's absence. Her household and estates were her legitimate sphere of influence,[1] and it was through them that she could exercise patronage, but no queen could function without an army of officers and servants to support her, headed by her councillors and her chamberlain; and all were answerable ultimately to the King.[2] They organised all her 'matters and businesses' for her, from managing her estates and maintaining standards in her household to buying clothing, providing entertainment and arranging pilgrimages and visits to her children. They were appointed by the Queen herself, or by the King or members of his Council.

The Queen had her own council to govern her affairs, which comprised her chief administrative officers – her chamberlain, chancellor, receiver-general (who collected her rents and revenues), secretary, attorney-general, sergeants-at-law, knights carver, the clerk to her council, and several noblemen. It probably met in the chamber in Westminster Palace that had been used since 1404 by the councils of previous queens. The function of the Queen's council was to give her advice, oversee the administration of her lands, deal with her legal business and act as a court of appeal.[3] These were areas in which she and her council enjoyed some autonomy and took their own internal decisions without reference to the King. The business they transacted would be administered by clerks and other officials. Elizabeth's chancellor, Edward Chaderton, had been Treasurer of the

Chamber to Richard III. Richard Eliot was her attorney, Richard Bedell her auditor, John Holland keeper of the council chamber, and John Mordant her sergeant-at-law.[4]

Sir Thomas Lovell, who had led the Commons when they petitioned the King to marry, was the first treasurer of the Queen's chamber, and treasurer of the King's Chamber and household. It was not uncommon for a man to serve both the King and the Queen in similar capacities. The Queen's treasurer, unlike her council, was accountable to the Exchequer.[5]

John Yotton was the Queen's secretary. Richard Deacons was her clerk of the signet, cofferer, accountant and surveyor of her lands. In 1503, his salary was £10 (£4,860). In addition, 'for his costs lying in London about the Queen's matters and business' and riding out to survey the Queen's lands, he received £16.13s.4d. (£8,100). Paper, ink and sealing wax was provided for him at an annual cost of £3.6s.8d. (£1,620).[6]

Elizabeth's most important personal servant was her chamberlain, to which office the King's friend, the wealthy Thomas Butler, Earl of Ormond, was appointed 'with the Queen's good grace'.[7] His task was to rule her privy chamber, and by August 1486 he had been rewarded for his 'good and acceptable service to the King and his consort, to their singular pleasure'.[8] His chief duty was to look to his mistress's welfare and comfort. He appointed and supervised her staff, ensured that due ceremonial was observed in her household and whenever she appeared in public, and made sure that she was properly attired at all times.[9] Much of his work was delegated, of course.

The Queen's chamberlain had under him a vice-chamberlain and many ladies, gentlemen, household officers, knights carver, esquires, valets, ushers, grooms, pages and porters. Menial servants, such as kitchen staff, were employed by the King's household, but the Queen had to pay their wages when her husband was away, and it has been estimated that Henry and Elizabeth were apart for an average of four or five months each year. When they were residing together she was obliged to pay £7 (£3,400) a day for their services. She also employed a personal chef, Brice, the 'cook of the Queen's mouth', and a 'gentleman of the pantry', Richard Brampton.[10]

Sir Roger Cotton, Elizabeth's master of horse, had responsibility not only for supplying and caring for the Queen's horses, but also for her travelling arrangements. Elizabeth journeyed widely around

England. Her main form of transport was a horse litter (also known as a chair or chariot), a covered but unsprung wagon, which was 'apparelled' in velvet at a cost of £22.9s.8d. (£11,000). She also owned 'palfreys and other horses',[11] and would have used the former for riding when she wasn't pregnant.

Cotton was assisted in his duties by John Reading, the clerk of the Queen's aviary – her 'avener'. In July 1486 Reading was paid £51 (£25,000) for various 'expenses of stable'; and later that year he received further payments of £50 'for his expenses in waiting upon the palfreys and other horses of the Queen', 'for the expenses of her horses and other necessaries of her stable' and 'for the expenses of the Queen's palfreys and offices'. Cotton himself received various payments for 'harness and other necessaries'. Nicholas Mayor was the Queen's saddler.[12] Elizabeth's privy purse expenses show that she had horses stabled at the royal stud at Stratfield Mortimer, Berkshire, Havering, Essex, Fotheringhay and Ham, near Richmond,[13] and no doubt others were stabled elsewhere. The King gave frequent payments to Elizabeth for the support of her horses, in which she evidently took a keen and affectionate interest, given the many references to them in the records.

Nicholas Gainsford and Arnold Chollerton were 'ushers of the chamber to the King's most dear consort', with responsibility for many tasks, the most important being controlling entrance to the Queen's apartments. Gainsford, who was granted an annuity of £20 (£10,000) in June 1486, had served Elizabeth Wydeville in the same capacity, and his wife, Margaret Sidney, was in the household of both Queen Elizabeths in turn. Nicholas Matthew was a yeoman of the Queen's chamber; in 1502 she recompensed him for the charges he had incurred after being injured by servants of Sir William Sandys. John Duffin, William Pole, John Field, Thomas Woodnote and John Staunton were grooms of the chamber, and Edmund and Edward Calvert, William Gentleman and John Bright pages of the chamber. Owen Whitstones was the Queen's messenger, receiving £2 (£970) per annum.[14]

'The boys and pages of the Queen's chamber' were sometimes handsomely rewarded with sums of £40 (£19,500); it was the responsibility of the pages of the chamber to keep Elizabeth's jewels securely.[15] Her portraits show that she owned many costly pieces. George Hamerton was groom porter. William Denton was the Queen's carver, as well as the King's, and his high salary of £26.13s.4d.

(£12,960) reflected the perception that carving meat was the attribute of a gentleman. Elizabeth also had her own cupbearers and servers.[16]

One grant from the King was made 'in consideration of the true and faithful service which our well-beloved Richard Smythe, the yeoman of the robes with our dearest wife, the Queen, hath done to us'.[17] The Queen's wardrobe of the robes, where her clothing and personal household stuff were stored, was headed by a yeoman, the aforementioned Richard Smythe, who was appointed on 20 June 1486,[18] and staffed by a groom, Ellis Hilton, and pages.[19] The pages were busy men, for the Queen's clothes, food hampers and other effects had frequently to be transported from one house to another, whenever she changed residences, and they also had to make each set of lodgings ready for her.[20] In 1502, Richard Justice, page of the robes, was dispatched from the Great Wardrobe at Blackfriars to Westminster to fetch a gown for the Queen. Richard Deacons gave him 8d. for hiring a boat; 5d. 'for conveying all the Queen's lined gowns from London to Westminster by water, and for men's labour that bare the same gowns' to and from the water; 5d. 'for bringing the Queen's furred gowns'; 4d. for conveying 'such stuff as remaineth there'; 4d. for 'going from Westminster to London for black damask, and for a frontlet of gold for the Queen'; and 6d. for making a new key for the 'great standard' at her wardrobe of the robes and mending two locks. His expenses totalled 2s.8d. (£70). His duties also included mending and hemming Elizabeth's clothes.[21]

John Coope was keeper 'of the Queen's stuff of her wardrobe of the beds' at Baynard's Castle. John Belly and William Hamerton (probably a relation of George) were 'yeomen of the Queen's stuff of her wardrobe of the beds', John Brown was groom of the beds, and Henry Roper, Benjamin Digby, Thomas Swan and William Paston were pages of the beds, and were each paid £1.13s.4d. (£810). Elizabeth bought William Paston his wedding clothes in 1502. The pages of the beds were responsible for seeing that the Queen's bed was properly arrayed and made up. Her wardrobes had a clerk to help with administration.[22]

Lewis Walter was the Queen's bargeman, with responsibility for the twenty-one oarsmen who rowed her barge – gaily decked out in her colours of blue and murrey – along the Thames, where most of the royal palaces were situated.[23] Transport by river through London was quicker, as the streets were so narrow and overcrowded.

Lewis Gough, John Rede, Richard Chollerton (probably a relation of Arnold) and Thomas Barton, who accompanied Elizabeth's daughter Margaret to Scotland in 1503, were the Queen's footmen. They wore gowns of tawny damask, doublets of yellow Bruges satin and jackets of black velvet.[24]

Elizabeth had her own medical team. She did not forget the debt she owed to Dr Lewis Caerleon, who had served her mother and been so active on their behalf during the dangerous days of 1483, and received him into her service as her physician.[25] He died around 1494–5.[26] Robert Taylor was her surgeon,[27] but the word then meant one who works with instruments, inferior to a physician, although surgery had for some time been a recognised branch of medicine. Many surgeons were also barbers, who acted as dentists and performed blood-letting, operations and amputations (the red and white barber's pole represents a limb in a bloody bandage), all of course without anaesthetic. John Pickenham and John Grice were the Queen's apothecaries.[28]

She had her own chaplains, who administered to her spiritual needs. One was Henry Haute, her maternal kinsman. Another, Jacques Haute, also related, was her servitor. One of Elizabeth's chaplains, Christopher Plummer, later became confessor to Katherine of Aragon.[29] Elizabeth's confessor in 1502 was Dr Edmund Underwood.[30] One example of the Queen operating within her permitted sphere occurred in the autumn of 1498, when, upon the death of Giovanni de' Gigli (who had written the epithalamium on her wedding), she put forward her confessor as a candidate for the vacant see of Worcester; when Pope Alexander VI wrote to the King suggesting his own nominee, Gigli's nephew, Silvestro, Henry replied that he had already promised the see to the Queen's confessor. In the end, however, it went to Silvestro de' Gigli.[31]

In 1501 Elizabeth took her half-brother, Arthur Plantagenet, Edward IV's illegitimate son by Elizabeth Lucy (née Waite), into her household, possibly through the good offices of Margaret Beaufort. That year Margaret mentioned doing the King's pleasure 'for the bastard of King Edward's', which, she said, she 'would be glad to fulfil to my little power'.[32] Older than Elizabeth by three to five years, Arthur was 'the gentlest heart living', according to the future Henry VIII, who liked him enormously – until Arthur fell foul of him in 1540. Elizabeth would have known him well in childhood, for he had been raised at her father's court. In 1472 the Exchequer accounts record that the King's tailor was paid for robes for 'my lord the bastard' – probably a reference to Arthur. But after that, he disappears from the record, and it may be that when his father died, he went to live with his mother's family near Southampton. The next mention of him occurs in 1501, when, as 'Arthur Waite', he entered Elizabeth's service as her carver.[33] He was probably the 'Master Arthur' (occupation not specified) who was paid a handsome salary of £26.13s.4d. (£12,960) in 1503.[34]

Most of the members of the Queen's household were men; the women who served her were those who kept her company or attended to her personal needs. Her life was governed by ceremonial and ritual, even in private. She was rarely alone; there was always someone in attendance or within earshot – usually her ladies, gentlewomen and female servants, who were naturally chosen from the higher ranks of society. These were the women whom the Queen saw daily, in whose company she spent much of her life, and who might, with luck, become her friends.[35] They had to be congenial to her, and virtuous, for their conduct would reflect upon her.

Places in the Queen's household were much sought after, for they provided women with status, an independent income as well as perquisites, pensions for good service on retirement, and privileged access to their mistress – and sometimes the King himself – from which could flow the lucrative benefits of patronage. Effectively they were career women, and if they were as efficient as they were well-connected, they could look forward to years in royal service.

Elizabeth's mother had had just five ladies-in-waiting, but Rodrigo de Puebla, the Spanish ambassador, was astonished to discover that 'the Queen has thirty-two ladies, very magnificent and in splendid style',[36] who attended her even in private. Eighteen of them were noblewomen.[37] In 1502–3 Elizabeth had seven maids of honour, who each received salaries of £6.13s.4d. (£3,300), while sixteen gentlewomen each got £3.6s.8d. (£1,620) per annum. There were also three chamberers – women who attended the Queen in her chamber or, more specifically, bedchamber.[38]

All the Queen's unmarried sisters waited on her. Cecily was her chief attendant until the latter's marriage in 1487, when she was replaced by Anne. Next in precedence came Lady Elizabeth Stafford (d. after 1544), who served as first lady of the bedchamber from 1494, at the latest. The daughter of Henry Stafford, Duke of Buckingham, by Katherine Wydeville, she was Elizabeth's first cousin.

She married firstly Sir Walter Herbert, who died in 1507, and secondly George Hastings, Earl of Huntingdon. She received a salary of £33.6s.8d. (£16,300), the highest paid to one of the Queen's female attendants.[39]

Another cousin was Margaret, Lady Pole. Her husband, Sir Richard Pole, was a kinsman of Margaret Beaufort and great-grandson of the poet Geoffrey Chaucer. He had been in the service of the future Edward V at Ludlow, and fought for his cousin Henry Tudor at Bosworth. His marriage to Margaret had been arranged to bind another Yorkist claimant to the royal House. Elizabeth's aunt, Mary FitzLewes, Lady Rivers, widow of the executed Anthony Wydeville, was also one of her favoured attendants.[40]

These close relations ranked above the ladies-in-waiting, married women who waited daily upon Elizabeth; some were there because their husbands served the King in his Privy Chamber. Impeccable courtesy, discretion and social skills would have been expected of them and, indeed, of all the women and girls who served the Queen. The ladies-in-waiting were her constant daily companions in her privy chamber; they attended her on ceremonial occasions and in private, and their function was to provide pleasant and decorous companionship at all times. They had to have 'a vigilant and reverent respect and eye', so that they might notice by their mistress's 'look or countenance what lacketh, or is her pleasure to be had or done'.[41]

Elizabeth's ladies were required to be accomplished in dancing, singing, playing musical instruments and other pastimes beloved by their royal mistress. Besides music and watching players and other entertainers, Elizabeth took pleasure in her gardens, and enjoyed gambling at games of chance, dice and cards.[42] Playing cards, which originated in China, became popular in Europe in the late fourteenth century. The four suits we know today originated in France around 1480, so would have been known at Henry VII's court. It was in the fifteenth century that kings, queens and knaves began to feature on the cards. The 'knave' derives from the German '*knabe*', meaning a male child or prince.

An old tradition, probably apocryphal, has it that the image of the Queen of Hearts in a pack of playing cards represents Elizabeth of York. It is said that, after her death, Henry VII ordered her image to appear on every deck of cards, in commemoration of the love they had shared. Certainly the long-lappeted gable headdress resembles the type she is known to have worn, and the Queen of Hearts is usually shown holding a Tudor rose. But others have claimed that the lady is meant to be Helen of Troy, and still others argue that the figures on playing cards represent no one in particular.

Dancing was often practised in the Queen's chamber in preparation for court entertainments, or just for its own sake. The ladies would also have been diverted by the antics of Elizabeth's fools, Patch and William. Henry VII once bought new shoes for Patch, and Elizabeth paid for William to be boarded out for several months while he was sick; she also bought coats, shirts and shoes for her fools.[43]

Every married woman in Elizabeth's train was expected to put the Queen's needs before those of her family, for royal service meant spending long periods at court. Time off was allowed for confinements, but once the baby was established with a nurse, the mother would return to court.

Next in rank after the ladies-in-waiting came the maids of honour, unmarried, well-born girls who were often appointed by the recommendation of the ladies-in-waiting, or through the influence of their relations or friends at court. The usual age for appointment was around sixteen. Since Edward IV's reign, beauty had been a prerequisite, since it would enhance the appearance of the Queen's entourage, and attract suitable husbands for the girls in question. Ambitious parents would compete to place their daughters in the Queen's household, for she and the King were better placed than anyone to arrange advantageous marriages for them, upon which they might be promoted to the rank of lady-in-waiting. Maids of honour were therefore expected to be virtuous, for their mistress was *in loco parentis*, and no scandal could reflect upon her name.

Also residing in the Queen's household, but not in her service, were the daughters and gentlewomen of her ladies, many of whom made good marriages through living at court. All the women attendant upon the Queen and her ladies had accommodation and board at court, as well as stabling for their horses. In addition to their salaries, they received new liveries and clothing at Christmas and Whitsun, and for coronations, royal weddings and funerals. They were given gifts by the King and Queen at New Year and at other times, often in recognition of good service, and if they were lucky they were granted annuities and pensions, which could be quite substantial.[44]

The names of many of Elizabeth's female attendants are known, although it is not possible to determine in what capacity they all served. They are listed in alphabetical order in Appendix II. Some had clearly been appointed at the behest of the King or Margaret Beaufort. Several served Elizabeth for many years, and were later rewarded for good service; some were entrusted with positions in the households of the royal children. The Queen's personal household, like the court, was composed of people who were often related to her and/or to each other, making it almost a familial organisation.

Elizabeth's female attendants would have dressed her, for help was essential, given the elaborate clothing worn by high-ranking ladies of the period. Queens were not expected to perform even personal tasks for themselves, so they also washed and bathed her, and attended her when she used the privy or close stool, wiping her with a clean cloth afterwards. It was taken for granted that body servants, who were required to be of gentle rank, would be in attendance even for the most intimate of functions.

It was a mark of rank to look clean and smell pleasant. Since the thirteenth century kings and queens had had the luxury of piped hot and cold water from a cistern, and Elizabeth was fortunate in that she had many servants, but not everyone at court was fastidious, and sanitation was poor: hers was a world scented with herbs, spices and flowers – variously spread or sprinkled on rush matting, napery, food, bedding and parts of the body – so that offensive smells might be camouflaged. Good manners dictated that the upper classes washed on rising, before and after meals, and on retiring for the night; the royal chamberlains would be at hand at those times with a basin and a towel of fine Holland cloth. Yet it is not known how often, or how thoroughly, people actually washed themselves. Elizabeth's father, Edward IV, had had his head, hands and feet washed every Saturday, which suggests there was a difference between the ideal and the reality. The rich did take baths fairly often, using a wooden tub lined with cloth and covered with a canopy. The bather sat on a bed of sponges, which were also used to wash her with herbs, rosewater and soap, and was attended by servants who spread mats for her to stand on and stood ready with towels. Toothpicks and cloths were used to clean and buff teeth, and Elizabeth's attendants would have tidied her hair with an ivory comb.

All the Queen's ladies were expected to be expert needlewomen, as much of their time was spent working with costly materials and threads of silk and gold, embroidering altar cloths, hangings, bedding and garments, or sewing clothing such as fine shirts. These might be given as New Year's gifts. Elizabeth Lock was the Queen's silk-woman, and also made items for the King. At Christmas 1502 Elizabeth paid her for 'certain bonnets, frontlets and other stuff of her occupation for her own wearing'.[45]

Like many aristocratic women, Elizabeth enjoyed embroidery. She employed a French embroiderer, Robinet, who got board and wages, and hired other embroiderers,[46] but herself embroidered the King's Garter robe, using Venetian gold that he had purchased himself,[47] and in 1502 she paid 8d. (£16) for an ell of linen cloth 'for a sampler'. A sampler at that time was an embroidery specimen or template that could be copied.[48]

Much time was devoted by the Queen and her ladies to making, mending, embellishing or trying on clothes. In an age of outward display, appearance counted for much, and it was expected of them that they enhance the splendour of the court by the resplendence of their attire. Elizabeth's ladies were required to dress almost as lavishly – and expensively – as she did: despite strict sumptuary laws restricting the wearing of certain materials to certain ranks, their dress was to reflect their employer's status rather than their family's. The rich materials and long trains worn at court reflected the wealth and status of their wearers, for such fabrics were dear. Needless to say, it cost a lot to equip a girl for royal service.

As queen, Elizabeth was expected to dress more magnificently than any other woman. The measure of a monarch's standing was judged by the conspicuous display he and his family maintained, and clothing was an outward sign of rank, which was why sumptuary laws were regularly – and sometimes ineffectively – passed, and anyone wearing apparel above their station was liable to a fine. The King instructed the Great Wardrobe and his own chamber to issue Elizabeth with the more expensive items that she needed, which was a great boon in view of her limited income. The Great Wardrobe also supplied clothing, normally of black or tawny, for the ladies and gentlewomen of the Queen's household, although peeresses in attend-ance were expected to wear their own rich attire. The King did not stint on such items, recognising the importance of outward display,[49] but Elizabeth had to pay the cost of transporting her clothes when-ever she changed residences.[50]

The chief item of dress worn by women was the gown, which had a fitted bodice, a natural waistline and a flowing skirt. Sleeves were usually narrow until *c.*1500–1, when they became fashionably wider; in 1502 Elizabeth ordered her tailor, Robert Ragdale, to line a gown of black velvet with wide sleeves with black sarcanet.[51] Narrow sleeves had cuffs, sometimes of fur, as can be seen in Elizabeth's portraits, and fur was often used to trim the neckline, or to line the gown, or as a border on the skirt. During Elizabeth's lifetime the square neck replaced the boat-shaped or V-shaped necklines of her younger years. She seems to have favoured black above other colours, black then being one of the costliest dyeing processes and therefore a symbol of status, but she also owned gowns of crimson, purple, gold and other hues.[52] Some of her gowns were of wool; some had a deep contrasting border at the hem, as can be seen in the Whitehall mural (see Appendix 1), where it is of ermine, or purfils, which were decorative edgings. One russet velvet gown had a purfil of cloth of gold and damask; another of purple velvet had a purfil of cloth of gold.[53]

Beneath the gown was worn an under-gown called a kirtle. Kirtles were not usually made of such rich fabrics as gowns, unless they were on display when trains were looped up at the back: they could be of silk or worsted and, like outer gowns, were often lined with wool. Elizabeth's privy purse expenses show payments for several kirtles and the hemming of one of damask.[54]

Gowns and kirtles were made for the Queen and her ladies by tailors of the Great Wardrobe, or by professional tailors. Elizabeth's tailors were Robert Johnson of the Merchant Adventurers' Company, Robert Ragdale, Stephen Higham and Robert Addington; Thomas Staunton was her cutter.[55] However, she and the women attendant on her made their own body-linen, which comprised smocks (the basic undergarment), kerchiefs (for the neck or nose) and head rails (coifs). Heavy fabrics could only be brushed or sponged, so smocks were worn next to the skin to preserve gowns and kirtles from sweat stains and keep them fresh. Smocks could be changed and laundered frequently, although that might have meant weekly. The Queen's laundress, Agnes Dean, was paid £3.6s.8d. (£1,620) a year.[56] In 1486 Thomas Fuller, mercer of London, provided Elizabeth with 'linen cloth' for body linen such as smocks; this cost £8.2s. (£4,000).[57] She also owned petticoats of scarlet and linen, and socks of white fustian.[58]

It has long been thought that women in this period wore no

undergarments apart from smocks and hose, but in 2012 well-preserved linen underclothing resembling a bra and a (male?) thong, thought to date from c.1480, were found in a vault in Lengberg Castle, East Tyrol. Hilary Davidson, fashion curator at the Museum of London, believes it is 'entirely probable' that similar garments were worn in late-medieval England.[59] If so, it is credible that Elizabeth might have owned something similar. One would not normally expect to find any surviving owing to their flimsy nature, so the Austrian undergarments are unique examples.

Coifs were worn beneath hoods, which were usually in the English gable style. At this period they had long lappets, frontlets and a black veil, and were usually of black velvet or silk with decorative, sometimes bejewelled, trims. 'Frontlets of gold' are itemised in Elizabeth's privy purse expenses,[60] and Henry VII once made her a gift of them.[61] Elizabeth's headdresses were usually bought from Mrs Lock, her silkwoman, who made her bonnets, hoods and frontlets. Joan Wilcock of Yorkshire, another silkwoman, supplied the Queen with a bonnet on 25 May 1502, and 'certain bonnets, frontlets and other stuff' in January 1503, for which she was paid £20 of a bill totalling £60.6s.5d. (£29,300), Elizabeth signing the bill with her own hand.[62]

Cloaks were worn as outer wear. Elizabeth owned several, and her privy purse accounts also mention stoles (large shawls). She also purchased laces, ribbon, and lengths of sarcanet in eight colours to make girdles and tippets (shoulder capes). Late in 1502 Richard Weston brought her 'certain harnesses of girdles' from France costing £4.10s. (£2,190).[63] The Queen's shoes were bought by the dozen, single- or double-soled pairs with tin or latten (copper alloy, like brass) buckles costing a shilling (£25). It is often claimed that she could not afford expensive buckles for her shoes, but in fact she bought the same kind as her wealthy mother-in-law. At Christmas 1502 she bought buskins, which were knee-high boots of leather or silk, usually with turned-down tops.[64]

In the first year of their marriage, Henry VII saw to it that Elizabeth was suitably accoutred as befitted a queen. On 10 February 1486 she was provided with ten yards of black velvet at 16s. (£400) a yard, and twelve yards of purple velvet at 21s. (£510) a yard, for two gowns. For the first Easter after her marriage, she was lavishly supplied with luxury fabrics and trimmings. Hildebrand Vannonhawe, furrier, was paid £44.2s. (£21,500) for '49 timbers of ermines, for the furring of one gown of the Lady Elizabeth, Queen of England, at 18s. [£440] the timber'. The Queen's skinner, Richard Story, was paid £31.14s. (£1,600) for powdering these ermines[65] and stitching them to the gown. Elizabeth had gowns and kirtles of white damask cloth of gold trimmed with powdered ermines.[66] In 1502 another of the Queen's skinners, Master Hayward, was paid for furring a crimson gown for Princess Margaret, and adding cuffs of pampilion, a fur that may have come from Pamplona, Navarre.[67] John Exnyng, grocer of London, supplied three yards of green cloth of gold 'for the use of the lady the Queen', for £13.10s. (£6,600); and Richard Smythe, yeoman of her wardrobe, bought Elizabeth 'black silk of damask and crimson satin' costing £11.5s.6d. (£5,500). Above this, the King commanded his wife to be given '10 verges [yards] of crimson velvet' and the sum of £90 (£44,000).[68] Such prices give us a good idea of how expensive – and sumptuous – the clothing of the upper classes was in Tudor times.

Four months later, in July, Elizabeth's wardrobe was further embellished. Hildebrand Vannonhawe received £42.2s. (£20,500) for 49 'timbers of ermines for a gown for the Queen', and another fifteen timbers were bought for the same gown for £10 (£4,860) from Gerard Venmar. Both were probably Flemish merchants. John Exnyng was paid £13.10s. (£6,600) for three yards of green cloth of gold, all 'to the Queen's use'. Richard Smythe bought 'divers silks' for £11.5s.6d. (£5,500). By 1487, there were 'divers workers and furriers working for the lady the Queen', all of whom were paid wages.[69]

Over the years, the King gave Elizabeth occasional, sometimes very personal, gifts of money, jewels, ornaments, furs, gowns, frontlets, crimson satin for a kirtle, robes furred with miniver, fur-lined night boots, gold wire for trimmings, a communion cloth, beds, and household essentials such as hammers. He also purchased a lion 'for the Queen's Grace', costing £2.13s.4d. (£1,300), which was no doubt sent straight to the royal menagerie in the Tower.[70] But, having outlaid a fortune on his wife's wardrobe, Henry evidently expected her to make things last, and her accounts show that her gowns were continually mended, turned, 'new-bodied' or newly trimmed, for which her tailor, Robert Addington, was paid 4d. (£8), and re-hemmed for 2d. (£4).[71] A degree of contriving must have gone into ensuring that she did not disappoint when she appeared in public.

13

'Unbounded Love'

Elizabeth was family-orientated to a high degree. She gave 'unbounded love'[1] and support to her children, her sisters and other relations, and always interested herself in their affairs. She kept her sisters with her at court before they wed, and sometimes after, and they were usually included in the royal celebrations of Christmas, Easter and Whitsun.

Cecily of York, who had played such a prominent role at the coronation, was the first of the Queen's sisters to marry. Henry VII was aware that, while Edward IV's daughters might be assets to him in terms of making advantageous marriages, they were also a threat by virtue of their Yorkist lineage. In 1486, determined to neutralise their dynastic claims by marrying them to his loyal supporters, Henry had had Cecily's marriage to Richard III's adherent Ralph Scrope dissolved, and between 25 November and 31 December 1487 she was married to Margaret Beaufort's half-brother, John, Viscount Welles. Probably Margaret, who was always to be a good friend to Cecily,[2] had a hand in brokering the marriage.

Welles had been in high favour with Edward IV and was one of those who watched over his body after his death.[3] An opponent of Richard III, he had joined Henry Tudor in Brittany after Buckingham's rebellion. He was a favourite of the King, and had been rewarded with his title in 1485. He was probably about thirty-seven, and his bride eighteen. The King and Queen attended their wedding.[4]

Cecily was described as being 'not so fortunate as fair'.[5] She got on well with the Lady Margaret, whom she took to visiting at Collyweston, and Margaret would later protect her from the consequences of an ill-advised second marriage, and pay towards her funeral expenses.[6] Sadly, Cecily's two daughters by Welles were to die young. After she married, her next sister, Anne of York, now twelve, became the Queen's chief lady-in-waiting, and was constantly in attendance on her.

In the months following her coronation, Elizabeth received various financial and material gifts. On 21 December Henry granted her 'the next presentation to the deanery of the College of St Stephen in the Palace of Westminster'.[7] Five days later 'our dearest wife the Queen' received a grant – backdated to 20 February – of some of Elizabeth Wydeville's lordships and manors that appear to have been overlooked earlier, namely 'Waltham Magna, Baddow, Mashbury, Dunmow, [Great] Leighs and Farnham, all in Essex', with the offices of feodary[8] and bailiff[9] in each. With that, the transfer of land from queen to queen was complete.[10]

On 6 March 1488 a charter was given 'to the King's very dear consort, that she may have and take for her life all the goods and chattels of all her men and tenants being either fugitives or felons, or persons condemned and convicted of felony'; she also received 'liberties and immunities in all her castles, lordships, etc.'. This charter was granted 'at the suit of the Queen herself'.[11] At Easter 100 marks (£15,500) were paid to her 'for the maintenance of her state'. She also received a tun of wine 'by way of reward'. On 8 May a royal writ was issued to the mayor and burgesses of Bristol 'requiring them to render to Elizabeth, the Queen Consort, the arrears, and also the half-yearly payments [of rents], as they become due'. Another writ was sent 'to the men of the town of Bedford in respect of an annuity of £20 [£10,000] out of the farm [rents] of the town, granted to the Queen from 20th February last past'.[12]

The Christmas of 1487 was kept 'full honourably' at Greenwich. The King presided over the customary feast in the great hall of the palace, while the Queen dined with her mother – clearly Elizabeth Wydeville was still welcome at court – and the Lady Margaret in her chamber. Cecily, 'the noble Princess, sister of the Queen, our sovereign lady', and her new husband, Viscount Welles, joined the festivities. The court stayed at Greenwich for a week after Christmas, and on New Year's Day, largesse was cried in the great hall, where Henry and Elizabeth distributed gifts to members of their households, with the Welleses following suit; and there was a banquet and 'a goodly disguising' in the evening.

When the King and Queen wore their crowns in public on Twelfth Day, 5 January, Elizabeth and Margaret Beaufort appeared in identical mantles and surcoats of estate, Margaret wearing 'a rich coronal' on her head. 'And when the High Mass was done, the King went to his chamber, and from thence to the hall, and there kept his estate, crowned with a rich crown of gold set with pearl and precious stones, and under [a] marvellous rich cloth of estate. The Queen, also crowned under a cloth of estate hanging somewhat lower than the King's, on his left hand, and my lady the King's mother on her left hand, with all four estates were served covered.' During the feast, the Earl of Ormond, Elizabeth's chamberlain, kneeling, held her crown, while the Earl of Oxford held the King's.[13]

In March 1488 negotiations were opened for the marriage of Prince Arthur to the Spanish Infanta, Katherine of Aragon. Katherine had been born on 16 December 1485. Her parents, King Ferdinand of Aragon and Queen Isabella of Castile, had not only united Spain by their marriage, but were now winning a centuries-long war to recapture the kingdom from the occupying Moors. For this, the Pope would award them the title 'Their Most Catholic Majesties', and they were already renowned and respected throughout Christendom. An alliance with Spain would undoubtedly bolster Henry VII's standing both at home and in Europe, for by agreeing to marry their daughter to his son, Ferdinand and Isabella were endorsing his right to the crown.

That spring, a new ambassador, Rodrigo de Puebla, was sent by the Spanish sovereigns to England, his first task being to inspect the two-year-old Prince Arthur. Puebla was much taken with the young Prince, reporting: 'We find in him so many excellent qualities as no one would believe.' He was a child 'of remarkable beauty and grace' and 'taller than his age would warrant'. Puebla also extolled Elizabeth's beauty and magnificence in his dispatches.[14]

But the ambassador had reservations about the match. 'Bearing in mind what happens every day to the kings of England, it is surprising that Ferdinand and Isabella should dare to give their daughter at all,' he observed, referring to the dynastic crises and rebellions of the past few years. Nevertheless, on 13 April his sovereigns authorised him to conclude a treaty of marriage between the Infanta and Prince Arthur, and thereafter negotiations proceeded.[15]

★

At Easter 1488 Henry and Elizabeth were at Windsor, staying in the old state apartments built by Edward III, which were now much outdated. Between 1497 and 1500, Henry VII was to extend them westward from the existing range towards the gatehouse, building for Elizabeth 'a new and elegant work of squared stones', a three-storeyed building that would be known as King Henry's Tower, which was constructed under the direction of Robert Janyns, who had designed St George's Chapel. The tower was surmounted by pairs of turreted oriel windows on the north and south facades, and its purpose was to provide extra accommodation for the Queen. Every provision was made by the King for her comfort and convenience.

Her apartments were established here and in the adjoining inner gatehouse, where her old bedchamber had been on the first floor; it had an anteroom that had served as a pallet chamber, where her female attendants slept. A gallery extended from her dining chamber (once Margaret of Anjou's bedchamber) in her old apartments to the pallet chamber outside her new bedchamber in the tower. A privy staircase led up from this pallet chamber to what was probably her jewel house, and the southern half of the gallery served as Elizabeth's closet. In the north-west corner of her new bedchamber was a deep oriel with tall windows on three sides, used as an 'arraying chamber', where Elizabeth was dressed each day.[16]

When a German, Paul Hentzner, visited Windsor in 1598, late in the reign of Elizabeth I, there were still to be seen the beds of the Queen's parents, Henry VIII and Anne Boleyn, and her grandparents, Henry VII and Elizabeth of York, 'each eleven feet square, covered with quilts shining with gold and silver'.[17] Probably Elizabeth's was made for her new bedchamber. The sheets in Henry VII's household ordinances were clearly large enough to have fitted the great beds mentioned by Hentzner.

Elizabeth had a prominent part to play in the customary religious observances at Easter. She distributed her own Maundy money and clothing to poor women, and on Easter Day her religious observances paralleled the King's.[18]

April 1488 witnessed the first Garter ceremonies to take place at Windsor in Henry VII's reign. For Elizabeth, the sight of Henry riding with his Knights Companions to the still-unfinished St George's Chapel on the Sunday after St George's Day must have brought back poignant memories of her father. She was there in company with Margaret Beaufort, who had just been made a Lady of the Garter – the last woman to be given that honour until 1901. Both were wearing 'gowns of the Garter of the same as the King and the lords wear'. These were gifts from Henry, from his Great Wardrobe, and of 'sanguine [red or rust colour] cloth in grain, furred with the wombs of miniver pure, gartered [banded] with letters of gold'. In providing his mother with identical clothes to those of his Queen, Henry proclaimed her importance. The significance of that would not have been lost on spectators. The poet Skelton praised Henry VII for his 'knightly Order, clothed in robes with Garter, the Queen's Grace and thy mother in the same'.[19]

That day Elizabeth and Margaret rode in procession through the precincts of Windsor Castle in a rich chariot covered in cloth of gold and drawn by six horses harnessed with gold. Their route took them from the royal lodgings through the narrow vaulted passageway of the Inner Gatehouse, then past the Round Tower down to the Inner Ward – the same path followed by Garter processions today. After them followed another Lady of the Garter, Anne of York, wearing a crimson velvet robe of the Order, Margaret Pole, Elizabeth's aunt, Lady Rivers, and eighteen other ladies similarly attired, all mounted on white palfreys bedecked with cloth-of-gold saddles and caparisons embroidered with the white roses of York in the Queen's honour. On arrival at the castle, the royal party attended Mass in St George's Chapel. At this special service, Elizabeth was the only one beside the King permitted to kiss the Gospel and the Pax.

Then the King, the Queen and 'my lady the King's mother' walked in procession around the cloister and attended a great feast in St George's Hall, with the ambassadors of Burgundy, Austria, Scotland and Brittany being present. The next day Elizabeth and Margaret Beaufort went with the King and the Garter Knights in procession to Mass and to Evensong, although they did not attend the feast held in the evening.[20]

The court was still at Windsor for the Whitsunday festival of 1488, which fell on 20 May, and again Elizabeth's sister Anne was with her. A Papal envoy had reported that on 9 May 'the mother of the Queen' had been present with the royal couple, the King's mother and many nobles and ambassadors, again proving that Elizabeth Wydeville was not *persona non grata* at court.[21] Her appearances there the previous Christmas and on this occasion suggest that she may have visited at other times when her presence was not recorded.

Much of the summer of 1488 was passed at Woodstock Palace

near Oxford,[22] a large, stone-built house decorated with heraldic emblems. It had been a favoured royal residence since the twelfth century, and Henry VII spent a lot of money upgrading it, enticed by the excellent hunting to be had nearby.

In July Rodrigo de Puebla, who had been busy debating the Infanta's dowry and jointure with the Privy Council, 'went at an unexpected hour to the Queen, whom we found with two and thirty companions of angelical appearance, and all we saw there seemed very magnificent, and in splendid style, as was suitable for the occasion'. He added: 'The King requests that from time to time Latin letters should be written to him from Spain, since he writes Latin letters to Spain. Neither the King, nor the Queen, are able to understand Spanish letters.'[23] It was important, of course, that Elizabeth was able to read the diplomatic correspondence concerning the marriage negotiations, because it was her role as a queen and a mother – and within her proper sphere of influence – to ensure that her children made good marriages.

It was probably in connection with these negotiations that Elizabeth wrote rather forcefully to the powerful and influential Lorenzo de' Medici, 'il Magnifico', of Florence. On 6 August 1488 Lorenzo informed Pope Innocent VIII that one 'Robert the Englishman, the bearer of the present letter, is going to his Holiness to obtain a brief to the King of England, for the purpose which his Holiness will learn from the Florentine ambassador and from Robert'. Lorenzo beseeched 'his Holiness to give Robert audience and grant his request, as the Queen has written very warmly on this matter'.[24]

Henry and Elizabeth spent All Hallows at Windsor and the rest of the autumn of 1488 at Westminster. When they went down the Thames by barge to the Bishop's Palace at St Paul's to receive the Papal chamberlain, there was 'so great a mist upon the Thames that there was no man could tell in what place the King was'. In the cathedral, Elizabeth watched as Archbishop Morton ceremonially girded Henry with a sword blessed by the Pope, and afterwards there was a lavish feast. The court removed to Sheen for Christmas, the Queen being attended by many great ladies, including her sisters, Lady Rivers, Margaret Beaufort and Margaret Pole.[25] This was the last occasion on which Margaret Pole was recorded at Henry VII's court.[26] She was becoming increasingly occupied with a series of pregnancies and the demands of a young family.

★

In March 1489 the marriage between Prince Arthur and Katherine of Aragon was finally agreed upon with the conclusion of the Treaty of Medina del Campo, which provided for the Infanta to bring to England a dowry of 200,000 crowns (£20 million). This treaty, which was ratified by the King on 23 September 1490,[27] was arguably Henry VII's greatest achievement in foreign policy, as it established the Tudor dynasty in the top rank of European monarchies – although it was to be many years before the marriage took place, and at times during those years it was to seem as if it might not take place at all.

Henry and Elizabeth were at Hertford Castle at Easter 1489, which fell on 31 March.[28] They were back at Windsor for the feast of St George and the annual Garter ceremonies. At this time Elizabeth was given 'cloth of black velvet, russet cloth', squirrel fur and shoes.[29] Shortly afterwards Henry received news that the Earl of Northumberland had been murdered whilst enforcing the collection of the King's taxes, and rode north to York to preside over the trials of the culprits.

By the time he returned to Windsor, Elizabeth knew she was to have another child. It was nearly three years since Arthur's birth, and in an era in which infant mortality was high, she must have felt under pressure to bear more children to ensure the succession. If she had had miscarriages in the interim period, they are not recorded. Maybe, having been so ill after her first confinement, she had delayed having another child for the sake of her health, or she had simply not managed to conceive.

The King was delighted to learn of his wife's pregnancy. He lavished gifts upon her against her coming confinement: bolts of black velvet, russet cloth, canaber (soft linen) cloth and white blanket, squirrel fur, cord, thread, tappet (tapestry) hooks, crochettes (pieces of crochet), iron hammers, a carpet, featherbeds filled with down and sheets of Holland cloth.[30]

The high ceremonial observed on 31 October suggests that the King was confidently expecting Elizabeth to present him with a second son. She was then eight months pregnant. 'On All-Hallows Eve, the Queen took to her chamber at Westminster, royally accompanied with ladies and gentlemen, that is to say, with my lady the King's mother, the Duchess of Norfolk and many other going before her, and besides greater part of the nobles of the realm assembled at Westminster at the Parliament. She was led by the Earl of Oxford and the Earl of Derby. The reverend father in God, the Bishop of Exeter, said Mass in his pontificals' in St Stephen's Chapel. 'The Earls of Shrewsbury and of Kent held the towels when the Queen received the Host, and the corners of the towels were golden, and the torches were holden by knights; and after *Agnus Dei* was sung, and the Bishop ceased, the Queen was led as before. When she was come unto her great chamber, she tarried in the anteroom before it, and stood under her cloth of estate. Then was ordained a void of spices and sweet wines. That done, my lord the Queen's chamberlain, in very good words, desired in the Queen's name all her people there present to pray that God would send her a good hour.'

Elizabeth now 'departed to her inner chamber, which was hanged and ceiled with rich cloth of blue arras with *fleurs-de-lis* of gold. In that chamber was a rich bed and pallet, the which pallet had a marvellous rich canopy of gold with a velvet pall garnished with bright red roses, embroidered with two rich panes of ermine covered with Rennes of lawn. Also there was an altar well furnished with relics, and a cupboard of nine stages, well and richly garnished.' It had been decreed that the tapestries in the birthing chamber were not to portray human figures, which were considered 'not convenient about women in such case', but pleasant subjects, so that the Queen and the newborn infant might not be 'affrighted by figures which gloomily stare'.

At the door to her chamber, the Queen 'recommended herself to the good praises of the lords; and my lord her chamberlain drew the traverse', the curtain that separated the bedchamber from the great chamber. 'From then forth no manner of officer came within the chamber but ladies and gentlewomen, after the old custom.'[31]

Elizabeth Wydeville came to court to support her daughter during her confinement, and a few days after the Queen had taken to her chamber an exception was made to the strict protocol prohibiting men from admittance to it. In the interests of good diplomatic relations, Elizabeth and her mother privately received the new French ambassador, their cousin, Francis, Sieur de Luxembourg, Viscount of Geneva, who had asked to see the Queen. Two other men were allowed to be present – Elizabeth's chamberlain and Garter King-at-Arms – as well as Margaret Beaufort, who was also in attendance on the Queen at this time. Elizabeth Wydeville deputised with Margaret Beaufort for her at another reception for the ambassadors.

On 29 November 1489 three-year-old Prince Arthur was brought to Westminster and dubbed a Knight of the Bath. While the ceremony of knighthood was in progress, Elizabeth went into labour. 'At that same season were all those of the King's Chapel reading a psalter for the good speed of the Queen, who then travailed; and upon nine of the clock of the same night, she was delivered of a princess.'[32] The midwife in attendance was 'our well beloved Alice Massey', who had been paid £10 (£5,000) for her services on 27 November,[33] and had probably assisted at Arthur's birth. She was to attend the Queen at all her later confinements, being paid the same sum for each.

On 30 November – the feast day of St Andrew, patron saint of Scotland, a most auspicious baptismal date for a child who would one day be Queen of Scots – the new-born Princess was collected by Anne Fiennes, Marchioness of Berkeley, from Elizabeth's chamber and carried into Westminster Hall, and thence to St Stephen's Chapel.[34] The officers-at-arms led the procession, followed by the High Constable, the Earl Marshal, the Earl of Kent, carrying two basins, Henry Bourchier, Earl of Essex, carrying an unlit taper, Viscount Welles with a gold salt cellar, 'my Lady Anne, the Queen's sister, [who] bare the chrisom with a marvellous rich cross-lace [cord]', and Lady Berkeley with the Princess, escorted by the earls of Arundel and Shrewsbury, and walking under a canopy borne by four knights; the baby's train of crimson velvet furred with ermine was carried by her great-aunt, Katherine Wydeville, Duchess of Buckingham, and George Stanley, Lord Strange.

John Alcock, Bishop of Ely, was waiting to receive her in the church porch, which was 'royally beseen' with a richly embroidered ceiling covering. He baptised her with the name Margaret, 'after my lady the King's mother', in Canterbury Cathedral's magnificent silver font, which had been brought to Westminster for the occasion and lined with cloth of Rennes. At that moment, the Earl of Essex lit his taper, and 120 knights, gentlemen and yeomen set their torches ablaze. Then Thomas Rotherham, 'the Lord Archbishop of York, being in pontificals, confirmed' the child at the high altar, with Lady Berkeley acting as sponsor. Wine and spices were served to the godparents: Margaret Beaufort, who gave the Princess a silver-gilt chest full of gold; George Talbot, Earl of Shrewsbury; the Duchess of Norfolk, who gave a rich cup, and Archbishop Morton, who gave two gilt flagons and a gold vessel for holy water. These gifts were borne before the child in the torchlit procession that carried her, with 'noise of trumpets [and] Christ's blessing', back to the palace to her parents. Having received their blessing also, she was carried off by her nurse and laid in an oak cradle lined with ermine and covered with a cloth-of-gold canopy.[35]

Margaret was probably given a separate, smaller nursery establishment from Arthur's. It would also have been ruled by a lady governess, but it was Alice Davy, the nurse, who looked after the child in her infancy, ably assisted by two rockers, Anne Mayland and Margaret Troughton, and by Prince Arthur's former rocker, Alison Bwimble, who became the Princess's 'day-wife', essentially a dairy maid who brought milk, cream and butter for the child.[36]

On the same day that Margaret was christened, Arthur was brought to the Parliament Chamber and created Prince of Wales and Earl of Chester, titles that had been borne by the heirs of English kings since 1301. During the ceremony Henry VII was lauded for restoring the pride of the Welsh, and as a British king capable of re-establishing order after the chaos of the Wars of the Roses. Afterwards the little Prince sat beneath the cloth of estate and presided over the feast held to celebrate the occasion.[37]

On 4 December 1489 King Ferdinand wrote triumphantly to Elizabeth to tell her that he had 'conquered the town of Baca, in the kingdom of Granada, and has made great progress in the war against the Moors. As his victory must interest all the Christian world, he thinks it his duty to inform the Queen of England of it.' If he wrote to Henry too, the letter has not survived, but it is possible that he wrote separately to Elizabeth because he recognised her status as the rightful Queen of England.[38]

Happy as this news was, Elizabeth had more immediate concerns on her mind. A virulent measles epidemic was raging and had claimed the lives of several ladies of her court. Consequently she had to miss the christening celebrations, which lasted into December, and some of the Christmas solemnities too, because her churching, which of necessity took place in private, had to be delayed until 27 December. Christmas was a subdued holiday, and on the 29th Henry moved the court to Greenwich to escape the contagion. 'There were no disguisings and but very few plays acted on account of [the] prevalent sickness, but there was an abbot of misrule, who made much sport.'[39]

By Candlemas, 2 February, the court was back at Westminster, where the King, the Queen, Margaret Beaufort and all the Lords Spiritual and Temporal went by custom in procession to Westminster Hall, and thence to Mass; and in the evening watched a play in the White Hall.[40] On 19 February 1490 Henry VII confirmed by Letters Patent the grant of Elizabeth Wydeville's dower lands to her daughter.[41] That year, the Queen Dowager's pension was increased to £400 (£195,570), further evidence that she was not out of favour.

On 26 February, near Kew, Prince Arthur boarded the King's state barge, which would bear him to Westminster for his investiture as Prince of Wales. Between Mortlake and Chelsea, other barges containing lords, bishops, knights, the Lord Mayor of London and the craft guilds waited to attend him; at Lambeth Stairs, the flotilla was joined by the Spanish ambassador's barge. To the sound of trumpets, and amidst colourful pageantry, the Prince alighted at the landing bridge at Westminster, and was carried to his father's presence. Many new knights were dubbed that day in his honour.

On Saturday, 27 February, the little boy was hoisted on a horse and led into Westminster Hall. Here, the King formally invested him as Prince of Wales and Earl of Chester, 'as accustomed. Then, the King departing, the Prince that day kept his state under a cloth of estate.' A banquet was served at which he 'licensed' the knights to enjoy their meat, while minstrels played. The celebrations were brought to a close by Garter King of Arms, who gave thanks to God. It was demanding ceremonial for such a young child, but Arthur bore himself commendably. In May the following year he would be made a Knight of the Garter.

In November 1490 Elizabeth was granted custody of the lordship and manor of Bretts, in West Ham, Essex. This may have been in response to her giving the King the glad news that she was expecting her third child, possibly conceived during a visit to Ewelme in Oxfordshire.[42] On St Peter's Eve, 28 June 1491, at Greenwich Palace, in the midst of a rainy summer, she bore a second son, called Henry after his father, and perhaps after Henry VI, whom the King hoped to have canonised. The child was red-haired and sturdy, a true Plantagenet who much resembled his grandfather, Edward IV. As Henry VIII, he was to become the most famous of Elizabeth's children.

Wrapped in 'a mantle of gold furred with ermine', and escorted by 200 men bearing torches, the new Prince was baptised a few days later in the nearby church of the Observant Friars. The church was hung with rich Arras and cloth of gold for the occasion, and carpets were laid in the chancel. Richard Fox, Bishop of Exeter, one of the King's chief ministers, officiated. The silver font in which this lusty infant was immersed was again borrowed from Canterbury Cathedral for the occasion, and 'the bottom [was] well-padded with soft linen'. Money was paid 'for sealing of a window where my Lord Henry was changed'. A nurse, Anne Oxenbridge,[43] was appointed to look after him during his early years; clearly he grew fond of her, as much later, after he became king, he would reward her with a pension of £20 (£9,670). In charge of his nursery was the King's 'dear and well-beloved Elizabeth Darcy, mistress to our dearest son the Prince'. Agnes Butler and Emmeline Hobbes were among the 'rockers to our said son'.[44]

When he was still quite young, Prince Henry's household was established at Eltham Palace in Kent, to the east of London. Although Prince Arthur was brought up away from the court, Elizabeth's younger children were largely reared in close proximity to their parents, at Eltham, or at Sheen (where she herself had spent part of her early childhood), Greenwich, or the Archbishop of Canterbury's palace at Croydon, Surrey – all well away from the unhealthy air of London.

Eltham Palace stood on a high hill with commanding views over the City, in a bracing location. There had been a moated manor house on the site as early as the thirteenth century; much extended, it became a favoured royal palace in the fourteenth century, boasting a bathroom, dancing chambers and beautiful gardens. Edward IV, who loved Eltham, had built its soaring great hall in the 1470s, adorning it with pairs of cinque-foil windows, battlements (now gone) and what is today the third-largest hammerbeam roof in England, after those at Westminster Hall and Christ Church, Oxford; and here his badges of the white rose and the sun in splendour still survive. Edward also built the stone bridge across the moat, the front courtyard, new kitchens at right angles to the hall, the service quarters of pantry and buttery at its screens' end, and new royal lodgings beyond for himself and Elizabeth Wydeville. The latter contained a novel and unique series of five-sided bay windows, and a new innovation, a gallery, built for the purpose of recreation – the earliest one of its kind known in England. Surrounding the palace was a forested hunting park. After Westminster, Eltham was the largest of the royal palaces – and it would have held happy associations for Elizabeth.

Henry VII built a new brick range of royal apartments with bays and oriel windows on the west side of the Great Court – 'a fair front over the moat'[45] – and rebuilt the chapel. From 1490 onwards, he and Elizabeth of York often resided at Eltham, and in their day the great hall was used as a dining hall for the court. Here they dined on the dais, while the officers of the court kept their tables at right angles to theirs.

The future Henry VIII and his siblings spent a large part of their childhood on Eltham's breezy heights,[46] their mother being a frequent visitor – often from nearby Greenwich – rather than a constant presence in their lives.[47] Margaret was weaned in 1491, probably around her second birthday, and her nurse, Alice Davy, dismissed. It is clear from Exchequer warrants that her household and Henry's were amalgamated before the end of that year, although each had their own attendants.[48] In time other infants would join them. The *Great Wardrobe Accounts* contain many payments for beautiful clothing for the royal children, who were clad in velvet, satin and damask, right from infancy, outward display being considered more important than practicality.[49]

Since 1489 there had been fresh and persistent rumours that at least one of the Princes in the Tower had survived. It is not known whence they originated, or if Elizabeth heard these rumours, or what she made of them. It is unlikely that she knew for certain what had happened to her brothers, so it is possible that hope sometimes sprang in her heart that one or both of them was alive. Conceivably she had long speculated as to their fate, and maybe this new crop of rumours gave her pause for thought.

But in the autumn of 1491, news came from Ireland that one of the Princes might be very much alive. A merchant of Brittany, Pregent Meno, had sailed into Cork with a youth on board. When this fair, blond young man appeared magnificently garbed in silks, bearing himself with great dignity, the citizens of Cork are said to have concluded at once that he must be of royal blood, and the Mayor, John Atwater, impressed by the youth's knowledge of the court, declared that he must be the Earl of Warwick, escaped from the Tower. It is likely that this plot had been hatched in advance.

What happened next is unclear, but soon afterwards it was announced that the handsome stranger was actually Richard, Duke of York, the younger of the vanished Princes. York would have reached sixteen in August 1491, and the stranger was about that age. In a drawing in the *Receuil d'Arras* he bears a strong resemblance to Edward IV, which was commented on by contemporaries, although he was 'not handsome' as Edward was.[50] Certainly the boy knew a lot about the Yorkist court. According to a third-hand report, Maximilian of Austria was to assert that he was Margaret of Burgundy's bastard son by Henri de Berghes, Bishop of Cambrai,[51] but there is no evidence to substantiate this.

By 1487 the boy had been taken into the service of Edward IV's godson, Sir Edward Brampton, a staunch Yorkist who had been knighted by Richard III. Brampton had gone to Portugal to negotiate the marriage between Richard and the Infanta Joana, but had fled into exile in the Netherlands after Bosworth. It could have been in his household that his protégé learned so much about the Yorkist court, knowledge that was to serve him well in the future. He might have been Edward IV's bastard; Bacon hints that there was something scandalous behind the employment of the boy by Edward's godson. Yet this lad, who claimed he had been brought up at the English court until he was ten, had clearly not yet mastered the English language.

Vergil believed that this was a new imposture, the brainchild of Margaret of Burgundy, who hated Henry VII and had probably been waiting for an opportunity to unseat him since the failure of the Simnel conspiracy. According to Vergil, Margaret had apparently come across the boy by chance, or he had been pushed into her path by Brampton. Impressed by his looks and sharp wits, and possibly struck by his resemblance to her brother, Edward IV, she was only too happy to recognise him as her lost nephew, whom she had last seen when he was seven. Bacon claimed that she had been looking out for such a handsome, graceful youth 'to make Plantagenets and dukes of York'. Vergil states that she kept him secretly in her household, and that it was she who taught him all he needed to know, 'so that afterwards he should convince all by his performance that he sprang from the Yorkist line'. Vergil believed that it was Margaret who had arranged for the lad to go to Ireland with a view to stirring up the Yorkist supporters there.

There is no evidence that Margaret ever met the pretender before

1492, when he fled to her court from France. Even so, it is likely that some conspiracy had been formed before he appeared in Ireland. Henry VII was convinced that it had its roots in Burgundy.[52] Certainly Margaret of Burgundy would not have hesitated to do everything in her power to overthrow Henry and Elizabeth and replace them with any 'male remnant' of the House of York who was remotely suitable.[53]

The news of York's apparent survival 'came blazing and thundering into England', arousing much excitement and speculation.[54] One wonders what Elizabeth felt on hearing it. Her Victorian biographers suspected that 'her mental sufferings were acute'[55] during the years and crises that followed, and that the emergence of this new pretender and his subsequent career filled her mind 'with gloomy forebodings'.[56] It seems that many wanted to believe that one of the Princes had survived. 'The King began again to be haunted by sprites, by the magic and curious arts of the Lady Margaret [of Burgundy], who raised up the ghost of Richard, Duke of York to walk and vex the King. This was a finer counterfeit stone than Lambert Simnel.' The youth who claimed to be York was so 'crafty and bewitching' that he could 'move pity and induce belief, as was like a kind of fascination and enchantment to those that saw or heard him'.[57]

Is it possible that he was the prince he claimed to be? His own account of how he was spared death after his brother had been killed lacks credibility, but there are inconsistencies in his confession, made much later when he was a captive, which cast doubt on its veracity. Even so, against the weight of evidence that the Princes were dead by October 1483, it would be hard to argue for the survival of one of them. But some were apparently convinced that he was York. He was to 'number kings among his friends',[58] convincing the monarchs of France, Denmark and Scotland, the Duke of Saxony, Maximilian of Austria and his son, the Archduke Philip; all claimed to be satisfied with the evidence of birthmarks, although each at some stage may have been glad of an opportunity to discountenance Henry VII.

The pretender was also a magnet for the dissident Irish lords. 'My masters of Ireland, you will crown apes at length!' Henry VII was to observe scathingly.[59] But it was no jesting matter: the King might dismiss him as 'this lad who calls himself Plantagenet',[60] but that lad was to be a constant thorn in Henry's side for the next eight years, and at first the King may have feared that he really was Richard of

York. The pretender could not have plagued him thus if he had discovered what had become of the Princes in the Tower. Had he been in possession of that information, he would surely have used it to counter the pretender's claims, as he had paraded Warwick in London to counteract Simnel's.

The question of the youth's true identity must at this stage have tormented Elizabeth, whose heart no doubt leapt at the news that her brother might be alive. Yet her hopes must have been tempered with dread and cruelly torn loyalties, for Richard of York had a better claim to the throne than she or Henry. Even if this pretender was her brother, he must be her husband's enemy, and therefore hers, a deadly threat to Henry's security and the safety of her children; and she herself would be placed in a most unenviable position.

Despite the sensation he had created in Cork, the pretender had little success in winning over many of the Irish to his cause, so in 1492 he went to France. Charles VIII's relations with Henry VII were dismal at that time, so predictably he warmly received the pretender as 'Richard IV'. Assigned royal apartments and a guard of honour, the young man 'thought himself in Heaven'.[61]

His advent had already subverted the loyalty of some of Henry's subjects, 'in some upon discontent, in some upon ambition, in some upon levity and desire of change, and in some few upon conscience and belief, but in most upon simplicity, and in divers out of dependence upon some of the better sort, who did in secret favour and nourish these bruits. And it was not long ere these rumours of novelty had begotten others of scandal and murmur against the King and his government, taxing him for a great taxer of his people. Chiefly they fell upon the wrong that he did his Queen, and that he did not reign in her right, wherefore they said that God had now brought to light a masculine branch of the House of York that would not be at his courtesy, however he did depress his poor lady.'[62] Unwittingly, Elizabeth had become a focus for discontent among her husband's subjects, and the existence of the pretender only fuelled the fire.

On 8 June 1492 Elizabeth Wydeville died at Bermondsey Abbey. She must have been unwell since at least 10 April, when she had made her will. Elizabeth could not be with her at the end, for 'at this same season', in the ninth month of her pregnancy, she had already taken to her chamber at Sheen,[63] knowing that her mother was very ill; but her sisters and her half-brother, the Marquess of Dorset, were present, with Grace, a bastard daughter of Edward IV. 'The said Queen desired on her deathbed that, as soon as she should be deceased, she should in all goodly haste, without any worldly pomp, by water be conveyed to Windsor, and there to be buried in the same vault that her husband was buried in, according to the will of my said lord and mine.'[64]

In her will, witnessed by Abbot John of Bermondsey, and Benedict Cun, 'doctor of physic', the Queen Dowager lamented: 'Where I have no worldly goods to do the Queen's Grace, my dearest daughter, a pleasure with, neither to reward any of my children, according to my heart and mind, I beseech Almighty God to bless her Grace, with all her noble issue, and with as good heart and mind as is to me possible, I give her Grace my blessing, and all the aforesaid my children . . . And I beseech my said dearest daughter, the Queen's Grace, and my son, Thomas, Marquess Dorset, to put their good wills and help for the performance of this my testament', and to ensure that her last requests were carried out. They were few.

Elizabeth Wydeville's wishes in regard to her interment were respected. Her body was 'wrapped in [fifty yards of] wax canvas' and, on the evening of Whitsunday (10 June), conveyed by barge from London to Windsor, with only the executors – the late Queen's chaplain, the Prior of the Charterhouse at Sheen, a Mr Haute, a clerk, Dr Brent, and 'Mistress Grace' in attendance. The coffin was borne 'privily through the little park and conveyed into the castle without ringing of any bells or receiving of the Dean and canons, but only by the Prior of the Charterhouse of Sheen and her chaplain. And so, privily, about eleven of the clock in the night, she was buried' in Edward IV's tomb in St George's Chapel, Windsor, 'without any solemn dirge or Mass done for her'.[65]

On the Tuesday following, Elizabeth's younger sisters, Anne, Katherine and Bridget, arrived by barge at Windsor for the Requiem Mass, Bridget having come from Dartford Priory. With them were several relatives, including Lord Dorset and John, Viscount Welles, husband of Cecily of York, who was not present, possibly because she was ill or pregnant, so Anne was chief mourner, deputising for Queen Elizabeth. They attended the ceremonies in St George's Chapel that evening and the next, and 'the officers of arms, there being present, went before the Lady Anne, which offered the Mass penny instead of the Queen, wherefore she had the carpet and the cushion laid', as would have happened had Elizabeth been present'.

There were murmurs that the obsequies were conducted cheaply and shabbily, because only the Poor Knights of St George, Garter officers and other servants were present, but they had been performed as Elizabeth Wydeville had directed.[66]

The death of her mother must have been a grievous blow to Elizabeth, coming as it did as she was about to give birth. An observer wrote that, because the Queen was confined to her chamber, 'I cannot tell what dolent [sad apparel] she goeth in, but I suppose she went in blue likewise as Queen Margaret, the wife of King Henry VI, went in when her mother the Queen of Sicily died.'[67] Henry VII's ordinances followed earlier precedents in laying down the colours to be used for royal mourning; blue was still to be worn,[68] although Elizabeth was also to don the traditional black after the death of one of her children.[69]

On 2 July she bore a second daughter, who was baptised Elizabeth in honour of her late grandmother as well as her mother.[70] According to the epitaph on her tomb, this child was exceptionally beautiful. She was brought up in the nursery household at Eltham Palace with her brother Henry and sister Margaret, in the care of her nurse, Cecilia Burbage, who was paid a salary of 100s. (£2,500). Her rockers each received 66s.8d. (£1,630). That the royal siblings were brought up together is attested by warrants dated September 1493 for payment to servants attending upon 'our right dearly well-beloved children, the Lord Henry and the Ladies Margaret and Elizabeth'.[71] The Wardrobe Accounts of the Lord Treasurer for the period 1491–5 contain orders for robes for 'Margaret and Elizabeth', the King's daughters.[72]

Henry VII's alliances with Ferdinand and Isabella and Maximilian had led to hostilities with Charles VIII. Early in October 1492 he departed for France, leaving Prince Arthur at Westminster to act as nominal regent in his absence. He arrived at Calais on 6 October, then joined his allies in besieging Boulogne. Elizabeth, left behind at Eltham in charge of her younger children, felt her husband's absence keenly, and wrote him many letters with 'tender, frequent and loving lines', begging him so persuasively to return that they were among the 'potent reasons' why he raised the siege, concluded a peace treaty with Charles VIII on 3 November at Étaples, and returned to England soon after 17 November.[73] This reveals how close the royal couple had become in nearly seven years of marriage – so close that they hated being apart.

The peace treaty put an end to Charles VIII's support of the pretender, but rather than surrender him to Henry VII, Charles merely banished him from France. Late that year the youth sought refuge at the court of Margaret of Burgundy. At first she showed herself dubious about his claims, but then said she had been persuaded, after questioning him, that he was indeed her nephew, 'raised from the dead', and publicly congratulated him on his preservation.[74] He was taken under the protection of the Archduke Philip, and was again treated like a king. Given a palatial house in Antwerp, he held court there seated under the royal arms of England, which enraged some English visitors. When he went abroad in the streets, he was escorted by a guard of thirty archers wearing his white rose badge. Philip's father, Maximilian, received him in Vienna as the rightful King of England.

Naturally, everyone wanted to know how 'York' had escaped from the Tower as a child. He told them he had narrowly avoided murder by a ruse, 'for that those who were employed in that barbarous fact, having destroyed the elder brother, were stricken with remorse and compassion towards the younger'. He had been delivered to 'a gentleman who had received orders to destroy him, but who, taking pity on his innocence, had preserved his life and made him swear on the sacraments not to disclose for a certain number of years his birth and lineage'.[75] It was an unlikely tale, since the assassins would surely have known that their remit was to do away with the Yorkist heirs who posed a threat to the King; it did not make sense – and indeed was perilous – for them to kill one and spare the other, however plaintively he pleaded for his life, for with his older brother dead, York would have been, in the eyes of many, the true King of England.

The pretender would never be drawn on the details of Edward V's murder or his own supposed escape from the Tower, saying only 'it is fit it should pass in silence, or at least in a more secret relation, for that it may concern some alive and the memory of some that are dead'.[76] That way he forestalled all discussion of the anomalies in his story. But the Duchess Margaret 'took pleasure in hearing him repeat the tale' and, following her example, the Flemings 'professed they believed the youth had escaped the hand of King Richard by divine intervention, and had been brought safely to his aunt'.[77]

'The rumour of so miraculous an occurrence rapidly spread into England, where the story was not merely believed by the common people, but where there were many important men who considered the matter as genuine.'[78] By now, one imagines, Elizabeth must have been desperate to get a look at, or at least obtain more knowledge of, this youth who insisted he was her brother. Frustratingly, we don't know what she made of the story of his escape.

Queens had little control over the lives of their eldest sons. Arthur was growing into a promising boy, 'blessed with such great charm, grace and goodness that he served as an example of unprecedented happiness to people oftimes', as André glowingly recorded. But when Arthur was six, Elizabeth had to bid him farewell, for by February 1493 he had been sent to live at Ludlow Castle on the Welsh Marches so that he could learn how to govern his principality of Wales. It was to be a practical apprenticeship for kingship. The precedent had been established by Edward IV, who had sent the future Edward V to be educated at Ludlow. Following in his uncle's footsteps, Arthur was nominally to preside over the Council of the Marches and Wales, which administered the principality. Thereafter Elizabeth would see him only intermittently.

His council was headed by his great-uncle, Jasper Tudor, Earl of Pembroke, and included his uncle, Dorset, Sir William Stanley, Thomas FitzAlan, now Earl of Arundel, Gerald FitzGerald, Earl of Kildare, who had been forgiven for helping to crown Lambert Simnel, and John Alcock, Bishop of Worcester, who served as President of the Council of the Marches, as he had done for the future Edward V; his appointment may have been made at the Queen's behest.

Early in 1493 Sir Richard Pole was appointed chamberlain of the Prince's household.[79] The other members of the Council of the Marches included Anthony Willoughby; Robert Ratcliffe, later Earl of Sussex; Maurice St John of Bletsoe, a favoured nephew of Margaret Beaufort who had entered royal service as a member of Henry VII's elite bodyguard; and Gruffydd ap Rhys, who was the son of an influential Welsh lord and became close friends with Arthur. An interesting appointment, probably also made by the Queen, was that of Dr John Argentine, former physician to Edward V, who was now to serve as Prince Arthur's doctor. Dr Argentine had been one of the last people to see the Princes in the Tower alive.[80] After Richard III was crowned, he had fled abroad. Probably he had been able to tell Elizabeth much about her vanished brothers, and possibly this appointment and the many other benefices and marks of royal favour he received under Henry VII were rewards for his loyalty to, and care for, them both.

Arthur's governor and comptroller was Sir Henry Vernon. In 1501 the Prince stayed at Vernon's house, Haddon Hall in Derbyshire, where a room adorned with his coat of arms was once called 'The Prince's Chamber'.

Arthur had commenced his formal education around 1490–1. His first tutor was his chaplain, John Rede, headmaster of Winchester College, who gave him a 'deep acquaintance with knowledge, without great labour on either side'.[81] When he was ten, Arthur twice stayed in the President's Lodgings at Magdalen College, Oxford, where he was served pike, tench, red wine, claret and sack (sweet fortified wine), presented with gloves (as were all distinguished guests) and amused by a marmoset; he came across as 'rather in the grave than in the gay aspect of youth'.[82]

Henry VII was the first English king to encourage the Renaissance culture of humanism, the study of ancient classical learning, at his court, and he was at the forefront of ideas in appointing humanist scholars to teach his sons. Around 1499 Rede was succeeded by the blind friar, Bernard André, who had been assisting Rede since 1496. Under André, Arthur studied classical and Renaissance literature, history and philosophy, reading numerous works by authors such as Homer, Virgil, Ovid, Thucydides, Livy, Tacitus and Erasmus. By 1501, according to André, Arthur 'had either committed to memory, or read with his own eyes and leafed with his own fingers' the best Latin and Greek authors. André was joined after 1499 by Dr Thomas Linacre, another humanist scholar, who had been in Italy and was a pioneer of the New Learning of the Renaissance as well as the King's physician. To him was entrusted 'the task of making the mind and body of Prince Arthur grow in wholesome vigour', and he dedicated his translation of a Greek text, *The Sphere*, to the Prince. Arthur was also instructed in music, horsemanship and the arts of warfare. Giles Dewes, who served Henry VII and Henry VIII as clerk of their libraries, was 'schoolmaster for the French tongue to Prince Arthur'.[83] Dewes also specialised in grammar and alchemy and was an accomplished lute player.

Thanks to his careful education, Arthur turned out to be studious, reserved and thoughtful, 'learned beyond his years, and beyond the custom of princes'.[84] Of the royal children, only he, the heir to the throne, was brought up so far away from his family. The younger ones were reared in households nearer the court, and consequently enjoyed a closer relationship with their parents, especially their mother, who customarily spent more time with them. Elizabeth's influence over her oldest son's upbringing would be far less than that she exerted over the lives of her other children.

By July 1493 Henry VII's intelligence had informed him that the young man whom he called 'the feigned lad' was Peter, commonly known as Perkin, Warbeck, the son of a boatman of Tournai, and not of royal blood at all,[85] whereupon he made a formal protest to Philip and Maximilian against harbouring such a dangerous rebel. When this failed, relations between England and Flanders, usually harmonious, quickly deteriorated, resulting in a temporary trade embargo by England.

Did Henry really believe this intelligence, or did it surface all too conveniently? His later conduct, as will be seen, suggests that there remained at least a grain of doubt. And if the King was uncertain, then Elizabeth must have been too. Maybe she and her sisters were entertaining a faint hope that their brother was indeed still alive.

But Warbeck's story had already spread, which was bad news for Henry VII. 'Conspiracies began to multiply. Desperadoes seeking refuge in sanctuaries broke forth to flock to Peter in Flanders. Many among the nobility turned to conspiracy. Some were actuated by mere foolhardiness; others, believing Peter to be Edward's son Richard, supported the claim of the Yorkist party. Others were moved partly by resentment and greed.'[86] One Edwards, the Queen's own yeoman, defected to the pretender. Elizabeth was unenviably in the middle. The very silence of the chroniclers on her role in all this strongly suggests that she did what was expected of her.

The Christmas season of 1493–4 saw lavish and unprecedented celebrations at Westminster. Henry and Elizabeth presided 'with great solemnity', and at 11 p.m. on Twelfth Night, after divine service and accompanied by the Queen's ladies and the Spanish ambassadors, they went in procession 'through both the halls' to Westminster Hall, which had been hung with tapestries for the occasion. Here they and their guests, including the Lord Mayor and aldermen of London, were entertained by an interlude (a short play) performed by the King's players; 'but ere they had finished came in riding one of the King's Chapel', the court composer and dramatist William Cornish, 'apparelled after the figure of St George; and after followed a fair virgin attired like unto a king's daughter and leading by a silken lace a terrible and huge red dragon, the which, in sundry places of the hall as he passed, spit fire at his mouth. And when Cornish was come before the King, he uttered a certain speech made in *ballade royal*,[87] after finishing thereof he began this anthem of St "*George, O Georgi deo Care*" ["O George, beloved of God"], whereunto the King's Chapel, which stood fast by, answered "*Salvatorem deprecare, ut gubernet Angliam*" ["Intercede with the Saviour, that He may govern England"], and so sang out the whole anthem with lusty courage. In pastime whereof the said Cornish avoided with the dragon, and the virgin was led unto the Queen's standing', to be taken under Elizabeth's protection.

Then there appeared 'twelve gentlemen leading by kerchiefs of pleasance twelve ladies, all goodly disguised, having before them a small tabret [tabor] and a subtle fiddle, the which gentlemen leaped and danced all the length of the hall as they came, and the ladies slid after them', looking as if 'they stood upon a frame running'. When they came before the King, they danced for an hour, and 'it was wonderful to behold the exceeding leaps'.

The King and Queen then entertained their guests to a private banquet, seating themselves at the King's direction at 'a table of stone garnished with napery, lights and other necessaries'. Then the disguised gentlemen came in 'bearing every each of them a dish, and after them as many knights and esquires as made the full number of sixty, the which sixty dishes were all served to the King's mess, and as many served unto the Queen'. All the dishes were 'confections of sundry fruits and conserves, and so soon as the King and the Queen and the other estates were served, then was brought unto the Mayor's stage twenty-four dishes of the same manner service, with sundry wines and ale in most plenteous wise. And finally, as all worldly pleasure hath an end, the board was reverently withdrawn, and the King and Queen with the other estates, with a great sort of lights [were] conveyed into the palace.' The Lord Mayor and aldermen of London did not get home until daybreak.[88]

In April 1492 Henry VII had appointed ten-month-old Prince Henry Lord Warden of the Cinque Ports, not only to honour him, but also to provide an income for his maintenance. The following year, to boost that income, Henry had been made Lord Lieutenant of Ireland

and Warden of the Scottish Marches. Now, in October 1494, in order to discountenance the pretender and proclaim him a fraud, the King created his three-year-old son Duke of York. Edward IV had given his second son that title; and henceforth, until the eighteenth century (and again today), the second sons of monarchs would customarily bear it. It is tempting to imagine that Henry created this precedent at Elizabeth's request, in memory of her father's House and perhaps of her brother Richard, Duke of York, but it is more likely that he did so to demonstrate that young Duke Richard was dead and that the title was now firmly vested in the Tudor dynasty.

On 27 October, the eve of the feast day of SS. Simon and Jude, 'the King, the Queen and my lady the King's mother came from Sheen to Westminster to dinner'. That same day, 'about three in the afternoon, Lord Henry came through the City. He sat on a courser and rode to Westminster to the King with a goodly company',[89] escorted by the Lord Mayor, the aldermen 'and all the crafts in their liveries'.[90] The King welcomed his son and 'kissed him, and from thence went into the Queen's closet'. There is a sketch of the child Henry at the age of two or three in the Bibliothèque de Méjanes, which shows him as a solid, placid infant with chubby cheeks and alert eyes.[91]

Three days later the little Prince waited upon his father with a towel while the King dined, then, having been signed with a cross by Henry and given Elizabeth's blessing, he and twenty-two other candidates received the customary ceremonial bath before keeping vigil in St Stephen's Chapel throughout the night — a long ordeal for so young a child. The next day he was dubbed a Knight of the Bath. The ceremony of ennoblement took place the following day, when he was formally created Duke of York in the presence of the whole court, both houses of Parliament, and the Lord Mayor and aldermen of London. 'My lord Shrewsbury bare my Lord Harry, Duke of York, in his arms, and ten bishops with mitres on their heads going before the King that day about Westminster Hall, with many others of great estate.' In the Prince's honour, the King created new Knights of the Bath. Elizabeth was not present at the ennobling, but afterwards she and Henry, crowned and robed in ermine, went with their son, who was wearing a miniature suit of armour, in procession to Westminster Abbey to attend a Mass celebrated by the Archbishop of Canterbury.[92] The following day was All Souls' Day, when, by tradition, the King kept a 'day of estate' at court and he and Elizabeth again wore their royal robes and crowns.

The celebrations in honour of the young Duke went on for at least two weeks. There were three days of 'jousts royal in the King's Palace of Westminster', where a special stand had been built for the royal party; 'it was the most triumphant place that ever I saw', wrote an observer. The people had flocked 'to see the King's Grace and the Queen so richly apparelled, his house and stage covered with cloth of Arras blue, enramplished with *fleurs de lis* of gold, and within hanged with rich cloth of Arras and two cloths of estate, one for the King, another for the Queen, and rich cushions of cloth of gold, accompanied with the great estates of this realm, as the Duke of York, the Duke of Bedford, the Duke of Buckingham and many other', and with them 'the fairest young Princess', 'the Lady Margaret, the King's oldest daughter'. On the first day the challengers wore the King's livery of green and white, the Tudor colours, but all sported a badge with the Queen's livery of blue and mulberry on their helmets. Other jousts were fought by lesser combatants, but were 'honourable and comfortable to the King and Queen and many other great people there to watch, and a great pleasure to the common people'. On the second day, the contestants wore Margaret Beaufort's blue-and-white livery, and 'by the advice of the King [and] the Queen, my lady the King's mother gave the prize'.[93]

On 11 November Henry and Elizabeth, sitting under their canopies of estate, presided over another tournament, which was followed by a comic display between mock knights. Two days later, there were more jousts before 'the King's Highness, for whose pleasure, the Queen's, and all the ladies' the contestants took part, 'especially for the pleasure of their redoubted lady and fairest young Princess', five-year-old Princess Margaret, who, prompted by her parents, presented the prizes. These were handed to her by three of her mother's ladies: Elizabeth Stafford, Anne Percy and Anne Neville, who, clad in white damask gowns with crimson velvet sleeves and gold circlets on their heads, had led three knights into the ring. By popular demand, more jousts were held on 12 November, and on the 13th 'the King [and] the Queen entered the field to their house'.[94]

In 1619 Paolo Sarpi, a Venetian scholar and church reformer, stated that Prince Henry, 'not being born the King's eldest son, had been destined by his father to be archbishop of Canterbury, and therefore in his youth was made to study'; this assertion was repeated by Lord

Herbert of Cherbury, Henry VIII's seventeenth-century biographer, who opined that a career in the Church was a 'cheap and glorious way' of advancing a younger son, and that the information came from a 'credible author'; yet there is no contemporary evidence to support it, and the fact that Henry was given a secular dukedom rather contradicts it.

That year the King held 'his royal feast of Christmas' at Greenwich, where he entertained the Lord Mayor of London; 'which disports being ended in the morning, the King, the Queen, the ambassadors . . . being sat at a table of stone, sixty knights and esquires served sixty dishes to the King's mess, and as many to the Queen's . . . And finally, the King and Queen were conveyed with great lights into the palace.'[95]

On 7 January 1495 the court moved to the Tower, where Elizabeth was a silent witness to the grim events that followed. Two years earlier a knight, Robert Clifford, had been secretly communicating with Sir William Stanley; then Clifford had gone to the court of Burgundy and espoused the cause of Perkin Warbeck. Mysteriously, in December 1494, he was granted a free pardon, upon which he returned to England. On 6 January, 'forewarned of his coming', the King went ahead to the Tower and had Clifford brought there so that he could question him himself. During that interview Clifford – who was probably a royal spy or a double agent – incriminated Sir William Stanley and others who enjoyed his confidence, apparently asserting that Stanley had said he would not fight against Warbeck if he was the true son of Edward IV.[96] Bacon asserts that resentment of Henry's rule, his taxes and his treatment of Elizabeth were at the root of Stanley's disaffection.

At first, according to Vergil, the King could not be persuaded to believe Clifford; he owed his crown to Stanley's intervention at Bosworth, and since then Stanley had held a position of great trust as chamberlain of the royal household, an office that brought him in daily contact with the King; and he had grown very rich in Henry's service. Elizabeth knew him well. He was also Margaret Beaufort's brother-in-law, so these allegations came close to home. In the end Clifford convinced Henry that Stanley was plotting treason, and left the Tower with a gift of £500.

Henry did not wish to alienate Thomas Stanley, but 'in the end, severity won and mercy was put behind'.[97] Sir William and his contacts were arrested, arraigned and condemned for aiding the cause of the pretender Warbeck and plotting the death and destruction of the King and the overthrow of his kingdom. Stanley was accused of passing on privileged information to the pretender, thus abusing the trust placed in him by the King. The allegiance he owed Henry VII may have been compromised by his resentment at not being awarded a peerage, and by Henry's curbs on the power of the nobility, but he must have known that he stood to lose more than most if Henry were overthrown; possibly he hoped for more from Warbeck. The twelve days of executions that followed, culminating with Stanley's beheading before dawn on 16 February on Tower Hill, caused a sensation.

Warbeck's cause was now 'as stone without lime' in England, and he knew it. In return for continuing financial support from Maximilian and Philip, he resorted to pledging them part of his kingdom if he died childless – and, of course, in possession of it; and he promised to give away all Henry VII's personal effects, even down to the toys of his children. Then he set about raising mercenaries to 'try his adventures in some exploit upon England, hoping still upon the affections of the common people towards the House of York'.[98]

With Warbeck at large on the Continent and Sir William Stanley proved guilty of treason, Henry VII was aware that his enemies might scheme to use Elizabeth's unmarried sisters against him. Wishing to avert that threat, he arranged marriages advantageous to himself for Anne and Katherine. On 4 February 1495, at Greenwich, Anne was married to Lord Thomas Howard, son of the Earl of Surrey, who had affirmed to the King that they had been betrothed since 1484.[99] The royal family attended the wedding and Henry VII gave the bride away, himself presenting the offering at the nuptial Mass.[100] The marriage marked the return to favour of the Howards: Thomas's father, the Earl of Surrey, had fought for Richard III at Bosworth and spent three years in prison in the Tower for it, but his refusal to seize an opportunity of escaping had marked him to Henry VII as an honourable, upright man, and secured his pardon and release, and the restoration of his estates and the earldom of Surrey. Since then Howard had proved his loyalty and worth to the new dynasty, paving the way for the marriage of his son to the Queen's sister, which would bind the Howards to the royal House by kinship as well as loyalty.

On 12 February Elizabeth met with Surrey to finalise Anne's

marriage settlement – which shows that she had been involved in arranging the match. The King had not advanced the marriage portion of 10,000 marks (£1.5 million) willed to Anne by Edward IV, so Elizabeth undertook in this indenture to provide the couple with an annuity of £120 (£58,300), to which the King had agreed to contribute £26 (£12,600, considerably less than Anne's father had willed) annually from the Crown lands; in addition, Elizabeth promised to pay allowances of 20s. (£500) a week for the upkeep of the couple's estate, food and drink; £51.11s.8d. (£25,000) for the wages of two female attendants, a maid, a gentleman, a yeoman and three grooms; and £15.11s.8d. (£7,600) a year to maintain seven horses. In addition, 'the said Queen's Grace, at her costs and charges, shall find unto the Lady Anne all her sufficient and convenient apparel for her body, at all times' until the couple came into their inheritance on Surrey's death.

In return, the cash-strapped Surrey settled on the couple, as jointure, four manors that would revert on Thomas Howard's death to Anne's half-brother, Dorset, her royal nephew, Henry, Duke of York, and others of the Queen's choosing. The indenture was signed in Elizabeth's own hand.[101] At her request and Surrey's, the settlement was approved by the King in Parliament in 1496, the Act being passed 'at the special desire' of the Queen, since it was 'her very will and mind' that the settlement be paid in full'.[102] This is another instance of Elizabeth exercising her authority within the conventional bounds permitted to queens.

After her marriage, Anne did not frequent the court: her name is not recorded there again. Tragically, her four children – Muriel, Katherine, Henry and Thomas – were all to die in infancy. They were buried in the Howard aisle in St Mary's Church at Lambeth.[103]

Later in 1495 (certainly by October) Elizabeth's other unwed sister, sixteen-year-old Katherine, was married to Lord William Courtenay. The Courtenays, who were descended from Edward I, had long supported the House of Lancaster. William's father, Edward Courtenay, had been one of Henry Tudor's adherents during Buckingham's rebellion; after being attainted he had defected to him in Brittany and fought for him at Bosworth, for which he had been rewarded with the earldom of Devon. His son William made a worthy and honourable match for a princess: Vergil praised his courage and his manly bearing, and Hall called him 'a man of great nobility, estimation and virtue'.[104]

Elizabeth almost certainly helped to arrange this marriage too, negotiating with the Earl of Devon a similar settlement to that which she had negotiated for her sister Anne and Thomas Howard; no indenture survives, but the Queen appointed the same men to hold the lands in question.[105] After the wedding, Katherine resided mainly at the castles of Tiverton, Colcombe and Powderham in Devon, or at her husband's London residence in Warwick Lane, Newgate. She bore Courtenay two sons and a daughter.

On 27 March 1495, to supplement her dower, Henry gave Elizabeth the castle, manor, lordship and town of Fotheringhay,[106] the chief seat of her Yorkist forebears, a gift that must have been very welcome to her. Strangely, given that so many members of her family were represented, her arms were missing from the lost heraldic glass in Fotheringhay Church and College, as described by William Dugdale in the seventeenth century.[107]

In April the King named Elizabeth Chief Lady of the Order of the Garter. Prince Henry, not quite four, was made a Knight of the Garter on 17 May, wearing a crimson velvet gown and cap for his investiture.[108]

Death carried off Elizabeth's grandmother, the eighty-year-old Cecily, Duchess of York, on 31 May 1495, at Berkhamsted Castle. Cecily, clothed in the black Benedictine habit she had worn for many years now, was buried with her husband, Richard Plantagenet, Duke of York, in the collegiate church at Fotheringhay, the ancestral mausoleum of the House of York. In her will, she bequeathed to Elizabeth a psalter with a relic of St Christopher;[109] Margaret Beaufort was left an exquisite breviary, which suggests that the two matriarchs had got on well.

On Cecily's death, her revenues reverted by inheritance to her granddaughter the Queen, bringing Elizabeth a further £1,399.6s.8d. (£680,200) a year, which considerably boosted her income and helped to clear the debts she had amassed. She also inherited Baynard's Castle, which fittingly made her the owner of the two great seats of the House of York. Baynard's Castle was a place she had known well from childhood, for it had been the London residence of Cecily Neville from 1461, and in 1461 and 1483 respectively, Edward IV and Richard III had been offered the crown of England in its great hall. A castle had stood on the site since Norman times, when, along with the Tower of London and Mountfichet's Tower, Baynard's Castle had been one of three fortresses guarding the City.

The house Elizabeth inherited was the third to be built on or near the site. It was 'situated right pleasantly on Thames' side, and full well garnished and arranged, and encompassed outside strongly with water',[110] its wall rising sheer from the river. It consisted of four wings built in a trapezoid shape around a double courtyard with lovely gardens, from which rose a hexagonal tower. It became Elizabeth's favourite London residence and she spent liberally on its gardens. In 1500–1 Henry VII 'repaired or rather new builded this house, not embattled, or so strongly fortified castle-like, but far more beautiful and commodious for the entertainment of any prince or great estate'.[111] His additions included five projecting towers between the two existing great octagonal corner towers on the riverfront. The principal chambers, which may have been located in these towers, were freshly decorated, with new glass in the windows, expensive ironwork and tapestries.[112]

On 1 July 1495 Henry and Elizabeth departed on a progress northwards, visiting Chipping Norton, Evesham, Tewkesbury and Worcester before arriving at Bewdley, the residence of Prince Arthur, on the 10th. They were with their son at Ludlow two days later;[113] he had travelled ahead to receive them. Entertainments had been laid on, and the Prince watched a play in the 'dry quarry', an amphitheatre on the site of the modern swimming pool. Henry and Elizabeth then left for Shrewsbury.

This progress came at a fraught time, as an invasion by Perkin Warbeck was expected daily. Sir William Stanley's execution had cost Henry much popularity in the north-west, where the Stanleys had a great affinity. In Lancashire, they were important landowners and commanded more respect than the monarch, and in this period they were steadily increasing their extensive land holdings in the county. It was not the most convenient time to be away, but the King felt it necessary that he should be seen in those parts with his popular Queen in order to regain the love of his subjects.

The royal couple rode northwards to Combermere Abbey, Shropshire, where they stayed in the lavish Abbot's Lodgings. From there they travelled via Holt to Chester, and thence to Hawarden in Wales, where Thomas Stanley, Earl of Derby, awaited them. On 27 July he accompanied the King and Queen to Vale Royal Abbey, then escorted them north to Lathom House,[114] his palatial mansion at Ormskirk, Lancashire. To ease the royal journey, Derby had had a fine stone bridge built at Warrington, which lasted until the nineteenth century.

Lathom had been in the possession of the Stanleys since 1390. It was set in a deer park bounded by the River Tawd, Eller Brook and Douglas Brook, and overlooked the town of Burscough and the marshlands of Martin Mere and Hoscar Mossit. The estate, part of the parish of Ormskirk, was mentioned in Domesday Book. Lathom House, begun by Derby in 1485, was a palatial mansion boasting eighteen towers and a moat eight yards wide; it is said that this splendid house, which was unique in the north-west, was Henry VII's inspiration for Richmond Palace. Derby was now busily converting Lathom into the chief administrative centre of the region, but it was still a peaceful retreat, far from the turmoil of the court.

In the early seventeenth century Samuel Rutter, Bishop of Sodor and Man, described Lathom before its destruction: 'Lathom House was encompassed with a strong wall of two yards thick; upon the walls were nine towers, flanking each other. Without the wall was a moat eight yards wide; upon the back of the moat was a strong row of palisades; beside these there was a high strong tower, called the Eagle Tower, in the midst of the house surrounding all the rest; and the gateway was also two high and strong buildings, with a strong tower on each side of it. There is something so particular and romantic in the general situation of this house, as if Nature herself had formed it for a stronghold or place of security.'[115] The names of seven of the towers were the Eagle Tower, the Tower of Madness, the Tower at the Kitchen Bridge, the little tower next it, the next tower to that in the corner, the Chapel Tower, and the Private Tower.[116]

Henry and Elizabeth stayed at Lathom for four days as guests of Derby and Margaret Beaufort. During their visit Henry rewarded 'the women that sang before the King and Queen'.[117] A tale persisted in the Stanley family that the King, after being shown over the house, was taken up to the leads by Derby to see the fine view of the countryside roundabouts. The Earl's fool had accompanied them, and seeing the King standing near the unguarded edge of the leads, he muttered to Derby, 'Tom, remember Will.' He was referring, of course, to Sir William Stanley. Henry heard his words and, perceiving what was meant, hastened back downstairs to Elizabeth and terminated his visit immediately, leaving the fool wishing that his master had had the courage to avenge the death of his brother.[118] But there is no historical evidence to back up the story.

Late in July, while Henry and Elizabeth were at Lathom, Warbeck and fourteen ships carrying his mercenary force of what Vergil called 'human dregs' finally anchored off Deal. The pretender sent his soldiers ashore to reconnoitre prior to invading, but the men of Kent were already on the alert, and summoned the King's forces, who cut them to pieces,[119] prompting Warbeck's fleet to scurry away to the west. By the end of July, Warbeck was in Ireland. His attempt to attack Waterford was fiercely repelled by the able Sir Edward Poynings, the King's Deputy. Driven off, Warbeck sailed towards Cork, disappeared for a time, then made his way north to Scotland.

On 3 August Henry and Elizabeth moved south to Derby's hunting lodge at Knowsley, east of Liverpool, where Derby had built for them a set of detached royal lodgings. He had perhaps also commissioned a new four-poster bed – the 'Paradise Bed' – which was very similar in size, design and ornamentation to another bed that he had had made for himself, either for Lathom or Knowsley. Both were probably built by the same craftsmen; the standard of carving is exceptionally high and reveals Burgundian influence. It is not known whether the Paradise Bed was installed at Lathom or Knowsley, or whether it was built some years before this visit, but it may have been specially made for the new royal apartments at Knowsley.

The royal bed has a triptych of panels set into the headboard; the central panel portrays the temptation of Adam and Eve in the Garden of Eden, and the side panels display the royal arms of France and England respectively, which are repeated on the footboard. The lion and the dragon, supporters of the Tudor arms, appear in the central panel. Tudor roses appear on the head posts and on shields supported by the heraldic lions surmounting the posts. The centre crest bears the royal arms of England and France quartered. The cross of St George – a saint much invoked by Henry VII – dominates the side crest of the bed, which is formed by a carved knotted cord that may symbolise the King's devotion to the Observant Friars. These symbols are all to be seen in the Henry VII Chapel in Westminster Abbey. The faces of Adam and Eve bear some resemblance to those of Henry and Elizabeth – especially as carved in the Sudbury Hutch (see Appendix 1) – and maybe Derby wanted a parallel drawn between the progenitors of humanity and the founders of the Tudor dynasty.[120]

If the Paradise Bed was at Knowsley, then Henry and Elizabeth slept in it for just one night. The next day they were in Manchester, then a market town, and on the 6th proceeded southwards, lodging at Macclesfield, Newcastle-under-Lyme, Stafford and Lichfield, before diverting north-east to Burton-on-Trent and Derby, then south via Loughborough to Collyweston, Margaret Beaufort's house. They continued south to Rockingham, and then to Northampton, Banbury and Woodstock, where they stayed for ten days. By now Elizabeth knew she was to have another child, so possibly she needed to rest. On 29 October she and Henry were at Ewelme, the Oxfordshire seat of her cousin, Edmund de la Pole, Earl of Suffolk, then they moved on to Bisham Priory, Berkshire, the burial place of many of her Neville ancestors. From there they went to Windsor Castle, and then to Sheen, arriving on 3 October.[121] They were to have four days in which to relax after their travels before calamity struck.

14

'Doubtful Drops of Royal Blood'

I nfant mortality was high in Tudor times, and in an age long before antibiotics even royal children succumbed to minor illnesses. Elizabeth faced tragedy when, on 7 October 1495,[1] when she was nearly five months pregnant, her three-year-old daughter Elizabeth died at Eltham Palace. Her death came at a time when her father was negotiating a marriage for her with the future King Francis I of France, then a year-old child. As the King and Queen were at Sheen when their daughter died,[2] her death was probably unexpected.

On 16 November 1495, bravely setting aside their grief, they honoured with their presence the traditional feast held by the newly appointed Serjeants-at-Law amid the splendours of Ely Place in Holborn,[3] Elizabeth and her ladies dining in one room, and Henry and his retinue in another, as was customary. Ely Place would have held a special relevance for both Henry and Elizabeth, for their common ancestor, John of Gaunt, Duke of Lancaster, had lived there with his third wife, Katherine Swynford, mother of his Beaufort children, in the late fourteenth century; but on this occasion Elizabeth's thoughts were far more likely to have been with the child she had lost.

The body of the infant Princess was brought from Eltham in a black 'chair', or chariot, drawn by six horses to the gate of Westminster Abbey, where the Prior was waiting to receive it. The King and Queen were nearby at Westminster Palace[4] but did not attend the obsequies, for which Henry had outlaid £318 (£155,480) on 26 October. The funeral was arranged by Cardinal Morton, Giles, Lord

Daubeney, the Lord Chamberlain and others. It took place on 26 November, and was conducted with great ceremony and attended by a hundred poor men who had been given black gowns for the occasion.[5] Soon afterwards the grieving parents raised to the memory of 'our daughter Elizabeth, late passed out of this transitory life', a small tomb chest of grey Lydian marble with a black marble cover 'on the right-hand side of the altar, just before St Edward's shrine, the foundation of which the foot of the grave almost touched'. It cost £371.0s.11d. (£181,400).[6]

Originally the tomb bore a copper-gilt effigy and inscription, but these have long disappeared, presumed stolen. Fortunately the inscription was copied and preserved by the Elizabethan antiquarian, John Stow. It read: 'Elizabeth, second daughter of Henry VII, the most illustrious King of England, France and Ireland, and of the Lady Elizabeth, his most serene wife . . . On whose soul God have mercy. Here, after death, lies in this tomb a descendant of royalty, the young and noble Elizabeth, an illustrious princess. Atropos, most merciless messenger of death, snatched her away. May she inherit eternal life in Heaven!'[7]

It is this reference to the goddess Atropos, the oldest of the Fates, that has led historians to conclude that Princess Elizabeth died of 'atrophy', a wasting disease that can have many causes, although the Tudor age understood it to be the result of poor nourishment. It is hard to imagine that Henry, Elizabeth or Margaret Beaufort would have allowed a child to perish through such neglect; however, the epitaph clearly referred not to a disease, but to the dread task of the severe and inflexible Atropos, which was to choose how a person would die and cut the thread of their life short with her shears. The Princess had probably succumbed rapidly to a childhood infection that would be easily treated today. There is nothing in the historical record to suggest that she was delicate or suffered a long illness.

Late that year Elizabeth, doubtless seeking spiritual comfort and wishing to pray for the blessing of a son, journeyed to the famous shrine dedicated to the Virgin Mary at Walsingham in Norfolk, where Christ's mother had reputedly appeared in 1061 to Richeldis de Faverches, a devout widow, and asked her to build a replica of the 'holy house of Nazareth' where she had received the Annunciation of the birth of Jesus. Angels were said to have assisted in the miraculous construction of what was to become one of the most important shrines in Christendom. In time, Augustinian and Franciscan monasteries had been founded nearby to look after the needs of the hordes of pilgrims, and over the centuries the 'holy house', known as 'Little Nazareth', had been visited by numerous kings and queens, and made rich by the offerings of the devout.

Our Lady of Walsingham, the patron saint of mothers, and indeed of all humanity, was said to bestow the gift of calm and serenity to those beset by troubles. Elizabeth would have passed several small chapels along the road leading to the shrine, but at the last, the fourteenth-century Slipper Chapel, dedicated to St Katherine, she would have removed her shoes and walked the remaining mile barefoot. Thus she reverently entered the holy sanctum of the incense-scented, candlelit Chapel of the Virgin to pray before the gilded and bejewelled image of St Mary. Nearby were displayed relics, among them a phial of the Virgin's milk, and a statue of her said to be of miraculous origin. Elizabeth would also have seen a kneeling silver-gilt statue of her husband, given during a pilgrimage made by Henry VII in 1487.

Elizabeth was also a patron of the shrine of Our Lady of Grace of Ipswich, which was first recorded in 1152 and now ranked only second in popularity to Our Lady of Walsingham. A daughter of Edward I had been married in the chapel of Our Lady of Grace in 1297. The shrine was closed down in 1538, during the Dissolution of the Monasteries, and no trace of the chapel survives; a bronze plaque in Lady Lane marks the site where it once stood. Almost certainly a statue of the Madonna in the sanctuary of Our Lady of Grace at Nettuno, Italy, is the original image that adorned the shrine in Ipswich, having been rescued from the pyre that awaited it in Chelsea, where it was to be burned with the statue of Our Lady of Walsingham.[8]

In November 1495 Perkin Warbeck surfaced in Scotland and was received with royal honours by King James IV at Stirling Castle. James took an instant liking to him, decked him out in clothes befitting a king, settled on him a very generous pension, and took him on a triumphal progress through his kingdom. News of this alarmed Henry VII, for he had been working to seal a peace alliance with Scotland through the marriage of his daughter Margaret to James.[9] James not only seemed determined to provoke his English neighbour, but clearly believed that Warbeck was indeed 'Prince Richard of England'. He held tournaments in his honour, and married him to his distant kinswoman, Katherine, daughter of George Gordon, Earl of Huntly, 'a young virgin of excellent beauty and virtue'.[10] If a love letter from Warbeck is genuine, he was deeply smitten. His bride's eyes were 'brilliant as the stars. Whoever sees her cannot choose but admire her; admiring, cannot choose but love her; loving, cannot choose but obey her.'[11]

This was all bad news for King Henry, for Ferdinand and Isabella were now stalling at concluding the marriage alliance with England while the pretender was at large. But the King was working to neutralise that threat. Fractured relations between England and the Low Countries were healed in February 1496, when he sealed a peace treaty with Maximilian, whereby each undertook not to support the other's rebels; the treaty was in both countries' interests, and effectively slammed the door to Flanders in Warbeck's face, for Margaret of Burgundy had been warned that she would be deprived of her dower lands if she did not honour its terms. Henry had also made peace with the French, so Warbeck was now isolated in Scotland.

Elizabeth's third daughter was born on 18 March 1496 at Sheen Palace.[12] The year is sometimes given as 1495, as Margaret Beaufort incorrectly recorded it in her book of hours. In true medieval fashion she dated the years from Lady Day, 25 March, and by that reckoning 18 March would have belonged to the previous year, 1495. Later Erasmus misleadingly stated that this child, Mary, was four in September 1499; however, he gave the ages of Prince Henry and Prince Margaret as a year older than they actually were, so it is likely that he gave Mary's age incorrectly too. The earliest extant document that mentions Mary is a payment to Anne (or Alice) Skern (or Skeron), her nurse, for one quarter ending June 1496, such payments normally being paid half-yearly. The fact that she was paid only from March confirms that Mary was born in 1496.[13]

The King and Queen possibly named their new baby after the sister Elizabeth had loved and lost, or after the Virgin Mary. Mary grew up to be very beautiful, much resembling her mother in portraits; like her, she had red-gold hair. The infant Princess was sent to Eltham to be brought up with Prince Henry and Princess Margaret.

By May Henry and Elizabeth had moved to Sheen and thence to Greenwich, where he gave her a gift of £30 (£14,600) to buy jewels.[14] That summer, their progress took them to the West Country. In June they left Sheen for Chertsey, then moved on to Guildford,

Farnham, Alresford, Bishops Waltham, Porchester and Southampton, arriving on 14 July. They stayed at Beaulieu Abbey and crossed the Solent to the Isle of Wight during their visit; then they travelled on to Christchurch, Poole and Corfe Castle. On 5 August they were at Salisbury, and on the 10th they visited Heytesbury, where Elizabeth had probably lived after she left sanctuary in 1484. John Nesfield, her former gaoler and host, had died in 1488, and the manor was now owned by Edward Hastings, Lord Hungerford; he was married to the heiress of the Hungerfords, who had been restored in blood by Henry VII.[15] During her visit Elizabeth may have reflected on how settled her life was now compared with the uncertainties of twelve years earlier when she had resided at Heytesbury during Richard III's reign.

The royal couple then travelled on to Bath, Bristol, Iron Acton, Malmesbury, Cirencester and Woodstock. On 10 September they returned via Wycombe to Windsor.[16]

In September 1496, Prince Henry – or 'my Lord Harry', as he was known[17] – performed his first public duty when he witnessed a charter granted by the King to the Abbot and convent of Glastonbury Abbey, a monastery he was to dissolve decades later.

Harry was now five, a boy of considerable intellect and talent, whom his grandmother called the King's 'fair sweet son'.[18] It was the King who drew up the rules by which the royal nursery was governed, but the Queen also had a say in the upbringing of her children, as – no doubt – did Margaret Beaufort. In 1496 Elizabeth appointed Elizabeth Denton, who had served her as wardrobe keeper since her marriage, as a replacement for the long-serving Elizabeth Darcy as lady mistress of the nursery to Prince Henry and his sisters at Eltham Palace.[19] Elizabeth Denton also continued to serve the Queen, and by February 1499 she had become governess to the princesses, and been replaced as mistress of the nursery by Anne Crowmer.[20] When Elizabeth Denton accompanied Princess Margaret to Scotland in 1503, Anne Crowmer took over as Mary's governess. Mistress Denton later served as lady governess and mistress of the nursery to Henry VIII's own children, Henry, Prince of Wales, and the future Mary I respectively, and in 1515 was in receipt of an annuity of £50 for good service rendered to the late King and Queen.[21]

By 1499 Jane Vaux, Lady Guildford, who had long served in the household of the Queen, was also employed as governess to the princesses; in 1503, she was paid a salary of £13.6s.8d. (£6,500).[22]

The nursery at Eltham was therefore dominated by women, and the young Prince Henry spent his childhood very much under female influence. The fact that Elizabeth Denton served both Prince Henry and his mother suggests that the Queen spent time with her younger son and his sisters,[23] taking a keen interest in their learning and accomplishments, as did the Lady Margaret. All the evidence suggests that Henry, Margaret and Mary grew up closer to their mother than was often the lot of royal children. It is likely that Elizabeth herself taught her younger children some of their early lessons. A literate woman who loved books and music, she imparted her passion for these things to the future Henry VIII and his sisters. David Starkey has noticed the similarities between the few extant examples of her handwriting and theirs, which suggests that she herself taught them to read and write.[24]

Prince Henry's formal education had begun the year before under the guidance of the Cambridge-educated poet laureate, John Skelton, a protégé of Margaret Beaufort, who was probably responsible for his appointment. Skelton, who was also a great satirist, now took up residence with his charge at Eltham Palace, and would remain in post until 1502. Erasmus told Prince Henry that Skelton was 'that incomparable light and ornament of British letters, who cannot only kindle your studies but bring them to a happy conclusion'.[25] Twenty years later, when Henry was king, the poet recalled:

> The honour of England I learned to spell
> In dignity royal that doth excel.
> I gave him drink of the sugared well.[26]

It was ever-frowning, frost-faced Skelton who encouraged the Prince's musical talents, inherited from and encouraged by both parents, and taught him to play the lute, organ and virginals, to read music, and to sing. Young Henry proved to be gifted musically, not only as a player but also as a composer: many pieces he was to compose as an adult survive and are still sung today. Skelton also fostered in his pupil a love of theology, and taught him Latin. Like all the Tudors, Henry had an aptitude for languages. Above all, Skelton instilled in the boy a love of learning and scholarship that lasted all his life; and he took delight in his charge's achievements, calling him 'a delightful small, new rose, worthy of its stock'. It was for Henry that he wrote his *Speculum Principis*, a manual for a future ruler, which advised him not to rely too heavily on his ministers, and to 'choose a wife for yourself, prize her always and uniquely' – advice that the adult Henry did not heed.

Much later – around the time of Elizabeth's death, as he was given mourning cloth to wear in her funeral procession – Skelton was succeeded as tutor by a Scottish schoolmaster, John Holt,[27] who in turn was replaced on his death in 1504 by William Hone, a Cambridge scholar who also taught Princess Mary.[28] The young Duke was also instructed by Bernard André, who wrote his *Vita Henrici VII* to teach him history, and probably schooled him in Latin. Arthur's former tutor, Giles Dewes, taught him French, and perhaps grammar and alchemy. It is possible that Thomas More, a humanist scholar like André, instructed the boy in mathematics, geometry and astronomy; it was probably More who had introduced the boy to the works of Erasmus. Later, Erasmus would assert that Henry's style of writing was like his own because he had been encouraged to read his books when young.

Of Margaret's education we know little, save that she could read and write, although not very competently; she was the first English princess whose signature survives. She loved music and dancing, and had minstrels among her personal servants. Elizabeth encouraged her to play the lute and clavichord, and the King purchased for her a lute costing 13s.4d. (£325).[29]

Despite all the care taken over their upbringing, Elizabeth's children grew up in a world overshadowed by insecurities, threats, intrigue and paranoia. Unsurprisingly that would take its toll – and now a new threat was brewing.

In September 1496 James IV invaded England with Warbeck, his support assured by Warbeck's promise of the return of Berwick, a town that had been much fought over by the Scots and the English, and which the future Richard III had taken in 1482. Henry VII prepared to confront the pretender, saying that 'he hoped now he should see the gentleman of whom he had heard so much'.[30] But James's army was more interested in looting and settling old border feuds than in securing a victory for Warbeck, and four miles into England the Scots King was obliged to cease raiding and retreat at the appearance of the royal army. Henry was now determined to force James to surrender Warbeck. Early in 1497 Parliament readily voted punishing taxes to finance a war against the Scots.

Elizabeth suffered a brief illness at Greenwich in the spring of 1497. On 25 April the Lady Margaret wrote to the Queen's chamberlain, acknowledging some gloves he had purchased for her: 'Blessed be God, the King, the Queen and all our sweet children be in good health. The Queen hath been a little crazed [broken down in health], but now she is well, God be thanked. Her sickness is not so good [amended] as I would, but I trust hastily it shall, with God's grace.'[31] It is clear from this letter that Margaret Beaufort took a proprietorial interest in her grandchildren – 'our sweet children' – and that she was genuinely concerned for her daughter-in-law, the Queen. It does not read as if this was merely the concern of a dynast for the royal bride her son had married. But by 12 June Elizabeth had recovered, as on that date Andrea Trevisano, the new Venetian ambassador, congratulated the King 'on his own wellbeing, and that of the Queen and his children'; Trevisano had also brought letters of credence to Elizabeth and Prince Arthur.[32]

Crippled and provoked by the new taxes, the 'brutish and rural' men of Cornwall rose against their sovereign and marched on London. Elizabeth was at Sheen with the King when news came that the rebels were on the march, and he paid her £10 (£4,860) 'for garnishing of a salett' – the helmet he would wear into battle – with jewels.[33]

Before departing on 5 June to deal with the threat, Henry furnished Elizabeth with a stout escort of lords and gentlemen, and she immediately hastened to Eltham Palace to collect Prince Henry and her daughters; although only Margaret is mentioned, the younger children lived together, so probably Elizabeth took Mary with her too. She entered London with them the next day, lodging at Margaret Beaufort's house, Coldharbour, within the protection of the City walls. They stayed there six days while the reports that filtered through from the west grew ever more alarming. The rebel army had been reinforced by malcontents from the shires. On 12 June it was known that their forces numbered 18,000 and that they were approaching Farnham in Surrey. On hearing this, the Queen hastened with her children into the Tower for safety, no doubt thanking God that Prince Arthur was far away in Ludlow and no longer living at Farnham.[34]

On 16 June the rebels reached Blackheath, four miles east of the City. Here they drew up their battalions, ready to attack. Their plan was to force an entry into the City and assault the Tower, because they thought the King was there. But Henry had now joined his forces with those of his Chamberlain, Lord Daubeney, and their 25,000 men were stationed at Lambeth, blocking access to London. The King was keeping his nerve, aware that the rebels were exhausted after their long march, and preparing to surround and overcome them. But he knew too that the situation was critical, for Elizabeth and his children were in the Tower.

'There was great fear throughout the City, and cries were made: "Every man to arms, to arms!" Some ran to the gates, others mounted the walls, so that no part was undefended; and the magistrates kept continual watch lest the rebels should descend from their camp and invade the City.'[35] For Elizabeth, this ordeal must have resurrected dim but frightening memories of Fauconberg's attack on the Tower in 1471, when she had been four years old. Once again she was trapped in the fortress while turmoil raged outside, and this time it was her own children who were at risk. Well-educated as she was, she was probably uncomfortably aware that, during the Peasants' Revolt of 1381, the mob had breached the Tower's defences, insulted the mother of Richard II, and dragged forth and beheaded the Archbishop of Canterbury and the Lord Treasurer. The Tower was no more heavily fortified now than it had been then.

But on 17 June the King 'delivered and purged' everyone's hearts of fear as he sent forces under the command of his nobles to surround the rebels. Then, 'with manly stomach and desire to fight', he himself led an army out of the City, sending Lord Daubeney ahead 'with a great company'.[36] Staunch Londoners hastened to the King's aid, and that day the Cornish insurgents were routed in a sharp skirmish at Blackheath, in which 2,000 of their number were slain. A victorious Henry returned to London to be welcomed by the Mayor and to give thanks in St Paul's Cathedral. Afterwards, he hastened to the Tower to be reunited with Elizabeth and their children. They were back at Sheen by 1 July.[37]

The following month Henry sent envoys to James IV to demand the surrender of Warbeck, and to offer peace terms. But James had pre-empted him, having already dispatched the pretender south – in a ship appropriately called *The Cuckoo* – to launch an offensive on the south-west. Simultaneously, despite having agreed a seven-year truce with Henry, James was planning another offensive across the Border. England stood in deep peril.

Warbeck, however, scuppered the fine timing of this strategy by making a detour to Cork to visit Sir James Ormond, his chief Irish supporter, in the hope of rallying more men to his banner. Learning that Ormond had been killed in a brawl, he had no choice but to flee across the sea to Cornwall, with four Irish ships in pursuit.

In July 1497 a new treaty was agreed with Spain, which provided for the Infanta to come to England when she was fourteen, an age she would reach in December 1499. That August, Prince Arthur was formally betrothed to Katherine of Aragon at Woodstock Palace, Henry and Elizabeth having travelled up to Oxfordshire to be present.[38] Arthur was now nearly eleven, 'but taller than his years would warrant, of remarkable beauty and grace, and very ready in speaking Latin'. The King and Queen 'celebrated with great triumph and festivities the marriage between Prince Arthur and Katherine, and in this good time they hope she will be brought to England with great splendour'.[39] But their hopes were destined to be frustrated.

On 3 September 1497, after the new Venetian ambassador, Andrea Trevisano, and his Milanese counterpart, Raimondo de Soncino, had had an audience of the King at Woodstock, they were presented to Queen Elizabeth, whom they 'found at the end of a hall, dressed in cloth of gold. On one side of her was the King's mother, on the other her son the Prince.' This was Henry, not Arthur, even though Arthur was present at Woodstock.[40] As David Starkey points out, by now, Arthur, the heir, was generally associated with the King, while Henry, the second son, was usually associated with the Queen[41] – a deliberate policy that may reflect personal affiliations within the royal family.

'The Queen is a handsome woman,' observed Trevisano. Being presented to the Queen was a privilege only permitted to ambassadors if the diplomatic business in question concerned a woman, in which case she would naturally take an interest. Trevisano and Soncino brought her letters from the Signory of Venice and from a lady whom Soncino called 'our queen'; this was probably the charming Beatrice d'Este, wife of Ludovico Sforza, Duke of Milan. Elizabeth's French was not fluent like her husband's, so the ambassadors addressed her in Italian, with Thomas Savage, Bishop of London, acting as interpreter.[42]

★

On 7 September 1497 Perkin Warbeck landed at Whitesand Bay near Land's End in Cornwall, a Cornwall still simmering with resentment against the King. But Henry had received reliable intelligence from Ireland of the pretender's aims, and was now making haste to assemble an army at Woodstock.

Having taken St Michael's Mount, and left his wife in the monastery there, Warbeck marched to Bodmin, recruiting 3,000 'part-naked men' of the 'rude people'[43] on the way. At Bodmin he had himself proclaimed Richard IV. On 17 September, having rallied at least 3,000 more supporters to his banner, 'this little cockatrice of a king'[44] and his army appeared before Exeter, to which they laid siege. Despite having few weapons, no armour and no artillery, they managed to breach one of the gates, but were firmly repelled by the King's brother-in-law, Lord William Courtenay, and the citizens, and cut to pieces.

Henry took the threat posed by Warbeck very seriously. In October Trevisano reported that the King had sent the Queen and the Prince (Henry) to a very strong castle on the coast, and commanded that vessels be made ready nearby to convey them away, if necessary; they had left London after 22 September, when Elizabeth was still in the capital.[45] In fact she had gone with her son and the Lady Margaret on a progress through East Anglia, well out of the way of the coming conflict. The presence of the true Duke of York in that region was intended to overturn the loyalty of Warbeck's supporters, who were influential there. Meanwhile the King had raised a large army to deal with the rebels.[46]

Warbeck had of necessity given up on Exeter. He pressed desperately on to Taunton, his remaining Cornishmen demoralised and deserting in droves. In the small hours of 22 September, warned that the King was twenty miles away at the head of his forces, Warbeck fled south to find a ship at Southampton, accompanied only by three of 'the chief officials of his court'. He had abandoned most of his remaining adherents, whom he left to flee or beg the King for mercy. Finding that the south coast was heavily guarded, Warbeck took sanctuary in Beaulieu Abbey. In no time, the abbey was surrounded by Henry's soldiers, who promised the pretender a pardon if he surrendered to the King and threw himself on his 'grace and pity'.[47] At this he capitulated.

Having dressed himself (somewhat inappropriately) in cloth of gold, he was brought to the royal headquarters at Taunton, where, on 5 October, Henry was finally brought face to face with the young man who had plagued him for six years. Confronted by nobles who had known the real Richard, Duke of York, Warbeck admitted he did not recognise anyone; kneeling, he confessed that he was not York, and pleaded for forgiveness. Henry made him write out his confession, which was to be printed and nailed to church doors throughout the land.

With Warbeck in his train, Henry rode to Exeter to celebrate his victory. He ordered only 'a few desperate persons' to be hanged, 'the better to set off his mercy to the rest'. 'He was never cruel when he was secure'.[48] From Exeter, Warbeck wrote to his real mother in Tournai.

Henry also took into custody Warbeck's wife, Lady Katherine Gordon. She had remained at St Michael's Mount, in mourning – possibly, it has credibly been conjectured, after losing a child.[49] There was some question of her being fit to travel, but when she was able, the King sent her a full outfit of black weeds. When she came before him she burst into tears, but Henry was gentle with her and relieved her fears, telling her she was more worthy to be among the captives of a general than a common foot soldier. He had been struck by her 'modest and graceful look' and the fact that this 'singularly beautiful' lady seemed as 'untouched' as a virgin.[50] According to Vergil, the King was much taken with her, while Hall goes as far as to say that he 'began a little to fantasise her person'. Bacon states 'it was commonly said' that he 'received her not only with compassion but with affection, pity giving more impression to her excellent beauty'; and when he comforted her, 'it was to serve his eye as well as his fame'. But that, probably, was as far as it went, for there survives no hint that Henry was ever actually unfaithful to Elizabeth, and events that were to unfold in less than six years show that his love for her was deep-seated.

Henry escorted Lady Katherine to Exeter, and when she arrived he permitted her to see Warbeck and made the pretender repeat his story in front of her, at which she wept and raged at her husband, 'soaked through with a fountain of tears'. But Henry had no quarrel with her. Doubtless relieved that she was not pregnant with a child who might live to challenge his title, he comforted her and dealt with her honourably, telling her that her 'whole body, beauty and dignity were crying out for a man of far greater superiority' than Warbeck. He assured her that her future would hold 'many possibilities' and that he desired to treat her as his sister. Then, 'because she was but a young woman', he sent her, under the protection of Windsor Herald and 'with a goodly sort of sad matrons and gentlewomen', to reside at the court of the Queen,[51] a most fitting arrangement given Katherine's rank. On 16 October Henry charged his 'trusty and well beloved servant, Thomas Stokes' with responsibility for 'the diet of Katherine, daughter to the Earl of Huntly, from Bodmin to our dearest wife the Queen, wheresoever she be'.[52] Henry also arranged for a pension to be paid to Katherine.

Nobly born she was, but the fact that Henry was prepared to allow the wife of the Yorkist pretender to associate with his Yorkist Queen is proof that he knew he had no need to suspect Elizabeth's loyalty, and strong evidence that he now had no doubts as to Warbeck's true identity. Had he entertained any lingering suspicion that Warbeck really was Richard of York, or that Katherine still believed he was, it is unlikely that he would have allowed the two women the freedom to exchange confidences, or Katherine the opportunity to use the Queen for her own ends. Even so, in setting six ladies to wait upon Katherine, he was probably placing her under surveillance.[53]

Elizabeth was then on pilgrimage, having taken the opportunity during her progress through Norfolk to visit the shrine of Our Lady of Walsingham, doubtless to pray for a happy outcome to the conflict, and perhaps for another child. It was at Walsingham that Elizabeth learned of Henry's triumph over Warbeck. Immediately she and her party hastened south, 'and upon St Luke's Even, the 17th day of October, came the Queen toward London from Walsingham, whereof the Mayor having knowledge met with her Grace at Bishopsgate. He with the aldermen being on horseback conveyed her Grace from that place unto the King's Wardrobe, the streets being garnished with the crafts [guilds] of the City standing in their best liveries as she passed by.' Elizabeth stayed the night at the Royal Wardrobe at Blackfriars, and the next day, 'being St Luke's Day, her Grace, after certain presents received from the Mayor, departed that afternoon to Sheen, where upon the Saturday [21 October] was presented to her Grace the wife of Perkin, which was a fair and goodly lady'.[54]

Elizabeth appointed Katherine Gordon a lady-in-waiting. Thanks to her noble birth, she ranked fifth of all women at court after the Queen, the Lady Margaret and the princesses.[55] Katherine won many hearts at court, not least the Queen's, and she was treated with much deference. Officially referred to as Lady Katherine Huntly, she became better known by her husband's former nickname, 'the White Rose', on account of her 'true beauty'. The King settled upon her 'a very honourable allowance for the support of her estate, which she enjoyed many years after'.[56] He also saw that she was dressed as splendidly as her rank merited, himself itemising each detail of the clothing ordered for her, even the hose of kersey lined with cypress lawn. In 1498 she received a black-velvet, mink-edged gown and other items of clothing worth the princely sum of £160 (£78,000) from the Great Wardrobe; in 1501–2 she was given several items of sumptuous apparel, and in 1502–3 Joan Wilcock, the silkwoman, supplied materials to the Great Wardrobe for Lady Katherine Gordon and Queen Elizabeth.[57]

In decking out Katherine so lavishly, Henry no doubt wished to impress her kinsman James IV, who had then just become betrothed to Margaret Tudor – and maybe it pleased him to adorn her beauty too, or even to fantasise about the body he was so bountifully decking out. If Elizabeth had any cause for disquiet over her husband's interest in Lady Katherine, there is no record of it, and later evidence suggests that husband and wife remained close. That Henry showed warm personal friendship towards Katherine is corroborated by speculation after Elizabeth's death that they would marry (see Chapter 19).

Warbeck had been sent under guard to London, paraded through streets crammed with people who had flocked to see him, and imprisoned in the Tower. The Milanese ambassador was moved to report that the Tudor throne was now 'most stable, even for the King's descendants, since there is no one who aspires to the crown'.

By the end of November Henry VII was back at Windsor[58] and Warbeck had made a long and detailed written confession, admitting he was not Richard of York. Some said this had been obtained by torture, and persisted in their belief that he was York, but there was no sign that he had been tortured. The confession, which contained several inconsistencies, was printed; copies were nailed to church doors across the length and breadth of the realm, and Warbeck was made to read it aloud before the lords of England. He was, it stated, the son of John Osbeck, customs controller of Tournai, and Katherine de Faro, his wife, both converted Jews, and thus a foreigner, which meant he could not technically be guilty of high treason against the King of England. He protested that he had been lured into his imposture against his will.[59]

Henry was astonishingly lenient with Warbeck, the rival who had posed such a serious threat to his kingdom for six years. He released him from the Tower and allowed him to live at court, shadowed by two guards and confined to the precincts of the palace. In November 1497 the Venetian ambassador reported that he had seen Warbeck 'in a chamber of the King's palace. He is a well-favoured young man, twenty-three years old, and his wife a very handsome woman. The King treats them well, but does not allow them to sleep together.'[60]

Henry VII had paraded Warwick before the Londoners and the court to give the lie to Lambert Simnel's claims, yet it has been asserted that he failed to confront Elizabeth with the man who had claimed to be her brother.[61] But Elizabeth must have met or seen Warbeck after he came to court, and presumably she had a view on his true identity. The likelihood is that seeing this young man put an end to years of secret hoping and fretting on her part. Henry's extraordinary magnanimity towards Warbeck was probably due to the fact that he was a foreigner and outside English jurisdiction; also his wife was the King of Scots' kinswoman and had aroused Henry's chivalry, if nothing else.

Edwards, the Queen's former yeoman, had been one of those taken with Warbeck. He was not so lucky. On 2 December he was tried at Westminster and found guilty. Three days later, he was conveyed from the Tower to Tyburn and there hanged.

On 3 December Elizabeth wrote a letter to Queen Isabella, which exemplifies the high formality and elaborate courtesy of communications between royalty:

> To the most serene and potent Princess, the Lady Elizabeth [*sic*], by God's grace Queen of Castile, Leon, Aragon, Sicily, Granada, etc., our cousin and dearest relation, Elizabeth, by the same grace Queen of England and France, and Lady of Ireland, wishes health and the most prosperous increase of her desires.
>
> Although we have before entertained singular love and regard to your Highness above all other queens in the world, as well for the consanguinity and necessary intercourse which mutually take place between us, as also for the eminent dignity and virtue by which your Majesty so shines and excels that your most celebrated name is noised abroad and diffused everywhere; yet

much more has this our love increased and accumulated by the accession of the most noble affinity which has recently been celebrated between the most illustrious Lord Arthur, Prince of Wales, our eldest son, and the most illustrious Princess, the Lady Katherine, the Infanta, your daughter. Hence it is that, amongst our other cares and cogitations, first and foremost we wish and desire from our heart that we may often and speedily hear of the health and safety of your Serenity, and of the health and safety of the aforesaid most illustrious Lady Katherine, whom we think of and esteem as our own daughter, than which nothing could be more grateful and acceptable to us. Therefore we request your Serenity to certify of your estate, and of that of the aforesaid most illustrious Lady Katherine, our common daughter. And if there be anything in our power which would be grateful or pleasant to your Majesty, use us and ours as freely as you would your own, for with most willing mind we offer all that we have to you, and wish to have all in common with you.

We should have written you the news of our state, and of that of this kingdom, but the most serene lord the King, our husband, will have written at length of these things to your Majesties. For the rest, may your Majesty fare most happily, according to your wishes.

From our Palace of Westminster, 3rd day of December, 1497.

Elizabeth R.

To the most serene and potent Princess, the Lady Elizabeth [sic], by God's grace Queen of Castile, Leon, Aragon, Sicily, Granada, our cousin and dearest kinswoman.[62]

This is one of several letters written by Elizabeth to survive, although there must have been many more. A similar letter, to King Ferdinand of Aragon, was written in 1498.

Another of Elizabeth's letters to Ferdinand and Isabella is dated 1 August 1499, and recommends one Henry Stile, 'who wishes to go and fight against the Infidels'. The Queen urged the Spanish sovereigns to agree to this, for 'though he is a very short man, he has the reputation of being a valiant soldier'.[63]

Another letter was written by Elizabeth to a member of the Arundell family of Trerice in Cornwall, who had once loyally supported her father. It bears her signature, and in it she announces the birth of one of her sons.

A further surviving letter was written on 6 June 1499 to Thomas
Goldstone, Prior of Christ Church, Canterbury, and must be a typical
example of many of the Queen's routine missives that have not
survived. It concerns her desire to present one of her chaplains to
the next vacancy in the living of All Saints, Lombard Street, London.
She had to apply to the Prior because Christ Church held the
advowson – the right of a patron to appoint a nominee to a benefice
– of that church. In this letter, Elizabeth demonstrated that she had
a talent for claiming her right with charm and tact:

> To our right trusty and well-beloved in God, the Prior of the
> monastery of Christ's Church at Canterbury.
> Right trusty and well-beloved in God, we greet you well,
> and as we recently in other letters desired you to grant unto
> us the living of the parish church of All Saints in Lombard
> Street in my lord's city of London, whenever it should fall
> vacant through the death of Sir Marques Husy [Mark Hussy],[64]
> the late incumbent; whereupon it pleased you, out of your
> loving and kindly heart, to grant us freedom of the said benefice
> in writing, to nominate it for whichever of our chaplains we
> should choose at its next vacancy, for which we heartily thank
> you. We have been informed that it is now the case, the said
> Sir Marques being recently departed out of this transitory life
> into the mercy of God, so that the said benefice is now vacant.
> We therefore request and require you that, in honouring the
> said promise, you shall send us under your usual seal the giving
> of the said benefice, with a blank space on it, with the inten-
> tion that we shall enter the name of whichever of our chaplains
> we shall think able and suitable to have charge of the curacy
> there. We sincerely trust that you will effect this desire of ours,
> whereby you will greatly deserve our special thanks, to be
> recalled in connection with any reasonable desires of your own
> concerning your well-being or that of your office in time to
> come.
> Given under our signet at my lord's city of London, the sixth
> day of June.
>   Elysabeth[65]

Henry VII had intended to spend the Christmas of 1497 at Sheen,
where he was staying 'with the Queen and the court',[66] but on the

evening of 21 or 23 December,[67] an alarm was cried because the palace was on fire. The blaze had broken out 'suddenly', either in the Queen's chamber[68] or the King's,[69] around nine o'clock. Raimondo de Soncino stated that it started 'by accident, and not by malice, catching a beam',[70] but Trevisano hinted that 'a fire was set', and that the culprit had been Perkin Warbeck, who was 'with the King'.[71] There is no evidence, however, that Perkin was held responsible by Henry.

The conflagration quickly spread and raged for three hours, resisting frantic attempts to put it out; and 'by violence whereof, much and great part of the old building was burnt', while hangings, beds, plate, apparel and many jewels were spoiled or destroyed.[72] The fire 'did a great deal of harm, and burned the chapel, excepting two large towers recently erected by his Majesty'.[73] Henry V's donjon tower – where it probably started – was certainly spared, although it is not known in what condition, or what other buildings survived.

King Henry, Queen Elizabeth, Margaret Beaufort, Princess Margaret, Prince Henry and other 'notable estates' were in residence at the time, but 'to the King's good comfort, the royal family escaped unhurt, and no man or Christian creature perished'. Even so, the King had been lucky, for a gallery had collapsed immediately after he sped along it to safety.

The damage, according to Soncino, was 'estimated at 60,000 ducats (£7.3 million). The King does not attach much importance to the loss. He purposes to rebuild the chapel all in stone, and much finer than before.'[74] Yet he was concerned about some of the crown jewels being lost in the fire, and offered a reward of £20 (£9,700) to anyone finding them in the smoking rubble.[75] Surveying the devastation, Henry decided to rebuild not only the chapel, but the palace itself, bigger and better than before.

Fortunately the old royal manor complex of Byfleet, moved to Sheen by Henry V, stood nearby, beyond the moat and gardens, and Henry and Elizabeth probably took up residence here for Christmas, as they were still at Sheen with the court on 30 January 1498, 'in good health and merry, thank God';[76] and they were at Sheen again the following July.[77]

Elizabeth's privy purse accounts record that on 6 June 1502 she paid out £3 (£1,450) to Nicholas Grey, clerk of works, 'towards such losses as he sustained at the burning of his house at Richmond', presumably in the same fire that wrecked the palace. On 7 February

1503 she paid £20 (£9,700) in partial compensation to Henry Coote, a London goldsmith, 'for certain plate delivered to the Queen's Grace at Richmond, and there lost and burnt at the burning of the palace there'.[78]

In April 1498 the King gave Elizabeth a gift of £6.13s.4d. (£3,250).[79] That year Prince Henry rode in great state into London, where the streets had been swept in his honour, and was presented with a gift by the City fathers, for which he made his first recorded speech, thanking them. On 23 May, not quite seven years old, he beat his father at cards, winning 3s.4d. (£80).[80] Four days later Henry VII paid out £3.6s.8d. (£1,620) to Robert Taylor, the Queen's surgeon,[81] possibly for drawing one of her teeth or letting blood. The generous payment reflects the King's concern for his wife's health.

There was alarm when, on 9 June 1498, Perkin Warbeck escaped from the Palace of Westminster. Evading his two warders, he climbed through a window in the wardrobe and set out for the coast, but the King sent men after him and gave orders for the roads to be closed, and Warbeck only made it as far as Sheen, where he took sanctuary at the Charterhouse.

On 12 June the Prior of the Charterhouse arrived at Westminster and informed the King of Warbeck's whereabouts. Henry immediately had the news conveyed to Puebla, who communicated it to Ferdinand and Isabella, to reassure them that the pretender had been speedily found. The Prior begged the King to spare Warbeck's life. Henry VII was not a bloodthirsty man, but he was no longer prepared to be lenient with Perkin. He had him put in the stocks in Cheapside and at Westminster, where he was again made to read aloud his confession, then he was marched under strong guard to the Tower and imprisoned in a cell where 'he sees neither sun nor moon'.[82] Bacon asserts that even now Warbeck was still insisting that he was Richard of York, and declaring that, when he was delivered from the Tower, he would wait for the King's death, 'then put myself into my sister's hands, who was next heir to the crown'. But Bacon was writing much later, and – as we have seen – tended to see intrigue where none probably existed, especially in regard to pretenders. It is highly unlikely that Elizabeth was harbouring sympathy for this young man, or that she still took his claim seriously.

Certainly Pedro de Ayala did not, and he assured Ferdinand and

Isabella that Henry VII's crown was now 'undisputed, and his government is strong in all respects'. But the years of uncertainty had taken their toll. Ayala added that Henry 'looks old for his years, but young for the sorrowful life he has led'.[83] Vergil too observed how Henry had aged: 'his teeth [were] few, poor and blackish; his hair was thin and grey; his complexion pale'. Worry and anxiety may have taken their toll on Elizabeth too: a portrait of her painted in the 1490s, now in the Royal Collection (see Appendix 1), shows her looking older than her years – she was thirty in 1496 – with pinched lips and a double chin.

But now, with Warbeck securely imprisoned, the outlook for the future appeared brighter, and the way seemed clear for preparations for Prince Arthur's wedding to the Infanta to proceed smoothly. It was what the King earnestly desired, and he 'swore by his royal faith that he and the Queen were more satisfied with this marriage than with any other'.[84]

On 7 July 1498 two Spanish diplomats, the Commander Sancho de Londoño and Juan de Matienzo, Sub-Prior of Santa Cruz, 'passed four hours with [King Henry] in conversation, at which the Queen and the mother of the King were present'. They reported to their sovereigns: 'To hear what they spoke of your Highnesses and of the Princess of Wales was like hearing the praise of God.' The envoys gave Elizabeth two letters from Ferdinand and Isabella and two letters from the Princess of Wales. 'The King had a dispute with the Queen because he wanted to have one of the said letters to carry continually about him, but the Queen did not like to part with hers, having sent the other to the Prince of Wales.'[85] It is hard to imagine Elizabeth defying Henry openly like this, and it is more likely that the dispute was staged to demonstrate to the Spanish envoys the enthusiasm of the royal pair for the marriage of their son to the Princess Katherine.[86]

When, on 25 August 1498, Rodrigo de Puebla brought Elizabeth letters from the Spanish sovereigns and Katherine of Aragon, 'and explained them, she was overjoyed'. She sent at once for her Latin secretary 'and ordered him to write, in her presence, two letters, one of them to the Queen of Spain, and the other to the Princess of Wales'. The secretary told Puebla afterwards 'that he was obliged to write the said letters three or four times, because the Queen had always found some defects in them', saying, 'They are not things of great importance themselves, but they show great and cordial love,' which had to be expressed in the proper fashion.[87] This testifies to

Elizabeth's keen desire for a successful outcome to the marriage negotiations, as do her efforts to cement good relations with Puebla by finding him an English bishopric or an English bride.

In February Henry VII had informed Ferdinand and Isabella that 'since Puebla could not be induced to accept a church preferment, he was asked whether he would also refuse an honourable marriage offered to him. After many excuses, he has at last been persuaded, principally by the Queen, to accept the marriage, but under the express condition that his King and Queen must first give him their consent. Wishing to marry Puebla well in England, he and his Queen beg them [the Spanish sovereigns] to grant their prayers, and to give their consent. The marriage will be of great advantage to the Princess Katherine when she comes to live in England.' Puebla dutifully but reluctantly relayed the proposal to his sovereigns, and it seems that Henry and Elizabeth continued to press him to accept the hand of an Englishwoman of their choosing.[88]

On the morning of Sunday, 18 July, the Commander Londoño and the Sub-Prior of Santa Cruz went to Sheen, accompanied by the Bishop of London and other great dignitaries of state, and there they saw the King and Queen walking in procession after hearing Mass in the chapel. 'The ladies of the Queen went in good order and were much adorned.' Later that day the envoys 'took leave, and went to kiss the hand of the Queen'.[89]

It was during this visit in July 1498 that the Commander Londoño and the Sub-Prior of Santa Cruz made their separate observations about Elizabeth resenting Margaret Beaufort's influence on the King. As discussed earlier, the envoys' conclusions were probably overstated, for Elizabeth and her mother-in-law continued to present a united and friendly front to the world, and until now there had been no hint of discord between them. Several times during 1498 alone we find them amicably working and playing together. They displayed a joint concern to prepare Katherine of Aragon for her marriage. On 17 July Puebla reported: 'The Queen and the mother of the King wish that the Princess of Wales should always speak French with the Princess Margaret [of Austria, wife of Katherine's brother, the Infante Juan, Prince of Asturias], who is now in Spain, in order to learn the language and to be able to converse in it when she comes to England. This is necessary, because these ladies do not understand Latin, and much less, Spanish. They also wish that the Princess of Wales should accustom herself to drink wine. The water of England is not drinkable, and even if it were, the climate would not allow the drinking of it.'[90]

That summer Margaret Beaufort accompanied the King and Queen on a progress into East Anglia, visiting Havering, Bury St Edmunds and Thetford on the way to Norwich, where they were received by the Mayor, who made an oration in their honour.[91] They again visited the shrine at Walsingham, and at Bishop's Lynn (later King's Lynn) they lodged in the Augustinian priory[92] before journeying westwards to Margaret's house at Collyweston.[93] Two years later Elizabeth collaborated with Margaret and Prince Arthur to secure the appointment of Thomas Pantry, a native of Calais, as Supreme Beadle of the Arts at the University of Oxford, although in 1501 they all supported rival claimants for the same post in Divinity, which shows that Elizabeth was not always swayed by her mother-in-law's opinions.[94]

In July 1498 Londoño and Santa Cruz reported an instance of the King, the Queen and Margaret Beaufort sharing a similar sense of humour. They had heard of it from 'a Spaniard, brought up and married in England', who was 'porter to the Queen of England. He said that some time ago the King was living at a palace about a quarter of a league distant from the town in which Puebla was staying. Puebla went every day, with all his servants, to dine at the palace, and continued his unasked-for visits during the space of four or five months. The Queen and the mother of the Queen sometimes asked him whether his masters in Castile did not provide him with food. On another occasion, when the King was staying at another palace, there was a report that Doctor de Puebla was coming. The King asked his courtiers, "For what purpose is he coming?" They answered, "To eat!" The King laughed at the answer.'[95] This is a revealing insight into a private joke shared by Elizabeth, her mother-in-law and her husband, which suggests that 'subjection' was quite the wrong word to describe her relations with the Lady Margaret.

There was a good reason to account for Elizabeth being out of sorts or looking strained or irritable during the ambassadors' visit: she was two months pregnant, and possibly suffering with it. The King paid out money to her physician, Lewis Caerleon, probably for consultations and treatment connected with her condition.[96]

In the summer of 1498, during a visit to London, the Bishop of Cambrai (once alleged to be Warbeck's real father) visited Henry VII and asked to see Perkin, who was duly produced for his inspection. Puebla observed that he was 'so much changed that I, and all other persons here, believe his life will be very short. He must pay for what he has done.' Puebla, doubtless acting on the orders of King Ferdinand, did not cease urging King Henry to rid himself of this embarrassment, hinting that Ferdinand was having second thoughts about marrying his daughter to a prince whose future throne might not be secure.[97]

On 11 September Bishop Fox was empowered to negotiate the marriage of Margaret Tudor and James IV. Henry was resolved upon cementing the peace between England and Scotland, and liked the prospect of his grandson sitting on the Scots throne. James too was eager for the marriage, and there was talk of an early wedding, but Henry revealed to Pedro de Ayala that his wife and his mother had worked in concert again, this time to protect Margaret from the perils of marrying too young. 'I have already told you more than once that a marriage between him and my daughter has many inconveniences,' he said. 'She has not yet completed the ninth year of her age, and is so delicate and female [i.e. weak] that she must be married much later than other young ladies. Thus it would be necessary to wait at least another nine years. Beside my own doubts, the Queen and my mother are very much against this marriage. They say, if [it] were concluded, we should be obliged to send the Princess directly to Scotland, in which case they fear the King of Scots would not wait, but injure her and endanger her health.'[98]

Margaret Beaufort probably spoke from bitter experience, for her husband had not waited, and the likelihood is that giving birth at thirteen had scarred her so badly, mentally as well as physically, that she had never borne another child. She and Elizabeth may also have heard reports of the Scots King's womanising, and been concerned for Margaret. Bowing to this pressure from his womenfolk, Henry compromised and made James agree not to demand his bride before September 1503, when she would be nearly fourteen.[99]

Early in 1499 a young Cambridge student, Ralph Wilford, the son of a London cordwainer, suddenly declared that he was the real Warwick. Like Lambert Simnel, he had been encouraged in his deception by an errant cleric, in this case a friar. He was speedily apprehended and 'confessed that he was sundry times stirred in his sleep that he should name himself to be the Duke of Clarence's son, and he should in process obtain such power that he should be king'. By now, Henry VII's patience was exhausted, and after personally interrogating the imposter, he did not hesitate to deal swiftly with him: on 12 February, Wilford was hanged.[100] Even so, the damage had been done, for the King was much disturbed by the appearance of yet another pretender, and – as he had probably feared – the Spanish sovereigns were dismayed when they heard of it.

Elizabeth was then in the last stages of pregnancy. The *Great Wardrobe Accounts* for January 1499 record payments for linen cloth for bearing sheets, 'headkerchiefs, biggins [bonnets for the baby] and breast kerchiefs', kersey for twelve couches (beds), and fustian 'for a bed for the nursery', all purchased for the Queen. On 20 January the King sent for the silver font from Canterbury Cathedral, paying the Prior £2 (£970), for the favour.

Around the time she took to her chamber, Elizabeth had to deal with more bad news. On 9 February 1499 her brother-in-law, John, Viscount Welles, the husband of her sister Cecily, died of pleurisy at his London home. In his will he had passed over his other heirs and directed that all his property should go to Cecily for the term of her life, and that his body should be interred wherever she, with the consent of the King and Queen and the King's mother, should deem appropriate. After his death Cecily sent to the King at Greenwich to discover his pleasure in the matter. He commanded that Welles be buried with great solemnity in the old Lady Chapel in Westminster Abbey. Cecily apparently returned to the Queen's household, where, given Elizabeth's love and care for her sisters, she was assured of a sympathetic welcome.[101]

By 19 February Anne Crown, mistress of the nursery (probably to be identified with Anne Crowmer), was installed and awaiting the arrival of her charge. Under her was Anne Skern, who had nursed Princess Mary, and 'five gentlewomen of the nursery'.[102]

Elizabeth bore her third son, her sixth child, on Thursday, 21 February 1499, at Greenwich.[103] He was baptised there in the church of the Observant Friars on 24 February. The Great Wardrobe provided linen for the silver font from Canterbury, cords for hanging the canopy that would be borne over the infant, red worsted, gilt nails and other items[104] against the christening, which was 'very splendid, and the festivities such as though an heir to the crown had been born'.[105] The baby was named Edmund, after Henry's father, Edmund Tudor, Earl of Richmond.

Margaret Beaufort was Edmund's godmother at the font, and gave him the generous gift of £100 (£48,600), as well as handsomely rewarding the midwife and the nurses.[106] Clearly she was relieved to see both mother and child safely delivered, for 'there had been much fear that the life of the Queen would be in danger, but the delivery, contrary to expectations, had been easy'.[107] A payment of 6s.8d. (£160) made by the King on the day after the birth to 'Wulf the Physician at two times'[108] may reflect the precautions put in place should something go wrong. We do not know why there were fears for the Queen's life, unless the shock of her brother-in-law's death and her sister's bereavement had affected her badly; but the ministrations of her doctors the previous year suggest she had had a difficult pregnancy.

Prince Edmund was styled Duke of Somerset,[109] a title that had been proudly borne by his Beaufort ancestors, although he was probably never formally ennobled since no enrolment of any patent can be traced.

Polydore Vergil recorded that 'by his wife Elizabeth, [Henry VII] was the father of eight children, four boys and as many girls'; and John Foxe, writing in the reign of Elizabeth I, stated that 'Henry VII had by Elizabeth four men children and of women children as many, of whom only three survived'. John Stow, the Elizabethan antiquarian, states that there was a fourth and youngest son called Edward. In the eighteenth century, Thomas Carte also asserted, in his history of England, that there was a fourth son who died in infancy, while in the nineteenth century, Arthur Stanley, Dean of Westminster, recorded a fourth son, Edward, who died very young and was buried in Westminster Abbey. However, the royal genealogist Francis Sandford, writing in the seventeenth century, says that Edmund was the third and youngest son.

Modern biographers[110] have put forward all kinds of theories about a fourth son. One names him George,[111] but most call him Edward. His birth date has variously been given as 1487–8,[112] 1495–6,[113] suggesting some confusion with Princess Mary, 1497,[114] or 1500–1.

There is no contemporary evidence to support any of these theories. Nor is there any record of Elizabeth having more than seven pregnancies. All are documented in one way or another, so it is unlikely that a prince called Edward ever existed. The most telling evidence in favour of the Queen having borne only three sons is to be found in two works of art. The St George altarpiece at Windsor, which depicts Henry and Elizabeth and their children adoring St George, and dates from 1505–9, shows four daughters and only three sons. An illumination in the 'Ordinances of the Confraternity of the Immaculate Conception', dating from 1503, also shows three sons and four daughters. Given that all the known children who died young are included in each of these groups, which were painted after Elizabeth's death, we might expect to see a fourth son – if there had been one – in both pictures.

There also exists in the British Library the 'Genealogical Chronicle of the Kings of England', dating from 1511, which has tiny circular images of Henry and Elizabeth with seven children, labelled Arthur, Edmund, Henry, Katherine, Margaret, Mary and Elizabeth. Margaret and Katherine are shown as boys – the other girls wear gable hoods.[115] The likelihood is that Vergil got it wrong and there were only three sons of the marriage. Claims by modern historians[116] that there were other children who died unnamed in infancy are not substantiated by any contemporary evidence.

In May 1499, with the portly Puebla standing in for the Infanta, Prince Arthur was married by proxy in a ceremony in the chapel at Tickenhill Palace, his house near Bewdley, Worcestershire. This was 'a fair manor place west of the town, standing in a goodly park well wooded' on a hill in the Severn Valley. Originally built in the fourteenth century, it had been enlarged by Edward IV for his son, the Prince of Wales, when the Council of the Marches was established, and Henry VII converted it into a palace for Prince Arthur.[117]

It was intimated by the King and Queen to the Spanish ambassador that the ladies Katherine brought with her to England should be 'of gentle birth' – for 'the English attach great importance to good connections' – and 'beautiful, or, at the least, by no means ugly'.[118]

From 1499 to 1501 Arthur and Katherine were encouraged to write frequently to each other. They corresponded in Latin in a formal style, no doubt supervised by their elders. Although the young couple had not yet met, they expressed the proper sentiments required by convention. One letter sent by Arthur on 5 October 1499 from Ludlow Castle is typical of how a royal courtship was conducted:

Most illustrious and most excellent lady, my dearest spouse, I wish you very much health, with my hearty commendations.

I have read the most sweet letters of your Highness lately given to me, from which I have easily perceived your most entire love to me. Truly, these your letters, traced by your own hand, have so delighted me, and have rendered me so cheerful and jocund, that I fancied I beheld your Highness, and conversed with and embraced my dearest wife. I cannot tell you what an earnest desire I feel to see your Highness, and how vexatious to me is this procrastination about your coming. I owe eternal thanks to your excellence that you so lovingly correspond to this, my so ardent love. Let it continue, I entreat, as it has begun; and, like as I cherish your sweet remembrance night and day, so do you preserve my name ever fresh in your breast. And let your coming to me be hastened, that instead of being absent we may be present with each other, and the love conceived between us and the wished-for joys may reap their proper fruit.

I have done as your illustrious Highness enjoined me in commending you to the most serene lord and lady, the King and Queen, my parents, and in declaring your filial regard towards them, which to them was most pleasing to hear.[119]

The expressions in the letter are those of an adult, and it seems unlikely that a thirteen-year-old boy would have written them; probably his words were dictated by his tutors.

In September, while the King and Queen were away on a progress in Hampshire,[120] the celebrated scholar Erasmus, then a guest of fellow humanist William Blount, Lord Mountjoy, was taken to meet their younger children at Eltham. Years later he recalled: 'Thomas More paid me a visit, and took me for recreation on a walk to a neighbouring country palace, where the royal infants were abiding, Prince Arthur excepted, who had completed his education. The princely children were assembled in the hall and were surrounded by their household, to whom Mountjoy's servants added themselves. In the middle of the circle stood Prince Henry, then only nine [*sic*] years old, and already having something of royalty in his demeanour, in which there was a certain dignity combined with a singular courtesy.' A painted terracotta bust by Guido Mazzoni in the Royal Collection, of a chubby-cheeked, mischievous-looking, laughing boy is thought to portray young Henry around this time (*c.*1498–1500), and may have been commissioned by Henry VII himself.

On Prince Henry's right hand 'stood the Princess Margaret, a child of eleven [*sic*] years, afterwards Queen of Scotland. On the other side was the Princess Mary, a little one of four [*sic*] years of age, engaged in her sports, whilst Edmund, an infant, was held in his nurse's arms.'[121]

Thomas More presented Prince Henry with some Latin verses he had composed especially for him, and that same evening, after they had returned to More's house, Erasmus received a request from the Prince for some verses of his own. 'I was angry with More for not having warned me,' he wrote, 'especially as the boy sent me a little note, while we were at dinner, to challenge something from my pen.' In fact the great scholar was so overcome with trepidation that it took him three days to come up with something he considered suitable, the *Prosopopoeia Britanniae;*[122] in this, he described the royal children in allegorical terms: the boys were red roses, for vigour, the girls white, for innocence.

Already, it seems, the future Henry VIII had a commanding and awe-inspiring demeanour, and to have read the verses dedicated to him he would have had to be highly proficient in Latin. Erasmus thought he was. His inscription read: 'We have dedicated these verses, like the gift of playthings, to your childhood, and shall be ready with more abundant offerings when your virtues, growing with your age, shall supply more abundant material for poetry.' Erasmus later recalled that Henry 'had a vivid and active mind, above measure to execute whatever tasks he undertook. You would say that he was a universal genius.'[123]

Erasmus was also much impressed by Lady Guildford, the princesses' governess, with whom he engaged in two conversations. By November 1501, however, Lady Guildford had returned to the Queen's service.

With their daughter due to come to England when she reached fourteen in December, Ferdinand and Isabella had expressed concern at the emergence of yet another pretender, and even though Ralph Wilford had been speedily dealt with, their faith in the security of the English throne had been shaken. They had seen over the years how it could be destabilised by imposters and the existence of Yorkist heirs who might yet challenge Henry VII's title. Now that Warbeck had been discredited, they regarded Warwick as the greatest threat to England's stability, as he had the strongest claim to the crown and was clearly a focus for malcontents. In the years to come, Katherine of Aragon was to say that her marriage to Prince Arthur had been made in blood,[124] which implies that it was conditional upon the removal of the hapless Warwick. Fifty years later Warwick's nephew, Cardinal Reginald Pole (the son of Margaret of Clarence), revealed that King Ferdinand was averse to giving his daughter to one who would not be secure in his own kingdom. The likelihood is that Ferdinand warned Henry VII that, while Warwick lived, the Infanta would not be coming to England.

Henry, like many of his contemporaries, was a superstitious man. In March, still perturbed by the Ralph Wilford affair, he heard of a priest who had accurately foretold the deaths of Edward IV and Richard III, and summoned him for a consultation. The soothsayer warned him that his life would be in danger all that year, for there were two parties with very different political creeds in the land – those who were loyal to the Tudor dynasty, and those who wanted to see the House of York restored – and that conspiracies against the throne would ensue. A fortnight later Pedro de Ayala reported that the King had aged twenty years in two weeks.[125]

Unnerved by the Ralph Wilford affair, and aware that Warwick would always remain a threat, Henry probably foresaw no end to the intrigues that had long undermined his security. Fearful as a result of the soothsayer's warning, he consulted his astrologer, Dr William Parron, several times. Later that year, Parron observed, 'It is expedient that one man should die for the people, and the whole nation perish not, for an insurrection cannot occur in any state without the deaths of a great part of the people and the destruction of many great families with their property.' This pragmatic view was shared by the King, and it was probably at this time that he began to come to the decision that Warwick must be eliminated.

Yet Warwick had never actually done anything to justify any legal process against him. Having him secretly murdered in the Tower, like the Princes, was clearly not Henry's way of doing things. The King had experienced, none better, what could ensue when an heir to the throne simply disappeared. Moral issues aside, Warwick had to be seen to be dead. The only sure way to remove him and eliminate any future claims of his survival was by the process of law.

What happened afterwards is still surrounded in mystery. We do not know the extent of official involvement – although the evidence suggests it was considerable – or how far the government drove or manipulated events. What was paramount, though, was that Henry secure his crown and safeguard the valuable Spanish alliance. Small wonder that he probably seized the chance to kill two birds with one shot.

One might have thought that high-security prisoners like Warwick and Warbeck would be kept isolated from each other lest they bred a further conspiracy together, but this was clearly not the case. On 2 August, according to Warwick's indictment, two gaolers – Thomas Astwood, one of Warbeck's former supporters who had been pardoned four years earlier, and Robert Cleymound – met with Warwick in his chamber in the Tower, and hatched a plot to fire and seize the Tower, thus facilitating his escape to Flanders, whence he would make war upon Henry VII, 'assume the royal dignity and make himself king'.[126]

Warwick may have been inveigled into colluding in what was nothing less than high treason; or he might, understandably, have leapt at the chance of being revenged upon the King who had so unjustly incarcerated him for fourteen years. Yet he may not fully have understood the enormity of what he thought he was about to do, or had the capacity to see it through. Vergil says he had been brought up in prison from his cradle, and although that was not strictly true of his earlier years, he had been a captive since 1485, 'out of sight of man or beast', and he was clearly not very bright. It is hard to imagine him seriously contemplating leading an armed rebellion.

Two days later the conspirators made contact with Warbeck, whose cell – somewhat conveniently – was below Warwick's, and drew him into the plot. Warwick, he was told, would set him at large and make him king of England – which was glaringly at variance with what Warwick had been promised, but was probably no more than an inducement to draw Warbeck into the plot. Given the sorry state Warbeck had been in the previous year, it could have been predicted that he was by now desperate to escape, and would seize any chance. Four other gaolers and two other prisoners, Yorkist dissidents, also became involved, as well as two citizens of London. Then suddenly Cleymound complained that Warbeck had betrayed the conspirators to the King and his Council, and fled into sanctuary.

This all suggests that the two prisoners had been enticed into the conspiracy, and that Cleymound was an *agent provocateur* placed in the Tower. No action was ever taken against him, and it seems suspicious that one of Warbeck's gaolers was his former adherent, and that Warwick and Warbeck were held close enough to communicate. Warwick is said to have knocked on the floor of his chamber, and even made a hole in it so that the two could speak, and to have sent Warbeck documents and tokens by Cleymound. This is even more suspicious, considering that the whereabouts of Warwick's chamber in the Tower had until now been a well-kept state secret for fear of rescue attempts. It is unlikely too that Warbeck would have revealed the conspiracy to the Council. Therefore the two prisoners probably were set up, and it is likely that the Earl of Oxford, the Constable of the Tower, and his deputy, John Digby, its Lieutenant, were parties to the deception; it is hard to imagine this conspiracy escaping their notice.

It seems implausible that Elizabeth knew anything of this. There is no official record of Spain's intervention, and if there was a policy to remove Warwick and Warbeck, it was kept highly secret. Henry and his advisers probably allowed the conspiracy to mature, and awaited their moment.

On 12 November the doomed plot came to light when John Fineux, Chief Justice of the King's Bench, reported to the Council 'certain treasons conspired of Edward, naming himself of Warwick, and Perkin and other within the Tower; which intendeth, as it appeareth by [their] confessions, to have deposed and destroyed the King's person and his blood. And over that the said Edward intended to have been king, and first to have holpen Perkin to the crown if he had been King Edward's son, and else to have had it himself.' Already the accused had been examined and it had been determined by the judges that they had committed treason 'and deserved death', while the King was already demanding what was to be done with them.

Did Elizabeth tremble at the thought of what might have befallen her husband and her children, or did she grieve for her guileless cousin? Did she suspect, from the sheer improbability of the charges, that Warwick had been led unwittingly into treason? More pertinently, was she startled by the revelation that Warwick had been willing to make Perkin king *if* he proved to be her brother? If this was true – and it may not have been – then Warwick had remained uncertain that Warbeck really was Richard of York. He had been brought up with the royal children from 1478 to 1483, so had known York, who was two years older, between the ages of four and nine. If York had survived, he would now be twenty-six. Even if Warwick had seen Perkin in the Tower, he might have found it difficult recognising the boy in the man – and may not have had the wits to do so. But on the face of it he had not ruled out the possibility that Warbeck was York. If Elizabeth did not know that the whole conspiracy was a fabrication – and it is hard to imagine her colluding in it – then she had cause to wonder.

The exposure of the conspiracy sealed the fate of both young men. Warbeck was arraigned at Westminster on 16 November and condemned to be hanged, drawn and quartered, the punishment meted out to traitors. Two days later, at London's Guildhall, eight people including Thomas Astwood were found guilty of conspiring to murder the Marshal of the Tower and free Warwick and Warbeck.

Warwick himself was tried the next day, 19 November, in Westminster Hall. 'Because of his innocency',[127] the simple young man pleaded guilty, and was also sentenced to a traitor's death. Later, Parliament attainted him for treason. We have no way of knowing if Elizabeth believed he had been justly condemned.

It was customary, in the case of peers of the realm, for the dread sentence handed down to traitors to be commuted by the King to beheading, so it is surprising to learn that Perkin Warbeck, a commoner, suffered only hanging on the public gallows at Tyburn. He certainly was drawn face-down on a hurdle to his execution, 'as being not worthy any more to tread upon the face of the Earth', but he was spared the full horrors of a traitor's death. Was there still, in the King's mind, and perhaps Elizabeth's too, some question that he might really be of royal blood? Or was Henry merely being merciful because Warbeck had unwittingly helped to send Warwick to a better world? Either way, on the scaffold, Warbeck swore on his death that he was not the son of Edward IV, and asked forgiveness of God and the King for his deception. Expecting to face divine judgement within minutes, he is unlikely to have been lying.

On 29 November Warwick, who was only twenty-four, was beheaded on Tower Hill. 'It was ordained that the winding ivy of a Plantagenet should kill the true tree itself,' observed Bacon. The King paid for the Earl's remains to be buried in Bisham Priory, Berkshire, near the tomb of his grandfather, Warwick the Kingmaker.[128] During the days that followed, Astwood and the other men involved in the plot were put to death. If they had all been seduced unwittingly into the conspiracy, then the government had made a ruthless and thorough job of it; but by willingly involving themselves, they had nevertheless committed treason.

Elizabeth and her ladies were left to comfort the popular Katherine Gordon for the loss of her husband. Universally applauded for her loyalty to Warbeck, she stayed on at court in Elizabeth's service, and in 1510 married the first of three more husbands, all gentlemen of Henry VIII's bedchamber.[129]

Henry VII fell ill after the executions, while staying at Wanstead, Essex, and was so poorly that his life was despaired of. But he had recovered by the middle of December, and in January 1500 Pedro de Ayala was able to assure Ferdinand and Isabella that 'this kingdom is at present so situated as has not been seen for the last five hundred years until now, because there were always brambles and thorns of such a kind that the English had occasion not to remain peacefully in obedience to their king, there being divers heirs of the kingdom. Now it has pleased God that all should be thoroughly and duly purged and cleansed, so that not a doubtful drop of royal blood remains in this kingdom, except the true blood of the King and Queen and, above all, that of the lord Prince Arthur'.[130]

15

'The Spanish Infanta'

Henry VII was now well established on his throne. His court poet, Pietro Carmeliano, observed that England's honour was 'in such wise now enhanced that all Christian regions pursue unto thee for alliance, confederation and unity'. In March, having satisfied Ferdinand and Isabella that his crown was secure, the King concluded the treaty with Spain, and within the next two years would make alliances with Scotland, Burgundy, the Holy Roman Empire and Flanders as well.

On 11 January 1500 Ferdinand and Isabella informed de Puebla that the Princess Katherine was to come to England 'as soon as the Prince of Wales shall have accomplished the fourteenth year of his age', which would be in the September following. But soon afterwards Don Juan Manuel, a servant of Philip of Burgundy, told Henry VII that the Princess would be sent in the spring, 'without waiting for the accomplishment of the fourteenth year of the age of the Prince of Wales, if the state of health of the Queen would permit it'. There is no other hint that Elizabeth was unwell at this time, so possibly there was speculation that she was pregnant again, which proved to be unfounded. Puebla added, 'The sums spent in preparation for the reception of the Princess are enormous.'

He was still fretting about the favours that the King and Queen of England were pressing on him. He 'did not like to accept the bishopric or the marriage offered to him because it seemed to him that a true servant of [Ferdinand and Isabella] ought not to do so'. It seemed the sovereigns agreed with him, because they failed to respond to the proposals, for which Puebla thanked them the following June, when he said he feared that Henry VII would still pursue the matter, and expressed his fears that the Sovereigns would no longer trust him 'if he were married by the Queen of England to a rich English lady'.[1] Evidently Elizabeth finally got the message that her offer was unwelcome, and dropped the matter.

From June 1499 England had suffered one of its worst-ever plague epidemics, which raged on through a mild winter into the late spring of 1500; in London alone, which suffered the most, it was said (probably with some exaggeration) that 30,000 died. After 'often change of places'[2] to escape contagion, Henry decided to take Elizabeth abroad to Calais, the last remaining outpost of England's continental territories. His intention was not only to avoid the pestilence but also to meet with the Archduke Philip.

With no pretenders left to challenge him, the King could safely go abroad at last, but not without anxiety, for it is clear his departure lacked fanfares. Puebla wrote: 'The internal peace of the kingdom is perfect. It is so great that the King and Queen left England. Until two days beforehand no one knew of their intended journey.'[3] The royal party travelled down from Greenwich to Dover with their households, attended by heralds and men-at-arms, and crossed the sea to Calais on 8 May,[4] arriving that night. This was the only time Elizabeth ever went abroad.

The next day the King and Queen put on a splendid show when, 'with many lords, ladies, knights, esquires, gentlemen and yeomen', they set out to greet the Archduke, who had married Juana of Castile, Katherine of Aragon's sister. Elizabeth was attended by fifty ladies of rank, all 'beautifully adorned', with Katherine Gordon prominent among them. The royal couple received the handsome but dissolute young Archduke with much pomp at Our Lady of St Peter's Church outside the city walls. The church had been 'richly hanged with arras' and 'parted with hangings into divers offices', including an area where a feast was served. 'And when they had all dined and communed, there was a rich banquet' of strawberries, cream, spice cakes and cherries. Afterwards, the Archduke 'danced with the ladies of England, and then took leave of the King and Queen'.[5]

Over the next few days Henry and Elizabeth entertained their guest with pageants, feasts and jousts. 'The King and the Archduke had a very long conversation, in which the Queen afterwards joined.

The interview was very solemn, and attended with great splendour.'[6] Elizabeth's presence was required because Henry and Philip had agreed that the Princess Mary, now four, should be betrothed to Philip's eldest son, Charles,[7] who had been born in February. Charles was the heir to the Habsburg territories and also to Spain, and in time he would be the master of vast domains, so this was a brilliant match for Mary.

Mary had recently been assigned a separate household with ladies-in-waiting, gentlewomen, a wardrobe keeper, a schoolmaster and a physician.[8] In 1499 the three-year-old had been provided with five beautiful gowns of green velvet edged with purple tinsel, black velvet edged with crimson, crimson velvet, blue velvet, and black velvet furred with ermine, as well as kirtles of tawny damask and black satin, both edged with black velvet, and two pairs of knitted hose.[9] In 1502 the King would order that Mary be assigned the same number of attendants as Katherine of Aragon, then Dowager Princess of Wales.[10]

Mary showed much greater promise intellectually than her sister Margaret, and was given the advantage of a good education. She learned French and Latin, music, dancing and embroidery. Her brothers' tutor, Giles Dewes, taught her French. Like most of her family, she was musical. Her father the King gave her a lute, and she also learned to play the clavichord and the regal, a small portable organ. In 1502, after the Borgia Pope, Alexander VI, had proclaimed a Catholic Jubilee year, Elizabeth paid 12d. (£25) so that Mary could have a 'letter of pardon'[11] – an indulgence that bought her remission from her sins. Possibly Elizabeth's youngest daughter was a high-spirited, headstrong child whom she thought was in need of such remission – or the lesson the indulgence would have taught her.

The King and Queen stayed for forty days in Calais. On 16 June, when the plague had abated, they sailed back to Dover[12] and journeyed directly to Greenwich. On, or before, their return, at a time when Prince Arthur's health was giving them cause for concern, they were brought the tragic news that the infant Prince Edmund had died at the episcopal palace at Hatfield, Hertfordshire.[13]

Edmund had lived for fifteen months. It is often stated that he died on 16 June, but Henry VII's privy purse expenses for May list £242.11s.8d. (£117,900) 'for the burial of my Lord Edmund',[14] and it would have taken longer than five days to arrange the ceremonial funeral. A payment on 14 February for 'hawk bells' for Prince Henry at Hatfield[15] suggests that all the younger royal children had been living there too, isolated from the pestilence, while their parents were abroad in Calais, and that Edmund did not die of plague but of some childhood ailment.

The little boy was given a state funeral. According to the provisions for the burial of a prince in Henry VII's ordinances, his tiny corpse was 'laid in a new chest covered with white damask, with a cross of red velvet thereon', and an image of him 'with a circlet on his head' was placed on top. The coffin and effigy were brought from Hatfield to London in 'a chariot covered with black' pulled by 'six horses trapped all in black', followed by the chief mourner, Edward Stafford, Duke of Buckingham, and other lords, all wearing mourning robes with 'their hoods fair hanging over their ears'. Torchbearers went before, and the Lord Mayor and guildsmen of London lined the streets as the cortège passed. The coffin was received by the grieving King at Westminster. Henry's ordinances provided for him to wear 'his robes of blue' for the occasion, and since those same ordinances make it clear that women were not barred,[16] Elizabeth was perhaps there too, trying to come to terms with the pain of losing a second child in five years, and watching the little coffin as it was borne on a hearse into the Abbey, where a dirge was sung over it and the lords kept watch overnight. The next day, 22 June, Mass was said, and the interment in the Confessor's chapel followed.[17] There is no record of a tomb being raised to mark Edmund's burial place.

Sheen was not the only royal residence to be updated by Henry VII. In 1500–1 the King demolished the old palace at Greenwich and began rebuilding it, facing the buildings with red brick in the Burgundian style much favoured by him and Elizabeth.

Accessed through an imposing gateway opposite Queen Margaret's Pier, the new Greenwich Palace was designed around three courtyards, known as Fountain Court, Cellar Court and Tennis Court. Its riverside façade boasted bay windows and an imposing five-storeyed tower, which probably housed Henry's privy chamber. Elizabeth's lodgings were in a parallel range that lay behind, the two suites being connected at one end by the hall and chapel. At the other end a gallery gave access to the convent of the Observant Friars, which had been re-founded by the King, who drew up elaborate instructions for a stained-glass window in the friars' church depicting himself and his family; it was completed around 1503.[18]

In 1500 the King and Queen visited Coventry, where they were admitted as members of the Holy Trinity Guild, and watched a mystery play portraying the story of the world from Creation to Judgement Day. They also visited Nottingham.

That year the King summoned Katherine of York and her husband, Lord William Courtenay, to court. By October they had settled in their house in Warwick Lane with their children, and thereafter were both often at court; early in 1501 William was granted an annuity for his daily diligent attendance on the King. Elizabeth must have been pleased to have her sister near at hand.

In Spain, Isabella and Ferdinand were preparing to send the Infanta Katherine to England. Notwithstanding the assurances given by Elizabeth, Isabella evidently was anxious about her youngest child. 'We ardently implore that the Princess shall be treated by [King Henry] and the Queen as their own daughter,' she wrote to Pedro de Ayala on 23 March 1501.[19] That month, Henry VII outlaid £14,000 (£6,800,000) for jewels from France 'against the marriage of my Lord Prince'.[20] No expense was to be spared for the wedding of his heir, which would reflect everything he had achieved in securing this crucial alliance.

In mid-April the King and Queen kept their Easter court at Eltham.[21] On 8 May the Portuguese ambassador in England reported to his master, King Manuel I, that 'the Queen was supposed to be with child, but her apothecary told me that a Genoese physician affirmed that she was pregnant, yet it was not so'. Nevertheless, it looked very much like it to the ambassador, for she had 'much *embonpoint* [plumpness] and large breasts'.[22] This report and the double chin evident in the contemporary portrait in the Royal Collection (see Appendix 1) suggest that Elizabeth, like her father before her, was becoming prematurely obese in her thirties – or she had retained a fuller figure after her previous pregnancies.

That month, accompanied by her duenna, Doña Elvira Manuel, and a train of sixty people, Katherine left the Alhambra Palace in Granada on the first stage of what was to prove a slow journey to England. In July Puebla reported: 'The King, the Queen and the Prince of Wales have great pleasure in hearing that the Princess Katherine is beginning to speak French. The Queen especially rejoices in the progress the Princess is making in the French language.'[23] It meant that she would be able to converse the more easily with the daughter-in-law whose arrival she so eagerly anticipated.

On 2 October Katherine of Aragon at last arrived in England, coming ashore at Plymouth after a stormy voyage. Ladies and officials had been appointed 'to give their attendance upon the Princess at her landing', summoned by letters sent by the Queen herself.[24] There was a formal reception, with 'the King's commendations made by my Lord Steward, the Queen's by her chamberlain'.[25] Elizabeth's officers were actively involved in all the preparations, for the marriage of her son was an event that came within her sphere of influence. Her master of horse provided five chariots and twenty palfreys for the Princess and her ladies, and henchmen to ride with them; her chamberlain was in charge of the etiquette to be observed and matters of precedence.[26]

When Katherine of Aragon set out on her journey eastwards to London, she received a rapturous welcome from the people who flocked to see her on the way. 'The Princess could not have been received with greater joy had she been the Saviour of the World,' a member of her suite reported to Queen Isabella.[27]

Henry and Elizabeth were then staying in the Tower of London, where they were preparing for the wedding celebrations. There were daily jousts on the tournament ground before the White Tower, and feasts in the King's Hall, the great hall in the Inmost Ward. But Henry had a more pressing matter on his mind: he wanted to see his son's bride and be reassured that she was as fit a mate for Arthur as he had been led to believe.

The Prince travelled from Ludlow, met up with his father, and rode with him to greet his bride. They caught up with the Princess at Dogmersfield, Hampshire, on 4 November. There was a tense altercation when Katherine appeared veiled and her duenna and the Spanish ambassador informed the King that Spanish protocol dictated she must remain so until she was married; but Henry, ever suspicious, and no doubt fearful that his son's bride was deformed or ugly, stood his ground. 'Tell the lords of Spain,' he commanded, 'that the King will see the Princess even were she in her bed.' The veil was lifted. Arthur later wrote to Ferdinand and Isabella that he 'had never felt so much joy in his life as when he beheld the sweet face of his bride', and he vowed to be 'a true and loving husband all his days'.[28] After the meeting he returned with his father to London to rejoin the Queen, with Katherine's procession following.

★

Elizabeth had gone to stay at the newly rebuilt and restored palace at Sheen. By November 1501 the King had 'finished much of his new building at his manor of Sheen, and again furnished and repaired that before was perished with fire'.[29] The renovated palace, which cost over £20,000 (£9.7 million), had only recently been made ready for occupation by the royal family. Built in late, ornate Perpendicular style around two broad, paved courtyards, it covered ten acres and faced the Thames to the south. It was dominated by Henry V's massive donjon tower, which had survived the fire and was completely restored. Now surmounted by fourteen turrets, pepper-pot domes and pinnacles, it contained the King's and Queen's suites of privy lodgings.

Lancaster Herald described the new palace as 'this earthly and second paradise of England, the spectacular and beauteous example of all proper lodgings'. He noted the towers, pinnacles and weather-vanes sporting the royal arms, painted and gilded, on every building in the complex; on windy days, the tinkling of the vanes was 'right marvellous'.[30]

The palace was approached through a massive gatehouse with an archway eighteen feet high and eleven feet wide, which gave access from the green in front to the Great Court. Above the archway was emblazoned the Tudor royal arms supported by the red dragon of Cadwaladr and the greyhound of Richmond. From the gatehouse extended 'a strong and mighty brick wall of great length', encircling the palace complex. Lancaster Herald described it as having 'towers in each corner and angle, and also in the midway', with several stout oak gates studded with nails and crossed with iron bars. 'Galleries with many windows full lightsome and commodious' overlooked the Great Court, where there were 'pleasant chambers for such lords and men of honour that wait upon the King's Grace'. A 200-foot-long gallery afforded excellent views of the gardens.

The smaller inner court – the River Court – was paved with marble and boasted a stone conduit and a drinking fountain sculpted with lions and red dragons guarding branches of red roses, from which the water ran clear and pure to a cistern beneath. This was where people washed their hands, for there was no running water inside the palace. To the west side was the great hall, 100 foot long and resplendent with a tiled floor, a central hearth and a timber roof lined with lead and decorated with hanging pendants and carved knots – all 'most glorious and joyful to behold'.[31] The walls were hung with rich cloths of Arras, including a fabulous one depicting 'The Destruction of Troy', and there were 'pictures' – probably statues – of 'the noble kings of this realm in their harness [armour] and robes of gold, like bold and valiant knights' – with Henry VII naturally prominent among them. Beneath the hall was a cellar, and next to it, on the ground floor, were to be found the royal wardrobe and domestic offices – 'the pantry, buttery, kitchen and scullery'. Coal and fuel were stored in the yards outside, well out of sight of the royal family.

On the opposite side of the courtyard to the hall, up a flight of stairs, was the chapel, 'well paved, glazed and hung with cloth of Arras' and gold, with an undercroft beneath it. The altar was set with jewels and relics and laden with rich plate, and pictures of virtuous and pious kings of England – doubtless including St Edward the Confessor and Henry VI – were displayed on the walls. A private closet to the left of the altar was shared by Elizabeth, her children, Margaret Beaufort and their attendants, while the King's closet was on the right side. Both closets were furnished with carpets, cushions and silk curtains. The chapel ceiling was 'chequered with timber lozenge-wise, painted azure, having between every check a red rose of gold or a portcullis'.[32]

From the chapel 'extended goodly passages and galleries, paved, glazed and painted', adorned with golden badges sporting Tudor roses and portcullises. These led to the three-storeyed donjon, which was accessed through an imposing arched doorway sculpted with the royal arms and the red dragon of Cadwaladr, and was notable for its many windows. Here, on the first floor, were the King's chambers, the first, second and third of which (watching chamber, presence chamber and privy chamber) were hung with costly cloth of Arras; each room had 'white-limed' and 'chequered' ceilings, and 'goodly bay windows' overlooking the river.

Below, connected by a great staircase, were 'divers and many more goodly chambers both for the Queen's Grace, the Prince and Princess, my lady the King's mother, the Duke of York and Lady Margaret, and all the King's noble kindred and progeny'. These suites contained 'pleasant dancing chambers and secret closets' and were 'most richly enhanged, decked and beseen'. More fine rooms were to be found in a new four-storeyed tower attached to the donjon.

Both the King's and Queen's apartments were on the south-east side of the donjon and overlooked 'most fair and pleasant' enclosed gardens and galleries with open loggias, a feature never before seen in England. There were kitchen gardens and orchards to the west, and a privy garden to the east. The latter had symmetrical railed beds with 'royal knots' of flowers, and lions and dragons on decorative poles; alleys led through the beds and beyond, to 'places of disport' and 'houses of pleasure' – bowling alleys, archery butts and tennis courts – another feature borrowed from the Burgundians.[33]

Henry VII gave the palace a new name: 'from this time, it was commanded by the King that it should be called Rich Mount', or Richmond, 'because his father and he were earls of Richmond' in Yorkshire.[34] It became his favourite residence, and remained the largest English royal palace until Hampton Court was built in 1514.

In 1499 Henry VII had founded, or re-founded, six English houses for Observant (Grey) Friars of the Order of St Francis, one of which was at Richmond. In May 1502 the King gave the friars the old manor buildings and chapel of Byfleet, and work began immediately on converting them into a convent. This was screened off from the palace by an orchard – no ordinary orchard, but a charming pleasaunce 'with royal knots alleyed and herbed'; along its alleys were set statues of 'many marvellous beasts, as lions, dragons and such other divers kind, with many vines, seeds and strange fruit right goodly beset'. And 'in the lower end of this garden beith pleasant galleries and houses of pleasure to disport in'. Galleries, beasts and houses of pleasure were all features of the Burgundian palaces.[35]

Richmond was not just a beautiful palace but a showpiece, a visual statement of Henry VII's achievements. Rampant with heraldry and resplendent with the very latest in Tudor taste, it was the flagship residence of the new dynasty, a treasure house packed with the symbols of power, wealth and majesty – the ultimate in conspicuous display. Sadly, Elizabeth did not live to see it completed.

As soon as he arrived at Greenwich, the King 'was met by the Queen's Grace, whom he ascertained and made privy to the acts and demeanour between himself, the Prince and the Princess, and how he liked her person and behaviour'.[36] Elizabeth must have been delighted to hear that her son's bride was pretty and golden-haired, with a pleasing dignity.

Preparations for the coming wedding advanced briskly. There was much discussion of the etiquette to be observed when Katherine was presented to the Queen. Elizabeth and Margaret Beaufort were drawing up lists of the ladies who were to attend her and the Princess during the reception celebrations;[37] Margaret would also arrange for Katherine to share several household officers with her. On 2 November Elizabeth appointed Agnes Tilney, Countess of Surrey, 'with certain ladies awaiting upon her', 'to meet and receive the Princess' at Amesbury.[38]

On 9 November Katherine was welcomed at Kingston-upon-Thames by Prince Henry, who escorted her to the Archbishop of Canterbury's palace at Lambeth, where she was to lodge before her marriage. Here awaited a letter for her from the King, expressing his great 'pleasure, joy and consolation' at her coming, and assuring her that he and the Queen would treat her 'like our own daughter'.

The next day the King and Queen were rowed to London in separate barges, Elizabeth being attended by a 'goodly company of ladies'. They took up residence in Baynard's Castle, where the Queen made 'ready for inducting the noble Princess of Spain'.[39] Margaret Beaufort was busily renovating nearby Coldharbour to make it a fit residence for Arthur and Katherine after their marriage.

On 12 November, as all the bells of London rang out, banners fluttered from windows, crowds packed the streets, music sounded from every side, and the conduits ran with free wine, Katherine made her formal entry into the City.[40] She was greeted by a series of lavish pageants in the Burgundian style as she passed along the processional route; all were designed to underline the success of the Tudor dynasty in obtaining such a high-born princess for the heir to the throne. In Cornhill, 'in a house wherein there dwelled William Geoffrey, haberdasher, stood the King, the Queen and many great estates of the realm', watching the procession with Prince Arthur. Henry, his son, Derby, Oxford, Shrewsbury and some French envoys were at one window, while 'in another chamber stood the Queen's good Grace, my lady the King's mother, my Lady Margaret, my lady [Mary] her sister, with many other ladies of the land, not in very open sight like as the King's Grace did with his manner and party'. The Londoners had displayed a somewhat excessive zeal for flattery, for nearby was a pageant portraying Henry VII as God the Father and Prince Arthur as God the Son. Henry also paid for a 'standing' in Cheapside from which to view the proceedings, but seems not to have used it, unless he moved by a circuitous route from Cornhill, ahead of the procession.

It was from her window in Cornhill that Elizabeth glimpsed her new daughter-in-law for the first time, as Katherine's procession passed below; looking out, she would have seen a young girl riding 'a great mule richly trapped after the manner of Spain', flanked by Prince Henry and the Papal legate, and wearing 'rich apparel' in the Spanish mode: 'a little hat fashioned like a cardinal's hat of pretty braid with a lace of gold to stay it, her hair hanging down about her shoulders, which is fair auburn, and a coif between her head and her hat of a carnation colour'. A little way behind walked the Queen's master of horse leading a spare palfrey with a side-saddle. At the climax of the procession, the bride-to-be was led by the Archbishop of Canterbury into St Paul's Cathedral, where she said her prayers and made an offering at the shrine of St Erkenwald before retiring to the adjacent Bishop's Palace for the night.

The following afternoon, on the eve of her wedding, the Princess went to Baynard's Castle to be presented to her mother-in-law. She was again accompanied by Elizabeth's master of horse and 'a right great assembly' of splendidly attired gentlemen and 'certain ladies: some of the Queen's, and some of the Princess's, at the Queen's nomination'. The Queen's chamberlain 'received her at the foot of the grece [stairs] that goes up to the Queen's chamber'. During her audience, she and Elizabeth both spoke in Latin, and they enjoyed 'pleasant and goodly communication, dancing and disports. Thus, with honour and mirth, this Saturday was expired and done', and it was late when Katherine departed for Lambeth Palace to make ready for her wedding day. Already Elizabeth had begun the process of preparing her successor for the role she would one day occupy, and probably Katherine was glad to have the guidance of a kindly mother-in-law who could initiate her into the realities and mysteries of English court life.

After Katherine left, Elizabeth rode to Lord Bergavenny's London house in Great St Bartholemew's by St Paul's, where she and the King were spending the night before the wedding. George Neville, Baron Bergavenny, had fought for Henry against the Cornish rebels and was Lord Warden of the Cinque Ports; he had accompanied Henry and Elizabeth to Calais the previous year. His first wife had been a granddaughter of Elizabeth's aunt, Joan Wydeville.[41] His house, which was burned down in the Great Fire of 1666, stood where the Stationers' and Newspaper Makers' Hall now stands in Stationers' Hall Court; its inner courtyard occupies the site of the garden of Abergavenny House.

★

On 14 November Arthur and Katherine were married in St Paul's Cathedral. The King had done his utmost to underline the importance of the nuptials. 'Within the church was erected a platform, or stage, six feet high and extending from the west door to the uppermost step of the choir; in the middle of this platform was a high stand, like a mountain, which was ascended on every side with steps covered over with red worsted. Against this mountain on the north side was ordained a standing for the King and his friends; and upon the south side was erected another standing, which was occupied by the Lord Mayor and aldermen of London.'

The royal standing – a 'high place set in the nave and body of the church', 'decked and trimmed for the King and Queen and such others as they appointed to have' – was a kind of private box above the consistory, which enabled Henry and Elizabeth privately to 'go out of the Bishop's Palace into the same consistory, and there hear and see the ceremonies of the marriage at their pleasure', watching 'in secret manner' from behind a lattice. The focus during the ceremony was to be on Arthur and Katherine, and Henry and Elizabeth 'would make no open show of appearance'.

On the morning of the wedding day, the royal entourages assembled at the Tower. Elizabeth was wearing an embroidered white satin gown and a purple velvet train. She travelled with the bride in an open chariot from the Tower to St Paul's, following behind the King, who rode a white horse and looked splendid in his red velvet robes, his breastplate studded with diamonds, rubies and pearls, and a belt of rubies at his waist. On arrival, the royal couple retired with the bride into the Bishop's Palace, whence Henry and Elizabeth discreetly entered the cathedral. Elizabeth's sister Katherine and Lord William Courtenay were among the illustrious guests, as was Margaret Beaufort, who 'wept marvellously' through the service.

Katherine emerged from the Bishop's Palace to the sound of trumpets, shawms and sackbuts, clad in white and gold satin. Beneath her wide-skirted gown she wore hoops – the first Spanish farthingale ever seen in England, which naturally drew much comment, as did her rich coronet and voluminous veil, or mantilla, of silk edged with a border of gold and precious stones, beneath which her long red-gold hair flowed loose down her back. She was escorted to her groom by her future brother-in-law (and husband), ten-year-old Henry, Duke of York, impressive in silver tissue embroidered with gold roses. Arthur, like his bride, was wearing white satin.

In the cathedral, the Prince and Princess 'ascended the mount, one on the north and the other on the south side, and were there married by [Henry Deane] the Archbishop of Canterbury, assisted by nineteen bishops and abbots. The King, the Queen and the King's mother stood in the place aforementioned, where they heard and beheld the solemnisation, which, being finished, the Archbishop and bishops took their way from the mountain across the platform, which was covered with blue ray cloth, into the choir, and so to the high altar. The prelates were followed by the bride and bridegroom. The Princess Cecily bore the train of the bride, and after her followed one hundred ladies and gentlewomen in right costly apparel. Then the Mayor, in a gown of crimson velvet, and his brethren, in scarlet, went and sat in the choir whilst Mass was said.' For this, the young couple processed through the rood screen and choir to the high altar. Mass being finished, they knelt to receive the blessing of the King and Queen, then proceeded to the church door, where Arthur publicly dowered his bride with one third of his income as Prince of Wales, as the crowds outside roared their approval, crying, 'King Henry! Prince Arthur!' and the trumpets, shawms and sackbuts blared out once more in celebration. Katherine was now second lady in the land after the Queen.

Afterwards the Prince and Princess of Wales were conducted in a grand procession led by Prince Henry to the Bishop's Palace, where a great feast was prepared, 'to which the Lord Mayor and aldermen were invited'. The latter had stationed themselves by the entrance so as to get a good view of the bride. The royal party and their guests were served on gold plate valued at £1,200 (£583,300), and the new Princess of Wales dined off plate of solid gold ornamented with pearls and precious stones worth £20,000 (£9.7 million). 'It was wonderful to behold the costly apparel and the massive chains of gold worn on that day.'

At the end of the day, the newly wedded couple were put to bed together in a ceremony witnessed by most of the court. The Prince was escorted by his lords and gentlemen to the nuptial chamber, 'wherein the Princess before his coming was reverently laid and disposed', and after the bed had been blessed and the newlyweds left alone to do their dynastic duty, the King and Queen departed for Baynard's Castle.

There then followed one of the most controversial wedding nights in history. It was stated years later that fifteen-year-old Arthur claimed beforehand that he felt 'lusty and amorous', and it was reported at the time, by the herald who wrote an account of the wedding celebrations, that 'thus these worthy persons concluded and consummated the effect and complement of matrimony'.

But did they? Doña Elvira stated some months later that they did not, and in 1503, King Ferdinand would tell his ambassador in Rome: 'The truth is that the marriage was not consummated, and that the Princess our daughter remained as whole as she was before she married.'[42] Years afterwards Katherine would swear that she and Arthur had spent just seven nights together, and that she emerged from her marriage 'as intact and undefiled as she had come from her mother's womb',[43] but Henry VIII, her second husband, professed to be not so sure about that. In 1529, when he was trying to move heaven and earth to have his marriage to Katherine dissolved, on the grounds that canon law forbade him to marry his brother's widow, Lady Guildford, who was present at the wedding celebrations in 1501, would depose in the legatine court that Arthur and Katherine spent their wedding night in bed together, and that Queen Katherine had afterwards told her that 'they lay together in bed as man and wife all alone five or six nights after the marriage'. William Thomas, a groom of Arthur's privy chamber, stated that he himself 'made Arthur ready for bed, and conducted him clad in his nightgown unto the Princess's bedchamber often and sundry times; and that at the morning he received him at the said doors and waited upon him to his own privy chamber'.[44]

None of this proved that the couple had actually had sex, but naturally Henry VIII needed testimony to show that the marriage had been consummated, and others were ready to come forward in 1529 to give evidence to that effect. The King's close friend, Charles Brandon, Duke of Suffolk, declared that he had heard from Maurice St John, the Prince's attendant, that Arthur's decline in 1502 'grew by reason that [he] lay with the Lady Katherine'. Sir Anthony Willoughby recalled that, the morning after his wedding, 'the Prince spoke before divers witnesses these words: "Willoughby, give me a cup of ale, for I have been this night in the midst of Spain. It is good pastime to have a wife!" Which words he repeated divers other times.' The fact he repeated them so often might suggest that Arthur was boasting to cover up his failure in bed, because he knew what was expected of him. St John had also mentioned Arthur's thirst to Robert Ratcliffe, now Viscount Fitzwalter, who recalled that St John asked the Prince why his throat was so dry, whereupon he replied, 'I have been in Spain this night.'[45]

Predictably the peers of England, in their scramble to ingratiate themselves with Henry VIII, were ready to brag about their own prowess at Arthur's age. George Talbot, Earl of Shrewsbury, affirmed that 'the Prince knew his lady carnally because he might be able to do so, as he himself had been, who knew his wife before he was sixteen'. That did not mean anything, of course. The Duke of Norfolk also boasted that he too 'at the same age did carnally know and use a woman', but also said he had heard 'from credible persons that Prince Arthur did lay with the Lady Katherine five or six nights after'. His wife the Duchess stated that the couple had been 'alone in bed together the next night after their marriage'.[46]

In 1531, however, at a hearing in Zaragoza, one of Katherine's attendants would testify that, on the day after the wedding, 'Francesca de Caceres, who was in charge of dressing and undressing [her], and whom she liked and confided in a lot, was looking sad and telling the other ladies that nothing had passed between Prince Arthur and his wife.'[47]

Nowadays many people find it hard to accept that two teenagers shared a bed and did not have sex. It was incumbent upon them, after all, to produce an heir to ensure the future of the Tudor dynasty: the consummation of their marriage was their duty. Others find it hard to believe that Katherine of Aragon, a devout woman of great integrity and principle, would vigorously maintain that her marriage to Arthur was not consummated if it had been. It has been said she might have lied to protect her position and her daughter's status, but for the avoidance of doubt, the Pope had actually issued two dispensations allowing her to marry Henry, one providing for the first marriage having been consummated. So she had no need to lie, for in the eyes of the Church her second marriage was valid anyway.

It is important to remember that Henry VIII's doubts of conscience came at a time when he was desperate to have a male heir – and to marry Anne Boleyn. But his adultery with Anne's sister Mary placed him in the same forbidden degree of affinity to Anne as he was to Katherine by virtue of her marriage to his brother. When Katherine publicly challenged him to deny in open court that she had come to him 'a true maid without touch of man', he remained silent; and when she vowed to Pope Clement VII that she would accept whatever he decided about her virginity if her husband would swear under oath that he knew her marriage to Arthur had been consummated, Henry failed to respond.[48]

There was a prevalent belief that early indulgence in sex by young people who were not physically mature was detrimental to health, and there had been a recent example that appeared to prove it. In 1497 Katherine's only surviving brother, the Infante Juan, Prince of Asturias, had died at nineteen – disastrously for the Spanish succession. The cause was possibly tuberculosis, but opinion generally held that overindulgence in the marriage bed had proved fatal. In 1533 Henry Fitzroy, Duke of Richmond, Henry VIII's bastard son, was married at fourteen but not permitted to live with his bride because he was considered to be too young.

Henry VII had good reason to be cautious. A despatch sent to Ferdinand of Aragon by his envoy, Gutierre Gomez de Fuensalida, in July 1500 reveals that the King had had concerns then about the health of Prince Arthur. Fuensalida had 'understood from a reliable source that the King has decided that the Prince will know his wife sexually on the day of the wedding, and then separate himself from her for two or three years, because it is said that in some way the Prince is frail, and the King told me that he wanted to have [Arthur and Katherine] with him for the first three years, so that the Prince should mature in strength'.[49] Evidence that emerged later about the state of Arthur's health in the months that followed (see Chapter 16) supports the theory that it was never consummated at all.

Twelve days of celebrations had been planned, and there was further excitement on 14 November, when envoys from James IV arrived in London to arrange their master's marriage to Princess Margaret. There were no entertainments on the day after the wedding, when Katherine and Arthur were allowed some privacy, but on Tuesday, 16 November, the King and Queen returned in state by river from Baynard's Castle and with the newly wedded Prince and Princess 'came to Paul's Church, where they made their offering, dined in the Bishop's Palace, and so returned'. Afterwards, the royal party went to Westminster by river, attended by the Lord Mayor, the aldermen and the sheriffs. 'For the more royalty of the going of the King and Queen, [and] of the Prince and Princess, unto Westminster by water', it had been decreed 'that the King and Queen and the

Prince have their barges apart and pompously rigged and dressed', and that minstrels should play for them as they sailed along the Thames.

On Thursday, 18 November, the first of the planned tournaments was held. The wide yard before Westminster Hall had been strewn with gravel and sand 'for the ease of the horses', and lists had been set up. Around the ground were flower displays and artificial trees heavy with fruit. To the south was a stand hung with cloth of gold and furnished with cushions of the same costly fabric. 'As soon as dinner was done in the court', the Queen, the Princess of Wales, Cecily, Viscountess Welles, the other princesses and a train of 'two or three hundred ladies and gentlewomen' entered this stand from the right, and the King, Prince Arthur, Prince Henry and many lords entered from the left.

'Round the whole area were stages built for the honest common people, which at their cost was hired by them in such numbers that nothing but visages presented themselves to the eye, without any appearance of bodies. And when the trumpets blew, the nobility and chivalry engaged to tilt appeared in the arena, riding under fanciful canopies borne by their retainers.' The Earl of Essex must have drawn many eyes, as he 'had a mountain of green carried over him as his pavilion, and upon it many trees, rocks and marvellous beasts climbing up the sides', and 'on the summit sat a goodly young lady, in her hair [with loose hair], pleasantly beseen'. The Queen's half-brother, Dorset, 'had borne over him a rich pavilion of cloth of gold, himself always riding within the same, dressed in his armour'. Elizabeth's brother-in-law, Lord William Courtenay, made his appearance 'riding on a red dragon led by a giant, with a great tree in his hand'.

Twenty or thirty contestants rode around the arena, cheered on by the commons, then the tournament began, and they engaged in the tilt 'with sharp spears, and in great jeopardy of their lives, breaking a great many lances on each other's bodies'. Fortunately, no one was killed. When the jousts were over, the royal party, followed by throngs of lords and Londoners, proceeded into Westminster Hall, where a royal dais had been erected, and a magnificent cupboard – which stretched the whole length of the wall of the Court of Chancery – was laden with a display of plate, mostly of solid gold. Elizabeth, Margaret Beaufort and the Princess Katherine sat down at elevated seats at the King's left hand, with their ladies and the royal children on their side of the hall, while Prince Arthur sat at his father's right hand, with the nobles seated according to degree on his side.

Stages with scenes of a castle, a fully rigged ship with sails, and a 'Mount of Love' were wheeled in, and pageants performed. The castle – representing Castile – was lit enticingly from inside, and eight gentlewomen could be seen looking out of its windows. At the top sat a lady wearing Spanish dress, representing Katherine of Aragon, and in the towers were the children of the King's Chapel in full chorus. The castle was drawn by 'marvellous beasts' – men dressed as gold and silver lions harnessed with huge gold chains. The ship was manned by mariners 'who took care to speak wholly in seafaring terms', and in it were men dressed as sailors and a girl playing a Spanish infanta. The princess in the castle was courted by 'two well-behaved and well-beseen gentlemen called Hope and Desire', who emerged from the ship, but she disdained them, at which point eight knights emerged from the 'Mount of Love' and stormed the fortress, forcing the ladies to surrender, whereupon they emerged from the castle, partnered the victors and danced with them 'goodly roundels and divers figures', before vanishing out of sight.

Arthur now led his aunt Cecily on to the floor, 'and danced two *basse* dances,[50] and then departed up again, the Prince to his father and Lady Cecily to the Queen her sister'. Next the Princess Katherine and one of her ladies, both wearing Spanish dress, danced two *basse* dances, then 'both departed up to the Queen'. After this things livened up. Ten-year-old 'Henry, Duke of York, having with him his sister, Lady Margaret, in his hand, came down and danced two dances, and went up to the Queen'. There was such applause that the pair came down again, and young Henry 'suddenly threw off his robe and danced in his jacket with the Lady Margaret in so goodly and pleasant a manner that it was to the King and Queen a great and singular pleasure. Then the Duke departed to the King and the Princess Margaret to the Queen.' At the end of the evening a hundred lords and knights paraded into the hall with gold cups of hippocras and gold plates of spices.

On the following Sunday, 21 November, there 'was laid out a table in the White Hall, or Parliament Chamber, for a lavish dinner. The King sat at the side table next to his own chamber, with Katherine at his right hand', her duenna beside her. The door to the King's chamber was open, and within 'the Queen sat at the table at the bed's feet, which was the table of most reputation of all the tables in the chamber', proclaiming to the world the esteem in which Henry held Elizabeth. Seated below the Queen were her sisters Cecily and Katherine, Margaret Beaufort and a Spanish bishop. Arthur presided over a third table, seated with his siblings, Margaret and Henry. After dinner Katherine presented the prizes won in the jousts. The Duke of Buckingham received a great diamond, Dorset got a ruby, and the rest rings set with precious stones. Then the King and Queen led their guests into Westminster Hall, where they watched an interlude and were diverted by disguisings and a pageant in which lords and ladies danced in celebration of the union of the Prince and Princess. Just before midnight eighty earls, barons and knights served a void of hippocras and comfits, offering the royal family golden plates of spices and gold cups, which were filled from a golden ewer by a lord of high rank.

The bridal pair spent the next few days at Baynard's Castle, during which period more tournaments took place, and there was a huge gathering in Westminster Hall for more disguisings and pageants, during which the King presented prizes to those who had been victorious in the jousts, and everyone departed 'with excellent mirth and gladness'. On Saturday, 27 November, the royal family and the court left London in sixty barges, among which numbered those of the Lord Mayor and the City livery companies, decorated with 'their standards and streamers, with their cognizances right well decked'. The journey was made delightful by 'the most goodly and pleasant mirths of trumpets, clarions, shawms, tabors, recorders and other diverse instruments, to whose noise upon the water hath not been heard the like'. At Mortlake everyone 'took horses and chariots, and so rode to Richmond', arriving late at night by torchlight. The King had arranged for the celebrations to continue in the great palace, 'the bright and shining star of building, the mirror and pattern of all palaces of delight, commodity and pleasure, there intending to finish, conclude and end the royalties of this most excellent wedding'.[51]

The next day being Sunday, the King and Queen attended Mass 'with pricked song and organs, and goodly ceremonies in the choir and altars'. 'After divine service, the King sped with the court through his goodly gardens to his gallery on the walls', where he and his family watched lords playing chess, backgammon, cards and dice. Later 'a framework with ropes was fixed in the garden, on which went up a Spaniard, and did many wondrous and delicious points of tumbling and dancing'. Afterwards the King led a hunt in Richmond Park, which Elizabeth did not attend.

In the evening, Henry, Elizabeth and Katherine took their places on the dais in the hall, which was lavishly furnished with carpets and gold cushions, and watched a pageant in the form of a rock drawn by three seahorses; on the rock sat models of mermaids, in which were hidden the children of the Chapel Royal, 'who sang sweetly with quaint harmony'. When the pageant reached the dais, 'instead of dancers were let out of the rock a great number of white doves and live rabbits, which creatures flew and ran about the hall, causing great mirth and disport'. At the end of the evening, after the void, the King distributed gifts to his Spanish guests, in gratitude for their having brought their Princess safely to England, and so ended the wedding celebrations.

The next day Katherine bade farewell to the Spanish lords, who returned home bearing letters from the Queen for Ferdinand and Isabella. Noticing that she was looking sad and pensive after their departure, Henry realised she was homesick. Kindly, he took her and her ladies to his new library and showed her 'many goodly pleasant books' to divert her; he even summoned a jeweller, from whose wares she was allowed to take her pick. The remaining jewels were given to her Spanish ladies.[52]

At the end of November the court moved to Windsor Castle. It had been decided that Arthur should return to Ludlow to resume his duties, but there was much debate as to whether Katherine would go with him, or stay with the Queen and Princess Margaret, at least for the winter. The King still felt that Arthur was not old enough to give free rein to 'the duties of a husband', and that the couple should wait a while before they lived together; others were worried that Katherine, coming from the warmer climate of Spain, would find it hard wintering on the Welsh border. Some councillors agreed that cohabitation should be delayed, on account of the 'tender age of our son', as Henry would explain to Ferdinand and Isabella in February.[53] The tragic memory of the Infante Juan had hovered like a spectre over the debate.

Doña Elvira and Ayala urged that the Princess remain behind, arguing that Ferdinand and Isabella would be 'rather pleased than dissatisfied' if the couple 'did not live together' for some time, on account of Arthur's tender age. Katherine herself declared to the

King that she had no other will than his in the matter. But her chaplain, backed by Dr de Puebla (who had fallen out with Doña Elvira), insisted that it was the true wish of Ferdinand and Isabella that the Prince and Princess should not be separated; if they were, the Spanish sovereigns would be displeased and the homesick Katherine 'in despair'. 'This indecision continued four days, during which [the King] caused the Prince to use his influence with Tudor Princess, and to persuade her to say that she preferred rather to go than to stay, and, as she refused to say it, the King, making show of great sorrow, decided that she should go to Wales, although nothing in the world he regretted more.' In this way Henry bowed to the perceived wishes of Katherine's parents, declaring that he was allowing her to go to Wales 'even to the danger of our own son'.[54] It was a decision he would soon come to rue. Elizabeth's wishes in the matter are not recorded, but she may well have felt some concern.

On 21 December Arthur and Katherine left together for Ludlow, where they set up their small court. Here, Arthur again presided over the Council of the Marches, learning how to govern his principality as a preparation for kingship, and continuing his studies with Dr Linacre. Henry, Elizabeth and their younger children spent Christmas at Richmond Palace.

Elizabeth was present when, on 24 January 1502, the treaty of marriage between Princess Margaret and James IV was concluded at Richmond,[55] and she played an important role in the ceremony of betrothal the following day, which was conducted with much pomp, and attended by many lords and high-ranking clergy, including Henry Deane, Archbishop of Canterbury, Thomas Savage, Archbishop of York, and Robert Blackadder, Archbishop of Glasgow. On this occasion Katherine Courtenay and Katherine Gordon were in attendance on the Queen, and the latter took precedence after the royal party.

Clarencieux King of Arms left an account of the ceremonies: 'First the King, the Queen, with their noble children, except the Prince [Arthur], heard the High Mass' in the royal chapel, after which Richard FitzJames, Bishop of Rochester, 'made a notable sermon'. Then 'the King and the Queen, accompanied with the Duke of York, the Lady Mary', the Papal legate, the ambassadors and the company of about ninety persons processed to the Queen's great chamber for the betrothal; the room had been newly decorated with entwined Tudor roses and Scottish thistles in honour of the occasion.

The King and Queen seated themselves beneath the canopy of estate, with Prince Henry and Princess Mary on stools at their feet. Princess Margaret stood before them, with all eyes upon her. During the ceremony, the Archbishop of Glasgow asked the King, the Queen and the Princess if they knew of any impediment, and all three assured him there was none.

Then the Archbishop turned to Margaret. 'Are you content without compulsion, and of your own free will?'

And Margaret, displaying none of the independence of spirit of her later years, replied dutifully, 'If it please my lord and father the King, and my lady my mother the Queen.' 'The King showed her that it was his will and pleasure, and then she had the King's and the Queen's blessing', whereupon the Archbishop proceeded to the betrothal ceremony, with Patrick Hepburn, Earl of Bothwell, standing proxy for the bridegroom.[56] Although she was not to go to Scotland until September 1503, Margaret was now Queen of Scots, and would henceforth be honoured as such at her father's court, and be assigned her own apartments at Westminster and Windsor.[57]

Trumpets sounded from the leads of the chamber and minstrels played 'in the best and most joyfullest manner' as 'the King went to his own chamber to dinner' with the Scots and English ambassadors, and 'the Queen took her daughter, the Queen of Scots, by the hand, and dined both at one mess, covered' – possibly meaning that both were now married and therefore they covered their heads – in Elizabeth's great chamber. Jousts followed in the afternoon, and in the evening there was 'a notable banquet', while in London *Te Deums* were sung in churches, bonfires were lit in celebration, and hogsheads of wine were passed round in the streets.

The next day the little Queen of Scots appeared in state in her mother's chamber, and 'by the voice of the principal officer there gave thanks to all those noble men who had taken pain to joust for her sake'. Prizes were presented to the winners in the lists, and afterwards 'there was in the hall a goodly pageant, curiously wrought with fenestrals [windows], having many lights burning in the same in manner of a lantern, out of which sorted various sorts [pairs] of morris [dancers]'. There followed 'a very goodly disguising of six gentlemen and six gentlewomen, which danced divers dances', then one more 'great and notable banquet'. The next day, there was another tournament, after which the King distributed gifts to the Scots envoys.[58]

Preparations were now put in hand for Margaret's departure for Scotland. The Queen took a personal interest in her daughter's trousseau, purchasing for her a gown of crimson velvet with cuffs of fur, white and orange sarcanet sleeves, three pewter basins, a brass chafer, two washing bowls, a fire-pan, 'a great trussing basket' and a pair of bellows; she also paid 'Giles the luter' for strings for the Queen of Scots' lute.[59] A painter, called 'Minour' — who was almost certainly Maynard Wewyck, the King's painter — was commissioned to execute portraits of the King, the Queen and the Princess, which he took to Scotland himself and presented to James IV.[60]

It might have seemed to Henry and Elizabeth that the high point of the King's reign had been reached with the culmination of his hard-negotiated treaties, and that all was set fair for a glorious future. Yet the euphoria surrounding the wedding and betrothal celebrations did not long endure. In February 1502 two new threats to the Tudor dynasty emerged, and both would impact badly on Elizabeth.

16

'Enduring Evil Things'

The year 1502 was to prove Elizabeth's *annus horribilis*. In 1500, after the elimination of Warwick and Warbeck, a Milanese envoy had observed of Henry VII: 'From this time forward, he is perfectly secure against Fortune.'[1] Alas, that prediction was shortly to be confounded, for now 'there suddenly came a lamentable loss and mischance to the King, the Queen and all the people'.[2]

'The Shrovetide following the marriage [the week ending 8 February 1502, which was Shrove Tuesday], Prince [Arthur] began to decay and grow feeble in body,' so the Duke of Suffolk recalled in 1529. He had heard the details from Maurice St John, who was of the opinion that the Prince's illness was the result of too much indulgence in the marriage bed. This testimony chimes with that of Sir Anthony Willoughby, who had 'heard say' that the Prince and Princess 'lay at Ludlow together the Shrovetide next following';[3] and it is supported by the contemporary account in *The Receyt of the Lady Katherine*, which dates Arthur's decline 'from the Feast of the Nativity of Christ unto the solemn feast of the Resurrection, at the which season grew and increased upon his body, whether it was by surfeit or cause natural, a lamentable and most pitiful disease and sickness'.

News of Arthur's illness reached the court within days, and must have occasioned the royal parents much concern. But that was not all they had to worry about, for there was a new threat to the Tudor throne. The King had restored the attainted Lincoln's younger brother, Edmund da la Pole, to the peerage, but only to the extent of making him earl of Suffolk – not duke, like his late father. Suffolk's resentment had smouldered. He was after all regarded by some malcontents as the rightful Yorkist claimant to the throne. A bold, rash man, he had murdered 'a mean person in rage and fury' the previous year. Henry VII had pardoned him, but he had long distrusted him, and with good reason. In the summer Suffolk, provocatively calling himself 'the White Rose', and his brother Richard had fled, with the aid of Sir James Tyrell, to the court of Maximilian of Austria, now Holy Roman Emperor. This had rightly been viewed by an alarmed Henry VII as a new threat to his security. It had 'vexed and misquieted' him, making him anxious lest 'some tumultuous business should be begun again', for Suffolk's claim to the throne was arguably better than his own. On 22 February 1502 Suffolk was publicly condemned in a sermon preached at Paul's Cross, and excommunicated.[4]

Suffolk was Elizabeth's first cousin, and he had played a prominent part at her coronation and in court ceremonials. He was part of a circle that included her brother-in-law, William Courtenay, and her kinsman, Henry Bourchier, Earl of Essex.[5] She was close to his mother, her aunt Elizabeth, Duchess of Suffolk, and possibly to him too, so his defection must have come as a shock to her.

Numerous people suspected of being in contact with the de la Poles had been under surveillance in recent months, and Henry had learned that Courtenay had banqueted and dined with Suffolk just prior to his defection. The King's agents had also uncovered disquieting intelligence that Courtenay had corresponded with Suffolk, and he was suspected of having invited the de la Poles to invade England in the west, where his family had their power base.

That was enough for Henry. Late in February Courtenay was suddenly seized – taken without night clothing, body linen or cloaks[6] – and imprisoned in the Tower on charges of conspiracy. But as Hall makes clear, Courtenay was 'rather taken of suspicion and jealousy than for any proved offence or crime'. Probably he was dealt with severely because he was married to a Yorkist princess and might conceivably have designs on the throne himself; his wife Katherine was said to have disparaged Henry VII's claim to the throne,[7] but this seems unlikely.

Courtenay was to be attainted for treason in 1503, and his estates given to his father, after whose death they were to revert to the Crown. He escaped the death penalty, perhaps because the King did not want his brother-in-law made a public spectacle on the scaffold.[8] But for

Katherine, his imprisonment was cataclysmic. She had as yet no guarantees that Henry would spare her husband. Impoverished by the confiscation of his property, with her children likely to be disinherited, the depths of her distress can be imagined. Despite her own trials, Elizabeth offered strong support to her sister during the coming difficult months, unhesitatingly welcoming Katherine into her household and succouring her both emotionally and financially.[9]

We know this from entries in Elizabeth's account book for the period 24 March 1502 to 15 March 1503, which survives in the National Archives and has many pages checked in her own hand.[10] It contains details of purchases made by her during that time, from minor items such as a pair of small enamelled knives, to payments to French embroiderers working all hours on hangings for her great bed of state. During this period Elizabeth kept herself solvent, which had not always been the case. Her chamber receipts amounted to £3,585.19s.10½d. (£1,743,150), and her expenditure was £3,411.5s.9 ¼d. (£1,658,230). Most fascinating of all, these accounts give us invaluable and detailed insights into the last months of her life and the daily existence of a queen.[11]

Elizabeth was already paying Katherine a pension of £50, but that she now augmented with gifts.[12] She must have had some warning of Courtenay's arrest – proof that Henry did confide some state secrets to her – because on 1 February, nearly a month beforehand, she had taken charge of the Courtenay children, Henry, Edward and Margaret, paying for them to be brought from Devon and installed in Sir John Hussey's country seat, Dagenham's Manor, a pretty moated courtyard house not far from the royal manor of Havering, Essex. Here Elizabeth established a nursery household under the care of a governess, Margaret, Lady Cotton, with nurses and rockers for Edward and Margaret, two women servants and a groom. Lady Cotton was already in charge of a child whom the Queen had taken under her wing, one Edward Pallet, whose schooling, diet and clothing Elizabeth funded; he was a companion for the Courtenay children. In June 1502 the Queen's accounts show that she was providing 4s.4d. (£110) a week for the children's food and servants, and that month she paid 4s. (£100) to her tailor for making two coats of black camlet (a valuable fabric woven from goat's hair) for her young nephews, and the same amount for velvet ones.[13]

How Elizabeth felt about the King's decision to imprison Courtenay and so plunge her sister into deep trouble when she herself was anxious about Arthur's health is unrecorded, but her kindness to all the Courtenays implies that she felt sympathy for her brother-in-law. Such charitable acts were expected of a queen, in emulation of Christ's exhortation to comfort those in prison, but – as subsequent events tend to suggest – Elizabeth may have resented Henry allowing mere suspicion to subvert family loyalties.

Sir James Tyrell was charged with treasonably corresponding with the disaffected Edmund de la Pole. Tyrell had prospered under Richard III, and at the time of Bosworth had been serving abroad as Governor of Guines in the English-held Pale of Calais; but soon afterwards he was deprived of his offices and estates by Henry VII. However, in 1486 he received two pardons and was re-appointed to his former post and given land in Calais, where he remained for the next sixteen years. Vergil suggests that Tyrell aided Edmund de la Pole, Edward IV's nephew, out of guilt at having murdered Edward's sons, the Princes in the Tower, whom he could easily, 'without danger to his own life, have spared, and carried to safety'.

Tyrell refused to obey the order recalling him to England in 1502 for questioning about his association with the de la Poles. At length he was lured out of Guines Castle on the promise of a safe conduct, but arrested once he had boarded ship. On arrival in England he was hauled off to the Tower.

Later evidence that will shortly be discussed shows that Prince Arthur's health was now in serious decline, and bulletins on his progress must have been sent to the King and Queen. In March Elizabeth paid two priests, Sir William Barton and Sir Richard Milner, to make pilgrimages and offerings on her behalf at no fewer than thirty-five important religious shrines.[14] The number of intercessions they were to make to the Virgin Mary, patron of mothers, bears testimony to the Queen's desperate fears for her son's health.

Barton was sent to 'Our Lady and St George' and 'the holy Cross' – the 'Cross Gneth', said to be a splinter of the True Cross – in St George's Chapel, Windsor, and to the tomb of Henry VI, who had a reputation for saintliness and whose tomb was already visited by many pilgrims. His pilgrimage continued to the college of 'Our Lady of Eton', and the 'Child of Grace' of Reading Abbey, an ancient image of the infant Christ given by Henry I in the twelfth century, of which it was said that 'everyone who prostrates himself in its chapel always obtains by the grace of God the fulfilment of his devout prayer in any trouble'.[15]

Barton also offered at the ancient, silver-plated image of Our Lady of Caversham; the shrine of the Holy Blood at Hailes Abbey, Gloucestershire; 'Prince Edward', meaning the grave of Henry VI's son, Edward of Lancaster, at Tewkesbury Abbey; Our Lady's shrine in Worcester Cathedral; the Holy Rood – a cross said to have been found buried at the site of the Crucifixion – in St Gregory's Church, Northampton; the image of Our Lady of Grace in the church of the Austin Friars, Northampton; Our Lady of Cockthorpe;[16] Our Lady of Walsingham, where the largest offering, 6s.8d. (£160) was made, demonstrating that shrine's importance to the Queen; Our Lady's shrine in the chapel of the College of St Gregory, Sudbury; the popular image of Our Lady of Woolpit, Suffolk; Our Lady of Grace of Ipswich; and the chapel of the Blessed Virgin in the College of Stoke-by-Clare, which was under the patronage of the queens of England. It took Barton twenty-seven days to visit all these shrines.[17]

At this time Henry VII was doing his best to have Henry VI canonised. Elizabeth's offerings at Eton College, Henry VI's own foundation, St George's Chapel, his burial place, and Tewkesbury Abbey, where his son's tomb was also attracting pilgrims at this time, were an acknowledgement of the legitimacy of the Lancastrian line that her husband represented, and a tribute to the sanctity of her father's rival. Ten years earlier Caxton had included an oration to Henry VI in his book, *The Fifteen Oes*, commissioned by Elizabeth and Margaret Beaufort.[18] Elizabeth, suffering anxiety and fear over her son's health, was perhaps haunted by thoughts of the last Lancastrian heir, who had met his untimely death at eighteen.

Father Milner spent thirteen days visiting the shrine of Our Lady of Crowham; the mechanically moving Rood of Grace in Boxley Abbey, Kent; the shrine of the martyred St Thomas Becket at Canterbury Cathedral, to whom, as we have seen, Elizabeth's devotion had been fostered in childhood by her mother; Our Lady of the Undercroft at Canterbury Cathedral; the shrines of St Augustine and St Adrian in St Augustine's Abbey, Canterbury; St Mary de Castro in Dover Castle; the great Rood over the north door of St Paul's Cathedral, London; the image of Our Lady of Grace in St Paul's; images of St Ignatius, St Dominic, St Peter of 'Melayn' and St Francis at unidentified locations in or near London; St Saviour's Abbey, Bermondsey; Our Lady of the Pew in Westminster Abbey; Barking

Abbey, Essex; and the shrine of the Black Madonna in St Mary's Church, Willesden[19] (now in north-west London), which had been founded in 938 by the Saxon King Athelstan. This image had been famed since before 1249 for working miracles, and was a popular destination of pilgrims throughout the later Middle Ages.[20] One day, less than forty years hence, Henry VIII would sweep away these shrines to which his mother had been so devoted, and in which she had invested so much faith.

Arthur was well enough to wash the feet of fifteen poor men on Maundy (or 'Shire') Thursday, which fell on 24 March 1502,[21] but thereafter his deterioration was rapid. Elizabeth must have been in torment when, on Maundy Thursday, at Westminster, she participated in the usual ceremonies, giving money and 105 yards of cloth to thirty-six poor women, to the number of her years. Bowls, baskets and flowers were bought for this occasion. Payment for the material was made on 1 December following, and for three yards of cloth delivered on an unspecified date 'by the commandment of the Queen to a woman that was nurse to the Prince, brother to the Queen's Grace' – probably Richard, Duke of York. Again, the untimely death of a royal heir was in Elizabeth's troubled mind. She was at Greenwich on Good Friday, when she made her offering in the chapel, and at Richmond for Easter Sunday; who knows with what fervency she offered to the Cross on the high altar after Mass?[22]

On Monday, 28 March, she paid the gifted composer, Dr Robert Fairfax, the princely sum of £1 (£490) 'for setting an Anthem of Our Lady and St Elizabeth',[23] which would invoke not only the protection of the Virgin Mother but, unusually, also that of the mother of the Virgin. Fairfax was the organist of St Alban's Abbey, and also the first Oxford scholar to obtain a doctorate in music; he had been a member of the Chapel Royal since 1497. The anthem, or votive antiphon, he composed for the Queen was a five-part motet entitled *Eterne laudis lilium*, in which the name Elizabeth features prominently, while the first letter of each line spells out the name ELISABETHA REGINA ANGLIE.[24]

That same day Elizabeth set out from Greenwich to stay for a few days at the Thames-side manor house of Hampton Court,[25] owned by the military Knights Hospitallers of St John of Jerusalem. It was on this site that Cardinal Thomas Wolsey would later build Hampton Court Palace. The Order of St John had been founded to succour wounded crusaders and protect the Holy Land from the

Turks, and had grown very wealthy. In the twelfth century the Hospitallers had maintained an agricultural estate office at Hampton, selling produce to increase revenue. The manor house had been built before 1338, and was now a substantial property in the middle of an 800-acre estate growing crops and supporting 2,000 sheep. From the fourteenth century, it served as a grand guest house for visitors to the court at Sheen and, later, Richmond, and it also provided accommodation for royal pensioners.

The Hospitallers' house stood in a walled enclosure surrounded by a rectangular moat. It boasted a great hall (traces of which remain beneath Henry VIII's great hall of the 1530s), a chamber block with a tower lodging, and a separate chapel; it also had a garden and a pigeon house. In 1494 the house was leased to Henry VII's loyal Chamberlain and friend, the powerful Giles, Lord Daubeney, who had been in exile with his master and fought valiantly for him at Bosworth. The lease gave Daubeney the right to 'take, alter, transpose, break, change, make and new build', and immediately he started converting Hampton Court into a great courtier house, making extensive changes. He erected a new courtyard range, a gatehouse and a great hall, all of brick. North of the hall he built a new kitchen with a massive fireplace, which survives today as the Great Kitchen at Hampton Court Palace. By the time Henry VII visited in October 1500 and July 1501, the house was a fashionable mansion sufficiently grand for entertaining royalty. Elizabeth had probably accompanied the King on these visits, and evidently she enjoyed the hospitality of Lord Daubeney, whose epitaph in Westminster Abbey describes him as 'a good man, prudent, just, honest and loved by all'.[26]

Elizabeth seems also to have regarded Hampton Court as a place of spiritual refuge, one to which she could retreat at times of trial, for it still retained aspects of its monastic past. Daubeney was required by the Knights Hospitallers to appoint a priest to 'sing and minister divine service' in the chapel on their behalf (the bell from the chapel tower is probably the one that survives today in Hampton Court's inner gatehouse). In 1503 Elizabeth would retreat into a 'cell' at Hampton for eight days, the word 'cell' then meaning a room in the monastic sense. It is likely that she went for the same purpose in 1502, so that she could pray for her son's restoration to health.

During her stay Elizabeth received visitors, and rewarded a poor woman who gave her some almond butter,[27] a welcome gift during Lent, when animal fats were eschewed by the devout.[28]

Elizabeth left Hampton Court on 2 April, when Lewis Walter, her bargeman, rowed her to Greenwich. Even at this anxious time she was thinking of others. On Friday, 4 April, she sent John Duffin, her groom of the chamber, to the Duchess of Norfolk 'to warn her to receive [Margaret Scrope] the wife of Edmund de la Pole, late Earl of Suffolk'. She also sent her barge to collect her gentlewoman, Elyn Brent, from Hampton Court, and row her to London. Possibly Mrs Brent had remained behind to pack up some of the Queen's stuff. On 12 May following payment was made to two men sent from Richmond to Hampton Court to collect Mrs Brent, which took two days.[29] This suggests that more of the Queen's belongings remained to be fetched. The delay is accounted for by the dreadful news that arrived during the night of 4 April.

'In all the devices and conceits of the triumphs of [Prince Arthur's] marriage,' there had been 'a great deal of astronomy', with jubilant predictions that the Prince would emulate his illustrious forebear, 'King Arthur the Briton. But,' reflected Bacon, 'it is not good to fetch fortune from the stars', for between six and seven o'clock on 2 April,[30] Arthur's 'lively spirits finally mortified', and 'the young Prince that drew upon him the hopes and affections of his country' commended 'with most fervent devotion his spirit and soul to the pleasure and hands of Almighty God,' aged fifteen years and seven months. 'His celebrated virtue equalled, if not surpassed, the fame of all former princes', lamented Bernard André. 'If only the Fates had granted him a longer stay in this world.'

It was said that Arthur expired 'of a malign vapour that proceeded from the constitution of the air'. A Spanish contemporary, Andres Bernaldez, curate of Los Palacios, wrote in his manuscript chronicle of the reigns of Ferdinand and Isabella that 'Prince Arthur died of the plague a little while after his nuptials, at a place they call Pudlo [sic]. In this house was Doña Catalina left a widow, when she had been married scarcely six months.' Arthur had not mentioned his wife in the will drawn up just before he died, in which he left all his robes and household stuff to his sister Margaret. This suggests that he and Katherine wre never close.

The contemporary herald's account in *The Receyt of the Lady Katherine* describes the Prince as suffering from 'the most pitiful disease and sickness that with so sore and great violence had battled and driven in the singular parts of him inward; that cruel and fervent enemy of nature, the deadly corruption, did utterly vanquish and overcome the pure and friendful blood, without all manner of physical help and remedy'.

In favour of the plague theory is the fact that Katherine fell ill too at this time, although she later recovered. But if Arthur had died of the plague, or the rarer but equally feared 'sweating sickness', there would surely be other reports of it.

In 1502 there are references to an epidemic in some parts of the country, but it is unlikely that this was the dreaded sweating sickness, because people regarded that as distinct from plague. The sweating sickness was a highly virulent disease that manifested itself in England in a series of epidemics between 1485 and 1551. The cause of it is still uncertain, but its onset was sudden and dramatic, unlike Arthur's illness, and it struck with deadly force: it was said that anyone who survived the first twenty-four hours would recover. Usually death occurred within hours; one could be 'merry at dinner and dead at supper'.[31]

But Arthur was ill for over seven weeks, and had been ailing for up to two months before that; there had been concerns about his frailty as far back as July 1500. Even without that new evidence, modern writers who state that his illness was sudden and brief have overlooked the testimony of Suffolk and St John in 1529, that the Prince had fallen sick at Shrovetide after sharing a bed with Katherine, and the account in *The Receyt* that he had been in a decline since Christmas. All were quite specific, and Suffolk and St John's evidence could have been corroborated – or disputed – by other witnesses who remembered Arthur's death. The Prince's capacity to bed his bride might have been exaggerated in 1529, but Suffolk had no reason to lie about the long duration of his final illness – rather the opposite, for it was in his, and his master Henry VIII's, interests to show that Arthur had been romping in bed with Katherine throughout the five months of his marriage.

There was no epidemic of the sweating sickness in 1502, but there was a 'great sickness' in the Ludlow area,[32] thought by some historians to have been plague. Although the great plague of 1499–1500 was over, evidence from local wills shows that, between harvest 1501 and harvest 1502, mortality was above average in the diocese of Hereford, with the most deaths – fifteen – occurring at Ludlow; the figures are even higher for the following year.[33]

The onset of the plague was sudden too. There were three types, bubonic, pneumonic and septicaemic; the latter two developed rapidly and invariably proved fatal. Few recovered from the commonest form, bubonic plague, either: untreated, it usually saw off its victims within five days; even today, eighty per cent of patients who do not receive antibiotics die within eight days. It was caused by the bite of an infected flea, or by contact with another sufferer. A disease of the lymphatic system, it first manifested itself by a headache, weakness, high fever, confusion, aches and chills. By the third day the lymph nodes in the neck and armpit would swell painfully, ooze pus and bleed. This was followed by gangrene of the fingers, toes, nose and lips, which turned black; it was this that gave bubonic plague its more common name, 'the Black Death'. The victim suffered pain, muscle cramps, seizures and lung infections, which might cause them to vomit blood incessantly; in the final stages, they lapsed into delirium and a coma as the nervous system collapsed. Death often occurred with terrifying suddenness.

There was no effective treatment. All the doctors could do was helplessly prescribe rest, good diet and a move to cleaner air. A fortunate few did survive; if they lived past the tenth day, they had a good chance of recovering. Non-fatal cases could last up to a month. There is one documented case of a fourteenth-century physician, Guy de Chauliac, suffering an attack of plague that lasted six weeks,[34] but he recovered, so for much of that period he would have been convalescent.

Arthur doesn't fit the pattern. His illness began with a decline, not a sudden escalation of symptoms like plague. Plague was a disease that manifested itself in warm weather and was largely absent in the winter months. We know that, as late as April 1502, the weather was cold and windy. Thus plague is unlikely.

Possibly it was an influenza-type virus that raged in the region and proved fatal to the Prince, especially if he was already ailing. The herald who wrote an account of his funeral states that very few citizens were present in Worcester Cathedral because of the great sickness that prevailed in those parts.[35] The fact that Arthur's body was buried at Worcester, and not taken back to London for burial in Westminster Abbey, strongly suggests that he was thought to have died of something contagious and that it was felt his body should be buried as soon as possible.

The most convincing theory is that Arthur had 'a consumption', or tuberculosis, perhaps contracted from his father, who would die of it at the age of fifty-two. In the nineteenth century there evolved the perception that this disease was the scourge of three young Tudor males; almost certainly it killed Arthur's nephew Edward VI, who was also fifteen when he died in 1553. But it did not kill another nephew, Henry VIII's bastard son, Henry Fitzroy, Duke of Richmond, who was evidently quite healthy until an acute pulmonary infection carried him off in 1536, aged seventeen.

Katherine's physician, Dr Alcaraz, later explained that she was still a virgin because 'the Prince had been denied the strength necessary to know a woman, as if he was a cold piece of stone, because he was in the final stages of phthisis [consumption]. He said his limbs were weak and that he had never seen a man whose legs and other bits of his body were so thin.'[36]

This might explain Henry VII's anxiety about allowing the couple to live together. Yet if Arthur had then been in such a decline, and so obviously weak and emaciated, it is surprising that no one else commented on it, and that the marriage had been allowed to go ahead. Had he been in that state before his departure for Ludlow, it is unlikely that the King would have allowed him to go so far from London, and equally unlikely that the Spanish ambassadors would not have known about his condition, or failed to warn the Spanish sovereigns about it.

The symptoms of pulmonary tuberculosis include coughing bloody sputum, breathing difficulties, fatigue, loss of appetite and weight, night sweats and chest pain. There was no treatment because antibiotics had yet to be invented. In the late medieval period the disease was common and Dr Alcaraz would easily have recognised it, so his diagnosis is almost certainly reliable. It is often contracted in childhood, from prolonged exposure to people with active tuberculosis, and symptoms may not appear for some years, if at all; but statistics show that, once they do manifest themselves, death occurs after about three years in untreated cases. The disease can also spread rapidly through both lungs and prove fatal, accounting for the short duration of Arthur's last illness, which might have been exacerbated by making the long journey from London in the depths of winter. Dr Alcaraz's report probably relates to the period between Christmas and April, when the Prince's decline would have been most evident. He must have known that Arthur and Katherine had not consummated their marriage prior to arriving at Ludlow, and it was probably obvious afterwards that Arthur was already too ill to play the husband.

An interesting theory has been put forward that he died of a less common form of the disease, testicular tuberculosis, which causes a fibrous mass that can mimic a cancerous tumour. The disease increases libido but inhibits sexual performance, which would explain why he was unable to consummate his marriage.[37] That Arthur's illness affected his testicles has been inferred from the description of his sickness affecting 'the singular parts of him inward' – which could mean any organ, however – and it has also been suggested that he died of testicular cancer, which can spread quickly in young victims.[38] Diabetes, asthma or pneumonia are other theories.[39]

The weight of evidence favours tuberculosis. The chances are that Arthur, a premature baby, had been of a weak constitution from birth, which made him susceptible to infection. Henry VII was already anxious about his health when he sent him to Ludlow, but maybe he had not suspected the nature of what ailed his heir; maybe he was in denial; probably Arthur did not show any alarming symptoms or lose weight so dramatically until he was at Ludlow.

According to an anonymous herald's account preserved by John Leland, 'immediately after [Arthur's] death, Sir Richard Pole, his chamberlain, wrote and sent letters to the King and Council at Greenwich, where his Grace, and the Queen lay, and certified him of the Prince's departure'. The Privy Council received the terrible news first, during the night, and 'discreetly sent for the King's ghostly father' and confessor, an Observant Friar, 'to whom they showed this most sorrowful and heavy tidings, and desired him in his best manner' to break it to their master. In the morning, the friar went to the King, arriving 'before the time accustomed', and knocked on the door of his chamber. On being admitted, he asked for everyone in attendance to be dismissed, and when he was alone with Henry, 'after due salutation', he gently quoted Job in Latin: '*Si bona de manu Dei suscipimus, mala autem quare non sustineamus?*' ('If we receive good things at the hands of God, why may we not endure evil things?') Then he 'showed his Grace that his dearest son was departed to God'.

For the stricken father, this was a devastating blow, and Henry VII must have struggled to confront the fact that his dream of a new Arthurian age lay in ruins. 'When the King understood these sorrowful, heavy tidings, he sent for the Queen, saying that he and his wife would take their powerful sorrow together.' Thus it was that

Elizabeth heard the shattering news that every parent dreads to hear, that her child was dead in the flower of his youth.

It is on this occasion that we are afforded a rare and touching glimpse of the private relationship between Henry and Elizabeth. The matrimonial career of Henry VIII had not yet made royal marriages legitimate objects of intense diplomatic interest, and information about the private lives of earlier kings and queens is often sparse. This account of the royal couple sharing their grief and striving to comfort each other gives one of the best insights into their relationship and shows them, after sixteen years of marriage, to have been loving, caring and mutually supportive. It shows Elizabeth taking the initiative in intimate matters and being quite firm with her husband, although, even in private, she still addressed him formally. And it reveals that she drew on an inner strength that enabled her selflessly to put his needs first, even at such a time. She would have been painfully aware that he had lost not just his son but also his heir and all the hopes he had invested in him, and that only one young life now stood between him and the loss of everything he had striven so carefully to build. Henry was now forty-five, well into middle age by Tudor standards, and may have feared he would not live to see his remaining heir grow to maturity, let alone a son born now, and he and Elizabeth had good reason for anxiety about the future for they knew, none better, what could happen to child kings. And so, setting aside her own grief, Elizabeth hastened to comfort him.

'After she was come and saw the King her lord in that natural and painful sorrow, she, with full great and constant and comfortable words, besought his Grace that he would first, after God, consider the weal of his own noble person, of the comfort of his realm, and of her.'

'And remember,' she said, 'that my lady your mother had never no more children but you only, yet God, by His Grace, has ever preserved you and brought you where you are now. Over and above, God has left you yet a fair prince and two fair princesses; and God is still where He was, and we are both young enough. As the prudence and wisdom of your Grace [is] sprung all over Christendom, you must now give proof of it by the manner of taking this misfortune.' Considering that her life had been feared for in her last pregnancy, it must have taken courage to assure Henry that they could have more heirs, but no doubt that was a bravado born of the need to console him – and herself.

Henry thanked Elizabeth for 'her good comfort'. But when she returned to her own chamber, she collapsed. The 'natural and motherly remembrance of that great loss smote her so sorrowfully to the heart that those who were about her were fain to send for the King to comfort her. Then his Grace, of true, gentle and faithful love, in good haste came and relieved her, and showed her how wise counsel she had given him before; and he for his part would thank God for his son, and would [that] she would do in like wise.'[40]

Elizabeth rallied. On 6 April, when she must have felt raw with grief, she paid for two of William Courtenay's former servants to ride to the West Country to see his father, the Earl of Devon,[41] no doubt to inform him of the tragic news, and perhaps to ask him to send her sister Katherine immediately to court, so that they could comfort each other.

Elizabeth's mourning attire conformed to the ordinances laid down by the King: 'The Queen shall wear a surcoat with a train before and behind, and a plain hood, and a tippet [shoulder cape] at the hood, lying a good length upon the train of the mantle. And after the first quarter of the year is past, if it be her pleasure, to have her mantle lined; it must be with black satin or double sarcenet; and if it be furred, it must be with ermine, furred at her pleasure.'[42]

On 19 April Richard Justice, page of the robes, was paid for mending a gown of black velvet. On 2 May black tinsel (taffeta) satin was purchased as edgings for another and a gown of crimson velvet. On 7 June six yards of black velvet for a gown and a yard of black buckram for stiffening the bodice were delivered for the Queen, and two days later Henry Bryan, a London mercer, supplied eight yards of black damask for a cloak, black sarcenet for the lining and black velvet for the edging. The bodice of a gown of black velvet of Princess Margaret's was relined, and 'a black satin gown for my Lady Mary'. On 21 June more black damask was bought for a gown for the Queen, and on 2 August payment was made for a black velvet mourning gown with wide sleeves lined with sarcenet.[43]

In November we find Elizabeth ordering sixty yards of blue velvet for her own use; this seems to have been used for 'the covering of a litter of blue velvet lined with sarcenet and bordered with satin figure[s] that was given to a lady of Spain', probably a member of Katherine of Aragon's household. Cushions of blue damask were made for the same litter. Elizabeth also bought seven yards of black velvet for a gown, and thirteen yards of black satin for a riding gown, as well as black velvet for the border and cuffs, black sarcenet for the 'vents' (slashes) and black buckram and canvas for the lining; she sent Richard Justice to fetch a gown of blue velvet and seven yards of black damask. In December she bought 8¾ yards of black velvet, and at the end of January 1503 blue worsted. Around that time she had a kirtle of black satin lined and hemmed. To pay for these and other items, she had once more to pawn her plate, and the King was obliged to give her money.[44]

The Queen remained in mourning for Arthur for most of 1502, although on state occasions she wore her normal queenly attire.[45] A contemporary composer, John Browne, wrote a Latin antiphon, 'Stabat iuxta Christi crucem', which speaks of the grief of the Virgin Mary for her crucified Son, evidently drawing a parallel with Elizabeth's grief for her own son.[46]

Elizabeth's health – she was reportedly well before the tragedy[47] – was undermined by the shock of Arthur's death. The first indication of this comes on 29 April, when she paid John Grice, her apothecary, the huge amount of £9.13.4d. (£4,700) for 'certain stuff of his occupation'.[48] What he supplied was clearly more than something to dull unbearable grief or help her to sleep. Given the other references to Elizabeth's poor health in the months to come, it would seem that there was some more fundamental medical problem.

'The calamity and the pitiful misfortune' of Arthur's unexpected death had 'touched the entire kingdom.'[49] It would have long-reaching repercussions that no one could have envisaged. He had been 'the delight of the Britons', 'the glorious hope of the realm' and 'the most renowned heir of our magnanimous King', but now he was no more, and England had perforce to weep 'since your hope now lies dead'.[50]

Arthur's corpse – disembowelled, boiled, cered and spiced[51] – lay in state in the great hall of Ludlow Castle until it was carried with mournful pageantry to St Laurence's Church nearby on 20 April. The Prince's heart and viscera are said to have been buried in the church, where his coffin lay before the altar for three days, but there is no contemporary evidence for this, and heart burial had been in decline in England since 1300.[52] On St George's Day, conducted by a vast cortège headed by Sir William Uvedale and Sir Richard Croft,

Arthur's body was conveyed to Worcester Cathedral. Katherine did not attend the funeral, as custom would not have allowed the widow to be present, and she was too ill anyway; neither did the King and Queen, Henry being represented by Thomas Howard, Earl of Surrey, as chief mourner. The black-draped hearse rested at Tickenhill Palace, Bewdley, on the way, brought there on 'the foulest cold windy and rainy day', and the escort was 'in some places fain to take oxen to draw the chair, so ill was the way'.

At his father's wish, the Prince was buried 'with great funeral obsequies'[53] on the right-hand side of the chancel. Gruffydd ap Rhys was chief mourner; he would later be buried near his young master. There was 'weeping and sore lamentation as Prince Arthur was laid to rest'. Thomas Writhe, Wallingford Pursuivant, 'weeping, took off his coat and cast it along over the chest right lamentably'.[54]

A beautiful chantry chapel was erected over Arthur's plain granite tomb, but Elizabeth did not live to see it built. Half a century after her death, her grandson Edward VI ordered it to be despoiled along with the other chantries that were swept away by the Reformation; but among the ruined stone carvings that remain can be seen Tudor roses, Beaufort portcullises, Katherine of Aragon's pomegranate, and the Yorkist falcon and fetterlock. The arms of Henry VII and Elizabeth of York appear on the south screen of the chantry.

The reaction of Arthur's siblings to his death is not recorded. Margaret was to name one of her sons after him, in the year when he would have succeeded his father to the throne. Possibly Henry did too: the names of two short-lived boys borne by Katherine of Aragon are unrecorded. But Henry cannot but have found some satisfaction in the knowledge that, with Arthur gone, he was now, as his father's next and only surviving son, heir to the throne. He was not imme-diately given his brother's titles since it was not yet known whether Katherine of Aragon was with child.[55] It is unlikely that the two boys had known each other well, or were close, as they had grown up apart, with Arthur at Ludlow and Henry usually at Eltham.

Cardinal Pole, the son of Margaret of Clarence, was later to claim that Henry VII disliked his second son intensely, 'having no affection or fancy unto him'.[56] Pole had little that was good to say about Henry VIII, so this may be an exaggeration, but his mother had known both kings, so there may be some truth in what he wrote. But in 1502 young Henry was barely eleven, and may not yet have aroused the antipathy of his father – unless Henry VII resented him for being alive when Arthur, in whom so many of his ambitious hopes had been vested, was dead.

Arthur's death did have an unfortunate consequence for his younger brother. The previous summer the King had considered giving young Henry his own household at Codnore Castle, Derbyshire (then vacant due to the death of its owner, Henry Grey), once Arthur was married,[57] which would have given him a degree of independence. The King, perhaps having the boy's measure, may also have reasoned that, living so far from court, his younger son would pose less of a threat to Arthur. What Elizabeth thought of this beloved child being sent to live such a distance from her is not recorded. But now the boy, the sole heir, would stay at court, or with his sisters, heavily protected, even isolated, and would not enjoy any independence while his father lived.

There were the Garter ceremonies to get through; the annual calendar of the court did not allow for private grief. Elizabeth paid 'Friar Hercules' £5 for golden fabric and silk from Venice, and gold damask, which he made into laces and buttons for the King's Garter mantle.[58]

On 27 April she left Greenwich by barge for the Tower, where she lodged for five days. During her visit she was in contact with Alice FitzLewes, Abbess of the Minoresses' convent at Aldgate; Alice had been a nun at 'the Minories' since about 1493, and had been elected abbess by 1501.[59] On 1 May Elizabeth rewarded her with 6s.8d. (£160) for sending a present of rosewater. She also gave 11s. (£270) for the succour of 'Dame Katherine and Dame Elizabeth, nuns of the Minories in almshouse, and to an old woman servant to the Abbess, and to a daughter of William Crowmer, also a nun there'.[60]

During her sojourn at the Tower Elizabeth may well have met with the Abbess, whose convent was a stone's throw away; this was probably how she learned of these needy cases. They must have known each other already, because Alice FitzLewes was cousin to Elizabeth's aunt, Mary FitzLewes, Lady Rivers, the widow of Anthony Wydeville, and Elizabeth appears to have been close to her aunt, who is known to have attended her on several occasions. Interestingly the Abbess's mother, Joan FitzSimon, widow of Philip FitzLewes, was a cousin of Sir James Tyrell, the man named by More as the murderer of the Princes in the Tower, who was then in the Tower awaiting trial for abetting the de la Poles.[61]

It seems significant that the Queen chose to visit the Tower at this time. The rosewater and the charitable gifts may have been genuinely intended, but they might also have been the cover for something of far greater import, because residing in a house within the precincts of the Minories at that time were several ladies who were well placed to know the truth about the fate of Elizabeth's brothers. Elizabeth Talbot, Duchess of Norfolk and mother-in-law of Richard, Duke of York, the younger of the Princes in the Tower, lived there until her death in 1506. With her was Elizabeth, daughter of Sir Robert Brackenbury, Constable of the Tower at the time of the Princes' disappearance, whose will of 1514 provides for her burial there; Mary, sister of Sir James Tyrell; and one of Tyrell's cousins, the daughter of John Tyrell.[62]

Also living in the house was Joyce Lee, a widow who took the veil and was interred in the church of the Minories in 1507. Her brother Edward later became archbishop of York, and he was friends with Thomas More; their families lived in the same London parish, and More was to dedicate a book to Joyce Lee in 1505.[63] It is conceivable that More visited her at the Minories when he was a young lawyer living at Bucklersbury in London, and that it was there that he first heard the truth about the fate of the Princes from people who had the means of knowing what had happened to them. Alice FitzLewes must have known Joyce Lee and all the other ladies in the house in the close. She could perhaps have told the Queen much about the fate of her brothers. But Elizabeth was probably at the Tower for another reason entirely.

She was back at Greenwich on 2 May; the next day, being Ascension Day, she made her offering at the altar.[64] During that first week of May those accused of conspiring treason with Edmund de la Pole were arraigned at Guildhall, and condemned for 'matters of treason'. Sir James Tyrell was beheaded on 6 May 1502 on Tower Hill.[65] Vergil observed that 'he paid by his own death the appropriate penalty for his previous crimes'.

Afterwards Henry VII 'gave out' that, while in the Tower, Tyrell was 'examined, and confessed' to murdering the Princes nineteen years earlier.[66] Either he let slip something compromising or he was already suspected of having been involved, although Henry was reluctant to believe any ill of him.[67] If the King gave out such information, it was probably by a proclamation[68] that does not survive. Of the sixty-two extant proclamations of Henry VII, some are lost,[69]

notably the one proclaiming his accession. Others that are missing
are referred to in contemporary documents, such as one issued in
1496 for expanding legislation on conditions of work for labourers;[70]
no one has ever disputed its existence, although rivers of ink have
been spilt in denying that Tyrell's confession was ever the subject of
a proclamation. It is true that no written confession or deposition
by Tyrell survives, but that is not unusual or necessarily significant
in Tudor treason cases.

It does seem more than coincidental that Elizabeth had chosen
to make a brief visit to the Tower at this particular time, just before
Tyrell's trial; it was perhaps significant too that she was in touch
with the Abbess of the Minories during her stay. It is possible that
her presence in the Tower had something to do with Tyrell's confession. Perhaps he made it to her in person, or the King and his
examiners deemed it useful to confront Tyrell with the sister of the
Princes. Or Tyrell, knowing that he almost certainly faced death,
asked if he could see the Queen, to confess to her his involvement
in the death of her brothers – perhaps insisting he would speak to
no other.

Conceivably Elizabeth's involvement, or perhaps her reaction, was
the reason why Henry VII did not make more of the confession.
Henry would surely have done much to secure confirmation that
the Princes really were dead, and would have sympathised with
Elizabeth's need to know the truth about her brothers. He may have
thought it fitting that she was the one to hear the truth. We know
she had had advance warning of Courtenay's arrest in February,
indicating that the King entrusted her with matters of state that
affected her; he might therefore secretly have involved her in this
delicate matter too. It does seem significant that Elizabeth had dealings with the Abbess of the Minories, Tyrell's cousin, who was
sheltering his sister and a mutual cousin; possibly they were all linked
to her visit in some way, even if it was only in their need for reas-
surance that Tyrell had at last unburdened his conscience before
facing divine judgement.

This is all purely hypothetical, of course. We will probably never
know the truth of the matter, although Elizabeth's presence in the
Tower at this particular time is surely grounds for speculation. More
wrote that Tyrell's horse-keeper, John Dighton, one of the murderers,
had also been examined and confessed to the murder, while Bacon
states that Dighton corroborated Tyrell's confession. More, whose

account was partly based on Tyrell's confession, probably tracked down and spoke with Dighton later on, for around 1513 he was able to state that 'Dighton yet walks on alive, in good possibility to be hanged' – an incorrigible criminal.

It has been argued that Henry's announcement of Tyrell's confession was a fabrication, or that the confession was forced. Certainly it was timely, especially in the wake of Prince Arthur's death, for a confession that the Princes had indeed been murdered must have undermined any new claims by would-be pretenders against Henry's sole remaining heir; and certainly no other pretenders claiming to be the sons of Edward IV emerged after this time. It is also true that Tyrell was dead, and could not refute what the King 'gave out'; Dighton, who escaped unpunished, was unlikely to talk. But if the confession was an invention, why had Henry waited until now, and not come up with something of the kind years earlier, when he was under threat from first Simnel, and then Warbeck, or even in 1499, after the execution of Warwick? It is not beyond the bounds of probability that a man facing death would want to lay bare his guilt in regard to such a crime.[71]

Then there is the evidence of More, who stated that he had learned about the murders from 'them that much knew and had little cause to lie' – a description that fits Tyrell and Dighton. If the story had not been true, what cause had Dighton to incriminate himself? And what cause had More – no yes-man of the Tudors – to make any of this up?

It is clear, though, that the bodies of the Princes were not found in the wake of Tyrell's confession, and that may have been the consequence of a deception. More, probably basing his tale on what Tyrell and Dighton had confessed, wrote that the murderers had buried the corpses 'at the stair foot, meetly deep in the ground, under a heap of stones' – which is precisely where a chest containing the skeletons of two children who were almost certainly the Princes was found in 1674 during demolition of a staircase in the entrance forebuilding to the White Tower. But More then says that Richard III had had the bodies dug up and 'secretly interred' elsewhere, and that he had taken the knowledge of the location to the grave with him. Tyrell, being close to Richard, might well have heard that, and disclosed it in 1502.

But the story was a fabrication: if they were those of the Princes, the bodies had not been moved at all. Without them Henry could not have proceeded against Dighton, for there was a legal presumption of 'no body, no murder' until the twentieth century. Bacon says that Dighton, 'who it seemeth spake best for the King, was forthwith set at liberty, and was the principal means of divulging this tradition' – which, again, explains how More got much of his information.

If Tyrell's confession was genuine – and there seems no good reason to doubt it – Elizabeth was probably shaken by it, whether she had heard it in person or not. Discovering the grim truth about how her brothers had met their end would have been traumatic, especially at a time when she was grieving for her own son (who had not been much older than Edward and Richard) and coping with the tragedy that had overtaken her sister. Was this the reason why she sent for her confessor on 17 May?[72] We can only speculate as to her frame of mind when she was rowed two days later to Richmond, where her lodgings had been made ready 'against the coming thither of the ambassadors of Hungary'. That day Richard Justice brought to her gowns of russet and purple velvet and a stole covered with scarlet;[73] it is unlikely that she was ready to put off her mourning garb so soon, and possible that these garments were to be lent to one of her sisters or ladies for the reception of the ambassadors.

In addition to Elizabeth's other burdens, she was concerned for her daughter-in-law, and seems to have felt – as the Spanish sovereigns would when they heard the news of Arthur's death – that Katherine of Aragon 'must be removed without loss of time from the unhealthy place where she is now'.[74] To this end she had sent an escort to bring the bereft and isolated young widow back to London as soon as she was well enough to travel, and herself provided a litter to convey her convalescent daughter-in-law. Her keeper of the beds, John Coope, had covered it with black velvet and black cloth, and fringed it with black valances, with the two head pieces bound with black ribbon and fringed with black cloth.[75]

In this mournful equipage Katherine was brought to Richmond, where the Queen evidently received her with much kindness. Queen Isabella told Ferdinand, Duke of Estrada, that she and King Ferdinand knew very well that, wherever King Henry and Queen Elizabeth were, their daughter 'would not lack either father or mother'.[76] After a short stay with the King and Queen, Katherine was given the choice of two residences: Durham House, the Bishop of Durham's palace on London's Strand, and Croydon Palace, the Archbishop of Canterbury's residence in Surrey. By 24 May she had taken up residence at Croydon.[77] The Queen was perhaps again unwell, for on that day her attendant Eleanor Ratcliffe, Lady Lovell, was dispatched from Richmond to the City to a 'Dr Lathis'; a London surgeon, John Johnson, also attended Elizabeth at Richmond on 28 May.[78] Katherine of Aragon was in the Queen's thoughts at this time, and she sent Edward Calvert, her page, to Croydon,[79] possibly to check on the Princess's health, and perhaps discreetly to ask her servants if there were any signs of a pregnancy. That there were not was soon to become clear.

On 15 April, unaware of the tragedy that had overtaken their daughter, Ferdinand and Isabella had written to Puebla of how glad they were 'to hear that the King and Queen of England, with the Prince and Princess of Wales, are in good health'. When they heard of Arthur's death they were quick to write again, telling Puebla that the news had caused them 'profound sorrow', painfully calling to mind 'the affliction caused' by the recent losses of their own son and eldest daughter. But, they added piously, 'the will of God must be obeyed'.[80]

The Spanish sovereigns were concerned, naturally, about their daughter. On 10 May they sent another ambassador to England with instructions to preserve the alliance and ask for the immediate return of Katherine and her dowry. 'We cannot endure that a daughter whom we love should be so far away from us in her trouble', they wrote, adding that, if possible, Puebla was to secure Katherine's betrothal to the new heir, Prince Henry,[81] who, at nearly eleven, was five and a half years her junior. Everyone was aware that, if Arthur and Katherine had consummated their marriage, her union with Henry would be incestuous and contravene canon law. Katherine's chaplain, Alessandro Geraldini, informed the Spanish ambassador that the marriage had been consummated; but Doña Elvira, Katherine's duenna, was adamant that it had not, and wrote to Queen Isabella insisting that the Princess remained a spotless virgin. Immediately Geraldini was recalled to Spain. In July Isabella informed Henry VII that the Princess remained a virgin.[82] But although he too wished to preserve the Spanish alliance, Henry was hesitant. Months – and momentous events – would pass before he reached a decision on the proposed betrothal between Katherine and his heir. Meanwhile, it had become clear that Katherine was not pregnant with Arthur's child,[83] and by 22 June, when he was made keeper of the forest of Galtres, young Henry Tudor was being styled Prince of Wales.

17

'The Hand of God'

Elizabeth had told Henry that they were still young enough to have other children, and he took her at her word. It was probably at Richmond, around the third or fourth week of May, that she conceived again, not two months after the death of Prince Arthur. At the time she had pressing concerns on her mind. On 30 May, doubtless responding to Katherine Courtenay's worries, she paid Ellis Hilton, her groom of the robes, for warm clothing she had commanded to be made for William Courtenay: Holland cloth for shirts, fox fur to line a gown of russet, and a night bonnet. She also paid out for black satin of Bruges and black velvet for covering Katherine Courtenay's saddle and sable trappings for her horse.[1]

The King and Queen were at Richmond for the feast of Corpus Christi, which fell on 5 June that year, and for the celebrations to mark it Elizabeth came briefly out of mourning, sending Richard Justice, her page of the robes, to London to fetch a cloth-of-gold gown trimmed with fur.[2]

The next day the court moved to Westminster. The Queen had bought orange sarcanet sleeves to enliven her daughter Mary's mourning gown, and clearly they were a favourite with the child. When it was found that the little Princess had left them behind at Baynard's Castle, Elizabeth sent her page of the robes from Westminster to collect them. Just before she departed from Westminster, she made an offering at the shrine of St Edward the Confessor in Westminster Abbey, kneeling beside the tombs of her dead infants; she also made offerings in the chapel of Our Lady of the Pew at Westminster and at the Norman shrine of Our Lady of Bow in London.[3]

Elizabeth was back at Richmond on 11 July, when there was a disguising at court. Her accounts record 56s.8d. (£1,380) paid to William Antyne, coppersmith, for 'spangles sets, square pieces, star drops and points after silver and gold for garnishing of jackets against the disguising'. This may have been 'the disguising in the year last past' for which Elizabeth provided coats of sarcenet in the Tudor colours of white and green for the King's minstrels and trumpeters, which were not paid for until December.[4]

By 17 June the Queen was at Windsor, having distributed alms on her journey there, as seems to have been her custom when she travelled. On St John's Eve, 23 June, she gave money to her grooms and pages for making the traditional bonfires. She made her offerings on St John's Day itself, and on 5 July she and her daughter Margaret made offerings before the Holy Cross, St George and Henry VI's tomb in St George's Chapel. The next day she sent 66s.8d. (£1,600) to the Abbess of Dartford 'towards such money as the Abbess hath laid out towards the charges of my Lady Bridget there'. An identical sum was also sent to Bridget herself. During her stay at Windsor Elizabeth enjoyed an outdoor banquet in the 'little park', where a 'harbour' had been made specially for her, and the King's painters were employed 'for making divers beasts and other pleasures for the Queen at Windsor'.[5]

That year the King's mason, Robert Vertue, was building a 'new platt [plan] of Greenwich which was devised by the Queen'.[6] She wanted a separate brick, battlemented residence for herself on the waterfront, with a great tower in the centre, a gallery, a privy kitchen, a garden and orchard, and building it would cost £1,330 (£650,000) over the next six years.[7] She would not, however, live to occupy it. Her involvement in the project probably reflects her love for Greenwich and an interest in Burgundian architecture and court culture that had no doubt been fostered by her father – but it may have had more significance than that.

Throughout her married life, Elizabeth had frequently resided with the King and accompanied him on his travels; apart from going on pilgrimage, there is no evidence for her travelling alone unless there was a pressing reason. Their mutual distress at being apart from each other had been a factor in bringing Henry home from a campaign in France. Yet on 12 July 1502 Elizabeth left Windsor in company with her sister Katherine for the royal palace of Woodstock in

Oxfordshire, on the first leg of a solo progress that would take her on a roundabout route to Wales – and away from Henry for much of the coming summer.[8] Had we her privy purse expenses for earlier years we might find details of other solo progresses, yet this is unlikely, as there would probably be some other evidence, however fragmentary, for them.

It is astonishing that a gravid woman in uncertain health, whose life had been despaired of in her previous pregnancy, should decide to travel so far at such a time, especially as it would mean being apart from her husband for two and a half months. It is possible that Elizabeth was not only unwell but in some distress of mind. Maybe Tyrell's confession had impacted badly on her, especially in the wake of Arthur's death. Her own loss must vividly have brought home to her what her mother had suffered after her brothers disappeared, while her ever-present grief for Arthur may have prompted a need to get away on her own for a time. Even so, to embark on such an arduous progress and thereby risk her uncertain health and that of her precious unborn child seems strange indeed.

Possibly there had been a rift between her and Henry. Her plans for a house for herself may reflect a need to have a residence where she could live apart from him. Grief may have led her to blame him for sending their son to Ludlow when he was ailing, although it is inconceivable that Henry would have done so had he known that Arthur was seriously ill. What is likely is that Elizabeth was finding it hard to forgive Henry for the devastation he had wrought upon her sister's life, for no apparent good reason – and at such a time. It is conceivable that the closeness that husband and wife had displayed in their shared grief had been fatally undermined by the continued imprisonment of Courtenay and the subsequent plight of Katherine of York – and by the King's harsh treatment of another of Elizabeth's sisters.

Sometime after 13 May 1502 (when Elizabeth repaid money Cecily had lent to her), Cecily made an illicit third marriage to an obscure man of low degree, Thomas Kyme (or Kymbe, or Keme) of Lincolnshire or the Isle of Wight. The date of their marriage is not recorded, and it is not until January 1504 that Cecily is first referred to as Kyme's wife, in the Parliament Roll of 1503–4.[9] As a princess of the blood, Cecily was not supposed to marry without the King's permission, still less disparage the royal lineage by throwing herself away on a mere esquire; and unsurprisingly, when Henry discovered what she had done, he banished her from court and angrily confiscated the Welles lands, in which she had a life interest. The fact that Margaret Beaufort, who was sympathetic towards Cecily in her plight, began taking a busy interest in those lands from 1502 strongly suggests that the marriage took place that year, after 13 May.[10]

There is no record of Elizabeth interceding with the King on her sister's behalf, but such a conversation would surely have taken place in private, and if it did, then her pleas fell on deaf ears. It may be that she was as shocked and angered at the marriage as the King, and that she did not intercede at all, but this seems out of character; the fact that Margaret Beaufort, who had often worked in concert with Elizabeth, was not afraid to help Cecily suggests not only that she was fond of her, but also that she knew she was better placed than Elizabeth to help her. Elizabeth was grieving for her son; she was pregnant and her health was precarious; she already had troubles enough with one sister's misfortune, and her marriage may have been under strain as a result of that, so she was probably not in the best position to help.

Margaret offered Cecily and Kyme shelter at Collyweston. From 1502 she took steps to assess the value of the Welles lands and drew up agreements with Cecily. By January 1504 she had negotiated a settlement with the King, whereupon Parliament restored Cecily's life interest in the Welles inheritance.[11]

Aside from resentment of Henry's impoverishment of her sisters, there is the possibility that Elizabeth was aware of his fancy for Katherine Gordon and that this was another cause of her distancing herself. Further than this we cannot speculate. The marriage of Henry and Elizabeth has always been seen as one of fidelity and mutual support, and there is no evidence that the King's interest in the beautiful Katherine went beyond chivalrous appreciation in Elizabeth's lifetime. But if that was as plain to his wife as it was to observers, then she had cause to feel threatened, and that could only have added to her resentment.

Elizabeth and her sister first travelled to Colnbrook, where Elizabeth rewarded a poor man who had guided them to St Mary's Chapel so that they could make an offering to Our Lady; she also gave alms to a hermit there. Then they boarded the ferry across the Thames at Datchet and rode northwards via Wycombe, arriving that night at Notley Abbey, an Augustinian monastery by Thame, Buckinghamshire;[12] their mother, Elizabeth Wydeville, had once owned lands nearby. The Abbot's house, where they lodged, still survives; its magnificent timber roof was recently revealed. While they were there, a messenger caught up with them with a letter from Lady Cotton at Havering bearing news of the sudden death of little Lord Edward Courtenay on 13 June, and seeking to know the Queen's pleasure as to where her nephew should be buried; that same day Elizabeth wrote to the Abbot of Westminster. Later she paid for the child's funeral and gifts for his nurse and his rocker.[13]

On 14 July Katherine having probably gone to Havering, Elizabeth rode north-east via Boarstall to Woodstock, where soon afterwards she fell 'sick'.[14] It is possible that she was suffering the discomforts of the early months of pregnancy, but this might have been a continuation of her illness of the spring, exacerbated by her condition; there is evidence to suggest that she did not enjoy good health through her pregnancy, and we know there had been fears that she would not survive her previous confinement. Either way, her malady may have been aggravated by grief for Arthur, revelations about her brothers' fate, and stress over her sisters' plight.

It has credibly been suggested that she was suffering from iron-deficiency anaemia as a result of repeated pregnancies,[15] which would have predisposed her to the condition, as each pregnancy can place a high demand on a woman's stores of iron. In such cases, the foetus and vital organs, such as the muscles that facilitate childbirth, can be starved of oxygen. Left untreated – and the condition was unknown in Elizabeth's day – iron-deficiency anaemia can have serious implications for the health of mother and child. The symptoms include breathlessness, tiredness, dizziness, fainting, pallor, palpitations and headaches; and the effects can be a lowering of resistance to infections, the exacerbation of minor disorders of pregnancy, a risk of premature labour, perinatal mortality, haemorrhaging before or after delivery and maternal death.[16]

Whatever the cause, Elizabeth's concern for her health – and probably for a successful outcome to her pregnancy – was manifested in the offerings she either made, or sent by proxy, to various shrines and churches: St Mary Magdalene's Church, Woodstock, St Frideswide's at Oxford, the Holy Rood at Northampton, Our Lady's Well at Linslade, Buckinghamshire, and Our Lady of Northampton, where she paid five priests to say five masses.[17]

By 4 August Elizabeth was well enough to travel on to the hunting lodge that Henry VII had built at Langley, Shipton-under-Wychwood, Oxfordshire; then it was on to Northleach, Coberley, 'the Rood beyond Gloucester' (probably the Holy Rood in the Saxon church at Daglingworth) and St Anne in the Wood, a holy well near Bristol. Here Elizabeth made an offering before proceeding to Over, where she stayed at the Vineyard, the Abbot of Gloucester's house, and gave alms to an anchoress of Gloucester. On 6 August she was at Flaxley Abbey in the Forest of Dean, a Cistercian monastery dating from the twelfth century (now a private house) that had welcomed several royal visitors since the time of King John. Here the Queen made another offering at the high altar. She had arrived in Wales by 14 August, when she was led by a local guide to Mitchel Troy, where she visited St Mary's Priory before travelling on to nearby Monmouth.[18]

A red chasuble with *opus Anglicanum* (fine English) embroidery, dating from *c*.1502, is owned by St Mary's Church, Monmouth; it was one of two vestments believed to have been donated by Elizabeth to Monmouth Priory during her visit. The other is the contemporary Skenfrith Cope, embroidered with the Assumption of the Virgin, encircled by angels and saints; it is now in the possession of St Bridget's Church, Skenfrith.[19]

From Monmouth Elizabeth journeyed to Raglan Castle, arriving by 19 August.[20] Here she was the guest of Charles Somerset, Lord Herbert, the illegitimate last male descendant of the Beauforts, who was cousin to the King and served him as a diplomat. It may be significant that Raglan had been the seat of William Herbert, Earl of Huntingdon, who had been close to Richard III, having married the latter's bastard daughter, Katherine Plantagenet. They were both dead now, but the castle had come to Charles Somerset in right of his wife, Huntingdon's daughter, Elizabeth Herbert; Henry VII and Elizabeth of York had attended their wedding on 2 June 1492.[21] Elizabeth Herbert was Huntingdon's child by his first wife, Mary Wydeville, and therefore the Queen's cousin. Elizabeth Herbert's uncle, Sir Walter Herbert, was married to another cousin, Anne Stafford, daughter of the late Duke of Buckingham by Katherine Wydeville; Anne's sister Elizabeth served the Queen as her chief lady-in-waiting.

This visit, therefore, was a family occasion, but during it Elizabeth might have had the fate of her brothers on her mind, possibly being in some turmoil in regard to Tyrell's confession; maybe she hoped to find some clarification at Raglan. Wales was a long way for an ailing, pregnant woman to travel, even to visit her relations, so there must have been a compelling reason for going so far – and it was not to visit Ludlow, where Arthur had died, for she did not venture near there. Did she hope that Elizabeth or Walter Herbert, who had known Huntingdon and Katherine Plantagenet, could tell her anything about the fate of her brothers?

During the Queen's stay a servant of Sir Walter Herbert brought her a goshawk, and a stranger came to deliver a pair of clavichords, purchased for her from a foreign craftsman by Hugh Denys, a courtier who was married to one of her ladies; they must have been fine instruments, for they cost £4 (£1,950). On 24 August she was gambling at 'tables', or backgammon, and during her visit her own minstrels entertained her.[22] It is possible that she gave one of several sets of beautifully worked vestments, perhaps made by Robinet, 'the Queen's broiderer', for use in the fifteenth-century galleried chapel in Raglan Castle, of which only ruins remain. A red-and-gold chasuble dating from c.1498, probably given by Elizabeth to St Mary's Priory, Abergavenny, during her visit to Raglan, now belongs to the Church of Our Lady and St Michael, Abergavenny.[23] While the Queen was in Wales, a Spanish servant came to her from Katherine of Aragon, and was given 20s. (£490).[24]

Elizabeth returned to England via Chepstow, where she arrived on 28 August, then rode through Woolaston before taking the ferry across the River Severn and making for Berkeley Castle, where she stayed from 29 August to 4 September as the guest of the elderly Maurice, Lord Berkeley, a former Knight of the Body to Edward IV, and his wife, Isabella Mead. The 'stuff of the wardrobe of her beds' was sent on from Raglan to Abingdon, and thence to London. While at Berkeley, Elizabeth received a servant of a Mr Esterfields of Bristol, who came with a costly gift of delicacies, oranges and suckets (candied fruits), for which she gave 2s. (£50) in reward. That same day, 29 August, she made an offering to the Virgin at the church at nearby Thornbury, and on 2 September she rewarded her minstrels for their performance at Berkeley. The next day she ordered that venison be sent on to London for her table; she feasted on venison while at Berkeley, and wine was bought for her in Bristol. During her stay her litter was repaired with silk points, pins and a yard of frieze.[25]

From Berkeley Elizabeth travelled to Beverstone Castle near Tetbury, another seat of the Berkeleys. She then stayed at Coates Place near Cirencester, and was escorted by a local guide on to Fairford, where she lodged from 10 to 14 September, and again dined on venison, and apples sent by Mary, Lady Hungerford, from Heytesbury. On 16 September the Queen was back at Langley, where she remained until 3 October. She may have needed to rest because of her condition or poor health, for on 17 September John Grice, her apothecary, was paid £10.19s.11d. (£5,350) for 'certain stuff of his occupation by him delivered to the use of the Queen'; and on 21 September she signed her accounts for the last time, after meticulously signing them daily for years, which suggests she was too sick or fatigued to attend to all her duties and had to let some things slide. But the Lord Mayor of London sent her two barrels of Rhenish wine, and venison was delivered to Langley for her table, so she was evidently not too ill to eat. The regular delivery of bucks and harts to the places where she stayed on her progress suggests that she may have had a craving for venison during this pregnancy.[26]

On 21 September Elizabeth gave 16s. (£390) to John Grice's servant 'towards his wedding gown', suggesting that the apothecary was still in attendance. Three days later, at her command, a messenger was dispatched from Windsor to her sister Bridget at Dartford, possibly to ask after her health and request her prayers. Again, Elizabeth was sending offerings and seeking intercessions at nearby shrines, notably Our Lady of Caversham and the Child of Grace at Reading, to which she gave a pleated lawn shirt.[27]

The King, who had been staying at Woodstock and was perhaps concerned about Elizabeth's health, joined her at Langley on 28 September,[28] and probably accompanied her for the rest of her progress. On 6 October, she visited Minster Lovell Hall, where William Hamerton built her a bedstead.[29] The hall was the former residence of Francis Lovell. He had disappeared in 1487 after fighting on the wrong side at Stoke,[30] and the manor was now nominally in the hands of Prince Henry. The Queen gave money to an old footman to the Prince who was now residing in an almshouse at Abingdon, where on 13 October she presented rich offerings to the silver effigy of Our Lady of Abingdon in the chapel of the Austin Friars.[31]

At Ewelme more memories of the House of York awaited her,

for the palatial house had been the seat of her kinsfolk, the de la Poles, so recently disgraced, and was now in royal hands. Here Elizabeth played dice and received messengers from Prince Henry and Margaret Beaufort; she also marked the feast of St Edward the Confessor. Three days later she had moved on via Henley to Easthampstead, Berkshire, a royal manor lying in the Forest of Windsor, where she rewarded a 'disare', or reciter, 'who played the shepherd before the Queen'.[32]

Elizabeth was back at Richmond Palace before 25 October, when rewards were paid out to those who had brought her gifts of apples and woodcocks. Two days later she was rowed to Westminster, where she stayed until 14 November. On the day of her arrival she sent her barge to Durham House to collect her daughter-in-law, Katherine, who stayed with her until 6 November. The Queen made her offering on the Feast of All Saints on 1 November, took communion and rewarded the young choristers of the King's Chapel for their singing. Later that day she visited Westminster Abbey with Henry to make more offerings in observation of the obit of his father, Edmund Tudor, Earl of Richmond, and to pray at the shrine of St Edward the Confessor. Around 4 November Elizabeth paid for fifty-two barrels of beer, which she gave annually in alms to the Observant friars of Greenwich, and two days later she sent 15s.8d. (£380) in alms to the Abbess of the Minories and the nuns she had succoured there in May.[33]

Her accounts show that in November and December her embroiderer, Robinet, and seven hired embroiderers were 'working upon the Queen's rich bed', probably at Richmond, in readiness for her coming confinement, for 'she intended to [be] delivered at Richmond';[34] the hangings were embroidered with white and red roses and clouds, and edged with red satin. Later that month Elizabeth paid out 33s.4d. (£810) for a new trussing bed with a ceiler, tester and counterpoint of crimson velvet with blue panes, and great rings for the bedcurtains; she also ordered a cloth of estate of rich crimson cloth of tissue (taffeta), a pile cloth (possibly a rug or a thick towel) of linen and matching curtains, together costing £46s.4d. (£1,130).[35]

Elizabeth was looking for suitable staff for her coming child's establishment. Dame Katherine Grey recommended a nurse, a Mistress Harcourt, who had an audience with the Queen at Westminster on 14 November, before Elizabeth left for Greenwich, but was dismissed with a gift of 6s.8d.(£160).[36]

From Greenwich, on 19 November, Elizabeth removed to Baynard's Castle, where she received several gifts on 23 November. Her cook, Brice, had bought chickens and larks prior to her coming.[37]

Elizabeth was still looking after the needs of the Courtenay children. In November, she paid a man to deliver messages from Lord Henry and Lady Margaret at Havering to the court, probably to their mother. She also paid for clothing for young Henry Courtenay: a gown of black damask lined with sarcanet, a gown of tawny medley bordered with sarcanet, a coat of murrey camlet, a bonnet and a petticoat (the little boy had not yet been breeched). She also reimbursed Margaret Cotton for hose, shoes, laces, soap and other necessaries for the children, including candlesticks and cloth to line a cupboard.[38]

On 24 November, a French nurse was interviewed by the Queen at Baynard's Castle; like the previous nurse, she too was sent away with 6s.8d. (£160). The next day Elizabeth gave alms to a poor man who had once served her father, and paid a messenger who had fetched bucks for the King from the estate of Sir John Seymour in Savernake Forest.[39] If there had been a coolness between the royal couple, it was probably thawing.

On 26 November Elizabeth returned to the Palace of Westminster. As the winter of 1502–3 drew on, she may still have been unwell or needed to rest, as she did not resume her daily checks on her account book. At the end of November her fool, Patch, was rewarded for bringing her pomegranates and apples. On 5 December, the eve of St Nicholas's Day, when custom dictated that 'boy bishops' be appointed in place of priests in churches, she made a generous gift of 40s. (£970) to 'the Bishop of the King's Chapel at Westminster'. Appropriately, on St Nicholas's Day itself , when gifts were given to children, the Queen outlaid 5s.6d. (£130) for the expenses of those who brought the Courtenay children 'from Sir John Hussey's place in Essex unto London', in time for Christmas. She made offerings on St Nicholas's Day and in the chapel of Our Lady of the Pew in Westminster Abbey on the eve of the feast of the Conception of the Virgin Mary, and on the feast day itself, 8 December. On 9 December she sent money to Henry Langton, another old servant of her father, and 12d. (£20) in reward to 'a man of Pomfret' in an almshouse, who claimed to have lodged her uncle, Earl Rivers, in his house when the latter had been on the way to execution at Pontefract in 1483.[40] It seems that her lost loved ones, and maybe the terrible events of 1483, were on her mind as Christmas approached.

On 12 December Elizabeth moved to the Tower. The next day she distributed £20 (£9,720) in rewards to the grooms and pages of her chamber 'against Christmas', and was no doubt grateful to receive a monk of Westminster Abbey, who brought her one of the Abbey's precious relics, 'Our Lady's girdle', and was rewarded with 8d. (£20).[41] 'Women with child were wont to girdle with' it,[42] and perhaps Elizabeth had found that the relic had helped – psychologically at least – during earlier deliveries, or felt that it would afford her special protection during her coming confinement. Given her poor health during the past year and her many offerings at shrines, it may be that she was anxious about the outcome of this pregnancy, as she had been before her previous labour, although there is much to suggest that she had good cause for concern this time: she had been unwell, on and off, for months.

On 21 December the Queen went by barge to Mortlake and thence to Richmond, and it was there that she spent her first Christmas without Arthur – and the last Christmas of her life. Six does were delivered for her table on Christmas Day. When she went in state with the King to Mass on that solemn feast, Prince Henry was with them. The children of the King's Chapel sang a new setting of a carol by William Cornish, for which Elizabeth rewarded him with 13s.4d. (£320). She also rewarded the King's minstrels with 40s. (£1,000) for their psalms. She made offerings on the feast days of St Stephen (26 December), St John the Apostle (27 December), the Holy Innocents, or Childermas, as it was known (28 December) and St Thomas of Canterbury (29 December), and sent a 'Doctor Uttoune' to offer on her behalf at Becket's shrine and other places in Canterbury.[43]

We learn of the cheering entertainments enjoyed by Elizabeth during the twelve days of Yuletide from her accounts and other sources. She drank Rhenish wine she had ordered, and was given 100s. (£2,450) for 'her disport at cards' on St Stephen's Day. She gave rewards to Princess Margaret's minstrels, who had entertained her, and to a Spanish dancing girl, who had probably come to England in the train of Katherine of Aragon. On New Year's Eve ten more does were brought to her from the park at Odiham, Rutland. She gave gifts on New Year's Day, rewards to those who had sent presents, among them the servant of Margaret Beaufort, and alms to the poor. The recipients of her gifts were numerous, and included several servants of the King, the royal minstrels, 'the children of the privy kitchen', and 'the lord of misrule', who traditionally held sway over the revels at court.[44] Henry gave her 10s. (£240) out of his privy purse, to pay for disguisings, and £20 (£9,700) for furs. His expenses also record rewards to 'the Abbot of Misrule', the players of St Albans and Essex, and 'the children of the King's Chapel for singing of *Gloria in excelsis*'.[45]

On 4 January 1503 Elizabeth made a donation to the fraternity (guild) of St Clement by Temple Bar, the western entrance to the City of London. Three days later, now heavy with child, she was conveyed with her ladies by her bargeman, Lewis Walter, 'in a great boat with twelve rowers' from Richmond to Hampton Court. Here she retreated to a 'cell', to spend time in private prayer before she was confined,[46] which suggests that her health was still giving her cause for concern. She was placing much faith in astrologers, who had promised her 'this year to live in wealth and delice'.[47] At New Year the court astrologer, Dr William Parron, had presented the King with his annual almanac; this year's was an exquisitely bound manuscript, the *Liber de optimo fato* (*Book of Fortunes*),[48] in which Parron prophesied that Elizabeth would live until she was eighty or ninety, and would bear the King many sons.

Elizabeth stayed at Hampton Court until 14 January, when Lewis Walter rowed her and her ladies back to Richmond.[49] Preparations were still apace for her confinement there, and on 20 January the King sent one of his grooms to fetch Robert Taylor, her surgeon, to Richmond,[50] possibly because she was again unwell. As male surgeons were excluded from obstetrics, Taylor may have performed bloodletting – a common function of his profession – to balance the humours in her body, according to the prevailing belief that an imbalance caused illness. Of course, if Elizabeth was anaemic, bleeding her would only have exacerbated the problem.

At this time Elizabeth was thinking of her aunt, Elizabeth, Duchess of Suffolk, mother of the unfortunate Edmund da la Pole, and the Courtenays. Her privy purse expenses record: 'Item, for a pair of buskins for the Duchess of Suffolk, 4s. [£100]. Item, to William Gentleman, page of the Queen's chamber, for carrying of two bucks from Windsor to London, the 24th Day of [January], one to the Duchess of Suffolk, &c., 5s.4d. [£130].' That month also, hearing that Lord Henry Courtenay had fallen sick, Elizabeth outlaid 10s. (£250) to a surgeon, Richard Bullock, for medicines.[51]

★

Henry VII, having a 'singular and special devotion' to the Virgin Mary, had decided to build a splendid new Lady Chapel at the east end of Westminster Abbey as a shrine for Henry VI, whom he had tried – so far unsuccessfully – to have canonised. It was not originally intended as a mausoleum for the Tudor dynasty, for from 1496 the King had made payments for the rebuilding of Henry III's thirteenth-century chapel of St Edward at Windsor Castle as a 'tomb house' for the anticipated shrine to Henry VI; and here, he had decided, he and his Queen and their royal descendants would be laid to rest. The old chapel at Windsor lay to the east of the new St George's Chapel, which had been begun by Elizabeth's father, Edward IV, and continued by Henry VII, who completed the choir and nave.

But in 1498, in response to a protest by the monks of Westminster, who wanted the relics of Henry VI moved from St George's Chapel, Windsor, to their Abbey, the King agreed that his uncle should be buried there. Between 1498 and 1502 he had the thirteenth-century Lady Chapel at Westminster demolished, along with the chapel of St Erasmus – founded two decades earlier by Elizabeth Wydeville – in which lay Anne Mowbray, Duchess of York.[52]

In July 1501 Henry commissioned his tomb at Windsor, and work proceeded there until January 1503, when he changed his mind and decided that he and Elizabeth would rest in a tomb in the centre of the new Lady Chapel at Westminster, before the principal altar; and that he would have Henry VI's remains translated to a new shrine at the east end as soon as the saintly King had been canonised.

In his will of 1509[53] Henry gave the reason for his change of heart as the fact that his grandmother, Katherine of Valois, widow of Henry V, was buried at Westminster: she had been laid to rest in the original Lady Chapel. Yet when that chapel was demolished, and her open coffin was placed above ground beside the tomb of Henry V, Henry VII made no effort to have it reburied or to erect a new monument. In fact, as Stow noted in 1598, her remains 'remaineth above ground in a coffin of boards behind the east end of the presbytery',[54] and they stayed on public view until 1777. But Henry VII had a more important reason for wishing to be buried in Westminster Abbey. It was the church in which English sovereigns had been crowned since 1066; it housed the shrine of the sainted King Edward the Confessor, around which many kings and queens were buried; and interment there would serve to reinforce the legitimacy of the Tudor dynasty. Here, according to a Latin inscription placed later around the tomb built for him, he 'established a sepulchre for himself, and for his wife, his children and his House', where he and his descendants would lie in glory for eternity.

Accordingly the building materials were moved from Windsor to Westminster, and here, on 24 January 1503, the foundation stone of the new Lady Chapel was laid on the King's behalf by Abbot John Islip, whereupon construction began, probably to the design of Robert Janyns and the brothers Robert and William Vertue, three of the King's most accomplished master masons.[55]

Henry took a great interest in his new chapel; he wanted it to be as sanctified a place as the chapel of St Edward the Confessor, which lay behind the high altar and housed the shrine and the Abbey's most precious relics. In his will, he gave orders that 'the walls, doors, windows, arches and vaults and images of our chapel, within and without, be painted, garnished and adorned with our arms, badges, cognisants and other convenient painting, in as goodly and rich a manner as such a work requireth';[56] these may be seen today – the leopards of England, Tudor roses, the red dragon of Cadwaladr, crowned *fleurs-de-lis*, Yorkist falcons and fetterlocks, Richmond greyhounds, Lancastrian collars of SS knots and broom-pods, Beaufort portcullises, crowned yales, antelopes and marguerites (for Margaret Beaufort), and hawthorn bushes to commemorate the finding of the crown on Bosworth field, indeed the whole panoply of contemporary royal imagery – adorning every surface. Elizabeth's badge is among the Tudor emblems that embellish the gates to the chapel. Henry obtained two relics, a piece of the True Cross and a leg bone of St George, for the small altar that originally stood at the foot of the tomb, but was destroyed in 1643.

No effort was spared to make the new Lady Chapel a magnificent resting place for the founder of the Tudor dynasty and his Queen. When it was finished – the main structure was completed by 1509, and the rest by *c.*1512 – it was a marvel of late-Perpendicular archi-tecture and one of the most splendid royal chapels ever built. Henry VII lavished great gifts on it – tapestries, furnishings, plate and crucifixes – making it a fittingly sumptuous burial place. Awed by its wondrous fan-vaulting, its intricate sculpture and its elegant bay windows filled with brilliant glass painted by the royal glazier, Bernard Flower, which echo the oriels in King Henry's Tower at

The two foremost residences of the House of York, which passed to Elizabeth in 1495. (*Left*) Baynard's Castle, on the Thames in London, where her father, Edward IV, and her uncle, Richard III, were in turn offered the crown. (*Below*) Fotheringhay Castle, a Yorkist stronghold since 1377 (modern reconstruction).

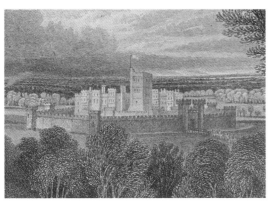

Lathom House, the seat of Thomas Stanley, Earl of Derby and Margaret Beaufort, where Henry and Elizabeth stayed in 1495. 'There is something so particular and romantic in the general situation of this house.'

The Paradise Bed, perhaps commissioned by Derby for the visit of the King and Queen to Lathom or Knowsley in 1495.

Margaret Tudor, Elizabeth's eldest daughter, in 1503.

The tomb of Elizabeth's second daughter and namesake in Westminster Abbey. 'Atropos, most merciless messenger of death, snatched her away' at the age of three.

Elizabeth's 'fair sweet son,' the future Henry VIII, in infancy.

'A delightful small, new rose, worthy of its stock.' Terracotta bust of a laughing child, possibly Prince Henry, by Guido Mazzoni, c.1498.

(*Above left*) Elizabeth of York, a portrait possibly painted in 1502, the year that may have witnessed a rift between the King and Queen. (*Above right*) Henry VII in later life: 'a dark prince and infinitely suspicious'. Terracotta bust by Pietro Torrigiano, *c.*1509–11.

Elizabeth of York, detail from Remigius van Leemput's copy of Hans Holbein's lost Whitehall Palace mural of 1537.

Stained glass windows depicting Henry VII and Elizabeth of York, dating from *c.*1537–40 and based on the Whitehall mural.

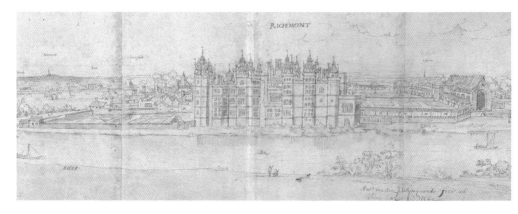

RICHMONT

Richmond Palace, 'this earthly and second paradise of England', built by Henry VII to showcase the Tudor dynasty. Drawing by Anthony van Wyngaerde, 1555.

'The delight of the Britons' and 'the glorious hope of the realm': Arthur Tudor, Prince of Wales, artist unknown, c.1520.

Katherine of Aragon, portrait by Miguel Sittow, c.1505. Arthur 'had never felt so much joy in his life as when he beheld the sweet face of his bride'.

Henry VII and Elizabeth of York kneeling with all their 'illustrious progeny' before St George. Votive altarpiece of c.1503-9, Flemish School.

Elizabeth and her four daughters. Nineteenth-century copy of a lost panel painting related to the St George altarpiece.

Henry and Elizabeth and their children in 'The Ordinances of the Confraternity of the Immaculate Conception', dating from March 1503.

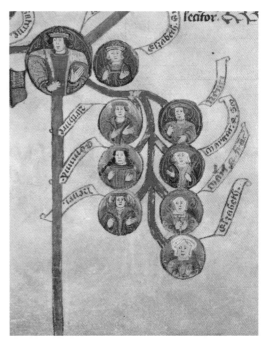

Henry and Elizabeth and their children from an early 16th century genealogy of the kings of England.

The Minoresses Convent at Aldgate, after the fire of 1797. Elizabeth was in touch with her kinswoman, the Abbess, when she visited the Tower in 1502, at the time Sir James Tyrell probably confessed to murdering her brothers, the Princes in the Tower.

Raglan Castle, Wales, where Elizabeth stayed on her long progress of 1502.

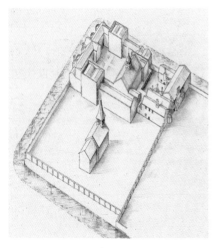

Reconstruction of Hampton Court as it was when Elizabeth visited in 1502 and 1503.

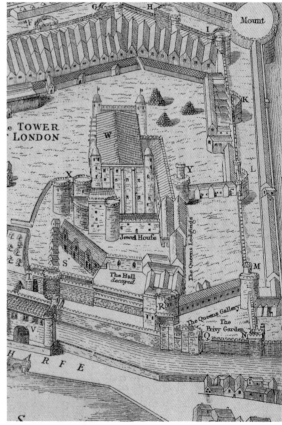

'Merciful God, this is a strange reckoning.' The Queen's lodgings at the Tower of London, where Elizabeth died, are clearly marked to the right of the White Tower on this plan of 1597 (detail).

Elizabeth's son, the future Henry VIII mourns her passing. 'Never since the death of my dearest mother hath there come to me more hateful intelligence.'

Remains of the wooden effigy of Elizabeth of York carried at her funeral: 'a image or personage like a queen, clothed in the very robes of estate of the Queen'.

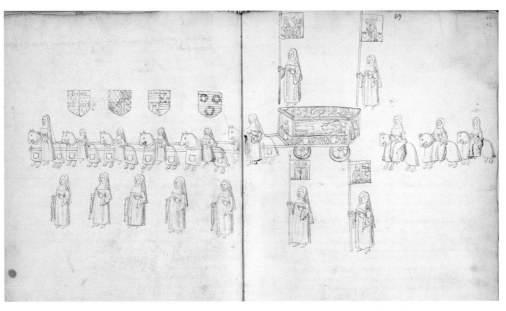

The funeral of Elizabeth of York. 'From Mark Lane to Temple Bar alone were five thousand torches, besides lights burning before all the parish churches.'

'This sumptuous sepulchre': the Henry VII Chapel in Westminster Abbey, with the tomb of Henry and Elizabeth in the centre.

Tomb effigies of Henry VII and Elizabeth of York by Pietro Torrigiano, 1512-19. 'Here is Henry VII, the glory of all the kings who lived in his time. Joined to him his sweet wife was very pretty, chaste and fruitful.'

The coffins in the vault below the tomb, as seen in 1869. Elizabeth's is in the centre, Henry VII's to the right, and James I's to the left.

Windsor, Leland was to call it 'this *orbis miraculum:*' this 'wonder of the world'.

But the Queen would not live to see it.

As Elizabeth's baby was not due until the middle of February, the King decided that they would spend Candlemas together at the Tower. On 26 January Elizabeth and her sister Katherine came by river from Richmond to Westminster,[57] where the King was waiting for them. Later that day they were all taken by barge to the Tower.[58]

The Tower must have held mixed memories for Elizabeth. It had been her father's favourite palace, and a place of refuge to her and her relatives in childhood and in recent years, yet it must also have been associated in her mind with danger and uncertainty – and with the disappearance of her brothers. Here, the previous May, Tyrell had made his confession before going to the scaffold. Here, on Tower Green, Lord Hastings had been done to death in that distant, turbulent summer of 1483. Here had been held doomed Stanley, Warbeck and her cousin Warwick. Here, now, her brother-in-law, Courtenay, was a prisoner.

The fourteenth-century royal apartments were in the Lanthorn Tower, and overlooked the River Thames. In 1501 Henry VII had begun extending these lodgings, adding a bedchamber, a privy closet and a square new tower – the 'King's Tower' – with a private chamber, a library and large windows over the river.[59] The medieval Queen's Lodgings, where Elizabeth stayed in 1503, lay at right angles to the Lanthorn Tower, extending south from the Wardrobe Tower by the White Tower. Timber-framed, with brick foundations and gable ends, they included a great chamber, a dining chamber, a bedchamber, and an outer chamber adjoining the jewel house to the west, with the Queen's arraying chamber next to it on the east side; at the north end steps led down to a privy and an outer entrance.[60] At the south end this range connected with the King's apartments and the new tower, which had been completed only six weeks before the royal couple's arrival.

The Queen was expected to pay £10 (£4,860) to the officers of the royal mint at the Tower, which was customary whenever a member of the royal family stayed there, but she did not have the money, so had to borrow it from one of the King's gentleman ushers.[61] A carpenter, William Trend, was paid 10s. (£240) for making a chest and '*armoire*' (cupboard) for Elizabeth's council chamber in the Tower, so that she could store her books and papers. Henry Roper, page of the Queen's beds, was paid 16d. (£30) for the work he did over two days to prepare her apartments for her coming. Her chamber was hung with blue tapestries embellished with *fleurs-de-lis* of gold.[62] On 31 January a poor woman came to the Tower with some fine capons for the Queen, and was rewarded with 3s.4d. (£80). Elizabeth gave her fool Patch 6s.8d. (£160) to buy some very costly oranges, pomegranates and other fruits. She sent a man to make an offering on her behalf to Our Lady of Willesden. Late in January she was at Coldharbour, where she paid the keeper for 'wine and fire'. Possibly she had hoped to see Margaret Beaufort, but had found her absent.[63]

Elizabeth was still at the Tower when her baby came ten days early, on 2 February 1503. It was Candlemas Day, when the King and Queen customarily donned robes of state and went in procession to Mass to celebrate this feast of the Purification of the Virgin Mary. Elizabeth's privy purse expenses record that she made her offering at the high altar, probably in the Norman chapel of St John the Evangelist in the White Tower, that morning, and that a doe had been delivered for her 'against Candlemas Day',[64] so it must have been later in the day that she 'travailed of child suddenly'.[65]

Her premature labour clearly took everyone by surprise, for 'she had intended to have been delivered at Richmond'.[66] It could have been a consequence of iron-deficiency anaemia, and it would account for the absence of any record of the Queen taking to her chamber. Fortunately, Alice Massey, her usual midwife, was able to attend her, having probably already been installed in her household. As usual, Alice received £10 (£4,860) for her services.[67] There was also a nurse in attendance, to whom the King paid £3.6s.8d. (£1,620). This was the first royal birth to take place in the Tower since that of Blanche de la Tour, a short-lived daughter of Edward III and Philippa of Hainault, in 1341, and no royal baby would be born there after this one.

Henry VII, who had lost two of his three sons in less than two years, must have been anxious to have another, but 'upon Candlemas Day, in the night following the day, the King and Queen then being lodged in the Tower of London, the Queen was delivered of a daughter'.[68] It had apparently been a difficult birth: Thomas More wrote soon afterwards that the Queen's pleasure in her honour and wealth was 'doubled with pain' and that she had 'endured more woe than wealth' in great sorrow and distress.[69] It is clear from the rest of his verses (reproduced in full in Chapter 18) that he was referring to her confinement, and not to her life in general, as he represents that as full of joy and prosperity.

On the day of his daughter's birth Henry VII made an offering of 6s.8d. (£160) to Our Lady of Barking[70] – the royal chapel of Our Lady in the churchyard of All Hallows Barking by the Tower, a church founded by Barking Abbey in Saxon times; the chapel had been founded by Richard I and made a royal chantry chapel by Elizabeth's father, Edward IV, and it contained a beautiful image of the Virgin Mary that was said to work miracles.[71]

The baby, who was evidently weak, was 'upon the Saturday following christened within the parish church of the Tower and named Katherine',[72] possibly after Katherine of York,[73] then in attendance on Elizabeth, or Katherine of Valois, the King's maternal grandmother, or Katherine of Aragon.[74] The new Princess's baptism in the chapel of St Peter ad Vincula is not described by any source, so was probably of necessity low-key. On 8 February the King ordered a woollen mattress and down pillows for the cradle of 'Katherine, our right dear daughter', as well as furnishings for the bedchambers of her nurse and rockers.[75]

On 9 February, a week after the birth, Elizabeth became ill. On the 10th the King summoned a physician all the way from Plymouth,[76] so evidently there was thought to be no urgency at this stage. The Queen was perhaps developing puerperal fever, then known as 'childbed fever', a common – and often dangerous – ailment of *post-partum* women in those days. It was a bacterial infection of the placental site caused by poor hygiene – dirty hands, instruments and cloths – during childbirth, and if untreated it could invade the bloodstream and cause puerperal sepsis, a form of septicaemia. Sufferers could experience severe pelvic pain, a rising or recurring fever, headaches, insomnia, an offensive discharge and increasing debility. Without antibiotics, there was no effective treatment. One could only wait for the crisis to pass.

Another possibility is that Elizabeth was suffering the consequences of iron-deficiency anaemia, which could have accounted for her premature labour and the fact that her baby was frail, and left her at risk of *post-partum* haemorrhage, another possible effect of the condition. This can occur up to six weeks after delivery, even if the mother is not anaemic; other causes are infection or retention of the products of conception. Anaemia can also cause fever, rigours and an abnormally accelerated heart rate. In those days – as in undeveloped countries today – it would have been a major cause of maternal mortality. Anaemia can also lead to circulatory shock and death in a newly delivered mother.

The Queen's condition quickly worsened. On the night of 10 February the King ordered one James Nattres to hasten down to Kent to summon her physician, Dr Hallysworth (or Aylesworth) from his home at Gravesend, and paid for boat hire, watermen to wait for him at Gravesend, and horses and guides 'by night and day' to speed his way with lighted torches.[77] Worsening fever, post-partum haemorrhage or the symptoms of shock would explain the desperate urgency suggested by these entries in the Queen's accounts. Hallysworth came hastening through the night, but he arrived too late. Elizabeth of York, 'the most virtuous princess and gracious Queen', died while 'lying in childbed' early in the morning of Saturday, 11 February, her thirty-seventh birthday.[78]

She would not have been alone at her passing: besides her husband, a chaplain would have been summoned to give her the last rites and read devotional texts, and her attendants and servants would have gathered around the bed, it being customary for the dying to be continuously watched over. But it is unlikely that her children were present.

The Queen's 'departing was as heavy and dolorous to the King as ever was seen or heard of, and likewise to all estates of his realm, as well citizens as commons, for she was one of the most gracious and best-beloved princesses in the world in her time being'.[79] Having delegated his mother, Thomas Howard, Earl of Surrey, and Sir Richard Guildford, Comptroller of the Household, to arrange the funeral,[80] Henry ordered a barge to convey him to Richmond. He 'took with him certain of his secretest, and privily departed to a solitary place to pass his sorrow, and would that no man should resort to him but such [as] his Grace appointed'.[81] Tradition dictated that he would not attend his wife's funeral. On 15 March he ordered a new velvet cloth of estate of blue, the colour of royal mourning. He had books bound in blue velvet, and mourning attire of blue and black, and he came only gradually out of mourning well after a year had passed.[82]

Coming just ten months after the death of his son, the loss of the wife who had comforted him, after bearing the child who was to have been their mutual consolation, was a heavy blow to bear.

And if there had indeed been a rift between them during the last months of her life, his grief may have been tinged with guilt or remorse. He would now abandon the Tower, where she had died, ensuring its decline as a royal residence; in the future, monarchs would only lodge there prior to their coronations, as tradition decreed. The ancient fortress became more of 'an armoury and house of munition, and a place for the safekeeping of offenders, than a palace royal for a king or queen to sojourn in',[83] and within a hundred years of Elizabeth's death the apartments she had occupied were ruinous. Only the remains of stone walls survive today, while the present Lanthorn Tower is a late-Victorian reconstruction, the original having been gutted by fire in 1774.

Presently the bells of St Paul's Cathedral tolled out for the Queen, and as their mournful chimes were taken up by all the London churches and religious houses, orders went out to every parish and monastery in the kingdom to have masses sung for the repose of her soul. Soon afterwards, 'throughout the realm' there were 'solemn dirges and Masses of requiems'. In London alone, on the day after her death, 636 masses were offered up for her on the King's orders, and at Walsingham fifty-six pounds of wax candles were burned as the monks prayed for her.[84] Knowing how beloved Elizabeth had been by her household, the King sent Charles Somerset, Lord Herbert and Sir Richard Guildford to afford 'the best comfort that hath been seen of a sovereign lord' to all the Queen's servants, 'with good words'.[85]

After Elizabeth's body had been washed, dressed in her robes of estate and laid out on her bed, her children were brought to pay their respects and say goodbye. On the day after her death, four yards of flannel for swaddling bands was purchased for her motherless infant, 'my Lady Katherine, the King's daughter', as well as a pair of black sarcanet mourning sleeves for the young Queen Margaret, who had evidently been close to her mother in these past months. According to the evidence in Elizabeth's accounts, they had offered together at Mass, and Margaret had walked only a pace behind Elizabeth at court.[86] Young Mary was dressed in mourning too; in June she was wearing dark blue damask banded with velvet, white stockings and tawny silk ribbons.[87] Prince Henry was provided with mourning attire of black cloth furred with lambskin, a cloak of black velvet, and black hose, shoes and gloves – twelve pairs of each.[88]

In 1494 Henry VII had drawn up ordinances for the mourning of a queen, and now, since he was incapacitated by grief, it may have been Margaret Beaufort who drew up new ones specifying in minute detail the size and design of hoods, trains and formal surcoats that were to be worn.[89] The court was plunged into black, with over 9,000 yards of black cloth being supplied by Richard Smythe, yeoman of the Queen's robes, Thomas Mounte, John Lewis, William Smith, John Kirkby and Thomas Spight, merchant tailors, William Bailly, mercer, Richard Conhill, John Copland and others to the Great Wardrobe for the households of the King, the Queen, their children, the nobility, and 200 'poor folk' who would each carry 'a weighty torch' in the funeral procession. It was said to be 'the greatest livery of black gowns that ever was seen in our day', and cost £1,483.15s.10d. (£721,270).[90]

On the day she died Elizabeth's body was embalmed by the Sergeant of the Chandlery, who had been supplied with 'sixty broad ells of Holland cloth, forty ells of lining Holland cloth for the cerecloth, gums, balms, spices, sweet wine' and 156 pounds of wax. The corpse would have been washed with wine and rosewater, anointed with balm and perfumed with spices, then 'cered' – wrapped tightly in cloth that had been cut into strips soaked in the molten wax. When that had set, 'the King's plumber closed her in lead, with an epitaph likewise in lead showing who and what she was. The whole was chested in boards [a wooden coffin] covered with black velvet with a cross of white damask.' The coffin was made of holly wood.[91]

The Queen's obsequies lasted for two weeks, and it was 'within the parish church of the Tower', the chapel of St Peter ad Vincula, that 'her corpse lay for eleven days',[92] having been carried there on Sunday, 12 February, the day after her death.[93] The coffin was borne by persons of the highest rank, with a canopy held over it by four knights; it was followed by Lady Elizabeth Stafford, first lady of the bedchamber, the ladies and maids of honour, and every member of the Queen's household, walking two by two, 'dressed in their plainest gowns', as their new mourning garments were not yet ready. The stained-glass windows of the chapel had been lined with black crêpe and its walls hung with black silk damask; it was lit by the flickering flames of 500 tall candles. The coffin was placed on a bier before the altar, then, acting as chief mourner, Katherine, Countess of Devon, entered the chapel with her brother-in-law, Thomas Howard, Earl of

Surrey. Katherine took her place at the head of Elizabeth's body, and remained there while Mass was celebrated and the offerings were made, after which she retired.[94] She must have been deeply grieved at the loss of the sister who had so generously succoured her through the past months, and to whom she was obviously close.

Cecily, the sister nearest to the Queen in age, who should have taken precedence before Anne and Katherine, and who had been prominent at court in 1501, was not present at Elizabeth's lying-in-state – but Cecily was still in disgrace. Neither she nor Anne had been in attendance on Elizabeth in the weeks leading up to her confinement, and although they were to attend her funeral, Katherine would again act as chief mourner. Cecily's presence in the funeral procession might suggest that the King had relented in their shared grief and allowed her to join her sisters on this occasion.

Surrounded by 800 burning tapers, the Queen's coffin lay in state, watched over by six ladies at all times, with Katherine Courtenay a constant presence during many of the vigils. They wore the 'most sad and simplest clothing that they had, on their heads threaden kerchiefs hanging on their shoulders and close under their chins, and this daily until their [mourning] slops [kirtles], mantles, hoods and paris [partlets?] were made' ready for the funeral.[95] Katherine's train, borne by Elizabeth Stafford, was as long as a duchess's, and she was always attended by Surrey and ladies and gentlemen of the court. 'The other gentlewomen gave way to their betters, but the chief mourner kneeled at the head [of the bier] alone, and thus they continued their watch.' Bishops said Mass on three consecutive days, and during the night watches an officer-at-arms recited a paternoster (the Lord's Prayer) for the soul of the Queen at every *Kyrie Eleison* (Lord have mercy, a prayer invoking God), at *Oremus* (the invitation to prayer), and before Collect (a short general prayer). At the offering, Katherine 'was led by two of the greatest estate present, and the noblest gave her the offering, the chamberlains and officers-at-arms marshalling her'.[96]

Not a stone's throw away from the chapel where Elizabeth reposed in state lay buried the chest in which the bones that almost certainly belonged to her lost brothers were rotting away.

18

'Here Lieth the Fresh Flower of Plantagenet'

The Queen was widely mourned. She had been 'one of the most gracious and best-loved princesses in the world'. 'The tidings,' wrote Ferdinand and Isabella, 'have, of a truth, caused us much grief.'[1] In Scotland, out of respect for his mother-in-law, James IV ordered dirges to be performed at the abbeys of Newbottle, Melrose, Dryburgh, Jedburgh, Kelso and many other places.[2] When Margaret Tudor arrived in Scotland later that year, James expressed his sympathy for the loss of her mother and brother, adding that he too had lost his own mother when he was young.[3] In Ireland, the *Annals of Ulster*, in which English affairs rarely featured, recorded: 'The wife of the King of the Saxons died, to wit, the daughter of King Edward, and Isabel [*sic*][4] was her name: a woman that was of the greatest charity and humanity from Italy to Ireland.' William Parron, who had predicted that Elizabeth would live to see eighty, fled the realm.

Thomas More, then a young London lawyer, was moved to write an elegy, 'A Rueful Lamentation on the Death of Queen Elizabeth':

> Oh ye that put your trust and confidence
> In worldly joy and frail prosperity,
> That so live here as ye should never hence,
> Remember death and look here on me.
> Example I think there may no better be.
> Yourself wot well that in this realm was I,
> Your Queen but late, and lo, now here I lie.

Was I not born of old worthy lineage?
Was not my mother Queen, my father King?
Was I not a king's fere [companion] in marriage?
Had I not plenty of every pleasant thing?
Merciful God, this is a strange reckoning:
Riches, honour, wealth and ancestry
Hath me forsaken, and lo, now here I lie.

If worship [worth, honour, renown] might have kept me,
   I had not gone;
If wit [intelligence] might have me saved, I needed not fear;
If money might have holp, I lacked none;
But oh, good God, what vaileth all this gear?
When Death is come, Thy mighty messenger,
Obey we must; there is no remedy;
Me hath he summoned, and lo, now here I lie.

Yet was I late promised otherwise,
This year to life in wealth and delice.
Lo! Whereto cometh thy blandishing promise
Of false astrology and divinatrice,
Of God's secrets, making thyself so wise?
How true is for this year thy prophecy?
The year yet lasteth, and lo, now here I lie.

O, brittle wealth, aye full of bitterness,
Thy single pleasure doubled is with pain.
Account my sorrow first, and my distress
In sundry wise, and reckon there again
The joy that I have had, and I dare sayn,
For all my honour, endured there have I
More woe than wealth, and lo, now here I lie.

Where are our castles now, where are our towers?
Goodly Richmond, soon art thou gone from me;
At Westminster, that costly work of yours,
Mine own dear lord, now shall I never see.
Almighty God vouchsafe to grant that these
For you and your children may well edify.
My palace builded is, and lo now here I lie.

Adieu, mine own spouse, my worthy lord!
The faithful love, that did us both combine
In marriage a peaceable concord,
Into your hands here I do clear resign,
To be bestowed on your children and mine;
Erst were ye father, now must ye supply
The mother's part also, for here I lie.

Farewell my daughter, Lady Margaret,
God wot full oft it grieved hath my mind
That ye should go where we might seldom meet;
Now I am gone, and have left you behind.
O mortal folk, but we be very blind:
What we least fear full oft it is most nigh –
From you depart I first, for lo, now here I lie.

Farewell, Madam, my lord's worthy mother;
Comfort your son, and be of good cheer,
Take all at worth, for it will be no other.
Farewell, my daughter Katherine, late the fere [companion]
Unto Prince Arthur, late my child so dear.
It booteth not for me to wail and cry;
Pray for my soul, for lo, now here I lie.

Adieu, Lord Henry, loving son, adieu!
Our Lord increase your honour and estate.
Adieu, my daughter Mary, bright of hue,
God make you virtuous, wise and fortunate.
Adieu, sweetheart, my little daughter Kate!
Thou shalt, sweet babe, such is thy destiny,
Thy mother never know, for lo, now here I lie.

Lady Cecily, Lady Anne and Lady Katherine,
Farewell, my well-beloved sisters three.
O Lady Bridget, other sister mine,
Lo, here the end of worldly vanity!
Now are you well who earthly folly flee
And heavenly things do praise and magnify.
Farewell, and pray for me, for lo, now here I lie.

Adieu my lords, adieu my ladies all,
Adieu my faithful servants every one,
Adieu my commons, whom I never shall
See in this world: wherefore to Thee alone,
Immortal God, verily Three in One,
I me commend; Thy infinity mercy
Show to Thy servant, for lo, now here I lie.[5]

More's poem, which was to be one of several epitaphs hung up on wooden boards near the Queen's burial place, reflects two popular contemporary themes: the fall of princes, and warnings from beyond the grave of mortality and the transience of life. Yet More's differs from late-medieval elegies, in that he shows Elizabeth not just as a sinner but as a Renaissance pattern of virtue.[6]

The elegy must have been written in the week after the Queen's death, for More speaks of the infant Princess Katherine as if she was still living. Tragically, she 'lived not long after'[7] and 'tarried but a small season after her mother' before being 'called unto a far better kingdom'. She died in the Tower on 18 February, and was buried in Westminster Abbey. The site of her grave is unknown; probably, like her brother Edmund, she was interred in the Confessor's chapel in an unmarked grave.[8]

Another epitaph, which may have been hung near Elizabeth's tomb, was also in verse form:

Here lieth the fresh flower of Plantagenet,
Here lieth the white rose in the red set . . .
God grant her now Heaven to increase
And our own King Harry long life and peace.[9]

Elizabeth was given a lavish funeral costing £2,832.7s.3d. (£1,381,000),[10] far in excess of the £600 spent on Prince Arthur's funeral, or on that of Edward IV even.[11] Her grieving widower spared no expense. Such open-handedness on the part of a miserly king might well have reflected Henry's feelings for his dead wife, but it was also a very public statement of her prime dynastic importance in the annals of English royalty.

On 22 February Mass was said early in the morning in St Peter ad Vincula. At noon 'the coffin was put in a carriage covered with black velvet, with a cross of white cloth of gold, very well fringed'.

Then, with the 200 poor men going before, followed by royal officers and clergy, it was borne in procession through London on a chariot 'drawn with six horses trapped with black velvet'. All the City churches were shrouded in black for the occasion.[12]

On the coffin lay 'a image or personage like a queen, clothed in the very robes of estate of the Queen, having her very rich crown on her head, her hair about her shoulders, her sceptre in her right hand and her fingers well garnished with gold rings and precious stones'.[13] As at Elizabeth's coronation, the virginal loose hair proclaimed her chastity. The effigy cost £2 (£970), and its clothing £5.2s.6d. (£2,500).[14]

From the thirteenth to the eighteenth century it was customary for funeral effigies of royal persons to be displayed at state funerals. Westminster Abbey possesses several such effigies, besides what is left of Elizabeth of York's; the earliest recorded, which does not survive, was that of Edward I; Henry V's effigy is also lost, as possibly are others. The oldest extant is that of Edward III (1377), and there are two others that pre-date Elizabeth's: those of Anne of Bohemia, queen of Richard II (1394) and Katherine of Valois, queen of Henry V (1437); and of course there are several later examples.

In the seventeenth century the poet John Dryden recorded that these effigies lay in open presses, where 'you may see them all a-row'. In the eighteenth century, around the time that the practice of making funeral effigies died out, John Dart recorded that they were 'sadly mangled, some with their faces broke, others broken in sunder, and most of them stripped of their robes' – by Oliver Cromwell's men, he supposed. They were a sorry sight – a 'ragged regiment'. But the face of Elizabeth of York, he noted, was still perfect. Later still, it was described as having 'a pleasant and slightly roguish, or boy-like, air'.[15]

The upper part of her painted effigy of soft Baltic wood, with a jointed left arm (the right is missing) beautifully carved from pear wood, and some beautiful gold satin from the original bodice, survives today in the Norman Undercroft Museum in Westminster Abbey. The rest of the effigy is either lost or in too poor a condition to display, much of the body having disintegrated after being saturated with water when Westminster Abbey was bombed in the Second World War. That also left the head and bust blackened and damaged, the wood split, the nose missing and the remains of the bodice stiff with filth – it was described, prior to cleaning in 1961, as an 'unpleasant-looking fabric of dirty grey with a shimmer of yellow'.[16]

The effigy was made by two Dutchmen, Laurence Wechon, 'the carver', and Hans van Hoof, and was five foot eleven tall, with a wooden head and bust, jointed wooden arms and fir poles for legs. The body – from the bust to the feet – was formed of hoops, stuffed with hay and covered in leather, which was secured with nails. Beneath the Queen's own robes of estate, it was clad in clothes specially made for it: a crimson satin square-necked 'garment' seamed and bordered with blue and black velvet, having a wider neckline than on bodices in the Queen's portraits (as appears from the outline on the wooden bust), and dark cloth stockings to the knees; the latter were still in place in 1890, but have since disappeared. The wig was hired and does not survive. The ears have holes, thought to have been for earrings,[17] but earrings were not commonly worn at this period, so perhaps they were for attaching the wig.

Almost certainly, the face, which so closely resembles Elizabeth's portraits, is a death mask, like the head of Henry VII's funeral effigy, which survives with it. Signs of the stroke that killed Edward III are evident in the face of his funeral effigy, so it is likely that the tradition of using death masks for such effigies dated from 1377 at the latest. The sunken aspect of the features of the effigy reflect the Queen as she looked in death. The accounts for Elizabeth's effigy record payments to 'two porters, for fetching of the coffin from the Princes' Wardrobe', to one John Scot 'for watching in the Tower a night', and to two more porters for bringing the effigy to the Tower, presumably so that the face could be modelled from Elizabeth's dead features.

At each corner of the funeral chariot 'sat a gentlewoman-usher kneeling on [beside] the coffin, which was in this manner conveyed from the Tower to Westminster. On the fore-horses rode two chariot men; and on the four others, four henchmen in black gowns. On the horses were lozenges with the Queen's escutcheon; by every horse walked a person in a mourning hood. At each corner of the chariot was a banner of Our Lady of the Assumption, of the Salutation, and of the Nativity', and these banners 'were all white in token that she died in childbed'. An early sixteenth-century drawing of the funeral procession made for Thomas Wriothesley, Garter King of Arms,[18] shows the wheeled chariot bearing a large coffin with hooded mourners at each corner carrying their banners. On the hearse lies the effigy with loose hair and a crown and sceptre.

The funeral route from the Tower to Westminster was the same as that followed at Elizabeth's coronation fifteen years earlier; now, as then, nobles, royal officers, citizens and clergy united together to pay their respects, and hundreds of painted escutcheons bearing the arms of the King and Queen were made, to be carried or displayed in the funeral procession. Following the chariot were 'eight palfreys saddled with black velvet, bearing eight ladies of honour, who rode singly after the corpse in their slops and mantles, every horse led by a man afoot without a hood but in a demi-black gown, followed by many lords. The Lord Mayor and citizens, all in mourning, brought up the rear, and at every door in the City a person stood bearing a torch.' Among the ladies were the Queen's four sisters, all wearing mourning attire with sweeping trains, even the nun Bridget. The principal mourner was Katherine, Countess of Devon, supported by Mary Say, Countess of Essex, Lady Elizabeth Stafford and Elizabeth, Lady Herbert.

As the cortège passed each church along the route, 'a solemn peal with all the bells was rung', and each curate came forward to cense the corpse, 'and thus was this gracious princess with the King's chapel and others singing all the way before her conveyed unto Charing cross'. 'At Fenchurch and Cheapside were set thirty-seven virgins all in white linen, having chaplets of white and green on their heads, and bearing lighted tapers' – each girl representing one year of the Queen's life, with their chaplets the colours of the Tudor royal livery. They were dressed as virgins because a woman who had died in childbed was honoured as a virgin. 'In Chepe the Lady Mayoress ordained also thirty-seven other virgins, in their hairs [i.e. with their hair loose], holding likewise pretty tapers, in the honour of Our Lady, and that the good Queen was in her thirty-seventh year [*sic*].'

The sombre pomp of the occasion impressed onlookers. 'From Mark Lane to Temple Bar alone were five thousand torches' carried by bearers wearing white woollen gowns and hoods, 'besides lights burning before all the parish churches, while processions of religious persons singing anthems and bearing crosses met the royal corpse from every fraternity [guild] in the City. And as for surplus of strangers, who had no torches, as Easterlings [Baltic traders], Frenchmen, Portugals, Venetians, Genoese and Lukeners [natives of Lucca], even they rode in black. All the surplus of citizens of London that rode out in black stood along Fenchurch to the end of Cheap[side].' The London craft guilds had paid for the black mourning clothes worn by their members, and also for white robes worn by those who stood with lighted torches beneath the Eleanor Cross at Charing as the coffin passed.

At Temple Bar the cortège was met by a procession of noblemen headed by Thomas Stanley, Earl of Derby, who had played such an important role in Elizabeth's life and was himself to die the following year. At Charing Cross the abbots of Westminster and Bermondsey, wearing black copes, met and censed the corpse, then preceded it to St Margaret's churchyard at Westminster, where it was received by eight bishops,[19] the abbots of Reading, St Albans, Winchcombe and Stratford, and the priors of All Hallows Barking by the Tower and Christ Church, Canterbury. Here the peers 'took their mantles' in readiness for the obsequies in the Abbey.

The body was 'censed and taken out of the chair', along with the effigy and banners. With Derby leading the procession, it was carried under a canopy 'with all due solemnity' on the shoulders of 'certain lords' to the door of Westminster Abbey. Inside the church it was laid on a grand catafalque hung with banners and covered in 'cloth of majesty' of black cloth of gold with a valance embroidered with the Queen's motto, 'Humble and reverent', and garnished with her coat of arms, gold roses, portcullises and *fleurs-de-lis*.[20] The wooden effigy of Elizabeth was laid on top. 'Then began the dirge.'

After the service Dorset and Derby escorted Katherine Courtenay and all the lords and ladies across to the Queen's great chamber in the Palace of Westminster, where Katherine presided over a supper at which fish was served. Meanwhile, in the Abbey, knights, ladies, squires and heralds kept watch over the body all night, their vigil illuminated by over 1,100 hearse candles, which were kept burning throughout the rest of the ceremonies.

Royal funerals at that period normally took place over two days, with the state obsequies on the first day and the interment on the second. At six o'clock the next morning, 23 February, the Dean of Westminster went to summon the female mourners to Our Lady's Mass at seven o'clock, and an hour later Katherine Courtenay and the Queen's other sisters assembled in the 'cathedral [sic] vast and dim'. The Abbey had been hung with black cloth, and was lit by the candles around the hearse and 273 tapers bearing escutcheons, placed high up above the hangings.

The Mass of the Trinity was celebrated. Afterwards the princesses and Lady Katherine Gordon, who took precedence immediately after them, were among the twenty ladies who presented thirty-seven palls of blue, red and green cloth of gold, one for each year of Elizabeth's life. The first pall was 'laid along the corpse' by Elizabeth Say, Lady Mountjoy, who made an obeisance as she approached and kissed her pall; the rest followed suit. The Queen's sisters, Katherine and Anne, each presented five palls.[21]

John Russell, Bishop of Lincoln, officiated at the final, requiem Mass, with Katherine of York, the chief mourner, making the only offering, in accordance with tradition. Then Richard FitzJames, Bishop of Rochester, preached the funeral sermon, taking as his text Job 19: *Miseremini mei, miseremini mei, saltem vos amici mei, quia manus Domini tetigit me* (Have pity, have pity on me, O ye my friends, for the hand of God hath touched me). 'These words he spake in the name of England, on account of the great loss the country had sustained of that virtuous Queen, her noble son, the Prince Arthur, and the recently deceased Archbishop of Canterbury [Henry Deane]' – three deaths that had left a nation bereft.

After the sermon the palls were removed from the coffin and the ladies left the Abbey, 'after whose departing the image with the crown and rich robes were had to a secret place by St Edward's shrine' and the men proceeded to the actual burial. Until the Lady Chapel was completed, Elizabeth was interred temporarily in a vault specially made for her in the crossing of the Abbey – 'the void space between the high altar and the choir', where monarchs were customarily crowned. Here 'her Grace was laid until the new chapel were fully edified and made'.[22] William Warham, Bishop of London, hallowed the vault with appropriate rites and ceremony, then the clergy and the King's chaplains approached the hearse and lifted the coffin, which was lowered into it, whereupon the Queen's chamberlain and her gentlemen ushers, weeping, broke their staves of office and cast them into the grave, to symbolise the termination of their service. It is possible that, like other early royal funeral effigies, Elizabeth's was laid on top of her temporary burial place. In his will of 1509, Henry VII left orders that her body be brought from here and interred beside him in the new Lady Chapel.[23]

To speed Elizabeth's passage through Purgatory, Henry VII had not only paid for those 636 Masses to be said for her soul, but also for at least £240 (£116,660) in alms to be distributed by her almoner to the bed-ridden, the blind, lepers and other unfortunates.[24] In 1504 Henry founded a chantry at Westminster for himself, Elizabeth, his parents and ancestors, and handsomely endowed it with a yearly income of £804.12s.8d. (£391,130).[25] In 1506 Margaret Beaufort founded another chantry in the new Lady Chapel for the souls of herself, her parents, her husbands, her deceased daughter-in-law, the Queen, and Elizabeth's deceased children.[26]

The King remained in seclusion at Richmond for six weeks after the funeral, prostrate with grief and so ill with quinsy – a complication of tonsillitis that can cause breathing difficulties – that it was said he was near death. He was unable to swallow and could barely open his mouth.[27] His mother came to nurse him, bringing sweet wine and ordering physic for him. It seems that the loss of Elizabeth – and of Arthur the year before – impacted badly on Henry, as for the remaining six years of his life, his health steadily declined.[28] By 1504 he had become 'a weak man and sickly, not likely to be no long-lived man'.[29]

He could not remain in solitude; life had to go on. The Emperor Maximilian, 'hearing that Queen Elizabeth had died, sent a solemn embassy to visit and comfort the King', whom he had heard was 'sorrowful and sad at the death of so good a queen and wife'. On Palm Sunday, 15 March, his wasted frame clad in blue velvet,[30] Henry rode to St Paul's Cathedral 'in great triumph' with the Imperial ambassador riding by his side. 'And there the Bishop made an excellent and comfortable oration to the King concerning the death of the Queen.'[31] Henry also wore blue mourning for the ceremonies of Maundy Thursday on 19 March.[32]

In April he paid off Elizabeth's ladies, gentlewomen and servants, and in May he settled her funeral expenses, and rewarded her dry nurse with £3.6s.8d. (£1,620).[33]

The sad news of the Queen's death had reached Spain by 11 April, when Queen Isabella wrote at once to her ambassador in England: 'We are informed of the death of the Queen of England, our sister. We have spoken of the audience you are to seek, and the consolation you are to administer upon our part to the King of England, our brother. He is suffering from the loss of the Queen his wife, who is in glory.'[34]

Henry VII never did secure the canonisation of Henry VI – Pope Julius II asked too high a price – so his plans for a shrine in the new Lady Chapel at Westminster were abandoned in favour of his own monument being built to the east of the altar. He had always envisaged a fine tomb for himself and his Queen. In 1506 he considered a design by Guido Mazzoni, based on the effigy of Charles VIII at St Denis. The following year he commissioned a black-and-white marble tomb chest with gilt effigies of himself and Elizabeth, which may have been designed by Mazzoni, although royal craftsmen were to execute the work; but these effigies were never made because Henry VIII 'disliked' the designs, according to a later note on the estimate.

It seems Henry VII did too. In his will of 1509 he left a lavish sum of money to be spent on his chapel and monument; the total eventual cost was at least £20,000 (£9.7 million), about £5,000 more than his son estimated. He also left minute instructions for a different tomb, still with a black-and-white marble chest; this was to have 'our and our wife's images' in gilt-bronze lying on it, side by side, 'as good or better than any of the other kings and queens in the Abbey'.[35] The new chapel was consecrated the day after the King's death in 1509, so that he could be buried there in the large vault that had been constructed at the east end. As he had ordered, he was laid next to Elizabeth; her body had been exhumed and placed in the vault so that it could rest beside his for eternity.

The vault measured 2.7 metres long, 1.5 metres wide and 1.4 metres high. Both bodies were encased in anthropoid lead coffins marked by Maltese crosses, with only the King's bearing a coffin plate. These were in turn chested in wooden outer coffins. Urns containing the entrails of the royal couple may have been buried with them. Bacon observed that Henry VII 'dwelleth more richly dead in the monument of his tomb than he did alive at Richmond or any of his palaces'.

In October 1512 Henry VIII commissioned the Florentine sculptor Pietro Torrigiano to build a Renaissance-style tomb for his parents over the vault. Torrigiano, a fearless, volatile man who had once broken the nose of Michelangelo during a fight, had worked under Pinturicchio on the Borgia apartments in the Vatican. Before 1507 he had travelled to England in the company of some Florentine merchants. By 1511 he had come to the attention of the young King, who asked him to design a fine tomb and effigy for Margaret Beaufort in the south aisle of the new Lady Chapel. In producing this outstanding sepulchre, which is reckoned to be his masterpiece (and on which Elizabeth of York's arms appear), Torrigiano proved himself to be superior to any sculptor then working in England, and so earned himself the honour of building a tomb for the founders of the Tudor dynasty. It was the first major Renaissance monument to be erected in England, and was designed as the centrepiece of the Lady Chapel, which would in time come colloquially to be known as 'the Henry VII Chapel'. In 1516 Torrigiano was also contracted to build the principal altar in the Chapel. He returned to Rome while these works were being executed, hoping to persuade Benvenuto Cellini to come to England to assist him, but Cellini refused on account of Torrigiano's arrogance and pride, and because he did not want to live among 'such beasts as the English'.[36]

Torrigiano's innovative marble tomb, one of the greatest sepulchres in Westminster Abbey, is considered to be 'the finest Renaissance tomb north of the Alps'.[37] It is of white and black touchstone work with elaborately decorated gilt-bronze pilasters with Corinthian capitals at each corner. Tudor roses, portcullises, dragons, greyhounds and crowns abound in the ornamentation of the monument. The tomb chest of Tournai marble is decorated with an exquisitely carved frieze, copper-gilt Italianate figures and gilt-bronze medallions with reliefs of the Virgin Mary and the King's patron saints; cherubs sit at the head and feet of the tomb, supporting the royal arms. The monument is surrounded by a massive intricate bronze grille by one Thomas the Dutchman, dating from 1505 and bearing royal badges and emblems. Originally it was adorned with thirty-two figures of saints, of which only six survive, and enclosed a chantry chapel with its own altar, long vanished, although the step on which it stood remains, along with the bar that once supported a canopy over the altar.

In 1512 Henry VIII commissioned Humphrey Walker and Nicholas Ewen, coppersmiths, to cast gilt-bronze effigies of his parents under the direction of Torrigiano. They took six years to complete, and rest on a white marble plinth. The tomb cost the King £1,500 (£569,400); it was finished on 5 January 1519.

It appears that the sculptors used the death masks from the funeral effigies of the King and Queen as models for their tomb effigies. The quality of their workmanship is superb, and the naturalism of the heads, hands and figures marks a departure from the stiff formalism of medieval effigies, and set a new standard for royal tomb sculpture. Elizabeth is portrayed with a slender figure, when in reality she was buxom and plump in her latter years; she and Henry lie side by side with their hands joined in prayer. They wear plain attire without any trappings of royalty, for their crowns – the only regalia ever to adorn the effigies – were lost or stolen after 1677, when they appear in an engraving of the tomb by John Dart in Francis Sandford's *A Genealogical History of the Kings and Queens of England*. It is this very simplicity that invests them with a realism that is at once majestic and pious, and in true Renaissance tradition shows the King to be a scholar, a humanist and a great prince. The serene figure of Elizabeth wears traditional ceremonial robes – a square-necked surcoat with a low-slung girdle over a gown with cuffs and a chemise inset, a mantle secured by tasselled cords, and her customary long gable hood, beneath which (unlike in portraits) her wavy hair is loose in token of her purity and her queenship. It bears a good resemblance to her portraits and her funeral effigy. Her head rests on two cushions and her feet on a lion.[38]

Henry VII's will made lavish and precise provision for perpetual daily Masses to be said at the tomb altar for his soul and that of his late wife. Four candles, each eleven feet high, were to be kept burning around the monument, and on feast days and solemn cereremonials of the Church thirty candles were to enclose it, each taller than a man. The candles were to be replaced when they had burned down to a height of three feet. Each year, on the anniversaries of the deaths of Henry and Elizabeth, no fewer than a hundred candles were to be lit in the chantry. Fines were to be imposed if the monks defaulted on these obligations.[39] Thus did the King hope to ensure the safe passage of his soul and Elizabeth's through Purgatory to eternal bliss. Alas, the dissolution of Westminster Abbey in 1540 put an end to these sacred rites.

The tomb survived with much of its splendour intact. Elizabeth, wrote Fuller, 'lieth buried with her husband in the chapel of his erection, and hath an equal share with him in the use and honour of that, his most magnificent monument'. Writing in the reign of her granddaughter, Elizabeth I, John Stow also found much to admire in this 'sumptuous sepulchre and chapel', with its breathtaking Perpendicular fan-vaulted roof, Tudor emblems and brilliant stained-glass windows that flooded the interior with light. It was, opined Bacon, the stateliest and daintiest chapel in Europe.

A white marble tablet inset in the bronze frieze to the right hand of the Queen's effigy bears the Latin inscription placed there on the order of Henry VIII:

Hic jacet regina Hellisabect,
Edwardi IIII quondam regis filia,
Edwardi V regis nominate soros,
Henrici VII olim regis conjux,
Atque Henrici VIII mater inclyta.
Obit autem suum diem turri Londiniarum,
Die Febrii 11, Anno Dom. 1502 [sic],
37 annorum etate functa.

This translates as: 'Here rests Queen Elizabeth, daughter of Edward IV, sometime king; sister of Edward V, who bore the name of king; formerly wedded to King Henry VII; and also the illustrious mother of Henry VIII; who closed her life in the palace of the Tower of London on February 11, in the year of Our Lord 1502 [*sic*], having completed her thirty-seventh year.' This recital of the Queen's royal connections was intended to proclaim the noble ancestry and connections of the Tudor dynasty, as was a further inscription around the tomb, also placed there by her son: 'Here is situated Henry VII, the glory of all the kings who lived in his time by reason of his intellect, his riches, and the fame of his exploits, to which were added the gifts of bountiful nature, a distinguished brow, an august face, an heroic stature. Joined to him his sweet wife was very pretty, chaste and fruitful. They were parents happy in their offspring, to whom, land of England, you owe Henry VIII.'

Impeccably connected, beautiful, ceremonious, fruitful, devout, compassionate, generous and kind, Elizabeth fulfilled every expectation of her contemporaries. Her goodness shines forth in the sources, and it is not surprising that she was greatly loved. She had overcome severe tragedies and setbacks, and emerged triumphant. We have seen how it is possible to reconcile her much-debated actions before her marriage with the gentle queen who emerges after it. Certainly the sources show that, as queen, she played a greater political role than that with which most historians have credited her, and that she was active within her traditional areas of influence. It is also clear that, far from being in subjection to Henry VII and Margaret Beaufort, she enjoyed a generally happy relationship with both of them – and with Henry at least up until the last year of her life.

Elizabeth is often unfairly overshadowed by her successors, the wives of Henry VIII, but she was more successful as queen than any of them. For this, and for her integrity, her sweet, good nature, and her many kindnesses, her memory deserves to be celebrated.

19

'As Long as the World Shall Endure'

In November 1504 Henry VII settled an annual payment of £10 (£4,860) on the University of Cambridge for holding a commemorative requiem service for Elizabeth in the church of St Mary the Great on the anniversary of her death, for 'as long as the world shall endure'. This was first marked on 11 February 1505, and continued up to the Reformation of the 1530s.[1]

Although Elizabeth's death left him free to make a profitable marriage alliance, Henry never took another wife. In the 1530s a Scots chronicler, Adam Abell, would recall that, in the aftermath of his bereavement, he kept Katherine Gordon so often in his company that 'some [thought] that they were married'.[2] Yet there is plenty of evidence that Henry's grief for Elizabeth was raw and genuine, and maybe Katherine Gordon, who had been close to her too on a daily basis, could offer some comfort at this time. His accounts show that she remained a support to him to the end of his life, partnering him at cards and obtaining medicines for him as his health declined; she even painted cloths of religious scenes to hold up before him as he lay dying, so maybe he did find solace with her.[3] But he did not marry her.

It would probably be fair to say that the loss of Prince Arthur and Queen Elizabeth aged Henry prematurely. But he was a pragmatic man with only one son to succeed him; just that one life stood between the continuance of his dynasty and the ruin of all he had worked for – and he had good reason to know how fragile young lives could be. At forty-six, he was young enough to sire more children – and doubtless lonely.

On hearing of the passing of Elizabeth, Queen Isabella expressed concern about propriety and the welfare of Katherine: 'Now that the Queen of England is dead, in whose society the Princess our daughter might have honourably remained as with a mother, it would not be right that the Princess should stay in England.'[4] So when, just weeks after Elizabeth's death, King Henry, reluctant to return Katherine's dowry, suggested he marry her himself, the Spanish sovereigns were horrified at the prospect of such an 'unnatural' union, and declined the honour. On 24 June 1503 Katherine was betrothed to Prince Henry, who was formally created Prince of Wales in 1504. Henry VII toyed with the idea of several other potential foreign brides, but in each case negotiations foundered.

It has been said that Elizabeth exerted a beneficial influence on him and that he became more miserly, suspicious and harsh after her death, while his court was a more sombre place, but the theory of 'an imaginary deterioration' in his character was dismissed years ago by G. R. Elton as being based 'only on insufficient knowledge of the facts'. However, it is inconceivable that the loss of his son and his wife, in the space of ten months, would not have left Henry a sadder man, and changed him in other ways too, not always for the better. The glory days were behind him now, and the last years of his reign also witnessed a decline in his health. Sentimentally he retained the services of Elizabeth's minstrels, who played for him at every New Year celebration up to his death; in their poignant melodies he could perhaps recapture happy memories of the years he had spent with his late wife, who had shared his love of music.[5]

After Queen Isabella's death in 1504, which left her widower Ferdinand as a mere king of Aragon, Henry would neither permit his heir to marry Katherine of Aragon, nor would he return Katherine or her dowry to Spain. He made young Henry secretly abjure his betrothal, and kept the Princess in England in increasing penury for the rest of his reign.

Isabella's passing reawakened Henry's fears about the legitimacy of his title. According to Bacon, after the death of Elizabeth he had fretted that there would be some question over his continuing to reign, and he had had cause, for one of his spies in Calais had reported speculation there that Edward Stafford, Duke of Buckingham, a descendant of Edward III, was the rightful successor of Elizabeth, whom some people still clearly regarded as the true Queen of England; Prince Henry was not even mentioned.[6]

Henry 'conceived that the case of Ferdinand of Aragon after the death of Queen Isabella was his own case after the death of his own Queen. For if both of the kings had their kingdoms in the right of their wives, they descended to the heirs and did not accrue to the husbands. And though his own case had both steel and parchment more than the other, that is to say a conquest in the field and an Act of Parliament, yet notwithstanding, that natural title of descent in blood did (in the imagination even of a wise man) breed a doubt that the other two were not safe nor sufficient. Wherefore he was wonderful diligent to inquire and observe what became of the King of Aragon in holding the kingdom of Castile',[7] which Ferdinand was soon successfully to wrest from his daughter Juana (who had succeeded her mother as queen) on the grounds that she was mad. Henry's concern shows he had always been aware that public opinion generally held that he was king in right of his wife. One pedigree roll showing the descent of Prince Arthur bypassed Henry and his immediate forebears completely, and showed Cadwaladr's line stretching down through the Mortimers to Edward IV and Elizabeth, through whom, it was made clear, Arthur derived his claim to the throne.[8]

This may explain why the King kept Prince Henry, his surviving son and heir, under such close supervision that the boy ended up isolated – 'locked away like a woman' and brought up more like a girl than a boy, as the Spanish ambassador Gutierre Gómez de Fuensalida put it, adding, 'He is so subjugated that he does not speak a word except in response to what the King asks him.' Henry's bedchamber could only be accessed through his father's,[9] and he was not allowed much freedom of movement, spending his formative years mainly with his tutors, 'sober and discreet' old men, and the noble boys who had been selected as his companions. He grew up to be learned and pious, but lacking in experience of life. Probably the King had fears for the succession and the health of this one remaining son, in whom were now vested all the hopes of his dynasty, which would explain why the Prince was never sent to Ludlow as Arthur had been.

Yet Henry VII also seemed reluctant to instruct his heir in the art of government or allow him to read state papers. It is possible that he had already assessed his son's character and potential and come to fear him, or that factions might form around him. On one occasion, the King got so angry with young Henry that it looked 'as if he sought to kill him'; instead, he locked him up until his anger had cooled.[10] This treatment may have proceeded from dread that those who were dissatisfied with his rule would rally around Elizabeth's son and clamour for his succession. It was perhaps for this reason that Henry was 'not greatly willing to cast any popular lustre' on his children,[11] although he had certainly given Arthur due prominence in happier days.

Henry VII died on 21 April 1509 at Richmond Palace, of tuberculosis. Despite his having brought peace and prosperity to England, and enhanced her reputation in Europe, he was not mourned. He was succeeded by seventeen-year-old Henry VIII, who became famous – or notorious – for marrying six wives, breaking with the Church of Rome, and founding the Church of England in the process, with himself as its Supreme Head. He died in 1547, and in the early seventeenth century there was still to be seen beside his vault in St George's Chapel, Windsor, a funeral banner bearing the arms of his parents, Henry VII and Elizabeth of York.[12] He was succeeded in turn by his three children, Edward VI (reigned 1547–53, on whose death Elizabeth of York's male descendants became extinct), Mary I (reigned 1553–8) and Elizabeth I (reigned 1558–1603). Seventy years after Elizabeth of York's right to succeed had been passed over virtually without comment, Henry VIII's lack of surviving sons had made it possible for a woman to rule in her own right.

It is almost certain that Henry VIII named the future Queen Elizabeth I, his daughter by Anne Boleyn, after his mother, Elizabeth of York, not only because of his fond remembrance of her, but also to proclaim his daughter's descent from the legitimist royal line. At Elizabeth's coronation procession in 1559, the figures of Henry VII and Elizabeth of York appeared in a pageant in Gracechurch Street, London, 'so set that one of them joined hands with th'other, with the ring of matrimony perceived on the finger',[13] and seated beneath a cloth of estate in their respective red and white roses symbolising the union of Lancaster and York, of which the Virgin Queen was now the embodiment:

The two princes that sit under one cloth of state,
The man in the red rose, the woman in the white:
Henry the VII and Queen Elizabeth, his mate,
By ring of marriage as man and wife unite.
Both heirs to both their bloods, to Lancaster the King,
The Queen to York, in one the two houses did knit,
Of whom, as heir to both, Henry the Eight did spring,
In whose seat his true heir, thou Queen Elizabeth, doth sit.[14]

The feisty and formidable Elizabeth I was the very antithesis of the mild and self-effacing grandmother whose name she bore. The Virgin Queen did not look to the gentler Elizabeth as a role model; she preferred to emulate her magnificent sire, Henry VIII. Proving that a woman could rule as capably as any man, she enjoyed a long and successful reign, but never married. She was the last of the Tudors.

Elizabeth's blood flowed on, however, through her daughter Margaret, the ancestress of the Stuart monarchs of Great Britain, and through them to the Hanoverians and the House of Windsor. Her namesake, Queen Elizabeth II, is her descendant in the sixteenth generation.

Of Elizabeth's surviving sisters, Cecily, who had perhaps borne Thomas Kyme two children,[15] died on 24 August 1507. Hall states that she was buried at Quarr Abbey, a Cistercian monastery on the Isle of Wight; if so, her tomb and its location was lost at the Reformation. Yet there is evidence in the Beaufort account books that she died at the Old Palace at Hatfield, Hertfordshire, after lodging there for three weeks, and was interred at 'the friars', which may have been the friary at King's Langley where her ancestor, Edmund of Langley, Duke of York, was buried.[16]

Anne (Lady Thomas Howard) died between November 1511 and 1513, and was buried in Thetford Priory, Norfolk. Her remains were later removed to Framlingham church.

After Elizabeth's death Henry VII sent Katherine and her children home to Tiverton in Devon, where she lived as a dependent of the Earl of Devon, her father-in-law. William Courtenay remained in prison until Henry VII's death in 1509, after which he was freed by Henry VIII, but he did not long enjoy his liberty, for he died in 1511. Katherine then took a vow of perpetual chastity. She passed away in November 1527 at Tiverton Castle, and was buried in Tiverton parish church, where her son, Henry Courtenay, Marquess of Exeter, erected a tomb to her memory, now gone.

Both John Speed and John Weaver, writing in the seventeenth century, state that the nun, Bridget, died in 1517, but Thomas More, writing in 1513, states that Elizabeth's *only* surviving sister, Katherine, was still living, which suggests that Bridget was then dead. She was buried in the priory church at Dartford, but her grave too was lost at the Dissolution.

More states that, 'representing the virtue of her whose name she bore, [Bridget] professed and observed a religious life in Dartford', and Speed says she 'spent her life in holy contemplation unto the day of her death'; but it has been suggested that she had a bastard daughter, Agnes of Eltham, who was born around 1498. It is possible that Agnes was an orphan whose wardship was administered by Dartford Priory, but until Elizabeth of York's death in 1503 she was maintained by the Crown, and when she married Adam Langstroth, a wealthy Yorkshire gentleman, in 1514, she had 'a considerable dowry'.[17] It is not inconceivable that the teenage Bridget, pushed into a convent at the age of seven, and perhaps not very bright anyway, had no vocation for the religious life and embarked on an affair that resulted in a child; and that the Queen supported that child, as she had supported her sisters. It is equally possible that Agnes was simply one of the children Elizabeth took pleasure in patronising. She died in 1530.

Margaret Beaufort, who was widowed in 1504, survived her son. She had played a mother's part to Henry and Mary, the grandchildren who were left to her, after Elizabeth's death and Margaret's departure for Scotland,[18] and in 1509 acted as unofficial regent for Henry VIII during his brief minority.[19] She died in the Abbot's House at Westminster Abbey on 29 June 1509, the day after her grandson reached eighteen. Her fine bronze tomb effigy by Torrigiano shows her in her customary widow's wimple.

Elizabeth's daughter Margaret married James IV on 8 August 1503 at Holyrood Abbey, Edinburgh, and was crowned Queen of Scots the same day. She bore six children, among them James V, father of Mary, Queen of Scots. James IV was killed at the Battle of Flodden in 1513. The following year, Margaret took a second husband, Archibald Douglas, Earl of Angus, to whom she bore a daughter, Margaret Douglas, later Countess of Lennox and mother of Henry

Stewart, Lord Darnley, who married Mary, Queen of Scots, and fathered the future James VI of Scotland. In 1603, James succeeded Elizabeth I as the first sovereign of the House of Stuart to reign over a united Great Britain. Margaret Tudor died of palsy in the autumn of 1541 at Methven Castle, and was buried in the Carthusian abbey of St John in Perth.

Her younger sister Mary, the beauty of the family, judging by all reports, was married in 1514 to the ailing King Louis XII of France. Widowed in 1515, she caused a scandal by marrying, for love, Charles Brandon, Duke of Suffolk. But when Henry VIII's anger had cooled, and the errant couple had agreed to pay a crippling fine, he received them back into favour. Mary bore four children, one of whom, Frances Brandon, became the mother of the ill-fated Lady Jane Grey, who was set up as a puppet queen for just nine days in 1553 and was beheaded on Mary I's orders the following year. Mary Tudor died on 25 June 1533 at Westhorpe Hall, Suffolk, and was buried in the abbey of Bury St Edmunds. Later, her remains were moved to St Mary's Church, where a white stone slab in the chancel marks her grave.

The future Henry VIII had not attended his mother's funeral; none of her children had, but Henry's tutor, chaplain and servants had walked in the procession and no doubt witnessed the obsequies and committal, and could have told him about the stark, mournful pageantry that surrounded that final act. The effect on an eleven-year-old who had been close to his mother was probably devastating.

That Henry was grief-stricken by his mother's death is attested on good evidence. A richly illuminated manuscript, the 'Vaux Passional' in the National Library of Wales in Aberystwyth,[20] dating from the early sixteenth century, is believed to have been in Henry VII's own library, and contains an illumination showing the presentation of a book to the King, who can be identified by his heraldic emblems. Behind the throne to one side is an empty black-draped bed, and kneeling beside it, his red-haired head buried in his arms, is a young boy in a green tunic. Almost certainly this image portrays the young Henry weeping for his mother. In front of the bed kneel two girls in black hoods who are probably his sisters, thirteen-year-old Margaret and seven-year-old Mary. The manuscript, which still has its original crimson-velvet binding, contains two French texts: 'La Passion de Nostre Seigneur', which invites the reader to reflect on the sufferings of Christ; and Georges Chastellain's poem *'Le miroir de la mort'*, an aid to meditation on the futility of worldly pleasures in the face of death. All the other illuminations show scenes from the Bible or classical history.

The manuscript was later owned by Jane Vaux, the wife of Sir Richard Guildford. She had served Elizabeth of York and was later governess to Margaret and Mary; she died in 1538. It is possible that the Passional was a gift to her from Henry VII or Henry VIII. The manuscript descended through the Vaux and Fermor families, from whom it was probably acquired by Sir Kenelm Digby in the seventeenth century. His decendants had it in their library at Peniarth, Merioneth. It was bought for the National Library of Wales in 1921.[21]

Thomas More, in his elegy of 1503, refers to Henry as Elizabeth's 'loving son'. This, and the portrayal of him in the illumination, suggests that his closeness to his mother was well known. There is too his own testimony to his grief at her loss: four years afterwards, in January 1507, in a letter to Erasmus about the untimely demise of the Archduke Philip, he wrote: 'Never since the death of my dearest mother hath there come to me more hateful intelligence. And to speak truth, I was the scanter well-disposed towards your letter than its singular grace demanded, because it seemed to tear open the wound to which time had brought insensibility. But indeed those things which are decreed by Heaven are so to be accepted by mortal men.'[22]

These heartfelt words show that Henry had grieved deeply for Elizabeth, and been close to her, and that at fifteen he was already familiar with the raw pain of loss when he learned of Philip's passing. The news of his mother's death must have come as a terrible shock. Already, in his short life, he had seen two brothers and a sister die young, and soon another sister would die too. The impact of these events on the young Henry should not be underestimated, and his misery can only have been compounded by the total withdrawal of his father, followed by the illness that threatened to deprive the boy of his other parent. It may well have been these terrible events that gave Henry VIII his lifelong fear of illness.

Elizabeth's influence on him is hard to gauge. Given Henry's chequered matrimonial career – six wives, two beheaded, three divorced, and only one son to show for it – post-Freudian historians have sometimes taken a psychological view, speculating that he was so traumatised by losing a mother he idolised that he developed an

Oedipus complex, which drew him irresistibly into incestuous relationships whilst being outraged by them; yet it has since been questioned whether such a condition as an Oedipus complex even exists.

It is tempting to speculate that, had Elizabeth lived, Henry's marital career would not have been so colourful. It is possible that his six marriages represented attempts to recreate the marital harmony of his parents, and mirror their example. The way he comforted Katherine of Aragon after the death of their son echoes the way his parents had consoled each other after Arthur died. Henry's eagerness to marry Katherine, six years his senior, may have stemmed partly from the fact that she had been beloved by his mother; possibly she appeared as a mother-substitute figure to him. Certainly the qualities he admired in his wives – fidelity, dignity, piety, virtue, fruitfulness, intelligence and docility – were those his mother had had in full measure. And, as Marie Louise Bruce has pointed out, he would have been too young to perceive any flaws in Elizabeth's character. For him, she probably remained the epitome of all that was desirable in a queen – with disastrous consequences for his own wives, who would suffer by comparison with such impossible perfection.

Henry inherited Elizabeth's books and manuscripts, as well as his father's, and would appoint the antiquarian John Leland, whom he made keeper of the King's books around 1530, to put them all in order in the new library at Whitehall Palace.[23] No doubt the King prized the cross his mother had given him – one 'set with a table diamond and three good pearls' – which had cost her £13.6s.8d. (£6,500).[24] He evidently cherished her memory. When he became king, he appointed to his service, and Queen Katherine's, several men and women who had served, or been related to, his mother, possibly for her sake, and rewarded many who had served her well[25] (see Appendix 11). The death of his third wife, Jane Seymour, in 1537 in childbed, twelve days after the birth of Henry's long-awaited son and heir, probably revived sad memories of his mother's passing, and his advisers consulted Garter Herald as to the ceremonial that had been observed at Queen Elizabeth's funeral so that it could be replicated at Jane's; a banner bearing the arms of Henry VII and Elizabeth of York was carried in the procession.[26]

By the end of Henry VIII's reign, it was generally accepted that Henry VII had owed his crown to Elizabeth of York. In 1533 the Imperial ambassador, Eustache Chapuys, observed that Henry VIII had 'received the principal title to his realm through the female line'.[27] In 1541 Henry's kinsman, Sir Anthony St Leger, was reported to him for saying that the King's father had had no just title to the crown till he married Edward IV's daughter. When questioned, St Leger insisted he had been misquoted, and had actually said that Henry VII's title was not perfect until he had married Elizabeth of York, because some of his advisers had urged him to claim the throne by right of conquest, 'but now, thanked be the Lord, all titles be in the King our master'. Henry VIII was satisfied with this line of reasoning.[28]

When, in 1674, workmen were dismantling the forebuilding to the White Tower during demolition of the old royal palace, they discovered – ten feet under the rubble infill of a spiral staircase, just as Sir Thomas More had described – a wooden chest containing the skeletons of two children. It was recorded that scraps of rag and velvet adhered to the bones. The velvet was evidence that these were children of high status, and it was assumed that they were the Princes in the Tower. On the orders of Charles II they were reburied as such in an urn in Westminster Abbey, just a few feet from where Elizabeth of York, the Princes' sister, lay at rest. The bones were examined in 1933, and the results, while not conclusive, were compatible with their being those of Elizabeth's lost brothers, Edward V and Richard, Duke of York. In 1965 dental tests on the remains of Anne Mowbray proved a familial link between her and the skeletons in the urn.[29]

However, in 1789, workmen restoring the tomb of Edward IV in St George's Chapel, Windsor, broke accidentally into the vault containing the coffins of the King and Elizabeth Wydeville, and discovered a small vault next to it, which held the bodies of two children. It was assumed that they were those of Princess Mary and George, Duke of Bedford, and their names were added to the inscription on the restored tomb. But in 1810, when Wolsey's tomb house was excavated to construct a burial vault for George III and his family, the coffin of George, clearly labelled '*serenissimus princeps Georgius filius tercius Christianissimi principis Edvardi iiij*', was found, and next to it one that was almost certainly Mary's, as the contemporary account of her funeral states she was buried beside her brother.[30] In 1813 both were moved into their parents' vault. Unfortunately, on neither of the occasions when Edward IV's vault was opened were the coffins of the two unidentified children opened, examined or even described.

It has been suggested that they could have been the Princes in the Tower, perhaps secretly laid to rest with their parents by a guilty Richard III, but until further investigations are made – and the Sovereign's permission would be required for that – there is too little evidence to say whose remains they are.[31] It is likely that the bones are those of royal children, but no other royal children are recorded as having been buried, with graves unaccounted for, in St George's Chapel prior to 1789.

A clue to the mystery may lie in Westminster Abbey. A history in the Abbey's library records that, when the sarcophagus of Elizabeth's infant sister Margaret was opened, it was found to be empty. At the Reformation the sarcophagus was moved from the steps of St Edward the Confessor's shrine to the side of his chapel, so it is possible that the body was removed at that time to Windsor. As to who the other child may be, that remains a mystery.

The full splendour of the incomparable and richly adorned chapel in which lay the remains of Henry VII and Elizabeth of York did not long outlive them. It was despoiled and stripped of some of its fittings during the Reformation that spanned the reigns of their son, Henry VIII, and their grandchildren, Edward VI and Elizabeth I, and more depredations took place later under Oliver Cromwell. The upper part of the fine screen around the tomb, most of the images of saints that adorned it, much of the wondrous glass of the chapel and the original altars, placed there with such veneration, were all destroyed, and the last of the glass was lost during the Blitz.

In 1625 the vault below Henry VII's tomb was opened for the burial of James I. At that time the large wooden outer coffins encasing the lead coffins of Henry and Elizabeth were removed to make space for the vault's new incumbent, leaving the bodies wrapped only in lead. They had originally been placed on either side of the vault, but were moved to one side to accommodate James I's coffin, and the head shell from Elizabeth of York's coffin was temporarily laid upon Henry VII's. It is possible that the visceral urns were removed and later placed in the nearby vault of General George Monck.

On 11 February 1869 the vault was again opened, on the instructions of Dean Stanley, who examined its contents. A drawing was made by Sir George Scharf, Director of the National Portrait Gallery, of the lead coffins lying in a row: James I's to the left, and the smaller ones of Elizabeth of York (centre), marked by a Maltese cross, and Henry VII (right).[32] Those of the two kings were identified by inscriptions.[33] The tomb has not been disturbed since, and Elizabeth sleeps on in peace.

Appendix I

Portraiture

Images as Princess

The earliest images of Elizabeth date from when she was fourteen at most. She appears with her parents and siblings in the magnificent stained-glass 'Royal Window' in the north-west transept of Canterbury Cathedral (above the site of St Thomas Becket's murder in 1170), executed probably by the King's glazier, William Neve, after Katherine's birth in 1479 and before November 1480, because the youngest sister, Bridget, who was born that month, does not appear. Elizabeth is shown kneeling behind her mother, at a prayer desk on which lies an open book. Between the King and Queen was a now-vanished Crucifixion, and above were once scenes showing the seven joys of the Virgin Mary. Behind Elizabeth – in a line, although not in order of age according to the later inscriptions below – kneel her four identically dressed sisters, who, according to those inscriptions, are Cecily, Anne, Katherine and Mary. Probably these are incorrect, and the princesses are actually depicted in their order of seniority, viz. Elizabeth, Mary, Cecily, Anne and Katherine. Elizabeth, like her sisters, wears a long purple damask gown with a golden girdle and a neckline trimmed with ermine, with a rich collar of gold studded with diamonds in quatrefoils; her long fair hair is loose nearly to her waist beneath a heavy coronet.

The window was partly destroyed in 1642, during the Civil War, by a Puritan fanatic, leaving only the royal figures. It was badly restored in the eighteenth century, after which Elizabeth's head was recorded as being too small; fortunately later restoration has used the surviving glass in as authentic a setting as possible. The only original heads are those of the King and Queen, but that of the princess in the end panel – probably Katherine – survives in the Burrell Collection in Glasgow, and from this we can see that the restored heads are all faithful copies of it. They are therefore unlikely to be true likenesses of the princesses.

It has been said that the naturalism in these stained-glass figures, and those at Little Malvern (see below) had not been seen in English art for a century, and that their rich design owes something to the influence of the Netherlandish painter Hugo van der Goes.[1]

Elizabeth is also depicted with her sisters Mary, Cecily and Anne in the remaining fragments of a stained-glass window in St Giles' Church – the tower and choir of which are all that remain of Little Malvern Priory, Worcestershire, a Benedictine cell of Westminster Abbey. It is one of a set of five windows depicting the royal family, which were crafted by local glaziers Richard Twygge and Thomas Woodshaw, and donated between 1480 and 1482 by Bishop Alcock, tutor to Edward, Prince of Wales, the subject of another window; the other three windows depicted Edward IV, Richard, Duke of York, both now lost, and Elizabeth Wydeville, whose head is missing.

Aged between fourteen and sixteen, Elizabeth kneels in front of her sisters at a prayer desk bearing books, beneath a rich canopy of estate. She wears a rather old-fashioned heart-shaped headdress adorned with an elaborate jewel, and a crimson mantle over a rich blue gown with a deep V-neckline edged with bands of gold. Her sisters are differently and less splendidly attired, reflecting the fact that, as the future Queen of France, Elizabeth was of far greater importance.[2]

Images as Queen

In the north transept of Great Malvern Priory, Worcestershire, another former daughter house of Westminster Abbey, can be seen the royal 'Magnificat' window, given by one of the donors it portrays between May 1499 and April 1502, according to the inscriptions and the evidence of the glazing.[3] It is inscribed: 'Pray for the good estate of the noble and most excellent King, Henry the Seventh, and of Elizabeth, Queen, and of the lord Prince Arthur, their son, and also of his most well-beloved consort.' At the bottom, below the lights depicting the joys of the Virgin (as in the Royal Window at Canterbury, which probably influenced that at Great Malvern), are the kneeling figures of the King (restored), Prince Arthur and three knights of the body: Sir Reginald Bray, Sir John Savage (gone, apart from his tabard) and Sir Thomas Lovell (reconstructed from fragments). The figure of Elizabeth of York is mostly missing, lost in a hotchpotch of glass fragments. It has been suggested that the window was the King's gift, prompted by Elizabeth, whose grandfather, Richard, Duke of York, had been active in the rebuilding of the priory in memory of his Beauchamp and Despenser relations; possibly she had mooted the idea after Warwick's execution in 1499, which left Henry VII undisputed lord of Malvern. However it could have been donated by any or all of the people portrayed in the glass.[4]

The earliest known surviving portrait of Elizabeth of York is a half-length in the Royal Collection (RC 403447). In 1974 tree-ring analysis of RC 403447 suggested that the panel dates from 1485–1500 and that it is from the same tree used for a portrait of Prince Arthur in the Royal Collection,[5] but further analysis in 2012 indicated 1480 as the earliest possible date of the panel, and the most likely date as the 1490s.[6] Examination under a microscope revealed an underdrawing that had been sketched, rather than one with straight traced lines. This strongly suggests that the portrait was painted from life.[7] Elizabeth wears a long-lappeted gable hood of black velvet or silk with frontlets embellished with precious stones and goldsmiths' work. Her gown is of crimson velvet with a front-fastening bodice, its neckline edged with a jewel-encrusted border and ermine; the long tight sleeves have ermine cuffs. Her beringed fingers hold a white rose. Her hair appears reddish-gold, parted in the centre, with plaits wound up over her head, which can just be seen beneath the hood, and she has a widow's peak, which is evident only in her early portraits. She wears a necklace of pearls and rubies. Another version of this picture hangs at Christ Church, Oxford.

A portrait of Elizabeth – which may well have been RC 403447 – is listed in Henry VIII's inventories of 1542 and 1547, and was almost certainly the one owned by his son, Edward VI.

Charles I had two portraits of Elizabeth. One was among 'nine old heads' on display in Whitehall Palace: 'King Henry the 7th his Queen in a black and golden dressing, holding in her hand a little white rose, in a blue-painted, gilded frame'. The other was 'among the 23 little heads, King Henry the 7th Queen picture with a little white rose in her hand and a black-and-gold dressing, in a red and gilded frame', which measured 14½ inches by 9 inches and hung beside a portrait of Henry VII.[8] Presumably (comparing the descriptions) the former picture was larger. The 'black-and-gold dressing' seen in both pictures was almost certainly Elizabeth's gable hood. Conceivably the smaller portrait owned by Charles I was the same as the one in Henry VIII's inventory, and is to be identified with RC 403447, which measures 14¾ inches by 10½ inches.

In 1537 Henry VIII commissioned from his court painter, Hans Holbein, a great mural for the privy chamber in Whitehall Palace, which was lost when the palace burned down in 1698, and is known only from two small copies painted *c.*1667–9 by Remigius van Leemput.[9] The 'Great Picture', as it was known, portrayed the full-length, life-sized figures of Henry VIII and his third wife, Jane Seymour, in the foreground, with Henry VII and Elizabeth of York standing behind on a raised carpeted platform. The figures are arranged around a large stone plinth bearing the date 1537 and a heroic inscription that makes no mention of Elizabeth or Jane Seymour, being concerned only with the achievements of the kings: 'If you enjoy seeing the illustrious figures of heroes, look on these: no painting ever bore greater . . .' A preliminary, full-size drawing by Holbein of the figures of the kings is in the National Portrait Gallery, but that of the queens is lost.

Probably Holbein took his likeness of Elizabeth from the portrait in Henry VIII's collection,[10] which was presumably offered as a good likeness of the King's mother. The features are strikingly similar to those in RC 403447, which lends to the theory that the latter was indeed the painting owned by Henry VIII. However, the necklace is different, as is the fabric of the gown, which is of cloth-of-gold damask.

It is possible that Holbein – probably at Henry VIII's request – chose to paint Elizabeth in a golden gown[11] with different jewels, rather than in the attire she wears in the portrait. It is not known where he got the details of the gown or its skirt, which do not appear in any portrait (full-length portraits prior to the mural are rare) or on Elizabeth's tomb effigy, but are accurate for the period. Possibly Holbein obtained descriptions of her dress from other sources. There would have been people at court who could remember her, not least the King himself. And possibly one of her surviving gowns was brought for him from the royal wardrobe at the Tower.

The only other portrait in which Elizabeth wears a gold damask gown is a seventeenth-century miniature painted by John Hoskins, now in the collection of the Duke of Buccleuch.[12] The miniature was one of several that Charles I commissioned of his forebears. In the seventeenth century Abraham van der Doort described it as a portrait of Elizabeth 'in a black dressing adorn'd with gold and pearls in a golden habit with white ermine', copied 'after an ancient old coloured piece'.[13] By 'piece' he evidently meant a panel – which was one of the meanings of the word in those days – and presumably a panel portrait; he is hardly likely to have referred to Holbein's magnificent and famed mural in such terms, so we might speculate that Hoskins based his miniature on the larger of Charles I's portraits of Elizabeth, which in turn was perhaps based on the mural. Several later images of Elizabeth (including numerous engravings from the eighteenth century onwards) derive from Holbein's image.

In the reign of Charles II, two portraits of Elizabeth – probably the same ones – were hanging at Whitehall:[14] one measured 22" by 17", the other, 'Henry 7ths Queen with a white rose in her hand', 14" by 10". It seems that both portraits had survived the sale of Charles I's goods, so the smaller picture may well have been RC 403447.

According to Oliver Millar, the larger picture in Charles II's collection had apparently left the Royal Collection by 1714. Perhaps it had perished when Whitehall Palace was burned down in 1698. In 1818 two paintings of Elizabeth were hanging at Kensington Palace. One was probably RC 403447, which presumably was the smaller portrait owned probably by Henry VIII, Charles I and Charles II. The other portrait recorded at Kensington was apparently part of a set of royal portraits bought by Queen Caroline of Ansbach, wife of George II, from Lord Cornwallis in the eighteenth century; it was later at Buckingham Palace, and is now at St James's Palace. Very similar to the image in the National Portrait Gallery, it measures 22¾" by 17½", and bears the inscription *ELIZABETH REGINA MATAR HENRICI OCTAV* (Queen Elizabeth, mother of Henry the Eighth). Millar describes it as a later derivation of the standard portrait type, part of a long gallery set of portraits of kings and queens, popular in late Elizabethan and Jacobean times among the owners of great houses; but it dates from 1550–1600, so may be one of the earliest surviving copies.[15]

A portrait of Elizabeth was painted around 1502 by Maynard Wewyck and sent to James IV in September that year.[16] Possibly it is to be identified with another early portrait, which was in the collection of the Duke of Hamilton at Holyroodhouse, Edinburgh before it was sold at Sotheby's in 2005. It was once thought to portray Margaret Tudor, but it is clearly Elizabeth, much as she is portrayed in RC 403447. Her attire is similar, but she looks older; she wears an elaborate heavy jewelled collar and holds, uniquely, a red rose. Her hair looks significantly darker, and dips to the widow's peak evident in early likenesses. What is different is the background, which is plain and dark in nearly every other portrait; here it is a luminous pale greenish-blue with a gold tracery canopy embellished with Tudor roses, *fleurs-de-lis* and portcullises. There has been speculation that the portrait dates from the early sixteenth century and was originally in Margaret's own collection[17] before being acquired by the Hamiltons.

A drawing called 'Margaret Tudor', probably by Jacques le Boucq, in the *Receuil d'Arras*, may depict her mother, Elizabeth of York, as it closely resembles the latter's portraits. It was once thought that it might be the lost original on which they are based,[18] and it is true that they are all versions deriving from a single type, but – given its early date and royal provenance – the original is far more likely to have been RC 403447.

The most famous – and the most widely reproduced – copy is that in the National Portrait Gallery, London, which has been tree-ring-dated to *c.*1590–1600. Its history prior to 1870 is not known, but it was probably originally part of a long gallery set. Like all versions, it shows the Queen in similar costume to that in RC 403447, but with minor variations. Here her gown is scarlet rather than crimson, and her hands rest on a parapet, a popular pose in portraits of the period; this parapet is draped with gold figured velvet, and her beringed fingers hold a white rose. She appears younger than in RC 403447. Around her neck hangs not a pearl necklace, but a ruby pendant in the form of a cross with pearls at each corner, suspended on a black cord; similar jewels appear in portraits of her sons, Arthur and Henry. The portrait is inscribed *ELIZABETHA UXOR HENRICI VII* – Elizabeth, wife of Henry VII. It has been said that this portrait makes her look 'bland and lacking in character',[19] but that could be said of many similar crudely executed, two-dimensional panel portraits of the period.

There are other versions of this standard portrait type at Anglesey Abbey; Hatfield House, Hertfordshire; the Old Deanery, Ripon; Dunham Massey, Manchester; Trinity College, Cambridge; Christ

Church College, Oxford; Nostell Priory, Yorkshire; Hever Castle, Kent; and in the Tyrwhitt-Drake collection. Another was recorded in 1866 in the collection of J. P. Bastard. A portrait from the Brocket Collection at Bramshill House, Hampshire, was sold first at Sotheby's in 1952 and again at Christie's in 1954; one from the Shelley-Rolls collection was sold at Christie's in 1961. A half-length, later version, showing Elizabeth in a high-necked gown with different, coarser features, was once at seventeenth-century Stanford Hall, Leicestershire, but is now in the Courtauld Institute of Art. An eighteenth-century version by a member of the circle of Michael Dahl, with the features painted in contemporary style, was sold by Priory Fine Arts in 2012.[20]

The Anglesey Abbey portrait, one of a pair with Henry VII in the collection of the National Trust, has been tree-ring-dated to 1512–20, and is one of the earliest surviving portraits of Elizabeth. Again her hair is darker than usual, and she wears a very rich, heavy gold collar not seen in other portraits, much in the style of the collars worn by her younger self and her sisters in the Royal Window at Canterbury. It has been described as 'a ponderous design typical of late-Gothic taste'.[21]

In the Nostell Priory and Dunham Massey portraits, Elizabeth's hands do not rest on a parapet, as in most of the others, but hover oddly in front of her, and she wears a simple cord necklace; the Nostell version is three-quarter length, showing a pointed bodice belonging to the later Tudor period, with a gathered skirt beneath; but we can see from the Holbein mural that Elizabeth's gown would actually have had a corded belt at waist level. The portrait at Hever Castle, said to date from *c.*1590 (although the style of painting, the lettering, and the oval inset suggest it is later), is inscribed *Elizabet Mater Henericus 8*, and shows her wearing a simple string of pearls.

Another slightly different version of the standard portrait, acquired by the art historian Philip Mould, was originally in the collection of the earls of Essex at Cassiobury Park (demolished 1927). Dating from the late sixteenth century, it probably once formed part of a long-gallery set, and shows Elizabeth in a looser gown with a much higher neck against a background of green damask. Several engravings derive from this portrait. The Hatfield portrait, in which the Queen wears a different jewelled collar of roses and knots, bears the date '1500' but was probably painted in the early seventeenth century, when it was first recorded in Robert Cecil's new house, built in 1611. It too has a green damask background, but darker than in the Cassiobury portrait.[22]

Elizabeth appears posthumously in a wood-panel painting in the Royal Collection at Windsor.[23] It was commissioned by Henry VII from an unknown Flemish painter around 1503–5, and depicts the King, the Queen and their children at prayer before England's patron saint, St George, who is vanquishing the dragon. In the background is the rescued princess, leading a lamb symbolising peace – the peace Henry Tudor had brought to England. St George appears as the family's protector, who will make suit to God to watch over this righteous king and his dynasty. The picture was almost certainly intended to emphasise the royal family's devotion to St George, whose cult Henry VII keenly promoted.

The King and Queen wear imperial crowns of the type adopted by Henry V, their children coronets. Henry's may be the new crown set with many precious stones that he had commissioned for the Feast of the Epiphany in 1488;[24] Elizabeth's crown sits on top of her hood. She kneels before a desk draped in rich cloth of gold patterned with red roses, and wears a long-lappeted gable hood of black velvet or silk and crimson robes of estate embellished with ermine, her daughters being attired in the same style. Behind the figures are canopies and royal tents decorated with the Tudor rose and the Beaufort portcullis. We know that this is a posthumous portrait of Elizabeth because all four of her children who had died young are included. In keeping with the artistic practice of those days, they are portrayed as children rather than infants – as if they were growing up in Heaven.[25]

Some of the figures may be likenesses. For example, Henry VII and Arthur are shown with straightish, lank hair, but Prince Henry has luxuriant curls and the high, hooked nose we see in later portraits. Henry VII's is an idealised representation. The likenesses of Arthur and Elizabeth were done from memory, and probably not very accurately. Those of Edmund, the younger Elizabeth and Katherine, all of whom died in infancy, are imaginary. Margaret and Mary are just recognisable.

Horace Walpole, who owned the picture in the eighteenth century, and published an engraving in his book, *Anecdotes of Painting in England*, incorrectly described it as Henry V and his family, but he was probably correct in claiming that it was a votive altarpiece, possibly commissioned by Henry VII for St George's Chapel, Windsor, or for the chapel royal at Richmond Palace. The earliest record of it is the engraver George Vertue's description *c.*1726, when it was at Tart Hall, St James's, London, in the collection of William Stafford, Earl of Stafford; it may have been one of the pictures that had come down to Stafford from Thomas Howard, Earl of Arundel, who had owned the Howard letter, another artefact connected with Elizabeth of York.[26]

At Syon House, Isleworth, there is a painting on canvas of Elizabeth and her daughters that derives from the St George altarpiece, although the costume and jewellery are different and the figures have a more realistic quality. Syon House also has a companion panel of the King and his sons. These are perhaps nineteenth-century copies of two lost panel paintings based on the figures in the altarpiece, last seen in 1863 when they were owned by Sir John Stephen Barrington Simeon of the Isle of Wight.[27] Again Elizabeth wears her beautiful imperial crown and the traditional robes of estate – a gown, high-necked surcoat with a furred stomacher, and a long mantle – the design of which dated from the fourteenth century. The background is a plain hanging, studded with Tudor roses and surmounted by banners bearing roses and portcullises.

A similar depiction of Henry and Elizabeth appears in an illuminated manuscript, 'The Ordinances of the Confraternity of the Immaculate Conception', and is dated 1503, the year the Confraternity was established in London; its ordinances were drawn up on 22 March.[28] It shows the King and Queen with their seven children, kneeling before the Immaculate Conception, represented by the figures of Joachim and Anna at the place where, according to medieval belief, they conceived the Virgin Mary – the Golden Gate of Heaven (which looks remarkably like a Beaufort portcullis). Again, this is a posthumous image of Elizabeth (her death is mentioned in the text), portraying her four infants who died young, who again are shown as grown children. Little attempt at accurate portraiture has been made.

Two carved wooden medallions in the window recess of the dining room of Haddon Hall in Derbyshire are possibly portraits of Henry VII and Elizabeth dating from *c.*1500, although it has also been suggested that they depict the then owner, Sir Henry Vernon, and his wife. Elizabeth's eldest son, Prince Arthur, stayed at Haddon Hall in 1501 as the guest of Sir Henry Vernon, his governor and treasurer.

A tiny sculpted figure of Elizabeth, encircled by a Tudor rose and surmounted by a crown, is to be seen in the south-west corner of the Antechapel of King's College Chapel, Cambridge; it is one of many early Tudor royal emblems decorating the chapel. Founded by Henry VI in 1446, the building was completed after 1508 by Henry VII and Henry VIII as a fitting memorial to their revered royal ancestor.

The Sudbury Hutch, a contemporary cupboard chest made *c.*1500 and named after retired vicar Thomas Sudbury, who presented it in 1503 to St James's Church, Louth, Lincolnshire (where it still reposes), bears carved medallions of Henry and Elizabeth, with a crowned Tudor rose between them. The arches surmounting the medallions are early examples of Renaissance carving in England. Elizabeth is portrayed in an open-arched crown with her hair loose; Henry wears an imperial (closed) crown.[29]

The full-length, stained-glass figures of Henry VII and Elizabeth of York appear, surrounded by Tudor heraldic symbols, in the east window of the chancel of St Nicholas's Church, Stanford-on-Avon, Northamptonshire, which dates from *c.*1537–40. Beneath the Queen is the label 'Elizabetha R.'. In the background the royal motto '*Dieu et mon droit*' appears in diagonals on a gold ground. The figures derive from Holbein's Whitehall mural. The window was at Stanford Hall until the 1880s, and it has been suggested that it was originally commissioned by Henry VIII for one of his palaces, and that there may have been other panels showing Henry VIII and Jane Seymour.[30] In support of that theory, the church organ in St Nicholas's is said by some sources to have been the one made in 1630 for the Chapel Royal of Whitehall Palace, which was removed by Oliver Cromwell and came into the possession of the Cave family, who had owned Stanford Hall since 1430; other sources claim that the organ came from Magdalen College, Oxford. Possibly the Caves acquired the glass panels from the palace; as has been noted, they owned a portrait of Elizabeth of York.

A full-length oil panel of Elizabeth in the Princes' Chamber in the Palace of Westminster was executed by Richard Burchett between 1854 and 1860; it too derives from the Holbein mural. A miniature portrait in the Royal Collection by William Essex is dated 1844, and is based – according to the artist – on the portrait at Hatfield House, but its similarity to RC 403447 is marked. A fanciful nineteenth-century portrait of Elizabeth by Edward Penstone was auctioned at Aylsham, Norfolk, in 2010.

Elizabeth appears in Victorian stained-glass windows in the Lady Chapel of Winchester Cathedral and Cardiff Castle.

It is sometimes said that the Queen in the historic tapestry dating from *c.*1500 in St Mary's Guildhall, Coventry, is Margaret of Anjou, and that the tapestry depicts her with Henry VI and their court, which was established at Coventry for three years in the 1450s. But it is possible that it is meant to show Henry VII and Elizabeth of York, who were admitted to the guild of the Holy Trinity in 1500. The tapestry was woven in Flanders around that time, and the costume and imagery give a vivid impression of the sumptuous attire of a queen of Elizabeth's time and her attendants. This is not a portrait, but the figure of Elizabeth (or Margaret), who kneels at a prie-dieu, wears a gorgeous gown of cloth of gold figured with red, a heavy collar and chain, and a shorter Flemish hood of red velvet topped with a fitted coronet.

Appendix II

Elizabeth of York's Ladies and Gentlewomen

Elizabeth's ladies and gentlewomen are listed below in alphabetical order. The records, however, are incomplete. Much of the inform-ation comes from Elizabeth's privy purse expenses of 1502–3; the rest, which is often of a fragmentary nature, has been pieced together from other sources.

Elizabeth Baptiste was in service in 1503.[1]

Frances Baptiste, who must have been related, was paid £2.13s.4d. (£1,300) in 1500, and was still in service in 1503.[2]

Margaret Belknap (d.1513), wife of John Boteler, was in service in 1503.[3]

Margaret Bone was in service in 1503.[4]

Mary Brandon (c.1466–c.1529), wife to John Reading, was sister to Sir William Brandon, Henry VII's standard-bearer, who had died defending the King at Bosworth. She later transferred to the house-hold of Elizabeth's son, the future Henry VIII, and in 1515 was granted an annuity of £50 for her service to Elizabeth of York and her daughter, Princess Mary.[5]

Elyn Brent, one of Elizabeth's gentlewomen, was probably the wife of Robert Brent, gentleman usher of the Queen's chamber, and was in service in 1502–3.[6]

Anne Browne, sister to Sir Anthony Browne (and later the first wife of Charles Brandon, Duke of Suffolk, who divorced her), was appointed a maid of honour at Michaelmas 1502, receiving the lowly salary of just £5 (£2,400) a year.[7]

Anne Buckenham was one of the Queen's gentlewomen in 1502.[8]

Elizabeth, wife of John Burton, was perhaps sister-in-law to Edmund Burton, a yeoman of the Queen's chamber; Henry VIII later bestowed on her an annuity of 20 marks (£2,350) in recognition of her good service.[9]

Elizabeth Catesby (c.1438–1514), wife of Roger Wake, was the sister of Richard III's adviser, Sir William Catesby, who was executed after Bosworth. She was in Elizabeth's household in 1503,[10] and later transferred to that of Princess Mary. In 1514 Henry VIII, describing her as his kinswoman, awarded her a pension for good service to his mother and sister.[11]

Elizabeth, wife of Edward Chamber of Dorset, went on to serve her mistress's daughter, Princess Mary. Henry VIII rewarded her with an annuity of £20 (£7,600) in 1515.[12]

Anne Crowmer (or Cromer) (c.1470–after 1520) received £10 (£5,000) in 1503,[13] by which time she had been appointed governess to Elizabeth's daughters and lady mistress of the royal nursery. Anne may have been the daughter of Sir James Crowmer who married William Whettenhall, Sheriff of Kent, in 1489.[14] A William Crowmer was one of the Queen's gentleman ushers and a servitor of the King; Elizabeth gave money to his daughter, a nun at the Minories, Aldgate.[15]

Margaret Ellerbeck married William Tendring around 1500, and later served Katherine of Aragon.

Elizabeth Fitzherbert was in service in 1503.[16]

Nothing is known of Margaret Gough apart from her name. She was perhaps related to Lewis Gough, the Queen's footman.

Anne Green (c.1489–1523) was another gentlewoman of honour. The daughter of Sir Thomas Green, she was an aunt of Katherine Parr, Henry VIII's sixth wife.

Anne Hubbard (b. c.1435), gentlewoman to Elizabeth and Margaret Beaufort, was rewarded in 1515 by Henry VIII with an annuity of 100s. (£2,000) for her good service.[17]

Elizabeth Hubbard is another attendant about whom nothing is known. She may have been a member of the Hobart family of Norfolk, Hubbard being a variation of their name.

Katherine Hussey (c.1461–1508) was the wife of the King's trusted adviser, Sir Reginald Bray, and almost certainly owed her position to his standing at court. A friend of the humanist John Colet, Dean of St Paul's, she had served Margaret Beaufort before joining Elizabeth's household, and she and her husband continued to maintain lodgings at Coldharbour, Margaret's London house. She was buried with Reginald in St George's Chapel, Windsor.[18]

Elizabeth Jerningham (d.c.1518), who served as Elizabeth's wardrobe keeper, was the wife of John Denton, of whom nothing is known. In July 1486, 'by the King's commandment, by the hands of Elizabeth Denton', £90 (£44,000) was delivered to the Queen.[19] In 1496 she became lady mistress of the nursery of Prince Henry. She received £20 (£10,000) in 1503,[20] and in 1515 was granted a pension of £50 per annum for 'service to the late King and Queen'.

Eleanor Johns, or Jones, was in service in 1502–3.[21]

Elizabeth Lee was also in service in 1502–3.[22]

Anne Neville (1468–after 1525) was probably the daughter of Ralph Neville, 3rd Earl of Westmorland, and married William, Lord Conyers, before 1498.[23]

Lady Anne Percy (before 1485–1552), who joined Elizabeth's household around 1495–6,[24] was the daughter of the 4th Earl of Northumberland, and was to marry William FitzAlan, Lord Maltravers, in 1510. She was lady-in-waiting to Elizabeth, and later served Princess Mary. Henry VII once gave her two gowns, a kirtle, a bonnet, a doublet and other items, valuable and costly additions to her wardrobe.[25]

Eleanor Pole, the wife of Sir Ralph Verney, was one of Elizabeth's favourite ladies. She was the daughter of Geoffrey Pole by Edith St John, and therefore Margaret Beaufort's half-sister. Later, she would serve Katherine of Aragon.[26] Henry VIII awarded her a pension for good service to his mother.[27]

Jane Popincourt – who was later to be at the centre of a scandal at the French court, thanks to her affair with a married royal duke – served in Elizabeth's household. She came from the nursery household at Eltham, where she was in post from at least 1500, when she had been provided with a black gown after the death of Prince Edmund. Elizabeth paid 8d. (£20) for repairs to Jane's gowns in 1502.[28] By then she was Princess Mary's maid. Possibly she had been engaged to help look after Princess Mary from infancy; certainly she taught her French. Later still Jane served Katherine of Aragon. There is no good evidence to substantiate modern assertions that she was an early mistress of Henry VIII.

Eleanor Ratcliffe (d.1518), who may have attended Elizabeth before her marriage, and was perhaps the 'Mrs Ratcliffe' later recorded in Margaret Beaufort's household, later married the Chancellor of the Exchequer, Sir Thomas Lovell of Elsynge Manor, Enfield, a house much visited by Henry VII.[29]

Mary Ratcliffe's salary in 1503 was £10 (£4,860).[30]

Mary Reading, gentlewoman, received a substantial annuity of £50 (£18,980) in 1515 from Henry VIII in gratitude for her service to Elizabeth, which must have been sterling to deserve such a lavish reward.[31]

Mary Roos (d. after 1540), granddaughter of Thomas, 9th Lord Roos of Hamlake, was closely related to Margaret Beaufort. Her brother, Thomas Roos, a staunch Lancastrian, had been beheaded in 1464. She married Hugh Denys, a prominent courtier and administrator of the Privy Chamber, and later served Katherine of Aragon. In 1496 Henry VII granted her an annuity of 40 marks (£1,050), which Henry VIII was still paying her in 1540.[32]

Anne Sandys married Richard Weston around 1502. He was also in Elizabeth's service and served the King as groom of the Privy Chamber. He was knighted in 1518. Their son, Francis Weston, would be executed in 1536 for adultery with Henry VIII's second queen, Anne Boleyn. Mrs Weston was in service in 1503.[33] Richard Weston was often involved in transactions between Henry and Elizabeth, once defraying her expenditure of £100 (£48,600) on 'Venice gold' for a gown for the King.[34]

Elizabeth Saxby ('Mrs Saxilby') had married into an old Lincolnshire family. She later served Princess Mary.[35] In 1514, when she is described as a widow, Henry VIII rewarded her with a pension of £20 (£9,680) for her services to his mother, father and sister.[36]

Anne Say was a gentlewoman to the Queen in 1502; when she fell ill at Woodstock during a progress, Elizabeth paid for her to be boarded out at Abingdon for several weeks until she recovered.[37]

Katherine (d. 1505), daughter of Lord Scales and wife of firstly Sir Thomas Grey, and secondly Sir Richard Lewkenor, was lady-in-waiting in succession to her kinswomen Elizabeth Wydeville and Elizabeth of York.[38]

Elizabeth Scrope (d. 1544) married Sir John Pechey around 1500. She was in service in 1503.[39] Henry VIII awarded her a pension for good service to his mother.[40]

Alice Skelling was in service in 1503 and received £5 (£2,400) per annum.[41]

Joan Steward was granted an annuity of £20 (£9,700) in 1511 by Henry VIII in consideration of her good service to his mother.[42]

Jane Vaux (*c.*1465–1538) had previously served Margaret Beaufort, and, before 1499, was appointed governess to Elizabeth's daughters.[43] The King and Queen attended her wedding to Sir Richard Guildford, Comptroller of Henry VII's household, before 1489. Henry VIII awarded her a pension for good service to his mother.[44]

Katherine Vaux (neé Peniston) (d. after 1509) was the mother of Jane Vaux, She had been lady-in-waiting to Margaret of Anjou from at least 1452, and was imprisoned with her in 1471 after the Battle of Tewkesbury, in which her husband, William Vaux, was killed. She returned to France with Margaret in 1476, and on the latter's death in 1482 she came back to England. Henry VII reversed the attainder on William Vaux, paving the way for Katherine to enter Elizabeth's service. She was present at the christening of Prince Arthur in 1486 and at Elizabeth's coronation.[45] Henry VIII awarded her a pension for good service to his mother.[46]

He did the same for Dorothy Verney.[47]

Anne Weston, sister-in-law of Anne Sandys, married Sir Ralph Verney around 1507–9. She features many times in the Queen's privy purse expenses for 1502–3, and was clearly a prominent member of Elizabeth's household. Her salary in March 1503 was £20 (£9,700).[48]

Margaret Wheathill (d. after 1518) was the wife of John Ratcliffe, Lord FitzWalter, and remained in Elizabeth's household even after her husband was beheaded in 1496 for his involvement in Perkin Warbeck's conspiracy.[49]

Margaret Wotton (1487–1541) seems to have been in attendance as a 'gentlewoman of honour' on a part-time basis, as in 1503 she received £2 (£970) for six months' service.[50] Her mother was Anne Belknap, sister of Margaret Belknap, who was also in Elizabeth's service. In 1509, Margaret Wotton would marry Elizabeth's nephew, Henry Grey, Marquess of Dorset.

Select Bibliography

Primary Sources

Abell, Adam: The riot or quheill of tyme (National Library of Scotland, Edinburgh, N.L.S. MS. 1746; ed. Stephanie Malone Thorson, PhD. thesis, University of St Andrews, 1998)

Acts of Court of the Mercers' Company, 1453–1527 (ed. L. Lyell and F.D. Watney, Cambridge, 1936)

Additional MSS (The British Library)

André, Bernard: *Hymi Christiani Bernardae Andreae poetae Regii* (Paris, 1517)

André, Bernard: 'Vita Henrici VII' (in *Memorials of King Henry VII*, ed. James Gairdner, Rolls Series, 1858; published as *The Life of Henry VII*, trans. and introd. by Daniel Hobbins, New York, 2011)

The Annals of Ulster (ed. B. MacCarthy, Dublin, 1895)

Anthology of Catholic Poets (compiled Shane Leslie, New York, 1926)

The Antiquarian Repertory: A Miscellany, intended to Preserve and Illustrate Several Valuable remains of Old Times (4 vols., ed. F. Grose and T. Astle, London, 1775–84, 1808)

Archaeologia, or Miscellaneous Tracts relating to Antiquity (102 vols., Society of Antiquaries of London, 1777–1969)

Articles ordained by King Henry VII for the Regulation of his Household, A.D. 1494 (British Library Harleian MS. 642, ff. 198–217)

Arundel MSS (The British Library)

The Babees' Book: Medieval Manners for the Young (trans. Edith Rickert and L.J. Naylor, Cambridge, Ontario, 2000)

Bacon, Sir Francis: *The History of the Reign of King Henry VII* (London, 1622; ed. Brian Vickers, Cambridge, 1998)

Balliol College Oxford MS. 354

The Beaufort Hours (B.L. Royal MSS 2A XVIII)

Bernaldez, Andres: *Historia de las Reyes Catolicos* (ed. J.M. Geofrin, Seville, 1870)

Bishop Percy's Folio Manuscript. Ballads and Romances (3 vols., ed. J.W. Hales and F.J. Furnivall, London, 1868)

Bodleian MSS (Bodleian Library, Oxford)

The Book of the Fraternity of Corpus Christi (Guildhall Library, London)

The Book of Howth (Carew MSS, Library of the Royal Irish Academy, Dublin)

Boucq, Jacques le: Le Receuil d'Arras (Bibliothèque Municipale, Arras)

British Library Harleian Manuscript 433 (4 vols., ed. Rosemary Horrox and P.W. Hammond, Upminster and London, 1979–83)

Buck, Sir George: *History of the Life and Reign of Richard III* (B.L. Cotton MS. Tiberius, E.X; 5 vols., ed. George Buck, nephew of the author, London, 1646; reprinted in *A Complete History of England, Vol. V*, ed. White Kennett, London, 1719; ed. as *The History of King Richard the Third by Sir George Buck, Master of the Revels* by A.N. Kincaid, Stroud, 1979, revised 1982)

Calendar of the Cecil Papers at Hatfield House, Vol. I: 1306–1571 (Historical Manuscripts Commission, 1883; (www.british-history.ac.uk)

Calendar of Close Rolls: Edward IV (www.british-history.ac.uk)

Calendar of Documents relating to Scotland, 1357–1509, Vol. 4 (ed. Joseph Bain, Edinburgh, 1888)

Calendar of Letters, Despatches and State Papers relating to Negotiations between England and Spain, preserved in the Archives at Simancas and Elsewhere (17 vols., ed. G.A. Bergenroth, P. de Goyangos, Garrett Mattingley, R. Tyler et al., H.M.S.O., London, 1862–1965)

Calendar of Papal Registers relating to Great Britain and Ireland (ed. W.H. Bliss, London, 1893)

Calendar of Patent Rolls: Edward IV: 1461–1467 (H.M.S.O., London, 1897)

Calendar of Patent Rolls: Edward IV: 1467–1477 (H.M.S.O., London, 1899)

Calendar of Patent Rolls: Edward IV, Edward V, Richard III: 1476–1485 (H.M.S.O., London, 1901)

Calendar of Patent Rolls: Henry VII: 1485–1509 (2 vols., H.M.S.O., London, 1914–16)

Calendar of State Papers and Manuscripts existing in the Archives and Collections of Milan, Vol. I, 1385–1618 (ed. Allen B. Hinds, London, 1912)

Calendar of State Papers and Manuscripts relating to English Affairs preserved in the Archives of Venice and in the other Libraries of Northern Italy

(7 vols., ed. L. Rawdon-Brown, Cavendish Bentinck *et al.*, H.M.S.O., London, 1864–1947)

Cambridge University Library Dd. 13.27

Camden, William: *Britannia* (London, 1588, 1607)

Capgrave, John: *The Book of the Illustrious Henries* (ed. F.C. Hingeston, London, 1858)

Caxton, William: *Caxton's Blanchardyn and Eglantine, c. 1489 : from Lord Spencer's unique imperfect copy, completed by the original French and the second English version of 1595* (ed. Leon Kellner, Ann Arbor, Michigan, 1997)

The Cely Letters, 1472–1488 (ed. Alison Hanham, Early English Texts Society, Oxford, 1875)

Cessolis, Jacobus de: *The Game and Play of the Chess* (William Caxton, Bruges, 1474; ed. W.E.A. Axon, St Leonards-on-Sea, 1967)

Chamber Receipts (E.101) (The National Archives)

Chapter Records XXIII to XXVI (The Chapter Library, St George's Chapel, Windsor; Chapel Archives and Chapter Library at www. stgeorges-windsor.org/archives

Charter Rolls (C.53) (The National Archives)

Christ Church Oxford MSS

The Chronicle of Calais in the Reigns of Henry VII and Henry VIII to the year 1540 (ed. John Gough Nichols, Camden Society, London, 1866)

Chronicle of the Grey Friars of London (ed. John Gough Nichols, Camden Society, Old Series 53, London, 1852)

Chronicles of London (ed. C.L. Kingsford, Oxford, 1905)

Cole MSS (The British Library)

A Collection of all the Wills, now known to be extant, of the Kings and Queens of England (ed. John Nichols, London, 1780)

A Collection of Ordinances and Regulations for the Government of the Royal Household made in Divers Reigns, from King Edward III to King William and Queen Mary (Society of Antiquaries, London, 1790)

College of Arms MSS (The College of Arms, London)

Commines, Philippe de: *Mémoires* (3 vols., ed. J.L.A. Calmette and G. Durville, Paris, 1824–5; trans. and ed. M. Jones, London, 1972)

Cotton MSS (The British Library)

Court Rolls (S.C.2) (The National Archives)

The Croyland Chronicle Continuation, 1459–1486 (ed. N. Pronay and J. Cox, Stroud, 1986; see also *Ingulph's Chronicle of the Abbey of Croyland, with the continuations by Peter of Blois and anonymous writers*, trans. and ed. Henry T. Riley, London, 1954)

Dineley, Thomas: *The Account of the Official Progress of His Grace Henry the first Duke of Beaufort* (1684; ed. Charles Baker, London, 1864)

Documents and objects extracted from the record series in Chancery Lane (EXT 6) (The National Archives)

Dodsworth, Roger, and Dugdale, William: *Monasticum Anglicanum* (2 vols., London, 1655, 1661)

Doort, Abraham van der: A Book of all such the King's Pictures, as are by His Majesty's especial appointment placed at this present time remaining in Whitehall in the several places following (1639–40, Bodleian Library Ashmole MS. 514; published as *Abraham van der Doort's Catalogue of the Collections of Charles I*, ed. Oliver Millar, Walpole Society, 37, Glasgow, 1960)

Dugdale, William: *Monasticon Anglicanum* (3 vols., London, 1693)

Dunbar, William: *Selected Poems* (ed. Harriet Harvey Wood, Manchester, 2003)

Egerton MSS (The British Library)

English Coronation Records (ed. Leopold G.W. Legg, Westminster, 1901)

Erasmus, Desiderius: *The Epistles of Erasmus* (ed. F.M. Nichols, New York, 1962)

Excerpta Historica (ed. S. Bentley and H. Nicolas, 1831)

Exchequer Records: Exchequer of Receipt: Warrants for Issues (E.404) (The National Archives)

Exchequer Records: Issue Rolls (E.403) (The National Archives)

Exchequer Records: King's Remembrancer, Accounts Various (E.101) (The National Archives)

Exchequer Records: King's Treasurer's Accounts (E.404) (The National Archives)

Exeter College MSS (University of Oxford)

Fabyan, Robert: *New Chronicles of England and France* (London, 1515; ed. Henry Ellis, London, 1811)

The Fifteen Oes and Other Prayers (printed by William Caxton, ed. S. Ayling, London, 1869)

Fisher, John: *The Funeral Sermon of Margaret, Countess of Richmond and Derby* (ed. T. Baker and J. Hymers, London, 1840)

Fisher MS. (University of Toronto)

Foedera, Conventiones, Et . . . Acta Publica inter Reges Angliae (ed. Thomas Rymer, London, 1704–17)

Formulare Anglicanum: Or, a Collection of Ancient Charters and Instruments of Divers Kinds, Taken from the Originals (ed. Thomas Madox, London, 1702)

Four English Political Tracts of the Later Middle Ages (ed. J.P. Genet, London, 1977)

Fuensalida, Gutierre Gómez de: *Correspondencia de Gutierre, Gómez de Fuensalida, embajador en Alemania, Flandes e Inglaterra (1496–1509)* *(Madrid, 1907)*

Fuller, Thomas: *History of the Worthies of England* (London, 1662)

Gainsford, Thomas: *The True and Wonderful History of Perkin Warbeck proclaiming himself Richard IV* (London, 1618)

Garrett MS. 168 (Princeton University Library)

Grafton, Richard: *Grafton's Chronicle, or History of England* (London, 1569; 2 vols., London, 1809)

The Great Chronicle of London (ed. A.H. Thomas and I.D. Thornley, Guildhall Library, London, 1938, privately printed)

The Great Wardrobe Accounts of Henry VII and Henry VIII (ed. Maria Hayward, London Record Society, 2012)

'Gregory's Chronicle': *The Historical Collections of a Citizen of London in the Fifteenth Century* (ed. James Gairdner, Camden Society, London, 1876)

Guildhall MSS (Guildhall Library, London)

Hall, Edward: *The Union of the Two Noble and Illustre Families of Lancaster and York* (ed. H. Ellis, London, 1809; published in facsimile 1970)

Halsbury's Laws of England (ed. James, Lord Mackay of Clashfern, London, 1998)

Harington, Sir John: *A New Discourse of a Stale Subject: The Metamorphosis of Ajax* (ed. E.S. Donno, London, 1962)

Harleian MSS (The British Library)

Hawes, Stephen: *A Joyful Meditation of the Coronation of King Henry the Eighth* (1509; Fili-Quarian Classics, 2010)

Hentzner, Paul: *A Journey into England in the Year MDXCVIII* (Strawberry Hill, 1757; reprinted Reading, 1807)

Herbert of Cherbury, Edward, Lord: *The Life and Reign of King Henry VIII* (London, 1649)

Hilton, Walter: *The Scale of Perfection* (ed. J.B. Dalgairns and Harry Plantinga, Oxford, 1995)

Historical Poems of the XIVth and XVth Centuries (ed. Rossell Hope Robbins, New York, 1959)

Historie of the Arrivall of King Edward IV in England and the final Recoverye of his Kingdomes from Henry VI, A.D. 1471 (ed. J. Bruce, Camden Society, London, 1838)

Holinshed, Raphael: *Chronicles of England, Scotland and Ireland* (London, 1577; 6 vols., ed. H. Ellis, London, 1807–8)

The Household of Edward IV: The Black Book and the Ordinance of 1478 (ed. A.R. Myers, Manchester, 1959)

Illustrations of Ancient State and Chivalry from Manuscripts preserved in the Ashmolean Museum (ed. W.H. Black, London, 1839)

Intimate Letters of England's Kings (ed. Margaret Sanders, Stroud, 1959)

King's MSS (The British Library)

Lambard, William: *A Perambulation of Kent* (London, 1576)

Lansdowne MSS (The British Library)

Leland, John: *Antiquarii de Rebus Britannicis Collectanea* (London, 1612; 6 vols., ed. Thomas Hearne, Chetham Society, Oxford, 1715, London, 1770)

Leland, John: *The Itinerary of John Leland, in or about the years 1535 to 1543* (5 vols., ed. Lucy Toulmin Smith, London, 1907–10)

The Letters of King Henry VIII (ed. Muriel St Clair Byrne, New York, 1968)

Letters of the Kings of England (2 vols., ed. J.O. Halliwell-Phillipps, London, 1848)

Letters and Papers, Foreign and Domestic, of the Reign of Henry VIII (21 vols. in 33 parts, ed. J.S. Brewer, James Gairdner, R. Brodie *et al.*, 1862–1932)

Letters and Papers Illustrative of the Reigns of Richard III and Henry VII (2 vols., ed. James Gairdner, London, 1861–3)

Letters of the Queens of England, 1100–1547 (ed. Anne Crawford, Stroud, 1994)

Letters of Royal and Illustrious Ladies of Great Britain (3 vols., ed. Mary Anne Everett Green, London, 1846)

Liber Regie Capelle (*The Book of the Chapel Royal*) (ed. Walter Ullman and Derek Howard Turner, Henry Bradshaw Society, 1961)

Linacre, Thomas: *Sphaira (The Sphere)* (Venice, 1499)

The Lisle Letters (ed. Muriel St Clare Byrne, London, 1983)

Lopes, Alvaro: *Alvaro Lopes de Chaves, Livro de Apontamentos, 1438–1489 códice 443 da colecção Pombalina da B.N.L.* (trans. Anastasia Mestrinho Salgado, Lisbon, 1983)

The Lord Chamberlain's Accounts (LC.9) (The National Archives)

Malory, Sir Thomas: *Le Morte d'Arthur* (ed. Helen Cooper, Oxford, 1998)

Mancini, Dominic: *De Occupatione Regni Anglie per Riccardum Tercium* (trans. and ed. as *The Usurpation of Richard III* by C.A.J. Armstrong, 2nd edition, Oxford, 1969)

Manners and Meals in Olden Time (ed. F.J. Furnivall, Early English Texts Society, 32, 1868)

Marche, Olivier de la: *Mémoires d'Olivier de la Marche* (ed. H. Beaune and J. Arbaumont, Paris, 1883)

Materials for a History of the Reign of Henry the Seventh (2 vols., ed. William Campbell, Rolls Series, London, 1873–7)

Memorials of King Henry VII (ed. James Gairdner, Rolls Series, 1858)

Miscellaneous Books (E.36) (The National Archives)

Molinet, Jean: *Chroniques de Jean Molinet, 1474–1506* (3 vols., ed. G. Doutrepont and O. Jodogne, Académie Royale Belgique, Brussels, 1935–7)

Monstrelet, Enguerran de: *Chroniques d'Enguerran de Monstrelet* (ed. L. Douet d'Arcq, Paris, 1857–62)

More, Sir Thomas: *The Complete Works of Sir Thomas More* (21 vols., ed. C.H. Miller *et al*, New Haven, 1963–97; Vol II contains 'The History of King Richard III', ed. Richard S. Sylvester, 1963; see also *The History of King Richard III/Historia Ricardi Tertius* (c.1513, ed. William Rastell, London, 1557; reprinted London, 2005, and *The History of King Richard the Third*, followed by *The Continuation of the History of Richard III from Grafton's Chronicle*, ed. S.W. Singer, London, 1821)

The Narrative of the Marriage of Richard, Duke of York with Anne of Norfolk, 1477 (ed. W.G. Searle, Cambridge, 1867)

'Narratives of the Arrival of Louis of Bruges, Lord of Gruthuyse' (ed. Sir Frederic Madden, *Archaeologia*, Vol. 26, 1836)

Original Letters Illustrative of English History (11 vols., ed. H. Ellis, London, 1824–46)

Original Letters, written during the reigns of Henry VI. Edward IV, and Richard III, by various persons of rank or consequence: containing many curious anecdotes, relative to that period of our history (5 vols., ed. Sir John Fenn, 1789–1823)

Palgrave, Francis: *The Antient Calendars and Inventories of the Treasury of His Majesty's Exchequer* (3 vols., Records Commissioners, London, 1836)

The Paston Letters, 1422–1509, Vol. VI (ed. James Gairdner, London, 1904); see also *Paston Letters and Papers of the Fifteenth Century* (2 vols., ed. N. Davis, Oxford, 1971–6)

The Plumpton Correspondence (ed. Thomas Stapleton and Keith Dockray, Stroud, 1990)

Political Poems and Songs relating to English History (2 vols., ed. T. Wright, London, 1859–61)

The Politics of Fifteenth-Century England: John Vale's Book (ed. M.L. Kekewich and others, Stroud, 1995)

The Popular Songs of Ireland (ed. Thomas Crofton Croker, London, 1839)

Prerogative Court of Canterbury Wills (PROB) (The National Archives)

The Private Lives of the Tudor Monarchs (ed. Christopher Falkus, London, 1974)

Privy Purse Expenses of Elizabeth of York; Wardrobe Accounts of Edward the Fourth. With a Memoir of Elizabeth of York, and Notes (ed. Nicholas Harris Nicolas, London, 1830)

Rastell, John: *The Pastime of People* (London, 1529)

Rawlinson MSS (The Bodleian Library, Oxford)

Real Academia de Historia MS. 9–4674 (Madrid)

The Receyt of the Lady Katherine (ed. G. Kipling, Early English Texts Society, 1990)

Records of the Borough of Nottingham (ed. W.H. Stevenson, London, 1998)

Records of the Court of King's Bench (KB) (The National Archives)

Records of the Keeper of the Privy Seal: Edward III to Henry VIII (PSO 1) (The National Archives)

Records of the Lord Chamberlain (LC) (The National Archives)

Records of the Skinners of London: Edward I to James I (ed. J.J. Lambert, London, 1933)

The Register of the Most Noble Order of the Garter, from its cover in black velvet usually called The Black Book (ed. John Anstis, London, 1724)

Registrum Thome Bourgchier, Cantuariensis Archiepiscopi, A.D. 1454–1486 (ed. F.R.H. DuBoulay, Canterbury and York Society, Liverpool, 1957)

The Reign of Henry VII from Contemporary Sources (ed. A.F. Pollard, London, 1913–14)

A Relation, or rather a True Account, of the Island of England, about the year 1500 (trans. and ed. Charlotte Augusta Sneyd, Camden Society, London, 1847)

Richard III: The Great Debate: Sir Thomas More's 'History of King Richard III'; Horace Walpole's 'Historic Doubts on the Life and Reign of King Richard III' (ed. Paul Murray Kendall, London, 1965)

Rotuli Parliamentorum (The Rolls of Parliament) (7 vols., ed. J. Strachey and others, Record Commissioners, 1767–83)

Rous, John: *The Rous Roll* (ed. Charles Ross and W. Courthope, Stroud, 1980)

Royal MSS (The British Library)

Roye, Jean de: *Journal de Jean de Roye connu sous le nom Chronique Scandaleuse, 1460–1483* (2 vols., ed. B. de Mandrot, Paris, 1894–6)

The Rutland Papers: Original Documents illustrating the Courts and Times of Henry VII and Henry VIII, selected from the private archives of His Grace the Duke of Rutland (ed. William Jordan, Camden Society, London, 1842)

Sarpi, Paolo: *Istoria del Concilio Tridentino (History of the Council of Trent)* (London, 1619)

Skelton, John: *The Poetical Works of John Skelton* (2 vols., ed. Alexander Dyce, London, 1843)

'The Song of Lady Bessy' (in *Bishop Percy's Folio Manuscript. Ballads and Romances*, (3 vols., ed. J.W. Hales and F.J.Furnivall, London, 1868; the later version was published as *The Most Pleasant Song of Lady Bessy*, ed. Thomas Heywood, London, 1829)

Special Collections (S.C.) (The National Archives)

Speed, John: *The History of Great Britain* (London, 1611)

The Stonor Letters and Papers (2 vols., ed. C.L. Kingsford, Camden Society, London, 1919; ed. Christine Carpenter as *Kingsford's Stonor Letters and Papers, 1290–1483*, Cambridge, 1996)

Stonyhurst MSS. (Stonyhurst College)

Stow, John: *The Annals of England* (1592; ed. C.L. Kingsford, 2 vols., Oxford, 1908)

Stow, John: *A Survey of London* (London, 1598; Stroud, 1994)

Stuart Royal Proclamations (ed. J.F. Larkin and P.L. Hughes, Oxford, 1973)

Tetzel, Gabriel: *The Travels of Leo of Rozmital through Germany, Flanders, England, France, Spain, Portugal and Italy, 1465–1467* (ed. Malcolm Letts, Hakluyt Society, Cambridge, 1957)

Treasurer's Accounts (Register House, Edinburgh)

Tudor Royal Proclamations (ed. P.L. Hughes and J.F. Larkin, New Haven, 1964–9)

The Vaux Passional, Peniarth MS. 482D (National Library of Wales, www.llgc.org.uk)

Vergil, Polydore: *The Anglica Historia of Polydore Vergil, A.D. 1485–1573* (trans. and ed. D. Hay, Camden Series, 1950; for an earlier edition of part of this work see *Three Books of Polydore Vergil's English History: Comprising the Reigns of Henry VI, Edward IV and Richard III*, ed. H. Ellis, Camden Society, London, 1844)

Vetusta Monumenta Vol. III (London, 1789)

The Voice of the Middle Ages in Personal Letters, 1100–1500 (ed. Catherine Moriarty, London, 1989)

Warkworth, John: *A Chronicle of the First Thirteen Years of the Reign of King Edward the Fourth* (ed. J.O. Halliwell, Camden Society, London, 1839)

Warrants for Issues (E.404) (The National Archives)

Waurin, Jean de: *Receuil des Chroniques et Anchiennes Istories de la Grant*

Bretagne, a present nomme Engleterre (5 vols., ed. Sir William Hardy and E.L.C.P. Hardy, Rolls Series, London, 1864–91)

Weinreich, Caspar: *Caspar Weinreichs Danziger Chronik, ein Beitrag zur Geschichte Danzigs, der Lande Preussen und Polen, des Hansabundes und der Nordischen Reiche* (ed. Theodor Hirsch and F.A. Vossberg, Berlin, 1855, reprinted 1973)

Westminster Abbey Muniments

Wills from Doctors' Commons: A Selection from the Wills of Eminent Persons proved in the Prerogative Court of Canterbury, 1495–1695 (ed. John Nichols and John Bruce, Camden Society, London, 1863)

Worcester, William: *Annales rerum Anglicarum* (in *Letters and Papers Illustrative of the Wars of the English in France during the Reign of Henry the Sixth*, 2 vols., ed. J. Stevenson, Rolls Series, London, 1860–1)

Wriothesley, Charles: *A Chronicle of England during the Reigns of the Tudors, from A.D. 1485 to 1559, Vol. 1* (ed. William Douglas Hamilton, Camden Society, London, 1875)

York Civic Records, Vols. I and II (ed. Angelo Raine, Yorkshire Archaeological Society, Record Series CIII, 1939–41)

Secondary Sources

Adair, John: *The Royal Palaces of Britain* (London, 1981)

Alberge, Dalya: 'Found in a castle vault, the scraps of lace that show lingerie was all the rage 500 years ago' (*Daily Mail*, 17 July 2012)

Anglo, Sydney: 'The Court Festivals of Henry VII: A study based upon the account books of John Heron, Treasurer of the Chamber' (*Bulletin of the John Rylands Library*, 43, 1960–1)

Anglo, Sydney: *Images of Tudor Kingship* (London, 1992)

Anglo, Sydney: *Spectacle, Pageantry and Early Tudor Policy* (Oxford, 1969, revised 1997)

Arch, Nigel, and Marschner, Joanna: *The Royal Wedding Dresses* (London, 1990)

Arthur Tudor, Prince of Wales: Life, Death and Commemoration (ed. Steven Gunn and Linda Monckton, Woodbridge, 2009)

Arthurson, Ian: *The Perkin Warbeck Conspiracy, 1491–1499* (Stroud, 1994)

Ashdown, Dulcie M.: *Princess of Wales* (London, 1979)

Ashdown, Dulcie M.: *Royal Children* (London, 1979)

Ashdown, Dulcie M.: *Royal Weddings* (London, 1981)

Ashdown-Hill, John: *Eleanor, the Secret Queen* (Stroud, 2009)

Ashdown-Hill, John: 'The Fate of Edward IV's Uncrowned Queen, the Lady Eleanor Talbot, Lady Butler' (*The Ricardian*, 2, 1997)

Ashdown-Hill, John: *The Fate of Richard III's Body* (www.bbc.co.uk/legacies/myths_legends/england/leicester/article_1.shtml)

Ashdown-Hill, John: *The Last Days of Richard III* (Stroud, 2010)

Ashdown-Hill, John: *Richard III's 'Beloved Cousyn': John Howard and the House of York* (Stroud, 2009)

Ashelford, Jane: *The Art of Dress: Clothes and Society 1500–1914* (The National Trust, London, 1996)

Ashley, Mike: *British Monarchs* (London, 1998)

Aslet, Clive: *The Story of Greenwich* (London, 1999)

Astle, T.: *The Will of King Henry VII* (London, 1775)

'Astonishing Portrait of the future Henry VIII at 11 found at Aberystwyth' (*Wales Online*, 18 October 2012, www.walesonline.co.uk)

Auerbach, Erna, and Adams, C. Kingsley: *Paintings and Sculpture at Hatfield House* (London, 1971)

Backhouse, Janet: 'Illuminated Manuscripts Associated with Henry VII and Members of his Immediate Family' (in *The Reign of Henry VII: Proceedings of the 1993 Harlaxton Symposium*, ed. Benjamin Thompson, Stamford, 1995)

Backhouse, Janet: *The Illuminated Page: Ten Centuries of Manuscript Painting in the British Library* (London, 1997)

Baldwin, David: *Elizabeth Woodville: Mother of the Princes in the Tower* (Stroud, 2002)

Baldwin, David: 'Elizabeth Woodville' (in *The Women of the Cousins' War*, London, 2011)

Baldwin, David: *The Kingmaker's Sisters* (Stroud, 2009)

Baldwin, David: *King Richard's Grave in Leicester* (www.le.ac.uk/lahs/downloads/BaldwinSmPagesfromvolumeLX-5.pdf)

Baldwin, David: *The Lost Prince: The Survival of Richard of York* (Stroud, 2007)

Baldwin, David: *Richard III* (Stroud, 2012)

Beauclerk-Dewar, Peter, and Powell, Roger: *Right Royal Bastards: The Fruits of Passion* (Burke's Peerage, 2006)

Bell, Michelle: *The Effects of Prematurity on Development* (www.prematurity.org)

Benham, H.: 'Prince Arthur (1486–1502), a Carol and a *Cantus Firmus*' (*Early Music*, 15, 1987)

Bennett, Michael: *The Battle of Bosworth* (Stroud, 1985, 2008)

Bevan, Bryan: *Henry VII: The First Tudor King* (London, 2000)

Billson, Charles James: *Medieval Leicester* (Leicester, 1920)

Black, Ira J.: A Study of Changing Historiographical Trends as illustrated in the Chronicles of Crowland Abbey (unpublished M.A. thesis, Ohio State University, 1965)

Body Parts and Bodies: Whole Changing Relations and Meanings (ed. Katharina Rebay-Salisbury, Marie Louise Stig Sørensen and Jessica Hughes, Oxford, 2010)

Bradley, E.T., and Bradley, M.C.: *Westminster Abbey* (London, 1953)

Bramley, Peter: *A Companion and Guide to the Wars of the Roses* (Stroud, 2007)

Brenan, Gerald, and Stratham, Edward Phillips: *The House of Howard* (2 vols., London, 1907)

Brigden, Susan: *New Worlds, Lost Worlds: The Rule of the Tudors, 1485–1603* (London, 2000)

Brook, Roy: *The Story of Eltham Palace* (London, 1960)

Brooke, Xanthe, and Crombie, David: *Henry VIII Revealed: Holbein's Portrait and its Legacy* (London, 2003)

Bruce, Marie Louise: *The Making of Henry VIII* (London, 1977)

Brysson-Morrison, N.: *The Private Life of Henry VIII* (London, 1964)

Buchanan, Patricia: *Margaret Tudor, Queen of Scots* (Edinburgh, 1985)

Buck, Stephanie, and Sander, Jochen: *Hans Holbein the Younger: Painter at the Court of Henry VIII* (London, 2003)

Buckland, Kirstie: 'The Skenfrith Cope and its Companion' (*Textile History*, 14, 1983)

Burton, Elizabeth: *The Early Tudors at Home, 1485–1558* (London, 1976)

Cannon, John, and Griffiths, Ralph: *The Oxford Illustrated History of the British Monarchy* (Oxford, 1988)

Cannon, John, and Hargreaves, Anne: *The Kings and Queens of Britain* (Oxford, 2001)

Carlson, D.: 'The Occasional Poetry of Pietro Carmeliano' (*Aevum*, 61,1987)

Carlton, Charles: *Royal Childhoods* (London, 1986)

Carson, Annette: *Richard III: The Maligned King* (Stroud, 2008)

Carte, Thomas: *A General History of England, Vol. 2* (London, 1750)

Catalogue of Illuminated Manuscripts (The British Library; www.bl.uk)

Catalogue of Western Manuscripts and Miniatures (Sotheby's, 1983)

The Catholic Encyclopaedia (www.oce.catholic.com)

The Caxton Project (www.citynet.net)

Challis, C.E.: *The Tudor Coinage* (Manchester, 1978)

Chambers, Raymond Wilson: *The Place of Saint Thomas More in English Literature and History* (London, 1937)

Chapman, Hester W.: *The Sisters of Henry VIII* (London, 1969)

Cheetham, Anthony: *The Life and Times of Richard III* (London, 1972)

Cheung, Vincent C.K.: 'Tudor Dedications to the Blessed Virgin: History, Style, and Analysis of Music from the Eton Choirbook' (2008, http://web.mit.edu/ckcheung)

Chrimes, S.B.: *Henry VII* (London, 1972)

Chronicle of the Royal Family (ed. Derrik Mercer, London, 1991)

Chronicles of the Tudor Kings (ed. David Loades, London, 1990)

The Chronicles of the Wars of the Roses (ed. Elizabeth Hallam, London, 1988)

The Church in Pre-Reformation Society (ed. C.M. Barron and C. Harper-Bill, Woodbridge, 1985)

City and Spectacle in Medieval Europe (ed. B.A. Hanawalt and K.L. Reyerson, Minneapolis, 1994)

Claremont, Francesca: *Catherine of Aragon* (London, 1939)

Clarke, Edward T.: *Bermondsey: Its Historic Memories and Associations* (London, 1902)

Clarke, Peter D.: 'English Royal Marriages and the Papal Penitentiary in the Fifteenth Century' (*English Historical Review*, 120, 2005)

Cleary, Brian: *Haddon Hall* (Wymondham, 2009)

Clive, Mary: *This Sun of York: A Biography of Edward IV* (London, 1973)

Cloake, John: *Palaces and Parks of Richmond and Kew* (Chichester, 1995)

Cloake, John: *Richmond Palace: Its History and its Plan* (Richmond Local History Society, 2001)

Cloake, John: 'Richmond's Great Monastery, The Charterhouse of Jesus of Bethlehem of Shene' (*Richmond Local History Society*, 6, 1990)

Cobbett, William: *Parliamentary History of England, from the Norman conquest in 1066 to the year 1803, Vol. II* (London, 1812)

Cokayne, George Edward: *The Complete Peerage* (8 vols., London, 1887–98; 13 vols., ed. Vicary Gibbs, H.A. Doubleday, Duncan Warrand, Lord Howard de Walden, Geoffrey H. White and R.S. Lea, 1910–59; microprint edition, 6 vols., with addenda and corrigenda by Peter Hammond, Stroud, 1982)

Cole, Hubert: *The Wars of the Roses* (London, 1973)

Cook, Petronelle: *Queen Consorts of England: The Power Behind the Throne* (New York, 1993)

Cooper, C.H.: *Memoir of Margaret, Countess of Richmond and Derby* (London, 1874)

Coulson, Ian: The Paradise State Bed (unpublished article of November 2012, sent to the author)

Cowie, L.W.: 'The Wedding of Prince Arthur and Katherine of Aragon' (*History Today*, November 2001)

Cracknell, Eleanor (Assistant Archivist): *The Princes in the Tower?* (Chapel Archives and Chapter Library, 2012, www.stgeorges-windsor.org)

Crawford, Anne: 'The King's Burden? The Consequences of Royal Marriage in Fifteenth-Century England' (in *Patronage, the Crown and the Provinces in Later Medieval England*, ed. Ralph A. Griffiths, Gloucester, 1981)

Crawford, Anne: 'The Piety of Late-Medieval English Queens' (in *The Church in Pre-Reformation Society*, ed. C.M. Barron and C. Harper-Bill, Woodbridge, 1985)

Crawford, Anne: 'The Queen's Council in the Middle Ages' (*English Historical Review*, vol. 116, 469, 2001)

Crawford, Anne: *The Yorkists: The History of a Dynasty* (London, 2007)

Cressy, David: 'Purification, Thanksgiving and the Churching of Women' (*Past and Present*, 141, 1993)

Crook, John: *Winchester Cathedral* (Andover, 2001)

Cunningham, Kevin: *The Bubonic Plague* (Edina, Minnesota, 2011)

Cunningham, Sean: *Henry VII* (London, 2007)

Cunningham, Sean: *Richard III: A Royal Enigma* (The National Archives, 2003)

Darracott, Anne: *Great Malvern Priory: Rebuilding of the Quire in the 15th Century* (Maidenhead, 2005, www.maidenheadcivicsociety.org.uk)

Dart, John: *Westmonasterium, or The History and Antiquities of the Abbey Church of St Peter's, Westminster* (2 vols., London, 1723)

Davey, Richard: *The Pageant of London* (2 vols., London, 1906)

Dictionary of National Biography (22 vols., ed. Leslie Stephen and Sidney Lee, Oxford, 1885–1901)

The Digital Index of Middle English Verse, http://www.cddc.vt.edu/host/imev/record.php?recID=1999

Dixon, William Hepworth: *History of Two Queens* (3 vols., Leipzig, 1873)

Dockray, Keith: *Richard III: Myth and Reality* (Bangor, 1992)

Dockray, Keith: *Richard III: A Source Book* (Stroud, 1997)

Dodson, Aidan: *The Royal Tombs of Great Britain: An Illustrated History* (London, 2004)

Doran, Susan: *The Tudor Chronicles* (London, 2008)

Dowle, Margaret: *The King's Mother: Memoir of Margaret Beaufort, Countess of Richmond and Derby* (London, 1899)

Dowsing, James: *Forgotten Tudor Palaces in the London Area* (London, undated)

Drake, Francis: *Eboracum* (York, 1736)

Draper, P.: *The House of Stanley* (Ormskirk, 1864)

Duffy, Eamonn: *The Stripping of the Altars: Traditional Religion in England, 1400–1580* (New Haven, 1992)

Duffy, Mark: *Royal Tombs of Medieval England* (Stroud, 2003)

Dunlop, David: 'The "Masked Comedian": Perkin Warbeck's Adventures in Scotland and England from 1495 to 1497' (*Scottish Historical Review*, vols. 70, 90, Oct. 1991)

Durant, Horatia: *'Sorrowful Captives': The Tudor Earls of Devon* (Pontypool, 1960)

Dutton, Ralph: *English Court Life from Henry VII to George II* (London, 1963)

Dynasties: Painting in Tudor and Jacobean England 1530–1630 (ed. Karen Hearn, Tate Gallery, London, 1995)

Eames, P.: *Furniture in England, France and the Netherlands from the Twelfth to the Fifteenth Century* (London, 1977)

Edwards, J.G.: 'The "Second" Continuation of the Crowland Chronicle' (*Bulletin of the Institute of Historical Research*, 39, 1966)

Edwards, Rhoda: *The Itinerary of King Richard III, 1483–1485* (London, 1983)

Eltham Palace (ed. Kate Jeffrey, London, 1999)

Elton, G.R.: *England under the Tudors* (London, 1955, revised edition 1969)

England in the Fifteenth Century (ed. D. Williams, Woodbridge, 1987)

Erickson, Carolly: *Great Harry* (London, 1980)

Erickson, Carolly: *Royal Panoply: Brief Lives of the English Monarchs* (New York, 2003)

Estrangement, Enterprise and Education in Fifteenth-Century England (ed. S.D. Michalove and A. Compton-Reeves, Stroud, 1998)

Falkus, Gila: *The Life and Times of Edward IV* (London, 1981)

Faraday, M.A.: 'Mortality in the Diocese of Hereford, 1442 to 1541' (*Transactions of the Woolhope Naturalists' Field Club*, 42, 1977)

Field, John: *Kingdom, Power and Glory: A Historical Guide to Westminster Abbey* (London, 1996)

Finch, Barbara Clay: *Lives of the Princesses of Wales* (3 vols., London, 1883)

Fletcher, Benton: *Royal Homes near London* (London, 1930)

Fletcher, John: 'Tree-Ring Dates for Some Panel Paintings in England' (*The Burlington Magazine*, CXVI, 1974)

Foister, Susan: *Holbein in England* (Tate Britain, London, 2006)

Fox, Julia: *Sisters, Queens: Katherine of Aragon and Juana, Queen of Castile* (London, 2011)

Fraser, Antonia: *The Six Wives of Henry VIII* (London, 1992)

Fraser, Antonia: *The Tudors* (London, 2000)

'Friaries: The Dominican nuns of Dartford' (in *A History of the County of Kent: Volume 2*, ed. William Page, *Victoria County Histories*, 1926)

The Funeral Effigies of Westminster Abbey (ed. Anthony Harvey and Richard Mortimer, Woodbridge, 1994)

Gainey, James: *The Princess of the Mary Rose* (East Wittering, 1986)
Gairdner, James: *History of the Life and Reign of Richard III* (Cambridge, 1898)
Gill, Louise: *Richard III and Buckingham's Rebellion* (Stroud, 1999)
Given-Hilson, Chris, and Curteis, Alice: *The Royal Bastards of Medieval England* (London, 1984)
Glasheen, Joan: *The Secret People of the Palaces: The Royal Household from the Plantagenets to Queen Victoria* (London, 1998)
Godfrey, Walter H., and Wagner, Sir Anthony: 'The College of Arms: Historical account to the Great Fire of 1666' (*Survey of London Monograph*, 16, College of Arms, 1963)
Goodall, John: *The English Castle* (Yale, New Haven and London, 2011)
Goodman, Anthony: The Fair Maid's Tale (forthcoming)
Goodman, Anthony: *A History of England from Edward II to James I* (London, 1977)
Goodman, Anthony: *The Wars of the Roses* (London, 1981)
Goodman, Anthony: *The Wars of the Roses: The Soldiers' Experience* (Stroud, 2005)
Gothic: Art for England 1400–1547 (ed. Richard Marks and Paul Williamson, Victoria and Albert Museum, London, 2003)
Green, Mary Anne Everett: *Lives of the Princesses of England from the Norman Conquest* (6 vols., London, 1849–1855)
Griffiths, Ralph A., and Thomas, Roger S.: *The Making of the Tudor Dynasty* (Stroud, 1993)
Gristwood, Sarah: *Blood Sisters: The Hidden Lives of the Women behind the Wars of the Roses* (London, 2012)

Halsted, Caroline Amelia: *Life of Margaret Beaufort, Countess of Richmond and Derby, Mother of Henry the Seventh* (London, 1839)
Halsted, Caroline Amelia: *Richard III* (London, 1844)
Hamilton, Jeffery: *The Plantagenets: A History of a Dynasty* (London, 2010)
Hammond, Peter: *Her Majesty's Royal Palace and Fortress of the Tower of London* (London, 1987)
Hammond, P.W., and Sutton, Anne F.: *Richard III: The Road to Bosworth Field* (London, 1985)
Hampton, W.E.: 'A Further Account of Robert Stillington' (*The Ricardian*, 27, 1976)
Hancock, Peter A.: *Richard III and the Murder in the Tower* (Stroud, 2009)
Handbook of British Chronology (ed. F. Maurice Powicke and E.B. Fryde, London, 1961)

Hanham, Alison: 'Sir George Buck and Princess Elizabeth's Letter: A Problem in Detection' (*The Ricardian*, 7, 1987)

Harris, Barbara J.: *English Aristocratic Women, 1450–1550* (Oxford, 2002)

Harrod, H.: 'Queen Elizabeth Woodville's visit to Norwich in 1469' (*Norfolk Archaeology*, 5, 1859)

Hassall, W.O.: *Who's Who in History, Vol. 1, 55 B.C. to 1485* (Oxford, 1960)

Hayward, Maria: *Dress at the Court of Henry VIII* (Leeds, 2007)

Hedley, Olwen: *Royal Palaces* (London, 1972)

Helmholz, R.H.: *Marriage Litigation in Medieval England* (Cambridge, 1974)

Henry VIII: A European Court in England (ed. David Starkey, The National Maritime Museum, London, 1991)

Henry VIII: Man and Monarch (ed. Susan Doran, The British Library, London, 2009)

Hepburn, F.: 'Arthur, Prince of Wales and his Training for Kingship' (*The Historian*, 55, 1997)

Herbert, Warren T.; Herbert, T.; and New, Edmund H.: *Magdalen College, Oxford* (Cambridge, 1907)

Herlihy, David: *Medieval Households* (Harvard, 1985).

Hervey, Mary F.S.: *The Life, Correspondence and Collections of Thomas Howard, Earl of Arundel, 'Father of Virtue in England'* (Cambridge, 1921)

Hichens, Mark: *Wives of the Kings of England, from Normans to Stuarts* (Brighton, 2008)

Hicks, Michael: *Anne Neville, Queen to Richard III* (Stroud, 2006)

Hicks, Michael: *Edward V: The Prince in the Tower* (Stroud, 2003)

Hicks, Michael: *False, Fleeting, Perjur'd Clarence: George, Duke of Clarence, 1449–78* (Gloucester, 1980)

Hicks, Michael: *Richard III: The Man behind the Myth* (London, 1991; revised edition Stroud, 2000)

Hicks, Michael: *Robert Stillington* (Oxford, 2004–8, www.ingilbyhistory. ripleycastle.co.uk/archives.html)

Higginbotham, Susan: *Medieval Woman* (www.susandhigginbothamblogspot. co.uk)

Hilliam, David: *Crown, Orb and Sceptre: The True Stories of English Coronations* (Stroud, 2001)

Hilton, Lisa: *Queens Consort: England's Medieval Queens* (London, 2008)

Hinde, Thomas: *Hinde's Courtiers: 900 Years of English Court Life* (London, 1986)

Hipshon, David: *Richard III and the Death of Chivalry* (Stroud, 2009)

A History of Fotheringhay (ed. S.J. Hunt, Peterborough, 1999)

Hoak, Dale: 'Rehabilitating the Duke of Northumberland: Politics and

Political Control, 1549–53' (in *The Mid-Tudor Polity c.1540–1560*, ed. Jennifer Loach and Robert Tittler, London, 1980)

Hope, Sir William St John: *Windsor Castle: An Architectural History* (2 vols., London, 1913)

Horrox, Rosemary: 'The History of King Richard III (1619) by Sir George Buck, Master of the Revels' (*English Historical Review*, 382, vol. 97, January 1982)

Howgrave-Graham, R.P.: 'The Earlier Royal Funeral Effigies: New Light on Portraiture in Westminster Abbey' (*Archaeologia*, 98, 1961)

Hughes, Jonathan: *Arthurian Myths and Alchemy: The Kingship of Edward IV* (Stroud, 2002)

Hutchinson, Robert: *House of Treason: The Rise and Fall of a Tudor Dynasty* (London, 2009)

Hutchinson, Robert: *Young Henry: The Rise to Power of Henry VIII* (London, 2011)

Impey, Edward, and Parnell, Geoffrey: *The Tower of London: The Official Illustrated History* (London, 2000, revised 2011)

Important British Paintings, 1500–1850 (Sotheby's Catalogue, 30 June 2005)

Ives, Eric: *The Life and Death of Anne Boleyn* (Oxford, 2004)

Jacob, E.F.: *The Fifteenth Century, 1399–1485* (Oxford, 1969)

James, M.R.: *Abbeys* (London, 1926)

Jenkins, Elizabeth: *The Princes in the Tower* (London, 1978)

Jenkyns, Richard: *Westminster Abbey* (London, 2004)

Jenner, Heather: *Royal Wives* (London, 1967)

Joelson, Annette: *Heirs to the Throne* (London, 1966)

Johnson, Caroline: *The Queen's Servants: Gentlewomen's dress at the accession of Henry VIII* (Lightwater, 2011)

Jones, Christopher: *The Great Palace: The Story of Parliament* (London, 1983)

Jones, Michael K.: 'Margaret Beaufort' (in *The Women of the Cousins' War*, London, 2011)

Jones, Michael K.: *Psychology of a Battle: Bosworth, 1485* (Stroud, 2002)

Jones, Michael K., and Underwood, M.G.: *The King's Mother: Lady Margaret Beaufort, Countess of Richmond and Derby* (Cambridge, 1992)

Jones, Nigel: *Tower* (London, 2011)

Keay, Anna: *The Elizabethan Tower of London* (London, 2001)

Keene, D.J., and Harding, Vanessa: *Historical gazetteer of London before the Great Fire: Cheapside; parishes of All Hallows Honey Lane, St Martin*

Pomary, St Mary le Bow, St Mary Colechurch and St Pancras Soper Lane (1987; www.british-history.ac.uk)

Kendall, Paul Murray: *Louis XI* (London, 1971)

Kendall, Paul Murray: *Richard the Third* (London, 1955)

Kincaid, A.N.: 'Buck and the Elizabeth of York Letter: A Reply to Dr Hanham' (*The Ricardian*, 8, 1988)

King, Edmund: *Medieval England* (Stroud, 1988)

Kings and Queens (The Queen's Gallery, Buckingham Palace, London, 1982)

Kings and Queens of England (ed. Antonia Fraser, London, 1975, revised edition 1998)

Kingsford, C.L.: *English Historical Literature in the Fifteenth Century* (Oxford, 1913)

Kingsford, C.L.: 'Historical Notes on Mediaeval London Houses' (*London Topographical Record*, vol. 10, 1916)

Köhler, Johann David: *Historische Münz-Belustigung, Vol. 12* (Nüremberg, 1729)

Lamb, V.B.: *The Betrayal of Richard III* (London, 1959; revised, with notes and an introduction by P.W. Hammond, Stroud, 1990)

Lancelott, Francis: *The Queens of England and their Times, Vol. I* (New York, 1858)

Lander, J.R.: *The Wars of the Roses* (Gloucester, 1990)

Lane, Henry Murray: *The Royal Daughters of England, Vol. 1* (London, 1910)

Lawrance, Hannah: *Historical Memoirs of the Queens of England, from the commencement of the twelfth to the close of the fifteenth century* (London, 1840)

Laynesmith, J.J.: *The Last Medieval Queens: English Queenship, 1445–1503* (Oxford, 2004)

Lee, Paul: *Nunneries, Learning and Spirituality in Late Medieval English Life: The Dominican Priory of Dartford* (York, 2001)

Lenz-Harvey, Nancy: *Elizabeth of York: Tudor Queen* (New York and London, 1973)

Lenz Harvey, Nancy: *The Rose and the Thorn: The Lives of Mary and Margaret Tudor* (London, 1975)

Letts, Ernest R.: 'The Stanley Chapel in Manchester Cathedral, and its Founder' (*Transactions of the Lancashire and Cheshire Antiquarian Society*, vol. 6, 1888)

Licence, Amy: *Elizabeth of York: The Forgotten Tudor Queen* (Stroud, 2013)

Licence, Amy: *In Bed with the Tudors* (Stroud, 2012)

Lindsey, Karen: *Divorced, Beheaded, Survived: A Feminist Reinterpretation of the Wives of Henry VIII* (New York, 1995)

Lingard, John: *The History of England, From the First Invasion by the Romans to the Accession of Henry VIII* (8 vols., London, 1819)

The Lives of the Kings and Queens of England (ed. Antonia Fraser, London, 1975, revised 1998)

Llewellyn, John F.M.: *The Chapels in the Tower of London* (St Ives, 1987)

Lloyd, Christopher, and Remington, Vanessa: *Masterpieces in Little: Portrait Miniatures from the Collection of Her Majesty Queen Elizabeth II* (London, 1996)

Lloyd, Christopher, and Thurley, Simon: *Henry VIII: Images of a Tudor King* (Oxford, 1990)

Lloyd, David: *Arthur, Prince of Wales* (Ludlow, 2002)

Lloyd, Stephen: *Portrait Miniatures from the Collection of the Duke of Buccleuch* (National Galleries of Scotland, Edinburgh, 1996)

Loades, David: *The Fighting Tudors* (Kew, 2009)

Loades, David: *Henry VIII* (Stroud, 2011)

Loades, David: *Henry VIII: Court, Church and Conflict* (Kew, 2007)

Loades, David: *Mary Rose* (Stroud, 2012)

Loades, David: *The Tudor Queens of England* (London, 2009)

Loades, David: *The Tudors: History of a Dynasty* (London, 2012)

Lofts, Norah: *Queens of Britain* (London, 1977)

Lowe, D.E.: 'Patronage and Politics: Edward IV, the Wydevilles and the Council of the Prince of Wales, 1471–83' (*Bulletin of the Board of Celtic Studies*, 29, 1981)

Luke, Mary M.: *Catherine the Queen* (London, 1968)

Lyte, Henry Churchill Maxwell: *A History of the University of Oxford from the earliest times to the year 1530* (London, 1886)

Macalpine, Joan: *The Shadow of the Tower: Henry VII and his England* (London, 1971)

MacGibbon, David: *Elizabeth Woodville (1437–1492): Her Life and Times* (London, 1938)

McIntosh, Marjorie Keniston: *Autonomy and Community: The Royal Manor of Havering, 1200 to 1500* (Cambridge, 1986)

McKelvey, Elaine Clark Beuchner: Thomas Stanley, First Earl of Derby, 1435–1504 (unpublished Ph.D. thesis, Pennsylvania State University, 1966)

McKendrick, Scot, and Doyle, Kathleen: *Royal Illuminated Manuscripts, from King Athelstan to Henry VIII* (The British Library, London, 2011)

McKendrick, Scot; Lowden, John; and Doyle, Kathleen, *et al.*: *Royal Manuscripts: The Genius of Illumination* (The British Library, London, 2011)

Mackie, J.D.: *The Earlier Tudors, 1485–1558* (Oxford, 1952, revised 1966)

Mcmahon, Phil: *The Archaeology of Wiltshire's Towns: An Extensive Urban Survey: Heytesbury* (Wiltshire County Archaeology Service, 2004, www.ahds.ac.uk)

MacNalty, Arthur Salusbury: *The Princes in the Tower and other Royal Mysteries* (London, 1955)

McSheffrey, Shannon: 'Sanctuary and the Legal Topography of Pre-Reformation London' (*Law and History Review*, 27.3, 2009)

Markham, Sir Clements R.: *Richard III: His Life and Character* (London, 1906)

Marks, Richard: *Stained Glass in England during the Middle Ages* (London, 1993)

Marques, A.S.: 'Alvaro Lopes de Cheves: a Portuguese source' (*Ricardian Bulletin*, Autumn, 2008)

Marsden, Jonathan, and Winterbottom, Matthew: *Windsor Castle* (London, 2008)

Mattingly, Garrett: *Catherine of Aragon* (London, 1944)

Meerson, Kate: *A Who's Who of Tudor Women* (www.katemeersonhistoricals.com)

Meyer, G.J.: *The Tudors* (New York, 2010)

Millar, Oliver: *The Tudor, Stuart and Early Georgian Pictures in the Collection of Her Majesty the Queen* (2 vols., London, 1963)

Milne, Graham: *Sir Roland de Velville: 'A Man of Kingly Line'* (www.cogent-comms.co.uk/roland.htm)

Mitchell, Dorothy: *Guide of Ricardian Yorkshire* (York, 1985)

Mitchell, Dorothy: *Richard III and York* (York, 1983)

Moorhen, W.E.A.: 'Four Weddings and a Conspiracy: The Life, Times and Loves of Lady Katherine Gordon, Part 1' (*The Ricardian*, 12, 156, 2002)

Morris, Christopher: *The Tudors* (London, 1955)

Mould, Philip: *Historical Portraits Image Library* (www.historicalportraits.com)

Mowat, A.J.: 'Robert Stillington' (*The Ricardian*, 4, 1976)

Mumby, Frank Arthur: *The Youth of Henry VIII: A Narrative in Contemporary Letters* (London, 1913)

Myers, A.R.: *Crown, Household and Parliament in Fifteenth-Century England* (London, 1985)

Myers, A.R.: 'The Household Accounts of Queen Margaret of Anjou, 1452–3' (*Bulletin of the John Rylands Library*, 40, 1957–8)

Myers, A.R.: 'The Princes in the Tower' (*The History of the English Speaking Peoples*, vol. 2, 1970)

National Portrait Gallery Archive

Neil, Nigel; Baldwin, Stephen; and Crosby, Alan: *The Medieval Deer Parks of Lathom in Lancashire* (The Lathom Park Trust Archive Research Group, 2004)

Nicolson, Adam: *Life in the Tudor Age* (London, 1995)

Norris, Herbert: *Tudor Costume and Fashion* (London, 1938)

Norton, Elizabeth: *England's Queens: The Biography* (Stroud, 2011)

Norton, Elizabeth: *Margaret Beaufort, Mother of the Tudor Dynasty* (Stroud, 2010)

Norton, Elizabeth: *She Wolves: The Notorious Queens of England* (Stroud, 2008)

Norwich, John Julius: *Shakespeare's Kings* (London, 1999)

Okerlund, Arlene: *Elizabeth Wydeville: The Slandered Queen* (Stroud, 2005)

Okerlund, Arlene: *Elizabeth of York* (New York, 2009)

Ormond, Richard: *The Face of Monarchy: British Royalty Portrayed* (Oxford, 1977)

The Oxford Book of Royal Anecdotes (ed. Elizabeth Longford, Oxford, 1989)

The Oxford Dictionary of National Biography (www.oxforddnb.com)

Painter, G.D.: *William Caxton: A Quincentenary Biography of England's First Printer* (London, 1976)

Palmer, Alan: *Princes of Wales* (London, 1979)

Palmer, Alan and Veronica: *Royal England: A Historical Gazetteer* (London, 1983)

Palmer, C.F.R.: 'History of the Priory of Dartford in Kent' (*Archaeological Journal*, 36, 1879)

Parrott, Kate: *Shakespeare's Queens (of England)* (Bloomington, 2007)

Parsons, John Carmi: 'Ritual and Symbol in English Medieval Queenship to 1500' (in *Women and Sovereignty*, ed. Louise Olga Fredenburg, Edinburgh, 1992)

Patronage, the Crown and the Provinces in Later Medieval England (ed. Ralph A. Griffiths, Gloucester, 1981)

Penn, Thomas: *Winter King: The Dawn of Tudor England* (London, 2011)

Perry, Francis: *A Series of English Medals* (London, 1762)

Perry, Maria: *Sisters to the King: The Tumultuous Lives of Henry VIII's Sisters – Margaret of Scotland and Mary of France* (London, 1998)

Pevsner, Nicholas: *The Buildings of England: Wiltshire* (London, 1975)

Phillips, Charles: *The Castles and Palaces of the Tudors and Stuarts* (London, 2009)

Pidgeon, Lynda: *The Burial Place of Richard III* (www.richardiii.net/r3_man_death_burial)

Pierce, Hazel: *Margaret Pole, Countess of Salisbury, 1473–1541: Loyalty, Lineage and Leadership* (Cardiff, 2009)

Plague, Poverty, Prayer (The York Archaeological Trust, 2009)

The Plantagenet Encyclopaedia (ed. Elizabeth Hallam, Twickenham, 1996)

Platt, Colin: *Medieval England: A Social History and Archaeology from the Conquest to 1600 A.D.* (London, 1978)

Plowden, Alison: *The House of Tudor* (London, 1976, revised edition 1998)

Plowden, Alison: *Tudor Women, Queens and Commoners* (London, 1979)

Plumb, J.H.: *Royal Heritage* (London, 1977)

Pollard, A.J.: *Richard III and the Princes in the Tower* (Stroud, 1991)

Priestley, John: *Eltham Palace* (Chichester, 2008)

Quaritch, Bernard: *Catalogue of Illuminated and Other Manuscripts* (London, 1931)

Rackham, Bernard: *The Stained-Glass Windows of Canterbury Cathedral* (Canterbury, 1957)

Randerson, James: 'Premature Birth has Long-Term Effects' (*The Guardian*, 26 March 2008)

Rawcliffe, Carole: *The Staffords: Earls of Stafford and Dukes of Buckingham, 1394–1521* (Cambridge, 1978)

Redstone, Lilian J.: 'The history of All Hallows Church: To *c.*1548' (*Survey of London: volume 12: The parish of All Hallows Barking, part I: The Church of All Hallows*, London, 1929)

The Reign of Henry VII: Proceedings of the 1993 Harlaxton Symposium (ed. Benjamin Thompson, Stamford, 1995)

The Renaissance at Sutton Place (The Sutton Place Heritage Trust, 1983)

Rex, Richard: *Henry VIII* (Stroud, 2009)

Rex, Richard: *The Tudors* (Stroud, 2002)

Reynolds, Graham: *English Portrait Miniatures* (Cambridge, 1988)

Reynolds, Graham: *The Sixteenth and Seventeenth-Century Miniatures in the Collection of Her Majesty the Queen* (The Royal Collection, London, 1999)

Ricci, Seymour de: *English Collectors of Books and Manuscripts (1550 to 1930)* (Cambridge, 1930)

Richard III: Crown and People (ed. J. Petre, London, 1985)

Richardson, Douglas: *Plantagenet Ancestry* (Salt Lake City, 2004)

Richardson, Geoffrey: *The Popinjays* (Shipley, 2000)

Richardson, Walter C.: *Mary Tudor, the White Queen* (London, 1970)

Ridley, Jasper: *Henry VIII* (London, 1984)

Ridley, Jasper: *The Tudor Age* (London, 1998)

Rivals in Power: Lives and Letters of the Great Tudor Dynasties (ed. David Starkey, London, 1991)

Robinson, John Martin: *The Dukes of Norfolk* (Oxford, 1983)

Robinson, John Martin: *Windsor Castle: Official Guide* (London, 1995, 1997)

Robinson, John Martin: *Windsor Castle: A Short History* (London, 1996)

Röhrkasten, Jens: *The Mendicant Houses of Medieval London, 1221–1539* (Munster, 2004)

Rose, Alexander: *Kings in the North: The House of Percy in British History* (London, 2002)

Rose, Tessa: *The Coronation Ceremony of the Kings and Queens of England and the Crown Jewels* (London, 1992)

Ross, Charles: *Edward IV* (London, 1974)

Ross, Charles: *Richard III* (Yale and London, 1981)

Ross, Charles: *The Wars of the Roses* (London, 1976)

Ross, Josephine: *The Tudors* (London, 1979)

Roulstone, Michael: *The Royal House of Tudor* (St Ives, 1974)

Routh, C.R.N.: *Who's Who in Tudor England* (Oxford, 1990)

Rowse, A.L.: *Bosworth Field and the Wars of the Roses* (London, 1966)

Rowse, A.L.: *The Tower of London in the History of the Nation* (London, 1972)

A Royal Miscellany, from the Royal Library, Windsor Castle (London, 1990)

Royal Palaces of England (ed. Robert S. Rait, London, 1911)

Royal River: Power, Pageantry and the Thames (ed. Susan Doran and Robert J. Blythe, London, 2012)

Rushforth, Gordon McNeill: *Medieval Christian imagery as illustrated by the painted windows of Great Malvern Priory Church, Worcestershire, together with a description and explanation of all the ancient glass in the church* (Oxford, 1936)

Rushton, Martin: 'The teeth of Anne Mowbray' (*British Dental Journal*, 19 October 1965)

St Aubyn, Giles: *The Year of Three Kings: 1483* (London, 1983)

St John Hope, W.H.: 'On the Funeral Effigies in Westminster Abbey' (*Archaeologia*, vol. 60, issue 2, 1907)

Sanceau, Elaine: *The Perfect Prince: A Biography of King Dom Joao II* (Porto, 1959)

Sandford, Francis: *A Genealogical History of the Kings and Queens of England, from the Conquest anno 1066 to 1677* (Savoy and London, 1677)

Santiusti, David: *Edward IV and the Wars of the Roses* (Barnsley, 2010)

Santos, Domingos Mauricio Gomes dos: *O Mosteiro de Jesus de Aviero* (3 vols., Lisbon, 1963)

Saunders, Hilary St George: *Westminster Hall* (London, 1951)

Scharf, George: 'On a Votive Painting of St George and the Dragon, with Kneeling Figures of Henry VII, his Queen and his Children, formerly at Strawberry Hill, and now in the possession of Her Majesty the Queen' (*Archaeologia*, vol. 49, 2, 1886)

Scofield, Cora L.: 'Elizabeth Wydeville in the Sanctuary at Westminster' (*English Historical Review*, 24, 1909)

Scofield, Cora L.: *The Life and Reign of Edward the Fourth* (2 vols., London, 1923)

Scott, A.F.: *Every One a Witness: The Plantagenet Age* (New York, 1976)

Scott, A.F.: *Every One a Witness: The Tudor Age* (New York, 1976)

Scott, Jennifer: 'Painting from Life? Comments on the Date and Function of the Early Portraits of Elizabeth Woodville and Elizabeth of York in the Royal Collection'

Scott, Jennifer: *The Royal Portrait: Image and Impact* (London, 2010)

Searle, W.G.: *The History of Queens' College of St Margaret and St Bernard in the University of Cambridge* (Cambridge, 1867–71)

Seward, Desmond: *The Last White Rose: Dynasty, Rebellion and Treason: The Secret Wars against the Tudors* (London, 2010)

Seward, Desmond: *Richard III, England's Black Legend* (London, 1982; revised London, 1997)

Sharpe, R.R.: *London and the Kingdom* (3 vols., London, 1894–5)

Shears, H.: *The Queen's Blood: A Study of Family Ties during the Wars of the Roses* (2010, www.soundideas.pugetsound.edu)

Sheppard-Routh, Pauline: '"Lady Scroop, Daughter of King Edward": an Enquiry' (*The Ricardian*, June, 1993)

The Shrine (www.stmarywillesden.org.uk)

Smith, Stanley: *The Madonna of Ipswich* (Ipswich, 1980)

Smyth, Martin: *John Nesfield's Retinue* (www.johannesfieldsretinue.com)

Softly, Barbara: *The Queens of England* (Newton Abbot and London, 1976)

Somerset, Anne: *Ladies in Waiting: From the Tudors to the Present Day* (London, 1984)

Southworth, John Van Duyn: *Monarch and Conspirators: The Wives and Woes of Henry VIII* (New York, 1973)

Stanley, Arthur Penrhyn: *Historical Memorials of Westminster Abbey* (London, 1867)

Starkey, David: *Henry, Virtuous Prince* (London, 2008)

Starkey, David: *Monarchy: From the Middle Ages to Modernity* (London, 2006)

Starkey, David: *Six Wives: The Queens of Henry VIII* (London, 2003)

Steane, John: *The Archaeology of the Medieval English Monarchy* (London, 1993)

Stevens, John: *Music and Poetry in the Early Tudor Court* (London, 1961)

Stevenson, Robert Louis: *Familiar Studies of Men and Books* (London, 1917)

Strickland, Agnes: *Lives of the Queens of England* (12 vols., London, 1840–48)

Strickland, Agnes: *Lives of the Tudor Princesses* (London, 1868)

Strong, Roy: *Coronation: A History of Kingship and the British Monarchy* (London, 2005)

Strong, Roy: *The House of Tudor* (H.M.S.O., London, 1967)

Strong, Roy: *Lost Treasures of Britain* (London, 1990)

Strong, Roy: *Tudor and Jacobean Portraits* (2 vols., London, 1969)

Struthers, Jane: *Royal Palaces of Britain* (London, 2004)

Sutton, Anne, and Visser-Fuchs, Livia: *The Hours of Richard III* (Stroud, 1990)

Sutton, Anne, and Visser-Fuchs, Livia: 'A "Most Benevolent Queen": Queen Elizabeth Woodville's Reputation, her Piety and her Books' (*The Ricardian*, 10, 1995)

Sutton, Anne, and Visser-Fuchs, Livia: *The Reburial of Richard, Duke of York, 21–30 July 1476* (London, 1996)

Sykes, N.: *Winchester Cathedral* (London, 1976)

Tanner, Lawrence E.: *The History and Treasures of Westminster Abbey* (London, 1953)

Thompson, Margaret E.: *The Carthusian Order in England* (London, 1930)

Thornton-Cook, Elsie: *Her Majesty: The Romance of the Queens of England, 1066–1910* (London, 1926)

Thornton-Cook, Elsie: *Royal Elizabeths: The Romance of Five Princesses, 1464–1840* (New York, 1929)

Thurley, Simon: *Hampton Court: A Social and Architectural History* (Yale and London, 2003)

Thurley, Simon: *Hampton Court Palace* (London, 1993)

Thurley, Simon: *The Royal Palaces of Tudor England* (Yale and London, 1993)

Todd, George W.: *Castellum Huttonicum: Some Account of Sheriff Hutton Castle* (York, 1824)

Tournoy-Thouen, Gilbert and Godelieve: 'Giovanni Gigli and the Renaissance of the Classical Epithalamium in England' (in *Myricae: Essays on Neo-Latin Literature in Memory of Jozef Ijsewijn*, ed. Dirk Sacré and Gilbert Tournoy, *Humanistica Lovaniensia* Supplement 16, 2000)

Trapp, J.B., and Herbruggen, Hubertus Scholte: '*The King's Good Servant*': *Sir Thomas More, 1477/8–1535* (The National Portrait Gallery, London, 1977)

Tremlett, Giles: *Catherine of Aragon, Henry's Spanish Queen* (London, 2010)

Tromly, Frederick B.: '"A Rueful Lamentation" of Elizabeth: Thomas More's Transformation of Didactic Lament' (*Moreana*, 53, March 1977)

Trowles, Tony: *Treasures of Westminster Abbey* (London, 2008)

Tudor-Craig, Pamela: *Richard III* (National Portrait Gallery, London, 1973, revised 1977)

Tytler, Sarah: *Tudor Queens and Princesses* (London, 1896)

Vail, Anne: *Shrines of Our Lady in England* (Leominster, 2004)

Vaughan, Richard: *Philip the Good* (London, 1970)

Victoria County Histories (www.british-history.ac.uk)

Visser-Fuchs, Livia: 'English Events in Caspar Weinreich's Danzig Chronicle, 1461–1495' (*The Ricardian*, 7, 1986)

Visser-Fuchs, Livia: 'Where did Elizabeth of York find consolation?' (*The Ricardian*, 9, 1993)

Walker, John: *Oxoniana: or Anecdotes relative to the University and City of Oxford, Vol. II* (Oxford, 1806)

Walpole, Horace: *Anecdotes of Painting in England* (London, 1782)

Warner, Marina: *From the Beast to the Blonde: On Fairytales and their Tellers* (London, 1995)

The Wars of the Roses (ed. Antonia Fraser, London, 2000)

Weightman, Christine: *Margaret of York, Duchess of Burgundy, 1446–1503* (Stroud, 1989)

Weir, Alison: Britain's Aristocratic Families, 1066–1603 (unpublished genealogical compendium)

Weir, Alison: *Britain's Royal Families: The Complete Genealogy* (London, 1989)

Weir, Alison: *Henry VIII: King and Court* (London, 2001)

Weir, Alison: *Lancaster and York: The Wars of the Roses* (London, 1995)

Weir, Alison: *The Princes in the Tower* (London, 1992)

Weir, Alison: *The Six Wives of Henry VIII* (London, 1991)

West, Ed.: 'Statue of Our Lady to stand on the Thames at Chelsea' (*Catholic Herald*, 26 October 2007)

West, Zita: *Acupuncture in Pregnancy and Childbirth* (Philadelphia, 2001)

Westervelt, T.: The Woodvilles in the Second Reign of Edward IV, 1471–83 (unpublished M.Phil. dissertation, Cambridge, 1997)

Wiesflächer, H.: *Kaiser Maximilian I* (2 vols., Munich, 1975)

Wilkins, Christopher: *The Last Knight Errant: Sir Edward Woodville and the Age of Chivalry* (London, 2010)

Wilkinson, James: *Henry VII's Lady Chapel in Westminster Abbey* (London, 2007)

Wilkinson, James: *Westminster Abbey: A Souvenir Guide* (London, 2006)

Wilkinson, James, and Knighton, C.S.: *Crown and Cloister: The Royal Story of Westminster Abbey* (London, 2010)

Wilkinson, Josephine: *Richard, the Young King to Be* (Stroud, 2008)

Williams, Barrie: 'The Portuguese Connection and the Significance of the "Holy Princess"' (*The Ricardian*, March, 1983)

Williams, Barrie: 'Rui de Sousa's embassy and the fate of Richard, Duke of York' (*The Ricardian*, June, 1981)

Williams, D.T.: *The Battle of Bosworth Field* (Leicester 1973, 1996)

Williams, Mary: 'French Manuscripts in the National Library of Wales'(*The National Library of Wales Journal*, 1, 1939–40)

Williams, Neville: *Henry VIII and his Court* (London, 1971)

Williams, Neville: *The Life and Times of Henry VII* (London, 1973)

Williams, Patrick: *Katharine of Aragon* (Stroud, 2013)

Williamson, Audrey: *The Mystery of the Princes* (Gloucester, 1978)

Williamson, David: *Brewer's British Royalty: A Phrase and Fable Dictionary* (London, 1996)

Williamson, David: *The National Portrait Gallery History of the Kings and Queens of England* (London, 1998)

Wilson, Derek: *Henry VIII: Reformer and Tyrant* (London, 2009)

Wilson, Derek: *Tudor England* (Oxford, 2010)

Wiltshire Community History: Heytesbury Search Results (www.wiltshire.gov.uk)

Women and the Book: Assessing the Visual Evidence (ed. L. Smith and J.H.M. Taylor, Toronto, 1996)

Women and Sovereignty (ed. Louise Olga Fredenburg, Edinburgh, 1992)

Wood, Charles T.: 'The First Two Queens Elizabeth' (in *Women and Sovereignty*, ed. Louise Olga Fredenburg, Edinburgh, 1992)

Woodward, G.W.O.: *Richard III* (London, 1977; reprinted, with additional material by Michael St John Parker, Andover, 1994, 1996)

Woolgar, C.M.: *The Great Household in Late Medieval England* (Yale and London, 1999)

Works of Art in the House of Lords (ed. Maurice Bond, London, 1980)

Worsley, Lucy, and Souden, David: *Hampton Court Palace: The Official History* (London, 2005)

Wroe, Ann: *Perkin: A Story of Deception* (London, 2003)

'The Yorkist Age' (ed. Hannes Kleineke and Christian Steer, Harlaxton Medieval Studies XXII, Proceedings of the 2011 Harlaxton Symposium, 2011)

Notes and References

Abbreviations

André	'Vita Henrici VII'
Arrivall	*Historie of the Arrivall of King Edward IV in England*
CSP Milan	*Calendar of State Papers and Manuscripts existing in the Archives and Collections of Milan*
CSP Spain	*Calendar of Letters, Despatches and State Papers relating to Negotiations between England and Spain*
CSP Venice	*Calendar of State Papers and Manuscripts relating to English Affairs preserved in the Archives of Venice*
HVIIPPE	Privy Purse Expenses of Henry VII, in *The Antiquarian Repertory*
Leland: *Collectanea*	Leland, John: *Antiquarii de Rebus Brittanicis Collectanea*
PPE	*Privy Purse Expenses of Elizabeth of York*
Strickland	*Lives of the Queens of England*

Introduction

1 Holinshed

Prologue: 'Now Take Heed What Love May Do'

1 I have adoped this spelling rather than the more commonly used and anachronistic Woodville, which is not contemporary. The name is spelt Wydeville on Elizabeth's coffin plate, and it is the way she

signed her name. In contemporary sources it is given variously as Wydvil, Wydvile, Wydevile or Widville.

2 William Monypenny, Louis IX's agent in Scotland, cited Scofield in *Life and Reign*

3 *CSP Milan*

4 *Calendar of Documents relating to Scotland*

5 *CSP Milan*

6 Vergil

7 Ibid.

8 Ibid.

9 Mancini

10 Commines

11 'Gregory's Chronicle'

12 Vergil

13 More

14 Hall

15 More

16 Ashdown-Hill: *Eleanor, the Secret Queen* suggests that her portraits show her with dark hair, but in the majority she is clearly blonde.

17 *Letters of Royal and Illustrious Ladies*

18 Mancini. For a discussion of this story, see Chapter 1.

19 Waurin

20 Worcester

21 Shears

22 Fabyan

1: 'The Most Illustrious Maid of York'

1 Much of the medieval palace, including the apartments where Elizabeth of York was born, was reduced to ruins in a devastating fire in 1512, and most of what was left was lost during a second conflagration in 1834. Only Westminster Hall, the crypt of St Stephen's Chapel and the Jewel Tower escaped unscathed. The Palace of Westminster, incorporating the Houses of Parliament, now occupies the site where the medieval palace once stood.

2 Fabyan. The date is confirmed in Elizabeth's tomb inscription in Westminster Abbey.

3 Ibid.

4 Ibid.; Jenkins

5 *Calendar of Papal Registers*

6 Tetzel

7 Ibid.

8 Daughter of Sir Richard Berners and wife of John Bourchier, Lord Berners, Constable of Windsor Castle.

9 *A Relation, or rather a True Account, of the Island of England*

10 Tetzel

11 *A Relation, or rather a True Account, of the Island of England*

12 Mancini

13 *A Relation, or rather a True Account, of the Island of England*

14 *Patronage, the Crown and the Provinces in Later Medieval England*

15 Mancini

16 *Letters and Papers Illustrative of the Reigns of Richard III and Henry VII*

17 Mancini

18 *CSP Milan*

19 Mancini

20 *Paston Letters*

21 Monstrelet

22 Ibid.

23 *Letters and Papers Illustrative of the Reigns of Richard III and Henry VII*

24 *Paston Letters*

25 When Mary's coffin was opened in 1810, when a vault was being constructed for the family of George III, her unembalmed body was found to be well-preserved, with long, pale-blonde hair and blue eyes, which were open, but quickly disintegrated when exposed to the air. Observers could see that she had been beautiful in life.

26 *Calendar of Patent Rolls: Edward IV, 1467–77; Wardrobe Accounts of Edward the Fourth*, in *PPE*

27 *Calendar of Patent Rolls: Edward IV, 1467–77*

28 *Calendar of Close Rolls: Edward IV; Foedera;* Exchequer Records: Issue Rolls E.403

29 *A Relation, or rather a True Account, of the Island of England*

30 Cited Brigden. These words were written by Edmund Dudley, who would become one of the foremost advisers to Elizabeth's future husband.

31 Civil and Uncivil Life, tract of 1579, cited Scott: *Every One a Witness: The Tudor Age*

32 Dowsing; Hedley; Cloake: *Palaces and Parks of Richmond and Kew* and *Richmond Palace*

33 *Collection of Ordinances; The Babees' Book*

34 Green

35 Harris

36 *Collection of Ordinances; The Babees' Book; Manners and Meals in Olden Time;* Woolgar
37 *The Plumpton Correspondence*
38 Brigden
39 Cited Brigden
40 *Collection of Ordinances*
41 *Paston Letters*
42 *CSP Milan*
43 *Great Chronicle of London*
44 *Croyland Chronicle*
45 Ibid.
46 Mancini
47 Jones: *Psychology of a Battle: Bosworth, 1485*
48 When Katherine Parr interceded with Henry VIII to spare the life of her adulterous sister-in-law, he would not do so unless her husband relented.
49 *CSP Milan*
50 Mancini
51 Ibid.
52 *Paston Letters*
53 *Wills from Doctors' Commons*
54 Okerlund: *Elizabeth Wydeville*; Okerlund: *Elizabeth of York*
55 Harrod
56 Weightman
57 *Croyland Chronicle*; Charter Rolls C.53/105
58 Warkworth
59 Geoffrey Richardson
60 *PPE*
61 The Manner and Guiding of the Earl of Warwick at Angers in July and August 1470, from the Harleian MS. 433, in *Original Letters Illustrative of English History*
62 John Neville was to be killed at Barnet in 1471. George Neville could not afford to support his dukedom of Bedford, and was deprived of it in January 1478. He died unmarried in 1483 and was buried in Sheriff Hutton Church, Yorkshire.
63 Hicks: *Anne Neville*
64 Warkworth
65 Ibid.; Fabyan
66 Hall
67 *Paston Letters*
68 Sharpe, citing records of the Court of Common Council of the City of London in the Guildhall archives.

69 *Paston Letters*
70 *The Politics of Fifteenth-Century England*; Scofield: 'Elizabeth Wydeville in the Sanctuary at Westminster'
71 Hall
72 Warkworth
73 These details are recorded in a letter written by Edward IV to the Lord Privy Seal in 1473; Additional MS. 4614, f.222
74 *Calendar of Patent Rolls: Edward IV*
75 *Croyland Chronicle*
76 Commines
77 *Croyland Chronicle*
78 *Arrivall*
79 Recovery of the Throne, Royal MSS; *Political Poems and Songs*
80 *Arrivall*
81 Ibid.
82 *Political Poems and Songs*
83 *Foedera*
84 *Arrivall*
85 Ibid.
86 Ibid.
87 Hall, corroborated by the illustrated version of the *Arrivall*, dating from 1471.
88 *Croyland Chronicle*
89 Ibid.
90 Mancini
91 *Arrivall*
92 *Croyland Chronicle*
93 Holinshed
94 He hastened to make peace with Edward IV, but in September was arrested and beheaded.
95 *Croyland Chronicle*
96 Warkworth
97 *Arrivall*
98 Warkworth
99 *Archaeologia*
100 *CSP Milan*
101 *Great Chronicle of London*
102 *Croyland Chronicle*
103 Cotton MS. Julius B, XII, 317; *Letters of Royal and Illustrious Ladies*
104 *Rotuli Parliamentorum*
105 Vergil
106 André

2: 'Madame la Dauphine'

1 Mancini
2 Commines
3 Mancini
4 *Croyland Chronicle*
5 More
6 Ibid.
7 Mancini
8 *CSP Milan*
9 Mancini
10 Ibid.
11 *Calendar of Patent Rolls: Edward IV, 1467–77*
12 *HVIIPPE*
13 Cotton MS. Vespasian, f. XIII
14 Pietro Carmeliano, cited in Anglo: *Spectacle, Pageantry and Early Tudor Policy*
15 An example is in Cotton MSS Vespasian, f. III, p.15, and probably comes from a book Cecily owned.
16 *CSP Spain*
17 *CSP Venice; CSP Milan*
18 *Collection of Ordinances*
19 In 1477 priests holding fellowships at Queens' College, Cambridge were instructed to offer daily prayers for 'our sovereign lady, Queen Elizabeth, foundress of the College, the Prince and all the King's childer'. The college had been founded by Andrew Dockett, a local rector, in 1446. Margaret of Anjou had become its patron in 1448.
20 Sutton and Visscher-Fuchs: 'A "Most Benevolent Queen"'; *Women and the Book*
21 Stonyhurst MS. 37; Tudor-Craig
22 Royal MS. 14, EIII; Wilkins; McKendrick, Lowden and Doyle
23 Garrett MS. 168; Quaritch; Okerlund: *Elizabeth of York*
24 Hinde
25 *Paston Letters*; Additional MS. 6113
26 *Croyland Chronicle*
27 Only some masonry and the vaulted undercroft, which housed the domestic offices, survives of Edward III's palace.
28 Hedley
29 'Narratives of the Arrival of Louis of Bruges'; Kingsford: *English Historical Literature in the Fifteenth Century*
30 Green

31 Brigden

32 Mancini

33 Rous

34 More

35 *Calendar of Patent Rolls: Edward IV, 1467–77*; B.L. Additional MS. 14289, f.12; Lowe

36 Shears

37 Hicks: *Edward V*; Exchequer Records E.101/412/9–11; Harleian MS. 158, ff.119v, 120v; Additional MS. 6113, ff.97–8v, 111–12

38 *Foedera*

39 Commines; *Foedera*

40 Commines

41 Cotton MSS

42 Commines

43 Additional MS. 6113

44 *Calendar of Close Rolls: Edward IV.* This infant was possibly named for her aunt, Anne of York, Duchess of Exeter, or for her great-grandmother, Anne Mortimer, Countess of Cambridge, through whom the House of York claimed its senior descent from Edward III. Edward IV also professed a special devotion to St Anne, mother of the Virgin Mary.

45 Cokayne

46 Leland: *Itinerary*

47 *Croyland Chronicle*

48 A detailed account of the proceedings by Thomas Whiting, Chester Herald, is in *Excerpta Historica*. See also Sutton and Visscher-Fuchs: *Reburial*

49 At the Reformation the college was dissolved and half the church dismantled. Visiting the ruined choir in 1573, Elizabeth I was appalled to see that the tombs were much decayed, and ordered that new Renaissance-style monuments be built in the church to house the remains of Edward, Duke of York, Richard, Duke of York, Cecily Neville (who had been buried at Fotheringhay in 1495) and Edmund, Earl of Rutland; these are the sepulchres that can be seen today in the sanctuary. The once-splendid castle, where Mary, Queen of Scots, was executed in 1587, was pulled down in 1627, and all that remain are the twelfth-century earthworks, and a fragment of masonry.

50 Plowden: *Tudor Women*. Holinshed, writing of Edward's later plan of 1483 to marry Elizabeth to Henry Tudor, states the marriage had been suggested some years earlier, but Elizabeth was betrothed to the Dauphin at the time.

51 André
52 Commines
53 *CSP Milan*
54 He was born at Windsor – Edward IV refers to him as 'our son, George of Windsor' (*Calendar of Close Rolls: Edward IV*) – not, as is sometimes stated, at the Dominican friary in Shrewsbury where his brother Richard had been born. The first mention of him is in a document of 6 July 1477, appointing him Lieutenant of Ireland.
55 *Calendar of Close Rolls: Edward IV*
56 *The Register of the Most Noble Order of the Garter*
57 Hedley
58 *Croyland Chronicle*
59 Ibid.
60 Anne Mowbray was reburied in the Poor Clares' convent at Stepney. Her coffin was found during excavations in 1965, and after examination her remains were reburied later that year as close as possible to her original burial place in Westminster Abbey. A photograph of her remarkably preserved hair is in the Museum of London.
61 *The Narrative of the Marriage of Richard, Duke of York; Illustrations of Ancient State and Chivalry*
62 *Rotuli Parliamentorum*
63 Mancini
64 Hicks: *False, Fleeting, Perjur'd Clarence*
65 Mancini; *Great Chronicle of London*; Commines; Molinet; Roye; Vergil; Stow: *Annals*
66 *Calendar of Patent Rolls: Edward IV, 1467–77*
67 *Wardrobe Accounts of Edward the Fourth*, in *PPE*
68 Hicks: *False, Fleeting, Perjur'd Clarence*
69 Cited Jones: *Psychology of a Battle: Bosworth, 1485*
70 Westervelt; Hicks: *Richard III*; Hicks: *False, Fleeting, Perjur'd Clarence*; Crawford: *The Yorkists*
71 *Croyland Chronicle*; Vergil; More
72 Vergil
73 Ibid.
74 Ross: *Edward IV*
75 *Calendar of Close Rolls: Edward IV*
76 Ibid.
77 *CSP Milan*
78 *CSP Venice*
79 Harleian MS. 336, in Leland: *Collectanea*
80 Warner

81 Harleian MS. 336, in Leland: *Collectanea*
82 Harleian MS. 4780
83 Green; Platt
84 Account of Garter King of Arms, in Additional MS. 6113, ff. 49, 74–74v; *PPE*
85 *Foedera*
86 Hall
87 *Foedera*
88 College of Arms MS I, 11, f.21r-v; Sandford.
89 Jones, in *Women of the Cousins' Wars*; André
90 Rous
91 *Foedera*
92 Kendall: *Louis XI*
93 *Croyland Chronicle*
94 *Wardrobe Accounts of Edward the Fourth*, in *PPE*
95 *Croyland Chronicle*
96 Ibid.

3: 'This Act of Usurpation'

1 More
2 *Croyland Chronicle*
3 Vergil
4 Commines
5 *Excerpta Historica*
6 McKelvey
7 *Calendar of Papal Registers*
8 Cotton MS. Cleopatra
9 Mancini; Vergil
10 Mancini
11 *Croyland Chronicle*; Mancini
12 Mancini
13 Ibid.
14 Ibid.
15 Vergil
16 Mancini
17 Ibid.
18 More
19 Mancini
20 Dockray: *Richard III: A Source Book*
21 Crawford: *The Yorkists*
22 Mancini

23 Vergil
24 *Croyland Chronicle*
25 Shears
26 Mancini
27 More
28 Mancini
29 More
30 Mancini
31 Fabyan
32 *Croyland Chronicle; Great Chronicle of London*; Fabyan; More; Vergil
33 Vergil
34 More; Hall
35 *Antiquarian Repertory*
36 Hall
37 More
38 *Stonor Letters*
39 Mancini
40 More; Hall. More relates a detailed conversation between the Queen and the Archbishop, but he almost certainly invented the speeches, basing them on what he knew had passed between them. This was a common practice in historical writing at that time.
41 More
42 Mancini
43 André
44 Rous
45 *Croyland Chronicle*
46 *Registrum Thome Bourgchier*
47 *Paston Letters*; McSheffrey
48 Warkworth
49 This Sir John Mortimer married, after 1485, Margaret, daughter of John Neville, Viscount Montagu, and sister of the George Neville who had at one time been affianced to Elizabeth; Margaret Neville later married Charles Brandon, Duke of Suffolk.
50 Tudor-Craig; *Catalogue of Western Manuscripts and Miniatures*. The manuscript was in the collection of Colonel Bradfer-Lawrence, but was sold at Sotheby's in 1983.
51 *Croyland Chronicle*
52 Guildhall MSS
53 *York Civic Records*
54 *Croyland Chronicle*
55 Ibid.

56 Mancini
57 Ibid.; *Croyland Chronicle*
58 Fabyan
59 André
60 Mancini
61 Buck, ed. Kincaid; Kendall: *Richard the Third*; Black; Edwards: 'The "Second" Continuation of the Crowland Chronicle'
62 Mancini
63 *Croyland Chronicle*
64 Commines
65 Okerlund: *Elizabeth Wydeville*
66 Ashdown-Hill: 'The Fate of Edward IV's Uncrowned Queen, the Lady Eleanor Talbot, Lady Butler'; Hampton; Mowat; *Calendar of Patent Rolls: Edward IV, 1467–77*; *Rotuli Parliamentorum*; Okerlund: *Elizabeth Wydeville*; Okerlund: *Elizabeth of York*. Ashdown-Hill argues that the story was true and that Edward did make a valid marriage with Eleanor Butler.
67 Helmholz. I am grateful to Professor Anthony Goodman for sending me this reference.
68 *Croyland Chronicle*
69 Ashdown-Hill: *Eleanor, the Secret Queen*
70 The *Croyland Chronicle* is the only source correctly to report Edward's supposed precontract with Eleanor Butler.
71 Crawford: *The Yorkists*
72 *Arrivall*
73 *Excerpta Historica*
74 Hicks: *Robert Stillington*
75 Mancini
76 Fabyan
77 Mancini
78 Rous
79 Fabyan
80 *Croyland Chronicle*
81 Ibid.
82 Mancini
83 *Croyland Chronicle*
84 Loades: *The Tudors*
85 Myers: 'The Princes in the Tower'
86 Brigden

4: 'The Whole Design of This Plot'

1　*Croyland Chronicle*
2　Ibid.
3　*Cely Letters*; Smyth
4　*Croyland Chronicle*
5　Ibid.
6　Dockray: *Richard III: A Source Book*
7　More
8　Mancini
9　More
10　Rawcliffe, citing D.1721/1/11, f.5–9, Staffordshire Record Office
11　Ross: *Richard III*
12　*Rotuli Parliamentorum*
13　*Croyland Chronicle*
14　The matter is discussed extensively, and the sources evaluated, in my book, *The Princes in the Tower* (1992); although my conclusions are substantially the same, I have revised some aspects in this book.
15　More; *Great Chronicle of London*; Vergil. For a balanced, academic view, see Hicks: *Edward V*, who points out that three sources are usually sufficient evidence for academic historians. For More's sources, see *The Princes in the Tower*.
16　The basis of the British Library.
17　For a full discussion of Buck's sources, see A. N. Kincaid's edition of his work.
18　Cited by Kincaid, in his edition of Buck.
19　Chambers; Markham
20　Hicks: *Edward V*
21　Ibid.
22　Cotton MS. Vitellius A XVI
23　*Croyland Chronicle*
24　Rowse: *Bosworth Field*
25　Hall
26　Jones, in *Women of the Cousins' Wars*
27　Vergil
28　*Calendar of Papal Registers*
29　Vergil
30　Ibid.
31　Ibid.
32　*Croyland Chronicle*
33　André
34　Caxton; *The Caxton Project*; Gill

35 *Dictionary of National Biography*

36 *Croyland Chronicle*

37 Ibid.

38 Ibid.

39 Baldwin: *Elizabeth Woodville*

40 *Croyland Chronicle*

41 Vergil

42 Stonyhurst MS. 37; Tudor-Craig

43 Vergil

44 Hicks: *Edward V*

45 Vergil

46 *Croyland Chronicle*. The original Parliament Roll was destroyed in 1485, but a transcript of the Act survives in the *Croyland Chronicle*.

47 Herlihy

48 Peter Clarke; Hicks: *Anne Neville*

49 *Croyland Chronicle*

50 St Aubyn. I can find no contemporary evidence to support this statement.

51 Harleian MS. 433, f.308; *Original Letters Illustrative of English History*

52 Cheetham

53 *Croyland Chronicle*

54 *Rotuli Parliamentorum*

55 Smyth

56 Baldwin: *Lost Prince*; Harleian MS. 433; Smyth

57 Mcmahon; Pevsner; *Wiltshire Community History*

58 *Victoria County History: North Yorkshire*

59 *PPE*

60 Smyth

61 Baldwin: *Lost Prince*; *Victoria County History: North Yorkshire*; Smyth. John Nesfield had died by April 1488, when his widow, Margaret Assheton, was granted letters of administration.

62 *Calendar of Patent Rolls: Edward IV, Edward V, Richard III*

63 For example, Kendall in *Richard the Third*

64 Harleian MS. 433, III

65 Ibid.

66 Pierce

67 *Richard III: Crown and People*

68 For example, Myers in 'The Princes in the Tower' and Kendall in *Richard the Third*

69 Pierce

70 Commines

71 Buck; Strickland

72 *Croyland Chronicle.* An empty tomb bearing the worn effigy of a
   boy in Sheriff Hutton Church, Yorkshire, has long been claimed to
   be Edward of Middleham's. It once bore the Neville arms (as Anne
   Neville is shown wearing in the contemporary Salisbury Roll) and
   the royal arms differenced, so the identification may be correct.
   Hicks: *Anne Neville.*
73 *Croyland Chronicle*
74 *Great Chronicle of London*
75 Gristwood
76 *Croyland Chronicle*

5: 'Her Only Joy and Maker'

1 *Croyland Chronicle*
2 Ibid.
3 Rous
4 *Croyland Chronicle*
5 The passage has also been translated to read that Queen Anne and
   Elizabeth were of similar colouring and shape, but that would
   hardly have given rise to such comments and speculation.
6 Hicks: *Anne Neville*
7 Letter of Thomas Langton, Bishop of St David's, cited by Ross:
   Richard III
8 Pollard
9 Dockray: *Richard III: A Source Book*
10 *Croyland Chronicle.* The words 'gratify an incestuous passion' can also
   be translated as 'gratify his incestuous passion' or 'complete his
   incestuous association'.
11 Peter Clarke: 'English Royal Marriages and the Papal Penitentiary
   in the Fifteenth Century'
12 Cited by Baldwin in *Richard III*
13 Baldwin: *Richard III*
14 Hicks: *Anne Neville*
15 Buck
16 Stow: *Annals*
17 *Croyland Chronicle*
18 Helmholz; Sheppard-Routh
19 *Croyland Chronicle*
20 *Acts of Court of the Mercers' Company*
21 *Croyland Chronicle*
22 Ibid.
23 Lopes

24 Warrants for Issues, E.404/78/3/47

25 For the Portuguese negotiations, see Wilkins; Sanceau; Barrie
    Williams: 'The Portuguese Connection and the Significance of the
    "Holy Princess"'; Lopes; Santos; Marques; Ashdown-Hill: *The Last
    Days of Richard III*; Baldwin: *Richard III*. Joana was canonised in 1693.

26 Lamb, citing Harleian MS. 433, states that Elizabeth was proposed
    as a bride for James FitzGerald, Earl of Desmond (1459–1487).
    Harley 433 does contain a letter sent in September 1484 by
    Richard III to the Earl, offering to find a suitable bride for
    Desmond if he ceased conducting himself violently in Munster,
    adopted English attire and returned to his allegiance – but
    Elizabeth is not mentioned. I am indebted to the historian
    Josephine Wilkinson, who double-checked this for me and
    confirmed that there is no reference at all to her in connection
    with Desmond.

27 Cited by Vergil's editor, Dennis Hay, from Vergil's unpublished
    manuscript. Buck's editor, A.N. Kincaid, suggests that the reason
    why this was omitted from Vergil's published history was that it
    reflected Elizabeth's views on marrying Henry Tudor rather than
    Richard III, but Vergil wasn't writing in reference to Henry VII,
    and it is more likely that he left out this passage because he knew
    his master was sensitive about the matter.

28 Reproduced by Kincaid in 'Buck and the Elizabeth of York Letter:
    A Reply to Dr Hanham'

29 Egerton MS. 2216; Bodleian MS. Malone 1; Fisher MS., University
    of Toronto; Additional MS. 27422

30 For a full discussion of these texts, see A.N. Kincaid, in Buck.

31 Kincaid: 'Buck and the Elizabeth of York Letter: A Reply to Dr
    Hanham'; Horrox

32 Buck, ed. Kincaid

33 Ibid.

34 Hicks: *Anne Neville*

35 Kincaid, in Buck

36 Hervey; Kincaid's edition of Buck; Ricci

37 Kincaid, in Buck

38 Memoir in *PPE*

39 Gairdner

40 For the debate see Kincaid, in Buck; Horrox; and the articles by
    Hanham and Kincaid in *The Ricardian*.

41 See also Okerlund: *Elizabeth of York*

42 Ashdown-Hill: *The Last Days of Richard III*; Ashdown-Hill: *Richard
    III's 'Beloved Cousyn'*

43 Kincaid: 'Buck and the Elizabeth of York Letter: A Reply to Dr Hanham'
44 Baldwin: *Elizabeth Woodville*
45 Baldwin: *Richard III*
46 For example, by me in *The Princes in the Tower*, although I have now revised that view in the light of further research.
47 *Croyland Chronicle*
48 Royal MS. 20, A, f.XIX
49 Harleian MS. 49
50 Gristwood
51 Weir: *The Princes in the Tower*; Visser-Fuchs: 'Where did Elizabeth of York find consolation?'; Baldwin: *Lost Prince*; Okerlund: *Elizabeth of York*
52 Vergil
53 Ibid.; Griffiths and Thomas
54 Gristwood
55 *Acts of Court of the Mercers' Company*
56 *York Civic Records*; *Letters of the Kings of England*
57 *Croyland Chronicle*

6: 'Purposing a Conquest'

1 Aside from Gairdner, who compared all the versions of the poem, most historians have based their assessments on Heywood's edition; however it differs considerably from the earlier texts.
2 Letts
3 Probably a reference to the Clare inheritance, which should have descended to Elizabeth as her father's heiress.
4 Meaning the common people of his affinity.
5 Cokayne
6 Leland: *Itinerary*
7 Ibid.; Todd; Camden. Sheriff Hutton Castle was much decayed by the reign of James I, when it was partially dismantled, and today only the stark ruins of two towers and the gatehouse remain on its grassy mound.
8 Bacon's work was based on printed sources that are still available today, and on manuscript sources, such as those in Sir Robert Cotton's library and documents in the records office in the Tower of London and the Crown Office. His contemporary, John Selden, praised his work as one of only two histories that contained 'either of the truth or plenty that may be gained from the records of this kingdom' (cited by Vickers in his edition of Bacon).

9 According to a near-contemporary pedigree roll drawn up for the family of Margaret of Clarence, Warwick's sister; see Philip Morgan: 'Those were the days: a Yorkist pedigree roll', in *Estrangement, Enterprise and Education in Fifteenth-Century England*; Jones: *Psychology of a Battle: Bosworth, 1485.*

10 *Original Letters Illustrative of English History*

11 *Croyland Chronicle*

12 Ibid.

13 Ross: *Wars of the Roses*

14 Ibid.

15 *Croyland Chronicle*

16 Most writers follow Kendall: *Richard the Third*, although he cites no source for this date.

17 *Croyland Chronicle*

18 Ibid.

19 Hall

20 Vergil

21 *Croyland Chronicle*

22 Ibid.

23 Ibid.; Vergil

24 Vergil is the only source to state it was Lord Stanley who retrieved the crown; the *Great Chronicle of London* states that it was Sir William Stanley. After Sir William's execution for treason in 1495, Vergil may have deemed it politic to assert that it was his brother.

25 Vergil; Hall

26 Vergil

27 Harleian MS. 542

28 *Croyland Chronicle*

29 Rous

30 HVIIPPE

31 Ashdown-Hill: *The Fate of Richard III's Body*; Pidgeon; Baldwin: *King Richard's Grave in Leicester*; Billson

32 Bacon; Francis Drake, in *Eboracum*, says that Halewell is mentioned in one of the warrants.

33 Vergil

34 Bacon

35 Vergil

36 Bacon

37 Ibid.

38 Laynesmith

39 Warrant of 24 February 1486 in Exchequer Records E.404/79

40 Godfrey and Wagner; Kingsford: 'Historical Notes on Mediaeval

London Houses'. Coldharbour was burned down in 1666 during the Great Fire of London.

7: 'Our Bridal Torch'

1   Chrimes; Professor Eric Ives, in conversation with the author, May 2012.
2   *Calendar of Papal Registers*. Henry's great-grandfather, John Beaufort, was the brother of Elizabeth's great-grandmother, Joan Beaufort.
3   Hicks: *Anne Neville*; Peter Clarke: 'English Royal Marriages and the Papal Penitentiary in the Fifteenth Century'
4   Rastell
5   *Rotuli Parliamentorum*
6   Bacon
7   Ross: *Wars of the Roses*
8   *Rotuli Parliamentorum*
9   Bacon
10 *CSP Spain*
11 Vergil
12 Hall
13 Gristwood; Jones and Underwood
14 *Calendar of Papal Registers*
15 *Materials for a History of the Reign of Henry the Seventh*
16 *Rutland Papers*
17 Fisher: *Funeral Sermon*
18 *Croyland Chronicle*
19 *Rotuli Parliamentorum*
20 *CSP: Spain*
21 Buck
22 *Rotuli Parliamentorum*
23 Anglo: *Spectacle, Pageantry and Early Tudor Policy*
24 In his dispensation of 1486 (*Foedera*) – see Chapter 9.
25 Leland: *Collectanea*
26 *Popular Songs of Ireland*
27 Mancini
28 Bacon
29 Ibid.
30 *Rotuli Parliamentorum*
31 Dockray: *Richard III: Myth and Reality*
32 Bacon
33 *Materials for a History of the Reign of Henry the Seventh*
34 *Rotuli Parliamentorum*

35 Vergil
36 Hall
37 Challis; Anglo: *Images of Tudor Kingship*
38 Mackie
39 Bacon
40 *Calendar of Papal Registers*
41 Weightman; Vaughan; Wiesflacker
42 Harleian MS. 336, in Leland: *Collectanea*. Gigli was rewarded with a prebendary stall in York; he would serve Henry VII as ambassador to Rome and become Bishop of Worcester (Tournoy-Thouen; Dixon).
43 *Calendar of Papal Registers*, January 1486
44 *PPE*
45 *Croyland Chronicle*
46 *Rotuli Parliamentorum*; *Materials for a History of the Reign of Henry the Seventh*; André
47 Mutilated document in Cotton MS. Cleopatra
48 *Calendar of Papal Registers*
49 Ibid.
50 Ibid.
51 Hall
52 *Rotuli Parliamentorum*
53 André
54 *CSP Venice*
55 *Calendar of Papal Registers*
56 *Letters and Papers Illustrative of the Reigns of Richard III and Henry VII*
57 Shears
58 *Calendar of Papal Registers*
59 Ibid.; Loades: *Mary Rose*
60 Bacon; Croyland also gives the date as 18 January.
61 André
62 Mutilated document in Cotton MS. Cleopatra
63 *Croyland Chronicle*
64 Meerson
65 Arch and Marschner
66 Harleian MS. 336, in Leland: *Collectanea*
67 Okerlund: *Elizabeth of York*; *Materials for a History of the Reign of Henry the Seventh*
68 Bacon
69 Ibid.
70 Harleian MS. 336, in *Leland Collectanea*
71 Cambridge University Library Dd. 13.27, f.31; Strickland
72 Hawes: *A Joyful Meditation*

73 *Stuart Royal Proclamations*
74 Kohler; Francis Perry; http://www.britishmuseum.org/research/
75 All cited by Wroe
76 *York Civic Records*
77 Cited by Hilliam
78 Anglo: *Images of Tudor Kingship*

8: 'In Blest Wedlock'

1 Woolgar
2 Harris
3 Laynesmith
4 Sandford; Laynesmith
5 *Great Chronicle of London*; Hall; Hayward
6 Hayward
7 *CSP Venice*
8 So called after the ceiling decoration in the room at the Palace of Westminster where it was held.
9 Exchequer Records E.101
10 Bacon
11 *CSP Venice*
12 *CSP Spain*
13 Cunningham: *Henry VII*
14 Erasmus: *The Epistles of Erasmus*; Bacon
15 *Gothic*. The book of hours is in the Devonshire Collection at Chatsworth House.
16 *Materials for a History of the Reign of Henry the Seventh*
17 *CSP Spain*
18 Jones and Underwood; Laynesmith; *Calendar of Patent Rolls: Henry VII*; Searle
19 Vickers, in his edition of Bacon
20 Bacon
21 *HVIIPPE*
22 *Memorials of King Henry VII*
23 Milne. He offers good evidence that Velville was Henry's son.
24 *CSP Spain*
25 *Four English Political Tracts of the Later Middle Ages*
26 *Oxford Dictionary of National Biography*
27 Cessolis
28 Norton: *She Wolves*
29 *Paston Letters*
30 Shears

31 *PPE*

32 Loades: *Tudor Queens*

33 *Paston Letters.* John Paston was knighted at the Battle of Stoke in June 1487, so the letters must have been written after that date, as he is referred to as Sir John in both of them. Daubeney, whose letter was written on the Saturday before St Lawrence's Day, 10 August, refers to Elizabeth having taken to her chamber. Only two of her children were born in the summer: Arthur in 1486, the year before Paston was knighted; and Elizabeth on 2 July 1492. The letters must therefore belong to 1492, when the Queen was still lying in after her confinement, in which case Daubeney's was written on 5 August.

34 *PPE*

35 *CSP Spain*

36 *PPE*

37 Okerlund: *Elizabeth of York*; Cloake: 'Richmond's Great Monastery'; Thompson

38 *PPE*

39 Ibid.

40 The device of Elizabeth Wydeville (Okerlund: *Elizabeth of York*)

41 Okerlund, in *Elizabeth of York*, suggests this is a reference to her being jilted by the Dauphin.

42 Additional MS. 5645, ff.8v–11; *Historical Poems of the XIVth and XVth Centuries*; Stevens

43 Cotton MS. Vitellius

44 *CSP Venice*

45 *PPE*

46 *Calendar of Papal Registers*

47 Cotton MS Vespasian F XIII, f.60

48 *Original Letters Illustrative of English History*

49 *Letters of Royal and Illustrious Ladies of Great Britain*

50 Harleian MS. 7039

51 Fisher: *Funeral Sermon*

52 Additional MSS

53 Fisher: *Funeral Sermon*

54 *Ibid.*

55 *Letters of the Queens of England*

56 Loades: *Tudor Queens*

57 *CSP Spain*

58 More

59 Gristwood

60 Laynesmith

61 *Records of the Borough of Nottingham*; Jones and Underwood; *City and Spectacle in Medieval Europe*

62 Gristwood

63 *Materials for a History of the Reign of Henry the Seventh*. Nothing remains of this chantry chapel today, as the church was mostly rebuilt in the eighteenth century; the only chantry chapel still to survive is that of Sir Richard Weston, the builder of nearby Sutton Place, who probably rose to prominence in the service of Elizabeth of York.

64 *Calendar of Patent Rolls: Henry VII*

65 Gristwood; *PPE*

66 *Collection of Ordinances*

67 Jones and Underwood

68 In Elizabeth's lifetime Margaret did not reside at Derby Place, the town residence built by her husband in 1503 on Peter's Hill, near Baynard's Castle. It later became the Heralds' College, but was burned down in the Great Fire of 1666. The present College of Arms occupies the site.

69 Jones and Underwood

70 *PPE*

71 *Collection of Ordinances*

72 *The Household of Edward IV*

73 Leland: *Collectanea*; *Collection of Ordinances*

74 *CSP Venice*. Foreign observers often referred to Henry VII as 'his Majesty', but that style was not adopted in England until the reign of Henry VIII; Henry VII used the traditional style, 'his Grace'.

75 *Collection of Ordinances*

76 *Materials for a History of the Reign of Henry the Seventh*; *PPE*; *HVIIPPE*

77 *PPE*

78 Ibid.

79 Ibid.

80 Additional MS. 50001, f.22; *England in the Fifteenth Century*; Sutton and Visser-Fuchs: 'A "Most Benevolent Queen"'; Backhouse: 'Illuminated Manuscripts associated with Henry VII'; *Gothic*; McKendrick, Lowden and Doyle

81 Exeter College MS. 47; *The Reign of Henry VII from Contemporary Sources*

82 Royal MS. 16, f.II

83 *Catalogue of Illuminated Manuscripts*; Backhouse: 'Illuminated Manuscripts associated with Henry VII'

84 Royal MS. 19B XVI

85 McKendrick, Lowden and Doyle

86 Royal MS. 20D VI

87 McKendrick, Lowden and Doyle

88 *Catalogue of Western Manuscripts and Miniatures*

89 Now in the British Library

90 Jones and Underwood

91 *PPE*

92 Yale Centre for British Art, Paul Mellon Collection. Painter;
     Okerlund: *Elizabeth of York*

93 *England in the Fifteenth Century*

94 Nicolas: Memoir, in *PPE*; Additional MS. 17, OX2

95 *CSP Spain*

96 *CSP Milan*

97 *CSP Venice*

98 *CSP Spain*

99 Ibid.

100 Vergil

101 'Lamentation', in More: *Complete Works*

102 *CSP Spain*

103 *Patronage, the Crown and the Provinces in Later Medieval England*

104 Crawford: 'The King's Burden?'

105 Loades: *Tudor Queens*

106 *Materials for a History of the Reign of Henry the Seventh*

107 *Rotuli Parliamentorum*; *Calendar of Patent Rolls: Henry VII*; Crawford:
     'The King's Burden?'

108 *Rotuli Parliamentorum*

109 *Halsbury's Laws of England*

110 *Calendar of Patent Rolls: Henry VII*

111 Myers: *Crown, Household and Parliament in Fifteenth-Century England*;
     Laynesmith; *Patronage, the Crown and the Provinces in Later Medieval
     England*

112 *Patronage, the Crown and the Provinces in Later Medieval England*

113 Special Collections S.C. 2/172/38, 40; McIntosh; Laynesmith

114 Additional MS. 46454

115 *PPE*

116 *Materials for a History of the Reign of Henry the Seventh*; *Calendar of
     Patent Rolls: Henry VII*; Westminster Abbey Muniments 12172–3 and
     12177; *PPE*; Laynesmith

117 HVIIPPE; *PPE*

118 *PPE*

119 'Lamentation', in More: *Complete Works*

120 *PPE*

121 *HVIIPPE*; Exchequer Records E.101/414/6; *PPE*
122 *Patronage, the Crown and the Provinces in Later Medieval England*; *PPE*
123 *PPE*
124 Ibid.; Laynesmith
125 *PPE*

9: 'Offspring of the Race of Kings'

1 *Materials for a History of the Reign of Henry the Seventh*
2 André
3 Ibid.
4 Hall
5 Ibid.
6 Rowse: *Bosworth Field and the Wars of the Roses*
7 Hedley
8 *Materials for a History of the Reign of Henry the Seventh*; Tudor-Craig.
   The original bull is in the possession of the Society of Antiquaries of
   London, and there are copies in the British Library, the National
   Archives and the John Rylands Library; the text is printed in *Foedera*.
9 William de Machlin: circular of the Papal Bull, in *Tudor Royal
   Proclamations*
10 Leland: *Collectanea*
11 *Materials for a History of the Reign of Henry the Seventh*
12 Hall
13 Macalpine
14 Ibid.
15 Rhoda Edwards; Macalpine; Hall
16 *Victoria County History: Hampshire*
17 Leland: *Collectanea*. The hall survives, but the interior of the
   Deanery has been much altered since Elizabeth stayed there.
18 Ibid.
19 *Materials for a History of the Reign of Henry the Seventh*
20 Ibid.
21 Articles ordained by King Henry VII for the Regulation of his
   Household, in Harleian MS. 642, f.198–217; *Collection of Ordinances*;
   Cotton MS. Julius B XII; Leland: *Collectanea*
22 *Antiquarian Repertory*
23 Eames; Laynesmith
24 *Antiquarian Repertory*
25 *Original Letters Illustrative of English History*
26 *Collection of Ordinances*
27 Ibid.

28 Harleian MS. 642, f.198–217; *Collection of Ordinances*; Leland: *Collectanea*

29 Leland: *Collectanea*

30 Okerlund: *Elizabeth of York*

31 *Collection of Ordinances*

32 Leland: *Collectanea*; *Collection of Ordinances*

33 *Collection of Ordinances*; Leland: *Collectanea*

34 *Plague, Poverty, Prayer*

35 *England in the Fifteenth Century*

36 Eamonn Duffy; *PPE*

37 *Plague, Poverty, Prayer*

38 Ibid.

39 The Beaufort Hours; Leland: *Collectanea*; McKendrick, Lowden and Doyle

40 Hall

41 Cotton MS. Julius EIV, f.10v

42 Hampshire Record Office, 11 M59, B1/211, cited by Jones in *Psychology of a Battle: Bosworth, 1485*

43 Leland: *Collectanea*

44 *Plague, Poverty, Prayer*

45 Bacon

46 Fuller

47 Hall

48 *Collection of Ordinances*

49 Leland: *Collectanea*; *Antiquarian Repertory*

50 *Collection of Ordinances*

51 Ibid.

52 Additional MS. 6113, f.77b; Leland: *Collectanea*; *Collection of Ordinances*; the Royal Book in *Antiquarian Repertory*

53 Leland: *Collectanea*

54 *Anthology of Catholic Poets*

55 *Materials for a History of the Reign of Henry the Seventh*; Anglo; *Spectacle, Pageantry and Early Tudor Policy*; Doran

56 Hughes

57 Additional MSS

58 Leland: *Collectanea*

59 Harris; Cressy

60 Leland: *Collectanea*

61 *Materials for a History of the Reign of Henry the Seventh*

62 Meaning attire, or a covering, in this case a veil.

63 *Collection of Ordinances*; Leland: *Collectanea*; Parsons

64 Cited by Hayward

65 Account of Norroy Herald in Additional MS. 6113; Leland: *Collectanea*; *Liber Regie Capelle*; Cressy; Harris; Brigden

66 *Collection of Ordinances*; *Materials for a History of the Reign of Henry the Seventh*; Exchequer Records E.404 and E.101; Gristwood; Hayward

67 Brigden

68 *Collection of Ordinances*

69 Ibid; Leland: *Collectanea*

70 Lansdowne MS. 278, f.26; Crawford: 'The Piety of Late-Medieval English Queens'. Elizabeth did not re-found the Lady Chapel, as is sometimes asserted.

71 Licence: *Elizabeth of York*

72 *Calendar of Patent Rolls: Henry VII*; *Materials for a History of the Reign of Henry the Seventh*

73 *Materials for a History of the Reign of Henry the Seventh*

74 Bell

75 Randerson

76 Starkey: *Henry, Virtuous Prince*, citing Leland: *Collectanea*; Hutchinson: *Young Henry*

10: 'Damnable Conspiracies'

1 *Materials for a History of the Reign of Henry the Seventh*

2 Ibid.; Okerlund: *Elizabeth of York*

3 Account of Norroy Herald in Additional MS. 6113; *Collection of Ordinances*; *PPE*

4 *Collection of Ordinances*

5 Vergil

6 Leland: *Collectanea*

7 Cotton MS. Julius, BXII, f.29

8 *Calendar of Papal Registers*

9 *Materials for a History of the Reign of Henry the Seventh*

10 *Foedera*

11 Vergil

12 *Materials for a History of the Reign of Henry the Seventh*

13 *Patronage, the Crown and the Provinces in Later Medieval England*

14 The site is now occupied by Bermondsey Square and Bermondsey Market.

15 Bacon

16 Okerlund: *Elizabeth Wydeville*

17 Okerlund: *Elizabeth of York*

18 For Bermondsey Abbey, see, for example, Okerlund: *Elizabeth Wydeville*; Edward Clarke

19 *Materials for a History of the Reign of Henry the Seventh*
20 Ibid.
21 Lee states that she entered the convent in 1490, when her mother entered Bermondsey, but that had been in 1487.
22 More
23 'Friaries: The Dominican nuns of Dartford'; Lee; C.F.R. Palmer
24 Vergil
25 Ibid.
26 Bacon
27 Okerlund: *Elizabeth of York*
28 *CSP Spain*
29 André
30 Bacon
31 *Calendar of Papal Registers*
32 *Original Letters Illustrative of English History*
33 Starkey: *Henry, Virtuous Prince*
34 Leland: *Collectanea*
35 *Materials for a History of the Reign of Henry the Seventh*
36 Bacon
37 Vergil
38 André
39 Bacon

11: 'Bright Elizabeth'

1 Bacon
2 Gristwood
3 Bacon
4 Ibid.
5 *Materials for a History of the Reign of Henry the Seventh*
6 Bacon
7 Rawlinson MS. 146, f.158, Bodleian Library; Leland: *Collectanea*
8 *Great Chronicle of London*
9 This account of Elizabeth's coronation and the attendant celebrations is based on the descriptions in Leland: *Collectanea*; Cotton MS. Julius B XII, f.39; Rawlinson MS. 146, f.161; Egerton MS. 985, f.19; *English Coronation Records*
10 Norris
11 Tessa Rose
12 Probably the same sceptre that Anne Neville is shown holding in the Rous Roll.
13 The King and Queen had attended Margaret's wedding (*HVIIPPE*),

which had taken place sometime after September 1486 (Pierce). Margaret was to bear Sir Richard five children before his death in 1505, and would name one Henry and another Arthur.

14 Parsons

15 Strong: *Lost Treasures of Britain*; Strong: *Coronation*; Tessa Rose

16 The Pageants of Richard Beauchamp, Earl of Warwick, B.L. Cotton MS Julius E IV

17 Hilliam

18 Strickland states that this poem, dated 1486, was found in an old chest at Gayton, Northamptonshire in the 1840s. It is also cited by Davey.

19 Leland: *Collectanea*

12: 'Elysabeth ye Quene'

1 Laynesmith

2 *Patronage, the Crown and the Provinces in Later Medieval England*

3 *Calendar of Patent Rolls: Henry VII*; Myers: *Crown, Household and Parliament in Fifteenth-Century England*; Myers: 'The Household Accounts of Queen Margaret of Anjou, 1452–3'; Laynesmith; *PPE*; Crawford: 'The Queen's Council in the Middle Ages'

4 Crawford: 'The Queen's Council in the Middle Ages'; *Patronage, the Crown and the Provinces in Later Medieval England*; *PPE*

5 Ibid.

6 *Materials for a History of the Reign of Henry the Seventh*; *PPE*

7 *Letters and Papers, Foreign and Domestic, of the Reign of Henry VIII*. Ormond's great-granddaughter, Anne Boleyn, became the second wife of Elizabeth's son, Henry VIII.

8 *Materials for a History of the Reign of Henry the Seventh*

9 Okerlund: *Elizabeth of York*

10 Crawford: 'The Queen's Council in the Middle Ages'; *Patronage, the Crown and the Provinces in Later Medieval England*; *The Household of Edward IV*; Myers: 'The Household Accounts of Queen Margaret of Anjou, 1452–3'; *PPE*

11 *Materials for a History of the Reign of Henry the Seventh*

12 Ibid.; *PPE*

13 *PPE*

14 Ibid.

15 Ibid.; Hayward

16 *PPE*

17 *Materials for a History of the Reign of Henry the Seventh*; *Great Wardrobe Accounts*

18 *Calendar of Patent Rolls: Henry VII*
19 *PPE*; Hayward
20 *PPE*
21 Ibid.
22 *Materials for a History of the Reign of Henry the Seventh*; *PPE*; Norris
23 *PPE*
24 *Materials for a History of the Reign of Henry the Seventh*; *PPE*
25 *HVIIPPE*
26 *Oxford Dictionary of National Biography*
27 *HVIIPPE*
28 *Materials for a History of the Reign of Henry the Seventh*; *PPE*
29 *England in the Fifteenth Century*
30 *PPE*
31 *The Reign of Henry VII from Contemporary Sources*; *Dictionary of National Biography*; *Handbook of British Chronology*
32 *Letters of Royal and Illustrious Ladies of Great Britain*; *Lisle Letters*
33 Given-Hilson; Beauclerk-Dewar and Powell; *Lisle Letters*
34 *PPE*
35 *Patronage, the Crown and the Provinces in Later Medieval England*
36 *CSP Spain*
37 *PPE*
38 Ibid. The later term 'chambermaid' derives from 'chamberer'.
39 *PPE*
40 Leland: *Collectanea*
41 *Collection of Ordinances*
42 *PPE*
43 Ibid.
44 Harris
45 *Great Wardrobe Accounts*; *PPE*
46 *PPE*
47 Exchequer Records E.101/415/3
48 *PPE*
49 Johnson
50 *PPE*
51 Ibid.
52 Ibid. I am indebted to historian Siobhan Clarke for the information on black clothing.
53 *PPE*; Hayward
54 *PPE*
55 *Great Wardrobe Accounts*; *PPE*; *Materials for a History of the Reign of Henry the Seventh*
56 *PPE*

57 *Materials for a History of the Reign of Henry the Seventh*; Johnson; Norris; Hayward
58 *PPE*
59 Alberge
60 *PPE*
61 *HVIIPPE*
62 *PPE*
63 Ibid.
64 Ibid.; Hayward
65 *Materials for a History of the Reign of Henry the Seventh*
66 Licence: *Elizabeth of York*
67 *PPE*
68 *Materials for a History of the Reign of Henry the Seventh*
69 Ibid.
70 *HVIIPPE*; *Great Wardrobe Accounts*; Exchequer Records E.101; Hayward; Gristwood
71 *PPE*

13: 'Unbounded Love'

1 André
2 See, for example, Jones and Underwood; Okerlund: *Elizabeth of York*
3 College of Arms MS. I, III, f.10
4 Additional MS. 38, 133, f.132b; Leland: *Collectanea*
5 Holinshed
6 *Letters of the Queens of England, 1100–1547*
7 *Materials for a History of the Reign of Henry the Seventh*
8 One who holds lands of an overlord in exchange for knight's service.
9 The official in charge of administration.
10 *Materials for a History of the Reign of Henry the Seventh*
11 Charter Rolls C.53
12 *Materials for a History of the Reign of Henry the Seventh*
13 Leland: *Collectanea*
14 *CSP Spain*
15 Ibid.
16 Hedley; Hope; Goodall. The eastern part of the gallery and the arraying chamber still survive, much altered. Elizabeth's dining chamber is now the Queen's Drawing Room. The site of her bedchamber is now occupied by the central room of the Royal Library. The old state apartments were extensively remodelled for Charles II in the seventeenth century, and for George IV in the nineteenth century.

17 Hentzner

18 Hayward

19 Leland: *Collectanea*

20 Ibid.

21 Gristwood

22 Licence: *Elizabeth of York*

23 *CSP Spain*

24 *CSP Venice*

25 Leland: *Collectanea*

26 Pierce

27 *CSP Spain*

28 Leland: *Collectanea*

29 *Materials for a History of the Reign of Henry the Seventh*

30 Licence: *Elizabeth of York*

31 Cotton MS. Julius B XII; Leland: *Collectanea*

32 Leland: *Collectanea*

33 *Materials for a History of the Reign of Henry the Seventh; PPE*

34 Leland: *Collectanea*; Green. Strickland, in her *Lives of the Queens of Scotland*, states incorrectly that the Princess was christened in St Margaret's Church, Westminster.

35 Leland: *Collectanea*

36 Exchequer Records E.404; *Collection of Ordinances; Original Letters Illustrative of English History;* Glasheen

37 Leland: *Collectanea*

38 *CSP Spain.* When Granada finally fell in 1492, completing the centuries-long Reconquest of Spain, *Te Deum* was sung in St Paul's Cathedral. The suggestion that Ferdinand wrote to Elizabeth because he recognised her title comes from the historian Sarah Gristwood, in correspondence with the author.

39 Leland: *Collectanea*

40 Ibid.

41 *Calendar of Patent Rolls: Henry VII*

42 *Materials for a History of the Reign of Henry the Seventh*; Starkey: *Six Wives*

43 Her surname is also given as Uxbridge. Later she married Walter Luke (or Locke).

44 Exchequer Records E.404

45 Lambard. These apartments do not survive.

46 Dowsing; Hedley; Thurley: *The Royal Palaces of Tudor England*

47 Starkey: *Monarchy*; Starkey: *Henry, Virtuous Prince*; Laynesmith

48 Starkey: *Henry, Virtuous Prince*; Exchequer Records E.404

49 In *Henry VIII: Man and Monarch* an engraving of 1748 by George

Vertue, incorrectly inscribed as Prince Henry, Prince Arthur and Princess Margaret, is said to be based on 'a no-longer-extant and possibly spurious painting of 1496'. But 'Henry' is clearly older than 'Margaret', and the painting, by Jan Gossaert, which is in the Royal Collection (a copy is in the collection of the Earl of Pembroke at Wilton House, Wiltshire), in fact portrays Dorothea, John and Christina, the children of Christian II, King of Denmark, and was painted in 1526. It is recorded in Henry VIII's collection, but in the eighteenth century was misidentified, perhaps by Queen Caroline of Ansbach, wife of George II, as the children of Henry VII.

50 *CSP: Milan*
51 *CSP: Spain*
52 Vergil; André
53 *CSP Spain*
54 Bacon
55 Strickland
56 Lancelott
57 Bacon
58 Vergil
59 Book of Howth
60 *Letters and Papers Illustrative of the Reigns of Richard III and Henry VII*
61 Bacon
62 Ibid.
63 Arundel MS. 26 f.29v
64 *A Collection of all the Wills, now known to be extant, of the Kings and Queens of England*
65 Arundel MS. 26 f.29v
66 Arundel MS. 26 f.30
67 Arundel MS. 26 f.29v
68 *Collection of Ordinances*
69 *PPE*
70 Leland: *Collectanea*
71 Exchequer Records E.404
72 Household book of Henry VII as kept by John Heron Treasurer of the Chamber, 1499–1505: Additional MS. 21, 480
73 André
74 Vergil
75 Bacon
76 Ibid.
77 Vergil
78 Ibid.

79 *Calendar of Patent Rolls: Henry VII*
80 Mancini
81 Hepburn
82 Herbert and New; Walker
83 Stow: *Annals*
84 Bacon
85 *Calendar of the Cecil Papers at Hatfield House*; *Original Letters Illustrative of English History*
86 Vergil
87 Four stanzas of seven lines each in iambic pentameter.
88 *Great Chronicle of London*
89 Hall
90 *Letters and Papers Illustrative of the Reigns of Richard III and Henry VII*
91 *Henry VIII: A European Court in England*; Hayward. The sketch is probably a copy, dating from *c*.1515–25, of a lost original. It is inscribed '*le roy Henry d'Angleterre*', but the identity of the sitter has been disputed on the grounds that the broad-brimmed feathered hat he wears over his coif is a fashion of a later date (*Henry VIII: Man and Monarch*). However there are many examples of this type of headgear in the 1490s, and the high square neckline of the Prince's paltock belongs also to that period (Norris).
92 Sir Thomas Tyng to Sir John Paston, in *Paston Letters*
93 Hall; Cotton MS. Julius A. XVI f.150, in *Letters and Papers Illustrative of the Reigns of Richard III and Henry VII*
94 Cotton MS. Julius A. XVI f.150, in *Letters and Papers Illustrative of the Reigns of Richard III and Henry VII*
95 Stow: *London*; *HVIIPPE*
96 Hall
97 Ibid.
98 Bacon
99 Strickland: Buck; Hutchinson: *House of Treason*
100 *HVIIPPE*
101 *Formulare Anglicanum*
102 *Rotuli Parliamentorum*
103 Meerson
104 Hall
105 *Rotuli Parliamentorum*
106 *Calendar of Patent Rolls: Henry VII*
107 Dugdale
108 *Letters and Papers Illustrative of the Reigns of Richard III and Henry VII*
109 Prerogative Court of Canterbury Wills, PROB 11/10 q.25
110 Cited by Finch

111 Stow: *London*
112 Thurley: *The Royal Palaces of Tudor England*. Baynard's Castle was largely destroyed in 1666 during the Great Fire of London; a single turret survived until 1720. The site was excavated in 1972–5.
113 *HVIIPPE*
114 Ibid.
115 Draper
116 Lathom House was to be slighted and destroyed in 1645 during the Civil War. A third house was erected in its place in the eighteenth century, but only the west wing stands today (*Victoria County History: Lancashire*; Neil, Baldwin and Crosby).
117 *HVIIPPE*
118 White Kennett's Collections in the Lansdowne MSS
119 Bacon
120 I am indebted to Ian Coulson for these details, and for kindly sending me his article detailing his research on the Paradise Bed, which he acquired in 2010. This research is still ongoing.
121 *HVIIPPE*

14: 'Doubtful Drops of Royal Blood'

1 Cotton MS. Vitellius A. XVI f.156 gives 7 October, but Stow: *London*, citing the tomb inscription, gives 14 November. This cannot be correct, as the warrant for the funeral expenses was issued on 26 October.
2 *HVIIPPE*
3 Ibid.; Bacon
4 *HVIIPPE*
5 Exchequer Records E.404; Egerton MS. 2, 642, f.185v
6 *Great Chronicle of London*; Cotton MS. Vitellius A. XVI f.156; Sandford; Lane; Strickland; Stow: *London*
7 Stow: *London*
8 PPE; Vail; Ashdown-Hill: *Richard III's 'Beloved Cousyn'*; Smith
9 *Foedera*
10 Bacon
11 *CSP Spain*
12 The King and Queen were in residence at Sheen from 26 February until they moved to Windsor on 14 April (*HVIIPPE*).
13 Records of the Keeper of the Privy Seal PSO 1; Exchequer Records E.101
14 *HVIIPPE*
15 Cokayne

16 *HVIIPPE*

17 Ibid.

18 *Letters of Royal and Illustrious Ladies of Great Britain*

19 Exchequer Records E.101; *PPE*

20 Miscellaneous Books E.36

21 Meerson

22 *PPE*

23 Starkey: *Henry, Virtuous Prince*

24 Ibid.

25 Erasmus: *The Epistles of Erasmus*

26 Skelton: *The Poetical Works*

27 Starkey: *Henry, Virtuous Prince*

28 Loades: *Tudor Queens*

29 *PPE*

30 Cited by Strickland

31 *HVIIPPE*; Special Collections S.C. 1/51/189

32 *CSP Venice*

33 *HVIIPPE*; Strickland; Wroe

34 *The Reign of Henry VII from Contemporary Sources*; Gristwood: Bruce

35 Hall

36 Ibid.

37 *HVIIPPE*

38 Ibid.

39 *CSP Milan*

40 Starkey: *Henry, Virtuous Prince*; Hutchinson: *Young Henry*

41 Starkey: *Henry, Virtuous Prince*

42 *CSP Venice*; *CSP Milan*

43 Bacon

44 Ibid.

45 *CSP Venice*

46 Ibid.

47 Letter of Henry VII in Lambeth Palace MS. 632 f.25

48 Bacon

49 Gristwood

50 André

51 Ibid.; Gristwood

52 *Letters and Papers Illustrative of the Reigns of Richard III and Henry VII*

53 Wroe; Gristwood

54 *Great Chronicle of London*; Cotton MS. Vitellius, A XVI, f.168; Moorhen

55 Wroe

56 Bacon

57 Meerson; *Calendar of Documents relating to Scotland*; Miscellaneous Books E.36; *HVIIPPE*; Wroe
58 *HVIIPPE*
59 Cotton MS. Vitellius A XVI, printed in *Chronicles of London*
60 *CSP Venice*
61 Baldwin: *Elizabeth Woodville*
62 Egerton MS 616, f.7
63 *CSP Spain*
64 Before the Reformation priests were customarily given the courtesy title 'Sir'.
65 *The Voice of the Middle Ages in Personal Letters*
66 *CSP Milan*
67 'St Thomas' night', according to *The Great Chronicle of London*, although *CSP Milan* says the night before Christmas Eve.
68 *CSP Venice*
69 *CSP Milan*
70 Ibid.
71 *CSP Venice*
72 Bacon
73 *CSP: Milan*
74 Ibid.
75 *Great Chronicle of London*
76 *CSP: Milan*
77 *CSP Spain*
78 *PPE*
79 *HVIIPPE*
80 Anglo: 'The Court Festivals of Henry VII'
81 *HVIIPPE*
82 *CSP Spain*
83 Ibid.
84 Ibid.
85 Ibid.
86 Gristwood
87 *CSP Spain*
88 Ibid.
89 Ibid.
90 Ibid.
91 *HVIIPPE*
92 Capgrave
93 *HVIIPPE*
94 Cooper; Lyte
95 *CSP Spain*

96   Licence: *Elizabeth of York*

97   *CSP Spain*

98   Ibid.

99   *Foedera*

100 *Great Chronicle of London*

101 Green

102 *Great Wardrobe Accounts*; Exchequer Records E.101; *HVIIPPE*

103 The date is recorded in the Beaufort Hours, which is more likely to be correct than Ayala, who wrote that the Queen 'was delivered of a son on Friday' (*CSP Spain*). Charles Wriothesley also gives the date incorrectly as 22 February.

104 *Great Wardrobe Accounts*; *HVIIPPE*

105 *CSP Spain*

106 Gristwood

107 *CSP Spain*

108 *HVIIPPE*

109 Wriothesley

110 Including your author in *Britain's Royal Families.*

111 Lenz Harvey: *The Rose and the Thorn*

112 Hutchinson: *Young Henry*; Gristwood

113 Lenz-Harvey, in *Elizabeth of York*, says that grief over Princess Elizabeth's death caused the Queen to give birth to a son too small to survive.

114 Loades: *Mary Rose*, although he says that Elizabeth had 'an abortive pregnancy'; Norton: *England's Queens*, but she incorrectly gives the date of Princess Elizabeth's death as 1497 and – like Lenz-Harvey in *Elizabeth of York* – the date of Princess Mary's birth as 1498, as Holinshed wrongly has it.

115 King's MS. 395, ff.32v-33

116 For example, Chrimes

117 Leland: *Itinerary.* The house was destroyed during the Civil War and rebuilt in the early eighteenth century.

118 *CSP Spain*

119 *Letters of Royal and Illustrious Ladies of Great Britain*

120 *HVIIPPE*

121 The occasion was immortalised in a fresco executed in 1910 in the Palace of Westminster by F.W. Cowper, although it was incorrectly set at Greenwich; and in stained glass made in 1881 for St Mary's Church, Bury St Edmunds.

122 'Britain Personified', in Erasmus: *The Epistles of Erasmus*

123 Erasmus: *The Epistles of Erasmus*

124 Letter of Cardinal Reginald Pole of 7 September 1549, in *CSP Venice*

125 *CSP Spain*
126 Records of the Court of King's Bench: Indictments Files KB 9/390, 84–6
127 Hall
128 *HVIIPPE*
129 Moorhen
130 *CSP Spain*

15: 'The Spanish Infanta'

1 *CSP Spain*
2 Bacon
3 *CSP Spain*
4 Ibid.
5 *Chronicle of Calais*; Wroe
6 *CSP Spain*
7 Bacon
8 *Great Wardrobe Accounts*
9 Ibid.; Wardrobe Indentures in Exchequer Records E.101
10 Chrimes; Loades: *Mary Rose*
11 *PPE*
12 Grafton; *Chronicle of Calais*; *CSP Spain*
13 This red-brick palace had been built around 1480–5 by Cardinal Morton when he was Bishop of Ely. It is famous as the palace where Prince Edmund's great-niece, Elizabeth I, spent much of her youth and learned of her accession. Only the great hall and one tower of the old palace remain today, the rest having been pulled down in 1607–8 when Robert Cecil was building Hatfield House. For Arthur's health, see page 356 and note 49.
14 *HVIIPPE*
15 Ibid.
16 *Collection of Ordinances*
17 *Chronicles of London*
18 Thurley: *The Royal Palaces of Tudor England*; *Victoria County History: Kent*; Jones and Underwood. Greenwich Palace and the Observants' church were demolished in the reign of Charles II. Today, the Queen's House and the National Maritime Museum occupy the site.
19 *CSP Spain*
20 *HVIIPPE*
21 Exchequer Records E.101
22 *Letters and Papers Illustrative of the Reigns of Richard III and Henry VII*
23 *CSP Spain*

24 Cotton MS. Vitellius A XVI
25 Harleian MS. 69
26 Orders of the Privy Council, cited Okerlund: *Elizabeth of York*
27 *CSP Spain*
28 Ibid.
29 *Great Chronicle of London*
30 Account of Lancaster Herald, in *Antiquarian Repertory*
31 Ibid.
32 Ibid.
33 Ibid.; *The Receyt of the Lady Katherine*; Thurley: *The Royal Palaces of Tudor England*; Dowsing; Hedley; Fletcher
34 *Great Chronicle of London*
35 *The Receyt of the Lady Katherine*; Thurley: *The Royal Palaces of Tudor England*; *Victoria County History: Surrey*. All that substantially remains of the palace today is the original gatehouse, which bears the arms of Henry VII above the entrance arch.
36 *The Receyt of the Lady Katherine*
37 Jones and Underwood
38 Harleian MS. 69
39 *The Receyt of the Lady Katherine*; Leland: *Collectanea*
40 This account of Katherine's reception, her wedding and the celebrations that followed is based on descriptions and information in *The Receyt of the Lady Katherine*; Hall; Cotton MS. Vitellius XVI; Cotton MS. Vitellius CXI; Harleian MS. 69; *Great Chronicle of London*; *HVIIPPE*; Leland: *Collectanea*; Cowie; Gristwood; Davey; Stow: *London*
41 Maria Perry; Cokayne
42 *CSP Spain*
43 *Letters and Papers, Foreign and Domestic, of the Reign of Henry VIII*
44 Ibid.
45 Ibid.
46 Ibid.
47 Real Academia de Historia MS 9–4674, cited by Tremlett
48 Cited by Tremlett
49 Fuensalida. Letter to Ferdinand and Isabella. 25 July 1500, cited Patrick Williams.
50 'Low' dances: elegant, measured dances in which there are no jumps or capers and the feet do not leave the floor.
51 *Antiquarian Repertory*
52 *The Receyt of the Lady Katherine*
53 *CSP: Spain*
54 Ibid.; Fraser: *The Six Wives of Henry VIII*; Starkey: *Six Wives*

55 *Foedera*
56 Account of Somerset Herald, in Leland: *Collectanea*
57 *PPE*
58 College of Arms MSS: Collection of Miscellany I, f.84b-91; Cotton MS. Vitellius A XVI, f.282; Leland: *Collectanea*
59 *PPE*
60 Treasurer's Accounts, September 1502, Register House, Edinburgh

16: 'Enduring Evil Things'

1   *CSP: Milan*
2   Grafton
3   *Letters and Papers, Foreign and Domestic, of the Reign of Henry VIII*
4   *Chronicle of the Grey Friars of London*; Seward: *The Last White Rose*
5   Cunningham: *Henry VII*
6   Durant
7   Ibid.
8   *Rotuli Parliamentorum*; Seward: *The Last White Rose*. Courtenay was to remain in the Tower for the rest of Henry VII's reign, and would not be released until 1509; he died in 1511.
9   *PPE*
10 It was published as *Privy Purse Expenses of Elizabeth of York* by Nicholas Harris Nicolas in 1830, and is referred to here as *PPE*.
11 Ibid.
12 Ibid.
13 Ibid.
14 *PPE*
15 Lambeth Palace MS. 371. Elizabeth's son, Henry VIII, would visit this shrine in 1521.
16 Probably St Mary's Priory, Binham, Norfolk.
17 *PPE; Victoria County History: Suffolk*
18 Tewkesbury Annals, in Kingsford: *English Historical Literature in the Fifteenth Century*; Laynesmith
19 *PPE*; Wriothesley; Laynesmith; Chapter Records
20 *PPE; The Catholic Encyclopaedia*; Ed West; The Shrine
21 Tremlett
22 *PPE*
23 Ibid.
24 Burton; *Gothic*
25 *PPE*
26 Ibid.; Worsley and Souden; Thurley: *Hampton Court Palace*. In 1505 Daubeney acquired a new lease on the property that effectively

conferred on him the rights of a freeholder. He lived at Hampton until his death in 1508. His house was leased in 1514 to Cardinal Wolsey and subsequently largely demolished to make way for the great palace. The outline of his courtyard range is marked out in red bricks in the courtyard of Clock Court. Hampton Court later came into the possession of Henry VIII, and became one of his favourite residences.

27 *PPE*
28 Gristwood
29 *PPE*
30 Leland: *Collectanea*; *Antiquarian Repertory*; Starkey: *Six Wives*. The time was recorded on a plaque in St Laurence's Church, Ludlow, which was seen by Thomas Dineley in 1684 (Dineley; David Lloyd).
31 Hall
32 Leland: *Collectanea*
33 Faraday; David Lloyd
34 Kevin Cunningham
35 Leland: *Collectanea*
36 Real Academia de Historia, MS. 9-4674, cited Tremlett
37 Licence: *Elizabeth of York*
38 Starkey: *Six Wives*
39 Loades: *The Tudors*
40 'An Account of the Death and Interment of Prince Arthur': anonymous herald's journal, in Leland: *Collectanea*
41 *PPE*
42 *Collection of Ordinances*
43 *PPE*
44 Ibid.
45 Ibid.
46 Benham; Cheung
47 *CSP Spain*: letter of Ferdinand and Isabella to de Puebla, dated 15 April, quoted further on in the text.
48 *PPE*
49 André
50 André: *Hymi Christiani Bernardae Andreae poetae Regii*
51 *The Receyt of the Lady Katherine*
52 *Body Parts and Bodies*
53 Grafton
54 'An Account of the Death and Interment of Prince Arthur': anonymous herald's journal, in Leland: *Collectanea*
55 Grafton

56 *Letters and Papers, Foreign and Domestic, of the Reign of Henry VIII*
57 Bruce
58 *PPE*
59 Röhrkasten
60 *PPE*
61 Keene and Harding; Röhrkasten
62 Brian Spencer, in Tudor-Craig; Rohrkasten
63 Ibid.
64 *PPE*
65 Hall, Stow: *Annals*
66 Bacon; More
67 *Letters and Papers Illustrative of the Reigns of Richard III and Henry VII*
68 Hicks: *Edward V*
69 Chrimes
70 *Chronicles of London*
71 Hicks: *Edward V*
72 *PPE*
73 Ibid.
74 *CSP Spain*
75 *PPE*
76 *CSP Spain*
77 *PPE*
78 Ibid.
79 Ibid.
80 *CSP Spain*
81 Ibid.
82 Ibid.
83 Fox

17: *'The Hand of God'*

 1 *PPE*
 2 Ibid.
 3 Ibid.
 4 Ibid.
 5 Ibid.
 6 Additional MS. 59,899 f.24
 7 Goodall; Thurley: *The Royal Palaces of Tudor England*; Laynesmith
 8 Ibid.
 9 *PPE*; Cokayne; *Rotuli Parliamentorum*
10 Jones and Underwood; *PPE*
11 Meerson; Jones and Underwood; Cokayne; *Rotuli Parliamentorum*

12 Ibid. Centuries later Notley would be the home of actors Sir Laurence Olivier and Vivien Leigh.

13 Ibid.

14 Ibid.

15 Cunningham: *Henry VII*

16 Zita West

17 *PPE*

18 Ibid.

19 See, for example, Buckland. The Monmouth and Skenfrith vestments are now at the Welsh Folk Museum at St Fagan's.

20 *PPE*

21 *HVIIPPE*

22 *PPE*

23 See, for example, Buckland

24 *PPE*

25 Ibid.

26 Ibid.

27 Ibid.

28 *HVIIPPE*

29 *PPE*

30 Around 1708, during repairs to the hall, the skeleton of a man found seated at a table in an underground vault was thought to be his.

31 *PPE; The Catholic Encyclopaedia*; Ed West

32 *PPE*; Palmer: *Royal England*

33 *PPE*

34 Herald's account in Cotton MS. Vitellius

35 *PPE*

36 Ibid.

37 Ibid.

38 Ibid.

39 Ibid. Seymour's daughter Jane was later to marry Henry VIII.

40 Ibid.

41 Ibid.

42 Wriothesley

43 *PPE*

44 Ibid.; Leland: *Collectanea*; Additional MS. 71009, f.15v; Penn

45 *HVIIPPE*

46 *PPE*

47 'Lamentation', in More: *Complete Works*

48 Royal MS. 12b VI

49 *PPE*

50 Cunningham: *Henry VII*

51 *PPE*

52 Anne's coffin was reburied in the Minoresses' convent at Stepney, where it was discovered during excavations in 1964. Examination of the teeth showed a familial link with the skeletons found in the Tower in 1674. The remains were then reburied in Westminster Abbey, as near as possible to their original resting place.

53 Astle

54 Stow: *London*

55 Henry VII's unfinished chapel at Windsor was to be lavishly completed by Cardinal Wolsey to house his own tomb. Later it was remodelled by Queen Victoria as the Albert Memorial Chapel.

56 Astle

57 *PPE*; Cloake: *Richmond Palace*; Thurley: *The Royal Palaces of Tudor England*

58 *PPE*

59 In 1506 Henry VII also built a gallery leading from the Lanthorn Tower to the Salt Tower, which appears on a 1597 plan of the Tower as 'the Queen's Gallery' – and created a privy garden below.

60 These were the rooms lavishly refurbished in 1533 for Anne Boleyn's sojourn prior to her coronation. Thurley: *The Royal Palaces of Tudor England*; Goodall; Impey and Parnell; Keay

61 *PPE*

62 Leland: *Collectanea*

63 *PPE*

64 Ibid.

65 Additional MS 45161, ff.41–2, reproduced in *Antiquarian Repertory*; *Great Chronicle of London*

66 Herald's account in Cotton MS. Vitellius

67 *PPE*

68 Cotton MS. Vitellius; *Great Chronicle of London*; Grafton

69 More: 'Lamentation', in *Complete Works*

70 *HVIIPPE*

71 Redstone. The chapel was demolished in 1547.

72 Grafton; *Great Chronicle of London*

73 Strickland

74 Sandford

75 Green

76 Cunningham: *Henry VII*

77 *PPE*

78 Wriothesley; *Great Chronicle of London*; Grafton

79 Additional MS. 45161, ff.41–2, reproduced in *Antiquarian Repertory; PPE*

80 Additional MS. 45161, ff.41–2, reproduced in *Antiquarian Repertory*

81 Ibid.

82 Exchequer Records E.101; Hayward

83 Holinshed

84 Additional MS. 45161, ff.41–2, reproduced in *Antiquarian Repertory*; Cunningham: *Henry VII*

85 Additional MS. 45161, ff.41–2, reproduced in *Antiquarian Repertory*

86 *PPE*

87 Richardson: *Mary Tudor, the White Queen*; Loades: *Mary Rose*

88 Hayward

89 Additional MS. 45133, f.141v; Jones and Underwood

90 Records of the Lord Chamberlain, LC 2/1, f.59–78; *Great Wardrobe Accounts*

91 Additional MS. 45161, ff.41–2, reproduced in *Antiquarian Repertory*

92 *Great Chronicle of London*

93 It is often stated that Elizabeth lay in state in the beautiful Norman chapel of St John the Evangelist, the chapel used by the monarch when in residence in the Tower. Dating from *c.*1078–80, it rises through two floors of the upper levels of the White Tower, the ancient keep. Its sanctuary and nave are encircled by Romanesque arches, a continuous ambulatory and flanking aisles. It is a rare survival, one of the most perfect Norman chapels still in existence. However, *The Great Chronicle of London* clearly states that Elizabeth lay in state in 'the parish church of the Tower', which is St Peter ad Vincula, where her daughter had been christened just eight days earlier. It would make sense that St Peter's was chosen, given the logistics of carrying the coffin up and down the spiral stairs to St John's Chapel.

94 Additional MS. 45161, ff.41–2, reproduced in *Antiquarian Repertory*

95 Ibid.

96 Herald's account in College of Arms MS. I, IX, f.27

18: 'Here Lieth the Fresh Flower of Plantagenet'

1 *CSP Spain*

2 Treasurer's Accounts, Register Office, Edinburgh

3 Buchanan

4 'Isabel' is the form of 'Elizabeth' in some countries.

5 Balliol College Oxford MS. 354, ff.175–6; B.L. Sloane MS. 1825, ff.88v–89; printed in More: *Complete Works*; Tromly

6 Tromly

7 Bacon

8 It has been suggested that she was buried with her mother (*Arthur Tudor, Prince of Wales*); if so, she was left undisturbed in Elizabeth's temporary grave (described further on in the chapter), for her coffin was not found in Henry VII's vault, and the anthropoid coffin of the Queen could not have accommodated the corpse of an infant.

9 Balliol College, Oxford MS. 354, f.176

10 *HVIIPPE*. The funeral accounts are in *Antiquarian Repertory*.

11 Gristwood

12 This account of the Queen's funeral is based on those in College of Arms MS. 1, ff. 27r–32r; Additional MS. 45131, ff. 41v–47, which includes the account of Charles Wriothesley, Windsor Herald; College of Arms MS. I, III, ff.23,24; Additional MS. 45161, ff.41–2, reproduced in *Antiquarian Repertory*; Fabyan; *Records of the Skinners of London*

13 Additional MS. 45161, ff.41–2, reproduced in *Antiquarian Repertory*.

14 The accounts for the effigy – in Records of the Lord Chamberlain, LC 2/1 f.46PRO LC/1/2, ff. 46v to 48v – are the first that survive for a royal funeral effigy.

15 Howgrave-Graham

16 Ibid.

17 Records of the Lord Chamberlain, LC 2/1 f.46PRO LC/1/2, ff. 46v to 48v; St John Hope

18 Additional MS. 45161, ff.41–2, reproduced in *Antiquarian Repertory*

19 Those of London, Salisbury, Lincoln, Exeter, Rochester, Norwich, Llandaff and Bangor.

20 Records of the Lord Chamberlain LC 2/1, f.48–9

21 Additional MS. 45161, ff.41–2, reproduced in *Antiquarian Repertory*; Records of the Lord Chamberlain, LC 2/1. F. 46, 52

22 Fabyan

23 Astle

24 Records of the Lord Chamberlain, LC 2/1, f.53

25 Westminster Abbey Muniments 6637, f.2–6

26 *A Collection of all the Wills, now known to be extant, of the Kings and Queens of England*; Astle

27 *CSP Spain*; Doran; Gristwood; Penn

28 Rex: *The Tudors*

29 *Letters and Papers Illustrative of the Reigns of Richard III and Henry VII*

30 Exchequer Records E.101

31 Grafton

32 Hayward
33 *HVIIPPE*
34 *CSP Spain*
35 Astle
36 Cited by Williams in *Henry VIII and his Court*
37 Cited by Cannon and Griffiths
38 Ormond; *Gothic*. An electrotype of Elizabeth's tomb effigy, cast by Domenico Brucciani in 1870, is in the National Portrait Gallery.
39 Wilkinson: *Henry VII's Lady Chapel in Westminster Abbey*; Wilkinson: *Westminster Abbey*

19: *'As Long as the World Shall Endure'*

1 Hayward
2 Abell; Wroe
3 Wroe; Dunlop
4 *CSP Spain*
5 Okerlund: *Elizabeth of York*; Anglo: 'The Court Festivals of Henry VII'
6 Rex: *Henry VIII*
7 Bacon
8 Anglo: *Images of Tudor Kingship*
9 *CSP Spain*
10 Ibid.
11 Bacon
12 Lansdowne MS. 874, f.49
13 Cited Anglo: *Images of Tudor Kingship*
14 Ibid.
15 Latin pedigree in the College of Arms; Harleian MS. 1139, f.37
16 Horrox
17 Meerson; Hamilton; Hōak
18 Jones and Underwood
19 Herbert of Cherbury
20 The Vaux Passional, Peniarth MS. 482D
21 Ibid.; Mary Williams
22 *The Letters of King Henry VIII*. When Philip had visited England in 1506, the late Queen Elizabeth's 'rich litters and chairs' were placed at his disposal (Starkey: *Henry, Virtuous Prince*)
23 Williams: *Henry VIII and his Court*
24 Palgrave
25 *Letters and Papers, Foreign and Domestic, of the Reign of Henry VIII*
26 Ibid.; Wriothesley; Additional MS. 71009, ff.37–44v

27 *CSP Spain*
28 *Letters and Papers, Foreign and Domestic, of the Reign of Henry VIII*
29 Rushton
30 College of Arms MS I,11, f.21r–v
31 Chapter Records; Hope; *Vetusta Monumenta*; Cracknell
32 National Portrait Gallery Archive
33 Stanley; Wilkinson: *Henry VII's Lady Chapel in Westminster Abbey*;
    Wilkinson: *Westminster Abbey*

Appendix I: Portraiture

1   Ormond; Rackham; Tudor-Craig; Jenkins; Marks; *Gothic*
2   Jenkins; *Gothic*
3   *Arthur Tudor, Prince of Wales*; Rushforth
4   Darracott; Rushforth; Jenkins; Chrimes; *Gothic*
5   Scott: 'Painting from Life?'; John Fletcher
6   This date reflects recent testing of the panel at the Royal
    Collection by Ian Tyers using dendrochronology.
7   I am indebted to Jennifer Scott, Curator of Paintings, The Royal
    Collection, for this information.
8   Doort
9   They are in the Royal Collection and at Petworth House, Sussex;
    the latter shows Edward VI standing in the centre foreground.
10 Strong: *Tudor and Jacobean Portraits*; Chrimes
11 Jennifer Scott, Curator of Paintings, The Royal Collection, in
    correspondence with the author.
12 Stephen Lloyd; Reynolds: *English Portrait Miniatures*. The features
    have been extensively repainted.
13 Doort
14 Inventory of Charles II's pictures at Whitehall, c.1666–7, MS. in 'the
    Surveyor's Office', cited Millar
15 Millar; Strong: *Tudor and Jacobean Portraits*; www.royalcollection.org.
    uk. I am indebted to Jennifer Scott, Curator of Paintings, The
    Royal Collection, for sending me information on this portrait and
    scans.
16 See notes at www.royalcollection.org.uk; Scott: 'Painting from Life?'
17 *Important British Paintings, 1500–1850*; Scott: 'Painting from Life?'
18 Tudor-Craig
19 Tudor-Craig; Strong: *Tudor and Jacobean Portraits*; Williamson: *The
    National Portrait Gallery History of the Kings and Queens of England*
20 Millar; Strong: *Tudor and Jacobean Portraits*; www.priory-fine-art.
    co.uk

21 Ashelford
22 Auerbach and Adams
23 It was purchased by Queen Victoria in 1883.
24 Leland: *Collectanea*
25 Laynesmith
26 Walpole; Scharf; Cloake: *Palaces and Parks of Richmond and Kew*; *The Reign of Henry VII: Proceedings of the 1993 Harlaxton Symposium*; *Arthur Tudor, Prince of Wales*; Scott: *The Royal Portrait: Image and Impact*; Millar; Hayward
27 Scharf
28 Christ Church Oxford MS. 179, f.lv; McKendrick, Lowden and Doyle
29 *The Renaissance at Sutton Place*
30 *Gothic*

Appendix II: Elizabeth of York's Ladies and Gentlewomen

1 *PPE*
2 Ibid.
3 Ibid.
4 Ibid.
5 Starkey: *Henry, Virtuous Prince*; Meerson
6 *PPE*
7 Ibid.
8 Ibid.
9 Ibid.; *Letters and Papers, Foreign and Domestic, of the Reign of Henry VIII*
10 *PPE*
11 *Letters and Papers, Foreign and Domestic, of the Reign of Henry VIII*
12 Ibid.
13 *PPE*
14 Richardson: *Plantagenet Ancestry*
15 *PPE*
16 Ibid.
17 *Letters and Papers, Foreign and Domestic, of the Reign of Henry VIII*
18 Cokayne; Meerson
19 *Materials for a History of the Reign of Henry the Seventh*
20 *PPE*
21 Ibid.
22 Ibid.
23 Cokayne
24 Exchequer Records E.101

25 Harris

26 Meerson; Glasheen

27 *Letters and Papers, Foreign and Domestic, of the Reign of Henry VIII*

28 *PPE*

29 Meerson

30 *PPE*

31 *Letters and Papers, Foreign and Domestic, of the Reign of Henry VIII*

32 *Calendar of Patent Rolls: Henry VII*; Exchequer Records E.101

33 *PPE*

34 Ibid.

35 Meerson

36 *Letters and Papers, Foreign and Domestic, of the Reign of Henry VIII*

37 *PPE*

38 Tomb inscription in St Swithun's Church, East Grinstead, Sussex.

39 *PPE*

40 *Letters and Papers, Foreign and Domestic, of the Reign of Henry VIII*

41 *PPE*

42 *Letters and Papers, Foreign and Domestic, of the Reign of Henry VIII*

43 Harris; Meerson

44 *Letters and Papers, Foreign and Domestic, of the Reign of Henry VIII*

45 Higginbotham

46 *Letters and Papers, Foreign and Domestic, of the Reign of Henry VIII*

47 Ibid.

48 *PPE*

49 Meerson; Cokayne; Weir: Britain's Aristocratic Families, 1066–1603

50 *Rivals in Power; PPE*

Elizabeth of York's family tree

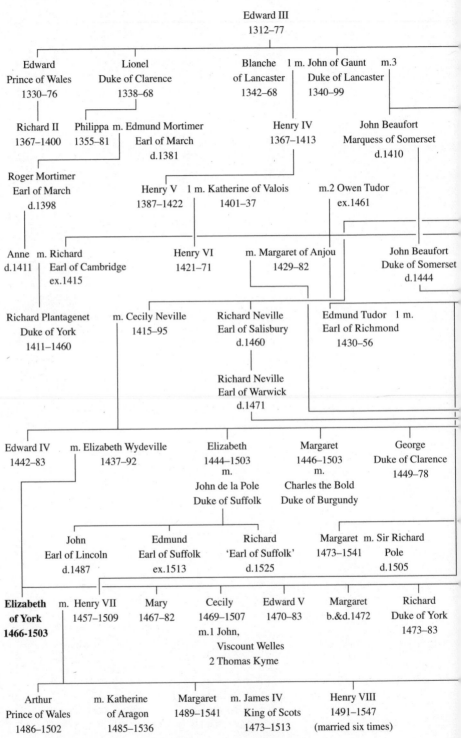

Edward III
1312–77

Edward
Prince of Wales
1330–76

Lionel
Duke of Clarence
1338–68

Blanche   1 m. John of Gaunt   m.3
of Lancaster   Duke of Lancaster
1342–68   1340–99

Richard II   Philippa m. Edmund Mortimer
1367–1400   1355–81   Earl of March
                                  d.1381

Henry IV
1367–1413

John Beaufort
Marquess of Somerset
d.1410

Roger Mortimer
Earl of March
d.1398

Henry V   1 m. Katherine of Valois
1387–1422   1401–37

m.2 Owen Tudor
ex.1461

Anne m. Richard
d.1411 | Earl of Cambridge
            ex.1415

Henry VI   m. Margaret of Anjou
1421–71   1429–82

John Beaufort
Duke of Somerset
d.1444

Richard Plantagenet
Duke of York
1411–1460

m. Cecily Neville
1415–95

Richard Neville
Earl of Salisbury
d.1460

Edmund Tudor   1 m.
Earl of Richmond
1430–56

Richard Neville
Earl of Warwick
d.1471

Edward IV   m. Elizabeth Wydeville
1442–83   1437–92

Elizabeth
1444–1503
m.
John de la Pole
Duke of Suffolk

Margaret
1446–1503
m.
Charles the Bold
Duke of Burgundy

George
Duke of Clarence
1449–78

John
Earl of Lincoln
d.1487

Edmund
Earl of Suffolk
ex.1513

Richard
'Earl of Suffolk'
d.1525

Margaret m. Sir Richard
1473–1541   Pole
                      d.1505

Elizabeth   m. Henry VII
of York   1457–1509
1466-1503

Mary
1467–82

Cecily
1469–1507
m.1 John,
Viscount Welles
2 Thomas Kyme

Edward V
1470–83

Margaret
b.&d.1472

Richard
Duke of York
1473–83

Arthur
Prince of Wales
1486–1502

m. Katherine
of Aragon
1485–1536

Margaret   m. James IV
1489–1541   King of Scots
                    1473–1513

Henry VIII
1491–1547
(married six times)

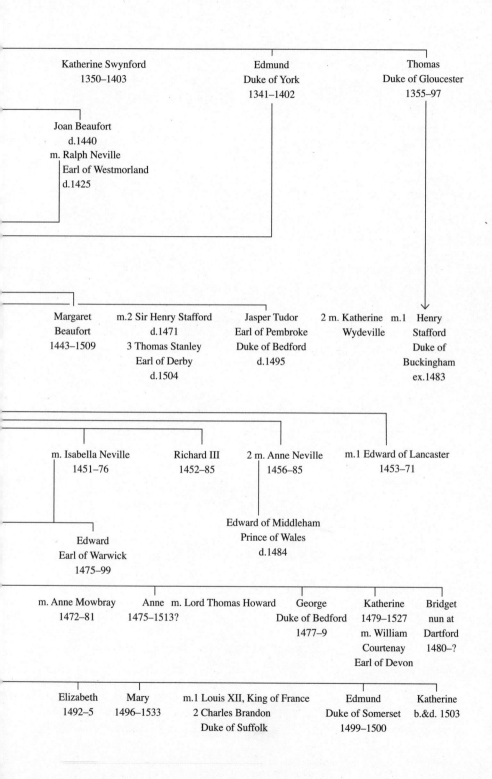

Katherine Swynford
1350–1403

Edmund
Duke of York
1341–1402

Thomas
Duke of Gloucester
1355–97

Joan Beaufort
d.1440
m. Ralph Neville
Earl of Westmorland
d.1425

Margaret
Beaufort
1443–1509

m.2 Sir Henry Stafford
d.1471
3 Thomas Stanley
Earl of Derby
d.1504

Jasper Tudor
Earl of Pembroke
Duke of Bedford
d.1495

2 m. Katherine
Wydeville

m.1 Henry
Stafford
Duke of
Buckingham
ex.1483

m. Isabella Neville
1451–76

Richard III
1452–85

2 m. Anne Neville
1456–85

m.1 Edward of Lancaster
1453–71

Edward
Earl of Warwick
1475–99

Edward of Middleham
Prince of Wales
d.1484

m. Anne Mowbray
1472–81

Anne m. Lord Thomas Howard
1475–1513?

George
Duke of Bedford
1477–9

Katherine
1479–1527
m. William
Courtenay
Earl of Devon

Bridget
nun at
Dartford
1480–?

Elizabeth
1492–5

Mary
1496–1533

m.1 Louis XII, King of France
2 Charles Brandon
Duke of Suffolk

Edmund
Duke of Somerset
1499–1500

Katherine
b.&d. 1503

Index